P9-CAN-180

HARCOURT HORIZONS

HARCOURT
HORIZONS

HARCOURT HORIZONS

HARCOURT HORIZONS

The Pledge of Allegiance

I pledge allegiance to the Flag

of the United States of America,

and to the Republic

for which it stands,

one Nation under God, indivisible,

with liberty and justice for all.

HARCOURT HORIZONS

United States History

Orlando   Austin   Chicago   New York   Toronto   London   San Diego

Visit *The Learning Site!*
www.harcourtschool.com

HARCOURT HORIZONS

UNITED STATES HISTORY

General Editor

Dr. Michael J. Berson
Associate Professor
Social Science Education
University of South Florida
Tampa, Florida

Contributing Authors

Dr. Robert P. Green, Jr.
Professor
School of Education
Clemson University
Clemson, South Carolina

Dr. Thomas M. McGowan
Chairperson and Professor
Center for Curriculum and Instruction
University of Nebraska
Lincoln, Nebraska

Dr. Linda Kerrigan Salvucci
Associate Professor
Department of History
Trinity University
San Antonio, Texas

Series Consultants

Dr. Robert Bednarz
Professor
Department of Geography
Texas A&M University
College Station, Texas

Dr. Barbara Caffee
Coordinator, K–12 Social Studies
Carrollton–Farmers Branch Independent
   School District
Carrollton, Texas

Dr. Asa Grant Hilliard III
Fuller E. Callaway Professor
   of Urban Education
Georgia State University
Atlanta, Georgia

Dr. Thomas M. McGowan
Chairperson and Professor
Center for Curriculum and Instruction
University of Nebraska
Lincoln, Nebraska

Dr. John J. Patrick
Professor of Education
Indiana University
Bloomington, Indiana

Dr. Cinthia Salinas
Assistant Professor
Department of Curriculum and Instruction
University of Texas at Austin
Austin, Texas

Dr. Philip VanFossen
Associate Professor,
   Social Studies Education,
   and Associate Director,
   Purdue Center for Economic Education
Purdue University
West Lafayette, Indiana

Dr. Hallie Kay Yopp
Professor
Department of Elementary, Bilingual, and
   Reading Education
California State University, Fullerton
Fullerton, California

Content Reviewers

United States Geography

Dr. Phillip Bacon
Professor Emeritus
Geography and Anthropology
University of Houston
Houston, Texas

Native Americans and European Exploration

Dr. Susan Deans-Smith
Associate Professor
Department of History
University of Texas at Austin
Austin, Texas

Dr. John Jeffries Martin
Professor
Department of History
Trinity University
San Antonio, Texas

Richard Nichols
President
Richard Nichols and Associates
Fairview, New Mexico

Early Settlement and the American Revolution

Dr. John W. Johnson
Professor and Head
Department of History
University of Northern Iowa
Cedar Falls, Iowa

Dr. John P. Kaminski
Director, Center for the Study of
   the American Constitution
Department of History
University of Wisconsin
Madison, Wisconsin

Dr. Elizabeth Mancke
Associate Professor of History
Department of History
University of Akron
Akron, Ohio

The Constitution and United States Government

Dr. James M. Banner, Jr.
Historian
Washington, D.C.

Carol Egbo
Social Studies Consultant
Waterford Schools
Waterford, Michigan

Dr. John P. Kaminski
Director, Center for the Study of
  the American Constitution
Department of History
University of Wisconsin
Madison, Wisconsin

Dr. John J. Patrick
Professor of Education
Indiana University
Bloomington, Indiana

The National Period and Westward Expansion

Dr. Ross Frank
Professor
Department of Ethnic Studies
University of California at San Diego
La Jolla, California

Civil War and Reconstruction

Dr. Judith Giesburg
Assistant Professor
Department of History
Northern Arizona University
Flagstaff, Arizona

The United States in the Twentieth Century

Dr. Carol McKibben
Visiting Professor
Monterey Institute of International Studies
Monterey, California

Dr. Albert Raboteau
Henry W. Putnam Professor
Department of Religion
Princeton University
Princeton, New Jersey

Classroom Reviewers

Kathleen Arseneau
Teacher
St. Matthew's School
Kalispell, Montana

Jane Blankenship
Teacher
Prestonwood Elementary School
Dallas, Texas

Portia F. Bohannon-Ramsey
Teacher and Social Studies Chair
James E. McDade Classical School
Chicago, Illinois

Judy S. Crawford
Teacher
Settlers Way Elementary School
Sugar Land, Texas

Lucille Ferragamo
Teacher
A. C. Whelan Elementary School
Revere, Massachusetts

Barbara Haack
Teacher
Perkins Academy
Des Moines, Iowa

Amy M. Krohn
Teacher
Tombaugh Elementary School
Las Cruces, New Mexico

Cindy Merchant
Teacher
Denver Place School
Wilmington, Ohio

Barbara Motzer
Teacher
General Wayne Elementary School
Malvern, Pennsylvania

Wendy Ogawa
Schoolwide Coordinator
Wheeler Elementary School
Wahiawa, Hawaii

Elma Schwartz
Teacher
Ascarate Elementary School
El Paso, Texas

Maps
researched and prepared by
MAPQUEST.COM

Readers
written and designed by
TIME FOR KIDS

Take a Field Trip
video tour segments provided by

CNN Turner Le@rning

Acknowledgments appear in the back of this book.

Printed in the United States of America

ISBN 0-15-320182-7

4 5 6 7 8 9 10 048 10 09 08 07 06 05 04 03

Contents

· UNIT ·

1

The Land and Early People

· UNIT ·
3

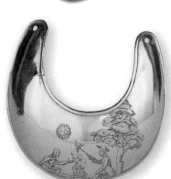

The English Colonies

· UNIT ·

4

The American Revolution

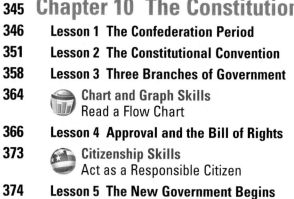
· UNIT ·

5

A New Nation

· UNIT ·

6

Civil War Times

· UNIT ·

7

The Twentieth Century

· UNIT ·

8

The United States and the World

Reference

Features You Can Use

Time Lines

Reading Your Textbook

Getting Started

Your textbook is divided into eight units.

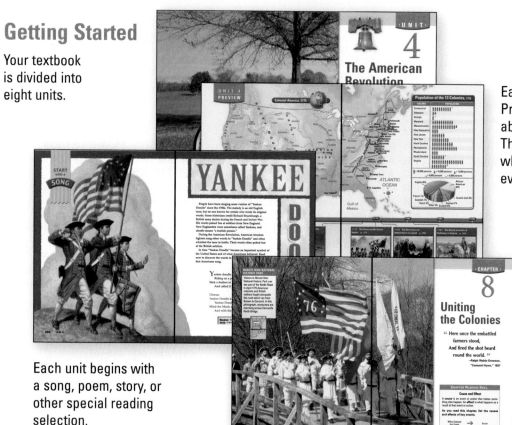

Each unit has a Unit Preview that gives facts about important events. The Preview also shows where and when those events took place.

Each unit is divided into chapters, and each chapter is divided into lessons.

Each unit begins with a song, poem, story, or other special reading selection.

The Parts of a Lesson

This statement gives you the lesson's main idea. It tells you what to look for as you read.

This statement tells you why it is important to read the lesson.

These are the new vocabulary terms you will learn in the lesson.

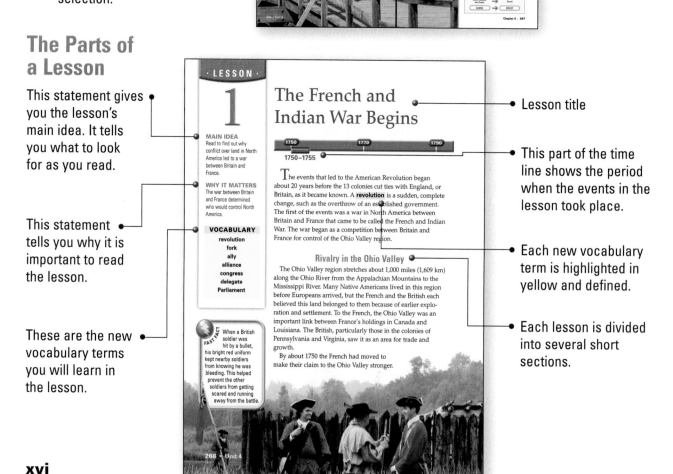

Lesson title

This part of the time line shows the period when the events in the lesson took place.

Each new vocabulary term is highlighted in yellow and defined.

Each lesson is divided into several short sections.

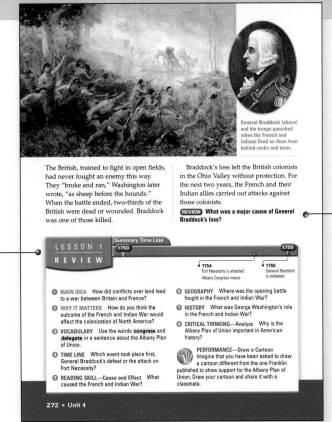

General Braddock (above) and his troops panicked when the French and Indians fired on them from behind rocks and trees.

The British, trained to fight in open fields, had never fought an enemy this way. They "broke and ran," Washington later wrote, "as sheep before the hounds." When the battle ended, two-thirds of the British were dead or wounded. Braddock was one of those killed.

Braddock's loss left the British colonists in the Ohio Valley without protection. For the next two years, the French and their Indian allies carried out attacks against those colonists.

REVIEW What was a major cause of General Braddock's loss?

Each lesson, like each chapter and each unit, ends with a review. There may be a Summary Time Line that shows the order of the events covered in the lesson. Questions and a performance activity help you check your understanding of the lesson.

Each short section ends with a **REVIEW** question that will help you check whether you under-stand what you have read. Be sure to answer this question before you continue reading the lesson.

LESSON 1 REVIEW

Summary Time Line
1750 — 1755
1754 Fort Necessity is attacked; Albany Congress meets
1755 General Braddock is defeated

① **MAIN IDEA** How did conflicts over land lead to a war between Britain and France?

② **WHY IT MATTERS** How do you think the outcome of the French and Indian War would affect the colonization of North America?

③ **VOCABULARY** Use the words **congress** and **delegate** in a sentence about the Albany Plan of Union.

④ **TIME LINE** Which event took place first, General Braddock's defeat or the attack on Fort Necessity?

⑤ **READING SKILL—Cause and Effect** What caused the French and Indian War?

⑥ **GEOGRAPHY** Where was the opening battle fought in the French and Indian War?

⑦ **HISTORY** What was George Washington's role in the French and Indian War?

⑧ **CRITICAL THINKING—Analyze** Why is the Albany Plan of Union important in American history?

PERFORMANCE—Draw a Cartoon Imagine that you have been asked to draw a cartoon different from the one Franklin published to show support for the Albany Plan of Union. Draw your cartoon and share it with a classmate.

272 ▪ Unit 4

Skills

Your textbook has lessons that will help you build your reading, citizenship, chart and graph, and map and globe skills.

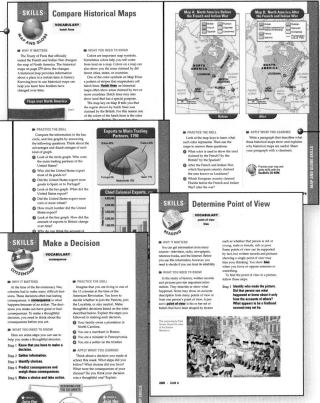

You will be able to practice and apply the skills you learn.

SKILLS — Compare Historical Maps

SKILLS — Compare Graphs

SKILLS — Make a Decision

SKILLS — Determine Point of View

This statement tells you why it is important to learn the skill.

xvii

Special Features

The feature called
Examine Primary
Sources shows
you ways to learn
about different kinds
of objects and
documents.

The Visit feature lets
you "visit" many
interesting places.

Atlas

The Atlas provides maps
and a list of geography
terms with illustrations.

For Your Reference

At the back of your textbook, you will find
the reference tools listed below.

- Almanac
- American Documents
- Biographical Dictionary
- Gazetteer
- Glossary
- Index

You can use these tools to look up words
and to find information about people,
places, and other topics.

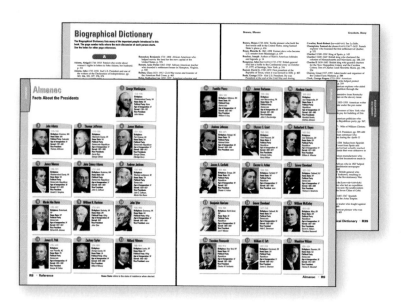

Atlas

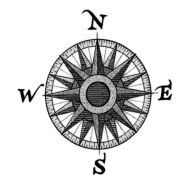

Read a Map

VOCABULARY

map title	grid system	compass rose
map key	locator	cardinal directions
inset map	map scale	intermediate directions

▶ WHY IT MATTERS

Maps provide many kinds of information about the world around you. Knowing how to read maps is an important social studies skill.

▶ WHAT YOU NEED TO KNOW

A map is a drawing that shows all of or part of the Earth on a flat surface. Mapmakers add certain features to most of the maps they draw.

Mapmakers sometimes need to show places marked on the map in greater detail or places that are beyond the area shown on the map. Find Alaska and Hawaii on the map of the United States on pages A10–A11. This map shows the location of those two states in relation to the rest of the country.

- A **map title** tells the subject of the map. It may also identify the kind of map.
  - Political maps show cities, states, and countries.
  - Physical maps show kinds of land and bodies of water.
  - Historical maps show parts of the world as they were in the past.

- A **map key**, or legend, explains the symbols used on a map. Symbols may be colors, patterns, lines, or other special marks.

- An **inset map** is a small map within a larger map.

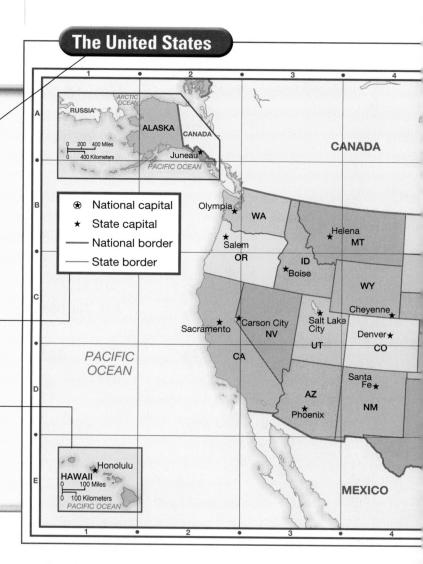

The United States

Now find Alaska and Hawaii on the map below. To show this much detail for these states and the rest of the country on one map, the map would have to be much larger. Instead, Alaska and Hawaii are each shown in a separate **inset map**, or a small map within a larger map.

To help people find places on a map, mapmakers sometimes add lines that cross each other to form a pattern of squares called a **grid system**. Look at the map of the United States below. Around the grid are letters and numbers. The columns, which run up and down, have numbers. The rows, which run left and right, have letters. Each square on the map can be identified by its letter and number. For example, the top row of squares in the map includes square A1, square A2, and square A3.

▶ PRACTICE THE SKILL

Use the map of the United States to answer the following questions.

1. What city can be found in square D3?
2. In which direction would you travel to go from Austin, Texas, to Richmond, Virginia?
3. About how many miles is it from Richmond, Virginia, to Albany, New York?
4. Which two oceans border Alaska?

▶ APPLY WHAT YOU LEARNED

Choose one of the maps in the Atlas. With a partner, identify the parts of the map and discuss what the map tells you. Ask each other questions that can be answered by reading the map.

- A **locator** is a small map or picture of a globe that shows where the place on the main map is located.

- A **map scale** compares a distance on the map to a distance in the real world. It helps you find the real distance between places on a map.

- A **compass rose**, or direction marker, shows directions.
  - The **cardinal directions**, or main directions, are north, south, east, and west.
  - The **intermediate directions**, or directions between the cardinal directions, are northeast, northwest, southeast, and southwest.

MAP AND GLOBE SKILLS

A3

The World
POLITICAL

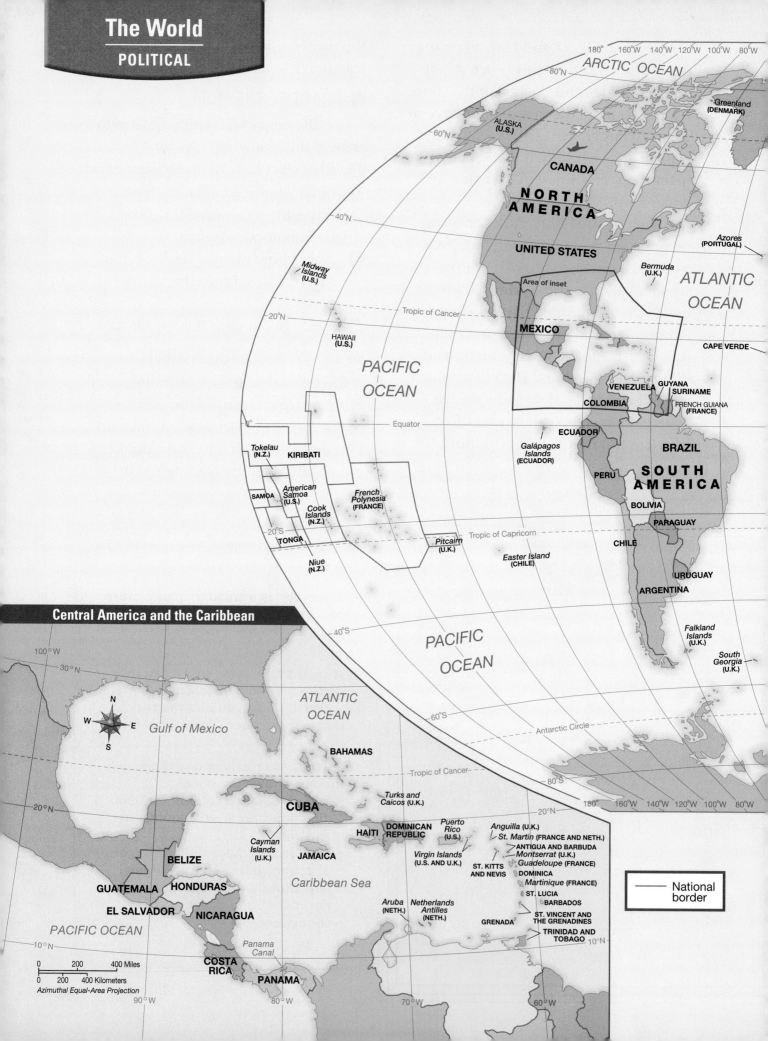

ARCTIC OCEAN

180° 160°W 140°W 120°W 100°W 80°W

80°N

Greenland (DENMARK)

ALASKA (U.S.)

60°N

CANADA

NORTH AMERICA

40°N

UNITED STATES

Azores (PORTUGAL)

Midway Islands (U.S.)

Bermuda (U.K.)

ATLANTIC OCEAN

Area of inset

20°N — Tropic of Cancer

MEXICO

CAPE VERDE

HAWAII (U.S.)

PACIFIC OCEAN

VENEZUELA GUYANA SURINAME

COLOMBIA FRENCH GUIANA (FRANCE)

Equator

ECUADOR

Galápagos Islands (ECUADOR)

BRAZIL

Tokelau (N.Z.)

KIRIBATI

PERU **SOUTH AMERICA**

SAMOA American Samoa (U.S.)

Cook Islands (N.Z.)

French Polynesia (FRANCE)

BOLIVIA

PARAGUAY

20°S

TONGA

Pitcairn (U.K.)

Tropic of Capricorn

CHILE

Niue (N.Z.)

Easter Island (CHILE)

URUGUAY

ARGENTINA

40°S

PACIFIC OCEAN

Falkland Islands (U.K.)

60°S

Antarctic Circle

South Georgia (U.K.)

80°S

180° 160°W 140°W 120°W 100°W 80°W

Central America and the Caribbean

100°W

30°N

Gulf of Mexico

ATLANTIC OCEAN

20°N

BAHAMAS

Tropic of Cancer

CUBA

Turks and Caicos (U.K.)

Cayman Islands (U.K.)

HAITI DOMINICAN REPUBLIC

Puerto Rico (U.S.)

Anguilla (U.K.)

St. Martin (FRANCE AND NETH.)

BELIZE

JAMAICA

Virgin Islands (U.S. AND U.K.)

ANTIGUA AND BARBUDA

Montserrat (U.K.)

GUATEMALA HONDURAS

Caribbean Sea

ST. KITTS AND NEVIS

Guadeloupe (FRANCE)

DOMINICA

Martinique (FRANCE)

EL SALVADOR NICARAGUA

Aruba (NETH.) Netherlands Antilles (NETH.)

ST. LUCIA

BARBADOS

PACIFIC OCEAN

GRENADA

ST. VINCENT AND THE GRENADINES

10°N

Panama Canal

TRINIDAD AND TOBAGO

10°N

0   200   400 Miles
0 200 400 Kilometers
Azimuthal Equal-Area Projection

COSTA RICA

PANAMA

90°W

80°W

70°W

60°W

| National border |

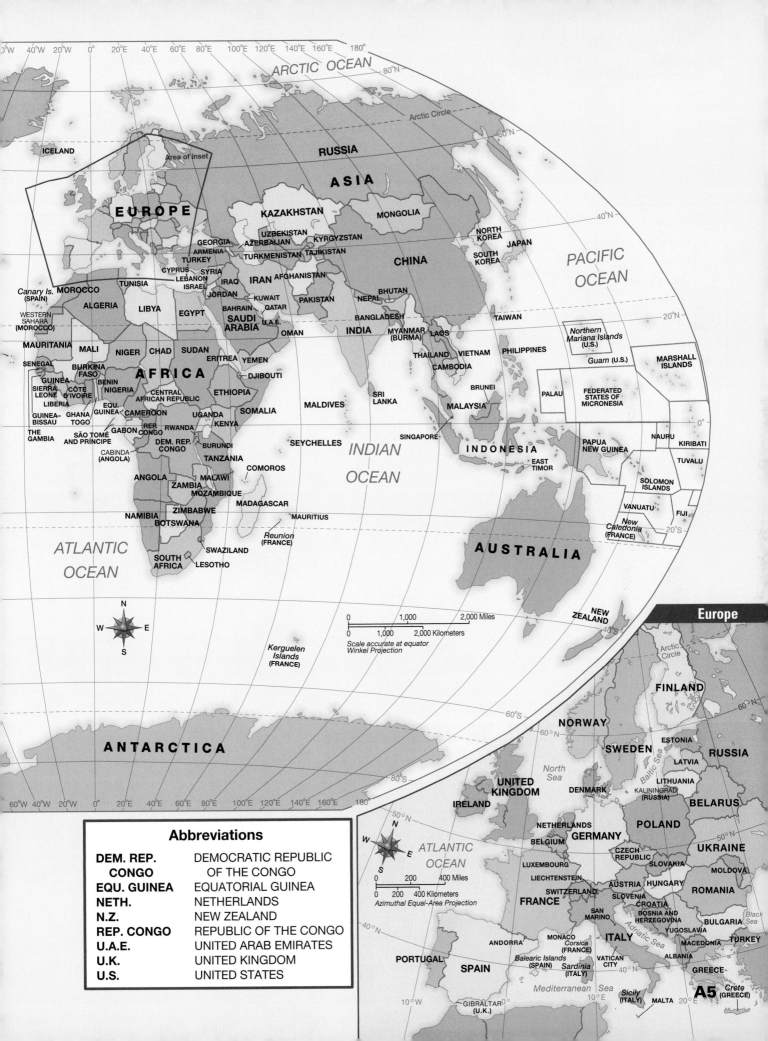

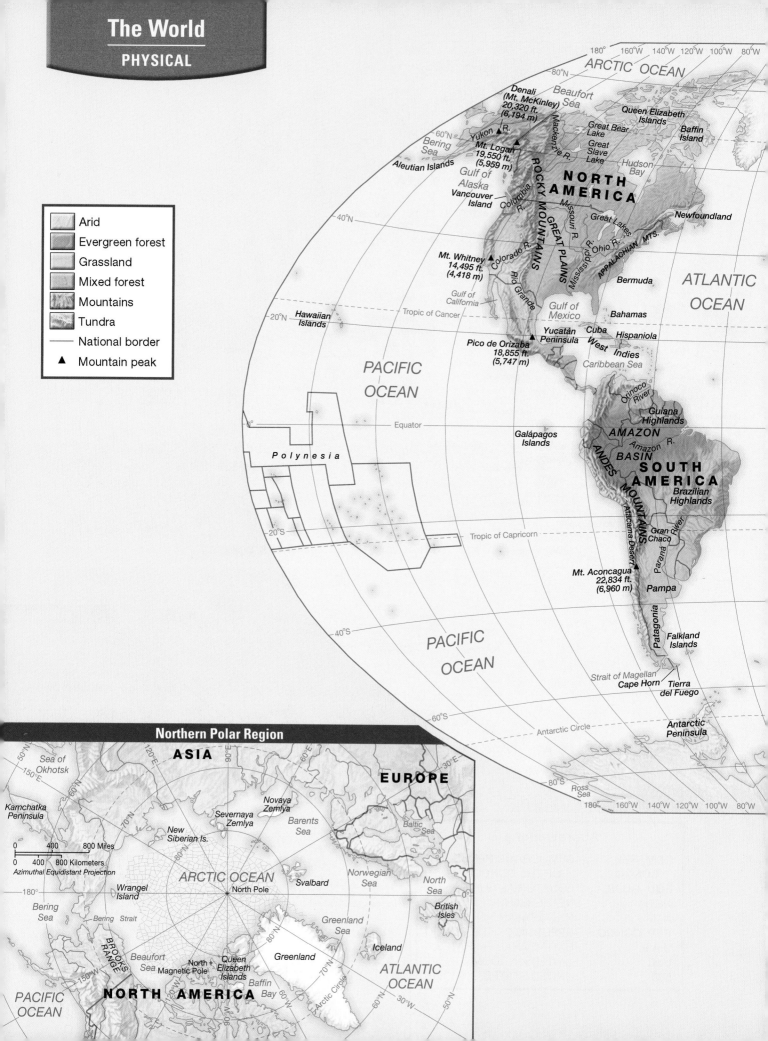

The World
PHYSICAL

Legend:
- Arid
- Evergreen forest
- Grassland
- Mixed forest
- Mountains
- Tundra
- National border
- ▲ Mountain peak

ARCTIC OCEAN

Beaufort Sea

Denali (Mt. McKinley) 20,320 ft. (6,194 m)

Queen Elizabeth Islands

Great Bear Lake

Baffin Island

Bering Sea

Yukon R.

Mt. Logan 19,550 ft. (5,959 m)

Mackenzie R.

Great Slave Lake

Hudson Bay

Aleutian Islands

Gulf of Alaska

Vancouver Island

Columbia R.

ROCKY MOUNTAINS

NORTH AMERICA

GREAT PLAINS

Missouri R.

Great Lakes

Newfoundland

Mt. Whitney 14,495 ft. (4,418 m)

Colorado R.

Mississippi R.

Ohio R.

APPALACHIAN MTS.

Bermuda

ATLANTIC OCEAN

Rio Grande

Gulf of California

Hawaiian Islands

Tropic of Cancer

Gulf of Mexico

Bahamas

Cuba

Hispaniola

Pico de Orizaba 18,855 ft. (5,747 m)

Yucatán Peninsula

West Indies

PACIFIC OCEAN

Caribbean Sea

Orinoco River

Guiana Highlands

Equator

Galápagos Islands

AMAZON

Amazon R.

SOUTH AMERICA

Polynesia

BASIN

Brazilian Highlands

ANDES MOUNTAINS

Atacama Desert

Tropic of Capricorn

Gran Chaco

Paraná River

Mt. Aconcagua 22,834 ft. (6,960 m)

Pampa

Patagonia

PACIFIC OCEAN

Falkland Islands

Strait of Magellan

Cape Horn

Tierra del Fuego

Antarctic Circle

Antarctic Peninsula

Ross Sea

Northern Polar Region

ASIA

EUROPE

Sea of Okhotsk

Novaya Zemlya

Severnaya Zemlya

Barents Sea

Baltic Sea

Kamchatka Peninsula

New Siberian Is.

0   400   800 Miles
0   400   800 Kilometers
Azimuthal Equidistant Projection

ARCTIC OCEAN

North Pole

Svalbard

Norwegian Sea

North Sea

Wrangel Island

Bering Strait

Bering Sea

BROOKS RANGE

Beaufort Sea

North Magnetic Pole

Queen Elizabeth Islands

Greenland

Greenland Sea

Iceland

British Isles

ATLANTIC OCEAN

NORTH AMERICA

Baffin Bay

Arctic Circle

PACIFIC OCEAN

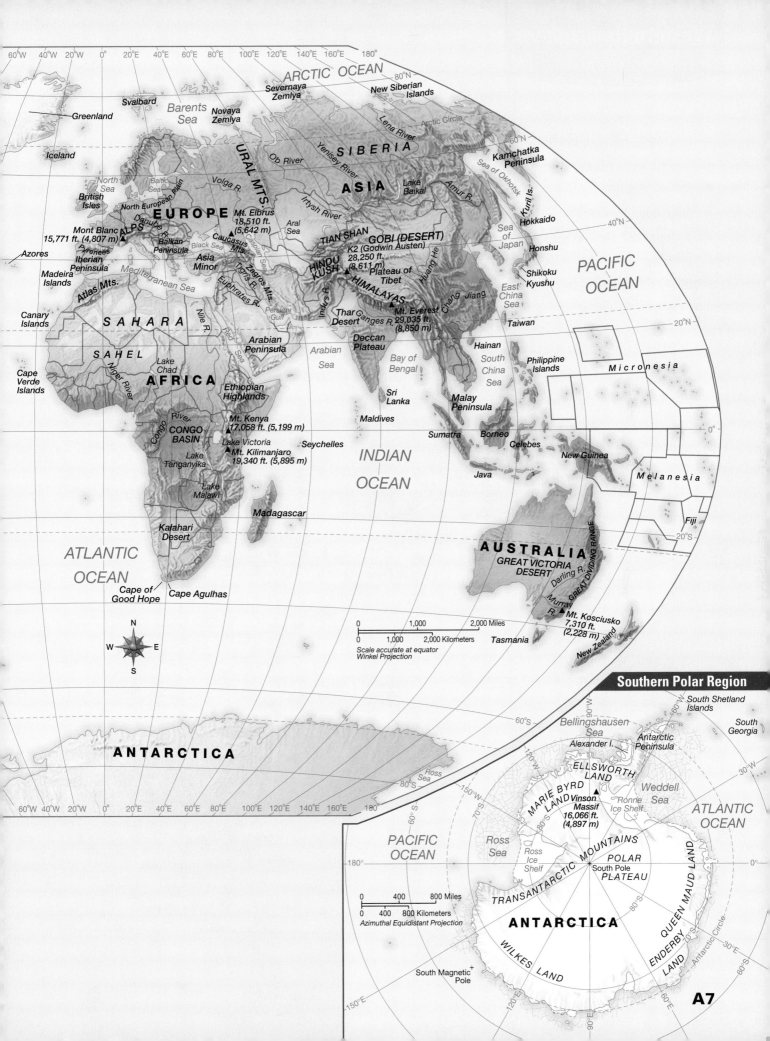

ARCTIC OCEAN

Greenland
Svalbard
Iceland
Barents Sea
Severnaya Zemlya
Novaya Zemlya
New Siberian Islands
Arctic Circle

North Sea
British Isles
Baltic Sea
North European Plain
EUROPE
Danube R.
ALPS
Mont Blanc 15,771 ft. (4,807 m)
Pyrenees
Iberian Peninsula
Balkan Peninsula
Azores
Madeira Islands
Atlas Mts.
Canary Islands
Mediterranean Sea

URAL MTS.
Ob River
Volga R.
Yenisey River
Irtysh River
Lena River
SIBERIA
ASIA
Kamchatka Peninsula
Sea of Okhotsk
Amur R.
Lake Baikal
Kuril Is.
Hokkaido

Mt. Elbrus 18,510 ft. (5,642 m)
Aral Sea
Caucasus Mts.
Black Sea
Caspian Sea
Asia Minor
Tigris R.
Euphrates R.
Zagros Mts.
Persian Gulf
TIAN SHAN
HINDU KUSH
GOBI (DESERT)
K2 (Godwin Austen) 28,250 ft. (8,611 m)
Plateau of Tibet
HIMALAYAS
Mt. Everest 29,035 ft. (8,850 m)
Huang He
Chang Jiang
Sea of Japan
Honshu
Shikoku
Kyushu
PACIFIC OCEAN
East China Sea
Taiwan

SAHARA
Nile R.
Red Sea
Arabian Peninsula
Arabian Sea
Indus R.
Thar Desert
Ganges R.
Deccan Plateau
Bay of Bengal
Sri Lanka
Maldives
Hainan
South China Sea
Philippine Islands
Micronesia

SAHEL
Lake Chad
Niger River
AFRICA
Ethiopian Highlands
Congo River
CONGO BASIN
Mt. Kenya 17,058 ft. (5,199 m)
Lake Victoria
Mt. Kilimanjaro 19,340 ft. (5,895 m)
Lake Tanganyika
Seychelles
INDIAN OCEAN
Malay Peninsula
Sumatra
Borneo
Celebes
New Guinea
Java
Melanesia
Fiji

Cape Verde Islands
Lake Malawi
Madagascar

ATLANTIC OCEAN
Kalahari Desert
Cape of Good Hope
Cape Agulhas

AUSTRALIA
GREAT VICTORIA DESERT
GREAT DIVIDING RANGE
Darling R.
Murray R.
Mt. Kosciusko 7,310 ft. (2,228 m)
Tasmania
New Zealand

N
W E
S

0   1,000   2,000 Miles
0   1,000   2,000 Kilometers
Scale accurate at equator
Winkel Projection

ANTARCTICA

Ross Sea

Southern Polar Region

South Shetland Islands
Bellingshausen Sea
Alexander I.
Antarctic Peninsula
South Georgia
ELLSWORTH LAND
MARIE BYRD LAND
Vinson Massif 16,066 ft. (4,897 m)
Ronne Ice Shelf
Weddell Sea
ATLANTIC OCEAN
PACIFIC OCEAN
Ross Sea
Ross Ice Shelf
TRANSANTARCTIC MOUNTAINS
POLAR PLATEAU
South Pole
QUEEN MAUD LAND
ENDERBY LAND
ANTARCTICA
WILKES LAND
South Magnetic Pole
Antarctic Circle

0   400   800 Miles
0   400   800 Kilometers
Azimuthal Equidistant Projection

A7

Western Hemisphere
POLITICAL

ARCTIC OCEAN

Bering Strait

Viscount Melville Sound

Beaufort Sea

Baffin Bay

Greenland
(DENMARK)

Arctic Circle

ALASKA
(U.S.)

Yukon River

Fairbanks

Great Bear Lake

Yellowknife

Great Slave Lake

Mackenzie River

Foxe Basin

Davis Strait

Anchorage

Whitehorse

Liard River

60°N

CANADA

Lake Athabasca

Hudson Strait

Juneau

Gulf of Alaska

Peace River

Hudson Bay

Labrador Sea

Bering Sea

Edmonton

Saskatoon

Saskatchewan R.

Lake Winnipeg

James Bay

Calgary

Regina

Winnipeg

St. Lawrence River

St. John's

Vancouver

Seattle

Puget Sound

Columbia R.

Portland

UNITED STATES

Thunder Bay

Great Lakes

Ottawa

Quebec

St. John

Gulf of St. Lawrence

Boise

Snake R.

Toronto

Montreal

Halifax

Missouri R.

Detroit

Albany

Boston

Salt Lake City

Chicago

Cleveland

New York City

Reno

Great Salt Lake

Denver

Indianapolis

Philadelphia

San Francisco

Las Vegas

Colorado R.

St. Louis

Richmond

Washington, D.C.

Memphis

Norfolk

ATLANTIC OCEAN

Los Angeles

Phoenix

Atlanta

Raleigh

San Diego

El Paso

Dallas

Charleston

Tucson

Houston

New Orleans

Savannah

30°N

Hermosillo

Rio Grande

San Antonio

Jacksonville

Chihuahua

Tampa

Orlando

Gulf of California

MEXICO

Monterrey

Gulf of Mexico

Miami

BAHAMAS

Tropic of Cancer

Durango

León

Tampico

Nassau

Havana

Honolulu

Guadalajara

Mexico City

Veracruz

CUBA

HAITI

Port-au-Prince

Santo Domingo

HAWAII
(U.S.)

Puebla

BELIZE

JAMAICA

Puerto Rico (U.S.)

PACIFIC OCEAN

Acapulco

GUATEMALA

Belmopan

Kingston

DOMINICAN REPUBLIC

Guatemala City

HONDURAS

San Salvador

Tegucigalpa

Caribbean Sea

EL SALVADOR

Managua

NICARAGUA

San José

Maracaibo

Panama City

Caracas

GUYANA

COSTA RICA

VENEZUELA

SURINAME

PANAMA

Paramaribo

Medellín

Cayenne

Cali

Bogotá

Georgetown

FRENCH GUIANA (FRANCE)

COLOMBIA

0°

Equator

Quito

Galápagos Islands
(ECUADOR)

Guayaquil

Rio Negro

Manaus

Amazon R.

Belém

ECUADOR

Iquitos

Fortaleza

French Polynesia
(FRANCE)

Trujillo

Tapajós R.

Xingu R.

Tocantins R.

Recife

Papeete

PERU

Lima

Cuzco

BRAZIL

Brasília

Salvador

Lake Titicaca

La Paz

Goiânia

São Francisco R.

Belo Horizonte

Arequipa

BOLIVIA

Rio de Janeiro

Sucre

Campo Grande

Tropic of Capricorn

Antofagasta

Paraguay R.

PARAGUAY

São Paulo

Curitiba

Asunción

0   1,000   2,000 Miles

Salta

0   1,000   2,000 Kilometers

San Miguel de Tucumán

Pôrto Alegre

Miller Cylindrical Projection

CHILE

Córdoba

URUGUAY

30°S

Valparaíso

Rosario

Santiago

Buenos Aires

Montevideo

La Plata

Concepción

Rio de la Plata

Mar del Plata

Valdivia

Bahía Blanca

—— National border

⊛ National capital

• City

ARGENTINA

N
W   E
S

A8

Punta Arenas

Falkland Islands
(U.K.)

South Georgia
(U.K.)

150°W   120°W   90°W   60°W   30°W

ARCTIC OCEAN

North Magnetic Pole +

Queen Elizabeth Islands

Ellesmere Island

Melville Island

Devon Island

Viscount Melville Sound

Baffin Bay

Greenland

Bering Strait

Point Barrow

Beaufort Sea

Banks Island

Victoria Island

Baffin Island

Foxe Basin

Davis Strait

Arctic Circle

Brooks Range

Mt. McKinley 20,320 ft. (6,194 m) ▲

Yukon River

Mackenzie Mts.

Great Bear Lake

Great Slave Lake

Hudson Strait

60°N

Cape Farewell

Alaska Range

Yukon Plateau

Liard R.

Mackenzie River

Peace River

Athabasca R.

Lake Athabasca

Hudson Bay

Labrador

Labrador Sea

Gulf of Alaska

Mt. Logan 19,550 ft. (5,959 m)

Coast Mountains

Saskatchewan River

Lake Winnipeg

James Bay

Kodiak Island

Alaska Peninsula

Bering Sea

Aleutian Islands

Queen Charlotte Islands

Vancouver Island

Puget Sound

Cascade Range

Coast Ranges

Sierra Nevada

CANADIAN

ROCKY

GREAT PLAINS

MOUNTAINS

SHIELD

NORTH AMERICA

Great Lakes

St. Lawrence R.

Newfoundland

Gulf of St. Lawrence

Nova Scotia

Bay of Fundy

Cape Cod

Long Island

Black Hills

Missouri R.

Mississippi R.

Ohio R.

APPALACHIAN MTS.

Great Salt Lake

GREAT BASIN

Snake R.

Platte R.

INTERIOR PLAINS

Arkansas R.

Ozark Plateau

Cape Hatteras

Mt. Whitney 14,495 ft. (4,418 m) ▲

Death Valley (lowest point in N.A.) -282 ft. (-86 m) ▼

Colorado R.

Sonoran Desert

Sierra Madre Occidental

Rio Grande

COASTAL PLAIN

ATLANTIC OCEAN

30°N

Baja California

Gulf of California

Sierra Madre Oriental

Gulf of Mexico

Bahamas

Tropic of Cancer

Hawaiian Islands

PACIFIC OCEAN

Pico de Orizaba 18,855 ft. (5,747 m) ▲

Yucatán Peninsula

Cuba

Greater Antilles

Hispaniola

Puerto Rico

Lesser Antilles

Caribbean Sea

Lake Maracaibo

Lake Nicaragua

Isthmus of Panama

Llanos

Orinoco R.

Guiana Highlands

Line Islands

Equator

Galápagos Islands

Chimborazo 20,702 ft. (6,310 m) ▲

Rio Negro

Amazon R.

Cape São Roque

ANDES

AMAZON BASIN

Marquesas Islands

Huascarán 22,205 ft. (6,768 m) ▲

Tapajós River

Xingu River

Tocantins R.

São Francisco River

Cook Islands

Tuamotu Archipelago

Society Islands

Mato Grosso Plateau

Brazilian Highlands

Lake Titicaca

Altiplano

SOUTH AMERICA

Tropic of Capricorn

Atacama Desert

MOUNTAINS

Gran Chaco

Paraguay R.

Iguazú Falls

0   1,000   2,000 Miles

0   1,000   2,000 Kilometers

Miller Cylindrical Projection

Mt. Aconcagua 22,834 ft. (6,960 m) ▲

Paraná R.

Uruguay R.

Rio de la Plata

Pampa

30°S

▲ Mountain peak

▼ Point below sea level

── National border

≈ Waterfall

N
W · E
S

Patagonia

Valdés Peninsula (lowest point in S.A.) -131 ft. (-40 m) ▼

Cape São Roque

Falkland Islands

South Georgia

A9

Strait of Magellan

Tierra del Fuego

Cape Horn

150°W   120°W   90°W   60°W   30°W

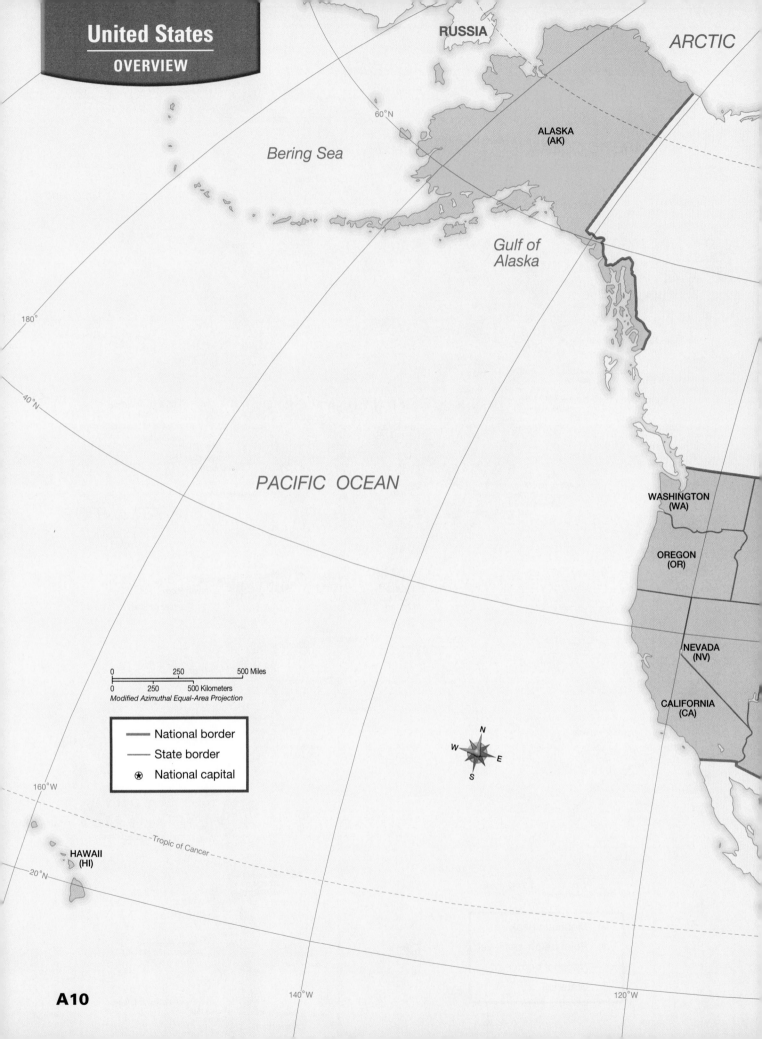

RUSSIA

ARCTIC

60°N

Bering Sea

ALASKA
(AK)

Gulf of
Alaska

180°

40°N

PACIFIC OCEAN

WASHINGTON
(WA)

OREGON
(OR)

NEVADA
(NV)

0	250	500 Miles
0	250	500 Kilometers

Modified Azimuthal Equal-Area Projection

CALIFORNIA
(CA)

——— National border
——— State border
⊛ National capital

N
W ✦ E
S

160°W

Tropic of Cancer

HAWAII
(HI)

20°N

140°W

120°W

United States
POLITICAL

CANADA

ARCTIC OCEAN

RUSSIA
170° E
70° N
120° W
60° N
ALASKA
CANADA
Arctic Circle
Yukon River
Fairbanks
Yukon River
Bering Sea
180°
60° N
Anchorage
Gulf of Alaska
Juneau
PACIFIC OCEAN
50° N
170° W
160° W
150° W
140° W
130° W

130° W
120° W
110° W

40° N

Northeast	⊛	National capital
South	★	State capital
Middle West	•	Major city
West	—	National border
	—	State border

Seattle
Tacoma
Olympia
Spokane
WASHINGTON
Portland
Columbia River
Salem
Eugene
OREGON
Great Falls
Helena MONTANA
Billings
Yellowstone R.
IDAHO
Boise
Snake River
Pocatello
WYOMING
Casper

PACIFIC
OCEAN

130° W

30° N

NEVADA
Lake Tahoe
Reno
Sacramento
Carson City
San Francisco
Oakland
San Jose
Fresno
CALIFORNIA
Bakersfield
Las Vegas
Los Angeles
San Bernardino
San Diego

Great Salt Lake
Ogden
Salt Lake City
Provo
UTAH
Colorado River
Cheyenne
Denver
Colorado Springs
COLORADO
Pueblo

Flagstaff
ARIZONA
Phoenix
Tucson
Santa Fe
Albuquerque
NEW MEXICO
Roswell
El Paso
Rio Grande

MEXICO

N
W E
S

160° W 155° W
PACIFIC OCEAN
Honolulu
HAWAII
Hilo
20° N

0 100 200 Miles
0 100 200 Kilometers

0 250 500 Miles
0 250 500 Kilometers
Albers Equal-Area Projection

120° W 110° W

20° N

A12

0 250 500 Miles
0 250 500 Kilometers

100°W 90°W 80°W 70°W

CANADA

MAINE

50°N

Lake of the Woods

Lake Superior

St. Lawrence River

Augusta

VERMONT

Lake Champlain

Burlington
Montpelier

NORTH DAKOTA   Grand Forks

Duluth

Sault Sainte Marie

Portland

NEW HAMPSHIRE

Bismarck   Fargo

MINNESOTA

MICHIGAN

Lake Huron

NEW YORK   Manchester   Concord

Boston

SOUTH DAKOTA

St. Paul
Minneapolis

Green Bay

WISCONSIN

Lake Michigan

Rapid City   Pierre

Sioux Falls

Madison

Milwaukee

Grand Rapids   Flint
Lansing

Syracuse

Albany

MASSACHUSETTS
Worcester   Providence

Rochester

RHODE ISLAND

Hartford   CONNECTICUT

Detroit

Lake St. Clair

Cleveland

Lake Erie

Buffalo

Bridgeport

40°N

Sioux City

IOWA   Cedar Rapids

Rockford

PENNSYLVANIA

Newark   New York City

NEBRASKA

Davenport

Chicago

Gary   South Bend

Toledo

Akron

Harrisburg

Trenton   NEW JERSEY
Philadelphia

Omaha

Des Moines

ILLINOIS

OHIO

Columbus

Wheeling

Pittsburgh

Wilmington
Dover

Lincoln

Peoria

INDIANA

Dayton

Baltimore

DELAWARE

70°N

Platte River

Decatur

Springfield

Indianapolis

Cincinnati

WEST VIRGINIA

Washington   Annapolis   D.C.   MARYLAND

Topeka

Missouri River

St. Louis

Louisville

Frankfort

Charleston

VIRGINIA   Richmond

KANSAS   Kansas City

Jefferson City

Ohio River   Lexington

Newport News

Norfolk

Wichita

MISSOURI

Evansville   KENTUCKY

Roanoke

Springfield

Greensboro

OKLAHOMA   Tulsa

Knoxville

Winston-Salem

Raleigh

Nashville

ATLANTIC OCEAN

ARKANSAS

TENNESSEE

Charlotte   NORTH CAROLINA

Amarillo   Oklahoma City

Arkansas River

Chattanooga

Fort Smith

Memphis

Huntsville

SOUTH CAROLINA

Lake Texoma

Little Rock

Atlanta

Columbia

Charleston

Lubbock

Red River

Birmingham

GEORGIA

Fort Worth

Mississippi River

Meridian

ALABAMA

Macon

Savannah

Abilene   Dallas

Shreveport

Columbus

30°N

Odessa

TEXAS

Jackson

MISSISSIPPI

Montgomery

Jacksonville

Tallahassee

Austin   Beaumont   Baton Rouge

LOUISIANA

Biloxi   Mobile

Houston

New Orleans

FLORIDA

San Antonio

Orlando

Rio Grande

Tampa

West Palm Beach

Laredo   Corpus Christi

St. Petersburg   Lake Okeechobee

BAHAMAS

Gulf of Mexico

Miami

80°W

CUBA

100°W   90°W

A13

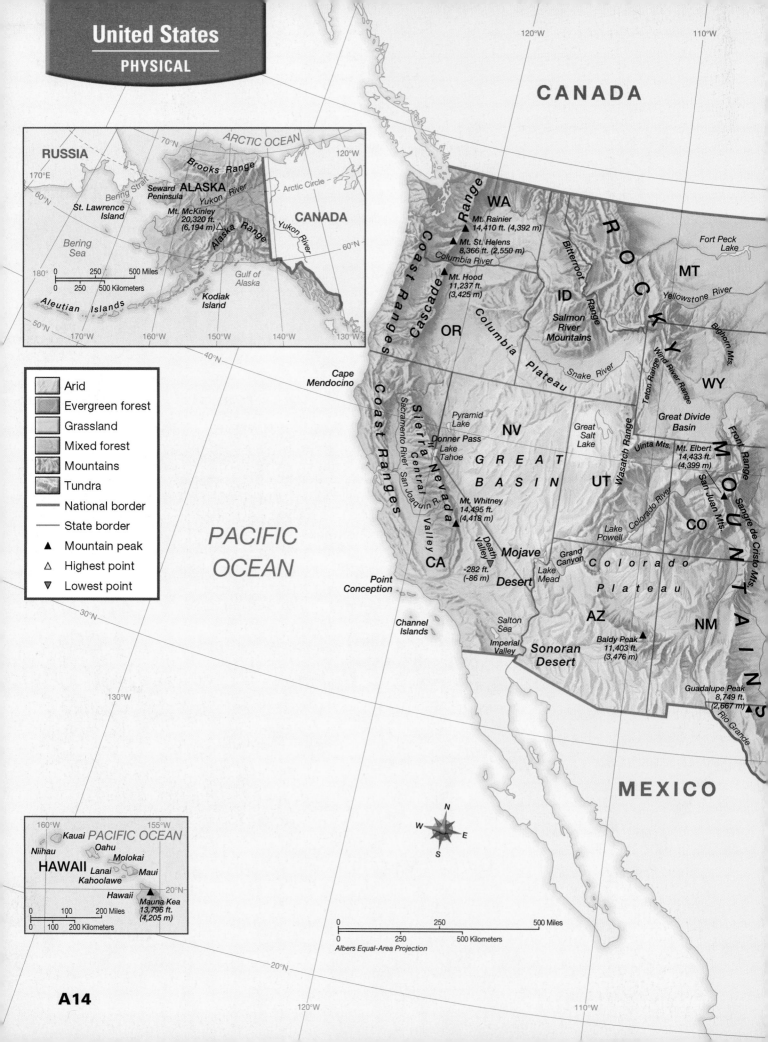

United States
PHYSICAL

CANADA

120°W   110°W

RUSSIA

ARCTIC OCEAN

170°E

70°N   Brooks   Range

Bering Strait

Seward Peninsula   ALASKA

Yukon River

60°N   St. Lawrence Island

Arctic Circle

120°W

CANADA

Mt. McKinley 20,320 ft. (6,194 m) △   Alaska   Range

Yukon River

60°N

Bering Sea

Gulf of Alaska

250   500 Miles

180°   0   250   500 Kilometers

Aleutian   Islands

Kodiak Island

50°N   170°W   160°W   150°W   140°W   130°W

40°N

Cape Mendocino

PACIFIC OCEAN

Legend
- Arid
- Evergreen forest
- Grassland
- Mixed forest
- Mountains
- Tundra
- ⎯ National border
- ⎯ State border
- ▲ Mountain peak
- △ Highest point
- ▽ Lowest point

30°N

Point Conception

Channel Islands

Coast Ranges

WA

Mt. Rainier 14,410 ft. (4,392 m) ▲

Mt. St. Helens 8,366 ft. (2,550 m) ▲

Columbia River

Mt. Hood 11,237 ft. (3,425 m) ▲

OR

Columbia Plateau

Bitterroot Range

ID

Salmon River Mountains

Snake River

Coast Ranges

Sierra Nevada

Sacramento River

San Joaquin R.

Central Valley

Pyramid Lake

Donner Pass
Lake Tahoe

NV

G R E A T

B A S I N

Great Salt Lake

Wasatch Range

Uinta Mts.

UT

Colorado River

Lake Powell

Mt. Whitney 14,495 ft. (4,418 m) ▲

Death Valley ▽ -282 ft. (-86 m)

Mojave

CA   Desert

Lake Mead

Grand Canyon

Salton Sea

Imperial Valley

Sonoran Desert

AZ

Colorado

Plateau

Baldy Peak 11,403 ft. (3,476 m) ▲

R O C K Y

Fort Peck Lake

MT

Yellowstone River

Bighorn Mts.

Teton Range   Wind River Range

WY

Great Divide Basin

Mt. Elbert 14,433 ft. (4,399 m) ▲

M O U N T A I N S

San Juan Mts.

CO

Front Range

Sangre de Cristo Mts.

NM

Guadalupe Peak 8,749 ft. (2,667 m) ▲

Rio Grande

MEXICO

N
W   E
S

250   500 Miles

0   250   500 Kilometers

Albers Equal-Area Projection

160°W   155°W

Kauai   PACIFIC OCEAN

Niihau   Oahu

Molokai

HAWAII   Lanai   Maui

Kahoolawe

Hawaii   20°N

Mauna Kea 13,796 ft. (4,205 m) ▲

0   100   200 Miles

0   100   200 Kilometers

30°N

20°N

130°W   120°W   110°W

A14

A15

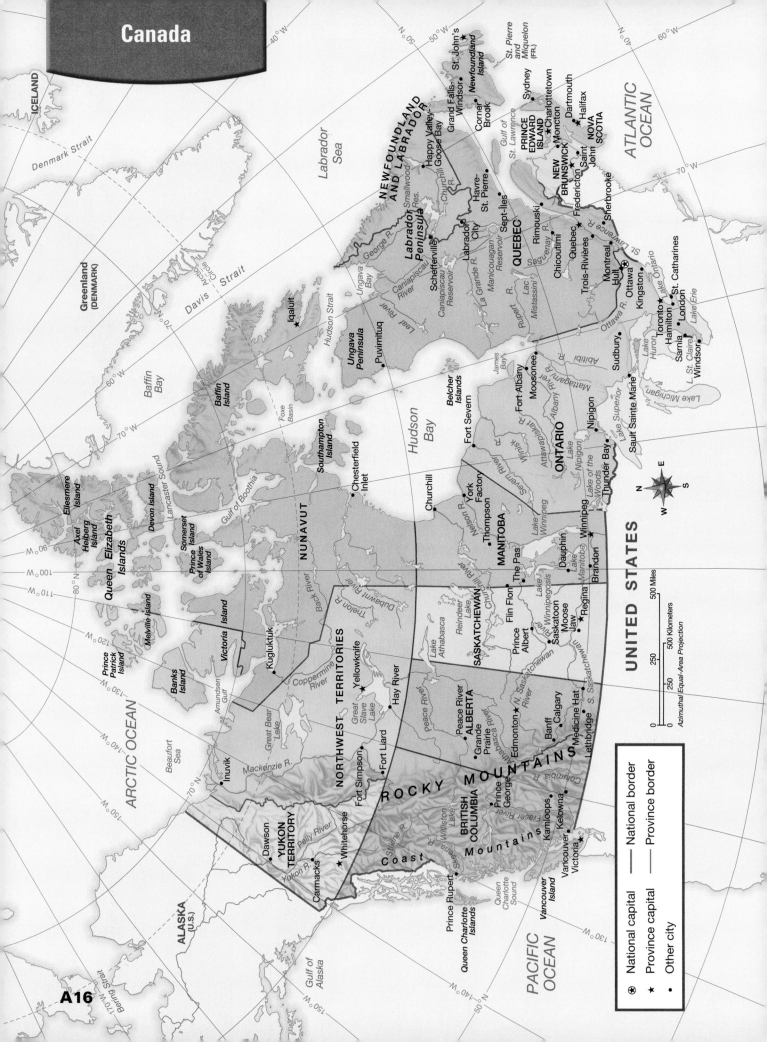

Canada

ICELAND

Denmark Strait

Greenland (DENMARK)

ARCTIC OCEAN

Baffin Bay

Davis Strait

Labrador Sea

ATLANTIC OCEAN

Ellesmere Island

Axel Heiberg Island

Queen Elizabeth Islands

Devon Island

Somerset Island

Prince of Wales Island

Baffin Island

Melville Island

Prince Patrick Island

Banks Island

Victoria Island

Amundsen Gulf

Great Bear Lake

Beaufort Sea

Gulf of Alaska

Bering Strait

ALASKA (U.S.)

Inuvik

Mackenzie R.

Dawson

YUKON TERRITORY

Whitehorse

Carmacks

Pelly River

Yukon R.

Stikine R.

Coast Mountains

Prince Rupert

Queen Charlotte Islands

Queen Charlotte Sound

Vancouver Island

PACIFIC OCEAN

Iqaluit

Foxe Basin

Southampton Island

Chesterfield Inlet

Gulf of Boothia

Lancaster Sound

Hudson Strait

NUNAVUT

Back River

Dubawnt River

Thelon R.

Kugluktuk

Coppermine River

Yellowknife

Great Slave Lake

Hay River

Fort Liard

Fort Simpson

NORTHWEST TERRITORIES

Ungava Bay

Ungava Peninsula

Puvirnituq

Belcher Islands

Hudson Bay

Fort Severn

Churchill

York Factory

Thompson

Nelson R.

The Pas

Flin Flon

Reindeer Lake

Lake Athabasca

Peace River

Peace River

Grande Prairie

Athabasca River

Edmonton

ALBERTA

Banff

Calgary

Medicine Hat

Lethbridge

ROCKY MOUNTAINS

BRITISH COLUMBIA

Prince George

Fraser River

Williston Lake

Columbia R.

Kamloops

Kelowna

Vancouver

Victoria

NEWFOUNDLAND AND LABRADOR

Labrador Peninsula

George R.

Smallwood Res.

Churchill R.

Happy Valley-Goose Bay

Grand Falls-Windsor

Corner Brook

Newfoundland Island

St. John's

St. Pierre and Miquelon (FR.)

Schefferville

Labrador City

Havre-St. Pierre

Sept-Îles

Caniapiscau Reservoir

Caniapiscau River

La Grande R.

Manicouagan Reservoir

Leaf River

QUEBEC

Rupert R.

Lac Mistassini

Saguenay R.

Chicoutimi

Quebec

Trois-Rivières

Rimouski

Gulf of St. Lawrence

PRINCE EDWARD ISLAND

Charlottetown

Sydney

NOVA SCOTIA

Halifax

Dartmouth

Moncton

NEW BRUNSWICK

Fredericton

Saint John

Sherbrooke

St. Lawrence R.

Montreal

Hull

Ottawa

Kingston

Ottawa R.

Lake Ontario

Toronto

Hamilton

St. Catharines

London

Sarnia

Windsor

Lake Erie

L. St. Claire

Lake Huron

Lake Michigan

Sudbury

ONTARIO

Moosonee

Fort Albany

Attawapiskat R.

Albany River

Mattagami R.

Abitibi R.

Nipigon

Lake Nipigon

Thunder Bay

Sault Sainte Marie

Lake Superior

Lake of the Woods

Winnipeg

Lake Winnipeg

Lake Manitoba

MANITOBA

Dauphin

Brandon

Lake Winnipegosis

Churchill R.

Severn River

Winisk

Winisk R.

SASKATCHEWAN

Prince Albert

Saskatoon

Moose Jaw

Regina

N. Saskatchewan River

S. Saskatchewan River

Medicine Hat

UNITED STATES

ATLANTIC OCEAN

Legend

- ⊛ National capital
- ★ Province capital
- • Other city

National border
Province border

500 Miles

500 Kilometers

250

250

0

Azimuthal/Equal-Area Projection

N E S W

A16

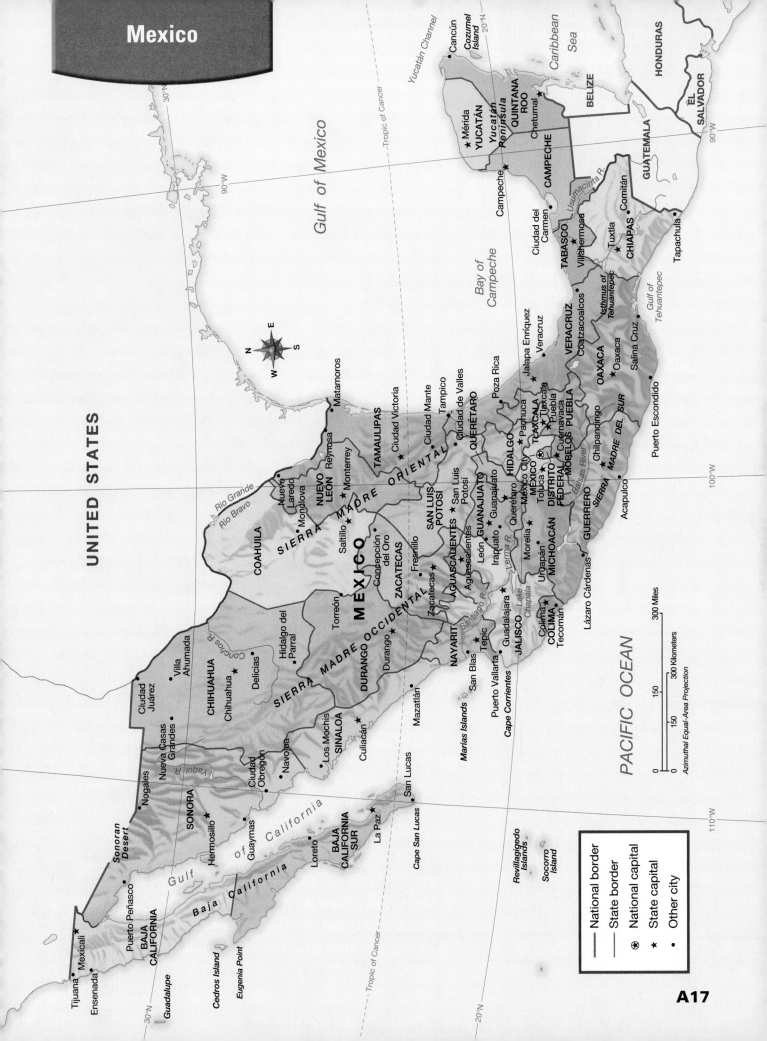

Mexico

UNITED STATES

Gulf of Mexico

Yucatán Channel

Caribbean Sea

HONDURAS

EL SALVADOR

BELIZE

GUATEMALA

Cancún
Cozumel Island
Mérida • YUCATÁN
Yucatán Peninsula
QUINTANA ROO
Chetumal
CAMPECHE
Campeche
Ciudad del Carmen
TABASCO
Villahermosa
Comitán
CHIAPAS
Tuxtla
Tapachula
Usumacinta R.

Bay of Campeche

VERACRUZ
Coatzacoalcos
Isthmus of Tehuantepec
Gulf of Tehuantepec
Jalapa Enríquez
Veracruz
OAXACA
Oaxaca
Salina Cruz
Puerto Escondido

Tropic of Cancer

Matamoros
Reynosa
Nuevo Laredo
Monclova
Monterrey
NUEVO LEÓN
Saltillo
COAHUILA
Concepción del Oro
SIERRA MADRE ORIENTAL
TAMAULIPAS
Ciudad Victoria
Ciudad Mante
Ciudad de Valles
Tampico
Poza Rica
Pachuca
HIDALGO
SAN LUIS POTOSÍ
San Luis Potosí
QUERÉTARO
Ciudad de Querétaro
MÉXICO
TLAXCALA
Tlaxcala
Puebla
Cuernavaca
MORELOS PUEBLA
Toluca
DISTRITO FEDERAL
MEXICO City
Balsas River
Chilpancingo
GUERRERO
SIERRA MADRE DEL SUR
Acapulco

Rio Grande
Rio Bravo

MEXICO

ZACATECAS
Zacatecas
Fresnillo
Concepción del Oro
AGUASCALIENTES
Aguascalientes
GUANAJUATO
León
Irapuato
Guanajuato
Querétaro
Lerma R.
Morelia
MICHOACÁN
Uruapan
Lázaro Cárdenas

DURANGO
Durango
Hidalgo del Parral
SIERRA MADRE OCCIDENTAL
Torreón
Santiago R.
Lake Chapala
JALISCO
Guadalajara
NAYARIT
Tepic
Colima
COLIMA
Tecomán

Concnos R.
CHIHUAHUA
Chihuahua
Delicias
Villa Ahumada
Ciudad Juárez
Nueva Casas Grandes
Mazatlán
SINALOA
Culiacán
Los Mochis
Navojoa
Ciudad Obregón
San Blas
Puerto Vallarta
Cape Corrientes

Yaqui R.
SONORA
Nogales
Hermosillo
Guaymas
Loreto
Gulf of California
BAJA CALIFORNIA SUR
La Paz
San Lucas
San Lucas
Cape San Lucas

Sonoran Desert
BAJA CALIFORNIA
Puerto Peñasco
Mexicali
Tijuana
Ensenada
Guadalupe
Cedros Island
Eugenia Point

Baja California

Marías Islands

Revillagigedo Islands
Socorro Island

PACIFIC OCEAN

300 Miles
300 Kilometers
150
150
0
0
Azimuthal Equal-Area Projection

Tropic of Cancer

30°N
20°N
110°W
100°W
90°W
30°W
20°N

N E S W

National border
State border
National capital
State capital
Other city

A17

Geography Terms

1. **basin** — bowl-shaped area of land surrounded by higher land
2. **bay** — an inlet of the sea or some other body of water, usually smaller than a gulf
3. **bluff** — high, steep face of rock or earth
4. **canyon** — deep, narrow valley with steep sides
5. **cape** — point of land that extends into water
6. **cataract** — large waterfall
7. **channel** — deepest part of a body of water
8. **cliff** — high, steep face of rock or earth
9. **coast** — land along a sea or ocean
10. **coastal plain** — area of flat land along a sea or ocean
11. **delta** — triangle-shaped area of land at the mouth of a river
12. **desert** — dry land with few plants
13. **dune** — hill of sand piled up by the wind

14. **fall line** — area along which rivers form waterfalls or rapids as the rivers drop to lower land
15. **floodplain** — flat land that is near the edges of a river and is formed by silt deposited by floods
16. **foothills** — hilly area at the base of a mountain
17. **glacier** — large ice mass that moves slowly down a mountain or across land
18. **gulf** — part of a sea or ocean extending into the land, usually larger than a bay
19. **hill** — land that rises above the land around it
20. **inlet** — any area of water extending into the land from a larger body of water
21. **island** — land that has water on all sides
22. **isthmus** — narrow strip of land connecting two larger areas of land
23. **lagoon** — body of shallow water
24. **lake** — body of water with land on all sides

26 **mesa** flat-topped mountain with steep sides	**40** **savanna** area of grassland and scattered trees
27 **mountain** highest kind of land	**41** **sea** body of salt water smaller than an ocean
28 **mountain pass** gap between mountains	**42** **sea level** the level of the surface of an ocean or a sea
29 **mountain range** row of mountains	
30 **mouth of river** place where a river empties into another body of water	**43** **slope** side of a hill or mountain
	44 **source of river** place where a river begins
31 **oasis** area of water and fertile land in a desert	**45** **strait** narrow channel of water connecting two larger bodies of water
32 **ocean** body of salt water larger than a sea	
33 **peak** top of a mountain	**46** **swamp** area of low, wet land with trees
34 **peninsula** land that is almost completely surrounded by water	**47** **timberline** line on a mountain above which it is too cold for trees to grow
35 **plain** area of flat or gently rolling low land	**48** **tributary** stream or river that flows into a larger stream or river
36 **plateau** area of high, mostly flat land	**49** **valley** low land between hills or mountains
37 **reef** ridge of sand, rock, or coral that lies at or near the surface of a sea or ocean	**50** **volcano** opening in the earth, often raised, through which lava, rock, ashes, and gases are forced out
38 **river** large stream of water that flows across the land	
39 **riverbank** land along a river	**51** **waterfall** steep drop from a high place to a lower place in a stream or river

A19

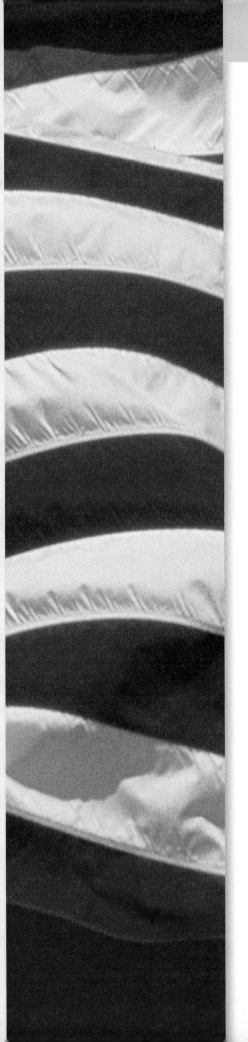

Introduction

"The history of every country begins with the heart of a man or a woman"

—Willa Cather, *O Pioneers!*, 1913

Learning About Our Country

This year in social studies, you will be studying the United States, past and present. You will learn about past events and the places where those events occurred. You will also read about people who helped shape our country. You will see how people have worked together to meet their needs and wants and to govern themselves. You will learn what it means to be a citizen of the United States.

Civics and Government

Culture and Society

What Is Social Studies?

History

Economics

Geography

Why History Matters

Studying **history**, or what happened in the past, helps you see how the past and the present are linked. Studying history also helps you understand how the events of today may be linked to the future. As you learn to recognize these links, you will begin to think more like a historian, a person who studies the past.

Measuring Time

One way historians see connections in history is by studying the order in which events happened. The order of events is called their **chronology** (kruh•NAH•luh•jee). By looking at the chronology of events, historians can learn how the past is connected to the present.

Finding Evidence

Historians study the past by looking for clues in the objects and documents that people have left behind. They read journal entries, newspaper articles, and other writings by people who experienced past events. They also listen to or read records of oral histories. An **oral history** is a story of an event or an experience told aloud by a person who did not have a written language or who did not write down what happened. Historians also look at photographs, films, and artwork. By examining such clues, historians can piece together what took place in the past and can better explain why they think events happened as they did.

In the past and the present, many people from other countries have chosen to immigrate to the United States.

In the past, many immigrants to the United States arrived by boat at Ellis Island in New York. The letters and diaries and oral histories of the immigrants tell much about their adventures.

2

Identifying Points of View

Historians examine people's points of view. A person's **point of view** is how he or she sees things. It can depend on whether that person is old or young, a man or a woman, rich or poor. A point of view is also shaped by a person's background and experiences. People with different points of view may see the same event differently.

Historians learn about the times and places in which people lived. They study how scientific discoveries and new ways of doing things affected people's lives. In that way, historians can understand earlier people's actions and feelings. This understanding is called **historical empathy** (EM•puh•thee).

Understanding Frames of Reference

Historians also work hard to understand people's **frames of reference**. A frame of reference includes where people were when an event took place and what part they took in it. Historians must be careful not to judge the actions of people in the past based on the way people of today would act.

Drawing Conclusions

Many events in history are connected to other events. To **analyze** an event, historians look closely at how the parts of it connect with one another and how the event is connected to other events. Analyzing an event allows historians to draw conclusions about how and why it happened.

REVIEW Why is it important to study history?

This display at Ellis Island shows a few of the people who arrived there. Immigrants to the United States have many different backgrounds and experiences. This may lead them to have different points of view.

Immigrants wait at Ellis Island. Historians use photographs like this one to draw conclusions about early United States immigration.

·SKILLS· Compare Primary and Secondary Sources

▶ WHY IT MATTERS

To know what really happened in the past, you need to find proof. You can do this by studying and comparing two kinds of sources—primary sources and secondary sources.

▶ WHAT YOU NEED TO KNOW

Primary sources are the records made by people who saw or took part in an event. These people may have written down their thoughts in a journal, or they may have told their story in a letter or a poem. They may have made a speech, produced a film, taken a photograph, or painted a picture. Primary sources may also be objects or official documents that give information about the time in which they were made or written. A primary source gives people of today a direct link to a past event.

This photograph **Ⓐ**, letter **Ⓑ**, and pen and ink bottle **Ⓒ** are all examples of primary sources from the time of the Civil War.

A **secondary source** is not a direct link to an event. It is a record of the event written by someone who was not there at the time. A magazine article, newspaper story, or book written by someone who only heard about or read about the event is a secondary source. So is an object made at a later time.

Some sources can be either primary or secondary, depending on how the event is reported. A newspaper might print the exact words of a person who saw the event take place. It might also print an article about the event, written by a reporter who was not there. Oral histories, textbooks, and online resources can also be either primary or secondary sources.

▶ **PRACTICE THE SKILL**

Look at the photographs of objects and printed materials that give information about the American Civil War. Then answer these questions.

1 How are items A and F alike and different?

2 What kind of information might be found in item B but not in item D?

3 Why might secondary sources D and E also be considered primary sources?

▶ **APPLY WHAT YOU LEARNED**

Look through your textbook for examples of primary and secondary sources. Explain to a classmate what makes each source you selected a primary source or a secondary source.

This newspaper **D**, Civil War Web site **E**, and recent photograph of people dressed as Civil War soldiers **F** are secondary sources.

Why Geography Matters

Every event you will read about in this book has a setting, and part of the setting is the place where the event happened. Learning about places is an important part of **geography**—the study of Earth's surface and the way people use it. People who study geography are called geographers.

The Five Themes of Geography

Geographers often speak of five main themes when they study a place. You will find that most of the maps in this book focus on one of these themes. Keeping these themes in mind as you read will help you think like a geographer.

Human-Environment Interactions

Humans and their surroundings interact, or affect each other. People's activities may **modify**, or change, the environment. The environment may affect people, causing them to **adapt**, or adjust, to their surroundings.

Location

Everything on Earth has its own **location**—the place where it can be found.

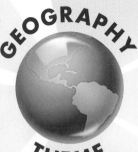

GEOGRAPHY THEME

Movement

Each day, people in different parts of the country and around the world exchange products and ideas.

Place

Every location has features that make it different from all other locations. **Physical features** are formed by nature. **Human features** are created by people.

Regions

Areas of Earth that share features that make them different from other areas are called **regions**. A region can be described by its physical features or human features.

Essential Elements of Geography

Geographers also use six other topics when they study a place. These six topics are called the six essential elements of geography. Thinking about them will help you understand the world around you.

• GEOGRAPHY •

The World in Spatial Terms

Geographers use maps and other kinds of information to study relationships among people and places. They want to know why things are located where they are.

Human Systems

People's activities include where they settle, how they earn a living, and the laws they make. All of these help shape Earth's surface.

Places and Regions

People are linked to the places and regions in which they live. Places and regions have both physical and human features.

Environment and Society

People's activities often affect the environment, and the environment affects people's activities.

Physical Systems

Physical processes, such as wind and rain, shape Earth's surface. Living things interact with physical features to create and change environments.

The Uses of Geography

Knowing how to use maps, globes, and other geography tools helps people in their everyday lives.

REVIEW What is geography?

Why Economics Matters

VOCABULARY

economy
economics

Have you ever earned money for doing chores? Did you use the money to buy something you needed or wanted? When you do these things, you are taking part in the economy. An **economy** is the way people of a state, a region, or a country use resources to meet their needs. The study of how people do this is called **economics**.

In this book you will read about how people in the past made, bought, sold, and traded goods to meet their needs. You will learn how the economy of the United States changed over time to become one in which businesses are free to sell many kinds of goods and services.

REVIEW How are resources important to a country's economy?

Farmland (above) is just one of the many resources people use to meet their needs. Paper money and coins (top right) are used in the economy to buy and sell goods. Children as well as adults find it wise to save money for the future (bottom right).

Why Civics and Government Matter

VOCABULARY

civics   civic participation   government

"Ask not what your country can do for you; ask what you can do for your country." When President John F. Kennedy said these words in 1961, he was talking about another key area of social studies—civics. **Civics** is the study of citizenship. In this textbook you will read about the rights and responsibilities of citizens of the United States. You will also learn about the importance of **civic participation**. Civic participation is being concerned with and involved in issues related to your community, state, or country or the entire world.

In the United States, citizens have an important part in making government work. A **government** is a system of leaders and laws that helps people live together in their community, state, or country. It protects citizens and settles disagreements among them. In this book you will read about the people and events that shaped government in the past. You will also find out how government works today.

REVIEW How is civics different from government?

The Constitution of the United States (below left) and the United States Capitol building (below right) are both symbols of American government.

Why Culture and Society Matter

In this book you will read about people of the past who helped shape the present. You will learn about their customs and beliefs, their families and communities, and the ways they made a living. All these things make up a **culture**, or way of life.

Each human group, or **society**, has a culture. This book will help you discover the many cultures of our country, both now and in the past. You will also learn about our country's **heritage**, or culture that has come from the past and continues today.

REVIEW How are the terms *culture* and *society* related?

The photograph above gives a glimpse of Mexican culture within the United States. The photograph below shows the many different heritages of the students in a Gary, Indiana, classroom of long ago.

The Land and Early People

A Cheyenne shield,
1860–1868

Paria Canyon, Vermillion Cliffs National Monument, Arizona

The Land and Early People

> 66 **And the People came to live in the Northern Mountains and on the Plains, in the Western Hills and on the Seacoasts, in the Southern Deserts and in the Canyons.** 99
>
> —Simon Ortiz, *The People Shall Continue*, 1977

Preview the Content

Scan the pictures in each chapter and lesson. Use them to create a list of topics you will learn about in Unit 1.

Preview the Vocabulary

Word Meanings   Write what you think each word below means and why. Use the Glossary to check your answers.

WORD	POSSIBLE MEANING	WHY
savanna		
tepee		
wampum		

Brooks Range

Beaufort Sea

Bering Sea

Yukon River

Victoria Island

Aleutian Islands

Alaska Range

Mount McKinley 20,320 ft (6,194 m)

Gulf of Alaska

Great Bear Lake

CANADIAN

Mackenzie River

Great Slave Lake

Hudson Bay

Lake Winnipeg

GREAT PLAINS

Vancouver Island

Columbia River

Coast Ranges

Cascade Range

ROCKY MOUNTAINS

Missouri River

Lake Superior

Mississippi River

Lake Michigan

PACIFIC OCEAN

Crater Lake

Great Salt Lake

GREAT BASIN

Sierra Nevada

Coast Ranges

Death Valley

Colorado River

Grand Canyon

Arkansas River

Sonoran Desert

Baja California

Gulf of California

Rio Grande

Sierra Madre Occidental

Sierra Madre Oriental

Yucatán Peninsula

Río Balsas

Hawaiian Islands

0   500   1,000 Miles
0   500   1,000 Kilometers
Modified Azimuthal Equal-Area Projection

N W E S

Key Events

12,000 years ago

8,000 years ago

About 10,000 years ago ancient Indians hunted large animals   p. 62

About 5,000 years ago ancient Indians begin farming   p. 64

About 3,500 years ago the Olmec civilization lived in North America   p. 65

12

North America

Baffin Bay
Baffin Island
Greenland
Labrador Sea
Labrador
SHIELD
Newfoundland
Lake Huron
St. Lawrence River
Lake Ontario
L. Erie
Ohio River
APPALACHIAN MOUNTAINS
Mammoth Cave
COASTAL PLAIN

ATLANTIC OCEAN

Gulf of Mexico
Bahamas
Cuba
Caribbean Sea
Hispaniola
Puerto Rico

Facts About United States Geography

PHYSICAL FEATURE	LOCATION
Largest Gorge	Grand Canyon, Nevada/Arizona
Largest Freshwater Lake	Lake Superior
Deepest Lake	Crater Lake, Oregon
Longest River	Mississippi River
Highest Mountain	Mount McKinley, Alaska
Lowest Point	Death Valley, California
Largest Cave	Mammoth Cave, Kentucky

United States Population

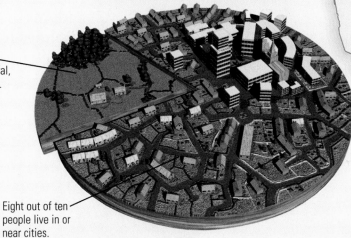

Two out of ten people live in rural, or country, areas.

Eight out of ten people live in or near cities.

4,000 years ago

PRESENT

About 1,000 years ago the Navajos moved to the Southwest p. 72

By 800 years ago more than 30,000 people lived in Cahokia p. 66

About 700 years ago the Iroquois lived in the Northeast p. 89

START with a POEM

Between Earth & Sky
LEGENDS OF NATIVE AMERICAN SACRED PLACES
Joseph Bruchac   Thomas Locker

IF WE SHOULD
TRAVEL

by Joseph Bruchac

Many people use poems, songs, or stories to tell about important events and people in their past. Some of these stories are legends. A legend is a story handed down by a group of people over time. Some legends tell about brave or heroic people. Others try to explain the origins of animals, plants, and physical features found in the world.

If we should travel
far to the South,
there in the land
of mountains and mist,
we might hear the story
of how Earth was first shaped.

Water Beetle came out
to see if it was ready,
but the ground was
still as wet as a swamp,
too soft for anyone to stand.

Great Buzzard said, "I will help dry the land."
He began to fly close above the new Earth.
Where his wings came down,
valleys were formed,
and where his wings lifted,
hills rose up through the mist.

So the many rolling valleys and hills
of that place called the Great Smokies
came into being there.
And so it is that the Cherokee people,
aware of how this land was given,
know that the Earth is a sacred gift
we all must respect and share.

Analyze the Literature

READ A BOOK

TIME FOR KIDS READERS
Meet a Weather Forecaster
by Terry Slevin
Harcourt

TIME FOR KIDS READERS
THE MIGHTY Mississippi
Harcourt

TIME FOR KIDS READERS
ONCE THERE WERE ANASAZI
Harcourt

START THE UNIT PROJECT

A Multimedia Presentation
Work with your classmates to create a multimedia presentation about the landforms and early people of the United States. As you study the unit, write down the landforms you read about and tell how early people used the natural resources around them.

USE TECHNOLOGY

Visit The Learning Site at

GRAND TETON NATIONAL PARK

The Grand Teton Mountain Range is located in the Cowboy State of Wyoming. In this photograph, the Snake River winds its way near the mountains. Twelve peaks in the mountain range reach above 12,000 feet (4 km).

LOCATE IT

Grand Teton National Park

Snake R.

WYOMING

1

Our Country's Geography

❝ O beautiful for spacious skies,
For amber waves of grain,
For purple mountain majesties
Above the fruited plain! ❞
—from the poem "America the Beautiful"
by Katharine Lee Bates, 1893

CHAPTER READING SKILL

Main Idea and Supporting Details

The **main idea** of a paragraph or lesson is what it is mostly about. The main idea may be stated in a sentence, or it may only be suggested. **Supporting details** give more information about the main idea.

As you read this chapter, list the main ideas and show how those ideas are supported with details.

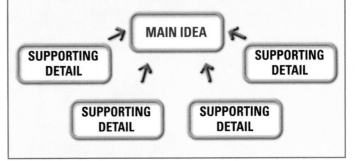

MAIN IDEA

Read to learn how the United States can be divided into regions based on different kinds of land.

WHY IT MATTERS

Learning about kinds of land will help you understand how areas of the country are similar and how they are different.

VOCABULARY

landform
mountain range
piedmont
sea level
plateau
basin
volcano

Land and Regions

In 1893 the poet Katharine Lee Bates saw the Rocky Mountains for the first time. She was in Colorado on a tour. "One day some of the other teachers and I decided to go on a trip to 14,000-foot (4,267-m) Pikes Peak," she later wrote. "We hired a prairie wagon. Near the top we had to leave the wagon and go the rest of the way on mules. I was very tired. But when I saw the view, I felt great joy. All the wonder of America seemed displayed there, with the sea-like expanse." By the time she left Colorado, Bates had written the opening lines to her poem "America the Beautiful." Her poem later became a well-known song when it was set to music.

Landform Regions

The United States is more than a land of beauty. It is also a land of many different places. To better study the land of the United States, geographers often divide it into landform regions. A landform region is a region that has similar land-forms throughout. **Landforms** are physical features on the Earth's surface, such as plains, mountains, hills, and valleys. Each landform is unique because of its shape and the way it came to be made.

All of the United States, except for the island state of Hawaii, is in North America. North America is one

LOCATE IT

COLORADO

Colorado
Springs

Pikes Peak

of the Earth's seven continents, or largest areas of land. In addition to sharing the continent of North America, the United States shares landform regions with its neighbors, Canada and Mexico.

REVIEW What are landform regions?

America's Largest Mountains

The two largest mountain ranges in the United States are the Appalachian (ap•uh•LAY•chee•uhn) Mountains and the Rocky Mountains. A **mountain range** is a group of connected mountains. The Appalachians cover much of the eastern United States. They stretch all the way from central Alabama to southeastern Canada. The Rocky Mountains cover much of the western United States. They extend north from Mexico through Canada and into Alaska.

Most scientists believe the Appalachian Mountains were formed more than 250 million years ago. Over time the mountains' peaks have been worn down. The highest peaks in the Appalachians are less than 7,000 feet (2,134 m) tall.

Most of the mountain peaks in the Appalachians are less than 3,500 feet (1,067 m) tall.

A large part of the Appalachians is made up of a series of ridges and valleys that run next to each other. Among these ridges are the Blue Ridge, Catskill, Pocono, and White Mountains. The area of high land on the eastern side of the Appalachians is called the Piedmont (PEED•mahnt). A **piedmont** is an area at or near the foot of a mountain. The Piedmont begins in New Jersey and stretches as far south as Alabama.

Pikes Peak (center) is one of many peaks that make up the Rocky Mountains.

FAST FACT

Pikes Peak was named for explorer Zebulon Pike. Because he did not have enough supplies, Pike was unable to climb to the top of the mountain he first saw in 1806. Today people can reach the top by using a highway or a mountain railway.

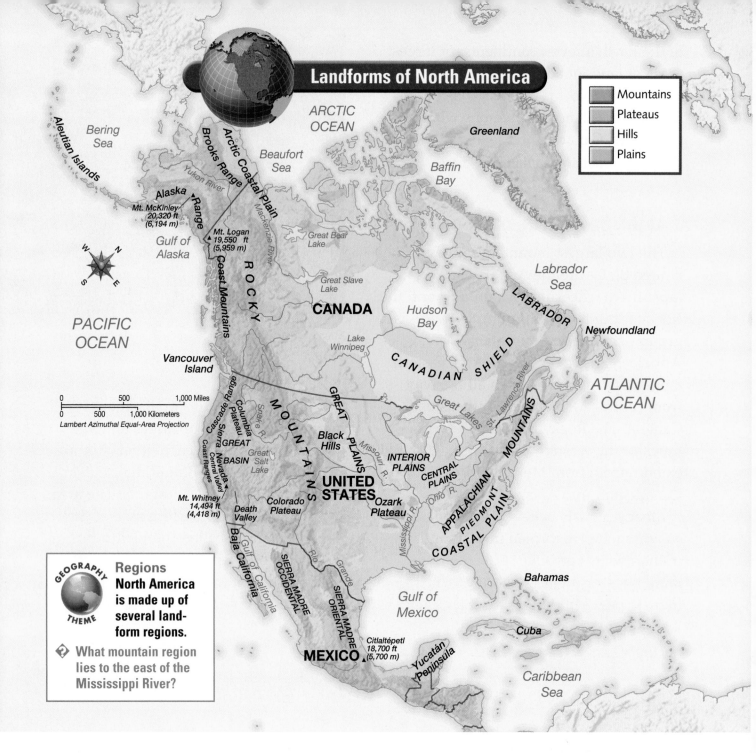

Landforms of North America

Mountains
Plateaus
Hills
Plains

ARCTIC OCEAN

Greenland

Bering Sea

Aleutian Islands

Brooks Range

Arctic Coastal Plain

Beaufort Sea

Baffin Bay

Yukon River

Alaska Range

Mt. McKinley 20,320 ft (6,194 m)

Mt. Logan 19,550 ft (5,959 m)

Gulf of Alaska

Great Bear Lake

Mackenzie River

ROCKY

Coast Mountains

Great Slave Lake

CANADA

Hudson Bay

Labrador Sea

LABRADOR

Newfoundland

PACIFIC OCEAN

Lake Winnipeg

CANADIAN SHIELD

ATLANTIC OCEAN

Vancouver Island

M O U N T A I N S

GREAT PLAINS

Great Lakes

St. Lawrence River

0   500   1,000 Miles
0   500   1,000 Kilometers
Lambert Azimuthal Equal-Area Projection

Cascade Range

Sierra Nevada

Columbia Plateau

Snake R.

GREAT BASIN

Great Salt Lake

Black Hills

Missouri R.

INTERIOR PLAINS

CENTRAL PLAINS

Ohio R.

APPALACHIAN MOUNTAINS

Coast Ranges

Central Valley

Mt. Whitney 14,494 ft (4,418 m)

Death Valley

Colorado Plateau

UNITED STATES

Ozark Plateau

PIEDMONT

COASTAL PLAIN

Baja California

Gulf of California

Rio Grande

SIERRA MADRE OCCIDENTAL

SIERRA MADRE ORIENTAL

Mississippi R.

Gulf of Mexico

Bahamas

Cuba

MEXICO

Citlaltépetl 18,700 ft (5,700 m)

Yucatán Peninsula

Caribbean Sea

GEOGRAPHY THEME

Regions
North America is made up of several land-form regions.

☑ What mountain region lies to the east of the Mississippi River?

Many scientists believe that most of the Rocky Mountains were formed more than 30 million years ago. Like the Appalachians, the Rocky Mountain Range is so large that it is made up of smaller ranges. Each range is separated from another by high plains and valleys.

Unlike the peaks of the Appalachians, the peaks of the Rockies appear sharp and jagged. They are also much higher

because they are newer and have not been worn down by wind and water for as long a time. More than 50 peaks in Colorado alone are higher than 14,000 feet (4,267 m). Because the Rockies are so high, many of the peaks are covered with snow all year.

REVIEW What mountain range covers much of the eastern United States? the western United States?

Regions of Plains

The two largest landform regions in the United States are plains—the Coastal Plain and the Interior Plains. A coastal plain is low, mostly flat land that lies along an ocean or another large body of water. The Coastal Plain stretches inland from the Atlantic Ocean and the Gulf of Mexico. The Interior Plains, also called the Interior Lowlands, extend across most of the center of the United States. The word *interior* means "the inside or inner part."

The Coastal Plain region begins along the Atlantic Ocean in Massachusetts. There it is only a narrow strip of land no more than 10 miles (16 km) wide. It gets wider—hundreds of miles wider—farther south toward Florida. From Florida the Coastal Plain extends west along the Gulf of Mexico into Texas and eastern Mexico. The land of the Coastal Plain region lies close to sea level and gradually rises inland. **Sea level** is the level of the surface of the oceans. It is used as a starting point in measuring the height and depth of landforms. Another, smaller coastal plain, the Arctic Coastal Plain, lies in northern Canada and Alaska.

The very large Interior Plains region stretches across the middle of North America, from the Appalachian Mountains in the east to the Rocky Mountains in the west. It extends north from Mexico, across the United States, and into Canada. In the eastern part of the Interior Plains, often called the Central Plains, the land is mostly flat to rolling with areas of forests to the east and grasslands to the west. Farther to the west, however, the land becomes much flatter and rises to meet the base of the Rocky Mountains. This western part of the Interior Plains is called the Great Plains. The Great Plains stretch from southern Texas into Canada.

While most of the land between the Appalachians and the Rockies is plains, there are areas with other kinds of landforms. To the north of the Interior Plains is the Canadian Shield. This rocky, horseshoe-shaped region wraps around Hudson Bay. There are hundreds of lakes in this region. In other places, such as the Black Hills of South Dakota and the Ozark Plateau (pla•TOH) in Missouri and Arkansas, the land rises very sharply to an area of hills and small mountains. A **plateau** is a broad area of high, mostly flat land.

REVIEW How is the location of the Coastal Plain different from that of the Interior Plains?

This wheat field in Kansas is a part of the miles and miles of flat land that makes up the Great Plains.

A Region of Basins, Ranges, and Plateaus

Between the Rocky Mountains and other mountain ranges farther west is a large area sometimes called the Intermountain Region. *Intermountain* means "between the mountains." Part of this land is the Great Basin, which includes Nevada and parts of five neighboring states. A **basin** is low, bowl-shaped land with higher ground all around it. At the southwestern edge of the Great Basin lies the lowest point on the continent of North America. Part of Death Valley in California lies more than 280 feet (85 m) below sea level.

Because the Intermountain Region has areas of low and high land, it is often called the Basin and Range Region. Not only basins and mountain ranges but other landforms mark this region. These include plateaus and canyons. The two largest plateaus in the region are the Columbia Plateau to the northwest of the Great Basin and the Colorado Plateau to the southeast.

The Grand Canyon, one of the world's natural wonders, cuts across part of the Colorado Plateau. Carved by the Colorado River over thousands of years, it extends 280 miles (451 km) through Arizona. It is up to 18 miles (29 km) wide and about a mile (1.6 km) deep.

REVIEW What kinds of landforms are found in the Intermountain Region?

More Mountains and Valleys

Lying west of the Intermountain Region and stretching to the Pacific Ocean is the Pacific Mountains and Valleys region. This region extends north from Mexico to Canada and Alaska. It is made up mainly of separate mountain ranges and a series of valleys between those mountain ranges.

On the eastern edge of the Pacific Mountains and Valleys region is the Sierra Nevada (see•AIR•ah neh•VAH•dah). *Sierra Nevada* is Spanish for "Snowy Mountain Range." The Sierra Nevada runs almost the length of California. Other mountains lie north of the Sierra Nevada. These are the Cascade Range in northern California, Oregon, and Washington, and the Coast Mountains in Canada. These ranges include some

Death Valley is about 140 miles (225 km) long and about 5 to 15 miles (8 to 24 km) wide.

LOCATE IT

Death Valley National Park

Sacramento
San Francisco
CALIFORNIA
Los Angeles

volcanoes. A **volcano** is an opening in the Earth through which hot lava, gases, ash, and rocks may pour out. When this happens, a volcano is erupting. Sometimes the lava and ash build up to form a mountain.

Farther north, in Alaska, is the Alaska Range. It has the highest mountain peak in North America, Mount McKinley. The peak, which is sometimes called by its Native American name, Denali (duh•NAH•lee), is 20,320 feet (6,194 m) high. *Denali* means "The Great One" or "The High One." The peak was first climbed in 1913.

Beside the Pacific Ocean in California, Oregon, and Washington are the Coast Ranges. These low mountains give much of the Pacific Coast a rocky, rugged look. At many places these mountains drop sharply into the ocean. Unlike the Atlantic Coast, the Pacific Coast has very little flat land along its coast.

Sandwiched between the Coast Ranges, the Sierra Nevada, and the Cascade Range are three large, fertile valleys. The largest is the more than 400-mile (644-km) long Central Valley in California. The others are the Puget Sound Lowland in Washington and the Willamette (wuh•LA•muht) Valley in Oregon.

REVIEW What region extends north from Mexico to Canada and Alaska?

In Big Sur, California, steep cliffs have formed where the Coast Ranges meet the Pacific Ocean.

LESSON 1 REVIEW

❶ **MAIN IDEA** What are the major kinds of land that determine the landform regions of the United States?

❷ **WHY IT MATTERS** How are the kinds of land in the United States different?

❸ **VOCABULARY** Write a paragraph that includes the terms **mountain range**, **piedmont**, and **sea level**.

❹ **READING SKILL—Main Idea and Supporting Details** What region extends across most of the center of the United States?

❺ **GEOGRAPHY** How do the Appalachian Mountains differ from the Rocky Mountains?

❻ **GEOGRAPHY** What are the two largest landform regions in the United States?

❼ **CRITICAL THINKING—Analysis** How might the similarities and differences of the land in different parts of the United States affect how people live in various regions?

PERFORMANCE—Draw a Map Draw a map of the United States that shows the main landform regions. Describe and label each region, and list some of the region's main physical features. Share your map with a classmate.

Use Elevation Maps

VOCABULARY

elevation

contour line

▶ WHY IT MATTERS

Different maps provide different kinds of information. If you want to know how high or how low the land is, you need to use an elevation (eh•luh•VAY•shuhn) map. **Elevation** is the height of the land in relation to sea level.

▶ WHAT YOU NEED TO KNOW

The elevation of land is measured from sea level, usually in feet or meters. The elevation of land at sea level is 0 feet (0 m). Find sea level on Drawing A. The lines on this drawing of a mountain are contour lines. A **contour line** connects all points of equal elevation. Find the contour line for 13,120 feet (4,000 m) on Drawing A.

This line connects all the points on the mountain that are 13,120 feet (4,000 m) above sea level.

Drawing B shows the hill as you look down on it from above. On the steeper side of the hill, the contour lines are closer together. On the sloping side of the hill, the lines are farther apart.

On Drawing C, color is added between the contour lines. A key is used instead of labels. The key for Drawing C shows that every place shown in green is between sea level and 655 feet (200 m). The border between green and yellow on the map is a contour line for 655 feet (200 m). The borders between the other colors are also contour lines.

Reading Contour Lines

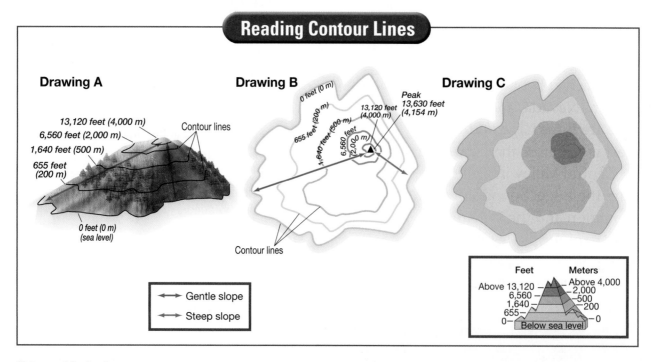

Drawing A

13,120 feet (4,000 m)
6,560 feet (2,000 m)
1,640 feet (500 m)
655 feet (200 m)
Contour lines
0 feet (0 m) (sea level)

←→ Gentle slope
←→ Steep slope

Drawing B

0 feet (0 m)
655 feet (200 m)
1,640 feet (500 m)
6,560 feet (2,000 m)
13,120 feet (4,000 m)
Peak 13,630 feet (4,154 m)
Contour lines

Drawing C

Feet	Meters
Above 13,120	Above 4,000
6,560	2,000
1,640	500
655	200
0	0
Below sea level	

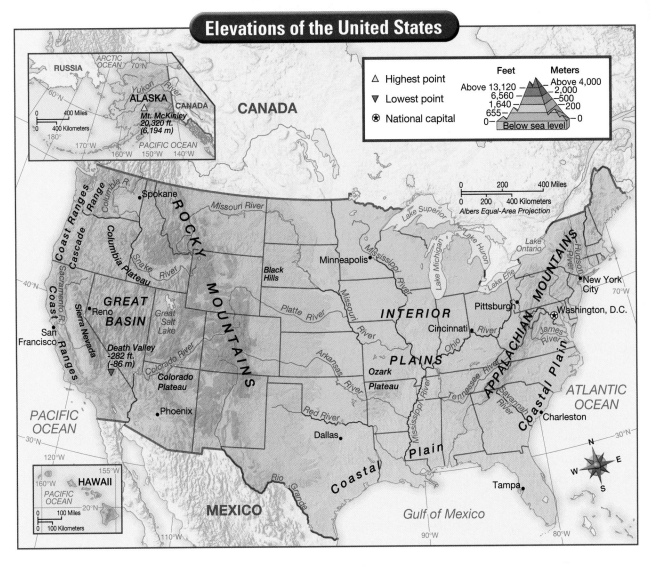

Elevations of the United States

Most elevation maps use only a few important contour lines, with colors added between the lines. Look at the elevation map of the United States on this page. The map does not show exact elevations. Instead, the key shows the range of elevation that each color stands for. On this map, green is used for land in the range between sea level and 655 feet (200 m).

➡ PRACTICE THE SKILL

Use the map to answer the following questions.

➊ Find the Coastal Plain on the map. What is the elevation of the land around Dallas, Texas?

➋ What range of elevations is shown by the color red?

➌ Which city has a higher elevation: Reno, Nevada, or Tampa, Florida?

➡ APPLY WHAT YOU LEARNED

Lay a ruler across the map on this page to connect any two cities. Describe the elevation of the land you would cross if you were to travel by car from one city to the other. Compare your description with that of a classmate.

Practice your map and globe skills with the **GeoSkills CD-ROM**.

MAP AND GLOBE SKILLS

MAIN IDEA
Read to learn about the different kinds of bodies of water.

WHY IT MATTERS
People use different bodies of water to meet their needs.

VOCABULARY

current
tide
inlet
sound
tributary
drainage basin
fall line

FAST FACT

Oceans cover almost three-fourths of the entire Earth's surface.

Bodies of Water

Bodies of water are important to life in the United States. Oceans help connect the United States to other countries of the world. Lakes and rivers provide fresh water for wildlife and, in many places, for people and their farms, factories, and cities. Large lakes and rivers also provide important transportation routes within the United States. Like landforms, bodies of water have different shapes and sizes.

Oceans

The largest bodies of water on Earth are the four oceans. From largest to smallest, they are the Pacific Ocean, the Atlantic Ocean, the Indian Ocean, and the Arctic Ocean. The Pacific Ocean alone covers nearly one-third of the Earth's surface, an area larger than all the continents put together.

These four oceans hold most of the Earth's water. They also separate most of the Earth's seven continents. From largest to smallest, these continents are Asia, Africa, North America, South America, Antarctica, Europe, and Australia. Geographers sometimes group Europe and Asia together and call them Eurasia (yu•RAY•zhuh).

Oceans form a natural boundary for a large part of the United States. On the northern coast of Alaska is the Arctic Ocean. On the eastern coast of the United States is the Atlantic Ocean. On the western coast and surrounding Hawaii is the Pacific Ocean.

Oceans move in the form of waves and currents. A **current** is that part of a body of water

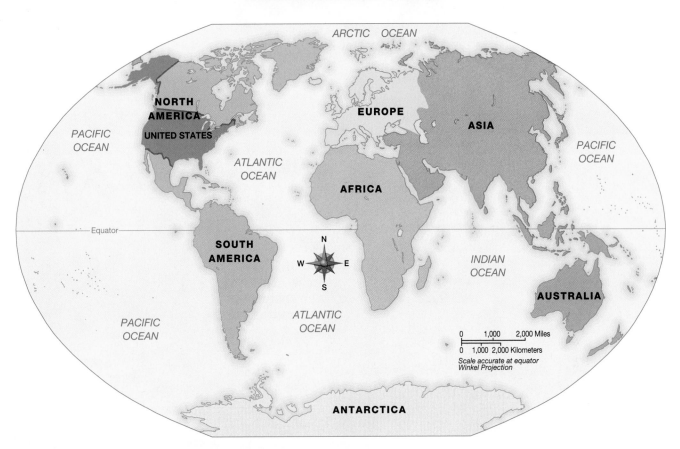

Movement **Oceans separate most of the continents.**

What ocean separates North America and Africa?

flowing in a certain direction. Ocean currents are caused mainly by the Earth's wind patterns.

Ocean water also moves in the form of tides. **Tides** are the regular rise and fall of an ocean and of the bodies of water connected to it. When the tide is high, some of the low-lying land near the ocean is covered with water.

REVIEW **What is the main cause of ocean currents?**

Gulfs, Bays, and Inlets

Hundreds of inlets along the Coastal Plain help define the shape of the United States. An **inlet** is any area of water extending into the land from a larger body of water. The largest of these inlets are called gulfs. The largest gulf bordering the United States is the Gulf of Mexico. Several states in the southeastern United States border this gulf. Another large gulf, the Gulf of Alaska, lies south of Alaska, along the Pacific Coast.

Hundreds of bays also shape the coastline. Many large bays provide harbors where ships can safely dock.

Most of the largest bays and other inlets in the United States are found along the Atlantic and Gulf Coasts. On the Atlantic Coast these include Chesapeake Bay between Maryland and Virginia, Delaware Bay between Delaware and New Jersey, and Albemarle (AL•buh•marl) Sound in North Carolina.

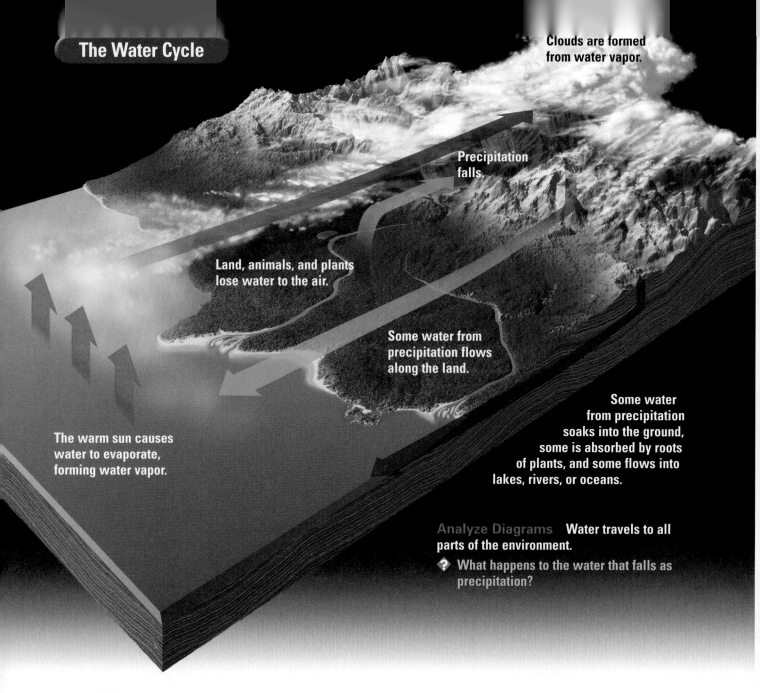

Clouds are formed from water vapor.

Precipitation falls.

Land, animals, and plants lose water to the air.

Some water from precipitation flows along the land.

Some water from precipitation soaks into the ground, some is absorbed by roots of plants, and some flows into lakes, rivers, or oceans.

The warm sun causes water to evaporate, forming water vapor.

Analyze Diagrams   Water travels to all parts of the environment.

❓ What happens to the water that falls as precipitation?

A **sound** is a long inlet that often separates offshore islands from the mainland.

Other large bays and inlets are found along the Gulf Coast. The largest of these are Tampa Bay in Florida, Mobile Bay in Alabama, and Galveston Bay in Texas. The largest bays and inlets on the Pacific Coast include San Francisco Bay near San Francisco, California, and Puget Sound in Washington State.

REVIEW What large bays can be found along the Gulf of Mexico?

Lakes

North America has more lakes than any other continent. The largest lakes in North America are together known as the Great Lakes. They are located along the border between the United States and Canada. These five lakes—Superior, Michigan, Huron, Erie, and Ontario—are among the world's largest freshwater lakes.

One-fifth of all the fresh water on Earth is found in the Great Lakes, and Lake Superior is the world's largest freshwater lake. It covers about 31,800 square miles (82,362 sq km), an area almost the size of South Carolina. Today the Great Lakes and the rivers connected to them form an important inland waterway for ships. This waterway links the Middle West region of the United States to the Atlantic Ocean. Other large freshwater lakes in the United States include Lake Okeechobee (oh•kuh•CHOH•bee) in Florida and Lake Tahoe on the California–Nevada border.

Most lakes in the United States are made up of fresh water, but the Great Salt Lake in Utah is as salty as any sea or ocean. Some people even consider it to be a sea—an inland body of salt water. Although freshwater streams feed the Great Salt Lake, they carry small amounts of salt. Because the lake lies in the Great Basin, surrounded by higher ground, the water coming into the lake has no way to escape. Over time, as water evaporates, salt is left behind. As a result, the lake is so salty that no fish can live in its water.

REVIEW **What is the world's largest group of freshwater lakes?**

Location **Lake Michigan is the only Great Lake that is completely in the United States.**

❖ What states border Lake Michigan?

Major Bodies of Water in the United States

Samuel Langhorne Clemens
1835–1910
Character Trait: Individualism

As a young man Samuel Clemens began his career by writing short, humorous stories for his brother's newspaper. At age 21 Clemens stopped writing for a while and took a job aboard a steamboat that traveled the Mississippi River. Clemens learned to guide a steamboat through the winding channels of the river and became a steamboat pilot. He traveled the Mississippi River for almost four years before ending his career as a pilot in 1861.

Clemens used his experiences to write about life along the Mississippi in his novels *The Adventures of Tom Sawyer* and *The Adventures of Huckleberry Finn* and in his autobiography, *Life on the Mississippi*. He wrote these books under his pen name, Mark Twain. The name Mark Twain comes from a term steamboat pilots used on the Mississippi. It meant that the river was at least 12 feet (about 4 m) deep, which was a safe depth for steamboats.

MULTIMEDIA BIOGRAPHIES **GO** ONLINE
Visit The Learning Site at
www.harcourtschool.com/biographies
to learn about other famous people.

The Mississippi River System

Rivers are bodies of fresh, moving water. Every river begins at a source and ends at a mouth, where it empties its water into an ocean or another body of water. As a river crosses the land, it may be joined by other streams or rivers. A stream or a river that flows into a larger stream or river is called a **tributary**. Tributaries are also called branches. Together, a river and its tributaries make up a river system.

River systems drain, or carry water away from, the land around them. The land drained by a river system is its

The Mississippi River drains all or parts of 31 states including Minnesota. It is also the largest river in North America.

LOCATE IT

Minneapolis

MINNESOTA

Mississippi River

Rivers East of the Appalachians

Many rivers cross the Coastal Plain and flow into the Atlantic Ocean. They include the Delaware, Hudson, James, Potomac, Roanoke, Savannah, and Susquehanna (suhs•kwuh•HAN•uh) Rivers. All of these rivers, or their tributaries, begin in the Appalachian Mountains.

Many cities in the United States have grown near where these rivers flow into ocean inlets. Philadelphia, for example, was built along the Delaware River near where it flows into Delaware Bay. New York City was built at the mouth of the Hudson River. Baltimore was built where the Patapsco River empties into Chesapeake Bay.

Cities such as Richmond and Raleigh were built farther inland on rivers where the Coastal Plain meets the Piedmont. These cities lie along the Fall Line. A **fall line** is a place where the elevation of the land drops sharply, causing rivers to form waterfalls or rapids. Cities grew along the Fall Line because people used the fast-moving water there to power machines in factories.

REVIEW Where is the source of many rivers in the eastern United States?

The Delaware River passes through the Kittatinny Mountains of Pennsylvania.

drainage basin. When a river is long, its drainage basin can be quite large. The Mississippi River, along with its largest tributaries—the Arkansas, Illinois, Missouri, Ohio, and Red Rivers—creates a gigantic drainage basin in the middle of North America. The mighty Mississippi and its tributaries drain most of the land between the Appalachian and Rocky Mountains.

The Mississippi River's source is Lake Itasca (eye•TAS•kuh) in Minnesota. From there the river flows more than 2,300 miles (3,701 km) south to the Gulf of Mexico.

REVIEW What is a drainage basin?

LOCATE IT

TEXAS
Dallas
Austin

Big Bend
National Park

The Pecos, Chama, and Puerco Rivers are some of the tributaries that flow into the Rio Grande.

Rivers in the West

An imaginary line runs north and south along the highest points of the Rocky Mountains. This line is called the Continental Divide. It divides the major river systems of North America into those that flow into the Gulf of Mexico and the Atlantic Ocean and those that flow into the Pacific Ocean. Western rivers that begin east of the Continental Divide empty into the Mississippi River or the Gulf of Mexico to reach the Atlantic Ocean. Rivers that begin west of the Continental Divide empty into the Pacific Ocean.

Many western rivers flow from sources on the eastern side of the Continental Divide. The largest of these include the Missouri and Arkansas Rivers and the Rio Grande. The Rio Grande forms part of the border between the United States and Mexico. In Mexico the river is known as the Río Bravo.

The major rivers on the western side of the Continental Divide include the Sacramento, San Joaquin (wah•KEEN), and Columbia Rivers. Another important western river is the Colorado. The Colorado River flows from the Rocky Mountains across the Colorado Plateau to Arizona before it empties into the Gulf of California in Mexico. The river passes through three national parks.

REVIEW What river forms part of the border between the United States and Mexico?

LESSON 2
REVIEW

1. **MAIN IDEA** Identify the major bodies of water in the United States.

2. **WHY IT MATTERS** Why are bodies of water important to life in the United States?

3. **VOCABULARY** Write a couple of sentences that explain how the terms **tributary** and **drainage basin** are related.

4. **READING SKILL—Main Idea and Supporting Details** What are the largest bodies of water on the Earth?

5. **HISTORY** Why did many cities grow along the Fall Line?

6. **CRITICAL THINKING—Synthesize** Why do you think it is important to have a waterway that links the states in the Middle West to the Atlantic Ocean?

 PERFORMANCE—Draw a Poster Find out what river is located nearest to where you live. Make a poster showing the river and its surrounding landforms. Label nearby cities and any tributaries the river may have. Share your poster with the class.

Climate and Vegetation Regions

At any time or place on Earth, the weather may change—sometimes quickly or violently. Weather is the day-to-day conditions in a place. **Climate** is the kind of weather a place has most often, year after year. The climate of a place can affect what people wear, what kinds of activities they do, and how they earn their living. Few countries in the world have as many different kinds of climate as the United States.

Climate and **natural vegetation**, or the plant life that grows naturally in a place, are closely related. The different climates in the United States influence the kinds of vegetation found in different parts of our country.

Factors Affecting Climate

The climate of a place depends partly on its distance from the equator. Usually, the closer a place is to the equator, the warmer it is. For example, average temperatures between Maine and Florida can vary greatly, especially in winter. That is because places closer to the equator, like Florida, receive more direct sunlight than places farther away. This causes higher average temperatures. Generally, the farther a place is from the equator, the cooler it is.

MAIN IDEA
The United States can be divided into regions based on different kinds of climate and vegetation.

WHY IT MATTERS
Learning about climate and natural vegetation will help you understand why people live differently in different parts of the country.

VOCABULARY
climate
natural vegetation
rain shadow
humidity
drought
arid
tundra
prairie
savanna

In places with high elevations, some mountains can have snow year-round.

Distance from oceans and other large bodies of water also affects climate. Water heats and cools more slowly than land does. Near the ocean, temperatures are usually not as hot in summer and not as cold in winter as they would be inland. The ocean often helps warm the land in winter and cool it in summer.

Ocean currents can also affect climate. The currents carry cold water from the North Pole and the South Pole toward the equator, and warm water from the equator toward the poles. The Gulf Stream, which carries warm water northward along the east coast of the United States, helps make winters there less cold than places farther inland. The California Current, which flows along the west coast of the United States, brings cold water southward from the Arctic Ocean. It helps keep places along the west coast cool in the summer.

Elevation affects climate, too. Places in the mountains are usually much cooler than places where the elevation of the land is closer to sea level. Temperatures drop about 3°F (about 2°C) for every 1,000 feet (305 m) above sea level. Because elevation can affect the temperature so greatly, even the tops of high mountains in tropical Hawaii are sometimes covered with snow.

Where a place is located on a continent can affect climate in other ways. In the West, mountain ranges such as the Sierra Nevada and the Rocky Mountains act like huge walls. When streams of air meet the mountains, they are forced to rise. As air rises, it cools. Because cool air cannot hold as much moisture as warm air, rain

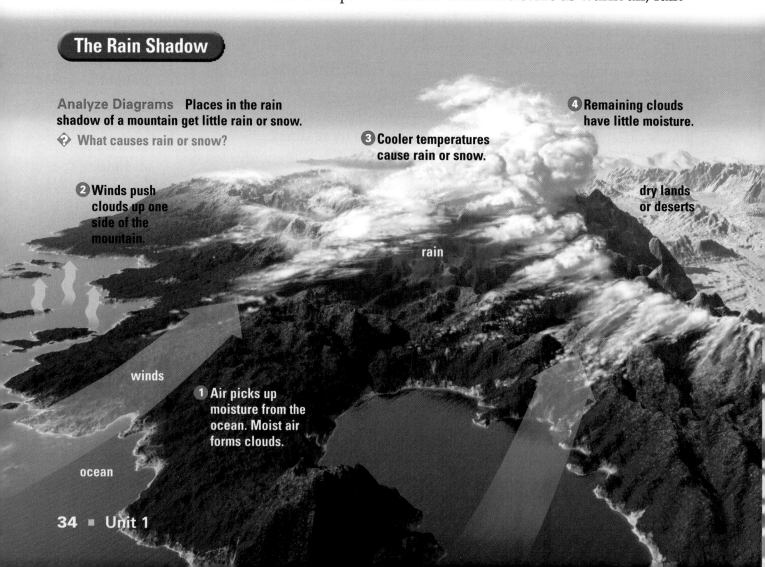

The Rain Shadow

Analyze Diagrams Places in the rain shadow of a mountain get little rain or snow.

❖ What causes rain or snow?

❷ Winds push clouds up one side of the mountain.

❸ Cooler temperatures cause rain or snow.

❹ Remaining clouds have little moisture.

dry lands or deserts

rain

❶ Air picks up moisture from the ocean. Moist air forms clouds.

winds

ocean

The Change of Seasons

MARCH 20 or 21
Spring in the Northern Hemisphere

DECEMBER 21 or 22
Winter in the
Northern
Hemisphere

Sun's rays

Sun

Equator

JUNE 21 or 22
Summer in the
Northern
Hemisphere

Earth's orbit

SEPTEMBER 22
or 23
Autumn in the
Northern
Hemisphere

Equator

Analyze Diagrams As the Earth moves around the sun, the seasons change.

◈ When does summer start in the Northern Hemisphere?

or snow falls on the mountains' western slopes. As the air begins to slide down the eastern side of the mountains, it gets warmer. The warm air can hold more moisture. As a result, places on the eastern sides of the mountains get little precipitation. They lie in the **rain shadow**, or on the drier side of a mountain.

Not having mountains can affect the climate almost as much as having them, but in a different way. Because there is no large mountain range in the central part of the United States to block the flow of air, bitter-cold air masses can move rapidly out of Canada across the plains. Called northers because they come from the north, these large, cold air masses can bring freezing temperatures to places as far south as the states of Texas and Florida.

REVIEW What factors affect the climate of a place?

Climate Regions

The United States has 11 climate regions. These climate regions vary from the mostly year-round cold in the *polar climate* and *subpolar climate* regions of Alaska to the mostly year-round heat in the *tropical wet climate* region of Hawaii and the *tropical wet and dry climate* region in South Florida. The change of seasons—summer, autumn, winter, and spring—is not very noticeable in those climate regions.

The *continental climate* region covers the northeast quarter of the United States. This region usually has four very different seasons, including a hot, wet summer and a cold winter. Most of the southeast quarter of the United States is in the *humid subtropical climate* region. This region also has four seasons, but its winters are milder and its summers are hotter than in the continental climate region.

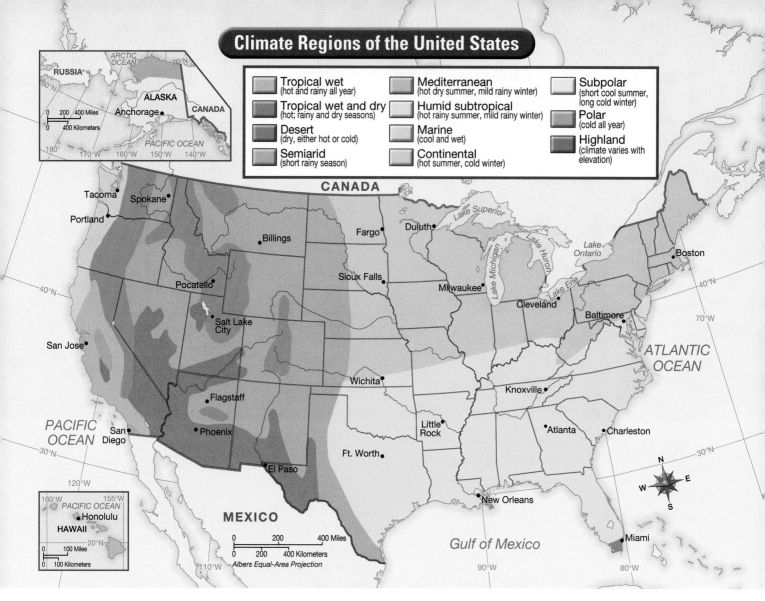

Climate Regions of the United States

Tropical wet (hot and rainy all year)

Tropical wet and dry (hot; rainy and dry seasons)

Desert (dry, either hot or cold)

Semiarid (short rainy season)

Mediterranean (hot dry summer, mild rainy winter)

Humid subtropical (hot rainy summer, mild rainy winter)

Marine (cool and wet)

Continental (hot summer, cold winter)

Subpolar (short cool summer, long cold winter)

Polar (cold all year)

Highland (climate varies with elevation)

Regions   There are 11 different climate regions in the United States.

In what climate region is your state located?

For most of the year, places in the humid subtropical region experience plenty of precipitation and high humidity. **Humidity** is the amount of moisture in the air. Like most other climate regions, however, this region does experience droughts (DROWTS). A **drought** is a long period with little or no rain.

Because the western United States is much more mountainous than the eastern part of the country, the climate varies more from place to place. The *semiarid climate* region covers much of the West. In

this region the climate is hot and **arid**, or dry, for most of the year with only a short rainy season. The writer Michael Grant once described the semiarid region with the words "hot, dry, wind, cold, sleet, thunder, puddles, drama." The "drama" was Grant's way to describe the huge thunderstorms that often form in the region during the spring and fall. These storms can drop hail that can damage crops as well as automobiles, roofs, and windows.

Mountainous areas in the western United States have a *highland climate*. In those areas, climate varies with elevation. Places at higher elevations have very cold winters with lots of snow.

The *desert climate* region covers a large part of the southwestern United States. Places with desert climates receive, on average, less than 10 inches (25 cm) of precipitation per year. The desert climate region receives little precipitation because much of it lies in the rain shadow of the western mountains. The land is part of a much larger desert region called the North American Desert, which extends southward into Mexico.

Most of the land near the Pacific Coast has one of two climates, a *marine climate* or a *Mediterranean* (meh•duh•tuh•RAY•nee•uhn) *climate.* A cool and wet marine climate can be found on the northern Pacific Coast west of the Cascade Mountains and is greatly affected by its location near the Pacific Ocean. The Mediterranean climate in central and southern California provides for long, sunny summers and mild, wet winters. This climate is called Mediterranean because it is very similar to the climate of some European countries located on the Mediterranean Sea.

REVIEW Why does the climate vary more from place to place in the western United States than in the eastern United States?

Vegetation Regions

The Earth is covered with different kinds of natural vegetation. The natural vegetation that grows in a place varies depending on whether the soil there is sand, clay, or loam. These are the three main kinds of soil. The natural vegetation also varies because of temperature and precipitation. In fact, the amount of precipitation in a place is the single most important factor affecting where different kinds of natural vegetation will grow.

Most of the United States can be divided into four main vegetation regions. These are forest, grassland, desert, and tundra. Tundra regions are found far to the north and high on mountains. A **tundra** is a cold, dry region where trees cannot grow.

The forest vegetation region is found in much of the eastern United States. Across the northern Coastal Plain, the Appalachian Mountains, and much of the Central Plains, forests have mostly evergreens, such as cedar and pine, and broadleaf trees, such as oak, ash, and birch. While evergreens stay green all year round, broadleaf trees change color in autumn and drop their leaves in winter.

Sequoias are some of the world's tallest trees.

Vegetation of the United States

Legend:
- Desert
- Forest
- Grassland
- Savanna
- Tundra

Regions Most of the nation can be divided into five vegetation regions.

What vegetation region can be found on both the east and west coasts of the United States?

Forests of evergreen pines and broadleaf oaks cover much of the southern Coastal Plain and the Gulf Coast.

Forests also cover areas of the western United States. In western Washington and Oregon and in northern California, rainfall amounts are often greater than 80 inches (203 cm) per year. Redwoods and giant sequoias, which are some of the world's oldest trees, grow in the forests there.

Trees need lots of water, but grasses can survive in much drier areas. The largest grassland region in the United States stretches across the middle of the country. It includes the western part of the Central Plains and all of the Great Plains. This part of the Central Plains is sometimes called a tall-grass prairie. A **prairie** is an area of flat or rolling land covered mostly by grasses and wildflowers. Left to grow, the grasses on this prairie would become as tall as people! Mostly short grasses cover the drier Great Plains. The land there has almost no trees and few rivers. As a result, it often looks the same, mile after mile.

Another vegetation region—savanna—is generally found between areas of grasslands and forests. A **savanna** is a kind of grassland that has areas with some trees. These trees are scattered, and the land is mostly covered with shrubs and bushes.

Only plants that can grow in a dry climate can grow in deserts. These plants include short grasses, low bushes, and cactuses. Cactuses store water in their thick stems so that they can survive until rain falls. A shrublike tree known as mesquite (muh•SKEET) sends its long roots 70 feet (21 m) into the ground to find water.

Small, hardy plants such as mosses, lichens (LY•kuhnz), herbs, and low shrubs grow in tundra regions. Tundra regions are covered by snow more than half the year. Yet there is not enough water for trees to grow because the water in the soil is frozen year-round.

Caribou and sheep feed on the plants that grow in the tundra.

There are two kinds of tundra regions. They are arctic and alpine. Arctic tundras lie near the Arctic Ocean. The only arctic tundra region in the United States is in northern Alaska. Alpine tundras can be found on mountains with elevations that make it too cold for trees to grow.

REVIEW **What four main vegetation regions cover most of the United States?**

LESSON 3
REVIEW

❶ **MAIN IDEA**   What are the main climate and vegetation regions found in the United States?

❷ **WHY IT MATTERS**   How do climate and natural vegetation affect how people live in different parts of the country?

❸ **VOCABULARY**   Write a description of a **savanna** region.

❹ **READING SKILL—Main Idea and Supporting Details**   In which climate region do people experience heavy precipitation, high humidity, and droughts?

❺ **GEOGRAPHY**   What are some kinds of plants that grow in the desert?

❻ **CRITICAL THINKING—Analyze**   How are winter weather in the continental climate region and winter weather in the humid subtropical climate region different?

PERFORMANCE—Write a Poem
Write a poem about the climate and vegetation of the region in which you live. Share your poem with classmates.

4

MAIN IDEA
Read to learn how people use the land and its resources to meet their needs and why people change their environment.

WHY IT MATTERS
People continue to use the land and change it to meet their needs. Some people also work to reduce the effects of the changes they make to the environment.

VOCABULARY
natural resource
modify
fertilizer
irrigation
nonrenewable
renewable
erosion
land use

Using the Land

The United States has many important natural resources. A **natural resource** is something found in nature that people can use. Natural resources include such things as soil, water, minerals, and vegetation.

Different physical environments and the natural resources found in them affect the way people live in different parts of the country. At the same time, people and their activities also affect their environment. People clear land to build houses and roads, and they use natural resources to meet their needs.

People and the Environment

The environment affects the activities of many people. It affects not only the kinds of activities people take part in for recreation, but also how they earn a living. That is because people often do work related to the resources around them.

People throughout time have used the land and its resources to meet their needs. However, not all resources are spread out equally around the Earth. Not every place has enough of every resource it needs. To meet their needs or to do their jobs, people must often **modify**, or change, their environment. People modify their environments based on how they value and use the Earth's resources.

Many people agree that water is one of the most important natural resources. Without it, crops would not grow and people could not live. To make sure they have enough water, people sometimes modify their environment by digging wells in the ground. They also build dams across rivers and streams. These dams form reservoirs (REH•zuh•vwarz) behind them. Both people and industries use the water stored in those reservoirs. Dams help make electricity, too. Water from large reservoirs can be used to turn large machines called generators, which make electricity. This hydroelectric power is an important source of electricity in many parts of the country.

This builder is modifying the environment.

Some natural resources are difficult to find. To reach coal and mineral resources such as copper, gold, and silver, people dig huge mines into the Earth's surface. To reach oil and natural gas resources, they must drill wells deep into the ground or down into the ocean floor.

Soil is another important natural resource. Without fertile soil, the United States could not grow food to feed its people or to sell to other countries. Before people can plant crops, however, they must often plow or disk the land to prepare it for planting. They may also add fertilizers. **Fertilizer** is material added to the soil to make it more fertile.

Many places in the United States have fertile soil, but sometimes the land is too dry for crops to grow well. Farmers in those areas have modified their environment by using irrigation. **Irrigation** is the use of canals, ditches, or pipes to move water to dry areas. With irrigation, many desert regions have been turned into productive farmland.

When people modify the environment for one purpose, they often change it in other ways. For example, if too much water is pumped from the ground for irrigation, then the amount of underground water available for other uses decreases. Once nonrenewable resources, such as minerals and fuels, are used up, there will be none left for future use. **Nonrenewable** means that a resource cannot be made again by nature or people. However, as people use these resources, they often find ways to use them more efficiently. They may also discover new resources to take their place.

Sometimes the results of changes to the environment may not be seen for years. At one time, forests covered almost all of the eastern United States. One early traveler told of spending "day after day among the trees of a hundred feet high, without a glimpse of the surrounding country." Over time, however, people cut down many of those trees and some of the forests disappeared.

People modify the environment when they lay pipes and build highways.

Land Use and Resources of the United States

Legend:
- Manufacturing
- Farming
- Grazing
- Forest
- Little-used land
- Fishing
- Oil or natural gas
- Coal
- Iron
- Copper
- Gold
- Silver
- Limestone
- Uranium
- Zinc

Human-Environment Interactions People in the United States use the land in many ways.

◈ Where is most of the land used for grazing?

In the past, many people thought that our supply of natural resources would last forever. However, Americans came to understand that the Earth does not have an endless supply of trees. People began planting new trees to replace the ones they cut down. They understood that trees are a renewable resource. **Renewable** means that a resource can be made again by nature or by people.

When people first plowed the grasslands of the Interior Plains, the topsoil—the fertile top layer of soil—was as deep as 16 inches (41 cm). Now, in many places, only 6 to 8 inches (15 to 20 cm) of topsoil are left. Plowing the land can speed up the process of erosion. **Erosion** is the wearing away of the Earth's surface, usually by wind and rain. Over time, people came to understand that they had to take action to protect soil and other natural resources.

REVIEW Why do people modify their environment?

Patterns of Land Use

People use the Earth's surface in a variety of ways. They divide it into nations, states, and other government units. They build communities, transportation systems, and businesses on it. They also gather natural resources from it. Some of the land is owned by the public, and some of it belongs to private property owners. People buy and sell the land and make laws to decide how it can be used.

In every place on Earth, landforms and climate influence **land use**, or how most of the land in a place is used. In the United States, about half of the land is used as farmland. Most farming takes place on the Coastal Plain, on the Interior Plains, and in the large valleys in the western part of the country. In those regions, the land is fertile and there is enough water for crops to grow. In more arid regions, most of the land is used for grazing cattle, sheep, and horses.

Forests cover about one-third of the land in the United States. The largest forests are found in mountain regions, along the Great Lakes, or on the Coastal Plain. Much of the mining in the United States also takes place in mountain regions, although mining may take place wherever there are ore or fuel deposits.

Cities also occupy large areas of the United States. There, most of the land is used for housing, transportation, and businesses. In cities, most people work in service industries, such as banking, education, or health care. Most manufacturing also takes place on land in or near cities.

REVIEW What factors influence land use?

This worker has a job in manufacturing. She is building computers.

LESSON 4 REVIEW

1. **MAIN IDEA** What are two ways that people use the land in the United States?

2. **WHY IT MATTERS** How can people minimize the effects of the changes they make to the land?

3. **VOCABULARY** Explain why the use of **fertilizers** and **irrigation** are examples of how people modify their environment.

4. **READING SKILL—Main Idea and Supporting Details** What are the two types of natural resources?

5. **GEOGRAPHY** Why do people dig wells or lay pipes that take water to dry places?

6. **GEOGRAPHY** What might people discover as they use resources?

7. **CRITICAL THINKING—Synthesize** How do the natural resources found in your community affect the way you live?

PERFORMANCE—Write a Paragraph Use sources from the Internet and the library to research land use in your state. Then write a paragraph describing the different ways the land is used.

5

MAIN IDEA
Read to learn about where people settle and how regions can be based on people's activities.

WHY IT MATTERS
The activities of people within a region help shape that region's identity.

VOCABULARY

relative location
political region
economic region
cultural region
population region
urban
suburban
rural
crossroads
metropolitan area

Newfane, Vermont, is typical of the small towns located in the Northeast.

Where People Live and Work

Regions can be based on physical features, such as land-forms, climate, and vegetation. But people can define a region by using just about any feature. Because the United States is such a large country with so many differences, there are many different kinds of regions.

Regions of the United States

To make it easier to talk about different areas of the country, people often group the 50 states into four large regions—the Northeast, the South, the Middle West, and the West. Each of these regions is based on its relative location in the United States. The **relative location** of a place is where it is, compared to one or more other places on the Earth. For example, the relative location of the Northeast region is in the northeastern part of the country.

The states in each of these regions are alike in many ways. In addition to being in the same part of the country, they often have the same kinds of landforms, climate, and natural resources. Because of that, the people who live there often earn their living in ways that are alike. The states in each region may also share a history and culture.

REVIEW What are the four large regions of the United States?

Regions of the United States

Regions People often divide the United States into four regions based on location.

❖ In which region is your state located?

Regions Based on People's Activities

Regions can also be based on patterns of human activity. Patterns of human activity include such factors as how people move from place to place and make settlements. These patterns also include how people work together to meet their needs and how they divide and share the land. Regions based on people's activities often form and change over time as people move and adopt new ways of living.

One kind of region based on patterns of human activity is a political region. A **political region** is a region in which people share a government and have the same leaders. Nations, states, counties, and cities are all political regions. Each political region has an exact boundary either set by law or agreed upon by the people in the neighboring areas. If people cannot agree on where a boundary is, conflict often results.

Other kinds of regions, known as **economic regions**, are based on the work people do or the products they make. In agricultural regions many people are farmers or ranchers. In manufacturing regions many people work in factories.

Another region based on human activity is a **cultural region**, a region based on culture. In a cultural region the main group of people who live there share customs and beliefs. The region may be based on the religion that most of the people follow or the language they speak.

Still another kind of region that is based on people is a population region. A **population region** is one based on where people live. Today, about three-fourths of the people in the United States live in **urban**, or city, regions. In urban regions many people live close together in cities.

Almost every large city has suburbs, or smaller cities and towns around it.

People who live in these **suburban** regions often work in the larger city nearby. Other people live in **rural**, or country, regions. Homes in rural regions are built farther apart, and people there often have to travel farther to go to school or work or to go shopping.

REVIEW What are the four kinds of regions that are based on people's activities?

Patterns of Settlement

Geographic factors, such as landforms, bodies of water, and climate, usually affect where people settle. Through most of human history, people have tended to settle in areas where the soil is fertile and good for farming. People have also settled where there is enough fresh water to meet their needs. Having waterways and other transportation routes nearby has always been important, too.

Geographic factors have also discouraged people from settling in areas. Most people have avoided settling in deserts, tundras, or high, mountainous areas. That is because building shelters, finding food and water, and meeting other basic human needs are more difficult in those areas. Today, however, people use tools and inventions to modify their environments and make living in some of those areas possible. In fact, some of the fastest-growing cities in the United States are in desert regions of the West.

When more and more people settle in a particular place, they tend to cluster, or group together, near harbors or crossroads. In the past, a **crossroads** was a place where two roads or railroads crossed and people met to buy and sell goods, communicate, and rest. Today, it is any place that connects people, goods, and ideas. A crossroads may be a shopping center or a business park.

Other people may create settlements that are more spread out. These settlements are often found along major rivers, roads, or railroads or along a coast. Wherever people settle, their settlements become part of the physical environment. Settlements change the land on which they are built, and they are in turn changed by the land.

REVIEW What are the leading influences on where people settle?

New York Harbor has helped to make New York City a busy crossroads.

LOCATE IT

Lake Ontario

NEW YORK

New York City

The Center of Population
Understanding Human Systems

Since the beginning of our nation, the center of population has gradually moved westward. A nation's center of population is the place within that nation where there are an equal number of people living to the north, south, east, and west. The center of population in the United States has shifted westward because over time people have moved farther west to settle the land and seek new opportunities. In 1790 the center of population was near Baltimore, Maryland. Today it is located at a point southwest of St. Louis, Missouri.

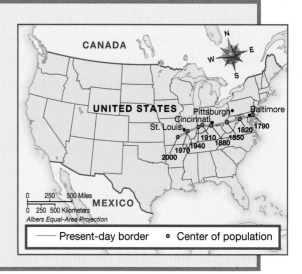

Types of Settlement

Settlements of many sizes can be found in the United States and around the world. Some are made up of single houses scattered far apart across the landscape. Others are clusters of houses neatly arranged in villages or towns. Still others are crowded cities. About half of all the people in the world live in cities.

Cities are the largest and the most crowded type of settlement. Together, a large city and its surrounding suburbs make up that city's **metropolitan area**.

Some metropolitan areas are so large that they stretch across state borders. The largest metropolitan area in the United States, the New York City metropolitan area, stretches across parts of three states.

Settlements also differ in how they are arranged and how they are used. The way settlements are arranged often depends on the background of the people who settled there or the leaders who planned the community. For example, many communities in the Northeast are built around a town square or common.

Many early settlers there were from England, where they used this kind of area to graze their farm animals.

The ways people organize their settlements reflect not only their past and their economic activities but also their culture and the way they govern themselves. If you flew over the Middle West in an airplane, for example, you could see that many places there were planned using a grid system. The roads are mostly straight, framing large, square plots of land. If you flew over parts of the West, however, you might see towns that are laid out a different way because of the culture of the people who first settled there. Many of the towns in the West were first settled by people from Spain and from Mexico, and other countries in Latin America. Like many towns in Latin America, some of the towns in the southwestern United States have a central plaza with a church surrounded by buildings that are made of stone or a clay-and-straw mixture known as adobe (ah•DOH•bee).

REVIEW What are the largest types of settlements?

The Location of American Cities

In the 1700s most people in our country lived in rural regions. At that time there were only 24 cities in the whole country. The biggest of these were port cities along the Atlantic Ocean.

Over time, new cities developed. Many grew up along the Mississippi River or its tributaries or along the shores of the Great Lakes. Other cities developed along railroad lines that were being built to connect different parts of the country. New cities also developed along the Pacific and Gulf Coasts.

Improvements in farm machinery, new methods of farming, and the growth of manufacturing encouraged people to move to cities. With new tools and new ways of growing food, farmers could produce more. That meant that not as many farmers were needed. Many people also moved to cities to find work in manufacturing and in other businesses.

Other factors have also caused the population to move from one area to another. Sometimes the importance of an industry

Santa Fe, the capital of New Mexico, is the oldest capital city in the United States. The buildings in Santa Fe reflect the city's heritage.

LOCATE IT

Santa Fe

NEW MEXICO

changes, and people may leave a place to get a job with a growing industry. For example, when oil was discovered in Texas, many people from across the country moved there to take jobs in the oil industry. People moving to the United States from other countries have also affected population in different areas of the country. They continue to do so today.

Today, most of the largest cities in the United States continue to be found near a coast, along rivers or the shores of the Great Lakes, or on other major transportation routes. In fact, the five largest cities in the country—New York City, Los Angeles, Chicago, Houston, and Philadelphia—are all located within 50 miles (80 km) of a coast or one of the Great Lakes.

Location also played a role in the selection of some cities as capitals. Often these cities were chosen because they were located near the central part of a state or country. Some state capitals were chosen because they were among the largest cities in their states or were located near the coast or near a major transportation route.

The Ten Largest Cities in the United States

CITY	POPULATION
New York City, NY	8,008,278
Los Angeles, CA	3,694,820
Chicago, IL	2,896,016
Houston, TX	1,953,631
Philadelphia, PA	1,517,550
Phoenix, AZ	1,321,045
San Diego, CA	1,223,400
Dallas, TX	1,188,580
San Antonio, TX	1,144,646
Detroit, MI	951,270

Analyze Tables Three of the country's largest cities are in the state of Texas.

❖ Which city has a larger population—Dallas or San Antonio?

At the time the site for our nation's capital was chosen, there were only 13 states. The capital, Washington, D.C., was built about halfway between the northernmost and southernmost states.

REVIEW Where are most of the largest cities in the United States?

LESSON 5 REVIEW

1 MAIN IDEA Describe regions in the United States that are based on human activity.

2 WHY IT MATTERS How do people's activities help shape a region's identity?

3 VOCABULARY Explain in a sentence or two how the terms **urban** and **suburban** are related.

4 READING SKILL—Main Idea and Supporting Details What features describe a political region?

5 ECONOMICS In what kind of region based on people's activities would a community of farmers live?

6 CRITICAL THINKING—Analyze Why do you think that people tend to live near crossroads?

PERFORMANCE—Make a Brochure Work with a partner to make a brochure about your community. Include information about the types of settlements there and the activities people do. Take the brochure home and share it with family members.

Use Latitude and Longitude

VOCABULARY		
absolute location	parallel	meridian
line of latitude	line of longitude	prime meridian

▶ WHY IT MATTERS

Lines of latitude and lines of longitude help you describe the **absolute location**, or exact location, of any place on Earth.

▶ WHAT YOU NEED TO KNOW

Mapmakers use a system of imaginary lines to form a grid system on maps and globes. The lines that run east and west are the **lines of latitude**. Lines of latitude are also called **parallels** (PAR•uh•lelz). This is because they are parallel, or always the same distance from each other.

Lines of latitude are measured in degrees north and south of the equator, which is labeled 0°, or *zero degrees*. The

parallels north of the equator are marked *N* for *north latitude*. This means that they are in the Northern Hemisphere. The parallels south of the equator are marked *S* for *south latitude*. This means they are in the Southern Hemisphere.

The lines that run north and south on a map or globe are the **lines of longitude**, or **meridians**. Each meridian runs from the North Pole to the South Pole. Unlike parallels, which never meet, meridians meet at the poles.

Meridians are numbered in much the same way that parallels are numbered. The meridian marked 0° is called the **prime meridian**. Lines of longitude to the west of the prime meridian are

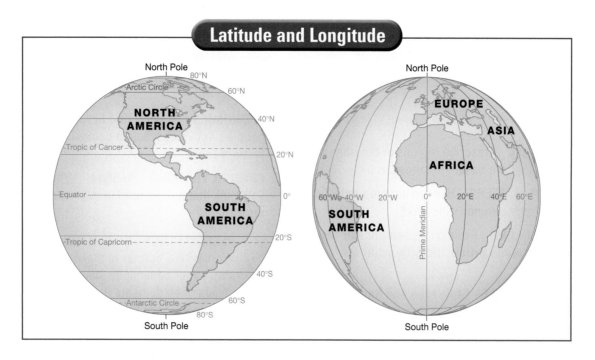

Latitude and Longitude

North Pole
80°N
Arctic Circle — 60°N
NORTH AMERICA — 40°N
Tropic of Cancer — 20°N
Equator — 0°
SOUTH AMERICA — 20°S
Tropic of Capricorn — 20°S
40°S
Antarctic Circle — 60°S
80°S
South Pole

North Pole
EUROPE
ASIA
AFRICA
60°W 40°W 20°W 0° 20°E 40°E 60°E
SOUTH AMERICA
Prime Meridian
South Pole

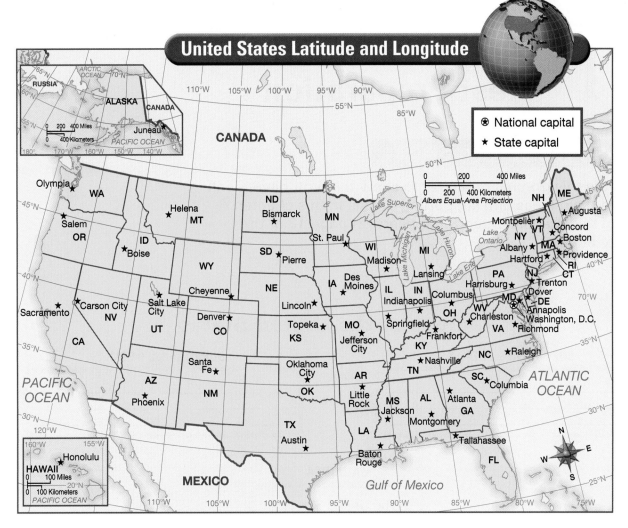

United States Latitude and Longitude

⊗ National capital
★ State capital

marked *W* for *west longitude*. They are in the Western Hemisphere. The meridians to the east of the prime meridian are marked *E* for *east longitude*. They are in the Eastern Hemisphere.

▶ PRACTICE THE SKILL

The map above, which shows the locations of state capitals in the United States, uses crossing lines of latitude and longitude to describe absolute location. On this map every fifth parallel is shown and every fifth meridian is shown.

At the left-hand side of the map, find 40°N. At the bottom, find 90°W. Use your fingers to trace these lines to the point where they cross. Springfield, Illinois, is not far from this point. So

you can say that Springfield is near 40°N, 90°W.

Now use the map to answer these questions.

1 What line of latitude is closest to Austin, Texas?

2 What line of longitude is closest to Denver, Colorado?

3 Which location is farther north—50°N, 80°W or 30°N, 90°W?

▶ APPLY WHAT YOU LEARNED

Use latitude and longitude to describe the location of your state's capital city. Write a paragraph to descibe how you found the capital's location.

Practice your map and globe skills with the **GeoSkills CD-ROM.**

Review and Test Preparation

USE YOUR READING SKILLS

Complete this graphic organizer to show that you have identified the main ideas and supporting details in this chapter. A copy of this graphic organizer appears on page 13 of the Activity Book.

Regions of the United States

SUPPORTING DETAILS

SUPPORTING DETAILS

MAIN IDEA

The United States can be divided into regions based on people's activities.

SUPPORTING DETAILS

SUPPORTING DETAILS

THINK & WRITE

Write a Letter   Imagine that you are traveling across the country, from New York City in New York to San Francisco in California. Write a letter to a friend that describes how the climate changes as you travel from east to west.

Write a Compare and Contrast Report   Write a report about the mountains in the United States. In your report, compare and contrast the mountains in the eastern United States with those in the western United States.

USE VOCABULARY

Identify the term that correctly matches each definition.

| landform (p. 18) |
| inlet (p. 27) |
| rain shadow (p. 35) |
| fertilizer (p. 41) |
| relative location (p. 44) |

1. where a place is, compared to other places

2. physical feature on Earth's surface

3. material added to soil to make it more fertile

4. any area of water that extends into the land from a larger body of water

5. the dry side of a mountain

RECALL FACTS

Answer these questions.

6. What group of lakes makes up the world's largest freshwater lakes?

7. What do river systems do?

8. What is the Continental Divide?

9. How do people today modify their environment?

10. How does erosion change the land?

Write the letter of the best choice.

11. **TEST PREP** Which of the following vegetation regions has low bushes and cactuses?
   A forest
   B grassland
   C desert
   D prairie

12. **TEST PREP** Cultural regions can be based on all of the following except—
   F the religion that people follow.
   G the language people speak.
   H the work that people do.
   J the customs of the people.

THINK CRITICALLY

13. What types of regions are based on people's activities?

14. What are some ways the land is used in the United States?

APPLY SKILLS

Use Elevation Maps
Use the map of the United States on page 25 to answer these questions.

15. How would you describe the land in the Great Basin?

16. What is the highest elevation in the Interior Plains?

17. Which mountain range has a higher elevation, the Rocky Mountains or the Appalachian Mountains?

Use Longitude and Latitude
Use the Latitude and Longitude map on page 51 to answer these questions.

18. What capital cities are located closest to 45°N?

19. Which is farther north, a city at 40°N, 85°W or a city at 35°N, 80°W?

20. What city is located closest to 40°N, 120°W?

21. What is the location of Denver, Colorado?

2

The Earliest Americans

" It is from this land that we obtained the timber and stone for our homes and kivas. "

—Hopi, quoted by Alvin M. Josephy, Jr. in *500 Nations*, 1994

MESA VERDE NATIONAL PARK

For more than 700 years, from A.D. 600 to A.D. 1300, many Native American peoples made their homes in the area that is today Mesa Verde National Park. These early Americans built sturdy stone villages carved directly into the canyon walls. This photograph shows the Cliff Palace in winter.

LOCATE IT

COLORADO

Mesa Verde
National Park

CHAPTER READING SKILL

Compare and Contrast

When you **compare** information you are showing how things are alike. Words such as *like, both, also,* and *similarly* indicate a **comparison**. When you **contrast** information, you are identifying how things are different. Words such as *instead, but,* and *however* signal a **contrast**.

As you read this chapter, compare and contrast information about the Native American tribes in what is now the United States.

DIFFERENCES | SIMILARITIES | DIFFERENCES

1

MAIN IDEA
Read to find out how people may have first come to live in North and South America.

WHY IT MATTERS
Over time, groups of early people spread out across North and South America, becoming the first Americans.

VOCABULARY
glacier
migration
theory
archaeologist
artifact
descendant
origin story
ancestor

The First Americans

The history of the United States of America begins long before there was a United States. It begins with the first people in North America many thousands of years ago. At that time, however, the continent was a far different place from what it is today.

At different times in its past, the Earth has experienced long periods of freezing cold. During these periods, known as the Ice Ages, the Earth's climate became so cold that huge, slow-moving sheets of ice called **glaciers** formed. These glaciers covered large parts of the Earth. So much of the Earth's water was trapped in glaciers that the level of the oceans dropped. At several different times this caused a "bridge" of dry land to appear between the continents of Asia and North America.

The Land Bridge Story

Scientists gave the name Beringia (buh•RIN•gee•uh) to this land bridge between Asia and North America. It was named for the Bering Strait, a narrow body of water that now separates Siberia, in present-day Russia, from Alaska. Some scientists believe that between 12,000 and 40,000 years ago, hunting groups from Asia began traveling across the Beringia land bridge.

FAST FACT
During the Ice Ages so much water was trapped in glaciers that the water level in the oceans dropped as much as 350 feet (107 m).

This **migration**, or movement of people, probably took place very slowly, with groups traveling only a few miles in an entire lifetime. Finally, after thousands of years, Asian hunters reached what is today Alaska. However, they and the animals they hunted could go no farther. Huge glaciers blocked their path.

About 12,000 years ago, the climate began to get warmer. Some of the glaciers started to melt. As a result, the oceans began to rise. Once again water covered Beringia. At the same time, a narrow path opened between two melting glaciers that covered what is now Canada.

The animals followed the path between the glaciers, and the hunters followed the animals. Slowly the hunters made their way farther into the Americas—North America and South America. These people became the first Americans.

REVIEW According to the land bridge story, why did the hunters make their way into the Americas?

New Discoveries

The land bridge story is one **theory**, or possible explanation, for when and how the first Americans arrived in the Americas. Scientists, however, continue to ask if the first Americans could have been here earlier, and if they could have come by some other means.

The scientists who study the cultures of people who lived long ago are known as **archaeologists** (ar•kee•AH•luh•jists). In recent years archaeologists have made discoveries that seem to support an "early arrival" theory. According to this theory, Beringia appeared during an earlier Ice Age.

Movement According to the land bridge story, it took thousands of years for people to spread out over North and South America.

❓ About how many miles is it from Asia to the tip of South America?

Land Routes of Early People

Land
Glacier
Sea ice
→ Land route

One of the most important discoveries that supports the early arrival theory was made at a dig, or an archaeological site, located in southwestern Pennsylvania. This site, known as the Meadowcroft Rock Shelter, appears to have been an Ice Age campsite. Archaeologists discovered **artifacts**, or objects made by early people, at the site. Most of the artifacts are 14,000 to 15,000 years old. A few are more than 19,000 years old.

Discoveries in South America also support the early arrival theory. In Monte Verde (MOHN•tay VAIR•day), Chile, archaeologists uncovered artifacts, animal bones, and even a child's footprint. This evidence, or proof, shows that people were there at least 13,000 years ago. In Brazil human-made stone chips were found that may be 30,000 years old.

Other discoveries, in California and Peru, support the theory that the first Americans did not cross the land bridge at all. Instead, they may have traveled to the Americas in boats. Some may have actually crossed the Pacific Ocean. On San Miguel Island, about 25 miles (40 km) off the coast of California, archaeologists found evidence that people lived there about 13,000 years ago. Archaeologists know that these people used oceangoing boats because they ate fish that could be caught only far from shore. In Peru archaeologists found two 12,000-year-old sites whose residents also ate foods only found in the deep ocean.

REVIEW **Why do many archaeologists believe that the first Americans arrived earlier than previously thought?**

Origin Stories

There are also people today who believe that the first Americans did not come from Asia or anywhere else. Many present-day Native Americans, or American Indians, the descendants of the first Americans, believe that their people have always lived in the Americas. A **descendant** is a person's child, grandchild, or later relative.

All Native American peoples use stories to tell about important events and people in their past. Some of these stories

Many archaeologists believe that these tools (above) found in Pennsylvania, and the cave paintings (left) at Pedra Furada, Brazil, are proof that people arrived in the Americas earlier than previously thought.

Native American storytellers, like this one, share stories of the past with young people.

tell about the origins, or beginnings, of Native American people. Such stories are called **origin stories**. Like the Creation story in the Bible, some Native American origin stories explain how the world was made. The Blackfoot people, for example, tell a story of Old Man the Creator. According to the story, he made the animals and plants and formed the prairies and mountains.

The Hurons tell an origin story that begins when water covered the Earth. According to the story, land was formed from a tiny bit of soil taken from the claws of a turtle. The turtle had picked up the soil from the bottom of the ocean. Because of this story and others like it, some Native Americans use the name Turtle Island to describe the Americas.

No one knows exactly when the first Americans arrived. However, it was so long ago that the descendants of the first Americans have no stories of distant homelands where their **ancestors**, or early family members, once lived. They tell only stories of the Americas.

REVIEW What do Native American origin stories tell?

LESSON 1 REVIEW

1 MAIN IDEA By what ways may early people have arrived in the Americas?

2 WHY IT MATTERS Why do you think the arrival of early people in the Americas caused many different cultures to form?

3 VOCABULARY What is a **theory**?

4 READING SKILL—Compare and Contrast How do Native Americans' views on how they arrived in the Americas differ from archaeologists' views?

5 HISTORY How did the artifacts found at Meadowcroft Rock Shelter change many archaeologists' theories?

6 CULTURE Why do many Native Americans believe that their people have always lived in the Americas?

7 CRITICAL THINKING—Evaluate Why do people disagree about when and how the first Americans came to the Americas?

 PERFORMANCE—Make a Chart With a classmate, make a chart that compares the points of view on how people first came to the Americas.

·SKILLS·
CHART AND GRAPH

Read Time Lines

▶ WHY IT MATTERS

An easy way to see relationships among events in history is to look at a **time line**. A time line is a diagram that shows events that took place during a certain period of time. Knowing how to read a time line can help you understand the order of the events and the amounts of time between events.

▶ WHAT YOU NEED TO KNOW

A time line looks like a ruler marked in dates instead of inches. Like inches marked on a ruler, the dates on a time line are equally spaced. However, not all time lines look the same or are read in the same way. Most time lines run horizontally, or across the page. But some run vertically, or down the page. Horizontal time lines, like the one shown below, are read from left to right. The earliest date is on the left end of the time line, and the most recent date is on the right end. The time line on page 61 is a vertical time line. It is read from top to bottom. The earliest date is at the top of the time line, and the most recent date is at the bottom.

Time lines can show events that took place during any period of time. Some time lines show events that took place over a **decade**, or a period of 10 years. Others show events that took place over a **century**, or a period of 100 years. Both a decade and centuries are shown on the horizontal time line below. Some time lines even show events that took place over a **millennium**, or a period of a thousand years. A millennium is shown on the vertical time line on page 61.

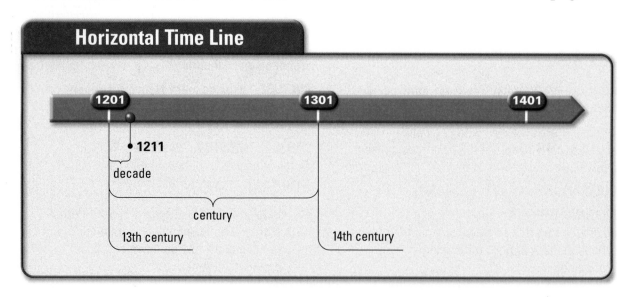

Horizontal Time Line

1201   1301   1401

• 1211

decade

century

13th century   14th century

The vertical time line here shows dates from the ancient past to today. Notice the letters B.C. and A.D. in the middle of the time line. Many people today identify years by whether they took place before or after the birth of Jesus Christ. The years before the birth of Christ are labeled B.C., which stands for "before Christ." Years after the birth of Christ are labeled A.D. This stands for the Latin words *Anno Domini,* which mean "in the year of the Lord."

An event that happened in 100 B.C. took place 100 years before the birth of Christ. An event that happened in A.D. 100 took place 100 years after the birth of Christ. Because every year in modern times is A.D., these letters are often not needed.

You may also see the letters B.C.E. or C.E. with dates. The abbreviation B.C.E. stands for "before the Common Era." It is sometimes used instead of B.C. The abbreviation C.E., which stands for "Common Era," is sometimes used in place of A.D.

▶ PRACTICE THE SKILL

Use the horizontal time line on page 60 to answer the following questions.

❶ How many centuries are shown on the time line?

❷ What were the first and last years of the thirteenth century?

Use the vertical time line on this page to answer the following questions.

❸ How many millenniums are shown on this time line?

❹ Which year came earlier, 1000 B.C. or A.D. 500?

▶ APPLY WHAT YOU LEARNED

Make a time line that shows the twentieth and twenty-first centuries. Label the first and last years of both centuries and the year you were born. Mark some other important events for you in the past and in the future. Display your time line in the classroom.

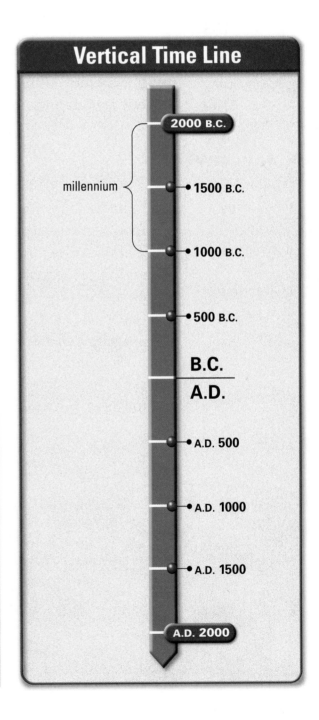

Vertical Time Line

2000 B.C.

millennium { 1500 B.C.

1000 B.C.

500 B.C.

B.C.
—
A.D.

A.D. 500

A.D. 1000

A.D. 1500

A.D. 2000

MAIN IDEA
Read to learn how changes
in the environment caused
the ancient Indians' ways
of life to change.

WHY IT MATTERS
As different cultures
developed among the
ancient Indians, North
America became a place
of great diversity.

VOCABULARY
nomad
technology
extinct
agriculture
tribe
civilization
class
slavery
pueblo

Ancient Indians

| 10,000 years ago | 5,000 years ago | Present |

10,000 years ago – 600 years ago

In many ways, the story of the first Americans, or ancient Indians, is filled with mystery. Just when archaeologists think they have some answers, they find new evidence that creates new questions. One thing, however, is known for certain. For many generations, the ancient Indians and their descendants slowly moved throughout the Americas. They settled in different regions and developed many different ways of life.

Hunters and Gatherers

After the last Ice Age, the climate of North America remained mostly cool and humid. Rich vegetation provided food for very large animals, including horses and camels. Giant mastodons and mammoths also roamed the vast grasslands and forests. Mastodons and mammoths looked like huge, hairy elephants. They stood 14 feet (4 m) tall, had tusks up to 14 feet (4 m) long, and weighed as much as 10,000 pounds (4,536 kg).

Many of the ancient Indians depended on these giant animals in order to survive. They ate the meat and used the fur, skins, and bones to make clothing, shelter, and tools. Daily life for these ancient Indians was spent mostly tracking and hunting

the animals and gathering fruits and nuts for food along the way. These people were mostly **nomads**, or wanderers who had no settled home. They built shelters in caves or in tents made from animal skins. The ancient Indians lived and hunted together in small groups or in families.

Compared to the animals they hunted, the ancient Indians were small and weak. Over time, however, they had learned to sharpen stones into spear points and tie them to wooden poles.

Some hunters also made and used clubs and axes with stone blades. From time to time, different groups of ancient Indians invented new tools or weapons. One such important weapon was the atlatl (AHT•lah•tuhl), or spear-thrower.

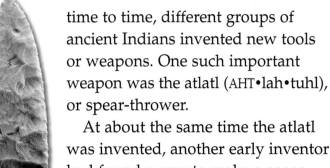

A Clovis point

At about the same time the atlatl was invented, another early inventor had found a way to make a spear point by a process scientists call flaking. Using a bone or a stone, the early inventor knocked off flakes, or small thin chips, from flint or another kind of stone. The inventor continued to flake the stone until a sharp point was formed. The point was then hollowed out and fastened tightly to a spear. These new spear points were razor-sharp, making them the best weapons early hunters had ever had.

These delicate yet deadly spear points are called Clovis points. They are named after the town of Clovis, New Mexico, where archaeologists first found them. Similar points have been found in places ranging from Alaska to the Andes Mountains, in South America.

The atlatl and Clovis points were two improvements in technology by ancient Indians. **Technology** is the use of scientific knowledge or tools to make or do something. These inventions were just as important to the ancient Indians as computers are to many people today.

REVIEW Why were Clovis points important to ancient Indians?

The ancient Indians moved from place to place to follow the animals they hunted.

Early farmers may have ground corn into flour by using a grinding stone (left) and may have stored kernels in containers like this one (above).

A Time of Change

Over thousands of years the environment of North America slowly changed. The climate became warmer and drier. As a result, much of the vegetation the giant animals ate could no longer grow. This may be one reason the giant animals became **extinct** (ik•STINGT), or died out. By about 10,000 years ago, most of them had disappeared from North America.

Life no longer centered around the hunting of giant animals. People began to fish and to hunt more of the smaller animals, such as deer and rabbits. To hunt them, the ancient Indians developed new hunting tools, such as the bow and arrow.

The ancient Indians also began to eat a greater variety of plants. In time they learned where certain plants grew best. They learned at what time of the year nuts, berries, and other plant parts became ripe. Each season the people traveled to places where they could gather food and hunt.

As the ancient Indians gathered more food than they could use at a time, they found ways to store the extra food. They made storage containers from reeds, vines, or strips of wood. Later, people learned to make storage containers out of other materials, such as clay.

Over time some ancient Indians changed their way of life even more. Some took the first steps toward producing their own food. They planted seeds and grew food crops. This was the beginning of **agriculture**, or farming.

Agriculture started at different times in different parts of the world. Ancient Indians in Mexico, however, were among the first to develop agriculture in North America. Some of the earliest farmers lived in the Tehuacán (tay•wah•KAHN) Valley in central Mexico. The early farmers of the valley grew at least 12 kinds of corn, as well as avocados, squash, and beans. Maize (MAYZ), or corn, became the most important crop for many ancient Indians living in North America.

Farming changed the lives of many of the ancient Indian groups. By about 5,000 years ago, some were building stronger homes and had started villages. Some groups also formed what are now called tribes. **Tribe** is a term often used to describe a group of Native Americans who share a language and customs. Over time each tribe came to have its own culture. A tribe's culture set it apart from other tribes.

REVIEW How did farming change the lives of many of the ancient Indians?

Early Civilizations

Having turned to a more settled way of life, some ancient Indian groups began to develop civilizations. A **civilization** is a culture that usually has cities and well-developed forms of government, religion, and learning. Among the most ancient American civilizations were the Olmecs (AHL•meks), the Maya (MY•ah), the Mound Builders, and the Anasazi (ah•nuh•SAH•zee).

From about 1500 B.C. to A.D. 300, the Olmecs lived in what is now southeastern Mexico. They developed their own calendar, number system, and form of writing. Because later groups learned so much from them, the Olmec culture came to be known as the "mother civilization" of the Americas. The Olmecs shared their ideas through trade with other groups.

One of these groups was the Maya, who lived south of the Olmecs. The Maya began to develop around 500 B.C. Building on what the Olmecs had done, the Maya slowly created their own civilization. They built more than 100 stone cities. Each city had its own ruler and government. Tikal, in what is now Guatemala, was the largest.

Like the Olmecs, the Maya were divided into social **classes**. Depending on what the people of a certain class did to make a living, its members were treated with different amounts of respect. At the top were the Mayan priests.

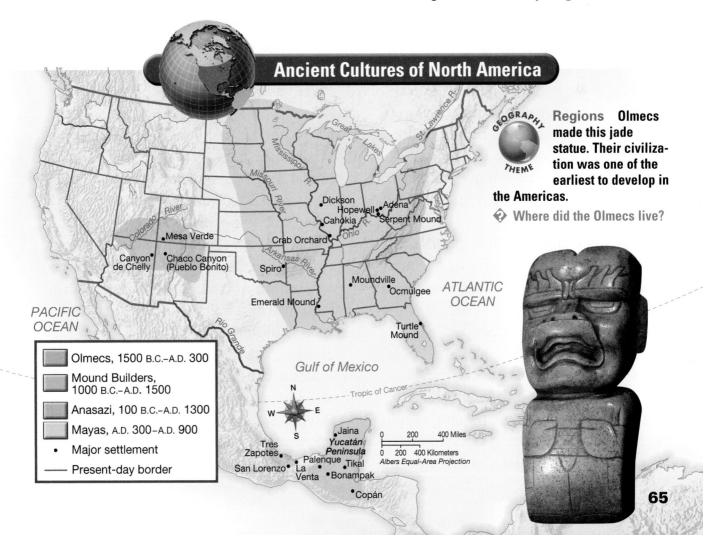

Ancient Cultures of North America

Great Lakes
St. Lawrence R.
Mississippi
Missouri River
Colorado River
Mesa Verde
Canyon de Chelly
Chaco Canyon (Pueblo Bonito)
Crab Orchard
Ohio R.
Spiro
Arkansas River
Dickson
Hopewell
Cahokia
Adena
Serpent Mound
Moundville
Ocmulgee
Emerald Mound
Turtle Mound

PACIFIC OCEAN

ATLANTIC OCEAN

Rio Grande

Gulf of Mexico

Tropic of Cancer

Tres Zapotes
San Lorenzo
La Venta
Palenque
Jaina
Yucatán Peninsula
Tikal
Bonampak
Copán

N W E S

0   200   400 Miles
0 200 400 Kilometers
Albers Equal-Area Projection

■ Olmecs, 1500 B.C.–A.D. 300
■ Mound Builders, 1000 B.C.–A.D. 1500
■ Anasazi, 100 B.C.–A.D. 1300
■ Mayas, A.D. 300–A.D. 900
• Major settlement
— Present-day border

GEOGRAPHY THEME

Regions Olmecs made this jade statue. Their civilization was one of the earliest to develop in the Americas.

❓ Where did the Olmecs live?

65

Then came the people from important families. Below them were the traders and craftspeople, the farmers, and finally the slaves. **Slavery** is the practice of holding people against their will and making them carry out orders. In Mayan society most slaves were people accused of crimes.

While cultures developed in Central America, other ancient civilizations grew in what is today the eastern half of the United States. These people became known as the Mound Builders because of the earthen mounds they built as burial sites or as places of worship.

The earliest of the Mound Builders were the Adenas (uh•DEE•nuhz), who lived in the Ohio River valley from about 1000 B.C. to A.D. 200. One of the most famous Adena mounds, Serpent Mound, is about 1,330 feet (405 m) long. When you look at it from the air, you can see that it forms the shape of a snake.

Around 300 B.C. a larger mound-building civilization known as the Hopewells developed in the central part of what is now the United States. The culture of the Hopewells was the strongest in the region for nearly 500 years. Hopewell goods and ideas spread far and wide through trade.

The greatest mound-building civilization was that of the Mississippian culture. It developed in the Mississippi River valley about A.D. 700. The Mississippians lived in hundreds of towns and several large cities. The largest Mississippian city was near where East St. Louis, Illinois, stands today. By A.D. 1200 more than 30,000 people lived in this city, called Cahokia (kuh•HOH•kee•uh).

From about 100 B.C. to A.D. 1300, the Anasazi, or "Ancient People," built a civilization in what is today the southwestern United States. They lived in groups of houses built next to or on top of one another, like apartment houses today. Spanish explorers later described these homes as pueblos (PWEH•blohz). **Pueblo** is the Spanish word for "village." Most pueblos were built on top of mesas, or high, flat-topped hills. Others were

Cahokia (left) had 85 mounds in all. One mound, now called Monk's Mound, stood 100 feet (30 m) high and covered 16 acres. People today can climb steps to reach the top of this mound (above).

built into the sides of high cliffs. The largest was Pueblo Bonito (boh•NEE•toh) in present-day New Mexico.

Over hundreds of years, the Anasazi and other early civilizations in North America gave way to new cultures and new civilizations. By about A.D. 1400, hundreds of different tribes of Native Americans lived throughout North America. North America was a land of great diversity—a land of many different peoples and cultures.

REVIEW **Which early civilization lived in what is now the eastern United States?**

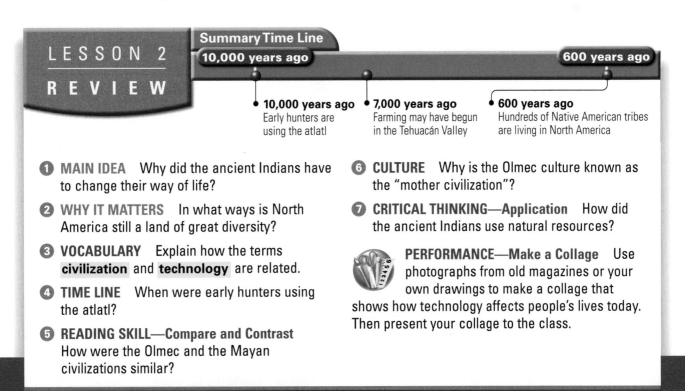

LESSON 2 REVIEW

Summary Time Line

10,000 years ago — 600 years ago

- **10,000 years ago** Early hunters are using the atlatl
- **7,000 years ago** Farming may have begun in the Tehuacán Valley
- **600 years ago** Hundreds of Native American tribes are living in North America

1 **MAIN IDEA** Why did the ancient Indians have to change their way of life?

2 **WHY IT MATTERS** In what ways is North America still a land of great diversity?

3 **VOCABULARY** Explain how the terms **civilization** and **technology** are related.

4 **TIME LINE** When were early hunters using the atlatl?

5 **READING SKILL—Compare and Contrast** How were the Olmec and the Mayan civilizations similar?

6 **CULTURE** Why is the Olmec culture known as the "mother civilization"?

7 **CRITICAL THINKING—Application** How did the ancient Indians use natural resources?

PERFORMANCE—Make a Collage Use photographs from old magazines or your own drawings to make a collage that shows how technology affects people's lives today. Then present your collage to the class.

Use a Cultural Map

VOCABULARY

generalization

This butterfly was made by a Crow Indian.

▶ WHY IT MATTERS

Some maps give you a general picture of the cultures of the people living in different regions. Maps showing cultural regions often use colors or symbols for places where most of the people speak a certain language or follow a certain way of life. Knowing about cultural regions can help you understand more about people and where they live.

▶ WHAT YOU NEED TO KNOW

Learning about the general picture of a place can help you make generalizations. A **generalization** is a statement that summarizes groups of facts and shows relationships among them. A generalization tells what is true most of the time.

The map on page 69 shows the early Native American cultural regions of North America. Each of the 11 regions is based on the unique location, landforms, climate, and vegetation that affected the cultures and traditions of Native Americans.

Within each cultural region are labels giving the names of some of the Native American tribes that lived there. The map also includes present-day state borders so you can better understand where these early cultures were located.

▶ PRACTICE THE SKILL

Use the following questions as a guide for making generalizations about the early cultures of North America.

1 Identify the color that covers most of the eastern half of what is today the United States. What generalization can you make about the way of life of the people who lived there?

2 Which three cultural regions included parts of present-day Texas?

3 What generalizations can you make about early Native American cultures in the present-day states of Arkansas, New Mexico, and Virginia?

▶ APPLY WHAT YOU LEARNED

Draw a cultural map of present-day North America based on the main languages spoken. Gather information for your map by using books or Internet sources. Use colors to show where different languages are generally spoken today. Have a classmate use your map to make generalizations about the cultures of North America.

Practice your map and globe skills with the **GeoSkills CD-ROM**.

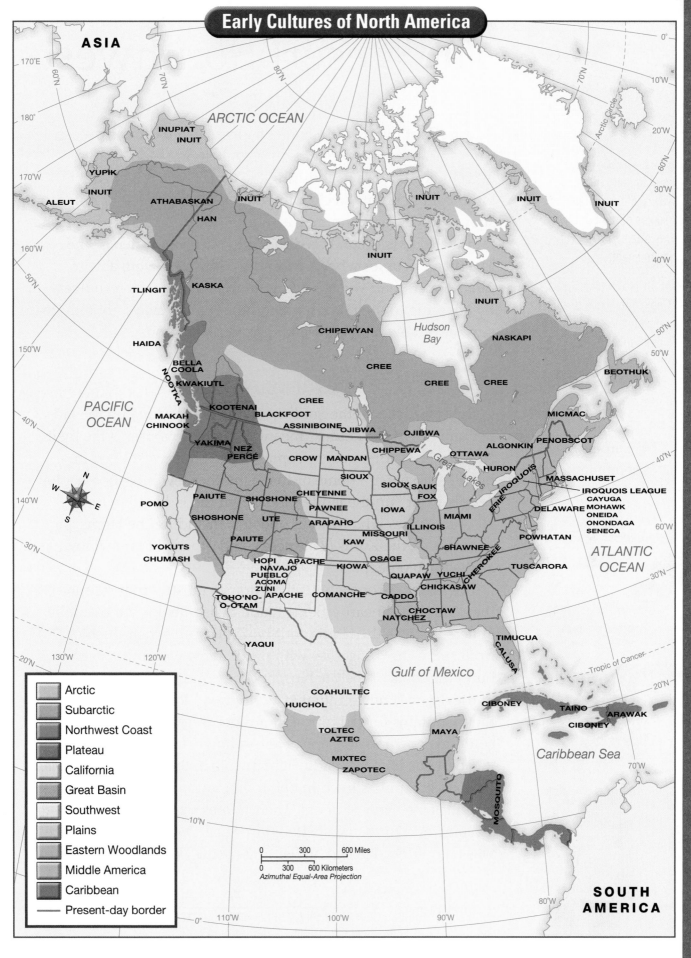

Early Cultures of North America

ASIA

ARCTIC OCEAN

INUPIAT
INUIT
YUPIK
INUIT
ALEUT
ATHABASKAN
HAN
INUIT
INUIT
INUIT
INUIT
INUIT
INUIT
TLINGIT
KASKA
HAIDA
BELLA
COOLA
NOOTKA
KWAKIUTL
MAKAH
CHINOOK
YAKIMA
NEZ
PERCÉ
KOOTENAI
BLACKFOOT
ASSINIBOINE
OJIBWA
CHIPEWYAN
CREE
CREE
CREE
CREE
NASKAPI
BEOTHUK
MICMAC
Hudson
Bay

PACIFIC
OCEAN

CROW
MANDAN
SIOUX
OJIBWA
CHIPPEWA
OTTAWA
HURON
ALGONKIN
PENOBSCOT
MASSACHUSET
POMO
PAIUTE
SHOSHONE
CHEYENNE
PAWNEE
IOWA
SIOUX
SAUK
FOX
MIAMI
ERIE
IROQUOIS
DELAWARE
IROQUOIS LEAGUE
CAYUGA
MOHAWK
ONEIDA
ONONDAGA
SENECA
SHOSHONE
UTE
ARAPAHO
MISSOURI
ILLINOIS
SHAWNEE
POWHATAN
YOKUTS
CHUMASH
PAIUTE
KAW
OSAGE
YUCHI
CHEROKEE
TUSCARORA
HOPI
NAVAJO
PUEBLO
ACOMA
ZUNI
APACHE
KIOWA
QUAPAW
CHICKASAW
CADDO
TOHO'NO-
O-OTAM
APACHE
COMANCHE
CHOCTAW
NATCHEZ
YAQUI
TIMUCUA
CALUSA

Gulf of Mexico

COAHUILTEC
HUICHOL
CIBONEY
TAINO
ARAWAK
CIBONEY
TOLTEC
AZTEC
MAYA
MIXTEC
ZAPOTEC
MOSQUITO
Caribbean Sea

SOUTH
AMERICA

Great
Lakes

ATLANTIC
OCEAN

Tropic of Cancer

Arctic Circle

Legend
- Arctic
- Subarctic
- Northwest Coast
- Plateau
- California
- Great Basin
- Southwest
- Plains
- Eastern Woodlands
- Middle America
- Caribbean
- Present-day border

0 300 600 Miles
0 300 600 Kilometers
Azimuthal Equal-Area Projection

MAIN IDEA
Read to learn how the way of life of Indian peoples of the Southwest was affected by the dry environment.

WHY IT MATTERS
People often have to adjust or modify their environment in order to live.

VOCABULARY
adapt
staple
surplus
ceremony
hogan

The Desert Southwest

The Southwest, with its rocky mesas, deep canyons, steep cliffs, and rugged mountains, is a challenging place to live, even today. Intense heat during the day can be followed by bitter cold at night. Weeks can go by without a drop of rain or snow. However, in summer, a sudden storm can bring so much rain that floods occur. It is difficult to survive in such a land. The many peoples who lived in the Southwest were able to **adapt**, or fit their ways of living to the land and its resources. By adapting to their environment, they found ways not only to survive but even to live well in the desert region.

The Pueblo Peoples

To the peoples of the Southwest, the expression "up the ladder and down the ladder" meant "to enter a house." Like their Anasazi ancestors, many peoples of the Southwest lived in pueblos. To enter a home or to reach other levels of the pueblo, people went "up the ladder and down the ladder." In time all of the tribes who lived in pueblos, including the Hopis (HOH•peez), the Zunis (ZOO•neez), and others, became known as the Pueblo peoples.

The Pueblo peoples built their homes mostly from resources they could find nearby. Some made their pueblos out of adobe. Others, such as the Hopis and the Zunis, built their pueblos from stones held together with mud. Some wood was used to build the roofs of the pueblos, but there are very few trees in the desert. Pueblo Indians had to travel long distances into the mountains to find pine and juniper trees from which they could make wooden beams. Here is how Charlotte and David Yue describe life in an early Hopi pueblo in their book *The Pueblo*.

"Pueblo families lived in one room, but most of the daily activities were out of doors. Their homes were used mainly for sleeping and for being sheltered from bad weather. The terrace was an outdoor kitchen and sitting room. The women went up

Pueblo families helped their children learn the names of the kachinas (kuh•CHEE•nuhz) by giving them kachina figures.

A CLOSER LOOK
Pueblo

Some pueblos had as many as five levels. The roof of one level was the floor of the next level above it.

1. kiva
2. pottery making
3. grinding corn
4. cooking
5. weaving
6. preparing food

❖ What activities are shown in this pueblo?

and down ladders to outside ovens on the terrace or down to the ground. The outdoor drying racks had to be tended, and baskets and pottery were often worked on outside."

The land of the Southwest also affected how the Pueblo Indians hunted and grew food. The **staple**, or main, foods of the Pueblos were corn, beans, and squash. As it was for most Native American groups, the most important of these was corn. The Pueblos also grew cotton, from which they made blankets and clothing. To grow these crops in the dry climate, the

Pueblos depended on water from rain and underground springs, which they used to irrigate the land. While the men tended the crops, the women spent hours each day grinding corn into meal, using smooth, flat stones. Part of every home was filled with containers of corn and cornmeal. A food **surplus**, or an amount more than what is needed, meant survival during times of drought.

The Hopis and other Pueblo peoples believed in gods of the sun, rain, and Earth. Spirits called kachinas (kuh•CHEE•nuhz) were an important part of the Hopis' religion.

The Hopis believed that kachinas visit the world of living people once a year and enter the bodies of kachina dancers. The kachina dancers were men who wore painted masks and dressed to look like the kachinas. Kachina dancers took part in many Hopi ceremonies. A **ceremony** is a series of actions performed during a special event, such as a religious service. Some of these ceremonies were held in special underground rooms called kivas (KEE•vuhz), and others were held in large meeting places outside. Today many Hopis continue to perform their traditional dances, some with kachina masks and some without.

REVIEW What kinds of natural resources did the Pueblo peoples use to build their homes?

Desert Newcomers

Not all of the people of the Southwest were Pueblo Indians. Before moving to the Southwest, peoples such as the Navajos (NA•vuh•hohz) lived mainly as nomads. They traveled in groups of families and did not have a formal leader.

The Navajos began moving into the Southwest about A.D. 1025. They settled in an area known today as the Four Corners. This is the place where the corners of the states of Arizona, Colorado, New Mexico, and Utah meet. The Navajo people still live in the Four Corners area today.

Some of this land was also Hopi land. In time the Navajos began learning Hopi ways of life. Soon they, too, were growing crops and making cotton clothing as the Hopis did.

In this land, the Navajos built shelters called hogans (HOH•gahnz). A **hogan** was usually cone-shaped. It was built by covering a log frame with bark and mud.

Rather than building their hogans close together, the Navajos built them in small, family-sized groups miles apart from one another.

REVIEW What ways of life did the Navajos learn from the Hopis?

• BIOGRAPHY •

Luci Tapahonso 1953–

Character Trait: Loyalty

Luci Tapahonso's writings help keep the Navajo culture alive. Tapahonso is the Navajo author of six books of poetry and short stories. She was born in Shiprock, New Mexico, and started writing poetry at the age of 9. She uses both the Navajo and the English languages in her writings, which are often about the landscape of the Southwest and the history of her people.

MULTIMEDIA BIOGRAPHIES **GO** ONLINE
Visit The Learning Site at
www.harcourtschool.com/biographies
to learn about other famous people.

Navajo Beliefs

The Navajos believed in gods they called the Holy People. Some gods, such as the Earth Mother, were kind. Others, such as the sun god, could cause crops to dry up. The Navajos believed that they needed to honor the gods so that the gods would not use their powers against the people.

The Navajos honored their gods in ceremonies. Navajo ceremonies were led by religious leaders and healers called medicine people. Medicine people called upon the gods to protect the Navajos' families, homes, and crops or to cure the sick. In healing ceremonies medicine people made sandpaintings, also called dry paintings, that were believed to help heal people. First, the medicine person created a pattern of symbols on the ground, using colored sand. Then, the sick person sat or lay on the sandpainting while the medicine person held a ceremony that the Navajos believed would help the sick person feel healing powers. The painting was always rubbed away after the ceremony.

REVIEW **What is a medicine person?**

Today some sandpaintings are preserved. This one was made by Michael Tsosie.

LOCATE IT

UTAH

ARIZONA

Monument Valley Tribal Park

The desert lands of Monument Valley are part of the Navajo lands.

LESSON 3 REVIEW

1. **MAIN IDEA** How did the dryness of the environment affect the Indian people of the Southwest?

2. **WHY IT MATTERS** In what ways do you think the environment affects how people in your community or state live?

3. **VOCABULARY** Use the term **ceremony** in a sentence to describe Hopi customs.

4. **READING SKILL—Compare and Contrast** In what ways were the Navajos different from the Hopis?

5. **HISTORY** Why was it important to the Pueblo peoples to store food?

6. **CRITICAL THINKING—Evaluate** How do you think the Navajos' way of life affected their need for a formal leader?

PERFORMANCE—Make a Graphic Organizer Using the information in the lesson, make a graphic organizer about the way of life of the Hopis. Then use your organizer to write a story about them.

PRIMARY SOURCES

Native American Pottery

For hundreds of years, pottery-making has been an important part of Native American cultures. Over time, products such as metal pans, glassware, and imported ceramics have changed the way traditional pottery is made and changed its uses. However, the designs and decoration of pottery continue to reflect themes that are important to Native American cultures.

This present-day potter makes pottery in the Native American tradition.

FROM THE PHILBROOK ART CENTER, THE MAXWELL MUSEUM OF ANTHROPOLOGY, AND THE NATIONAL MUSEUM OF AMERICAN HISTORY AT THE SMITHSONIAN INSTITUTION

1990

This traditionally styled Pueblo seed pot shows contemporary images of the space shuttle and an astronaut.

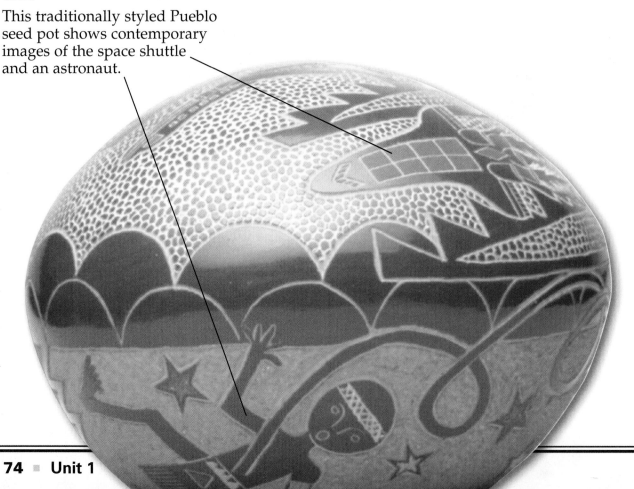

Analyze the Primary Source

❶ How do you think these pots are similarly decorated? How are their decorations different?

❷ What differences do you see in the pottery of different time periods? How do you think each vessel would be used today?

About 1300

The paints used to decorate pots were made from plants.

About 1000

Bowls like this may have been used to store grain.

Middle 1800s

Jars like this were made for storing food and water. By the late 1800s, however, glass jars were often used instead.

ACTIVITY

Compare and Contrast Make a list of uses that you might have for a clay pot. Then select designs that you would like to show on your pot. Use your information to draw a picture showing what your pot will look like. Share your drawing with your classmates. How are your pottery designs alike? How are they different?

RESEARCH

Visit The Learning Site at **www.harcourtschool.com/primarysources** to research other primary sources.

MAIN IDEA
Read to learn how the environment of the Northwest Coast and Arctic regions made life different for the peoples who lived there.

WHY IT MATTERS
The environment continues to affect the unique ways of life of peoples in different parts of the world.

VOCABULARY
dugout
barter
potlatch
clan
pit house
harpoon
totem pole

The people of the Northwest Coast traveled from place to place in dugouts.

The Northwest Coast and the Arctic

The Indians of the Northwest Coast and the Arctic lived in a place that was very different from the deserts of the Southwest. The Northwest Coast is a strip of land that stretches along the Pacific Ocean from northern California to Alaska. Nestled between the ocean and rugged mountains, it is a land of rivers and forests filled with fish and game. The Arctic region is much colder, and the land is frozen for most of the year.

River Traders

Along the Northwest Coast there was little agriculture. But there were plenty of fish, especially salmon. There were also plenty of deer, bears, and other animals. Therefore, instead of growing their own food, the Indians of the Northwest Coast met their need for food by fishing, hunting, and gathering plants. The enormous trees that grew in the forests provided them with wood for boats, houses, and tools.

If the Indians of the Northwest Coast needed items they could not make, they could get them through trade. Although the region's mountains made overland travel difficult, people could travel long distances on its waterways. In fact, the Columbia River became the "highway" of the Northwest. People used it to travel from place to place in wooden dugouts. A **dugout** is a boat made from a large, hollowed-out log.

One of the greatest trading centers located on the Columbia River was called The Dalles (DALZ). People would travel hundreds of miles to trade there. Dozens of tribes, some speaking languages as different from each other as English is from Chinese, took part in the trading through the mild summer months.

REVIEW **What was one of the greatest trading centers on the Columbia River?**

The Chinooks made people pay them for the right to travel on the Columbia River.

Making a Dugout

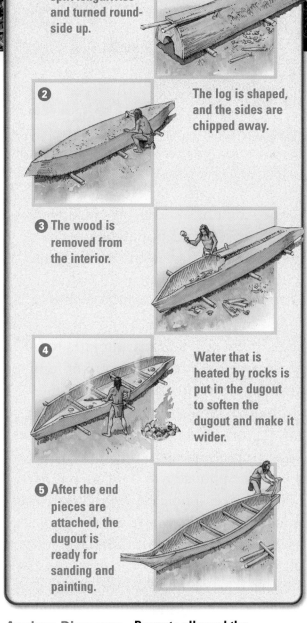

1 A cedar log is split lengthwise and turned round-side up.

2 The log is shaped, and the sides are chipped away.

3 The wood is removed from the interior.

4 Water that is heated by rocks is put in the dugout to soften the dugout and make it wider.

5 After the end pieces are attached, the dugout is ready for sanding and painting.

The Chinooks

The best-known traders among the Northwest Coast Indians were the Chinooks (shih•NUKS). The Chinooks, who lived at the mouth of the Columbia River, controlled the river from the coast all the way to The Dalles—about 200 miles (322 km) upstream.

Because many tribes gathered at The Dalles to trade, the different languages they spoke made communication difficult. To help solve the problem, the Chinooks developed a language for trading. It was made up of Chinook words and words borrowed from other languages. This language made it easier for people of different tribes to talk to each other and to **barter**, or exchange goods. People traded dried fish, shells, furs, whale products, seal oil, cedar, dugouts, masks, jewelry, baskets, copper, and even prisoners.

Wealth was important to the people of the Northwest Coast. Tribes often attacked one another to gain wealth and, in turn, respect. Prisoners, a sign of wealth, were frequently taken as slaves during the many wars.

Analyze Diagrams Dugouts allowed the Northwest Coast Indians to travel on the many rivers in the region.

◆ How were the dugouts made wider?

During a whale hunt the chief harpooner showed his respect for the huge animal by singing a special song, promising to give the whale gifts if it allowed itself to be killed.

The Chinooks and other Northwest Coast people held **potlatches** to show their wealth. These were celebrations with feasting and dancing. During a potlatch, the hosts gave away gifts as a sign of their wealth. Members of some clans spent years preparing gifts to be given away. A **clan** is a group of families that are related to one another.

Chinook villages were made up of rows of long wooden houses. The houses were built of boards and had no windows. Each house was built so that part of it was over a hole dug in the earth and some of its rooms were partially underground. Such a house is called a **pit house**.

In each house lived several families belonging to the same clan. Each clan was headed by its oldest member. The Chinooks traced their clans through the mother's family line. The people of the clan had the same mother, grandmother, or great-grandmother.

REVIEW What were potlatches?

The Makahs and the Kwakiutls

Most peoples of the Northwest found plenty of food in rivers and nearby coastal waters. Salmon and other fish and whales were in good supply. The Makahs (mah•KAWZ), who lived in what is now the state of Washington, were one of the many coastal peoples who built dugouts to hunt whales at sea. Some other coastal tribes, such as the Kwakiutls (KWAH•kee•oo•tuhlz), captured whales only if they became stranded on the shore. The Kwakiutls lived north of the Makahs on what is now Vancouver Island and western Canada.

Whale hunts were very important to the Makahs. Makah whale hunters often spent months preparing for a whale hunt. They fasted and prayed to their gods to favor them. They made new wooden **harpoons**—long spears with sharp shell points. They repaired their canoes and paddles. Made of wood, their canoes were 6 feet (about 2 m) wide and carried up to 60 people. They were built to travel over the open ocean. However, they still could be tipped over by an angry whale.

Imagine one group of whale hunters setting out to sea. The chief harpooner leads the hunters. Once they get close enough to the whale, the chief harpooner throws his harpoon. The whale is hit! Sealskin floats tied to the harpoon line make it difficult for the whale to dive down into the water and escape. Harpooners from nearby canoes throw

their weapons, too. When the whale dies, the hunters start towing it to shore.

It takes hours of paddling for the hunters to reach their village. Wooden houses line the narrow beach between the water and the forest. Outside each house stands a tall wooden post called a **totem pole**. Each totem pole is carved with shapes of people and animals.

Some of the best woodcarvers in the Northwest Coast were the Kwakiutls. Like the Makahs, the Kwakiutls lived in wooden houses along the shore. Some houses were huge, up to 60 feet (18 m) long. Like others in the region, the Kwakiutls ate plants, shellfish, salmon, elk, and deer. They also held the most lavish potlatches of all the Northwest Coast Indians.

REVIEW How did the Makahs prepare for a whale hunt?

· HERITAGE ·

Family Heritage

In the past the Indian tribes of the Northwest Coast had no written language. Because of this, they passed on their family and tribal histories in other ways. One way was through expertly carved and painted masks and totem poles. Masks were used in elaborate dances and ceremonies to act out stories of important events in the Indians' lives, such as births, deaths, and marriages. Totem poles were used to represent their ancestors and to tell the history of their people.

The carvings on a totem pole show a family's history and importance.

These Inuit sisters are wearing traditional dress.

The Inuit

The native peoples of the Arctic lived mostly north and east of the Northwest Coast Indians. Among them were the Inuit, who first settled in the harsh environment of the Arctic region of present-day northern Alaska and Canada only about 4,000 years ago. Since much of this land was frozen tundra, it was much too cold for farming. The early Inuit, like the early Northwest Coast Indians, got most of their food and made most of their clothing, shelters, and tools from the animals they hunted. Although resources were scarce in the Arctic, the Inuit developed the skills necessary to survive in a land of ice and snow.

To survive in the harsh environment, the Inuit had to be skilled hunters and fishers. They hunted seal, walrus, and caribou. They used the meat for food, the bones for tools, and the skins for clothing. Like the Makahs, the Inuit along the Alaskan coast hunted whales.

The Inuit made many kinds of shelters. Some built igloos—dwellings made of ice—in which they lived during the winter months. Igloos were made from large blocks of ice stacked into a dome shape. A hole in the top allowed the smoke from cooking fires to escape, and blocks of clear ice served as windows. During the summer the Inuit lived in tents made of animal skins. Other Inuit lived in tents and huts year-round.

REVIEW How did the Inuit use the environment to meet their needs?

LESSON 4
REVIEW

1 MAIN IDEA How was life in the Northwest Coast region different from life in other regions?

2 WHY IT MATTERS How does the environment cause people today to have a unique way of life?

3 VOCABULARY Use the term **barter** in a paragraph about trade on the Northwest Coast.

4 READING SKILL—Compare and Contrast In what ways were the Makahs and the Kwakiutls similar?

5 CULTURE Who was the head of a Chinook clan?

6 HISTORY Why did the Makahs build canoes that could travel on the open ocean?

7 CRITICAL THINKING—Synthesize What do you think the Northwest Coast Indians learned from each other by trading at The Dalles?

PERFORMANCE—Write a Description Using facts from the lesson, write a paragraph that describes what life was like for the Indians of the Northwest Coast or the Arctic. Then read your paragraph to a classmate.

The Plains

Millions of buffalo, or American bison, as scientists call them, once roamed the grassy lands of the Interior Plains. These hairy, cowlike beasts moved in huge herds made up of thousands of animals. The herds were so large that they were said to blacken the horizon. To the Plains Indians, who lived on the Interior Plains between the Mississippi River and the Rocky Mountains, the buffalo were second only to water as the region's most important resource.

MAIN IDEA
Read to learn how the Plains Indians used natural resources to live in their environment.

WHY IT MATTERS
People continue to depend on natural resources to live in their environment.

VOCABULARY
lodge
sod
tepee
travois

Life on the Plains

Imagine a Native American hunting party coming upon a herd of buffalo. Wearing animal skins as disguises, the hunters creep into position around some of the buffalo. At a signal, the hunters all shout together. The frightened buffalo run, and the hunters drive them toward a steep cliff. The buffalo fall over the cliff and are killed.

Most of the women of the tribe were not hunters. Their job was to skin the buffalo and prepare them for many uses. Some of the meat was eaten right away. The rest was dried and saved for winter or a time when there were no buffalo nearby to hunt. Dried meat, which people today call jerky, can be kept for many months.

This painting by George Catlin shows two hunters hiding under wolf skins.

The Plains Indians used every part of the buffalo they hunted. They made clothing, blankets, and moccasins from the skins. They carried water in bags made from the stomachs. They twisted the hair into cord. They made needles and other tools from the bones and horns.

REVIEW What did the peoples of the plains make from buffalo skins?

Farmers and Hunters

Among the many Plains Indians who lived on the tall-grass prairies of the Interior Plains were the Mandans, Pawnees, Wichitas (WICH•ih•tawz), and some bands, or groups, of Sioux (SOO). These groups lived mostly in the eastern part of the Plains cultural region. They were both farmers and hunters. They farmed the rich land in the valleys along rivers such as the Missouri, Mississippi, and Platte. They also hunted deer, elk, and buffalo.

These people lived in villages made up of circular houses called **lodges**. Each lodge was built over a shallow pit. On the northern prairies of the Interior Plains, the lodges were covered with sod. **Sod** is earth cut into blocks or mats and held together by the grass and its roots. Because these houses were covered with earth, they are often called earth lodges. On the southern prairies, the earth lodges were covered with grass or animal skins.

Each earth lodge was home to several families. Sometimes as many as 60 people, plus their dogs, lived in one lodge. Each family had its own bed or beds next to the outer wall. In the center of the earth lodge was a shared fireplace under a hole in the roof for letting out smoke. The earth lodge was warm, and it protected the people during the cold winters.

Buffalo were a very important resource to the Indians of the western Plains. Buffalo hides were used to make much of their clothing, such as dresses and moccasins (right).

This painting by Karl Bodmer shows the Mandan lodges and the boats the Mandans used. To make the boats, they stretched buffalo skins around a wooden frame.

About twice a year the villages on the prairies emptied, as men, women, and children took part in a great buffalo hunt. The people walked for several days from their villages in the river valleys and forests to the grassy hunting areas.

When they were not hunting, the Indians on the prairies farmed. Their farms were small—more like gardens than farms. Their crops were mainly beans, corn, squash, and sunflowers. The farmers often traded their crops for goods that other tribes brought to them. Some of the villages along the Missouri River became trade centers for Native Americans from faraway places. The present-day site of Pierre (PIR), South Dakota, for example, was once the capital of the Arikara (uh•RIK•uh•ruh) Indian nation and a center for trade for more than 400 years.

REVIEW In what ways did the Plains Indians get their food?

The Great Plains Nomads

Many of the people who lived on the Great Plains, the western part of the Plains cultural region, did not farm or live in villages. Groups such as the Crows, the Cheyennes (shy•ANZ), the Kiowas (KY•uh•wuhz), and the Comanches (kuh•MAN•cheez) were nomads. They moved from place to place because they followed herds of buffalo. They did not grow crops because the flat grasslands on which they roamed had no rich river valleys. The roots of the short grass were so tough that it was almost impossible to break the soil with a digging stick.

Although these nomads had no permanent dwellings, they claimed certain areas as their own hunting lands. They followed specific routes within their lands. These routes usually depended on the movement of the herds of buffalo.

A Calendar Robe

Analyze Primary Sources

Many Plains Indians kept the history of their tribe on what is now called a calendar robe. Each year leaders met to decide what event should be recorded on the robe. The drawings of the events could be read from left to right, right to left, or outward in a spiral from the center. This calendar robe was drawn by a Dakota Indian named Lone Dog. It covers the period 1800–1871.

1 1837–1838: A successful elk hunt was held.

2 1840–1841: The Dakotas and the Cheyennes made peace.

3 1845–1846: Buffalo meat was plentiful.

◆ Why is it important to record historical events?

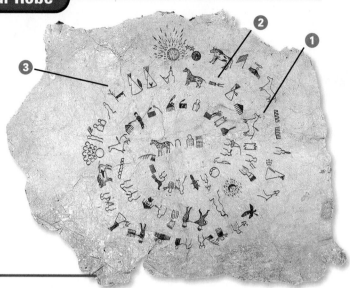

They depended on the buffalo as one of their most important resources. Houses, clothing, food, and even fuel for fire came from the buffalo. For fuel they used dried buffalo droppings, called chips.

Because the nomads had no permanent home, they built shelters that were easy to move. One kind was a cone-shaped tent called a **tepee** (TEE•pee). The nomads set wooden poles in a circle and tied them together at the top. They covered the poles with buffalo skins, leaving a hole at the top to let out the smoke from their fires.

Wood was hard to find because few trees grew on the Great Plains. The early Native Americans made double use of their wooden tepee poles by turning them into a kind of carrier called a **travois** (truh•VOY). A travois was made up of two poles fastened to a harness on a dog. Goods were carried on a skin tied between the poles.

In the Plains Indian way of life, each person was equal in the group. No one person was born more important than anyone else. Any man could become chief by proving himself a good hunter and a good leader of people. He was chief because his people chose and trusted him.

Women were responsible for sewing buffalo hides together to make tepee coverings. They also set up the tepees. Tepees were usually set up so that the entrance faced east. This kept the strong western winds on the Great Plains from blowing inside.

In some nomadic tribes, members who did not follow the ways of their group were free to live on their own. Sometimes a leader and his followers would start a new group. In this way, one tribe often had many subgroups. Each subgroup was made up of families who worked together.

REVIEW How could a man become chief of a Plains Indian tribe?

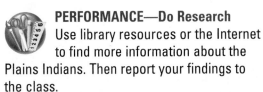

LESSON 5 REVIEW

❶ **MAIN IDEA** How did the peoples of the Plains use natural resources to live in their environment?

❷ **WHY IT MATTERS** In what ways do people today depend on natural resources to live in their environment?

❸ **VOCABULARY** Write a sentence that compares and contrasts a **lodge** and a **tepee**.

❹ **READING SKILL—Compare and Contrast** How were the Great Plains nomads different from the Indians who lived along the rivers in the eastern part of the Interior Plains?

❺ **GEOGRAPHY** What were the two most important resources to the Plains Indians?

❻ **CULTURE** How did the Plains Indians divide the work that went into a buffalo hunt?

❼ **CRITICAL THINKING—Analyze** How did the way of life of the Plains Indians affect the type of shelters they built?

PERFORMANCE—Do Research Use library resources or the Internet to find more information about the Plains Indians. Then report your findings to the class.

The Eastern Woodlands

MAIN IDEA
Read to find out how the people of the Eastern Woodlands shared similar ways of life even though they spoke different languages and had different governments.

WHY IT MATTERS
Like the peoples of the Eastern Woodlands, the people of the United States today come from different backgrounds, but they share similar ways of life.

VOCABULARY
palisade
slash-and-burn
wigwam
wampum
longhouse
confederation
council

The cultural region known as the Eastern Woodlands covers most of the present-day United States east of the Mississippi River. Its name comes from the dense forests that once blanketed the land and that were the region's main natural resource. In some places, it was said, the forests were so thick with trees in the Eastern Woodlands that only a little sunlight could reach the ground.

Life in the Eastern Woodlands

The people of the Eastern Woodlands had many uses for trees. They used trees and tree bark to make canoes and shelters. Some trees even provided food. Nuts came from trees such as the walnut, the hickory, and the American chestnut. In the northern part of the Eastern Woodlands, maple sugar was made from the sap of maple trees.

Eastern Woodlands people were farmers, gatherers, and hunters. However, the Eastern Woodlands was a huge region of great diversity. In the northeastern part of the Woodlands, where the soil was rocky and there were many mountains, the people did more gathering and hunting than farming. In

FAST FACT
The sugar maple tree of the northeastern part of North America is one of the most valuable trees on the continent. Its sap is used to make maple syrup, and the wood is used for lumber.

The rich forests of the northeastern United States were home to the Eastern Woodlands people.

The people of the Eastern Woodlands used resources like deer hides and clay to make storage containers, such as this bag (left) and this pot (right).

southern areas, the soil and climate were better for growing crops. In their fields, the Eastern Woodlands people raised corn, beans, squash, and other plants.

Because they farmed and got enough food where they lived, the Eastern Woodlands people settled in villages. The villages often included a community building for meetings and ceremonies. Surrounding many villages was a wall, called a **palisade**, made of sharpened tree trunks. The palisade was built to protect the village from enemies and wild animals. The farm fields were located outside the palisade.

The Eastern Woodlands people made clearings in the forests for their fields. They cleared the land by cutting away a circle of bark on selected trees in the fall. By spring the tree was dead. With the leaves gone, the sun shone through the branches to the ground. Among the dead trees, the Woodlands people planted crops. After a year or two the dead trees were burned. After several more years, a field might be completely cleared. This method of clearing fields and growing crops is called **slash-and-burn** agriculture.

Some people in the Eastern Woodlands used fish as fertilizer. Others did not. Without fertilizer a field wore out in about ten years and no longer grew good crops. As a result some peoples had to move to new places, build new villages, and start clearing new fields.

Although Eastern Woodlands people raised much of their food, they also gathered and hunted. They gathered nuts, berries, wild fruits, greens, and shellfish. They caught fish and hunted beavers, porcupines, deer, and birds. They also hunted to get animal skins for clothing. Furry beaver and bear skins made warm robes, capes, and blankets. Scraped and tanned deer hides made soft buckskin for lighter clothing.

The peoples of the northeastern part of the Eastern Woodlands included two main language groups, the Algonquian (al•GAHN•kwee•uhn) and the Iroquoian (ir•uh•KWOY•uhn). Most of the Native Americans who spoke the Algonquian languages generally lived on the Coastal Plain. Most of the Iroquoian people, or Iroquois (IR•uh•kwoy), lived farther inland.

REVIEW How did Eastern Woodlands people get their food?

The Algonquians

Among the Algonquian tribes were peoples such as the Delawares, Wampanoags (wam•puh•NOH•agz), and Powhatans (pow•uh•TANZ), who lived along the Coastal Plain. Some of the Algonquian tribes lived farther inland, around the Great Lakes. These tribes included peoples such as the Algonkins (al•GAHN•kuhnz), the Chippewas (CHIP•uh•wahz), and the Miamis.

Each Algonquian tribe had anywhere from 1 to 20 villages. In most villages, 10 to 20 round, bark-covered shelters called **wigwams** were grouped around a village common. Most Algonquian tribes built their villages along the banks of rivers or streams. Some were built where two rivers or streams met. In wetland areas, villages were built on high ground to keep them safe from flooding.

The Algonquian peoples built birch-bark canoes to fish in the rivers and along the coast. They used animal bones and wood to make fishing tools, such as hooks, lines, and fishing traps. Fish was a very important food source in winter, when crops would not grow. Near the coast, many tribes also made strings of beads that were cut from seashells. These beads, which they called **wampum** (WAHM•puhm), were used to keep records and send messages to other tribes. Algonquian peoples sometimes gave belts of wampum beads as gifts or in exchange for bartered goods.

Many Algonquian tribes had leaders who governed groups of villages. These villages traded together and helped one another during times of war. Other Algonquian peoples had two chiefs. One chief ruled during times of peace. The other chief ruled during times of war. Some tribes had a third leader, who was in charge of religious ceremonies.

REVIEW **What were some of the uses of wampum?**

This scene (below) shows an Algonquian village. The shirt (right) was worn by an Algonquian chief.

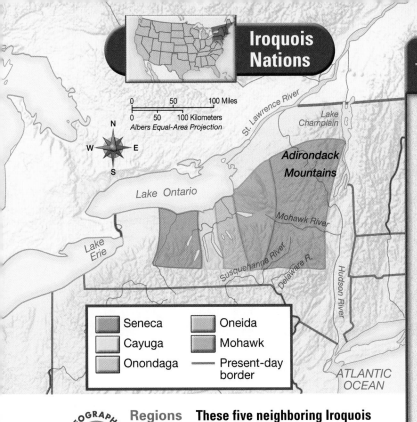

Iroquois Nations

0 50 100 Miles
0 50 100 Kilometers
Albers Equal-Area Projection

Adirondack Mountains

St. Lawrence River

Lake Champlain

Lake Ontario

Mohawk River

Lake Erie

Susquehanna River

Delaware R.

Hudson River

ATLANTIC OCEAN

Seneca   Oneida
Cayuga   Mohawk
Onondaga   Present-day border

GEOGRAPHY THEME

Regions These five neighboring Iroquois nations shared a government.

❖ How did the locations of the tribes help make working together so important?

DEMOCRATIC VALUES
The Common Good

The leaders of the five Iroquois nations agreed to stop fighting and unite so that together they could defend their lands against attacks from others. They recognized that they had more to gain by working together for the common good than by continuing to fight one another. The people worked together for the good of their village. To make it easier for the village to meet its needs, the work was usually divided among different workers. Some members of the village might have worked at making pots, while others made arrow points. Like the people of the Iroquois League, people living in the United States today often work together for the common good of all the citizens.

Analyze the Value

❶ Why was it important for the Iroquois to work together as one?

❷ **Make It Relevant** Identify some examples of people who are working for the common good of your school. Then write a paragraph that explains why their work is important.

The Iroquois

Like the Algonquians, the Iroquois were not one tribe but a group of tribes that lived near each other and spoke a common language. Five of the largest Iroquois tribes were the Senecas (SEN•uh•kuhz), Cayugas (ky•YOO•guhz), Onondagas (aw•nuhn•DAG•uhz), Oneidas (oh•NY•duhz), and Mohawks. These tribes, known as the Five Nations, were the most common groups in what is now upstate New York and the Lake Ontario region of Canada.

Also like the Algonquians, the Iroquois tribes farmed and lived in villages. The Iroquois lived in dwellings called longhouses. A **longhouse** was a long wooden building in which several related Iroquois families lived together. It was made of elm bark and had a large entrance at each end.

The longhouse was also a symbol for the Iroquois. Just as several families shared a longhouse, the five largest Iroquois tribes shared a government. It became known as the Iroquois League and acted as a **confederation** (kuhn•feh•duh•RAY•shuhn), or a loose group of governments working together. In *The Law of the Great Peace,* the Iroquois described the League. "Five arrows shall be bound together very strong and each arrow shall represent one nation each. As the five arrows are strongly bound this shall symbolize [represent] the complete union of the nations."

This computer-generated picture shows what an Iroquois village may have looked like.

Each tribe in the League governed itself. However, matters that were important to all of the tribes, such as war and trade, were decided by the Great Council. A **council** is a group that makes laws.

For many years before the League came into being, the Iroquois had fought with each other and with neighboring tribes. The fighting often began over land.

In one Iroquois legend, a man named Deganawida (deh•gahn•uh•WIH•duh) spoke out against the fighting. He said that the Iroquois must come together "by taking hold of each other's hands so firmly and forming a circle so strong that if a tree should fall upon it, it could not shake nor break it . . ."

A Mohawk leader named Hiawatha (hy•uh•WAH•thuh) shared Deganawida's hopes for peace. Hiawatha visited each of the Iroquois tribes, asking for an end to the fighting. The tribes finally agreed to work together in the Iroquois League.

REVIEW What was the Iroquois League?

LESSON 6
REVIEW

1. **MAIN IDEA** What ways of life did the peoples of the Eastern Woodlands share?

2. **WHY IT MATTERS** What are some ways of life that people of the United States share today?

3. **VOCABULARY** Use the terms **confederation** and **council** in a report about the Iroquois.

4. **READING SKILL—Compare and Contrast** In what ways were the Algonquians and the Iroquois different?

5. **GEOGRAPHY** Why was fish an important food source in winter for the Algonquian peoples?

6. **CULTURE** Why did the Iroquois form the Iroquois League?

7. **CRITICAL THINKING—Analyze** How was the Iroquois longhouse a symbol of the Iroquois League?

PERFORMANCE—Deliver a Speech Write and deliver a speech to persuade Iroquois leaders to join the Iroquois League. Be sure to include the benefits of working together.

·SKILLS· CITIZENSHIP

Resolve Conflict

VOCABULARY
compromise
resolve

▶ WHY IT MATTERS

The Iroquois resolved the conflicts over land by forming the Iroquois League. In forming the Iroquois League, it is likely that the different tribes had to compromise to reach an agreement. You **compromise** when you give up some of what you want in order to reach an agreement. Knowing how to compromise gives you another way to **resolve**, or settle, conflicts.

▶ WHAT YOU NEED TO KNOW

Here are some steps that can help you resolve conflicts through compromise.

Step 1 Tell the other person clearly what you want.

Step 2 Decide which of the things you want are most important to you.

Step 3 Present a plan for a possible compromise, and listen to the other person's plan.

Step 4 Talk about any differences in the two plans.

Step 5 Present another plan, this time giving up one of the things that is important to you.

Step 6 Continue talking until the two of you agree on a plan. If either of you becomes angry, take a break and calm down.

Step 7 Plan a compromise so that it will work for a long time.

▶ PRACTICE THE SKILL

Think of a disagreement that your class or your community might be facing. Form groups to discuss it. Using the steps listed in this skill, vote on a compromise plan.

▶ APPLY WHAT YOU LEARNED

With your classmates, choose an issue that you do not all agree on. Form sides and discuss the issue, using the steps in What You Need to Know.

This staff was used to list the members of the Iroquois League. The pegs in the staff stood for each tribe's representatives.

CITIZENSHIP SKILLS

2 Review and Test Preparation

USE YOUR READING SKILLS

Complete this graphic organizer to compare and contrast the Indians of the Plains and the Indians of the Northwest Coast. A copy of this graphic organizer appears on page 24 of the Activity Book.

Compare and Contrast

The Plains Indians

The Northwest Coast Indians

DIFFERENCES

1. _____
   _____
   _____

2. _____
   _____
   _____

3. _____
   _____

SIMILARITIES

Both groups used natural resources to meet their needs.

DIFFERENCES

1. _____
   _____
   _____

2. _____
   _____
   _____

3. _____
   _____

THINK & WRITE

Write an Article   Imagine that you are one of the archaeologists that uncovered artifacts at the Meadowcroft Rock Shelter in Pennsylvania. Write an article that explains why this evidence supports the early arrival theory.

Write a Journal Entry   Suppose that you are an early traveler on the Columbia River. Write a journal entry about your journey as you travel to The Dalles. Describe your experiences as you travel the river and at the trading center.

USE VOCABULARY

Use each of the following terms in a sentence that will help explain its meaning.

archaeologist (p. 57)

technology (p. 63)

civilization (p. 65)

adapt (p. 70)

barter (p. 77)

travois (p. 85)

confederation (p. 89)

RECALL FACTS

Answer these questions.

1 What connected the continents of Asia and North America long ago?

2 Why were the ancient Indians nomads?

3 How did changes in the environment affect the way of life of the ancient Indians?

4 How were the Olmecs and the Maya divided?

5 What was the purpose of Navajo sandpaintings?

Write the letter of the best choice.

6 TEST PREP   The Pueblo peoples modified their environment by—
A traveling long distances to gather wood.
B irrigating land for farming.
C storing food in containers.
D making kachinas.

7 TEST PREP   One of the most important resources for the Plains Indians was—
F the forest.
G the buffalo.
H the river.
J the whale.

8 TEST PREP   The Iroquois tried to make peace by—
A forming a confederation.
B leaving the Eastern Woodlands.
C building a longhouse.
D building palisades around the villages.

THINK CRITICALLY

9 How did the environment affect the ways of life of people across North America?

10 How is North America a place of great diversity today?

APPLY SKILLS

Read Time Lines
Use the time lines on pages 60–61 to answer the following questions.

11 Between which years did the fourteenth century take place?

12 Which year was earlier, 200 B.C. or A.D. 2000?

Use a Cultural Map
Use the map on page 69 to answer the following questions.

13 What is the largest cultural region in North America?

14 Do you think more people relied on fishing in the Northwest Coast or in the Plains?

Resolve Conflict

15 Think of an issue that you and a friend disagree about. Make a list of the steps that you might follow to resolve the conflict. Include a compromise that could resolve the conflict.

VISIT THE HOPI NATION

GET READY

WHAT TO SEE

The Hopi Nation is made up of 12 villages. The villages are located at the tops and at the bases of three mesas in northeastern Arizona. Many Hopis still follow their traditional way of life. They perform Kachina ceremonies, produce traditional craft work, and farm the land as they have done for hundreds of years. On a visit to the Hopi Nation, you can learn about Hopi culture and see examples of how Hopis keep their traditions alive.

Visitors to the Hopi Nation may have the chance to see a Kachina ceremony. The Kachina dances express prayers for rain, health, and bountiful harvests.

LOCATE IT

ARIZONA

Hopi Nation

This young girl is dressed for the Butterfly Dance, which celebrates the harvest.

Hopi artists create jewelry, baskets, and pottery. They use patterns and styles that have been passed down from generation to generation.

TAKE A FIELD TRIP

GO ONLINE

A VIRTUAL TOUR
Visit The Learning Site at www.harcourtschool.com/tours to take virtual tours of other cultures.

CNN Turner Le@rning

A VIDEO TOUR
Check your media center or classroom library for a videotape tour of the Hopi Nation.

1 Review and Test Preparation

VISUAL SUMMARY

Write a News Story Imagine that you are a news reporter. Your job is to review the Visual Summary below and choose one of the events to write a news story about. Tell when and where the event took place and its importance.

USE VOCABULARY

Use the words from the list to complete the sentences below.

> sea level (p. 21)
>
> tributary (p. 30)
>
> nonrenewable (p. 41)

1. A resource that cannot be made again by nature or people is called ____.

2. The land of the Coastal Plain region lies close to ____.

3. A stream or river that flows into a larger stream or river is called a ____.

RECALL FACTS

Answer these questions.

4. Name the seven continents, from largest to smallest.

5. Why are oceans, lakes, and rivers important to life in the United States?

6. What are the similarities between the desert and tundra regions of the United States?

7. **TEST PREP** Which of these ancient cultures developed first?
   A Anasazi
   B Olmec
   C Mound Builder
   D Maya

8. **TEST PREP** Which groups of Native Americans call the Northwest Coast and the Arctic home?
   F Hopis, Zunis, Chinooks
   G Comanches, Kiowas, Cheyennes
   H Chinooks, Makahs, Inuit
   J Maya, Olmecs, Makahs

Visual Summary

12,000 years ago   8,000 years ago

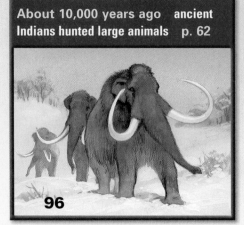

About 10,000 years ago ancient Indians hunted large animals p. 62

About 5,000 years ago ancient Indians begin farming p. 64

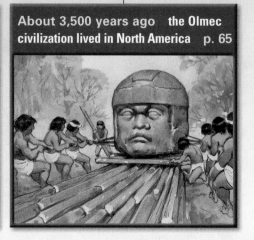

About 3,500 years ago the Olmec civilization lived in North America p. 65

9 **TEST PREP**   Navajo religious ceremonies are led by a religious leader known as a—

A totem pole.

B kachina.

C kiva.

D medicine person.

THINK CRITICALLY

10 Why do you think there are different ideas as to how people may have come to live in North and South America?

11 What role do you think farming had in the development of civilizations in North and South America? Explain.

12 Do you think the Iroquois Nations could have survived without the Iroquois League? Why or why not?

APPLY SKILLS

Use Longitude and Latitude
Use the map of the Great Plains region on this page to answer the following questions.

13 Which location is farther north, 35°N, 100°W or 45°N, 95°W?

14 What line of latitude is closest to the borders of North and South Dakota?

15 What state capital is located closest to 40°N, 105°W?

Great Plains

— Present-day border

Great Plains region

★ State capital

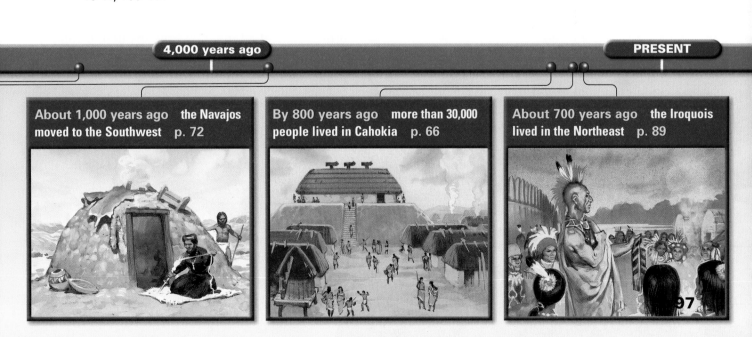

4,000 years ago

PRESENT

About 1,000 years ago   the Navajos moved to the Southwest   p. 72

By 800 years ago   more than 30,000 people lived in Cahokia   p. 66

About 700 years ago   the Iroquois lived in the Northeast   p. 89

Unit Activities

 Visit The Learning Site at www.harcourtschool.com/socialstudies/activities for additional activities.

Draw a Map

In a group, work together to draw a map of the United States. Include the present-day borders of all 50 states. Using a different color to represent each of these regions—the Desert Southwest, the Northwest Coast and Arctic, the Plains, and the Eastern Woodlands—divide your map into sections. Label each section with the names of the Native American tribes that lived in that region.

Write a Short Story

Imagine that you are a member of an ancient Indian tribe living in North America. Write a short story explaining what your everyday life is like. Include the kind of food you eat, the clothing you wear, and what type of shelter you live in.

VISIT YOUR LIBRARY

- *Squish! A Wetland Walk* by Nancy Luenn. Atheneum.

- *Anasazi* by Leonard Everett Fisher. Simon & Schuster.

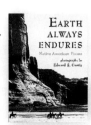

- *Earth Always Endures: Native American Poems.* Edited by Neil Philip and Edward S. Curtis. Viking.

COMPLETE THE UNIT PROJECT

A Multimedia Presentation Work with a group of classmates to complete the unit project—a multimedia presentation. Decide on a topic and what information you want to include. Next, create a variety of visual and written aids to help your group present information from the unit. Invite students from other classes to see your presentation.

Time of Encounters

A compass, 1570

Trunk Bay, United States Virgin Islands

Time of Encounters

❝ I saw so many islands I could not count them all . . . ❞

—Christopher Columbus, November 14, 1492

Preview the Content

Skim the unit. When you have finished, answer the following—
Who and *What* is the unit about? *Where* are the places you will
learn about? *When* did the events happen? *Why* are these events
important? Make a graphic organizer and fill in your responses.

WHO	→	_____
WHAT	→	_____
WHERE	→	_____
WHEN	→	_____
WHY	→	_____

Preview the Vocabulary

Related Words   Use the Glossary to look up the vocabulary
words below. What do these words have in common?

colony   hacienda   presidio   mission

Early European Settlements

PACIFIC
OCEAN

NORTH AMERICA

SEKANI
CARRIER
NOOTKA
CHINOOK YAKIMA
SIUSLAW
MODOC
POMO
MIWOK
YOKUTS
PAIUTE
CHUMASH
CAHUILLA
YUMA
PIMA
YAQUI
MAYO

SARCEE
SARCEE
SHUSWAP
CREE
BLACKFOOT
KUTENAI
NEZ PERCE
BANNOCK
SHOSHONI
PAIUTE
UTE
NAVAJO
MOHAVE
HOPI
ZUNI
PUEBLOS
APACHE
CONCHO
TEPEHUAN
ZACATECA

Columbia R.
ROCKY MOUNTAINS
Colorado R.

CREE
CREE
CHIPPEWA
ATSINA
MANDAN
CROW
SIOUX
CHEYENNE
OMAHA
IOWA
ARAPAHO
PAWNEE
MISSOURI
KIOWA
WICHITA
COMANCHE
WACO
ATAKAPA
COAHUILTEC

Mississippi R.
L. Superior
L. Michigan
SAUK
WINNEBA
FOX
MIAMI
ILLINOIS
OSAGE
SHAWNEE
CHICKASAW
QUAPAW
CADDO
NATCHEZ
CHOCTAW
BILOXI
APPALACH
CRE

Rio Grande

NEW SPAIN

● Mexico City
(1522)

N W E S

0   250   500 Miles
0   250   500 Kilometers
Lambert Equal-Area Projection

▨	French
☐	Spanish
●	Settlement
FOX	Name of Native American tribe
—	Present-day border

Key Events

1200 — 1300 — 1400

1275 Marco Polo reaches China p. 109

1492 Christopher Columbus lands at San Salvador p. 122

1498 Vasco Da Gama reaches India by sea p. 118

NASKAPI

MONTAGNAIS

CREE

MICMAC

ALGONKIN

Quebec
(1608)

ABNAKI

MAHICAN

HURON

NEW
FRANCE

MASSACHUSET

IROQUOIS

PEQUOT

Plymouth
(1620)

SUSQUEHANNA

DELAWARE

ERIE

POWHATAN

Jamestown
(1607)

TUSCARORA

CHEROKEE

YAMASEE

St. Augustine
(1565)

SEMINOLE

CALUSA

**ATLANTIC
OCEAN**

First Explorers to the Americas,
1492–1542

COUNTRY	EXPLORER	DATES OF EXPLORATION	AREA EXPLORED
Spain	Christopher Columbus	1492	Caribbean
England	Giovanni Caboto	1497	Newfoundland
Spain	Amerigo Vespucci	1499–1501	eastern South America
Portugal	Pedro Alvarez Cabral	1500	Brazil
Spain	Vasco Núñez de Balboa	1513	Isthmus of Panama
Spain	Juan Ponce de León	1513	Puerto Rico and Florida
Spain	Ferdinand Magellan	1519–1522	Brazil, eastern South America
Spain	Hernando Cortés	1519–1536	Mexico, California
France	Giovanni da Verrazano	1524	northeast North America
Spain	Panfilo de Narvaez	1528	Gulf of Mexico
Spain	Álvar Núñez Cabeza de Vaca	1528–1536	Texas, New Mexico, Mexico
Spain	Francisco Pizarro	1531–1535	western South America
France	Jacques Cartier	1534–1541	eastern Canada
Spain	Hernando de Soto	1539–1542	southeastern North America
Spain	Francisco Vásquez de Coronado	1540–1542	southwestern North America
Spain	Juan Rodriguez Cabrillo	1542	California

1500   1600   1700

1519 Hernando Cortés arrives in Tenochtitlán p. 129

1607 English colonists settle Jamestown p. 161

1620 English colonists settle Plymouth p. 167

San Salvador

from *The World in 1492* by Jamake Highwater

San Salvador is among the many tropical islands of the Bahamas, off the coast of Florida. Before the arrival of the Europeans, who gave the island its present-day name, people known as the Tainos (TY·nohz) lived there. The Tainos grew crops in the warm climate. They hunted small animals and birds, and they fished. They also traded with the tribes living on other islands and in other coastal regions around the Caribbean Sea.

Nothing in their experience, however, prepared them for what they saw one day in the year the Europeans called 1492.

On that morning of October 12, 1492, a miraculous sight is seen by the people of a little island, now called High Cay, that lies just off the coast of San Salvador in the Caribbean Sea. There in the twilight, as they climb from their hammocks and come out of their palm-leaf-covered houses, they see three moving islands that gradually make their way across the water, coming out of the great unknown and moving ever closer to the astonished people on the shore. In the first light, the floating islands give birth to small rafts that float away from their mothers and drift toward the beach, carrying the most unbelievable creatures. They look like people made of bright colors. Their faces are covered with bushy hair, as if they are holding squirrels in their mouths.

Despite the strangeness of these creatures, the people are delighted and astounded to see them, and they run toward the water to greet them. At close range, the people realize that the strangers from the sea look like real men, except they have very pale faces covered with bunches of curly hair. They are terribly ugly and have a dreadful smell of spoiled milk. Yet they seem harmless, despite the strange gray and black weapons they carry. The people smile happily when the strangers admire their spears made of reeds and the lovely little ornaments of gold they wear on their ears and nostrils. The people cannot understand why the yellow metal is so fascinating to them. To make them happy, they bring their strange guests many gifts—green parrots and bundles of precious cotton—in return for which they are given beautiful colored beads and small bells that make a delightful sound. These strangers, who completely hide themselves behind clothing, seem ill at ease with the nakedness of the people of the island, who do not cover their handsome bodies except for lavish painted designs of black, white and red.

Then a man with a scarlet chest steps forward and tries to talk to the people, though he does not know how to speak properly and can only make strange noises and wave his arms in the air. Despite this strange behavior, the people smile at him respectfully. Hoping to teach him how to speak, they gesture across the landscape, and they tell the scarlet man that their island is called Guanahani. He seems to understand. Then the man points to himself and repeatedly tells the people his name. At this the people of the island begin to laugh. For this stranger has a most peculiar name!

Christopher Columbus.

Analyze the Literature

1 Why do you think the Tainos were so surprised by the Europeans?

2 Write about how Columbus may have viewed the Tainos.

READ A BOOK

START THE UNIT PROJECT

An Exploration Map With your classmates, create a map that shows the exploration of North America. As you read, take notes about the key explorers and the routes they traveled. Your notes will help you decide which routes to show on your map.

USE TECHNOLOGY

Visit The Learning Site at **www.harcourtschool.com/ socialstudies** for additional activities, primary sources, and other resources to use in this unit.

A Time of Exploration

LOCATE IT

BAHAMAS

San Salvador

" *Lumbre! Tierra!* "

(Light! Land!)

—Pedro Yzquierdo, member of Columbus's first expedition to America, midnight, October 11, 1492

CHAPTER READING SKILL

Sequence

A **sequence** is the order in which one event comes after another. Words like *first, then, next, before, after,* and *later* can help you recognize a sequence.

As you read this chapter, try to put events related to exploration in the correct sequence.

EVENT → EVENT → EVENT

The World in the 1400s

1200   1475   1700

1400–1500

MAIN IDEA
Read to learn how the world's cultures became connected in the 1400s.

WHY IT MATTERS
As people learned more about the world, they began to trade with faraway places.

VOCABULARY

encounter
empire
monarch
Renaissance
compass
city-state

When the Tainos welcomed Christopher Columbus in 1492, almost 500 years had passed since the last **encounter**, or meeting, between Europeans and Native Americans. In about A.D. 1000 a group of people known as Vikings had come to North America from what is today the country of Norway. The Vikings did not stay long, and they met few people. The memory of their visit soon faded. As a result, Native Americans knew nothing about Europe.

In the 1400s Europeans knew nothing about the Americas and very little about the rest of the world. That was beginning to change, however, as new trade routes connected Europe with parts of Asia and Africa.

The Americas

Long before Columbus arrived in the Americas, some groups of Native Americans had established powerful empires. An **empire** is a collection of lands ruled by the nation that conquered them. One of the largest and richest of these empires was ruled by the Incas of South America. Their empire covered about 3,000 miles (4,828 km) of the western coast of South America, including

FAST FACT Legend says that the Aztecs built their capital where they saw what they believed to be a sign from the gods—an eagle with a snake in its mouth, sitting on a cactus. Today the eagle with the snake appears on the Mexican flag.

Analyze Illustrations The Aztecs built causeways, or land bridges, to connect the island capital of Tenochtitlán to the mainland. They also built pyramids (right).

❖ How would having water on all sides of the capital help keep it safe from attacks?

parts of what are now the countries of Ecuador, Peru, Bolivia, Chile, and Argentina.

The Incas expanded their empire by using force to take over other peoples' land. In time, they ruled as many as 12 million people, most of whom lived in villages along the coast, in the Andes Mountains, and in the rain forests along the Amazon River. The Incas' capital city was Cuzco (KOOS•koh), in what is now Peru.

A system of roads connected Cuzco to all areas of the Inca Empire. In fact, two major roads—one along the coast and one through the Andes Mountains—ran the length of the empire. These roads led to great cities whose grand buildings were made of stones. These stones were cut by hand to fit together. This way of building can still be seen today in the ruins of the Inca city of Machu Picchu (MAH•choo PEEK•choo).

The Incas kept records on groups of colored, knotted strings known as quipus (KEE•pooz). The different-colored knots stood for words or ideas. For example, a knot made from yellow string represented the word *gold*. A knot made from white string stood for *peace*. Although archaeologists have found many quipus, most of what is known about the Incas was written down by Spanish explorers after they arrived in the Americas.

North of the Incas lived the Mexicas, a tribe later known as the Aztecs. For many years the Aztecs moved from place to place in search of food. In about A.D. 1200 they began to settle in the Valley of Mexico, in the central part of present-day Mexico. By the late 1400s the Aztecs had taken control of much of central and southern Mexico. They ruled over a huge empire that covered about 200,000 square miles (518,000 sq km) and included more than 5 million people.

The Aztecs built their capital city, Tenochtitlán (tay•nawch•teet•LAHN), on two islands in the middle of Lake Texcoco (tays•KOH•koh). Today Mexico City, the capital of Mexico, stands on this same spot.

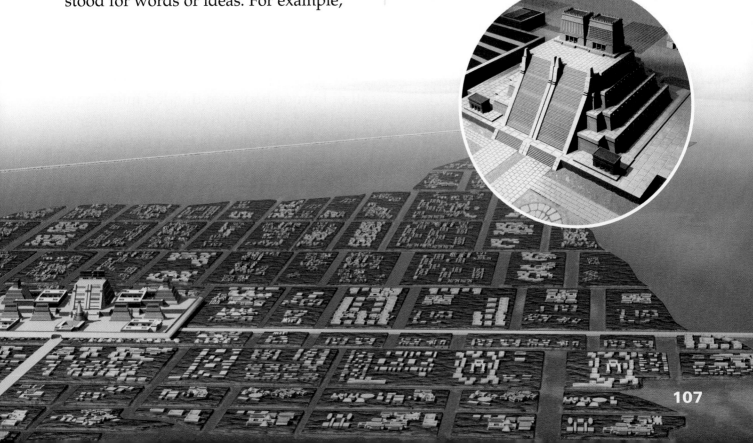

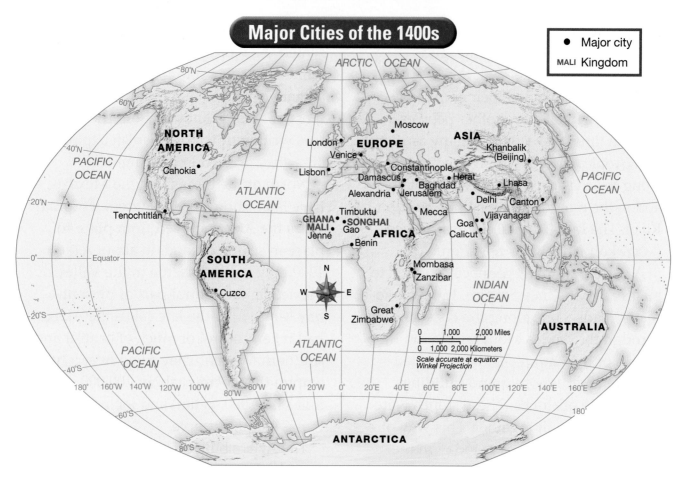

● Major city
MALI Kingdom

Location In the early 1400s most people knew little or nothing about cities on other continents.

❓ What major cities were located in North America?

In the very center of Tenochtitlán, huge flat-topped pyramids rose toward the sky. On top of the pyramids stood the great stone temples that were built to honor the Aztecs' gods. Past the temples was a large, open area where a daily market was held.

The Aztecs recorded information by using pictures of objects and symbols to represent words and syllables. They used these pictures and symbols to make calendars and keep records. This system of communication made the Aztec Empire one of the most advanced civilizations in the Americas at that time.

REVIEW How did the Incas expand their empire?

Europe

In the 1400s many changes were taking place in Europe. In earlier times, almost all of Europe had been divided into many small land areas, each owned by a different noble. Over time, some of these separate land areas had been joined to form countries. Portugal, Spain, France, England, and other European countries were now ruled by **monarchs**, or kings and queens.

Europeans at this time were making big improvements in science and technology. With this new knowledge, they entered into an age of thought, learning, art, and science. This period lasted through the 1400s and 1500s and was known as the **Renaissance** (REH•nuh•SAHNS). *Renaissance* is a French word meaning "rebirth." During this time people were eager to explore unknown lands.

Knowledge of the Renaissance spread with the help of Johannes Gutenberg. In about 1450 he invented a new way to print books that was easier and less costly. As a result, more books were printed. In addition to the Bible, one of the most popular books of the Renaissance was *The Travels of Marco Polo.* Written almost 200 years earlier, this book described what the traveler from Venice, Italy, had seen on his journey to Asia in the late 1200s. When he was just 17 years old, Marco Polo, his father, Nicolò Polo, and his uncle, Maffeo Polo, set out to explore Asia. Four years later the Polos reached Cathay, as China was then called. They also traveled to the Indies, the islands off the China coast, as well as to Myanmar (Burma), India, and Southwest Asia.

The Polos were impressed by everything they saw, especially in China. They were amazed by Chinese inventions such as gunpowder and the **compass**— an instrument for finding direction. They also held paper money for the first time and saw the palace of Kublai Khan (KOO•bluh KAHN), China's ruler.

As Europeans read Marco Polo's accounts, they became interested in the lands he had visited. They wanted to share in the great wealth he described and buy Asian goods such as silks and spices. Soon, traders from Europe were traveling the long, difficult land routes that connected Europe and Asia.

REVIEW How did people react when they heard Marco Polo's stories?

Asia

Some Asian countries began to explore the world by sailing the oceans. The Chinese ruler Yong Le (YUHNG LEH) paid for the ocean voyages of Admiral Zheng He (JUHNG HUH). Zheng He made at least seven voyages between 1405 and 1433.

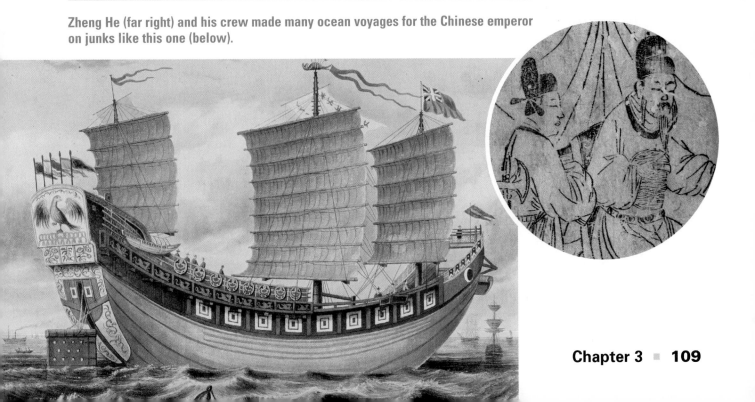

Zheng He (far right) and his crew made many ocean voyages for the Chinese emperor on junks like this one (below).

Timbuktu became a center of learning as well as a trading center.

The admiral and his crews sailed in junks, Chinese wooden boats with four-sided sails. Zheng He sailed to Southeast Asia and to present-day Sri Lanka (SREE LAHNG•kuh). He also visited several ports along the Persian Gulf, the Red Sea, and the eastern coast of Africa.

After Yong Le's death, new Chinese rulers decided to keep China apart from other civilizations. They stopped all ocean voyages and limited trading out-side of China's borders. They later ordered that the records of Zheng He's voyages be destroyed.

While China moved to limit its contact with the rest of the world, other places in Asia, such as India, Korea, and Japan, continued to develop trading centers. In the southern part of India, Vijayanagar (vih•juh•yuh•NUH•ger) became an important trading center for Asian and European countries. It was also known for its art, writing, and buildings.

REVIEW How did China limit its contact with other countries?

Africa

For centuries, groups in Africa traded with one another. In time, African trading centers grew. As early as the eighth century, Ghana in western Africa had become a great African empire. Ghana had grown from just a small town into a grand walled city with palaces and busy market centers. The capital of Ghana was Kumbi Saleh (koom•BY sah•LAY), a large market center that stood in what is now a desert region of Senegal.

In the 1100s, the powerful trading cen-ters of Ghana began to move east to the cities of Gao (GOW), Timbuktu (tim•buhk•TOO), and Jenné (jeh•NAY). The great empire of Mali (MAH•lee) formed from these growing market cities. By the 1300s Mali had become one of the most powerful empires in Africa.

In the 1400s these market centers broke away from Mali rule. Gao became the head of a new empire known as Songhay (SAWNG•hy).

A Chinese vase traded in Africa.

Benin was known for its brass and bronze sculptures. This statue was made in the 1500s.

The Songhay Empire controlled many of the market cities. This gave the Soninkes (sawn•IN•kayz), the people of Songhay, control of much of the trade across the Sahara to the north where they traded gold for European goods.

One of the best-known leaders of the Soninkes was Sunni Ali. He ruled from 1464 to 1492. Under his rule the Songhay Empire stretched more than 1,000 miles (1,609 km). Sunni Ali also encouraged more trade, which helped Songhay remain a strong empire until the end of the 1500s.

Also in western Africa was the kingdom of Benin. Benin was located in what is now southern Nigeria, near the mouth of the Niger River. Benin was an artistic center where sculptors carved ivory and worked with brass and bronze.

On the eastern coast of Africa, groups of people called the Swahili (swah•HEE•lee) lived in several city-states. A **city-state** included a city and the surrounding area. These city-states grew from the trading centers that Arab settlers had started at ports along the coast. Trade centered around gold and ivory, which were exchanged for goods from China, India, and Southwest Asia.

REVIEW How did Emperor Sunni Ali keep Songhay a strong empire?

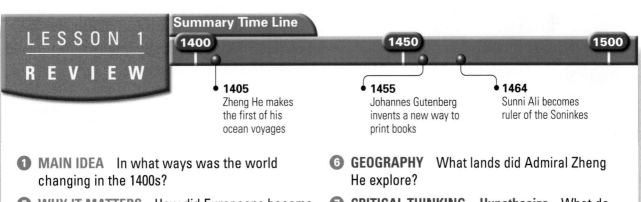

LESSON 1 REVIEW

Summary Time Line

1400 — 1450 — 1500

1405 Zheng He makes the first of his ocean voyages

1455 Johannes Gutenberg invents a new way to print books

1464 Sunni Ali becomes ruler of the Soninkes

1. **MAIN IDEA** In what ways was the world changing in the 1400s?

2. **WHY IT MATTERS** How did Europeans become interested in trading with people in Asia?

3. **VOCABULARY** Use the words **monarch** and **Renaissance** in a sentence about early exploration and trade.

4. **TIME LINE** Did Gutenberg invent a new way of printing before or after Sunni Ali became ruler of the Soninkes?

5. **READING SKILL—Sequence** Whose travels led to more European interest in Asia?

6. **GEOGRAPHY** What lands did Admiral Zheng He explore?

7. **CRITICAL THINKING—Hypothesize** What do you think might have happened if China had not stopped its ocean exploration?

PERFORMANCE—Write a Diary Entry Imagine that you are an early trader on a journey across Africa or Asia. Write a diary entry that describes some of the civilizations you encounter. Share your diary entry with your classmates.

Follow Routes on a Map

VOCABULARY
historical map

▶ WHY IT MATTERS

Marco Polo's book *The Travels of Marco Polo* inspired other Europeans to go to Asia. You can learn more about Marco Polo, and about other people and events, by using historical maps. A **historical map** gives information about a place as it was in the past. It may show where a historical event took place. It may show where cities or towns were once located. It may also show the

routes that people followed as they traveled from one place to another. Knowing how to follow a route on a historical map can help you better understand the past and gather information about it.

▶ WHAT YOU NEED TO KNOW

The map on page 113 shows the routes followed by Marco Polo on his journey to and around Asia. Notice on the map key that the colored arrows represent the different routes he used during his adventure. These include the route to China, the route to Pagan, and the route back to Venice. The map also shows the lands and cities he visited along these routes. The dates of his journey are included in the map title.

▶ PRACTICE THE SKILL

Look at the map key to learn about the routes Marco Polo used during his exploration of Asia. Use the information provided on the map to answer the following questions about Marco Polo's journey.

1 What color shows the route Marco Polo followed to China?

Marco Polo wrote about Asia in *The Travels of Marco Polo*. This copy was printed in 1577.

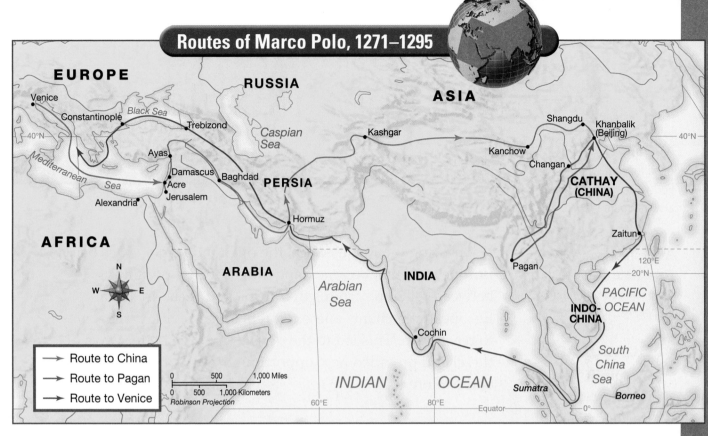

Routes of Marco Polo, 1271–1295

EUROPE
RUSSIA
ASIA

Venice
40°N
Constantinople
Black Sea
Trebizond
Caspian Sea
Kashgar
Shangdu
Khanbalik (Beijing)
40°N
Kanchow
Changan
Ayas
Mediterranean Sea
Damascus
Acre
Baghdad
PERSIA
CATHAY (CHINA)
Alexandria
Jerusalem

AFRICA
Hormuz
Zaitun
120°E
20°N

ARABIA
Arabian Sea
INDIA
Pagan
PACIFIC OCEAN
INDO-CHINA

Cochin
South China Sea

INDIAN OCEAN
Sumatra
Borneo

→ Route to China
→ Route to Pagan
→ Route to Venice

0   500   1,000 Miles
0   500   1,000 Kilometers
Robinson Projection
60°E
80°E
Equator
0°

2 What lands did he visit on his way to China?

3 What lands did he visit on his way home to Venice?

4 What geographic features did Marco Polo come across on his journey to China?

5 What geographic features did Marco Polo come across on his journey back to Venice?

➡ APPLY WHAT YOU LEARNED

Imagine that the ruler of Italy has given you money to explore Asia. Like Marco Polo, you will begin your journey from Venice. Draw a map like the one on this page. Show the routes you would take on your expedition to Asia and the lands you would

visit along the way. Use a map key to explain what the symbols on your map stand for. You can use both land and sea routes to get to and from Asia.

MAP AND GLOBE SKILLS

Practice your map and globe skills with the **GeoSkills CD-ROM.**

Many travelers used camels to carry their supplies on overland journeys.

2

MAIN IDEA
Read to learn why the Portuguese wanted to find a water route to Asia.

WHY IT MATTERS
Portugal's discovery of a water route to Asia led to more ocean exploration by Europeans.

VOCABULARY

profit
navigation
cartographer
astrolabe
caravel
expedition

Background to European Exploration

1200   **1475**   **1700**

1450–1500

During the Renaissance, the overland trade routes between Europe and Asia became dangerous because of fighting between religious groups in Europe and Asia. As a result, European merchants and explorers looked for less risky ways to reach Asia. This led to the development of better ways of travel and provided new opportunities for European merchants and explorers.

An End to East-West Trade

For hundreds of years Europeans carried on a busy trade with people from Asia. To get goods from China and other places in Asia, merchants set off on the ancient Silk Road. The Silk Road, also known as the Silk Route, was not really a road, but a group of overland trade routes between China and Italy.

The Silk Road stretched over the mountains and deserts of Asia, so travel was often difficult and slow. Instead of going all the way to the Far East, as the Europeans called Asia, most European merchants traveled only part of the way. They went to trading cities in North Africa and in Southwest Asia, which the Europeans called the Middle East. The major trading cities included Alexandria (a•lig•ZAN•dree•uh) in North Africa and Baghdad (BAG•dad) and Constantinople (kahn•stant•uhn•OH•puhl) in Southwest Asia. There, European merchants exchanged their goods for goods that had been brought there from Asia.

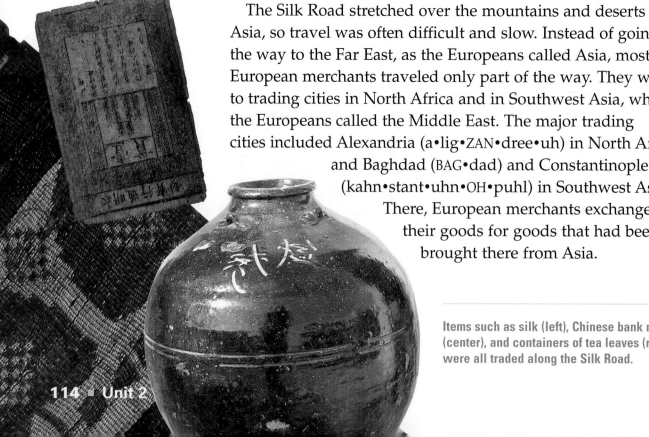

Items such as silk (left), Chinese bank notes (center), and containers of tea leaves (right) were all traded along the Silk Road.

These people are traveling on what was once a part of the Silk Road.

LOCATE IT

Pamir Plateau
TAJIKISTAN | CHINA

The Asian goods that Europeans wanted most included gold, jewels, silks, perfumes, and spices. Spices such as pepper, cloves, cinnamon, and nutmeg were used to help add flavor to food and keep it fresh.

Asian goods were usually expensive because Europeans could not easily get them. Europeans, however, were willing to pay high prices to have them. As a result, merchants made huge profits from selling these goods. A **profit** is money left over after the goods and the costs of getting them have been paid for.

European merchants continued to enjoy these huge profits until 1453, when trade with Asia was suddenly stopped. In that year the Turks, a people from a land called the Ottoman Empire in the Middle East, captured the important trading city of Constantinople. This gave the Turks control of the Middle East, and they closed the trade routes to Asia. Now there was no way for Europeans to get Asian goods.

REVIEW What was the Silk Road?

Portugal Leads the Way

By the time the city of Constantinople was captured, Portugal's monarch, King John I, had already decided to spend as much money as needed to find a new route to Asia. King John asked his son Henry to direct the country's search for a water route to Asia. Prince Henry soon set up a school for training sailors in navigation (na•vuh•GAY•shuhn). **Navigation** is the skill of controlling the course of a ship.

Prince Henry started his school at Sagres (SAH•gresh), a town on the southwestern tip of Europe. There he brought together sailors, shipbuilders, and **cartographers** (kar•TAH•gruh•ferz), or mapmakers. The cartographers drew up new, more accurate maps. Many were based on information from the journals of early travelers.

Prince Henry also hired people who helped improve two important navigation tools—the compass and the astrolabe (AS•truh•layb).

Prince Henry later became known as Henry the Navigator.

An **astrolabe** is an instrument used to calculate the positions of the sun, moon, and stars. The astrolabe helped sailors find their location by using the position of the sun or the North Star.

Sailors at Prince Henry's school learned how to sail a new kind of ship, the **caravel**. This ship used square or triangular sails to travel long distances quickly. It also was able to survive heavy seas. Since the caravel was easier to sail and could carry more cargo than older types of ships, it was the preferred ship for ocean exploration.

Prince Henry believed that the most direct way to reach Asia from Europe by sea would be to go south around Africa and then sail east across the Indian Ocean. Under his direction, dozens of Portuguese ships made their way down Africa's west coast. Altogether, Henry organized more than 50 voyages, but he did not go on any of them. For this reason he is sometimes called "the explorer who stayed at home."

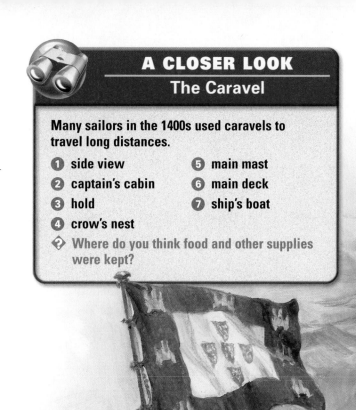

A CLOSER LOOK
The Caravel

Many sailors in the 1400s used caravels to travel long distances.

1. side view
2. captain's cabin
3. hold
4. crow's nest
5. main mast
6. main deck
7. ship's boat

❓ Where do you think food and other supplies were kept?

· SCIENCE AND TECHNOLOGY ·

Navigational Tools

In the 1400s sailors used the compass and the astrolabe to help determine their location at sea. In the 1700s, however, they used more advanced instruments, such as the sextant and the chronometer, to help find a ship's position. The sextant was used to determine the altitude, or the height above the horizon, of the sun or stars. The chronometer (kruh•NAHM•uh•ter) kept very accurate time. It was used to measure the positions of certain stars based on the time. Today, radar and other electronic systems have replaced these tools.

An astrolabe

Ahmad Ibn Majid
1432–1500
Character Trait: Inventiveness

Ahmad Ibn Majid (AH•mahd IH•bihn ma•JEED) was born in what is today the United Arab Emirates. He learned navigation skills, geography, astronomy, and Arabic literature at an early age.

In 1498, Majid helped Vasco da Gama sail around the Cape of Good Hope and on to India. He is considered by many to be a great contributor to the study of navigation.

MULTIMEDIA BIOGRAPHIES
Visit The Learning Site at
www.harcourtschool.com/biographies
to learn about other famous people.

As the Portuguese explored the western coast of Africa, they found new markets where they could trade European goods for nuts, fruits, and gold. They also discovered that they could trade their goods for slaves. Like Native Americans and other groups throughout history, Africans had long used prisoners of war as slaves. Traders from Portugal saw that they could make money by buying slaves in Africa and taking them to Europe to be sold as servants. By 1460 Portuguese traders were buying about 800 slaves from African traders each year.

REVIEW How did Prince Henry contribute to ocean exploration?

Dias and Da Gama

After Prince Henry's death, the Portuguese continued to explore the west coast of Africa. King John II of Portugal ordered Bartolomeu Dias (DEE•ahsh) to sail to the southern tip of Africa. The king wanted to know for sure that ships could reach Asia by sailing around Africa. Earlier **expeditions**, or journeys of exploration, had failed because of the rough ocean currents along the southern coast of Africa.

Dias commanded a fleet of three ships. In 1488 the ships reached southern Africa, and a storm blew them out to sea. When the winds died down and the sky cleared, Dias realized that the storm had blown the ships around to the east coast of the continent. He and his crew had become the first Europeans to sail around the southern tip of Africa!

On their way back around the tip of Africa, Dias sighted what is now called the Cape of Good Hope. Some historians believe that Dias originally named it the Cape of Storms but that King John later renamed it the Cape of Good Hope. To King John the discovery of the cape meant that a sea route to India would soon be found.

Almost ten years later Vasco da Gama (dah GA•muh) reached India. He sailed around the Cape of Good Hope with four

FAST FACT Vasco da Gama returned to Portugal in 1499 with Indian spices and jewels. The sale of the items brought 60 times what the trip had cost!

ships. He brought back to Portugal perfumes, silks, spices, and other goods that he had traded for in India. The expedition returned to Lisbon, Portugal's capital, in September 1499. Many of da Gama's crew, however, did not survive the long voyage. Of the 170 crew members who started the voyage, only 55 lived to return home.

As a reward for his successful expedition, da Gama was given the title Admiral of the Sea of India. His voyage opened the Cape Route to India and led to the regular sailing of ships between Europe and Asia. The trade that resulted helped Portugal become wealthier and more powerful. It also spread Portuguese influence and culture to Africa and Asia. Portugal quickly became one of the most important trading powers in the Indian Ocean.

REVIEW What led to the regular sailing of ships from Europe to Asia?

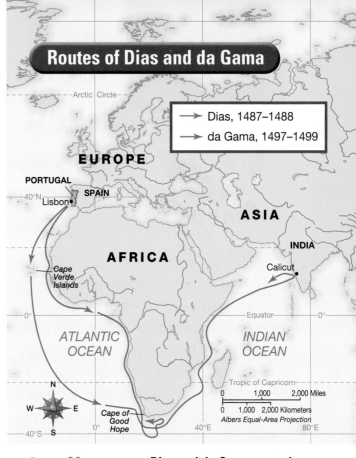

Routes of Dias and da Gama

→ Dias, 1487–1488
→ da Gama, 1497–1499

Movement Dias and da Gama were the first Europeans to sail around the Cape of Good Hope.

In what direction did da Gama sail after he sailed around the Cape of Good Hope?

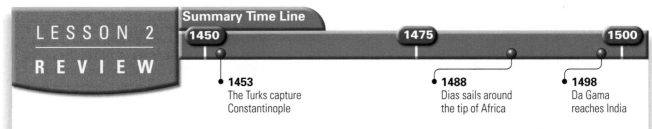

LESSON 2 REVIEW

Summary Time Line

1450 — 1475 — 1500

1453
The Turks capture Constantinople

1488
Dias sails around the tip of Africa

1498
Da Gama reaches India

1 MAIN IDEA Why did Portugal want to find a water route to Asia?

2 WHY IT MATTERS Why do you think a water route to Asia would lead to more ocean exploration by Europeans?

3 VOCABULARY Use the words **navigation** and **astrolabe** in a sentence about early Portuguese exploration.

4 TIME LINE How long after the Turks captured Constantinople did da Gama reach India?

5 READING SKILL—Sequence How did European merchants get Asian goods before sailing to India was possible?

6 SCIENCE AND TECHNOLOGY What instrument made it possible for sailors to calculate their position by the sun and stars?

7 CRITICAL THINKING—Evaluate Why do you think Henry the Navigator believed European exploration was so important?

PERFORMANCE—Write a Persuasive Letter Imagine that you are a Portuguese sailor. Write a persuasive letter to King John I, explaining why he should pay for an ocean voyage you want to make to Asia. Explain why your journey would be good for the Portuguese.

Identify Causes and Their Effects

VOCABULARY	
cause	effect

➡ WHY IT MATTERS

To find the links between events in history, you need to identify cause-and-effect relationships. A **cause** is an event or action that makes something else happen. An **effect** is what happens as a result of that event or action. Knowing about causes and effects can help you predict likely outcomes so that you can make more thoughtful decisions.

➡ WHAT YOU NEED TO KNOW

Events in history can have more than one effect. You can use these steps to help you identify the causes and the effects of events.

Step 1 Look for the effects.

Step 2 Look for the causes of those effects.

Step 3 Think about how the causes relate to the effects.

➡ PRACTICE THE SKILL

The following cause-and-effect chart lists the effects of the Turks taking over Constantinople and closing the trade routes between Europe and Asia. Use the chart to answer these questions.

❶ The capture of what city caused Europeans to begin searching for water routes to Asia?

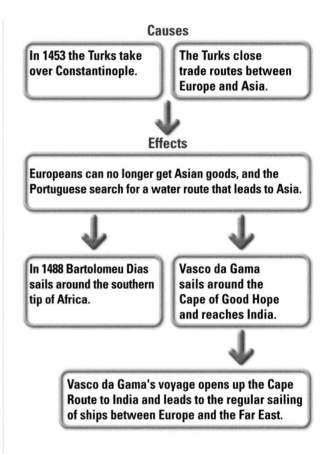

Causes

In 1453 the Turks take over Constantinople.

The Turks close trade routes between Europe and Asia.

Effects

Europeans can no longer get Asian goods, and the Portuguese search for a water route that leads to Asia.

In 1488 Bartolomeu Dias sails around the southern tip of Africa.

Vasco da Gama sails around the Cape of Good Hope and reaches India.

Vasco da Gama's voyage opens up the Cape Route to India and leads to the regular sailing of ships between Europe and the Far East.

❷ What was the immediate effect of the Turks closing these trade routes?

❸ Name an event that took place as a result of da Gama sailing around the Cape of Good Hope to India.

➡ APPLY WHAT YOU LEARNED

Look through pages 114–119 of your textbook, and identify at least two other cause-and-effect relationships in this lesson. Then share your findings with a classmate.

Europeans Explore the World

· LESSON ·

3

MAIN IDEA
Read to learn about the European attempts to find a western route to Asia.

WHY IT MATTERS
The attempts to find a western route to Asia led the Europeans to the Americas.

VOCABULARY
claim
isthmus
demarcation
treaty

1200   **1475**   **1700**

1482–1522

Portugal and other European countries, such as Spain, Denmark, England, Holland, and France, were determined to find new and faster water routes to Asia. These nations also hoped to **claim**, or declare they owned, new lands in the hope of building their empires and discovering new riches.

Christopher Columbus

Born and raised in Italy, Christopher Columbus had sailed to all parts of the world that were known to Europeans, including the Mediterranean Sea, England and the European coast, the Canary Islands, and the coast of Africa. He was fascinated by the stories he had heard of the wealth in Asia, especially in China and on the islands of Southeast Asia, then a part of what was known as the Indies.

For years Columbus had worked on a plan to reach Asia by sailing west across the Ocean Sea, as the Atlantic Ocean was then known. He believed that sailing west was a more direct route to Asia than going around Africa. Columbus first took his plan to the king of Portugal in 1482. The Portuguese king turned him down. Three years later, in 1485, Columbus asked Spain's monarchs, King Ferdinand and Queen Isabella, to support his plan.

At the time, Spain's monarchs were more interested in life at home than in paying for an ocean expedition. Ferdinand and Isabella believed that Spain could be united as a nation only if all its people were Catholic. Their plan to make Spain all Catholic was called the Reconquista (ray•kohn•KEES•tah), or Reconquest.

Christopher Columbus was determined to reach Asia by sailing west across the Ocean Sea.

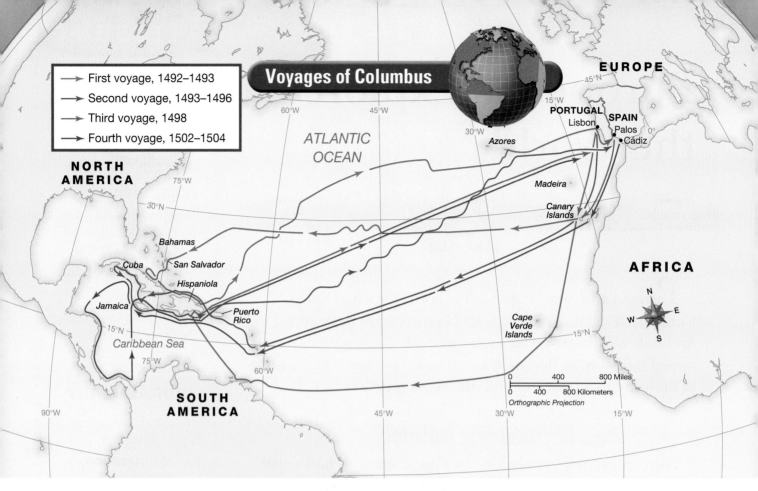

Voyages of Columbus

→ First voyage, 1492–1493
→ Second voyage, 1493–1496
→ Third voyage, 1498
→ Fourth voyage, 1502–1504

EUROPE

ATLANTIC OCEAN

NORTH AMERICA

PORTUGAL
Lisbon
SPAIN
Palos
Cádiz

Azores

Madeira

Canary Islands

AFRICA

Bahamas
Cuba
San Salvador
Hispaniola
Jamaica
Puerto Rico
Caribbean Sea

Cape Verde Islands

SOUTH AMERICA

0   400   800 Miles
0   400   800 Kilometers
Orthographic Projection

GEOGRAPHY THEME

Movement **The King and Queen of Spain declared Columbus Admiral of the Ocean Sea and governor of any lands he discovered.**

◆ In which voyage did Columbus reach the islands off the coast of South America?

By 1492 the Spanish monarchs had forced the Muslims, who would not become Catholic, out of Spain. They also forced all Jewish people to leave Spain.

When Spain was united under one religion, Columbus again asked Ferdinand and Isabella to support his expedition. He promised the monarchs great wealth and new lands. Columbus also said that he would take the Catholic religion to the people of Asia. The king and queen agreed to support his plan.

On August 3, 1492, Columbus and a crew of 90 sailors set forth on three ships—the *Niña* (NEEN•yuh), the *Pinta* (PEEN•tuh), and the *Santa María*. On October 12 they anchored off an island

that Columbus named San Salvador, which in Spanish means "Holy Savior." He claimed the island for Spain.

Columbus believed he had reached Asia and was now in the Indies. For this reason he called the people of the island Indians. The name West Indies is still used to refer to the islands Columbus visited in the Caribbean Sea.

News of Columbus's voyage stirred an excitement to explore. Columbus himself made three more voyages to the "new world." Today, his arrival in the Americas is remembered in many cities in the United States on Columbus Day.

REVIEW Why did King Ferdinand and Queen Isabella support Columbus's expedition?

An Unknown Continent

Soon after Columbus's first voyage, most European monarchs wanted to send ships across the Atlantic to China and the Indies. In 1497 the king of England paid an Italian sailor named Giovanni Caboto (kah•BOH•toh) to lead an expedition.

Caboto's course across the Atlantic Ocean was far north of Columbus's course. Many believe that Caboto reached the coast of present-day Newfoundland, a part of Canada. When Caboto returned to England, he said he had found Cathay, and it was a place so rich in fish that a person could simply lower baskets into the water and draw them up filled with fish. Caboto became a hero. In England he was given the English name John Cabot.

Not everyone believed that Columbus had found the Indies or that Caboto had found Cathay. Amerigo Vespucci (veh•SPOO•chee) of Italy was one who had doubts. In 1499 Vespucci sailed to a place just south of where Columbus had landed. Two years later Vespucci sailed on an expedition down the coast of South America.

Vespucci looked for signs that he had reached Asia, but he could find none. Something else did not make sense. Years earlier he had studied the work of Ptolemy (TAH•luh•mee), an astronomer in ancient Egypt, and had learned that Earth was larger and Asia was smaller than most people had thought. If Asia were as far east as Columbus claimed, it would cover half the Earth.

Vespucci came to realize that he, Columbus, and Caboto had found an unknown continent. In 1507 a mapmaker named Martin Waldseemüller (VAHLT•zay•mool•er) published a world map that included this unknown continent. He named the new lands for Amerigo Vespucci, calling them America.

The first to prove Vespucci's idea was the Spaniard Vasco Núñez de Balboa (NOON•yays day bahl•BOH•uh), who crossed the Isthmus of Panama in 1513. An **isthmus** (IS•muhs) is a narrow strip of land that connects two larger land areas.

• HERITAGE •

Columbus Day

The first Columbus Day celebration was held in 1792, when New York City celebrated the three-hundredth anniversary of Columbus's landing at San Salvador. Columbus Day became a legal federal holiday in 1971. It is celebrated on the second Monday in October. Today, many cities and organizations hold parades and banquets to honor this early explorer.

Many cities, like Chicago, hold parades to celebrate Columbus Day.

POINTS OF VIEW
An Unknown Land?

CHRISTOPHER COLUMBUS, from a letter he wrote to his friend Doña Juana de Torres in 1500

❝I should be judged as a captain who went from Spain to the Indies . . . ❞

AMERIGO VESPUCCI, from a letter to his friend Lorenzo Medici announcing the discovery of a new continent

❝Those new regions [America] which we found and explored with the fleet . . . we may rightly call a New World . . . a continent more densely peopled and abounding in animals than our Europe or Asia, or Africa . . . ❞

Analyze the Viewpoints

❶ What view about his discovery did each explorer hold?

❷ **Make It Relevant** Look at the Letters to the Editor section of your newspaper. Find two letters that express different viewpoints about the same topic. Then write a paragraph that summarizes each viewpoint.

The Isthmus of Panama connects the continents known today as North America and South America. Balboa's explorers landed on the east coast of the isthmus and marched west. They eventually reached a huge, unfamiliar ocean known today as the Pacific Ocean.

REVIEW Why was Amerigo Vespucci's discovery important?

First Voyage Around the World

In 1522 a Spanish expedition headed by the Portuguese explorer Ferdinand Magellan (muh•JEH•luhn) also proved Vespucci was correct. That same expedition proved that Columbus's dream was possible and that Europeans could reach Asia by sailing west. First, however, the explorers had to sail around the Americas. That proved to be a long and dangerous task.

Magellan set sail from Spain in September 1519, in command of about 250 sailors on five ships. He sailed to what is now Brazil and then south along South America's eastern coast. For many months he sailed up rivers into the middle of the continent, hoping to find a river that would lead to the ocean on the other side. However, he never did, and each time he had to sail back down the rivers, to the coast. As the ships fought their way through huge, pounding waves and against howling winds, one ship and many of its crew were lost. Finally, in the fall of 1520, the rest of Magellan's ships sailed through what is now called the Strait of Magellan, near the southern tip of South America. The sailors found themselves in the same ocean that Balboa had seen. Magellan named it Pacific, which means

When Vasco Núñez de Balboa crossed the Isthmus of Panama he proved that Vespucci was right about an unknown continent.

"peaceful," because it seemed so still and quiet compared with the Atlantic.

For more than three months, the ships sailed across the Pacific Ocean toward Asia. The voyage around the world was full of hardship—disease, shipwreck, and hunger. Four of the ships were lost. The small amount of food that was left quickly spoiled, and there was no place to stop for fresh food. Many sailors died of hunger and illness. Magellan himself was killed in the spring of 1521 during a battle with the people of one of the Philippine Islands in Southeast Asia.

Despite the terrible losses, the last of Magellan's ships, with just 18 sailors aboard, finally made it around the world.

In September 1522, the *Victoria* limped into the Spanish port of Seville.

REVIEW **What did Ferdinand Magellan and his crew prove?**

Spain Challenges Portugal

In the early days of European exploration, explorers always claimed the lands they visited for the country they represented. Sometimes more than one country claimed the same land. Spain and Portugal often disagreed about the ownership of the lands they had been exploring. Since the monarchs of both nations were Catholic, they asked Pope Alexander VI to settle their argument.

Movement **Caboto, Vespucci, Balboa, and Magellan were among the first Europeans to sail across the Atlantic.**

❖ **Where did Vespucci sail in 1501–1502?**

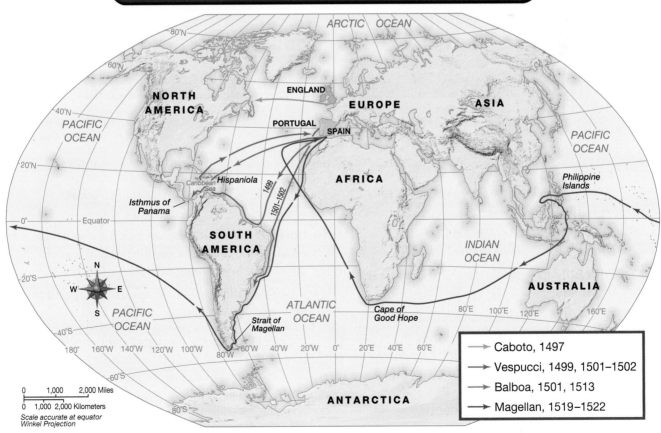

Routes of Caboto, Vespucci, Balboa, and Magellan

→ Caboto, 1497
→ Vespucci, 1499, 1501–1502
→ Balboa, 1501, 1513
→ Magellan, 1519–1522

0   1,000   2,000 Miles
0   1,000 2,000 Kilometers
Scale accurate at equator
Winkel Projection

Chapter 3 ■ **125**

The pope is the leader of the Catholic Church.

In 1493 the pope drew on a map a line of **demarcation**, or a line that marks a boundary. The line divided the world as he knew it. Portugal had the right to all lands east of the line. Spain got all lands west of the line. This included both North America and South America.

A year later, in 1494, Portugal and Spain signed the Treaty of Tordesillas (tawr•day•SEE•yahs). A **treaty** is an agreement between nations about peace, trade, or other matters. This treaty moved the Pope's line of demarcation farther west, allowing Portuguese explorer Pedro Álvares Cabral (kuh•BRAHL) to claim Brazil for Portugal when his expedition landed there in 1500. Spain claimed the rest of the Americas.

REVIEW What role did the pope play in settling the argument over land ownership?

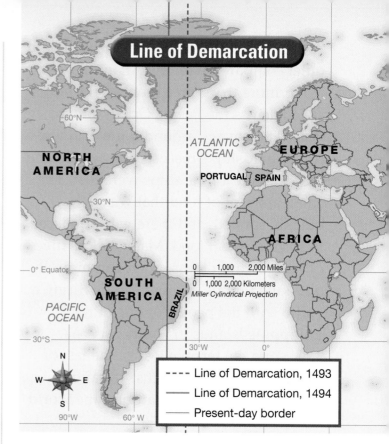

Line of Demarcation

- - - - Line of Demarcation, 1493
——— Line of Demarcation, 1494
——— Present-day border

Regions Portugal could claim lands east of the line of demarcation, and Spain could claim lands west of the line.

❓ Who would be able to claim an island off the coast of Africa?

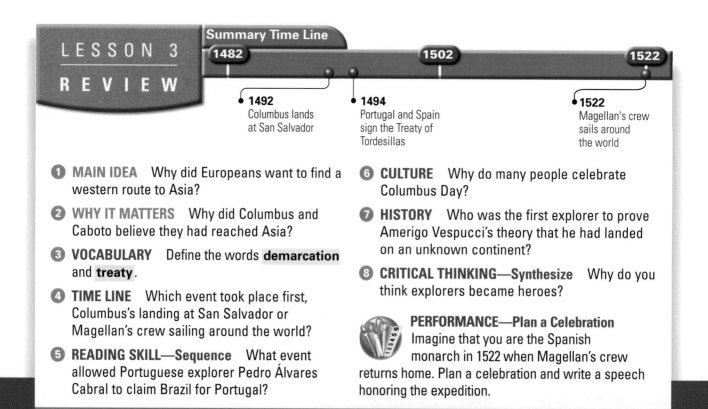

LESSON 3 REVIEW

Summary Time Line

1482 — 1502 — 1522

1492 Columbus lands at San Salvador

1494 Portugal and Spain sign the Treaty of Tordesillas

1522 Magellan's crew sails around the world

1. **MAIN IDEA** Why did Europeans want to find a western route to Asia?

2. **WHY IT MATTERS** Why did Columbus and Caboto believe they had reached Asia?

3. **VOCABULARY** Define the words **demarcation** and **treaty**.

4. **TIME LINE** Which event took place first, Columbus's landing at San Salvador or Magellan's crew sailing around the world?

5. **READING SKILL—Sequence** What event allowed Portuguese explorer Pedro Álvares Cabral to claim Brazil for Portugal?

6. **CULTURE** Why do many people celebrate Columbus Day?

7. **HISTORY** Who was the first explorer to prove Amerigo Vespucci's theory that he had landed on an unknown continent?

8. **CRITICAL THINKING—Synthesize** Why do you think explorers became heroes?

PERFORMANCE—Plan a Celebration Imagine that you are the Spanish monarch in 1522 when Magellan's crew returns home. Plan a celebration and write a speech honoring the expedition.

The Spanish Conquerors

1200   **1475**   **1700**

1505–1545

MAIN IDEA
Read to learn how the desire for wealth led to exploration of the Americas by Europeans.

WHY IT MATTERS
Further exploration of the Americas caused conflict between the European explorers and the Native Americans.

VOCABULARY
grant
conquistador
desertion

Once Spain had claim to the Americas, explorers and soldiers from Spain soon sailed there. Some were driven by their desire to serve their country and win fame. Some dreamed of finding gold and other riches. Others wanted to change the beliefs of Native Americans, or convert them, to Christianity. To encourage the explorers, the Spanish king offered grants to those who would lead expeditions. A **grant** is a sum of money or other payment given for a particular reason.

The explorers and soldiers eventually pushed deep into North America and South America. Along the way they conquered many of the native peoples who were already living there. Among the Europeans, these explorers and soldiers came to be known as **conquistadors** (kahn•KEES•tuh•dawrz), or "conquerors."

Juan Ponce de León

By 1508 the island of Hispaniola (ees•pah•NYOH•lah), in the Caribbean, had become the center from which the Spanish directed their conquest of the Americas. Today, Hispaniola is made up of the countries of Haiti and the Dominican Republic. From Hispaniola, the conquistadors soon conquered Puerto Rico, Jamaica, and Cuba. Eager to add to their growing empire, Spain's rulers urged the conquistadors to go farther. One of the first to do so was Juan Ponce de León (POHN•say day lay•OHN).

Ponce de León had sailed with Christopher Columbus on his second voyage and had later helped take over Puerto Rico.

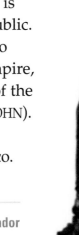

Juan Ponce de León was the first conquistador known to arrive in Florida.

From the Native Americans who lived there, Ponce de León had heard about an island to the north called Bimini (BIH•muh•nee). Legend says he also may have heard about a special spring on the island. This "Fountain of Youth" was said to have water that made old people young again!

In 1513 Ponce de León set out to find Bimini. Instead, he landed on the mainland of North America in what is now the state of Florida. He claimed the land for Spain and named it *La Florida,* Spanish for "flowery." To the Spanish, La Florida came to refer to all of what is now the Southeast United States. Though Ponce de León never found a fountain of youth, he was the first Spanish explorer to set foot on territory that became part of the United States.

This Aztec pendant is made of gold.

REVIEW When Ponce de León discovered Florida, what was he really looking for?

Cortés in Mexico

Ponce de León never found the great riches he was looking for, but the dramatic fight for what is today Mexico would bring Spain a great deal of wealth. Spain's fight for Mexico began in 1519 when the Spanish sent Hernando Cortés, a Spanish noble, on an expedition to find gold in the land of the Aztecs.

Cortés had heard stories about the great wealth of the Aztec Empire. Before setting out from Cuba, Cortés told his soldiers,

> ❝We are waging a just and good war which will bring us fame. . . . If you do not abandon me, as I shall not abandon you, I shall make you the richest men who ever crossed the seas.❞

In the spring of 1519, Cortés landed on the east coast of Mexico with more than

This painting shows the meeting of Motecuhzoma (left) and Cortés (right). Malintzin (next to Cortés) helped translate for the conquistadors.

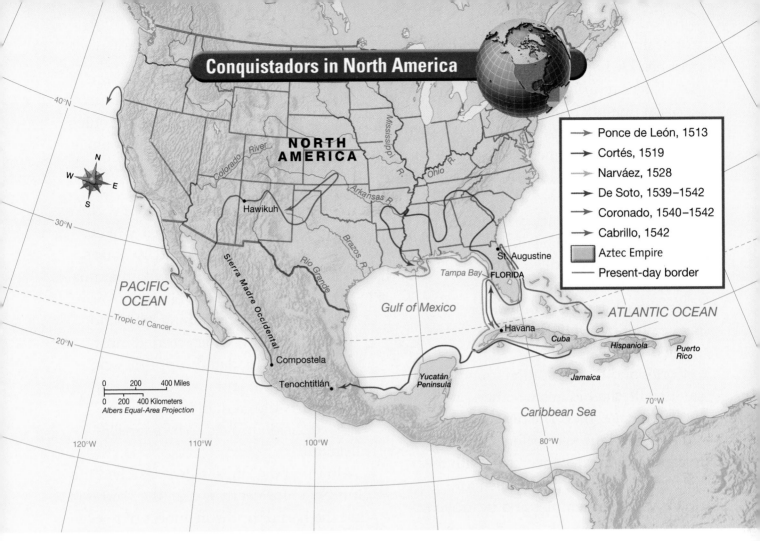

Conquistadors in North America

NORTH AMERICA

PACIFIC OCEAN

ATLANTIC OCEAN

Gulf of Mexico

Caribbean Sea

Colorado River
Rio Grande
Sierra Madre Occidental
Brazos R.
Arkansas R.
Mississippi R.
Ohio R.

Hawikuh
Compostela
Tenochtitlán
St. Augustine
Tampa Bay
FLORIDA
Havana
Cuba
Hispaniola
Puerto Rico
Jamaica
Yucatán Peninsula

Tropic of Cancer

→ Ponce de León, 1513
→ Cortés, 1519
→ Narváez, 1528
→ De Soto, 1539–1542
→ Coronado, 1540–1542
→ Cabrillo, 1542
▭ Aztec Empire
— Present-day border

0   200   400 Miles
0   200   400 Kilometers
Albers Equal-Area Projection

40°N
30°N
20°N
120°W
110°W
100°W
80°W
70°W

GEOGRAPHY THEME

Movement **Many conquistadors set out to the Americas in search of gold and other riches.**

❓ **Which conquistador traveled through part of what is now Texas?**

650 soldiers and 16 horses—the first horses in the Americas for thousands of years. Nearby he founded the settlement of Veracruz (vair•ah•KROOS). To make turning back impossible, Cortés destroyed all but the one ship he sent back to Cuba. He then led a march from the coast, over the mountains, and into the Valley of Mexico. After several months, the expedition reached the Aztec capital of Tenochtitlán. There the Spaniards saw the treasures they were seeking.

Along the way, the Spanish had been joined by groups of Indians who were unhappy with Aztec rule. They gave food to the Spanish and even agreed to help them fight the Aztecs. Yet perhaps the greatest help to Cortés came from the Aztecs' belief in a god named Quetzalcoatl (ket•zahl•KOH•ah•tuhl). According to legend, this god had sailed away years before but had promised to return. The Aztecs believed that the light-skinned Quetzalcoatl would one day return to rule his people. Thinking that Cortés might be Quetzalcoatl, Motecuhzoma (maw•tay•kwah•SOH•mah), the Aztec emperor, welcomed Cortés and offered him housing and gifts of gold.

Cortés, however, took Motecuhzoma prisoner. He hoped to rule the Aztecs by capturing their king.

When fighting broke out, Motecuhzoma tried to stop it by speaking to his people. While he was talking, someone threw a stone at him. The stone struck Motecuhzoma in the head, and the injury soon killed him. The Spanish were forced to leave Tenochtitlán, but only after heavy fighting. Half of Cortés's soldiers died.

Cortés and his expedition found safety with the Indians who had helped them earlier. The next year, in 1521, Cortés returned to Tenochtitlán to capture the Aztec treasures. With the help of the Indians, the Spanish tore down the Aztec temples and destroyed the great city. Cortés believed that only by destroying the city would he be able to break the power of the Aztecs. On the ruins of the Aztec capital, the conquistadors built Mexico City, which was officially recognized by Spain in 1522. Mexico City later became the capital of Spain's new empire in the Americas.

REVIEW Why did Cortés and his men try to conquer the Aztecs?

Pánfilo de Narváez

Following the success in Mexico, Spain once again turned its attention to Florida. In 1528 Pánfilo de Narváez (PAHN•fee•loh day nar•VAH•ays) led another Spanish expedition there. The purpose of Narváez's expedition was to conquer all the lands along the Gulf of Mexico.

This ceramic figure is of an Aztec eagle warrior.

Narváez and his ships arrived near Tampa Bay, on the west coast of Florida, in April 1528. He went ashore with a landing party of 300 soldiers and 40 horses. Narváez decided that this group would travel north over land. The remaining crew and the ships, which carried most of the food and supplies, would sail north and meet the landing party at a certain harbor. This decision proved to be a terrible mistake.

Although the ships' crews searched the Gulf Coast for nearly a year, they did not find the harbor or the members of the landing party. Meanwhile, when Narváez and the landing party reached the place where they expected to find the ships, the ships were not there. Tired and hungry, the 242 survivors in the landing party decided to build small rafts and sail along the Gulf Coast until they reached Spanish lands in Mexico.

Having built their rafts by splitting pine trees into thick boards and sewing together their shirts to make sails, the survivors set sail on the Gulf of Mexico. After 31 days at sea, their rafts were wrecked in a storm off the coast of what is now Texas. The 80 men who reached shore set out to walk to Mexico City, however poor health and lack of food killed all but four of them.

REVIEW What was the purpose of Pánfilo de Narváez's expedition?

Golden Cities

In 1536 the four survivors from the Narváez expedition arrived in Mexico City. They were three Spanish explorers, including Álvar Núñez Cabeza de Vaca (kah•BAY•sah day VAH•kah), and an African named Estevanico (es•tay•vahn•EE•koh), also called Esteban (es•TAY•bahn). Cabeza de Vaca told the survivors' story to Spanish leaders in Mexico City. He explained that during their long overland journey from the Texas coast to Mexico City, they had met Native Americans along the way who told them about seven cities rich in gold, silver, and jewels. The Spanish listened to the story with great interest.

In 1539 the Spanish leaders sent Esteban and a priest named Marcos de Niza (day NEE•sah) on an expedition to see if the story about the Seven Cities of Gold was in fact true. During the expedition, Esteban was killed by a group of Zuni Indians after he approached the Zuni pueblo.

De Niza, however, returned safely, saying he had seen a golden city during his travels.

After hearing about de Niza's expedition, Francisco Vásquez de Coronado (kawr•oh•NAH•doh) set out in 1540 with more than 300 Spaniards, several Africans, and more than 1,000 American Indians to find the seven cities. The expedition traveled through lands that are now parts of Arizona, New Mexico, Texas, Oklahoma, and Kansas. They marched through the Zuni town of Hawikuh (hah•we•KOO) and other Pueblo Indian towns, but they did not find any trace of the Seven Cities of Gold. Terribly disappointed, Coronado began the long journey home. The route he took would later become the Santa Fe Trail, one of the most traveled overland trade routes in North America before the time of the railroad.

Coronado arrived back in Mexico City in June 1542. Only 100 of his party returned. Many had died. Others had run away.

Cabeza de Vaca, Esteban, and two others were the only survivors of the Narváez expedition to North America.

Although Coronado failed to find any riches, he had explored vast areas of New Spain and claimed lands in what is now the southwestern United States for Spain.

REVIEW Why were the Spanish leaders interested in finding the seven cities?

De Soto in the Southeast

At about the same time that Coronado was planning his expedition, another Spanish conquistador, Hernando de Soto (day SOH•toh), was beginning one in what is now the Southeast United States. In May of 1539 de Soto and more than 600 soldiers landed near Tampa Bay. From there, they traveled north and reached what is now Georgia. Finding no gold, they moved on through parts of South Carolina and North Carolina, crossed the Smoky Mountains of Tennessee, and turned south into Alabama.

De Soto and his soldiers met many Native American peoples during this expedition. These encounters often ended in brutal battles. One of the worst took place in Alabama. There the Spanish fought the Mobile people, who were led by Tuscalusa (tuhs•kuh•LOO•suh).

A Spanish soldier who witnessed the battle wrote later that the number of Native Americans killed may have been as high as 11,000. The Spanish lost most of their supplies during the fighting. Because of this, de Soto's army was soon reduced in size by starvation and **desertions**, as soldiers ran away to save themselves.

De Soto and those who remained marched on, reaching the banks of the Mississippi River in May 1541. They were the first

De Soto brought these bells to trade for Native American goods.

Conquest of the Incas
Understanding Places and Regions

In 1531 Francisco Pizarro and a group of 80 soldiers explored the west coast of South America. They went in search of the riches of the Inca Empire. For months they traveled the Andes Mountains collecting gold and riches from the Native Americans they encountered. Pizarro later met with the Inca emperor, Atahuallpa (ah•tah•WAHL•pah). When Atahuallpa refused to accept Christianity and to accept the king of Spain as his ruler, Pizarro captured him and later had him killed. The Spanish then conquered the Inca Empire.

ROUTE OF PIZARRO

Panama

Quito

Tumbes

Chachapoyas

Cajamarca

SOUTH AMERICA

Amazon R.

Machu Picchu

Cuzco

Nazca

Tiahuanaco

Potosí

PACIFIC OCEAN

INCA EMPIRE

0   500   1,000 Miles
0   500 1,000 Kilometers

Talca

ATLANTIC OCEAN

Europeans to see the great river. The Spanish built rafts to cross it and continued their search for gold on the other side of the river in what is now Arkansas and Louisiana. Then in May 1542 de Soto died of fever. The soldiers buried their leader in the Mississippi River to hide his death from the Native Americans. Then they made their way to Mexico.

Although de Soto and his soldiers found no gold, de Soto claimed for Spain much of the land his expedition had explored. The Spanish had now claimed all of what is today the Southeast United States.

REVIEW How did the battle against the Mobile people hurt de Soto's army?

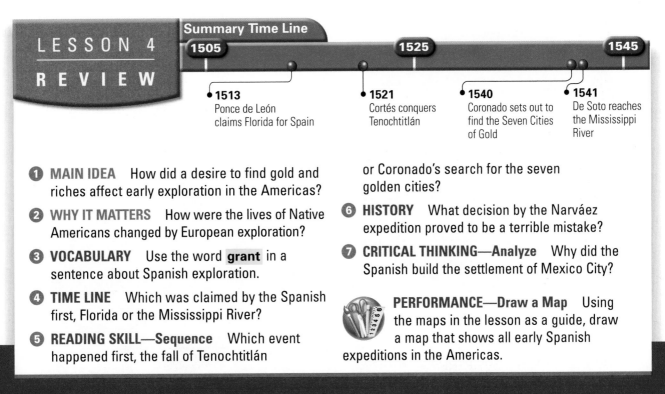

LESSON 4 REVIEW

Summary Time Line

1505   1525   1545

1513
Ponce de León claims Florida for Spain

1521
Cortés conquers Tenochtitlán

1540
Coronado sets out to find the Seven Cities of Gold

1541
De Soto reaches the Mississippi River

① **MAIN IDEA** How did a desire to find gold and riches affect early exploration in the Americas?

② **WHY IT MATTERS** How were the lives of Native Americans changed by European exploration?

③ **VOCABULARY** Use the word **grant** in a sentence about Spanish exploration.

④ **TIME LINE** Which was claimed by the Spanish first, Florida or the Mississippi River?

⑤ **READING SKILL—Sequence** Which event happened first, the fall of Tenochtitlán

or Coronado's search for the seven golden cities?

⑥ **HISTORY** What decision by the Narváez expedition proved to be a terrible mistake?

⑦ **CRITICAL THINKING—Analyze** Why did the Spanish build the settlement of Mexico City?

PERFORMANCE—Draw a Map Using the maps in the lesson as a guide, draw a map that shows all early Spanish expeditions in the Americas.

Conquistador Armor

Like most other soldiers, Spanish conquistadors wore suits of armor to protect themselves in battle. The armor, called plate armor, was made of large pieces of steel. The armor was often designed to cover and protect the entire body. Some armor-makers, or armorers, made very decorative armor that they engraved with special designs or scenes. Although the armor was a highly effective means of protection, it was very heavy, weighing up to 60 pounds (27 kg), and very hot. It was also expensive. A full suit of armor would sometimes cost as much as an entire farm!

This portrait of Hernando Cortés shows that he wore the armor of Spanish nobility.

FROM THE NATIONAL MUSEUM OF ARMS AND ARMOUR AND THE HIGGINS ARMORY

In the 1400s a Spanish conquistador wore this helmet.

Helmets were styled in various ways. Their function, however, was always the same—to protect the peoples' heads.

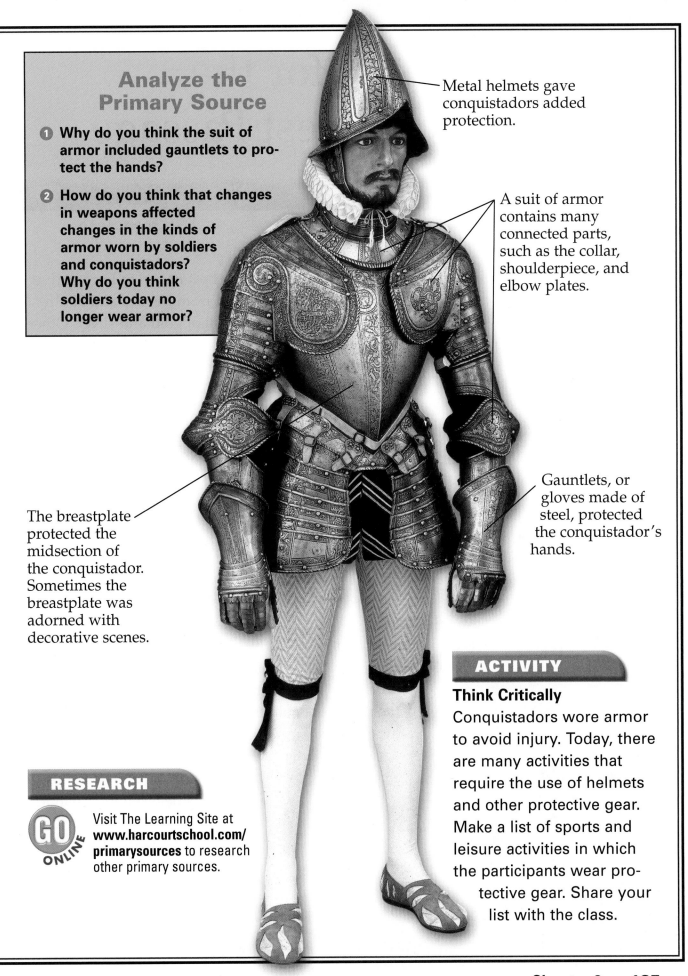

Analyze the Primary Source

1. Why do you think the suit of armor included gauntlets to protect the hands?

2. How do you think that changes in weapons affected changes in the kinds of armor worn by soldiers and conquistadors? Why do you think soldiers today no longer wear armor?

Metal helmets gave conquistadors added protection.

A suit of armor contains many connected parts, such as the collar, shoulderpiece, and elbow plates.

Gauntlets, or gloves made of steel, protected the conquistador's hands.

The breastplate protected the midsection of the conquistador. Sometimes the breastplate was adorned with decorative scenes.

RESEARCH

GO ONLINE Visit The Learning Site at **www.harcourtschool.com/primarysources** to research other primary sources.

ACTIVITY

Think Critically
Conquistadors wore armor to avoid injury. Today, there are many activities that require the use of helmets and other protective gear. Make a list of sports and leisure activities in which the participants wear protective gear. Share your list with the class.

Search for the Northwest Passage

MAIN IDEA
Read to learn why some explorers were searching for a northern route to Asia.

WHY IT MATTERS
The search for a northern route to Asia led to the exploration of much of what is today Canada and the northeast United States.

VOCABULARY
Northwest Passage
estuary
rapid
company
mutiny

1200   1475   1700

1520–1610

In the 1500s Spain became the richest nation in Europe due to its conquests. Spanish ships sailed from Mexico and South America with their treasure chests full of gold and silver. Other countries in Europe believed that if they could find a new trade route to Asia, they might also gain such wealth. The route followed by Ferdinand Magellan around South America to Asia was long and difficult. Other European explorers looked for what they called the **Northwest Passage**, a waterway along the north coast of North America connecting the Atlantic Ocean and the Pacific Ocean. The search for such a route between Europe and Asia began in the early 1500s.

Verrazano Leads the Way

The French king Francis I was one of the many European rulers who wanted to find a Northwest Passage through North America. In 1524 he sent an Italian, Giovanni da Verrazano (ver•uh•ZAH•noh), to find it. The king gave Verrazano ships, sailors, food, and other supplies. Verrazano set sail for North America in January 1524 on his ship, the *Dauphine* (doh•FEEN). A few months later he reached what is now the Cape Fear River on the North Carolina coast.

After sailing farther north, Verrazano saw that only a narrow strip of land—perhaps a mile wide—lay between the Atlantic Ocean and another great body of water to the west.

Giovanni da Verrazano (left) sailed the *Dauphine* (right) into what is now New York Bay.

He thought that body of water might be the Pacific Ocean. It was actually what we call today the Pamlico (PAM•lih•koh) Sound. From Pamlico Sound, Verrazano sailed northward along the Atlantic coast to what is now New York Bay.

Verrazano sailed into the bay and landed the *Dauphine* on the north end of present-day Staten Island. He was given a warm welcome by the native people, who had never had contact with a European before. Verrazano developed a strong friendship with these Native Americans and described them in his report to King Francis I.

> 66 These people are the most beautiful and have the most civil customs we have seen on this voyage. They are taller than we are. They are of a bronze color and some tend to whiteness, others to a tawny color. The face is clear-cut, the hair is long and black, and they take great care to decorate it . . . 99

From New York Bay Verrazano sailed as far north as present-day Nova Scotia before returning to France. He made two more voyages to the Americas to try to find a water route to Asia. On these voyages, he searched the coastlines of North America and South America and still found no passage.

REVIEW Who did King Francis I send to find a Northwest Passage?

Cartier Moves Inland

Ten years after Verrazano sailed into New York Bay, a French navigator named Jacques Cartier (ZHAHK kar•TYAY) also tried to find the Northwest Passage for France. Between 1534 and 1541, Cartier made three voyages and claimed land for France in North America.

In 1534 King Francis I sent Cartier to North America to search for gold and other valuable metals. The explorer left France with two ships to search the northern Atlantic coast. On this first voyage, he sailed up the estuary of the St. Lawrence River. An **estuary** is the wide mouth of a river where the ocean tide flows in. He landed on the Gaspé (ga•SPAY) Peninsula and claimed the land for France.

Jacques Cartier (right) wrote about his second voyage to North America in this journal (left).

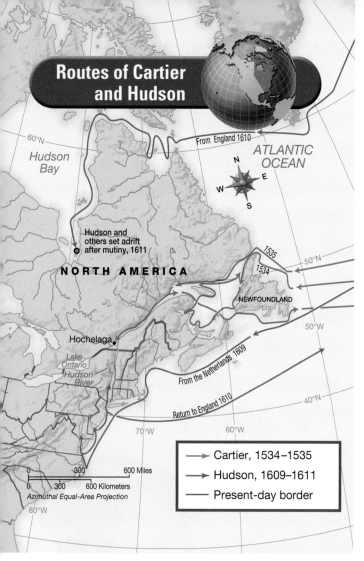

Routes of Cartier and Hudson

From England 1610

ATLANTIC OCEAN

60°N

Hudson Bay

Hudson and others set adrift after mutiny, 1611

NORTH AMERICA

1535

1534

50°N

NEWFOUNDLAND

50°W

Hochelaga

Lake Ontario

Hudson River

From the Netherlands 1609

Return to England 1610

40°N

70°W

60°W

0   300   600 Miles
0   300   600 Kilometers
Azimuthal Equal-Area Projection

80°W

	Cartier, 1534–1535
	Hudson, 1609–1611
	Present-day border

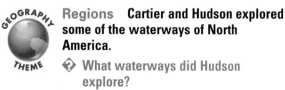

Regions **Cartier and Hudson explored some of the waterways of North America.**

◆ What waterways did Hudson explore?

During this expedition, Cartier was told by a group of Iroquois that jewels and metals could be found farther northwest. The French became friendly with the Iroquois and gave them gifts. When Cartier left to return to France, he carried a supply of corn that was given to him by the Iroquois. The corn was well received by northern Europeans, many of whom had never seen this vegetable before.

The following year, on his second voyage, Cartier became the first European to reach the inland of what is now Canada.

He sailed up the St. Lawrence River, hoping to find a water route through the continent. But his hopes disappeared when he came upon great **rapids**. No boat could travel through the fast-moving water. The expedition was forced to turn back. It had gone as far as what is now Montreal (mahn•tree•AWL), where a Huron Indian village called Hochelaga (hah•shuh•LA•guh) was located.

Cartier made a third journey in 1541, but he was never able to find the Northwest Passage. He sailed up the St. Lawrence near to what is now Quebec City. Some of his men remained there and built a camp while Cartier and the others searched for gold. They traveled even farther west but found nothing. Cartier returned to the camp and eventually returned to France.

REVIEW **What stopped Cartier from searching for a water route through the North American continent?**

The Voyages of Henry Hudson

After Verrazano and Cartier, other Europeans continued to look for the Northwest Passage. Henry Hudson, an English sea captain, was one of them. In 1608, on his first expedition, he reached an island east of Greenland. He then sailed farther north by way of the Arctic Ocean but failed to find the Northwest Passage. The following year Hudson searched by way of the Barents Sea, an arm of the Arctic Ocean.

For his third voyage, Hudson had been hired by the Dutch East India Company to find the Northwest Passage. The **company**, or business, gave him a ship, the *Half Moon*, and a crew of about 20 sailors. They set sail in 1609 for the Arctic Ocean, but his crew soon **mutinied**, or rebelled. Hudson was forced to head south along the North American coast.

Hudson's journey led him to the coast of Maine, where members of the crew went ashore. They fished and traded with the Native Americans and soon went south to the Delaware and Chesapeake Bays. Hudson then sailed north to the mouth of the Hudson River. He spent a month exploring the river, which he named for himself. Hudson's voyage gave the Dutch rulers in Holland control of the whole Hudson River valley.

In 1610 Hudson set out on his final search for the Northwest Passage. This time he was sailing for an English company. On this voyage Hudson reached the bay that also carries his name—Hudson Bay.

He spent three months exploring the huge bay, located in east central Canada, north of present-day Ontario and Quebec. By November his ship was frozen in the ice, and after a cold winter and much

Henry Hudson, his son, and some of his crew were set adrift on Hudson Bay.

suffering, his crew again mutinied. They put Hudson, his son, and seven others into a small boat and left them drifting on the bay. They were never seen again.

REVIEW What area of North America did Henry Hudson claim for the Dutch?

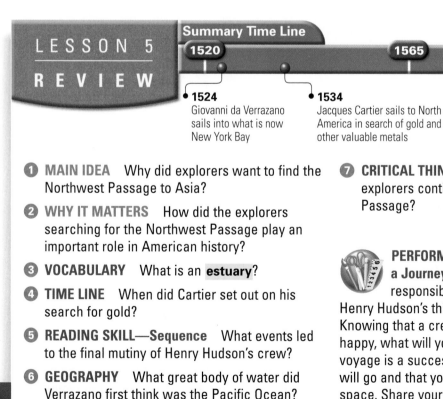

LESSON 5 REVIEW

Summary Time Line

1520 — 1565 — 1610

1524
Giovanni da Verrazano sails into what is now New York Bay

1534
Jacques Cartier sails to North America in search of gold and other valuable metals

1611
Henry Hudson is set adrift on Hudson Bay while searching for the Northwest Passage

1 **MAIN IDEA** Why did explorers want to find the Northwest Passage to Asia?

2 **WHY IT MATTERS** How did the explorers searching for the Northwest Passage play an important role in American history?

3 **VOCABULARY** What is an **estuary**?

4 **TIME LINE** When did Cartier set out on his search for gold?

5 **READING SKILL—Sequence** What events led to the final mutiny of Henry Hudson's crew?

6 **GEOGRAPHY** What great body of water did Verrazano first think was the Pacific Ocean?

7 **CRITICAL THINKING—Evaluate** Why did explorers continue to search for the Northwest Passage?

PERFORMANCE—Write a "Packing for a Journey" List Imagine that you are responsible for getting the supplies for Henry Hudson's third voyage to Hudson Bay. Knowing that a crew might mutiny if they are not happy, what will you put on the list to make sure the voyage is a success? Consider where the expedition will go and that you have a limited amount of cargo space. Share your list with your classmates.

Review and Test Preparation

Summary Time Line

1400

1405
Zheng He makes
the first of his
ocean voyages

1453
The Turks
capture
Constantinople

USE YOUR READING SKILLS

Complete this graphic organizer to show that you understand the sequence of some of the key events that encouraged exploration and led to the discovery of the Americas. A copy of this graphic organizer appears on page 33 of the Activity Book.

European Exploration

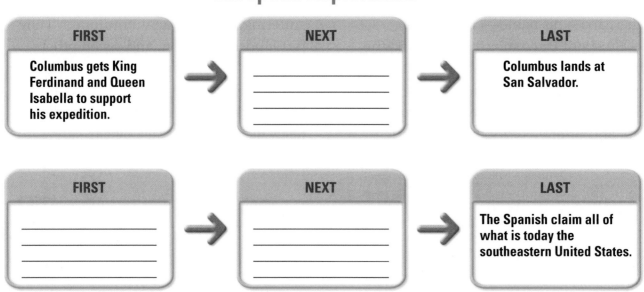

FIRST	NEXT	LAST
Columbus gets King Ferdinand and Queen Isabella to support his expedition.	_____ _____ _____	Columbus lands at San Salvador.

FIRST	NEXT	LAST
_____ _____ _____	_____ _____ _____	The Spanish claim all of what is today the southeastern United States.

THINK & WRITE

Write a Letter Imagine that you are Prince Henry of Portugal and that you have set up your navigation school in Sagres, Portugal. Write a letter to your father, King John I, describing how you are successfully training sailors to find new ocean routes to Asia.

Write a News Story Suppose that you are a Spanish newspaper reporter who has been sent along with Hernando Cortés's expedition to write about the Aztec Empire. Write a short newspaper article in which you describe the Aztecs and their culture.

1475   1550   1625

● **1492**
Columbus lands
at San Salvador

● **1498**
Da Gama
reaches India

● **1541**
De Soto reaches
the Mississippi River

● **1608**
Hudson sails to find
the Northwest Passage

USE THE TIME LINE

Use the chapter summary time line to answer these questions.

1 What happened first, the Turks' capture of Constantinople or Zheng He's voyages?

2 How many years after Columbus landed at San Salvador did de Soto reach the Mississippi River?

USE VOCABULARY

Identify the term that correctly matches each definition.

empire (p. 106)

astrolabe (p. 116)

claim (p. 121)

grant (p. 127)

estuary (p. 137)

3 to declare you own

4 a collection of lands ruled by the nation that conquered them

5 the wide mouth of a river where the ocean tide flows in

6 a sum of money or other payment given for a particular reason

7 an instrument used to calculate the positions of the sun, moon, and stars

RECALL FACTS

Answer these questions.

8 Why did King John I of Portugal decide to spend as much money as needed on ocean exploration?

9 How did Balboa prove Amerigo Vespucci's theory that Columbus had landed on an unknown continent?

10 Why did the Aztecs welcome Cortés with gifts of gold?

Write the letter of the best choice.

11 **TEST PREP** Prince Henry helped Portugal lead the way in ocean exploration by—

A giving explorers money.

B encouraging people to read Marco Polo's book.

C setting up a school for training sailors in navigation.

D inventing the astrolabe.

12 **TEST PREP** Hernando Cortés was sent to Mexico to—

F convert the Indians to Catholicism.

G make maps.

H build a city.

J find gold.

THINK CRITICALLY

13 How did trade play an important role in the growth of exploration?

14 How might history have been different if the Turks had not captured Constantinople in 1453?

APPLY SKILLS

Follow Routes on a Map
Use the map on page 113 to answer the following questions.

15 What city did Marco Polo visit after visiting Baghdad?

16 What two cities on the Black Sea did Polo visit on his way back to Venice?

Identify Causes and Their Effects

17 Think again about the Northwest Passage. Draw a cause-and-effect chart similar to the one on page 120. Show the causes that led to the French exploration of North America.

European Settlement

" . . . the front and vanguard of all my West Indies . . . the most important of them all—and the most coveted by my enemies. "

—King Philip IV of Spain, 1645, on the importance of Puerto Rico to Spain

EL MORRO

El Morro, or "headland" in Spanish, was Spain's first military fort in the Americas. The fort, started in 1539, served as a base to guard the valuable port of San Juan, Puerto Rico. Much of the fort was built from sandstone that has lasted for centuries. In 1961, El Morro became part of the National Parks System.

LOCATE IT

El Morro
San Juan
PUERTO RICO
Ponce

CHAPTER READING SKILL

Categorize

To **categorize** is to group information, or sort information by category. You can place people, places, and events into categories to make it easier to find facts.

As you read this chapter, put information into the categories of key people, key settlements, and key events.

| KEY PEOPLE | KEY SETTLEMENTS | KEY EVENTS |

1

MAIN IDEA
Read to learn about early Spanish settlements in the Americas.

WHY IT MATTERS
A Spanish influence can still be seen in parts of the United States.

VOCABULARY

colony
colonist
buffer zone
borderlands
presidio
permanent
hacienda
self-sufficient
missionary
mission

New Spain

1200   1475   1700

1500–1600

By the 1500s several European nations had sent explorers to claim land in the Americas. Often more than one country claimed the same land because an explorer had no way of knowing that another explorer had already claimed it. In those days of exploration, people claimed the land and moved on, leaving no one to protect the claim.

Over time, Spain decided it needed to protect its claims in the Americas. To protect the land in its growing empire and govern the people there, Spain formed colonies. A **colony** is a land ruled by another country. The colony of New Spain was formed in 1535, with most of its land in Mexico and its capital at Mexico City. New Spain included mostly the Spanish lands north of the Isthmus of Panama and the many islands of the Caribbean Sea.

Building New Spain

At first very few Spanish people settled in New Spain. Many of those who did were conquistadors. After news spread of the discovery of gold, silver, and other treasures, however, many colonists came to seek their fortunes. The people who go to live in a colony are called **colonists**.

Many of the colonists worked in the gold and silver mines. Others brought oxen and plows to work the land and horses to ride. They brought cattle and sheep, fruit trees, grain, and vegetable seeds. Over time, the Spanish began to build cities, and tens of thousands more colonists came to live in them.

The Spanish colonists needed many workers to grow their crops, to mine gold and silver, and to build and provide services in their cities. So they made slaves of the American Indian peoples they had conquered.

FAST FACT These irregularly shaped gold doubloons were called cobs, meaning "cut of the bar."

Bartolomé de Las Casas 1474–1566

Character Trait: Fairness

Bartolomé de Las Casas was one of the first Europeans to work to improve the treatment of American Indian workers. He became known as the Apostle to the Indians and wrote many essays questioning the Spanish colonists' treatment of the enslaved Indians.

Las Casas became bishop of Chiapas in Mexico in 1544. In 1547 he returned to Spain, where he continued to work for better treatment of the Indians until his death in 1566.

MULTIMEDIA BIOGRAPHIES
Visit The Learning Site at **www.harcourtschool.com/ biographies** to learn about other famous people.

American Indians were forced to mine gold and silver for the Spanish (left).

Thousands of Indians had already died fighting the conquistadors. Now thousands more died of hunger, overwork, and disease. The diseases the settlers unknowingly brought from Europe, such as measles, influenza, and smallpox, sometimes killed whole tribes.

In time, some colonists grew concerned about the cruel treatment of the Indians. One such colonist was Bartolomé de Las Casas (bar•toh•loh•MAY day lahs KAH•sahs). Las Casas settled on the island of Hispaniola in 1502 and became a successful plantation owner.

Las Casas used American Indians as enslaved workers, but came to believe that making the Indians slaves was wrong. In 1509 he freed his slaves and began to work to get better treatment for

them. Las Casas spoke out so strongly that the king of Spain, Charles I, agreed to pass laws to protect the Indians. In 1550 the king ordered that the Spanish could no longer enslave the Indians. These orders, however, were not always carried out.

As more Indians died, the number of Indian workers fell sharply. The colonists now looked for other workers. They began to bring Africans to the colony as slaves. Even Bartolomé de Las Casas thought that Africans could be used to do the work. It was an idea he came to regret. Soon Africans were working under the same terrible conditions that the Indians had worked under.

REVIEW Why did the Spanish colonists need many workers?

The Spanish Borderlands

As other European countries started colonies in North America, Spain believed it needed to protect its own. To do so, the Spanish created a buffer zone. A **buffer zone** is an area of land that serves as a barrier. The buffer zone north of New Spain came to be known as the **borderlands**. The borderlands stretched across what are today northern Mexico and the southern United States from Florida to California.

Spanish soldiers led the way into the borderlands, where they built **presidios** (pray•SEE•dee•ohz), or forts, and places for the settlers to live. In 1565 Pedro Menéndez de Avilés (may•NAYN•days day ah•vee•LAYS) and 1,500 soldiers, sailors, and settlers set sail from Spain. After several ships were lost in storms, the surviving members of the expedition reached the location of present-day St. Augustine, Florida. There they built the first **permanent**, or long-lasting, European settlement in what is now the United States.

Analyze Diagrams Once the coquina was brought to St. Augustine from a nearby island, workers shaped it into blocks.

❖ How did workers transport heavy materials?

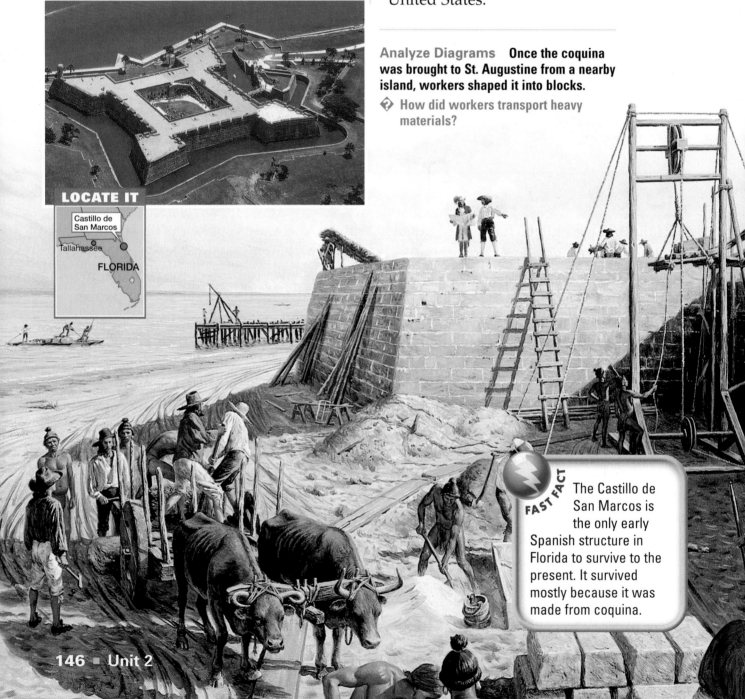

LOCATE IT

Castillo de San Marcos

Tallahassee

FLORIDA

FAST FACT

The Castillo de San Marcos is the only early Spanish structure in Florida to survive to the present. It survived mostly because it was made from coquina.

In 1672, after years of attacks by European pirates and American Indian raiders, the queen of Spain sent money to pay for the building of a strong stone fort. Workers built the fort with coquina (koh•KEE•nuh), a type of stone formed of broken seashells. After 23 years of work, the Castillo (kah•STEE•yoh) de San Marcos, as the presidio was called, was strong enough to protect Spanish settlers from any attackers. It was one of a line of hundreds of presidios stretching from Florida to California that protected the colonists in New Spain.

REVIEW Why did the Spanish build the Castillo de San Marcos in St. Augustine?

Ranches and Haciendas

The Spanish realized that gold and silver were hard to find in the borderlands. They also knew that in many places the land was so hot and dry "that even the cactus pads appeared to be toasted." But settlers moved there anyway. Most made money by raising livestock and by selling the hides to markets in the colonies and in Spain. They often traded for things they needed with Indian tribes who lived in the borderlands. In what is now the southwestern United States, for example, they traded with the Pueblos for corn, pottery, and cotton cloth.

The Spanish—and the animals they brought with them—changed life for many of the Indians living in the borderlands. Horses, long extinct in the Americas, once again roamed the land. The Plains Indians learned to tame horses and use them in hunting and in war. In what today is the southwestern United States, the Navajos learned to raise sheep. They also began weaving sheep's wool into clothing and blankets.

Some ranchers in the borderlands of northern Mexico built large estates called **haciendas** (ah•see•EN•dahs). There they raised cattle and sheep by the thousands. In what are now Texas and California, cattle were the most important kind of livestock. Ranchers who lived on the haciendas raised their own livestock, grew their own crops, and made most of what they needed to live. These **self-sufficient**, or self-supporting, communities began to grow far from the markets of Mexico City and the other large cities of New Spain.

REVIEW How did horses change the Indians' way of life?

Missions

Spain's main interest in settling the borderlands was to protect its empire and to expand its economy. However, the Spanish king also said he wanted to "bring the people of that land to our Holy Catholic faith." To do this, missionaries were sent to turn the American Indians into Catholics as well as loyal Spanish subjects. A **missionary** is a person sent by a church to teach its religion.

The first successful missionaries in the borderlands were the Franciscans, members of a Catholic religious order. They built **missions**, or small religious settlements, in what are now the states of Georgia, Florida, Texas, New Mexico, Arizona, and California. Their first mission was Nombre de Dios (NOHM•bray day DEE•ohs), or "Name of God." It was built near St. Augustine as the first in a chain of missions that would eventually connect the Atlantic and Pacific coasts. On the Pacific coast of New Spain, a Franciscan priest named Junípero Serra

(hoo•NEE•pay•roh SEH•rah) later helped build a string of 9 missions in California.

When missionaries came to the borderlands, the missions they built included ranch and farm buildings as well as churches. Some of the missions were built near Indian villages. In other places, Indians settled around the missions.

The coming of the missions changed the way many Indians lived and worked. It also changed something more important to the Indians—the way they worshipped. While many Indians kept to their traditional religions, others became Catholics.

At first some of the Native Americans welcomed living at the missions. Like the missionaries, they were learning new ways. The missionaries and soldiers also protected them from enemies. Problems developed, however. Many Indians had to work on mission farms and ranches against

---

Father Junípero Serra (below right) founded the mission of San Carlos Borromeo del Rio Carmelo (below left) in 1770. It was the second of nine missions started by Father Serra along what is now the California coast.

LOCATE IT

Mission San Carlos Borromeo del Rio Carmelo

CALIFORNIA

their will. Some missionaries also treated the Indians cruelly.

Some Indians fought back. They destroyed churches and other mission buildings. To protect its missions, the Spanish government built roads linking them with nearby presidios. This road system was called *El Camino Real* (el kah•MEE•noh ray•AHL), or "The Royal Road." One road stretched for more than 600 miles (966 km) from San Diego to Sonoma in what is today California.

The government of New Spain, and later the Mexican government, continued to build missions in the borderlands until the 1830s. Many cities in the western and southwestern areas of the United States—such as San Antonio, Texas, and San Diego, California, began as missions.

REVIEW Why did the Spanish send missionaries to the borderlands?

Major Missions of New Spain

New Spain
El Camino Real
⌂ Mission

0 300 600 Miles
0 300 600 Kilometers
Azimuthal Equal-Area Projection

NORTH AMERICA

San Francisco
CALIFORNIA
Colorado River
San Diego
Santa Fe
Tucson
El Paso del Norte
Rio Grande
Los Adaes
Mississippi River
ATLANTIC OCEAN
St. Augustine
FLORIDA
PACIFIC OCEAN
Gulf of Mexico
CUBA
Mexico City
Caribbean Sea

GEOGRAPHY THEME

Movement **El Camino Real connected most of the missions and presidios in New Spain.**

❓ How did this system of roads help the Spanish missionaries?

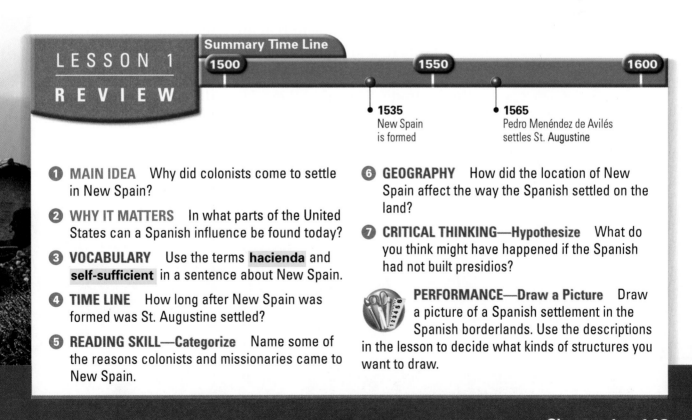

LESSON 1 REVIEW

Summary Time Line

1500 — 1550 — 1600

1535 New Spain is formed

1565 Pedro Menéndez de Avilés settles St. Augustine

❶ **MAIN IDEA** Why did colonists come to settle in New Spain?

❷ **WHY IT MATTERS** In what parts of the United States can a Spanish influence be found today?

❸ **VOCABULARY** Use the terms **hacienda** and **self-sufficient** in a sentence about New Spain.

❹ **TIME LINE** How long after New Spain was formed was St. Augustine settled?

❺ **READING SKILL—Categorize** Name some of the reasons colonists and missionaries came to New Spain.

❻ **GEOGRAPHY** How did the location of New Spain affect the way the Spanish settled on the land?

❼ **CRITICAL THINKING—Hypothesize** What do you think might have happened if the Spanish had not built presidios?

PERFORMANCE—Draw a Picture Draw a picture of a Spanish settlement in the Spanish borderlands. Use the descriptions in the lesson to decide what kinds of structures you want to draw.

New France

1200   1475   1700

1600–1700

While the Spanish were growing rich in New Spain, the French were making their own claims in what is today Canada and the northeastern United States. They found good fishing waters along the coast, and farther inland they began to trade with the Native Americans. They traded for a good that became nearly as valuable in Europe as gold—fur.

French Settlement in North America

The fur trade between the French and the American Indians grew following Jacques Cartier's trips up the St. Lawrence River. Cartier had begun to trade with the Huron Indians. The Hurons were as eager for European goods as the French were for furs the Hurons had. Beaver fur, from which hats were made, was especially popular among the French.

By 1600, trade with the Indians was important for many Europeans, especially for French merchants. Knowing this, the French king, Henry IV, said that any merchant who wanted to trade in furs had to build a colony in North America.

French merchants jumped at the chance to get rich from the fur trade. Several of them formed a company to start a colony. In 1603 the company sent a cartographer named

Europeans (below) traded items, such as glass beads (left), for beaver furs.

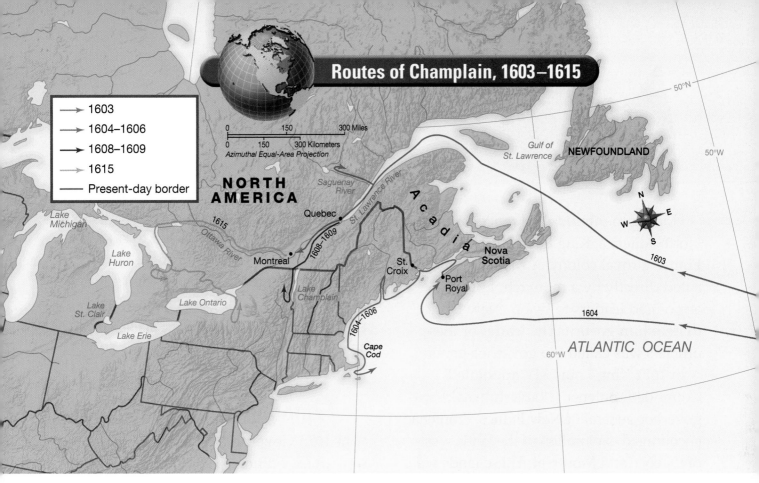

Routes of Champlain, 1603–1615

→ 1603
→ 1604–1606
→ 1608–1609
→ 1615
— Present-day border

0   150   300 Miles
0   150   300 Kilometers
Azimuthal Equal-Area Projection

NORTH AMERICA

Lake Michigan
Lake Huron
Lake St. Clair
Lake Erie
Lake Ontario

1615
Ottawa River
Montreal
1608–1609
Quebec
Saguenay River
St. Lawrence River
Acadia
Lake Champlain
St. Croix
Port Royal
Nova Scotia
Gulf of St. Lawrence
NEWFOUNDLAND

1604–1606
Cape Cod

1603
1604
ATLANTIC OCEAN

50°N
50°W
60°W

Movement   **Champlain explored inland waterways in North America.**

◆ In what waterway did Champlain travel to reach Quebec?

Samuel de Champlain (sham•PLAYN) to North America to map the places where beavers were found.

Champlain explored the forests of what is now eastern Canada, which he called New France. When he returned to Europe, Champlain's reports made more people want to go there. He himself went again.

For the next five years, Champlain explored the lands along the St. Lawrence River. He also built a settlement on the St. Lawrence River at a place that the Hurons called *kebec*. In 1608 Kebec became Quebec (kwih•BEK), the first important French settlement in North America.

REVIEW Why were the French eager to build colonies in New France?

The Growth of New France

The early French settlements grew very slowly. One reason for this slow growth was trouble in France. In the early 1600s, civil war kept many people from leaving France. A **civil war** is a war between two groups in the same country.

In North America, English and Dutch colonists began settling the southern coast of New France. Soon disagreements over the fur trade broke out among the French, the English, and the Dutch, as well as between the Iroquois and the Hurons. By the 1660s the French fur trade was nearly destroyed, and the French hold in North America was crumbling.

Hoping to rebuild the French empire in North America, King Louis XIV made New France a royal colony. A **royal colony** is ruled directly by a monarch. Louis XIV appointed leaders to live in New France to help him govern. The leader of these officials was called the governor-general.

In 1672 King Louis XIV appointed Count de Frontenac (FRAHN•tuh•nak) governor-general of New France. Frontenac encouraged exploration of the lands west of Quebec and Montreal. These lands were not easy to reach, however. Rapids and shallow waters prevented French ships from traveling very far inland. To travel the rivers, the French had to learn from their Native American trading partners how to build and use birchbark canoes. These boats could navigate in very shallow water. They also could be carried around waterfalls and rapids or overland between rivers.

The Native Americans often spoke of a great river to the west, larger than all the others. The Algonkins called it the *Mississippi*, which means "Father of Waters." Ever since the days of Jacques Cartier, the French had hoped to find the Northwest Passage through North America. Frontenac believed the Mississippi River might be that route.

REVIEW Why was New France made a royal colony?

Exploring the Mississippi

In 1673 Governor-General de Frontenac sent an expedition to explore the rivers and lakes that he hoped would lead them to the Mississippi River. One member of the expedition was Jacques Marquette (mahr•KET), a Catholic missionary who spoke several Indian languages. The other members were Louis Joliet (zhohl•YAY), a fur trader and explorer, and five other adventurers.

The explorers set out from northern Lake Michigan in two birchbark canoes.

This painting by George Catlin shows La Salle and his expedition entering the Mississippi River.

They crossed the huge lake, entered the Fox River, and then traveled to the Wisconsin River. When they reached the mouth of the Wisconsin River, they saw the Mississippi River for the first time.

The explorers followed the river but soon realized that it could not be the Northwest Passage because it flowed south. As they neared the mouth of the Arkansas River, they met some Indian peoples who told them that Europeans lived farther south. The French feared that the Europeans might be Spanish soldiers so they turned back.

Marquette and Joliet had traveled about 2,500 miles (4,023 km). Their expedition opened the Mississippi River valley to French settlement and trade. In time, the French also built trading posts that later grew into towns with such names as St. Louis, Des Moines, and Louisville.

REVIEW How did Marquette and Joliet know the Mississippi River could not be the Northwest Passage?

Founding Louisiana

Soon another French explorer set out, this time to find the mouth of the Mississippi River. This explorer was René-Robert Cavelier (ka•vuhl•YAY), known as Sieur de la Salle, or "Sir" La Salle. In February 1682 La Salle and an expedition of about 50 French and Indian people traveled south from the mouth of the Illinois River. Two months later the explorers reached the mouth of the Mississippi at the Gulf of Mexico. With shouts of "Long live the king!" they claimed all the Mississippi River valley for France. This claim included all the river's tributaries. It reached from the Appalachians in the east to the

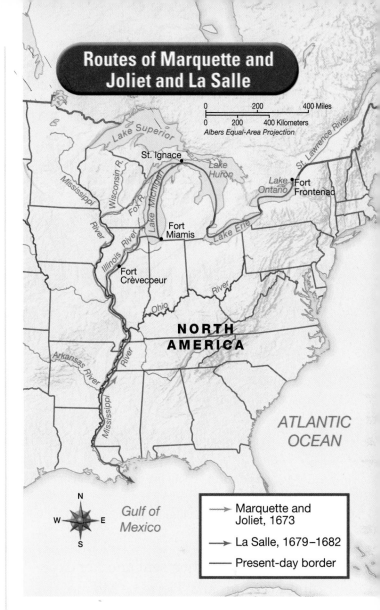

Routes of Marquette and Joliet and La Salle

Marquette and Joliet, 1673

La Salle, 1679–1682

Present-day border

Movement Early French explorers led expeditions down the Mississippi River.

❖ In what waterways did La Salle travel to reach the Mississippi River?

Rockies in the west and from the Great Lakes in the north to the Gulf of Mexico in the south. La Salle named the region Louisiana in honor of King Louis XIV.

In 1684 La Salle tried to start a settlement near the mouth of the Mississippi River. However, it was difficult in the hot, swampy land. Hardships led to disagreements among the settlers, and three years later one of them killed La Salle. Without a strong leader, the settlement failed.

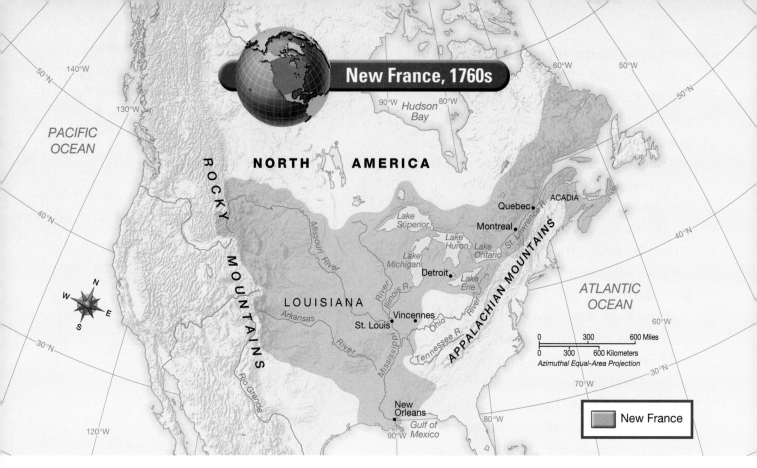

New France, 1760s

PACIFIC OCEAN

NORTH AMERICA

Hudson Bay

ROCKY MOUNTAINS

Lake Superior
Lake Huron
Lake Michigan
Lake Ontario
Lake Erie

Quebec
ACADIA
Montreal
St. Lawrence R.

Detroit

Missouri River
Illinois R.

LOUISIANA
Arkansas
St. Louis
Vincennes
Ohio
Tennessee R.

APPALACHIAN MOUNTAINS

ATLANTIC OCEAN

Mississippi River
Rio Grande

New Orleans
Gulf of Mexico

0   300   600 Miles
0   300   600 Kilometers
Azimuthal Equal-Area Projection

New France

Location **With the claim to Louisiana, New France greatly increased in size.**

❓ **What mountain ranges bordered New France?**

The French king then sent another expedition to Louisiana. Pierre Le Moyne (luh•MWAHN), known as Sieur d'Iberville (dee•ber•VEEL), and his brother Jean-Baptiste (ZHAHN ba•TEEST), known as Sieur de Bienville (duh bee•EN•vil), reached the northern coast of the Gulf of Mexico in 1699. Their ships entered the mouth of a great river and sailed upstream. The brothers were not sure they were traveling on the Mississippi River until they met Mongoulacha (mahn•goo•LAY•chah), a Taensa (TYN•suh) Indian. He was wearing a French-made coat and carrying a letter addressed to La Salle. Mongoulacha told the Europeans his coat was a gift from Henri de Tonti (ahn•REE duh TOHN•tee). Tonti had stayed in Louisiana after traveling with La Salle years earlier. Mongoulacha said that Tonti had asked him to give the letter to a white man who would come from the sea. The brothers then knew they had found La Salle's river.

The members of the Iberville and Bienville expedition built a settlement along the river and, in time, more settlers arrived. The settlers experienced many of the same hardships that the La Salle expedition had faced.

After claiming Louisiana for France, La Salle attempted to start a settlement.

154 ■ **Unit 2**

In 1712 the king made Louisiana a **proprietary colony** (pruh•PRY•uh•ter•ee). This meant that the king gave ownership of the land to one person and allowed that person to rule it. In 1717 John Law, a Scottish banker, became Louisiana's **proprietor**, or owner. Law formed a company to build more towns and to start farms. More settlers came, and Louisiana finally started to grow. In 1718 the town of New Orleans was founded, and four years later it became Louisiana's capital.

Despite Law's efforts, the colony still needed workers—especially on the large farms called **plantations**. Many settlers began to bring in Africans to do the work as slaves.

Louisiana, like the rest of New France, failed to attract enough people for it to do well. By 1754 only

Many streets in the French Quarter have French names.

about 55,000 French colonists lived in the area that stretched from the St. Lawrence River to the Gulf of Mexico. That same year, more than 1,200,000 English colonists lived in North America.

REVIEW **Why was it difficult to settle in Louisiana?**

LESSON 2 REVIEW

Summary Time Line

| 1600 | 1650 | 1700 |

1608
Quebec is founded

1673
Jacques Marquette and Louis Joliet explore the Mississippi River

1682
Sieur de la Salle claims Louisiana for the French

1. **MAIN IDEA** How did Henry IV get merchants to build colonies in North America?

2. **WHY IT MATTERS** What cities grew from French settlements?

3. **VOCABULARY** Explain the difference between a **royal colony** and a **proprietary colony**.

4. **TIME LINE** When was Quebec founded?

5. **READING SKILL—Categorize** Name some French explorers who helped expand New France.

6. **HISTORY** Why was the Marquette and Joliet expedition important to the French?

7. **CRITICAL THINKING—Analyze** What were the economic reasons behind the exploration and settlement of New France?

PERFORMANCE—Make a Poster
Suppose that you are a French citizen who is asked by the French government to get people to settle in New France. Make a poster that persuades people to move to New France. Use words and pictures in your poster to show people the benefits of moving to New France. Compare your poster with those of your classmates.

MAIN IDEA

Read to learn how the English began to explore and start colonies in North America.

WHY IT MATTERS

Although early settlements failed, English settlers were determined to start colonies in North America.

VOCABULARY

sea dog
raw material
armada

The English in the Americas

1200	1475	1700

1550–1600

The English had been sailing to North America since John Cabot made his first voyage there in 1497. Unlike the Spanish or the French, most of the English who first came to North America did not come in search of gold or the riches of the fur trade. Instead, they came mostly for the rich fishing found at the Grand Banks, off the coast of Newfoundland. However, by the late 1500s, the English rulers began taking more of an interest in the Americas.

England Challenges Spain

England saw that Spain had become very wealthy as a result of its colonies in the Americas. Its gold and silver mines and the sale of products from its ranches in the Americas had filled Spain's treasury. England was not as wealthy as Spain, but it did have fast ships and skilled ocean sailors. At first the English sailors went to catch fish in the Grand Banks. Then they went to capture Spanish treasure ships.

England's queen, Elizabeth I, encouraged English sea captains to attack Spanish treasure ships carrying riches to Spain. English merchants and sea captains used their own money to build ships, hoping to capture Spanish treasure. When they succeeded, they had money to build more ships. The commanders of these English warships were known as **sea dogs**. They were pirates, but Queen Elizabeth protected them

Sailing in the *Golden Hind*, Drake captured a Spanish treasure ship.

Drake's Voyage Around the World, 1577–1580

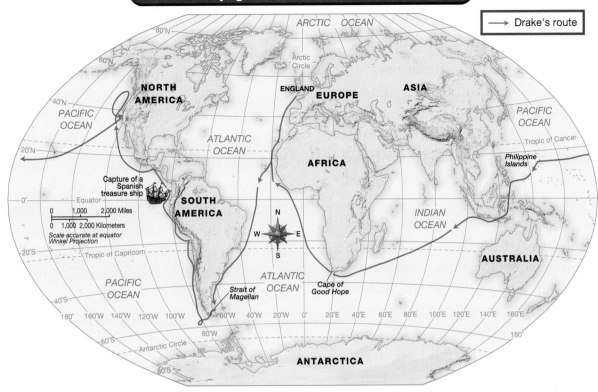

→ Drake's route

Movement   Before sailing back to England, Drake may have sailed as far north as Vancouver Island, Canada.

❖ Which ocean did Drake cross to reach Asia?

because they shared their wealth with the government.

England's best-known sea dog was Francis Drake. In 1577 Drake started his most famous voyage. He sailed through the Strait of Magellan at the southern tip of South America to the Pacific Ocean. Off the western coast of South America, he captured a Spanish treasure ship so loaded with riches that it took the crew four days to transfer all the gold and boxes of jewels to Drake's ship.

Worried that Spanish warships would come after him, Drake decided not to follow the same route home. Instead,

he continued north along the Pacific coast of North America. He stopped near San Francisco Bay in what is now California and claimed the land for England. Drake eventually returned to England by sailing westward. In doing so, Drake and his men became the second crew to sail around the world. Upon Drake's return, Queen Elizabeth made him a knight, and he became known as Sir Francis Drake.

REVIEW Why did Queen Elizabeth I protect the English pirates known as sea dogs?

When Drake returned to England, he was made a knight.

Chapter 4 ▪ 157

England Starts a Colony

The treasure captured by sea dogs increased England's wealth. With that wealth, England built a strong navy and became a powerful country. At that time, Europe's most powerful countries had colonies. So in 1584 Queen Elizabeth gave Sir Walter Raleigh (RAW•lee) permission to set up England's first colony in North America.

Raleigh sent two sea captains, Philip Amadas and Arthur Barlowe, to explore the Atlantic coast to find a good place for a settlement. Upon their return, Barlowe told Raleigh that they had "found such plenty" in what is now North Carolina. The good news led Raleigh to set up his colony there. He named the area that he chose Virginia. He hoped the colony would provide lumber and other raw materials for England. A **raw material** is a resource that can be used to make a product.

Raleigh sent about 100 colonists to North America but did not go himself. In the late summer of 1585, the colonists landed on an island, which the Hatteras Indians called Roanoke (ROH•uh•nohk), just off the coast. Under the leadership of Ralph Lane, the colony's governor, the colonists built a fort and several houses, but they stayed on Roanoke Island less than a year.

The ship that had brought the colonists to Roanoke Island sailed back to England for more food and supplies. By spring, however, it had not returned. Food ran low, and the colonists wanted to go home. So when Sir Francis Drake visited the colonists, they went back to England on his ship.

REVIEW Why did the English set up a colony on Roanoke Island?

The Lost Colony

In 1587 Sir Walter Raleigh sent a second group of colonists to settle a colony in Virginia. This time Raleigh chose John White to be their governor.

The English colonists reached Roanoke Island in July. They quickly rebuilt the fort

John White's Map

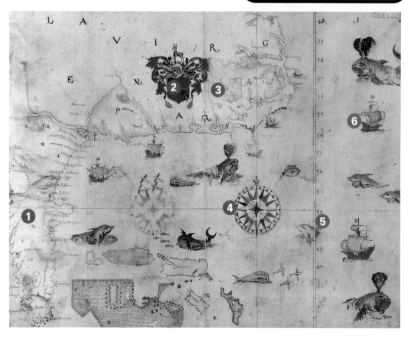

Analyze Primary Sources

This map drawn by John White shows the eastern region of North America.

1. Florida
2. Sir Walter Raleigh's coat of arms
3. Virginia
4. a compass rose
5. measurements that may have indicated longitude
6. English ships

❖ Why do you think ships are shown along the coastline?

and repaired the old houses and built new ones. However, they arrived too late in the year to plant crops. White decided to return to England for food and other supplies.

When White reached England, he wanted to gather supplies and return quickly to his family, but he could not get a ship. England was at war with Spain and needed all of its ships for battle. Three years later, after English ships had defeated Spain's **armada**, or a fleet of warships, John White returned to Roanoke—only to find everyone gone. All that was left were some of his books with the covers torn off, maps ruined by rain, and armor covered with rust.

White did make a puzzling discovery. He found the letters *CRO* carved on a tree and the word *CROATOAN* carved on a wooden post. No trace, however, was ever found of the Roanoke Island settlers. Some people believe they went to live

When John White returned to Roanoke Island, he found that the settlers were gone and that the word *CROATOAN* had been carved into a post.

with the Croatoan Indians, who later became known as the Lumbees. Many Lumbee Indians today have the same English last names as the missing colonists from the "lost colony."

REVIEW Why did John White return to England?

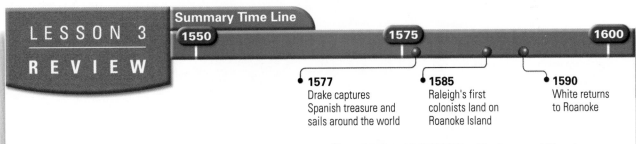

LESSON 3 REVIEW

Summary Time Line

1550 — 1575 — 1600

1577 Drake captures Spanish treasure and sails around the world

1585 Raleigh's first colonists land on Roanoke Island

1590 White returns to Roanoke

1. **MAIN IDEA** Why did the English begin to settle in North America?

2. **WHY IT MATTERS** Why was it difficult for the first English settlers to colonize in North America?

3. **VOCABULARY** Define the terms **sea dog** and **raw material.**

4. **TIME LINE** In what year did Raleigh's first colonists land on Roanoke Island?

5. **READING SKILL—Categorize** Who might you put into the category of "English pirate"?

6. **HISTORY** Where did the English first set up a colony?

7. **CRITICAL THINKING—Evaluate** Why do you think it would be important that the English colonists reached Roanoke Island in time to plant crops?

PERFORMANCE—Write a Journal Entry Imagine that you are John White. Write a journal entry describing why you decided to leave your family and go back to England to get supplies for the colonists. Then write another journal entry about returning three years later to find everyone missing. Describe what you think may have happened to them. Share your journal entries with your classmates.

The Jamestown Colony

MAIN IDEA

Read to learn how the English settlers overcame many hardships to make the Virginia Colony of Jamestown a success.

WHY IT MATTERS

England's power and influence grew as more English settlers moved to North America.

VOCABULARY

stock
prosperity
cash crop
legislature
burgess
authority

1200   1475   1700

1600–1625

Although English settlements at Roanoke Island had failed, the idea of settling an English colony in North America lived on. A group of English merchants decided to try again. To establish a new colony in Virginia, they needed permission from England's monarch. The English believed that the king or queen controlled all land claimed by England. With the permission of King James I, the merchants organized the Virginia Company. The aim of these merchants was to make money by starting trading posts in Virginia. Despite the company's plans, however, most of the colonists went to look for gold.

FAST FACT By the end of the first year at Jamestown, over half of the colonists had died.

LOCATE IT

VIRGINIA

James R.

Jamestown

The Founding of Jamestown

The Virginia Company was owned by many people. Each owner had given money to organize the company. In return, each one had received **stock**, or a share of ownership, in the company. The owners hoped that over time the company would make a profit. If it did, each stock owner would make money.

In the spring of 1607, three ships sent by the Virginia Company sailed into the deep bay now called Chesapeake Bay. The 105 men and boys aboard sailed up a river that they named the James River to honor their king. They chose a spot along the shore and began to build a settlement they called Jamestown.

The location of Jamestown turned out to be a poor choice for a settlement. The land was wet and full of disease-carrying mosquitoes. The water in the wells that the colonists dug was foul, or bad.

Many of the colonists were not used to working with their hands, and they did not know how to farm or fish in this new land. They had come to Virginia to get rich, and they spent so much of their time searching for gold that no one bothered to plant or gather food for the winter. As a result, many of the colonists starved that first winter. One survivor later wrote, "Our men were destroyed with cruel diseases, . . . burning fevers, and by wars."

Jamestown might have become another lost colony, like the earlier settlement at Roanoke, if it had not had a strong leader like Captain John Smith. Smith was a soldier, an explorer, and a writer. Smith made an important rule for the colonists: Anyone who did not work did not eat. The colonists were soon very busy planting gardens and building shelters.

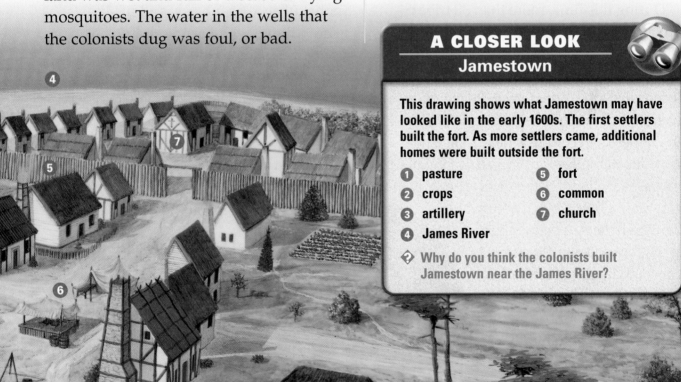

A CLOSER LOOK
Jamestown

This drawing shows what Jamestown may have looked like in the early 1600s. The first settlers built the fort. As more settlers came, additional homes were built outside the fort.

1. pasture
2. crops
3. artillery
4. James River
5. fort
6. common
7. church

❓ Why do you think the colonists built Jamestown near the James River?

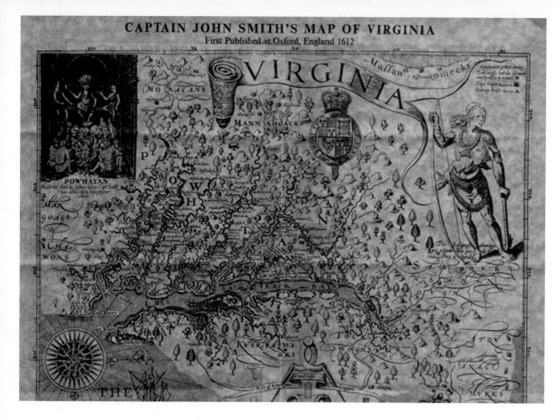

This map, drawn by Captain John Smith, shows the locations of the Virginia Colony and the Powhatan Confederacy. The chief of the Powhatans is also shown (top left).

They also put up fences to protect the settlement from attack by Indians.

During this time, more than 30 tribes of Eastern Woodlands Indians lived in Virginia. Most were members of a confederation known as the Powhatan (pow•uh•TAN) Confederacy. Its members were united under one main chief. When the Jamestown colonists heard this, they gave the name *Powhatan* to all the member tribes, as well as to their chief. The way the colonists behaved toward the Powhatans—seizing their crops for food—put them in constant danger of attack.

One day, while in the countryside around Jamestown, Captain Smith was captured by the Powhatans. A legend says that the chief ordered

This portrait of Pocahontas shows her after she moved to England.

Captain Smith to be put to death but that the chief's daughter, Pocahontas (poh•kuh•HAHN•tuhs), saved his life. It is not known whether this story is true or not, but it is known that fighting continued between the colonists and the Powhatan Confederacy. Jamestown remained a dangerous place to live.

REVIEW How did Captain John Smith help the colonists at Jamestown?

Prosperity and Growth

Despite Jamestown's troubles, the colony survived. In time, it prospered, or did well. This **prosperity**, or economic success, began when the colonists finally found the "gold" they had hoped would make them rich. Their "gold" was not a precious metal but a crop called tobacco.

A Jamestown leader named John Rolfe experimented with various kinds of tobacco and ways of drying it. By 1613 Rolfe had developed a kind of tobacco that the English liked. The colonists at Jamestown were soon growing tobacco as a **cash crop**, or a crop that people raise to sell rather than to use themselves. The Virginia Company sold its tobacco all over Europe and made huge profits.

Jamestown saw even more success when the Virginia Company began to give land to those who stayed in the colony seven years. Until then, there had been no private ownership of land. Everyone was supposed to work for the benefit of the company. After receiving land of their own, the colonists worked harder. Now individual colonists, as well as the company, enjoyed prosperity.

Most of the early colonists had planned to make money in Virginia and return to England. To encourage people to settle permanently, the company allowed the first women to become colonists in 1619.

The first Africans also arrived that year. They came as free laborers paid to work in the tobacco fields. As more workers were needed, more Africans were brought to the colony. Instead of paying these workers, however, colonial leaders enslaved them. Later, all Africans arriving in Virginia were made slaves.

By 1619 Virginia had more than 1,000 colonists. With so many people, the colony needed laws to keep order. The Virginia Company said that the English in the colony would live under English laws and have the same rights as the people living in England. One of these was the right to set up a lawmaking assembly, or legislature. A **legislature** is the branch of a government that makes laws.

Virginia's legislature, called the House of Burgesses (BUHR•juhs•iz), first met in 1619. A **burgess** is a representative who is chosen by and speaks for other people. The Virginia House of Burgesses was the first legislature in the English colonies.

REVIEW **What was the House of Burgesses?**

CITIZENSHIP

DEMOCRATIC VALUES
Representative Government

The House of Burgesses was modeled after the English Parliament. Burgesses would meet once a year with the royal governor to make local laws and decide on taxes. These representatives were wealthy landowners who were elected by the people to speak for them. Electing leaders to make decisions continues to be an important right that Americans have today.

Analyze the Value

1 What was the House of Burgesses modeled after?

2 **Make It Relevant** Identify a present-day example of representative government.

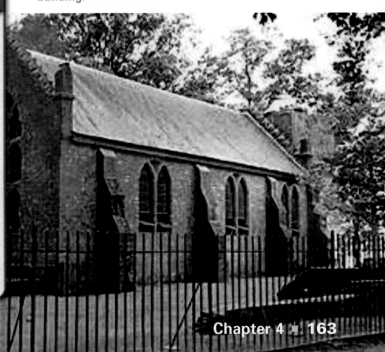

The House of Burgesses met in the Jamestown church. The tower from the original church is part of this building.

The End of Company Control

King James I

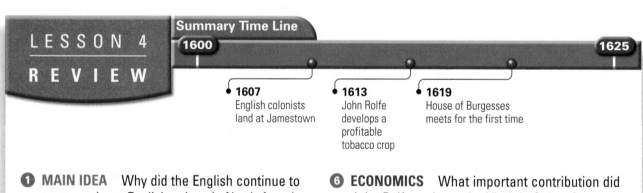

For the Virginia Colony to continue to prosper, the settlers had to grow and sell more and more tobacco. This meant that they needed to clear more land to grow it. As a result, the Indians of the Powhatan Confederacy lost much of the land they had used for hunting and farming. In 1622 the Powhatans attacked and killed more than 340 colonists. Having lost nearly one-third of their people, the Virginia colonists fought back in an all-out war. They defeated the Powhatans and took over their remaining lands.

After the fighting ended, King James took away the charter of the Virginia Company and made Virginia a royal colony. The king, rather than business people, now held direct control over the colony.

The king knew that he ruled from too far away to look after all of Virginia's concerns and problems. As a result, he appointed a royal governor to represent him. The royal governor of Virginia shared ruling authority with the House of Burgesses. **Authority** is the right to control and make decisions. The king instructed the royal governor to meet with the burgesses "once a year or oftener."

REVIEW Who did King James appoint to represent him in Virginia?

LESSON 4 REVIEW

Summary Time Line

1600 — 1625

1607 English colonists land at Jamestown

1613 John Rolfe develops a profitable tobacco crop

1619 House of Burgesses meets for the first time

1. **MAIN IDEA** Why did the English continue to try to settle an English colony in North America despite the hardships?

2. **WHY IT MATTERS** How do you think the Virginia Colony's success would benefit England?

3. **VOCABULARY** Use the words **legislature** and **burgess** in a sentence about Jamestown.

4. **TIME LINE** Which happened first, John Rolfe developing a profitable tobacco crop or the House of Burgesses meeting for the first time?

5. **READING SKILL—Categorize** In what category would you put John Smith and John Rolfe?

6. **ECONOMICS** What important contribution did John Rolfe make to the Virginia Colony?

7. **CRITICAL THINKING—Evaluate** How did the success of the Virginia Colony lead to the development of the House of Burgesses?

PERFORMANCE—Write a Letter Expressing Your Opinion Imagine that you are a Jamestown colonist. Write a letter to Captain John Smith expressing your opinion about his leadership abilities. Do you approve or disapprove of his rule?

·SKILLS·

Solve a Problem

CITIZENSHIP

➡ WHY IT MATTERS

People everywhere face problems at one time or another. Many people face more than one problem at the same time. Think about a problem you have faced recently. Were you able to solve it? Did you wish you could have found a better way to solve the problem? Knowing how to solve problems is a skill that you will use all your life.

➡ WHAT YOU NEED TO KNOW

Here are some steps you can use to help you solve a problem.

Step 1 Identify the problem.

Step 2 Gather information.

Step 3 Think of and list possible options.

Step 4 Consider advantages and disadvantages of possible options.

Step 5 Choose the best solution.

Step 6 Try your solution.

Step 7 Think about how well your solution helps solve the problem.

➡ PRACTICE THE SKILL

You have read about the problems that made life in Jamestown difficult. Colonists did not have enough food, and they were often attacked by Indians. Captain John Smith wanted to solve these problems. Think again about the problems Captain Smith saw and the way he tried to solve them.

1 What problems did Captain Smith see in Jamestown?

2 What did Captain Smith decide was a good way to solve the problems?

3 How did Captain Smith carry out his solution?

4 How did Captain Smith's solution help solve the colonists' problems?

5 Do you think Captain Smith's solution was the best way to solve these problems?

➡ APPLY WHAT YOU LEARNED

Identify a problem in your community or school. Use the steps shown to write a plan for solving the problem. What solution did you choose?

Why do you think that your solution will help solve the problem?

Captain John Smith

CITIZENSHIP SKILLS

Chapter 4 ■ 165

The Plymouth Colony

1200   1475   1700

1600–1700

MAIN IDEA

Read to learn how the desire for religious freedom led to the colonization of the Plymouth Colony.

WHY IT MATTERS

The success of Plymouth led to more English settlements in North America.

VOCABULARY

pilgrim
compact
self-rule
majority rule

Tobacco profits and the private ownership of land led more English settlers to North America. So did a book written by Captain John Smith after he explored the Atlantic coast in 1614. In *A Description of New England*, published in 1616, Smith mapped the coastline, described its landscape, and named the region that today includes the states of Connecticut, Maine, Massachusetts, New Hampshire, Rhode Island, and Vermont.

The Mayflower Compact

Among those who read Smith's description of New England was a group of English people who were living in Holland. They were known as Separatists, because they had left, or separated from, the Church of England. At the time, everyone in England had to belong to the Church of England. Those who refused were not safe. In 1608 the Separatists had moved to Holland, where they could follow their own religion freely.

In Holland the Separatists had religious freedom, but they soon worried that their children would not learn English ways. So they decided to go to the Americas, where they would live among English colonists and still be able to follow their own religion. In time, these Separatists came to be known as Pilgrims. A **pilgrim** is a person who makes a journey for religious reasons.

Items such as this beaver-fur hat and these eyeglasses were worn by settlers on the *Mayflower*.

Early in 1620 a group in England invited the Pilgrims to join them in their journey to North America. The Virginia Company agreed to pay for the colonists' voyage. In return, the colonists would send the company furs, fish, and lumber.

The Mayflower Compact

In the name of God, Amen. We, whose names are underwritten, the loyal subjects of our dread sovereign Lord, King James, by the grace of God, of Great Britain, France, and Ireland, King, defender of the faith, etc.

Having undertaken for the Glory of God, and Advancement of the Christian Faith, and the Honour of our King and Country, a voyage to plant the first colony in the northern Parts of Virginia; do by these Presents, solemnly and mutually in the Presence of God and of one another, covenant [enter into an agreement] and combine ourselves together into a civil Body Politick, for our better Ordering and Preservation, and Furtherance of the Ends aforesaid; And by Virtue hereof to enact, constitute, and frame, such just and equal Laws, Ordinances, Acts, Constitutions, and Offices, from time to time, as shall be thought most meet [proper] and convenient for the General good of the Colony; unto which we promise all due Submission and Obedience.

In witness whereof we have hereunder subscribed our names at Cape Cod the eleventh of November, in the year of the reign of our sovereign Lord, King James of England, France, and Ireland the eighteenth, and of Scotland the fifty-fourth. Anno Domini, 1620.

On a cold day late in 1620, a ship called the *Mayflower* set sail for North America. It carried 101 passengers, including Captain Miles Standish, who had been hired as the new colony's military leader. Fewer than half of the passengers on the *Mayflower* were Pilgrims. Some of them were servants and workers hired by the Virginia Company to help build the new colony.

The *Mayflower* had a long and troubled journey. Violent storms drove the ship off course, and the Pilgrims ended up far north of the lands governed by the Virginia Company. They had reached Cape Cod in what is now Massachusetts.

The people had landed in a place without a government. To keep order, all the men aboard the *Mayflower* signed an agreement, or **compact**. This agreement became known as the Mayflower Compact. The signers agreed that "just and equal laws" would be made for the common good of the colony and promised to obey these laws. In other words, they would govern themselves.

At a time when monarchs ruled, **self-rule**, or governing oneself, was a very new idea. The Mayflower Compact gave everyone who signed it the right to share in the making of laws. It also recognized the right of the majority to rule. **Majority rule** means that more than half of the people have to agree for a decision to be made. The Mayflower Compact was the first example of self-rule and majority rule in the English colonies.

REVIEW What is self-rule?

• HERITAGE •

Thanksgiving Day

In the fall of 1621, the Pilgrims gathered their first harvest. William Bradford, governor of Plymouth Colony, decided they should have a celebration so that the people could "rejoice together" to give thanks to God. He invited the neighboring Wampanoag Indians to join the Pilgrims for a festival that lasted for three days.

This is what many people today think of as the first Thanksgiving. Some people think the first European Thanksgiving in the Americas took place in 1598, when Spanish settlers gave thanks for safely reaching the Rio Grande.

Thanksgiving became a national holiday in 1863, when President Abraham Lincoln declared the last Thursday in November as "a day of thanksgiving and praise to our beneficent Father."

LOCATE IT

Boston
MASSACHUSETTS

Plymouth Colony

Plymouth Colony

For more than four weeks, Captain Miles Standish and the colonists explored what is now Massachusetts Bay, looking for a suitable place to settle. Finally, on December 25, 1620, they chose a place near Cape Cod with a harbor, open fields nearby, and fresh water. John Smith had called it Plymouth. William Bradford, one of the Pilgrim leaders, described the scene that day. "Being thus arrived in a good harbor, and brought safe to land, they fell upon their knees and blessed the God of Heaven, who had brought them over the vast and furious ocean, and delivered them from all the perils and miseries thereof, again to set their feet on the firm and stable earth, their proper element."

The first winter was hard for the colonists. The weather was cold, and there was not enough food. Many people became ill, and about half of them died. Help, however, came in the spring, when a Native American who spoke English walked into their settlement.

"Welcome, Englishmen," the Indian said. He was an Abenaki (AH•beh•nah•kee) Indian named Samoset who had been visiting the neighboring Wampanoags (wam•puh•NOH•agz). Samoset had learned English from sailors who fished along the Atlantic coast.

Several days later Samoset returned to Plymouth with a Wampanoag who spoke English better than he did. This was Tisquantum, or Squanto, as the English called him. Years before, Tisquantum had been taken and sold as a slave in Spain. He had escaped and spent several years in England before returning to his homeland.

Tisquantum stayed with the Plymouth colonists, showing them where to fish and how to plant squash, pumpkins, and corn. For a time the Pilgrims lived in peace with the Wampanoags, who were led by their chief, Massasoit (ma•suh•SOYT). However, as more English colonists came to settle in Massachusetts, the situation changed. Many of the new colonists were not friendly toward the Indians and settled on more and more of their lands. This caused many quarrels between the Wampanoags and the English colonists. Over time, these quarrels became fights and eventually grew into terrible wars.

REVIEW Who was Tisquantum?

Plymouth Colony Prospers

When the Plymouth colonists first arrived, there was no private ownership of land. Everyone worked for the community, and the harvest was divided equally among the families. Some complained about this system because they felt they were working harder than others.

People today can visit this re-creation of the Plymouth Colony (below) in Massachusetts. Actors there take on colonial roles in which they chop wood (right), sew (far right), and plant crops (bottom right).

In 1623 the colonial leaders divided the land among the colonists. The result was the same as it had been at Jamestown—the people worked harder when they owned the land. However, the idea of community sharing remained strong. Large areas of land in Plymouth were set aside for common use.

The Plymouth colonists, including the Pilgrims, began to prosper with their fishing, farming, and fur trading. As new colonists arrived, the earlier ones had extra goods ready to sell or trade. They sold or traded milk, meat, fruit, and vegetables to the newcomers.

William Bradford was a governor of the Plymouth Colony.

Colonists like William Bradford provided the strong, steady leadership that kept the community alive. Bradford fought for the religious ideals of Plymouth's founders and kept the colony separate from any neighboring settlements. Bradford was so popular with the colonists that he was reelected governor of Plymouth 30 times! After a hard beginning, Plymouth continued to prosper. In 1691 Plymouth became a part of the Massachusetts Bay Colony, a larger colony that was formed later.

REVIEW **What helped the Plymouth colonists prosper?**

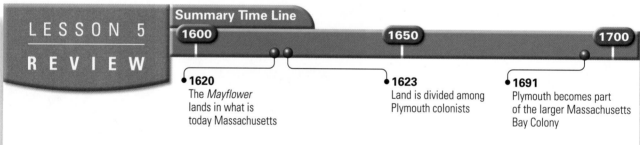

LESSON 5 REVIEW

Summary Time Line

1600 — 1650 — 1700

1620
The *Mayflower* lands in what is today Massachusetts

1623
Land is divided among Plymouth colonists

1691
Plymouth becomes part of the larger Massachusetts Bay Colony

1. **MAIN IDEA** Why did many settlers come to the Plymouth Colony?

2. **WHY IT MATTERS** How do you think the success of Plymouth might have influenced more people to come to North America?

3. **VOCABULARY** Describe the difference between **self-rule** and **majority rule**.

4. **TIME LINE** When did Plymouth become part of the Massachusetts Bay Colony?

5. **READING SKILL—Categorize** What were the names of some of the Indians who had contact with the first Plymouth colonists?

6. **CIVICS AND GOVERNMENT** Describe the Mayflower Compact and tell why you think it would serve as a model for later documents.

7. **CRITICAL THINKING—Hypothesize** What do you think might have happened if Tisquantum had not helped the Pilgrims?

PERFORMANCE—Write a List of Questions Write a list of questions you might ask people who want to join you in starting a colony. As you write the questions, think about the personal qualities and skills people need in order to start a successful colony. Compare your questions with those of your classmates.

Compare Tables to Classify Information

VOCABULARY

classify

➤ WHY IT MATTERS

Information can be easier to find if you **classify**, or group it. Knowing how to classify information can make facts easier to find.

➤ WHAT YOU NEED TO KNOW

When you read about European settlement in the Americas, you were given a lot of information. You learned where, when, and why the Spanish, French, and English set up colonies. This and other information can be classified by using a table.

The tables below classify information about European settlement in the Americas in two different ways. In Table A, the settlements are classified according to when they were founded. Table B gives the same information as Table A, but the information is

classified according to what countries founded the settlements.

➤ PRACTICE THE SKILL

Use the tables below to answer the following questions.

❶ Which table makes it easier to find out when the first European settlement in the Americas was founded?

❷ Which table makes it easier to find out the number of settlements founded by the French?

❸ When was Roanoke founded? Explain which table you used to find this information.

➤ APPLY WHAT YOU LEARNED

Make a table to show information about European explorers. Choose some headings under which to classify the information by topic. Then compare your table with a classmate's table.

Table A: European Settlements in the Americas

DATE FOUNDED	SETTLEMENT	COUNTRY
1521	Mexico City	Spain
1565	St. Augustine	Spain
1585	Fort Raleigh (Roanoke)	England
1607	Jamestown	England
1608	Quebec	France
1620	Plymouth	England

Table B: European Settlements in the Americas

COUNTRY	SETTLEMENT	DATE FOUNDED
England	Fort Raleigh (Roanoke)	1585
England	Jamestown	1607
England	Plymouth	1620
France	Quebec	1608
Spain	Mexico City	1521
Spain	St. Augustine	1565

4 Review and Test Preparation

Summary Time Line

1500   1550

1535
The colony of
New Spain
is formed

USE YOUR READING SKILLS

Complete this graphic organizer by categorizing people and settlements with the countries they are associated with. A copy of this graphic organizer appears on page 42 of the Activity Book.

Key Settlements in North America

SPANISH SETTLEMENTS

↓

KEY PEOPLE

1. Bartolomé de las Casas

2. _____

3. _____

KEY SETTLEMENTS

1. Hispaniola

2. _____

3. _____

FRENCH SETTLEMENTS

↓

KEY PEOPLE

1. Samuel de Champlain

2. _____

3. _____

KEY SETTLEMENTS

1. Quebec

2. _____

3. _____

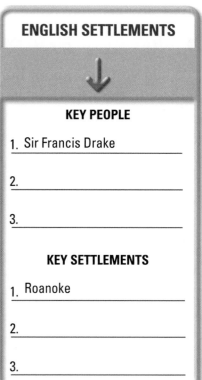

ENGLISH SETTLEMENTS

↓

KEY PEOPLE

1. Sir Francis Drake

2. _____

3. _____

KEY SETTLEMENTS

1. Roanoke

2. _____

3. _____

THINK & WRITE

Write a Classroom Compact The Mayflower Compact set up rules designed to help the Plymouth settlers. Write a classroom compact that lists rules for your class. Explain how this compact will benefit the members of your class.

Write a Letter Imagine that the year is 1620 and you have just moved to the Plymouth Colony with your family. Write a letter to a friend in England about your new life. Describe your new environment and the challenges you and your family face.

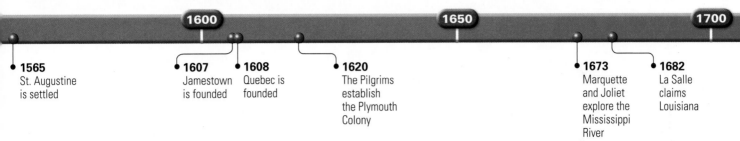

1600 **1650** **1700**

1565
St. Augustine
is settled

1607
Jamestown
is founded

1608
Quebec is
founded

1620
The Pilgrims
establish
the Plymouth
Colony

1673
Marquette
and Joliet
explore the
Mississippi
River

1682
La Salle
claims
Louisiana

USE THE TIME LINE

Use the chapter summary time line to answer these questions.

1 When was the Jamestown Colony founded?

2 Was St. Augustine settled before Quebec?

USE VOCABULARY

Identify the term that correctly matches each definition.

> colony (p. 144)
>
> proprietor (p. 155)
>
> burgess (p. 163)
>
> compact (p. 167)

3 an owner

4 a representative who speaks for other people

5 a signed agreement

6 a settlement ruled by another country

RECALL FACTS

Answer these questions.

7 What group of people did Bartolomé de Las Casas work to protect?

8 What early problems did the Jamestown colonists face?

9 How was the government of a royal colony different from that of a proprietary colony?

Write the letter of the best choice.

10 **TEST PREP** The forts built by Spanish soldiers were known as—
  A haciendas.
  B plantations.
  C presidios.
  D missions.

11 **TEST PREP** After leaders of the Plymouth Colony divided the land among the colonists—
  F many people starved.
  G people stopped immigrating to Plymouth.
  H people lost their sense of community.
  J people worked harder and the colony began to prosper.

THINK CRITICALLY

12 Why do you think problems developed between Native Americans and Spanish missionaries?

13 How do you think English pirates such as Francis Drake would have been treated by Queen Elizabeth I if they had not shared their wealth?

APPLY SKILLS

Solve a Problem

14 Imagine that you are a Jamestown colonist in 1622. What ideas would you offer to solve the problems between the colonists and the Powhatan Indians?

Compare Tables to Classify Information

15 Choose a lesson from this chapter and make a table about the explorers discussed in that lesson. Make sure to list the places the explorers visited and the dates of their travels. Compare your table to a classmate's table.

Chapter 4 ▪ **173**

VISIT The Mission San Diego de Alcalá

GET READY

High on a hill overlooking the city of San Diego, California, sits the Mission San Diego de Alcalá. It was the first in a string of 21 missions that stretched across the Spanish borderlands of California. San Diego de Alcalá was founded by Father Junípero Serra on July 16, 1769. In time, the city of San Diego grew around the mission. Today, many people visit to learn about mission life hundreds of years ago. At San Diego de Alcalá, you can see artifacts that belonged to Native Americans, early Spanish settlers, soldiers, and missionaries. Experience life in another time as you walk where they once walked.

LOCATE IT

San Diego

CALIFORNIA

WHAT TO SEE

Visitors can spend time in the mission's scenic gardens.

People still attend church services at the Mission San Diego de Alcalá.

This songbook, on display at the mission, was used more than 200 years ago.

A statue of Father Junípero Serra stands on the mission grounds.

TAKE A FIELD TRIP

GO ONLINE

A VIRTUAL TOUR
Visit The Learning Site at **www.harcourtschool.com/tours** to find virtual tours of historic sites in the United States.

CNN Turner Le@rning®

A VIDEO TOUR
Check your media center or classroom library for a videotape tour of the Mission San Diego de Alcalá.

2 Review and Test Preparation

Write a Journal Entry Choose one of the events shown below. Write a journal entry from the perspective of a person present at one of the events.

USE VOCABULARY

Use each of the following words in a sentence about exploration.

1 **compass** (p. 109)

2 **claim** (p. 121)

3 **Northwest Passage** (p. 136)

4 **missionary** (p. 148)

RECALL FACTS

Answer these questions.

5 Why did Prince Henry set up a school for navigators?

6 What Native American group was one of the first to trade furs with the French?

7 How did the Jamestown Colony finally achieve prosperity?

Write the letter of the best choice.

8 **TEST PREP** The Inca Empire covered thousands of miles on the western coast of—
A Europe.
B Asia.
C South America.
D Africa.

9 **TEST PREP** One of the first Spanish explorers to journey through what is now the state of Texas was—
F Hernando Cortés.
G Álvar Núñez Cabeza de Vaca.
H Juan Ponce de León.
J Hernando de Soto.

10 **TEST PREP** Sieur de la Salle set out to find—
A the Northwest Passage.
B the mouth of the Mississippi River.
C El Dorado.
D the Fountain of Youth.

Visual Summary

1200   1300   1400

1275 Marco Polo reaches China p. 109

1492 Christopher Columbus lands at San Salvador p. 122

1498 Vasco da Gama reaches India by sea p. 118

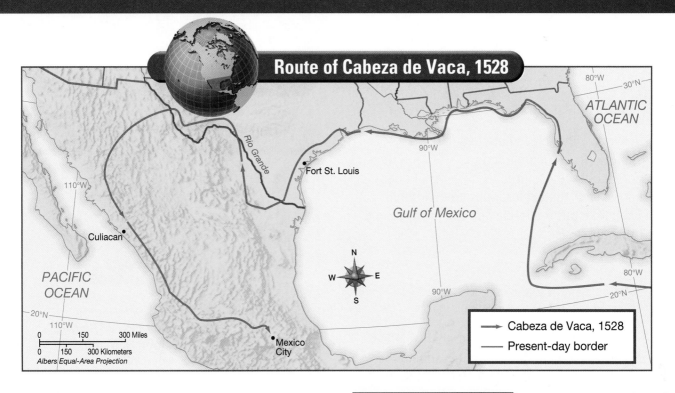

Route of Cabeza de Vaca, 1528

ATLANTIC OCEAN

Rio Grande

Fort St. Louis

Gulf of Mexico

Culiacan

PACIFIC OCEAN

Mexico City

N W E S

0 150 300 Miles
0 150 300 Kilometers
Albers Equal-Area Projection

→ Cabeza de Vaca, 1528
— Present-day border

11 **TEST PREP** The Mayflower Compact allowed the colonists to—
F govern themselves.
G trade.
H grow tobacco.
J join the Virginia Company.

THINK CRITICALLY

12 Why do you think *The Travels of Marco Polo* was such a popular book?

13 Do you think Francisco Vasquez de Coronado's 1540 expedition was a success or a failure? Explain.

APPLY SKILLS

Follow Routes on a Map

Use the map on this page to answer the following questions.

14 For the most part, did Cabeza de Vaca travel east or west on his expedition?

15 Where did Cabeza de Vaca end his expedition?

16 How many times did Cabeza de Vaca cross the Rio Grande on his way to Mexico City?

1500   1600   1700

1519 Hernando Cortés arrives in Tenochtitlán p. 129

1607 English colonists settle Jamestown p. 161

1620 English colonists settle Plymouth p. 167

177

Unit Activities

 GO ONLINE Visit The Learning Site at www.harcourtschool.com/socialstudies/activities for additional activities.

Conduct an Interview

Work with a classmate to select an explorer from the unit and research information about the explorer. Write a list of questions to ask the explorer during an interview. Then take turns role-playing the explorer and the interviewer.

Make a Display

Work in a group to create a chart titled *Daily Life in America*. Your chart should feature Spanish missions, French settlements, and the Jamestown and Plymouth Colonies. For each settlement or colony, list the location, climate, foods available, and buildings. To illustrate the chart, draw pictures, cut them out of magazines, or print them out from the Internet.

VISIT YOUR LIBRARY

 ■ *If you Were There in 1492* by Barbara Brenner. Macmillan.

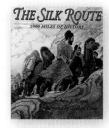 ■ *The Silk Route: 7,000 Miles of History* by John S. Major. HarperCollins.

■ *The History News: Explorers* by Michael Johnstone. Candlewick.

COMPLETE THE UNIT PROJECT

An Exploration Map Work with a group of your classmates to complete the unit project—a map that shows exploration of North America. Decide which key explorers' routes you want to include on your map. Start by drawing a map of North America on posterboard. Then draw the routes of the explorers you have chosen. Use a different color for each route. Also label each route with the correct explorer's name and the dates of the exploration.

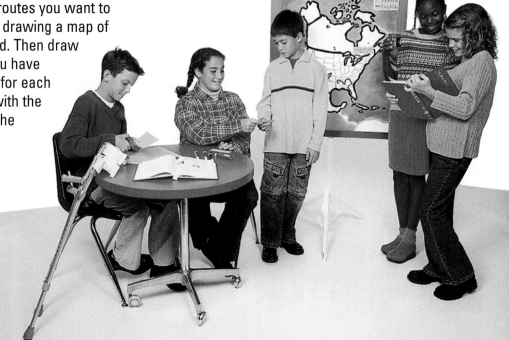

The English Colonies

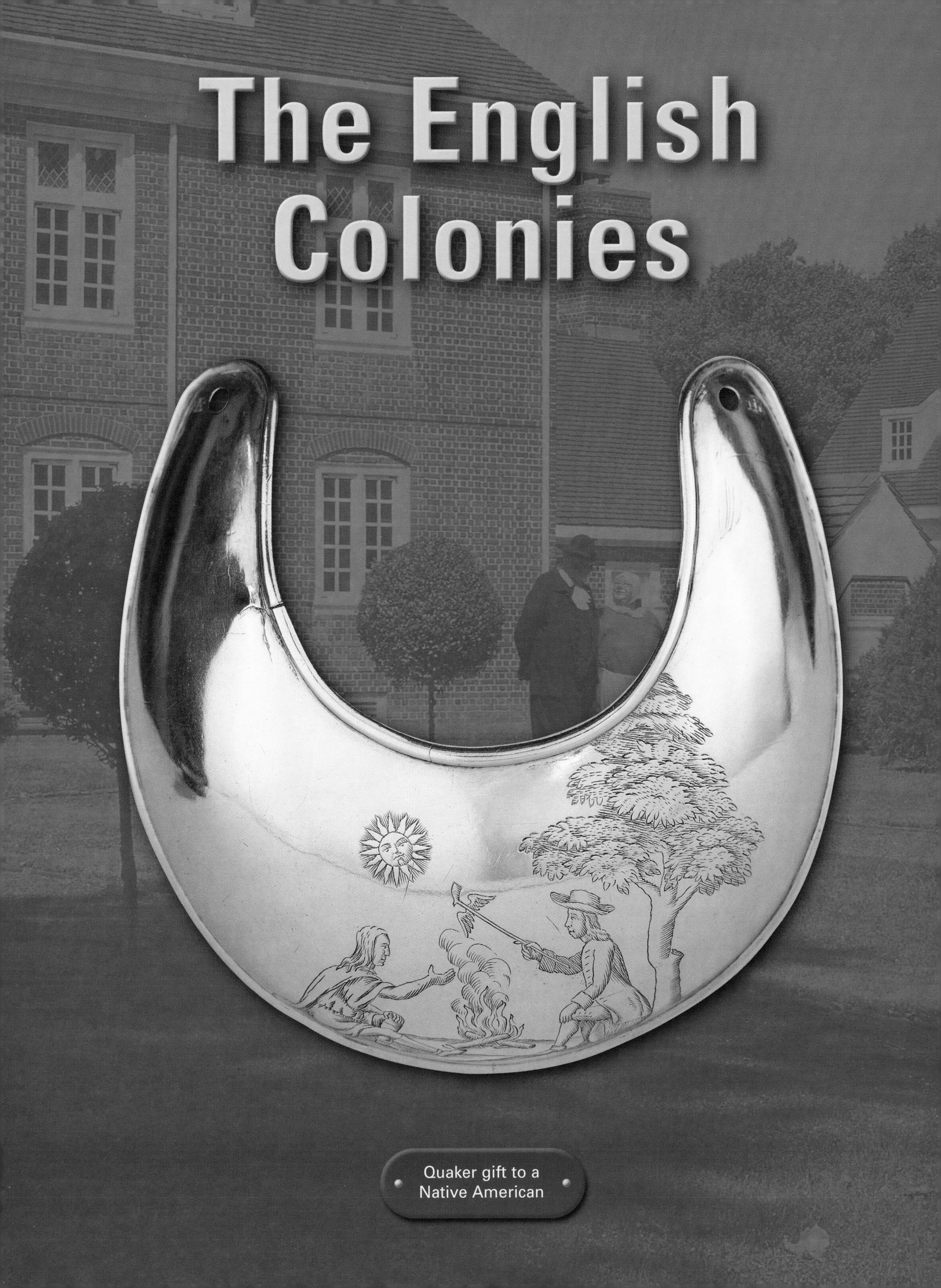

Quaker gift to a
Native American

The home of William Penn, Pennsbury Manor, Pennsylvania

The English Colonies

> **Any government is free to the people under it where the laws rule and the people are a party to the laws.**
>
> —William Penn, Frame of Government of Pennsylvania, 1682

Preview the Content

Scan the unit. Then make a K-W-L chart. First, write what you have learned about the 13 colonies. Next, write what you would like to know about them. As you read, fill in details.

Preview the Vocabulary

Synonyms Synonyms are words with similar meanings. Look in the unit to find vocabulary words you can match to the synonyms below. Then use each word in a sentence.

SYNONYM	VOCABULARY WORD	SENTENCE
1. setting up 2. shelter 3. army	charter	

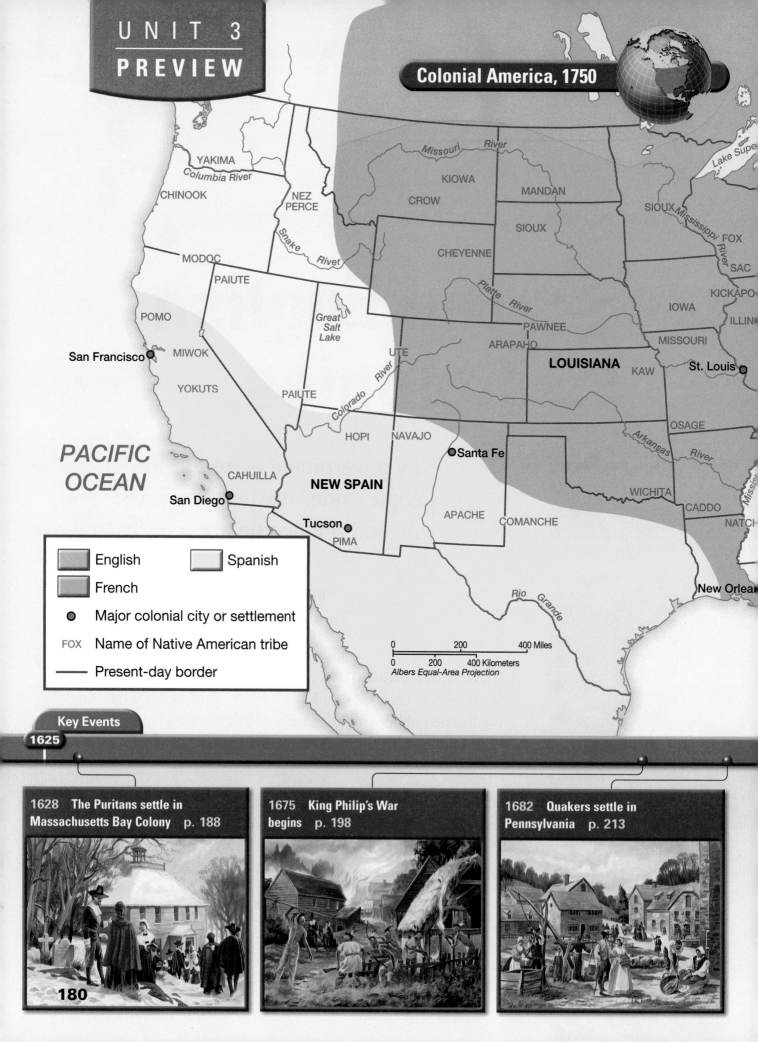

Colonial America, 1750

PACIFIC
OCEAN

YAKIMA
Columbia River
CHINOOK
NEZ
PERCE
MODOC
Snake River
PAIUTE
POMO
Great
Salt
Lake
San Francisco
MIWOK
YOKUTS
PAIUTE
Colorado River
UTE
HOPI   NAVAJO
CAHUILLA
San Diego
NEW SPAIN
Santa Fe
Tucson
PIMA
APACHE   COMANCHE

Missouri   River
KIOWA
CROW   MANDAN
SIOUX
CHEYENNE
Platte   River
PAWNEE
ARAPAHO
LOUISIANA   KAW
St. Louis
OSAGE
Arkansas   River
WICHITA
CADDO
NATCH
Rio   Grande
New Orlea

Lake Supe
SIOUX Mississippi River FOX
SAC
KICKAPO
IOWA   ILLIN
MISSOURI
Missi

English   **Spanish**
French
● Major colonial city or settlement
FOX   Name of Native American tribe
— Present-day border

0   200   400 Miles
0   200   400 Kilometers
Albers Equal-Area Projection

Key Events

1625

1628 The Puritans settle in
Massachusetts Bay Colony p. 188

1675 King Philip's War
begins p. 198

1682 Quakers settle in
Pennsylvania p. 213

180

The 13 Colonies

COLONY	LOCATION	DATE FOUNDED
Massachusetts	New England Colony	1630
Connecticut	New England Colony	1636
Rhode Island	New England Colony	1647
New Hampshire	New England Colony	1680
Delaware	Middle Atlantic Colony	1638
New Jersey	Middle Atlantic Colony	1664
New York	Middle Atlantic Colony	1664
Pennsylvania	Middle Atlantic Colony	1681
Virginia	Southern Colony	1607
Maryland	Southern Colony	1632
North Carolina	Southern Colony	1663
South Carolina	Southern Colony	1712
Georgia	Southern Colony	1733

ATLANTIC OCEAN

1750

1730s The Great Awakening spreads throughout the colonies p. 215

1733 James Oglethorpe settles the Georgia Colony p. 236

1750s Williamsburg, Virginia becomes a large city p. 238

181

Stranded at Plimoth Plantation
—1626—

words and woodcuts by Gary Bowen

On October 12, 1626, a ship bound for the Jamestown colony set sail from England. The actual name of the ship is unknown, but the Pilgrims called it the *Sparrowhawk*. On November 6, the ship crashed in the fog along the New England coast near the Pilgrim colony at Plimoth Plantation, known today as Plymouth, Massachusetts. Rescued by the

colonists, the ship's passengers remained stranded there for nine months until another ship arrived to take them to Jamestown. The following is a fictional journal based on the wreck of the *Sparrowhawk*. The writer is one of the passengers, 13-year-old Christopher Sears. After being rescued, Sears stayed with the family of William Brewster, a Pilgrim church leader. Also living with the Brewsters at that time was another boy, Richard More, whose parents had died during the first years of the Pilgrim colony. The entries from Sears's fictional journal, accompanied by woodcut engravings, tell what life was like in the early New England colonies. Read now about Christopher Sears's experiences at Plimoth Plantation.

November 24, 1626

His worship the Governor [William Bradford] met at the fort this afternoon with all of us who crossed on the *Sparrowhawk*. He told us that 21 other ships have arrived in Plimoth in six years, and said it may be months before another anchors again.

We are to earn our board by working for the families with whom we reside. Our labors are to be reported weekly to Captain Sibsey or Master Fells.

I am happy that Richard lives and works here, too. When he was six years old, he came over on the *Mayflower* with two brothers and a sister who did not survive their first year here. Richard says they had been told their mother and father died, but he does not remember their illnesses or any funeral service. He says his parents did not like each other.

My knee aches and I am cold because my garments are not warm enough for this climate.

December 23, 1626

Governor Bradford talked with me today and showed me the notes that he has been keeping since he arrived in 1620. He commended me for recording my experiences here and said that I am participating in a "great event, which is the founding of God's community."

His Worship suggested that I make larger woodcuts and consider using color. The physician gave me these mixtures.

December 30, 1626

I was measured for new woolen breeches as my old ones are too small. The Mistress plans to sew them from fabric that once was her skirt. She will re-dye the cloth with agrimony roots and nutshells because all textiles are imported and are difficult to come by here.

It is surprising that I have seen no spinning wheels or looms in Plimoth since they are so common in England.

January 23, 1627

Master Brewster will include me in his tutoring of Richard, Oceanus Hopkins (who was born aboard the *Mayflower*), and Peregrine White, who Master Brewster says is the first Anglo-Saxon born in New England.

We had cold eel pie in a <u>coffin</u> for dinner.

<u>**coffin**</u> a pastry crust

February 3, 1627

I am happy that my schooling continues.

Each evening Master Brewster works with me on herb lore, farming, reading, and scriptures. He says the Plimoth people are more learned than in most English villages, as all parents must educate their children, even if that requires tutoring in another home.

March 3, 1627

I was with a group of men organized by the Governor, cutting timbers in the forest.

Indians approached us, wanting to trade some furs, three turkeys, and a deer for grain. His Worship agreed to the barter, and the Indians will receive a bushel of corn.

April 5, 1627

I carried in 24 buckets of springwater to heat. Each member of the Brewster household had a bath today. It felt good to wash.

Love [the Brewster's son] cautioned me that it is unhealthy to have more than three or four baths a year because, if done too often, all the body's natural protection against disease is washed away.

Tomorrow we will be fishing for herring, which is plentiful this month and next.

June 1, 1627

Because Master Brewster predicts rainy weather is coming, we worked doubly hard to sow our seeds for peas, beans, wheat, rye, barley, and turkey corn. Not all families have planted their crops yet.

Mistress Priscilla Alden gave birth to baby John. Master John Alden, her husband, was very pleased.

Love prepared mussels again.

July 1, 1627

The weather has been hot and dry and our garden has suffered. Richard and I carried buckets of water to give the crops a drink.

Since there is no rain in sight, we plan to cut a field of grain tomorrow. After it is turned over to dry thoroughly in the sun, we will stack the barley in the shape of cones.

I boiled seawater to replenish the Brewsters' salt supply.

Love says I am growing like a weed!

August 18, 1627

Today when we returned from the Indian settlement, I learned that two barks had arrived from Jamestown to transport the *Sparrowhawk* passengers to Virginia. For me it was not a welcome sight.

August 22, 1627

Since the ship will depart Thursday at sunrise, tomorrow will be my last full day here.

I feel very sad.

Analyze the Literature

1 How did people at Plimoth Plantation get goods that they needed?

2 Compare Christopher Sears's daily activities with your own. How are they alike and how are they different?

READ A BOOK

START THE UNIT PROJECT

A Book on Colonial America With your classmates, create a book on the 13 colonies. As you read, take notes about why different colonies were started, key people, economic practices, and how the colonies were governed. These notes will help you decide what to include in your book.

USE TECHNOLOGY

Visit The Learning Site at **www.harcourtschool.com/ socialstudies** for additional activities, primary sources, and other resources to use in this unit.

A NEW ENGLAND CHURCH

Religion was the center of life for most early New England colonists. As a result, nearly every town had its own church, or meetinghouse. A town's church was usually among the first major structures built. In the case of Thetford Hill, Vermont, the building of the meetinghouse marked the beginning of the village itself.

LOCATE IT

VERMONT

Thetford Hill

5

The New England Colonies

" The New Englanders are a people of God. . . . "
—Cotton Mather,
Wonders of the Invisible World, 1693

Summarize

When you **summarize,** you tell a shortened version of what you have just read.

As you read this chapter, summarize the sections within each lesson.

FACTS SUMMARY

MAIN IDEA
Read to find out why a group of English colonists founded the Massachusetts Bay Colony.

WHY IT MATTERS
The Massachusetts Bay colonists' thoughts about government and education helped shape our present-day systems of government and education.

VOCABULARY
Puritan
charter
common
specialize
town meeting
public office

The Massachusetts Bay Colony

1625 ——————————————————————— 1750

1625–1645

Less than ten years after the Pilgrims founded Plymouth, another group of religious settlers founded an English colony in North America. Like the Pilgrims, these settlers disagreed with many practices of the Church of England. Unlike the Pilgrims, however, they did not want to separate from the church. They wanted to change some religious practices in order to make the Church of England more "pure." For this reason, they were called **Puritans**. The Puritans set up a community in North America so they could make money, freely practice their beliefs, and live by their Christian ideas.

A City on a Hill

In 1628 a group of Puritans joined other people in England to form the New England Company. That year King Charles I granted the company a charter. A **charter** is an official paper in which certain rights are given by a government to a person or business. The king's charter allowed the Puritans to settle in the region Captain John Smith had named New England.

In 1628 John Endecott led the first group of Puritans to sail to New England. There they built a settlement named Salem on a bay they called Massachusetts Bay. The word *Massachusetts* means "at the big hill" in the Algonquian language. The following year the company became the Massachusetts Bay Company, and the king granted a new charter.

FAST FACT
Salem was the Puritans' first settlement in the Massachusetts Bay area. Its name comes from the Hebrew word *shalom*, which means "peace."

King Charles I is shown in the top left corner of the Massachusetts Bay Company Charter.

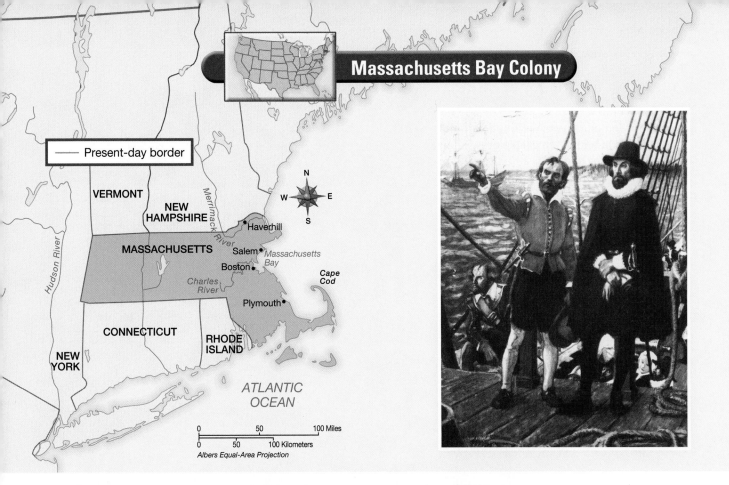

— Present-day border

VERMONT
NEW HAMPSHIRE
• Haverhill
MASSACHUSETTS
Salem •
Boston •
Massachusetts Bay
Charles River
Merrimack River
Hudson River
Plymouth •
Cape Cod
CONNECTICUT
RHODE ISLAND
NEW YORK
ATLANTIC OCEAN

N
W E
S

0   50   100 Miles
0   50   100 Kilometers
Albers Equal-Area Projection

GEOGRAPHY THEME

Location   In 1630 John Winthrop (far right) led more than 700 Puritans to Massachusetts Bay. They soon settled on the Massachusetts coast north of Plymouth.

❖ Why do you think most of the settlements in Massachusetts were located near the coast?

In 1630 John Winthrop brought a second and much larger group of Puritans from England to settle along Massachusetts Bay. Winthrop served as the governor of the Massachusetts Bay Colony. In fact, he would serve as governor of the colony several times during the next 20 years. In that time more than 20,000 newcomers, mostly Puritans, settled in the colony.

Winthrop said that Puritan cities should be models for Christian living.

❝For we must consider that we shall be as a city upon a hill. The eyes of all people are upon us. . . .❞

The Puritans hoped that all their communities would become models for good living. They built new villages, many of which were near Boston.

In 1637 Winthrop worked at forming a confederation among the people of New England. He believed a confederation would help them better defend themselves in case they were attacked by nearby Indian groups or by the Dutch, who had started settlements to the south of New England. Winthrop became the first president of the confederation when it was formed in 1643.

REVIEW   What did John Winthrop accomplish as leader of the Puritans?

Most New England towns were self-sufficient communities in which the people grew or made most of what they needed.

1. houses
2. general store
3. mill
4. fields
5. cooper
6. blacksmith
7. common
8. well
9. cobbler
10. minister's house
11. meetinghouse
12. school
13. minister

Why do you think the common was in the center of the town?

A Puritan Village

At the center of each Puritan village was the **common**, or village green. This was a parklike area shared by all the villagers and used for grazing their animals. At one end of the common was the church, called the meetinghouse. Houses and other buildings lined the other sides of the common.

In time, other buildings that might be found around the common were a general store, a sawmill, and a blacksmith shop. Blacksmithing is one particular craft in which a person in a village may have specialized. To **specialize** is to become skilled at one kind of job.

A blacksmith might make nails for a neighbor. In exchange, the neighbor might make barrels for the blacksmith. In the early days of the Massachusetts Bay Colony, the Puritans bartered for goods and did not spend money very often.

Another building that might be found near the common was a school. Schools were important because the Puritans wanted every person to be able to read the Bible. At first, Puritan children went to schools that were run by women in their homes. Later, villagers began to build schools after the Puritans passed a law stating that every village of 50 families or more must have a school.

Puritan schools were the first community schools in the English colonies. Some of these schools still exist. They include Boston Latin School, which was founded in 1635, and Harvard College, now Harvard University, which was founded in 1636. Harvard was the first college in England's North American colonies.

The small size of a Puritan village made people feel they belonged to a community and made it easier for them to help each other. Village life also made it easier for church ministers to keep their authority in the village. The duty of the minister was to make sure people lived their lives in ways that the Puritan leaders thought were right.

REVIEW How did the small size of villages help the Puritans?

The Meetinghouse

The meetinghouse was at the center of village life because it was where church services were held. The most important part of the Puritan church service was the minister's sermon, or his explanation of the Bible's teachings. The sermon often lasted for several hours. The whole service lasted for most of the day, with a break for a meal at noon.

The meetinghouse was also where the Puritans conducted all town business. Everyone in the town could attend a **town meeting**, but only men who owned property could vote. They voted on laws and on matters that affected the whole community. At first, a man had to be a member of the Puritan church to vote. By the end of the 1600s, however, any man who owned property could vote.

Each year at a town meeting, some people were elected to **public offices**, or jobs for the community. Offices in a Puritan town included constable, town crier, digger of graves, drummer, sweeper of the meetinghouse, and fence viewer. The constable was in charge of maintaining order and keeping the peace. The town crier walked around and called out important news and other announcements. The fence viewer made sure that the fences around the crops were kept in good repair.

A town meeting held in Haverhill, Massachusetts, once elected a man to run a ferry across the Merrimack River. He could not charge passengers any price he wanted, however. The town meeting set the charges.

REVIEW What were some of the public offices that the Puritans could be elected to?

Home and Farm Life

The main room of a Puritan home contained a large fireplace, where a fire was always kept burning. All cooking was done in the fireplace. Baking was done in a small oven inside the fireplace. Most food was roasted over the fire or simmered in large iron kettles hung in the fireplace. Kettles were also used to heat water for cooking and washing.

Women and girls spent many hours preparing food for the rest of the family. They used churns to turn cream into butter. They dried and preserved fruits. They pickled cabbages and other vegetables grown in the gardens they tended. Pickled vegetables could be eaten throughout the cold, hard winter.

The women and girls also made all the clothing for the family. Sometimes pieces of worn-out clothing were used to make

This reenactment shows how Puritan women prepared meals.

This scene shows a New England farm.

new clothing and patchwork quilts for bedding. Nothing useful went to waste.

The men and boys spent many hours each day working in the nearby fields. Despite the rocky soil, Puritan farmers were able to grow corn, rye, barley, and wheat. They traded some of these crops for sugar from English colonists on the Caribbean islands. Farmers also grew pumpkins and other kinds of squash among the corn. This method of farming was first used by the Wampanoag Indians.

The Puritans also raised livestock as sources of food, leather, and wool. Cattle, hogs, and sheep often grazed on the town common. The Puritans used pig bristles, or hair, to make brushes. They turned animal fat into soap and candles. The Puritans made their own tools from wood and their own shoes from leather. They also wore warm clothing from sheep's wool.

REVIEW **What kinds of crops were grown on New England farms?**

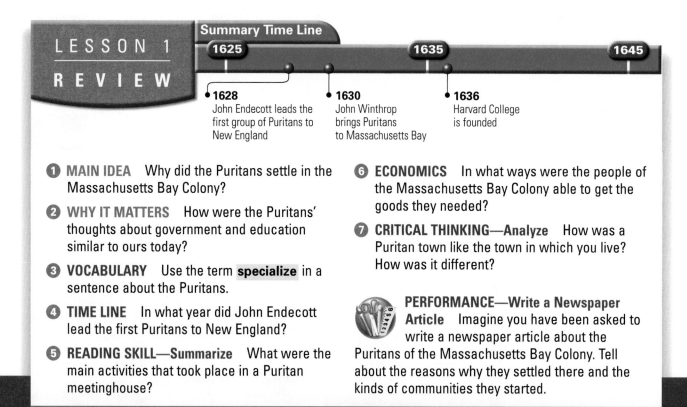

LESSON 1 REVIEW

Summary Time Line

1625 — 1635 — 1645

1628
John Endecott leads the first group of Puritans to New England

1630
John Winthrop brings Puritans to Massachusetts Bay

1636
Harvard College is founded

1. **MAIN IDEA** Why did the Puritans settle in the Massachusetts Bay Colony?

2. **WHY IT MATTERS** How were the Puritans' thoughts about government and education similar to ours today?

3. **VOCABULARY** Use the term **specialize** in a sentence about the Puritans.

4. **TIME LINE** In what year did John Endecott lead the first Puritans to New England?

5. **READING SKILL—Summarize** What were the main activities that took place in a Puritan meetinghouse?

6. **ECONOMICS** In what ways were the people of the Massachusetts Bay Colony able to get the goods they needed?

7. **CRITICAL THINKING—Analyze** How was a Puritan town like the town in which you live? How was it different?

PERFORMANCE—Write a Newspaper Article Imagine you have been asked to write a newspaper article about the Puritans of the Massachusetts Bay Colony. Tell about the reasons why they settled there and the kinds of communities they started.

New Ideas, New Colonies

MAIN IDEA
Read to find out what led some Massachusetts Bay colonists to form new colonies nearby.

WHY IT MATTERS
As the English colonies attracted even more settlers, their people expanded the ideas of freedom of speech and freedom of religion.

VOCABULARY
expel
consent
sedition
fundamental
frontier

1625 ———————————————— 1750

1630–1680

The lives of the Puritans in the Massachusetts Bay Colony centered around religion. In fact, religion was so important to the Puritans that they expected all newcomers to follow the Puritans' beliefs. They did not welcome people whose ideas were different from theirs. When the Puritan leaders disapproved of someone's ideas, they sent that person back to England or to another English colony. Some colonists who left the Massachusetts Bay Colony started new colonies nearby.

Roger Williams and Rhode Island

In 1631 Roger Williams and his family arrived in the Massachusetts Bay Colony from England. They settled in the village of Salem, where Roger Williams became a minister.

Roger Williams lived with the Narragansett Indians before starting a settlement he called Providence.

Williams was a popular minister because he and many people in Salem shared the same beliefs. They believed that their church should be separate from the colonial government and free from the rule of the Church of England. They also believed that people should not be punished if their beliefs were different from those of the Puritan leaders.

Roger Williams often stated his beliefs in his sermons and in letters that he wrote to Governor John Winthrop. Before long his ideas became unpopular with other ministers and with Winthrop. In 1635 the Puritan leaders voted to **expel** him, or to force him to leave. This meant that he was no longer allowed to live in the Massachusetts Bay Colony.

From Salem, Williams and his family fled beyond the border of the colony south to Narragansett (nar•uh•GAN•suht) Bay. There they received food and protection from the Narragansett Indians. In 1636 many of Williams' followers also left Salem and joined him. He bought land from the Narragansetts and founded a settlement he called Providence. It later became the capital of the present-day state of Rhode Island.

Williams set up a government based on the **consent**, or agreement, of the settlers. The new government of what would later become the Rhode Island Colony gave its people the freedom to follow any religion they chose.

REVIEW What did Roger Williams accomplish after he left the Massachusetts Bay Colony?

Anne Hutchinson on Trial

Not long after the Puritan leaders expelled Roger Williams from the Massachusetts Bay Colony, they faced

Anne Hutchinson was put on trial for causing people to work against the government.

other challenges to their leadership. One such challenge came from a colonist named Anne Marbury Hutchinson.

Hutchinson and her husband, William, moved to North America in 1634. They settled in Boston and attended church services there. Hutchinson soon began to question the authority of the Puritan ministers and their teachings. Her strong and spirited personality attracted many followers. She started holding her own religious meetings at home and stated her own beliefs during these services.

The Puritan leaders said Hutchinson was "a woman not fit for our society." In 1637 they brought her to trial.

This painting by Fredric Edwin Church shows Thomas Hooker and his followers arriving in what became Hartford.

She stood trial before a Puritan court on charges of **sedition**, or the use of speech or behavior that causes people to work against a government. She was found guilty, and the Puritan leaders ordered her to leave the colony. A year later they also expelled her from the Puritan church.

With her family and many followers, Anne Hutchinson moved to Narragansett Bay. There they founded a settlement on an island near Providence. Hutchinson's settlement later united with the one founded by Roger Williams under the charter that formed the Rhode Island Colony.

REVIEW What were some of Anne Hutchinson's accomplishments?

Thomas Hooker

Connecticut

Other settlers also left the Massachusetts Bay Colony, but not for religious reasons. They wanted to leave the rocky fields of Massachusetts to find better farmland. By the early 1630s people began moving into the fertile Connecticut River valley. The first permanent settlement, Windsor, was founded in the river valley in 1633. It was soon followed by the Wethersfield settlement.

Most early Connecticut settlers came to find better farmland, but many also came in search of religious freedom. The best-known of these settlers was a minister named Thomas Hooker. Hooker had left the Massachusetts Bay Colony because he did not like the way the colony's Puritan leaders tried to influence the lives of the colonists. Hooker thought that a colony's government should be based on what its people wanted, not on what its leaders wanted. Many of Hooker's followers went with him to the Connecticut River valley, where they founded the settlement of Hartford. Hartford, along with Windsor and Wethersfield, united in 1636 to become the Connecticut Colony. The name *Connecticut* comes from the Mohegan (moh•HEE•guhn) Indian word *quinnitukqut,* which means "at the long tidal river."

In 1638 Hooker preached a sermon calling for a government that would be based on the consent of the people. In 1639 the Connecticut Colony adopted Hooker's idea in the form of the Fundamental Orders. The word **fundamental** means "basic." The Fundamental Orders were the first written plan of government in North America. They allowed Connecticut's voters—all landowning male colonists—to elect their leaders.

REVIEW Why did Thomas Hooker leave the Massachusetts Bay Colony?

New Hampshire

The Connecticut River valley was not the only place where Massachusetts Bay colonists went in search of more fertile land and greater economic opportunity. Some settlers moved north of the Merrimack River into what is now New Hampshire in search of these things.

The earliest permanent settlements in New Hampshire were started in the

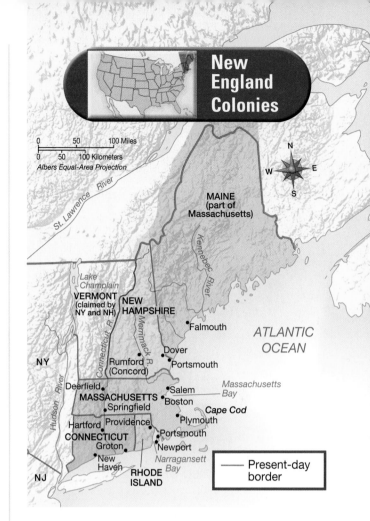

New England Colonies

Location Most towns in the New England Colonies were located near a body of water.

❓ Which two rivers ran through parts of New Hampshire and Massachusetts?

1620s. In 1623 David Thomson founded the first settlement near the mouth of the Piscataqua (pi•SKA•tuh•kwaw) River. In 1630 the settlement moved to a site near a thick growth of trees and wild berries. The settlers cut down the trees and shipped them as lumber to England. The settlement was renamed Strawberry Banke. Today it is the city of Portsmouth. In 1679 the town of Strawberry Banke and other settlements in the area were united under a charter from King Charles II as the New Hampshire Colony.

REVIEW Why did some settlers move north into what is now New Hampshire?

Metacomet (left) led the Wampanoags in the fight to keep their lands. Some historians believe this club (below) was Metacomet's.

Indian Wars

As settlers moved beyond the Massachusetts Bay Colony, they tried to keep peace with the region's many Indian groups. In the Connecticut River valley, however, fighting broke out between the colonists and the Pequots (PEE•kwahts). The Pequots wanted to stop the colonists from taking over Indian lands. With the help of some soldiers from the Massachusetts Bay Colony, the Connecticut settlers defeated the Pequots in the 1630s. The conflict became known as the Pequot War.

Most of the disagreements between the Native Americans and the settlers were over land ownership. The Wampanoags, Narragansetts, Mohegans, Podunks (POH•duhnks), and Nipmucs (NIP•muhks) felt that no one could "own" land. When they "sold" land to the settlers, they thought they were agreeing to share it. The English, however, expected the Indians to leave the land when they sold it.

In 1675 bad feelings between the Indians and the settlers started an all-out war. The settlers called it King Philip's War. Metacomet, known to the English as King Philip, was the leader of the Wampanoags.

After the Indian wars settlers moved into areas like northern New Hampshire.

Metacomet was also the son of Massasoit, who years earlier had helped the Pilgrims.

The war began when the Indians attacked and destroyed the town of Swansea. To get back at the Indians, the English settlers destroyed a nearby Indian settlement and took the Indians' lands. The war quickly spread as far north as present-day Maine and as far south as Connecticut. Both sides suffered terrible losses in the fighting. At least 3,000 Indians, including Metacomet, died. Among the colonists, 1 out of every 16 men of military age died.

As a result of King Philip's War, some Native American tribes were forced off their lands and very few Indians

Buckets like this were often used by settlers who lived on the frontier.

remained along the eastern coast of New England. Because many of the Indians had left, waves of settlers began pushing farther north up the Connecticut River valley into the Berkshire Hills in what is now western Massachusetts. Others moved even farther north into areas of present-day Vermont, northern New Hampshire, and Maine. The frontier was being pushed farther west as well. A **frontier** is land that lies beyond settled areas. The New England frontier separated the land settled by Europeans from the land lived on by Native Americans.

REVIEW What started King Philip's War?

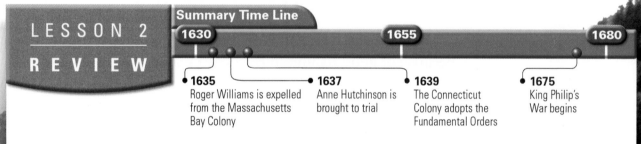

LESSON 2 REVIEW

Summary Time Line

1630 — 1655 — 1680

1635 Roger Williams is expelled from the Massachusetts Bay Colony

1637 Anne Hutchinson is brought to trial

1639 The Connecticut Colony adopts the Fundamental Orders

1675 King Philip's War begins

1 MAIN IDEA What led some Massachusetts Bay colonists to form new colonies nearby?

2 WHY IT MATTERS How did the people of the new colonies expand the ideas of freedom of speech and freedom of religion in the English colonies?

3 VOCABULARY Write a sentence about Roger Williams, using the words **expel** and **consent**.

4 TIME LINE When was Anne Hutchinson brought to trial?

5 READING SKILL—Summarize Why did Massachusetts Bay colonists settle Connecticut and New Hampshire?

6 HISTORY What were the effects of King Philip's War?

7 CRITICAL THINKING—Evaluate Do you think the beliefs of leaders such as Roger Williams, Anne Hutchinson, and Thomas Hooker helped bring positive changes to the New England Colonies? Explain your answer.

PERFORMANCE—Write a Letter Imagine that you are a follower of Thomas Hooker who has just moved to the settlement of Hartford. Write a letter to a friend in England that explains why Hooker disagreed with the leaders of the Massachusetts Bay Colony.

New England's Economy

MAIN IDEA
Read to find out how
New England's economy
depended mostly on
resources found in the
ocean and in the forests.

WHY IT MATTERS
New England's economic
successes helped the
English colonies depend
less on England for their
supplies.

VOCABULARY
industry
export
import
triangular trade
route
naval store

1625   1750

1700–1750

As time passed, life in New England became less difficult.
Many people, especially those who lived in the coastal towns,
had to struggle less to make a living. By the 1700s the great-
grandchildren of the early colonists lived much more
comfortable lives. This prosperity, or economic success, was
based mainly on the sea and the region's dense forests. Many
colonists in New England had built successful fishing, whaling,
trading, and shipbuilding industries. An **industry** includes all
the businesses that make one kind of product or provide one
kind of service.

Fishing and Whaling

Many coastal towns in New England Colonies prospered
because of good fishing in the ocean waters. Because New
Englanders could catch more fish than they needed, they had a
surplus. The surplus catch could be dried and then sold or
traded to people in Europe or to other English colonists in the
West Indies.

The town of New Bedford, in Massachusetts, prospered
in the 1700s because some of its settlers began catching
whales in addition to hunting.
Colonial whalers used methods
brought from England. They
launched small rowboats from
beaches and hunted for whales in
the waters not far from the shore.
Once they captured a whale, they
killed it and towed it to shore.
The whalers then cut up and
boiled the whale's blubber, or
fat, to obtain oil.

FAST FACT In one year,
during the peak of
colonial whaling,
at least 350 whale-
hunting ships sailed
from colonial ports.

Oil made from whale blubber
was used to fuel lamps.

New Englanders fished and hunted whales in the waters of the Grand Banks, near Newfoundland, and off the Greenland coast.

Oil made from whale blubber was very popular at that time because it burned brightly without an unpleasant odor. One lamp filled with burning whale oil gave as much light as, and much less smoke than, three candles.

So many New England whalers hunted close to shore that after a while the number of whales in those waters started to decline. As a result, the New England whalers began hunting in bigger ships and sailed farther out into the ocean. As the years passed, whaling trips became longer and longer. Some whaling ships left their home ports on ocean voyages that lasted for several months or even years.

REVIEW What industries helped New England coastal towns prosper?

Trading

In addition to fishing and whaling, many New England fortunes were made in trade. Ships owned by New England merchants carried trade goods to and from ports in the Caribbean, southern Europe, and England.

Many ships owned by the colonial merchants followed a direct trade route between the New England ports and England. They followed this route because the English government insisted. It wanted the colonists to send their **exports**, or goods leaving a country, only to England or to other English colonies. The English government also expected the colonists to buy only English-made **imports**, or goods brought into a country.

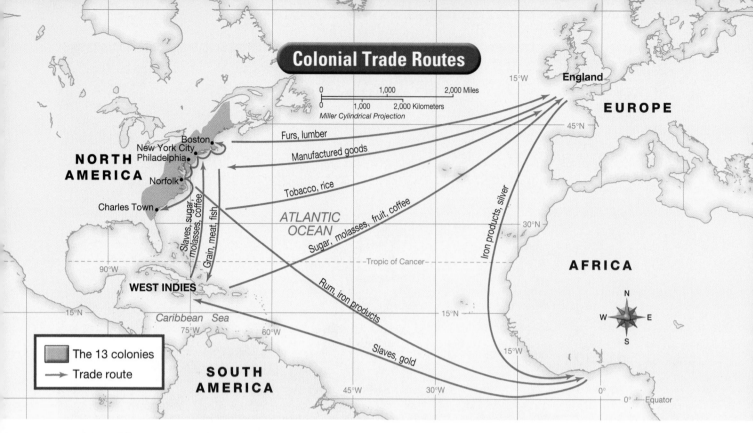

Colonial Trade Routes

England

EUROPE

NORTH AMERICA

Boston
New York City
Philadelphia
Norfolk
Charles Town

Furs, lumber

Manufactured goods

Tobacco, rice

Slaves, sugar, molasses, coffee

Grain, meat, fish

ATLANTIC OCEAN

Sugar, molasses, fruit, coffee

Iron products, silver

AFRICA

Tropic of Cancer

Rum, iron products

Caribbean Sea

WEST INDIES

Slaves, gold

SOUTH AMERICA

Equator

0   1,000   2,000 Miles
0   1,000   2,000 Kilometers
Miller Cylindrical Projection

The 13 colonies
Trade route

GEOGRAPHY THEME

Movement England, Africa, the West Indies, and the English colonies were connected by trade routes.

◆ What goods did the colonies get from England?

Along this direct trade route, colonial ships from ports such as Boston and New Haven, in Connecticut, and Newport, in Rhode Island, carried exports of furs, lumber, and dried fish to England. The ships returned to the colonies with imports of tea and spices, as well as manufactured goods, such as buttons, cloth, and shoes.

Other New England trading ships followed what came to be known as **triangular trade routes**. These routes connected England, the

English colonies in North America, and the west coast of Africa. They formed great imaginary triangles on the Atlantic Ocean. Trading ships carried goods from England and raw materials from the English colonies and the West Indies. Slave ships also carried enslaved people from central and western Africa. These people were used as workers in the English colonies. During this time, millions of enslaved Africans were forced to voyage across the Atlantic Ocean. The voyage across the Atlantic Ocean from Africa to the West Indies came to be known as the Middle Passage.

Barrels were used to ship goods.

The Africans suffered greatly on the slave ships. Many of them died during the Middle Passage. Their long voyage in overcrowded ships with cramped quarters was part of a large and cruel slave trade business. During the 1700s some of the people in the colonies became alarmed by the cruelty of the slave trade. Later, some of the New England colonists began to form groups that worked to end slavery.

REVIEW What were the triangular trade routes?

Shipbuilding

Fishing, whaling, and trading encouraged the shipbuilding industry in New England. The forests of New England provided the raw materials needed for building ships in colonial times. Logs cut in inland forests were floated down rivers to the coastal towns. There, skilled craftworkers used the logs to produce **naval stores**, the products that were used to build and repair ships. Workers used oak trees to make planks, or thick boards, for shaping ships' hulls. They used tall pines to make the masts. Pine trees also provided tar and turpentine to make pitch, a coating that is used to seal the wood and to help make a ship watertight.

Workers called coopers used wood to make barrels and casks. A cooper was a regular member of a merchant ship's crew. It was the cooper's responsibility to put together and repair barrels and casks for the long ocean voyages. Merchants used barrels to store grain, dried fish, salted meats, and other foods they traded. Casks held molasses, whale oil, and other liquids.

By the late 1700s nearly one-third of all the ships sailing under the English flag were built in the New England Colonies.

This harbor scene shows the city of Portsmouth, New Hampshire in the 1700s. Portsmouth was one of the busy ports in the New England Colonies.

This painting by Ashley Bowen, a sailor, shows a newly built ship ready to be launched.

One reason was the low cost of building ships there. Ships that were built in New England cost merchants only half of what they might have to pay for them in Europe. The shipbuilding industry contributed greatly to the growth and prosperity of many coastal towns in the New England Colonies. Some of these towns became cities. By 1750 more than 15,000 people lived in Boston. It was one of the largest cities in the North American colonies.

REVIEW In what ways did people in the shipbuilding industry earn a living?

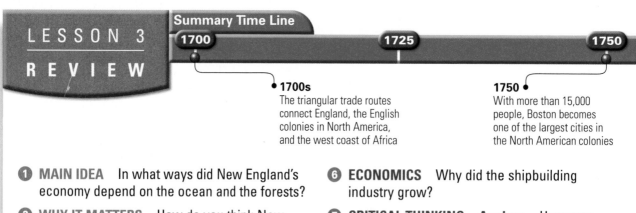

LESSON 3 REVIEW

Summary Time Line

1700   **1725**   **1750**

1700s
The triangular trade routes connect England, the English colonies in North America, and the west coast of Africa

1750
With more than 15,000 people, Boston becomes one of the largest cities in the North American colonies

1. **MAIN IDEA** In what ways did New England's economy depend on the ocean and the forests?

2. **WHY IT MATTERS** How do you think New England's economic successes helped the English colonies in North America depend less on England?

3. **VOCABULARY** Use the terms **export** and **import** to explain the **triangular trade routes**.

4. **TIME LINE** What happened by 1750?

5. **READING SKILL—Summarize** How did industries in New England help its economy prosper?

6. **ECONOMICS** Why did the shipbuilding industry grow?

7. **CRITICAL THINKING—Analyze** How was colonial whaling similar to the whaling done by the Makah Indians, whom you read about in Chapter 2? How was it different?

PERFORMANCE—Draw a Poster Draw a poster that shows the products that New England colonists made from the resources found in the ocean and in the forests. Label the products, and indicate each product's connection to the ocean or the forests. Share your poster with the class.

·SKILLS·

Use a Line Graph

VOCABULARY
line graph

▶ WHY IT MATTERS

Soon there were 13 English colonies along the Atlantic Coast. The value of exports that these colonies sent away to England changed during the years from 1700 to 1750. The numbers that show how the value of these exports changed are very large. These numbers are easier to understand if they are placed on a line graph. A **line graph** is a graph that uses a line to show changes over time.

▶ WHAT YOU NEED TO KNOW

This line graph shows the changes in the value of colonial exports to England from 1700 to 1750. The numbers along the left side of the graph show the value of

colonial exports. Across the bottom of the graph are years. As you read the red line from left to right, you see how the value changed.

▶ PRACTICE THE SKILL

Use this line graph to answer the following questions.

1 Find the year 1700 at the bottom of the graph. Move your finger up from that date until you reach the red dot. Then move your finger left to the value numbers. Your finger will be a little below 500,000, so you will need to estimate the value. To *estimate* is to make a close guess. The value of the exports was worth about 375,000 English pounds in 1700. Pounds are the name of the English currency.

2 Now find 1740 at the bottom of the graph. Repeat the process. About how many pounds was the value of exports in that year?

3 Look at the red line on the graph. How did the value of exports change?

▶ APPLY WHAT YOU LEARNED

Think about the change shown on this graph. Notice that the value of exports decreased between 1700 and 1710. What factors could have caused the value to decrease during those years?

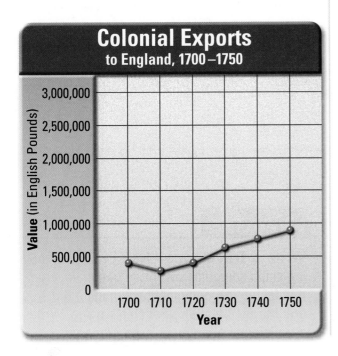

Colonial Exports
to England, 1700–1750

Value (in English Pounds): 3,000,000 / 2,500,000 / 2,000,000 / 1,500,000 / 1,000,000 / 500,000 / 0

Year: 1700 1710 1720 1730 1740 1750

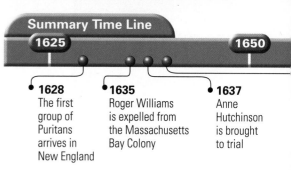

Summary Time Line

1625 — 1650

1628
The first
group of
Puritans
arrives in
New England

1635
Roger Williams
is expelled from
the Massachusetts
Bay Colony

1637
Anne
Hutchinson
is brought
to trial

USE YOUR READING SKILLS

Complete this graphic organizer by summarizing the following
facts about the Massachusetts Bay Colony. A copy of this
graphic organizer appears on page 52 of the Activity Book.

The Massachusetts Bay Colony

(FACTS) → (SUMMARY)

1. The Puritans built many villages in North
   America.
2. The most important building in a Puritan
   village was the meetinghouse.
3. The village meetinghouse served as a
   church and a place to hold town meetings.

1. Roger Williams was forced to leave the
   Massachusetts Bay Colony.
2. Anne Hutchinson was also forced to leave
   the colony.
3. Roger Williams and Anne Hutchinson
   established their own settlements.

1. Trading goods made many people wealthy
   in New England.
2. Goods were traded between the colonies,
   England, and the west coast of Africa.
3. Trade brought the first African slaves
   to the English Colonies.

THINK & WRITE

Write a Folktale Every New England
town had several public-office jobs. These
jobs included constable, town crier, and
fence viewer. Write a folktale about a person
who held one of these jobs.

Write a Travelogue New England whaling ships sometimes went on ocean voyages
that lasted for many months. Imagine that you
are a crew member on such a voyage. Write
a travelogue about your experiences.

1639
The Fundamental Orders are adopted by the Connecticut Colony

1675
King Philip's War begins

1750
Boston becomes one of the largest cities in North America

USE THE TIME LINE

Use the chapter summary time line to answer these questions.

1 When did the first group of Puritans arrive in New England?

2 When did King Philip's War begin?

USE VOCABULARY

Use a term from this list to complete each of the following sentences.

> town meeting (p. 192)
>
> consent (p. 195)
>
> sedition (p. 196)
>
> industry (p. 200)
>
> naval stores (p. 203)

3 The government of Providence was based on the _____ of the settlers.

4 The _____ was where public officers were elected.

5 Anne Hutchinson was brought to trial on charges of _____.

6 A major _____ in New England was ship-building.

7 Logs from New England forests were used to produce _____.

RECALL FACTS

Answer these questions.

8 What group of settlers set up the first community schools in the New England Colonies?

9 What were some of the results of King Philip's War?

10 Why was New England a good location for the shipbuilding industry?

Write the letter of the best choice.

11 **TEST PREP** Problems developed between the New England colonists and Native Americans because—

A the colonists forced Native Americans to work on their farms.

B Native Americans refused to trade furs with the colonists.

C the two groups had different understandings of land ownership.

D Native Americans never offered the colonists any help.

12 **TEST PREP** The New England colonists used whale blubber to make—

F tar.

G turpentine.

H molasses.

J lamp oil.

THINK CRITICALLY

13 Compare the system of government of the Connecticut Colony to that of the Massachusetts Bay Colony.

14 How might history have been different if King Philip's War had not taken place?

APPLY SKILLS

Use a Line Graph

15 Look in newspapers or magazines for a line graph that shows a trend. Cut out the graph and tape it to a sheet of paper. Below the graph, identify the trend shown. How does the trend change over time?

LANCASTER COUNTY

Many early immigrants settled in Pennsylvania because of its rich farmland. Today, areas such as Lancaster County continue to produce a variety of crops. Among the Amish and Mennonite families who make their homes here, many live and work in the same manner as their eighteenth century ancestors.

LOCATE IT

PENNSYLVANIA

Lancaster County

The Middle Atlantic Colonies

❝ The Fields, most beautiful, yield such Crops of Wheat, And other things most excellent to eat. ❞

—Richard Frame, *A Short Description of Pennsylvania,* 1692

CHAPTER READING SKILL

Make Inferences

When you make an **inference,** you use facts and your experiences to come to a conclusion.

As you read this chapter, make inferences about people, places, and events associated with the Middle Atlantic Colonies.

WHAT YOU HAVE READ WHAT YOU KNOW

INFERENCE

Chapter 6 ■ **209**

1

MAIN IDEA

Read to find out why the Middle Atlantic Colonies attracted people of many different cultures and religions.

WHY IT MATTERS

As in the Middle Atlantic Colonies, people from many different cultures and religions contribute to the United States today.

VOCABULARY

refuge
trial by jury
justice
farm produce
Great Awakening

Breadbasket Colonies

1625 ━━━━━━━━━━━━━━━━━━━━━━━━━━━━━━ 1750

1625–1700

While the Puritans were building settlements in New England, other settlers were establishing colonies to the south. This region, which included present-day New York, New Jersey, Delaware, and Pennsylvania, came to be known as the Middle Atlantic Colonies.

The first settlers in the Middle Atlantic region discovered that when the land was cleared of trees and rocks, it was good for farming. The climate was also good for growing crops. The summers were long, and the amount of rain each year was just right for crops such as wheat, corn, and rye. In fact, the Middle Atlantic Colonies produced so many crops used in making bread that they came to be called the "breadbasket" colonies. The region's rich resources attracted people from many European countries and people of various religions.

New Netherland

Not long after the English started colonies in North America, the Dutch began to build settlements in their own colony, called New Netherland. They settled in parts of what are today New York, New Jersey, and Delaware. The Dutch came to the

FAST FACT Manhattan Island was bought from the Manhattan Indians for goods worth 60 Dutch guilders, or about $24.

area because the explorer Henry Hudson had claimed it for their country, Holland, in 1609.

A few years after Hudson's visit, the New Netherland Company established several trading posts in the Hudson River valley. In 1621 the Dutch West India Company took control of trade in the area. The first Dutch settlers arrived three years later. Some were sent to a fort on the Delaware River, and others sailed to a fort on the Hudson River.

In 1626 the Dutch began building a fort and laying out a town on Manhattan Island in New York Bay. They called the settlement New Amsterdam. In that same year Peter Minuit (MIN•yuh•wuht), one of the directors of the New Netherland Colony, bought Manhattan Island from the Manhattan Indians. During the next few years, New Amsterdam grew and became the capital of New Netherland. The Dutch built other settlements that would one day become Brooklyn, Kingston,

Rensselaer (ren•suh•LIR), and Schenectady (skuh•NEK•tuh•dee), New York.

The Dutch welcomed settlers to New Amsterdam from many countries. People from Belgium, Denmark, France, Italy, and Spain all made their homes there. Among these newcomers was the first group of Jews to settle in North America. However, the Jews in New Amsterdam did not have many of the same rights as Christian colonists had. Under Dutch rule, Jews could not work at certain jobs and could not freely practice their religion.

REVIEW Where did the Dutch first settle in North America?

GEOGRAPHY THEME

Place New Amsterdam was the capital of New Netherland. The Dutch and Swedish colonies eventually became English colonies.

❖ What natural resources do you think the colonists used?

Dutch and Swedish Colonies, 1654

New Netherland
New Sweden
—— Present-day border

VT
Beverwyck (Albany)
MA
Esopus (Kingston)
NY
CT
Manhattan Island
PA
Vriesendael (Tappan)
New Amsterdam (New York)
ATLANTIC OCEAN
NJ
Fort New Gothenburg (near Philadelphia)
Fort Christina (Wilmington)
MD
DE
Hudson River
Delaware River

0   40   80 Miles
0   40   80 Kilometers
Albers Equal-Area Projection

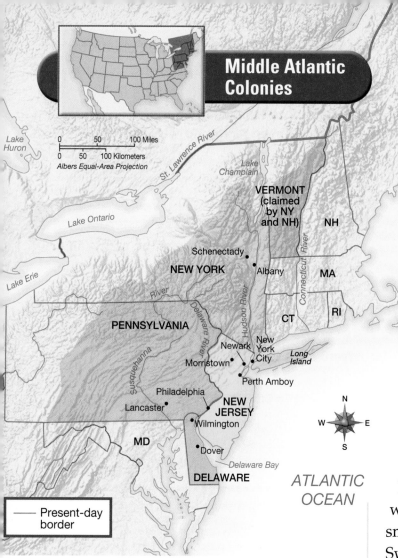

Middle Atlantic Colonies

Lake Huron

Lake Ontario

Lake Erie

0   50   100 Miles
0   50   100 Kilometers
Albers Equal-Area Projection

St. Lawrence River

Lake Champlain

VERMONT (claimed by NY and NH)

NH

Schenectady

NEW YORK

Albany

MA

Connecticut River

River

PENNSYLVANIA

Delaware River

Hudson River

CT

RI

Susquehanna

Newark
New York City
Morristown
Perth Amboy

Long Island

Philadelphia
Lancaster

NEW JERSEY

Wilmington

MD

Dover

Delaware Bay

DELAWARE

ATLANTIC OCEAN

N
W   E
S

Present-day border

GEOGRAPHY THEME

Regions Many towns in the Middle Atlantic Colonies were located near waterways.

❖ What were some of the waterways in the Middle Atlantic Colonies?

New Netherland Becomes New York

In 1646 the Dutch West India Company appointed Peter Stuyvesant (STY•vuh•suhnt) as director general of New Netherland. When Stuyvesant arrived in New Amsterdam the following year, he found New Netherland in trouble. The government was having problems. The settlers were fighting over land with the neighboring Delaware and Wappinger (WAHP•ihn•jer) Indians and with other European colonists. Not long after he arrived, however, Stuyvesant helped resolve the conflicts over land.

Stuyvesant's strong way of ruling helped solve some problems, but it created new problems between him and the colonists. The colonists wanted more voice in their government, which Stuyvesant would not allow.

Despite such disagreements, the colony prospered under Stuyvesant's leadership. He expanded New Netherland into what is now New Jersey. Then he pushed south into what is now Delaware, taking over the small colony of New Sweden in 1655. Swedish settlers had founded the colony in 1638. It was chiefly a group of trading posts built around Fort Christina, where today Wilmington, Delaware, stands.

Even though the population of New Netherland remained small, the English still thought that the Dutch colony prevented their own colonies from expanding. This was one reason King Charles II of England declared war on Holland. The king then told his brother, James, the Duke of York, that he could have the Dutch colonies if he could seize them.

Peter Stuyvesant

This Quaker meetinghouse was located in New Jersey. Chests (above) like this one could often be found in Quaker homes.

In 1664 English warships sailed into the harbor at New Amsterdam. Stuyvesant tried to get the Dutch settlers to fight the English, but they refused. Stuyvesant had to give up the colony. The English split up New Netherland, giving it the present-day names of New Jersey and New York. New York City grew from the Dutch capital, New Amsterdam.

REVIEW What were some of Peter Stuyvesant's accomplishments?

New Jersey

Not long after the English divided New Netherland, the Duke of York gave New Jersey and part of New York to John Berkeley and George Carteret. The two offered to sell the land at low prices to anyone in England willing to settle in North America. The offer attracted many settlers to New Jersey. Among them were numerous members of the Society of Friends, a religious group also known as the Quakers. In 1674 a group of Quakers led by Edward Byllinge bought Berkeley's share of New Jersey. They started the first colony in North America founded by Quakers.

The Quakers believe that all people are equal and basically good. Because they think that violence is always wrong, they refuse to carry guns or to fight. They also believe in solving all problems peacefully. In England, Quakers often were treated poorly because of their beliefs, particularly their refusal to fight for the king. In New Jersey, they hoped to find a **refuge**, or safe place, where they could live and worship as they pleased.

REVIEW Why did many Quakers want to settle in New Jersey?

Pennsylvania and Delaware

While New Jersey was being sold to groups of Quakers, King Charles II gave a charter to William Penn, who had become a Quaker. The charter made Penn the proprietor, or owner, of what is now Pennsylvania. The English king granted him the region because the king owed a debt to Penn's father. Penn wanted to call his new colony *Sylvania*, which means "woods." King Charles asked that the land be named Pennsylvania.

DEMOCRATIC VALUES
Justice

In his Frame of Government of Pennsylvania, William Penn included the idea that all citizens of the Pennsylvania Colony were to be treated equally by the law.

Penn's Frame of Government guaranteed everyone the right to a trial by jury. This right was important because it allowed a group of citizens, instead of a single judge, to decide whether or not someone had broken the law. This method is a more democratic way of making this kind of decision. It gives decision-making control to the people. In most countries there was no right to trial by jury.

Today the United States government upholds the idea of equal justice for all. All people in the United States have the right to a fair trial and to equal treatment under the law.

William Penn with Indian leaders

Analyze the Value

1 How did Penn make sure people in the colony would be treated equally under the law?

2 **Make It Relevant** Imagine that a student in your school has been accused of breaking a school rule. With some classmates, decide whether one person or a group should determine whether the student really broke the rule.

The new name, which means "Penn's woods," honored William's father.

Before coming to Pennsylvania, William Penn planned his colony's government. In 1682 he wrote a document called the Frame of Government of Pennsylvania. It provided for a legislature called the General Assembly to make the laws for the colony. Penn's Frame of Government also provided for the citizens of Pennsylvania to have freedom of speech, freedom of worship, and trial by jury. **Trial by jury** guarantees a person accused of breaking the law the right to be tried by a jury of fellow citizens.

When Penn arrived in Pennsylvania, he met with many of the leaders of the local Delaware Indian tribes. He paid them for

most of the land King Charles II had given him. A legend says that Penn and Tamenend (TAM•uh•nehnd), a chief of the Delaware people, exchanged wampum belts as a sign of friendship. Indian leaders came to respect Penn and believed he was their friend. Penn had said, "Let them have justice, and you win them." Penn also ensured that his colonists were ruled with **justice**, or fairness.

Penn also became the owner of what is now Delaware. When colonists in Delaware asked for their own general assembly, Penn granted it to them. The first Delaware General Assembly met in 1704.

REVIEW What did the right of trial by jury guarantee a person?

Market Towns

Most people in the Middle Atlantic Colonies made their living by farming. Because the soil was fertile and the land was not too mountainous, many were able to develop large farms. On these farms they were able to grow enough food to feed their families and also have a surplus.

Farmers depended on market towns as places to trade their livestock and their surplus **farm produce**—grains, fruits, and vegetables—for goods and services. Market towns became a common sight throughout the Middle Atlantic Colonies.

In most market towns a general store sold goods, such as tools, cloth, shoes, stockings, and buttons. Near the general store there was often the shop of a cobbler, who made and repaired shoes. Nearby there was also a gristmill, where grain was ground into flour and meal, and a sawmill, where logs were sawed into lumber.

Unlike the New England Colonies, the Middle Atlantic Colonies welcomed people of different religions. Towns in these colonies often had more than one kind of church. A Presbyterian church, for example, might be only a block away from a Methodist church and a Quaker meetinghouse.

Interest in religion led to the **Great Awakening**, a movement that called for a rebirth of religious ways of life. This way of thinking quickly spread through other English colonies during the 1730s and 1740s.

Wheat was traded in market towns.

REVIEW What kinds of goods were bought and sold in market towns?

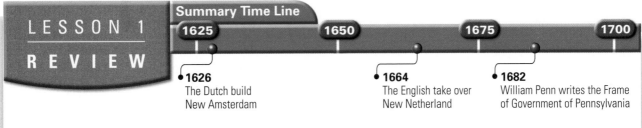

LESSON 1 REVIEW

Summary Time Line

| 1625 | 1650 | 1675 | 1700 |

•**1626**
The Dutch build New Amsterdam

•**1664**
The English take over New Netherland

•**1682**
William Penn writes the Frame of Government of Pennsylvania

1. **MAIN IDEA** Why did people of many different cultures and religions settle the Middle Atlantic Colonies?

2. **WHY IT MATTERS** In what ways do people of different cultures and religions contribute to the United States today?

3. **VOCABULARY** Use the term **refuge** in a sentence.

4. **TIME LINE** In what year did the English take over New Netherland?

5. **READING SKILL—Make Inferences** Why do you think the Dutch settlers refused to fight when the English arrived to take over New Netherland?

6. **GEOGRAPHY** Where was the first Quaker colony in North America located?

7. **CRITICAL THINKING—Hypothesize** What might New York City be like today if the Dutch had kept control of New Amsterdam?

PERFORMANCE—Draw a Picture On a large piece of paper, draw a picture of a scene showing life in one of the Middle Atlantic Colonies. Make sure your scene includes examples of things that attracted people to these colonies.

Great Awakening Sermons

In the 1730s and 1740s, The Great Awakening swept the English-speaking world. The Great Awakening was a revival, or rebirth, of the importance of religion in people's lives. In the colonies of North America, it was led at first by a minister named George Whitefield. He traveled from Maine to Georgia preaching sermons. Whitefield and The Great Awakening were not popular with all people. In the end, however, The Great Awakening contributed to a new sense of unity among all the English colonists.

 FROM THE LIBRARY OF CONGRESS ONLINE EXHIBIT "RELIGION AND FOUNDING OF THE AMERICAN REPUBLIC"

George Whitefield

George Whitefield used this collapsible field pulpit for open-air preaching.

Many sermons delivered by the preachers of the Great Awakening were later published as books.

THE DANGER OF An Unconverted MINISTRY,

Considered in a

SERMON

On MARK VI. 34.

Preached at *Nottingham*, in *Pennsylvania*,
March 8. ANNO 1739,40.

By *GILBERT TENNENT*, A. M.
And Minister of the Gospel in *New-Brunswick*,
New-Jersey.

Jerem. V. 30, 31. *A wonderful and horrible Thing
is committed in the Land : The Prophets prophesy
falsely, and the Priests bear Rule by their Means,
and my People love to have it so ; and what will
they do in the End thereof ?*

PHILADELPHIA:
Printed by BENJAMIN FRANKLIN,
In *Market-street*, 1740.

Gilbert
Tennent

Analyze the Primary Source

❶ **In which colonies did Gilbert Tennent and Jonathan Edwards live?**

❷ **When and where were the original sermons delivered?**

❸ **When and where were the sermons published as books?**

❹ **Who printed Tennent's sermon?**

ACTIVITY

Write to Explain Make a list of the kinds of things that people might learn from sermons. Then use your list to help you write a paragraph about why you think sermons were important to the people in the colonies.

Jonathan
Edwards

RESEARCH

GO ONLINE Visit The Learning Site at **www.harcourtschool.com/primarysources** to research other primary sources.

A Faithful NARRATIVE OF THE Surprizing Work of GOD IN THE CONVERSION OF

Many HUNDRED Souls in *Northampton*,
and the Neighbouring Towns and
Villages of *New-Hampshire* in *New-England*.

In a LETTER to the Revᵈ. Dr. BENJAMIN
COLMAN of *Boston*.

Written by the Revᵈ. Mr. EDWARDS, Minister of
Northampton, on *Nov.* 6. 1736.

And Published,

With a Large PREFACE,
By Dr. WATTS and Dr. GUYSE.

MAIN IDEA
Read to find out why Philadelphia became the Pennsylvania Colony's main port.

WHY IT MATTERS
Port cities are important to the growth and prosperity of countries.

VOCABULARY
township
immigrant
militia
almanac

Colonial Philadelphia

1625   1750

1700–1750

As proprietor of the Pennsylvania Colony, William Penn planned not only its government but also its settlements. One of them, Philadelphia, became the largest and wealthiest city in all the English colonies of North America. By 1770 it had more than 28,000 people—a small population by today's city standards but very large for that time.

Early Colonial Days

William Penn named his colony's chief city Philadelphia, a word meaning "brotherly love" in Greek. Like all of Pennsylvania, Philadelphia was founded on the idea that people of diverse backgrounds could get along with each other.

That idea was reflected in the layout of most of the colony's settlements. Penn wanted to divide his colony into townships. Each **township**, or area of land, would be 5,000 acres—a space large enough for ten families. Land belonging to individual families would be carved out of the township in giant pie-like slices. Penn wanted settlers to build their homes at the tips of the slices so that every family would be within walking distance of one another and of whatever church they chose to build.

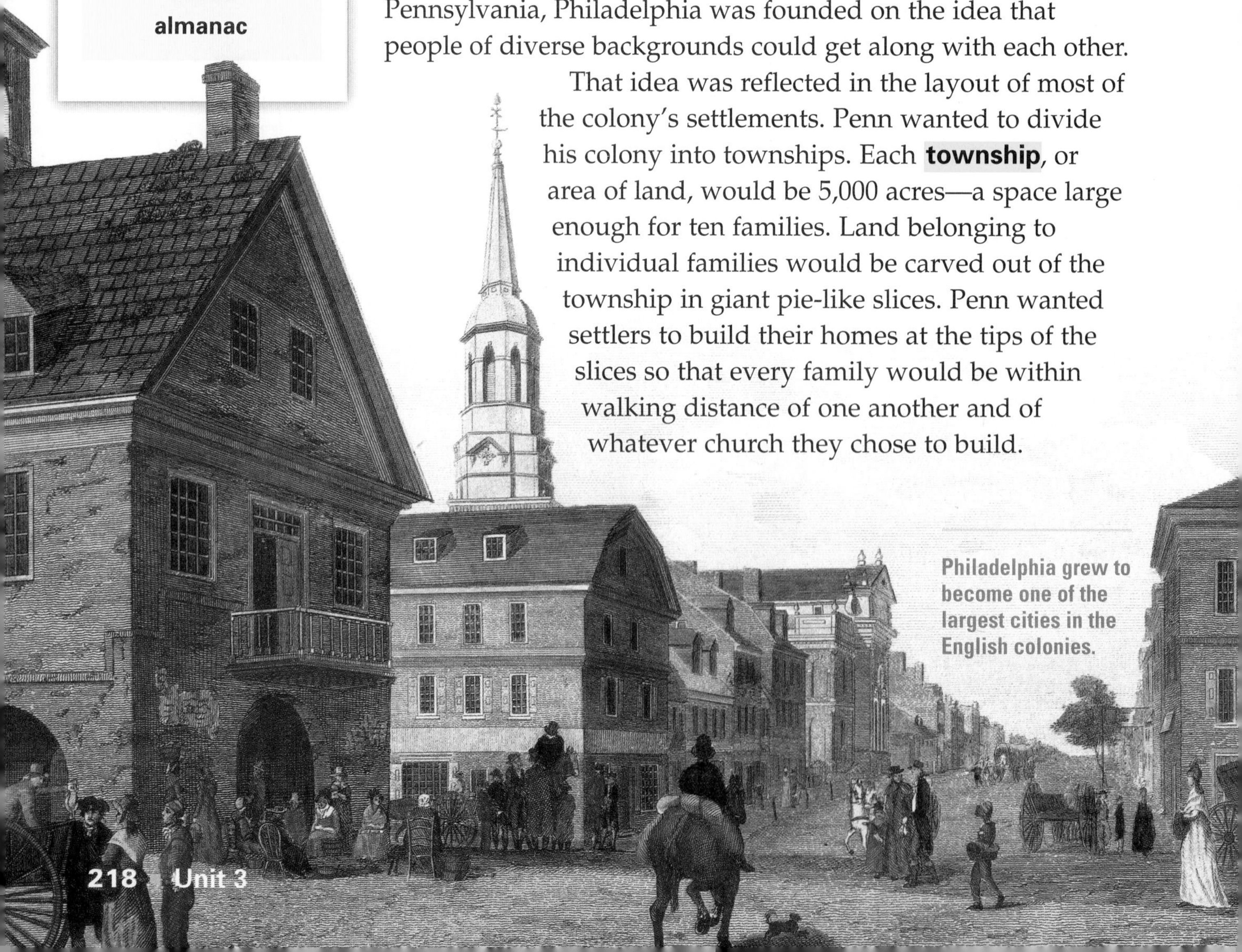

Philadelphia grew to become one of the largest cities in the English colonies.

William Penn had a different layout in mind for Philadelphia, his colony's most important town. It covered a strip of land between the Schuylkill (SKOO•kuhl) River on the west and the Delaware River on the east. Early drawings of one plan looked like a checkerboard, with straight streets laid out in great squares. Public parks added open spaces to the city that Penn called "a green country town."

Philadelphia's location near good land and waterways contributed to growth in shipping and trading. During the 1700s Philadelphia developed into one of the busiest ports in the English colonies. By 1710 it had become the largest city in the colonies. Chief among its exports were farm products such as wheat, corn, rye, hemp, and flax. Imports consisted mostly of manufactured goods from England, which were then sent all over the Middle Atlantic Colonies.

REVIEW What did William Penn accomplish as leader of the Pennsylvania Colony?

The People of Philadelphia

Philadelphia soon became the main port in Pennsylvania for receiving not only imports but also immigrants. An **immigrant** is a person who comes into a country to make a new home there. According to Reverend William Smith, Philadelphians in the 1700s were "a people, thrown together from various quarters of the world, differing in all things—language, manners and sentiment [attitude]."

The largest group in Philadelphia was made up of English and Welsh Quakers.

GEOGRAPHY THEME

Place   As shown on this present-day map of Center City (right), the checkerboard pattern of William Penn's city plan can still be seen.

◆ What rivers form the east and west boundaries of Center City?

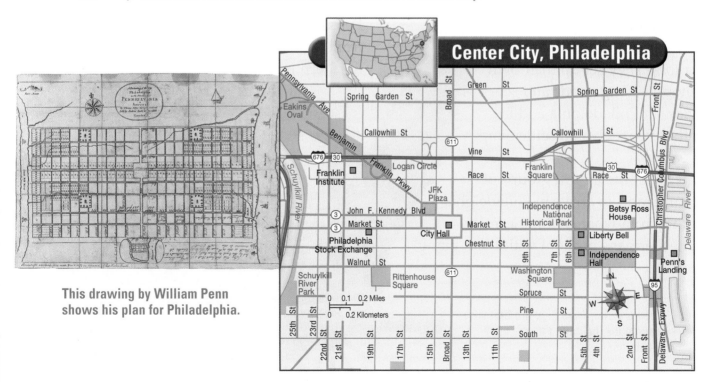

This drawing by William Penn shows his plan for Philadelphia.

Center City, Philadelphia

Das erste Farmhaus

They had arrived with William Penn. Later, Irish Catholics, German Lutherans, and Jews from many countries arrived. Free Africans came, too.

Some immigrants came to Philadelphia to find refuge from war and famine, or shortage of food, in their homelands. Many sought religious freedom. Others came because Philadelphia quickly gained a reputation for offering economic opportunity. Immigrants arriving in the city included farmers and skilled workers, such as bakers, blacksmiths, butchers, carpenters, shoemakers, and tailors. They set up their own shops, selling goods and services in Philadelphia and in other Pennsylvania settlements nearby.

One of the largest groups of immigrants to arrive in Philadelphia came from what is now Germany. The Germans brought with them many of their customs and traditions, including barn raising. First, a farmer dug his barn's foundation and prepared a frame made of lumber. He then invited his friends and neighbors and their families to help raise the frame into place. To feed all the people, the families prepared huge meals.

German immigrant gunmakers developed the long-barrel gun called the Pennsylvania rifle. In the 1700s it was the most accurate rifle in the world. It was particularly valued on the frontier, where accurate weapons were needed for hunting. German craftworkers also designed a deep-bellied wagon known as the Conestoga. Conestoga wagons were larger than regular wagons and were first used mainly by farmers to carry produce to market.

Scotch-Irish settlers also came to Pennsylvania. These were people from Scotland who had settled in northern Ireland in the 1600s.

When a visitor from England first saw Conestogas, he called them "huge moving houses."

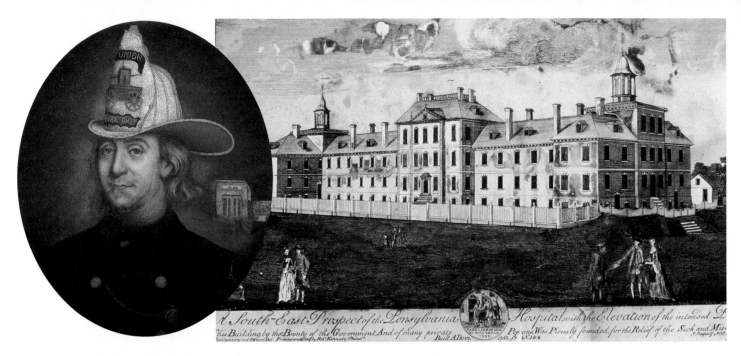

The Union Fire Company was, according to Benjamin Franklin (left), the first group of firefighters he organized. After Franklin raised money to build a hospital, others were soon built (right).

Many of them and their descendants came to the English colonies. Like other immigrants to Pennsylvania, they entered the colony through the port of Philadelphia. Then they moved into the hilly frontier areas located near the Appalachian Mountains.

REVIEW **For what reasons did immigrants come to Philadelphia?**

Benjamin Franklin and His City

The story of Benjamin Franklin's rise to wealth and fame matches colonial Philadelphia's rise to become one of the most prosperous cities in the English colonies. As a citizen, Franklin left a strong mark on the growing city. He organized the first trained firefighting company in the 13 colonies and the first fire insurance company. He worked to have Philadelphia's streets paved and lit at night. He raised money to help build the first hospital in Philadelphia. He also organized a **militia**, or volunteer army, to protect Philadelphia and the frontier settlements.

As a scientist, Franklin is best known for his experiments with electricity. It is believed that he proved that lightning is a form of electricity by tying a metal key to the string on his childhood kite and flying the kite in a thunderstorm. Using what he learned from his experiments, Franklin invented the lightning rod. A lightning rod is a straight, thin bar of metal attached to the top of a house or barn. It conducts, or guides, lightning into the ground. As a result, the building will not be damaged if it is struck. Until the invention of the lightning rod, buildings struck by lightning were likely to burst into flames.

Benjamin Franklin's interest in learning included the education of others. He even helped establish the first library in the colonies which people could subscribe to.

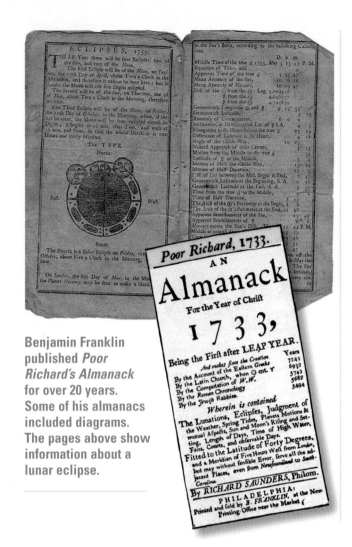

Benjamin Franklin published *Poor Richard's Almanack* for over 20 years. Some of his almanacs included diagrams. The pages above show information about a lunar eclipse.

Colonists could borrow books after paying a small fee to become a member of the library. As a result, people seeking knowledge did not have to pay much money. Franklin's opinions on education were used, too, when a school called the Philadelphia Academy was founded.

As a printer, Benjamin Franklin helped make Philadelphia a major publishing center in the English colonies. In 1729 he started printing a newspaper, the *Pennsylvania Gazette*. In 1732 he began publishing *Poor Richard's Almanack*. An **almanac** is a book issued only once each year. Franklin's had a calendar and a yearly weather forecast, which helped farmers know the best time to plant crops. It also had stories, jokes, and witty sayings, such as "Early to bed and early to rise, makes a man healthy, wealthy, and wise."

REVIEW **What were some of Benjamin Franklin's contributions as a scientist and inventor?**

LESSON 2 REVIEW

Summary Time Line

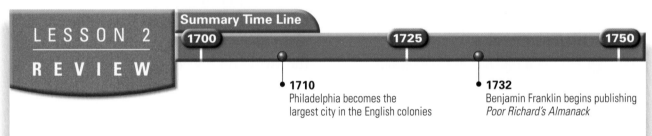

| 1700 | | 1725 | | 1750 |

1710 Philadelphia becomes the largest city in the English colonies

1732 Benjamin Franklin begins publishing *Poor Richard's Almanack*

1. **MAIN IDEA**   Why did Philadelphia become the Pennsylvania Colony's main port?

2. **WHY IT MATTERS**   How are port cities important to the growth and prosperity of countries?

3. **VOCABULARY**   Use the term **immigrant** in a sentence to describe why some people settled in Philadelphia.

4. **TIME LINE**   When did Philadelphia become the largest city in the English colonies?

5. **READING SKILL—Make Inferences**   How do you think Benjamin Franklin's lightning rod might have helped with the growth of Philadelphia?

6. **ECONOMICS**   What were some of Philadelphia's chief exports?

7. **CULTURE**   What did German immigrants contribute to the Pennsylvania Colony?

8. **CRITICAL THINKING—Analyze**   In what ways did William Penn lead his colony most like a leader in the United States today?

PERFORMANCE—Plan a Community Work with a group of classmates to draw a plan for a community. Then, write a paragraph describing the plan and display it in the classroom.

Use a Circle Graph

VOCABULARY

circle graph

WHY IT MATTERS

Suppose you want to show in a simple, clear way how the population of the 13 colonies was divided between the New England, Middle Atlantic, and Southern Colonies. One way to show the information is by making a **circle graph**. A circle graph is sometimes called a pie graph because it is round and is divided into pieces, or parts, like a pie is.

WHAT YOU NEED TO KNOW

The circle graph below shows the population of the 13 English colonies in the year 1750. The graph's parts are the colonial regions that made up the population.

A percent, shown by the symbol % in the graph, is given to each part of the graph. A percent is one-hundredth of something. For example, if you cut a pie into 100 pieces, those 100 pieces together equal the whole pie, or 100 percent (100%) of it. Fifty pieces would be one-half of the pie, or 50% of it. Ten pieces would be one-tenth of the pie, or 10% of it. Each piece would be one-hundredth, or 1%, of the pie.

PRACTICE THE SKILL

Use the circle graph to answer the following questions.

1 In which region did the largest part of the population in the 13 colonies live in 1750?

2 What percent of the total population did the region with the largest population make up?

3 What percent of the total population did the Middle Atlantic Colonies make up?

4 What percent was made up by the New England Colonies?

APPLY WHAT YOU LEARNED

Use information from the circle graph to write a paragraph about the different colonial regions in the 13 colonies. Compare the population sizes of the regions.

Population of the 13 Colonies, 1750

44% Southern Colonies

31% New England Colonies

25% Middle Atlantic Colonies

MAIN IDEA
Read to find out the many challenges colonists faced as they settled on lands farther west.

WHY IT MATTERS
People today often meet challenges when they move to new places.

VOCABULARY
backcountry
loft

This forested land in Virginia was once a part of the backcountry.

Moving West

Settlers from Pennsylvania, especially the Germans and the Scotch-Irish, were among the first to settle farther inland, away from the Atlantic coast. There they claimed what they saw as open land, even though American Indians lived there. They hoped to make a piece of the frontier into a farm, where they could build a house and raise a family. They felt that moving to the frontier would give them a chance for a better life.

The Great Wagon Road

In the early 1700s most cities, towns, farms, and plantations in the 13 English colonies were located near the coast, in the Coastal Plain region. At that time, few colonists had settled in the Piedmont—the land between the Coastal Plain and the Appalachian Mountains. Settlers called this frontier region the **backcountry** because it was beyond, or "in back of," the area settled by Europeans.

The waterfalls in the rivers along the Fall Line and the lack of roads made travel to the backcountry difficult. To get around the waterfalls, settlers had to portage, or carry overland, their boats and supplies. This kind of travel was so difficult that it discouraged many settlers from moving inland.

By the mid-1700s many settlers in the 13 colonies began to settle in areas west of the Coastal Plain. From Pennsylvania large numbers of German and Scotch-Irish immigrants had begun moving into the backcountry of western Virginia, North Carolina, and South Carolina. To get there, the settlers followed an old Indian trail. As more and more settlers used the trail, it became wider and wider. Finally, wagons could travel on it, and it became known as the Great Wagon Road.

From Pennsylvania the Great Wagon Road passed through the Shenandoah Valley of Virginia and along the eastern side of the Blue Ridge Mountains. The land there was hilly, and travel on the road was difficult. "[In places] it was so slippery the horses could not keep their footing but fell . . . to their knees," wrote one early traveler. However, the Great Wagon Road was the only way to get wagons loaded with household goods to the backcountry.

Thousands of people followed the Great Wagon Road to move inland from Pennsylvania. Among them was a young man named Daniel Boone. When Boone was 16 years old, his family followed the Great Wagon Road to settle in the Yadkin Valley in North Carolina. The journey took more than a year. Later, Boone would become a well-known explorer who made new trails that took settlers even farther west.

REVIEW Why was the Great Wagon Road important to the settlement of the frontier?

Movement **Thousands of settlers moved to the backcountry to start farms.**

❖ By what year had settlers moved the farthest west?

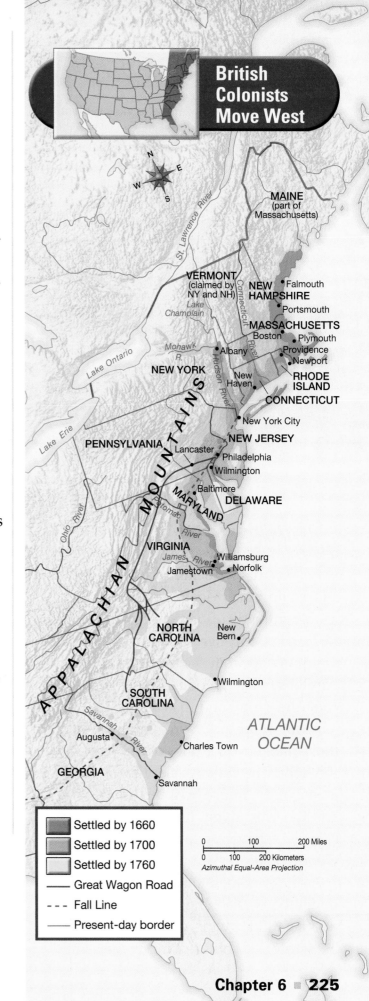

British Colonists Move West

Settled by 1660
Settled by 1700
Settled by 1760
Great Wagon Road
Fall Line
Present-day border

A CLOSER LOOK
Frontier Life

Life was hard and often lonely for early settlers in the backcountry. Family members had to work together to provide all the items they might need.

1. chopping wood
2. farming
3. cleared land
4. candle making
5. churning butter
6. fire used for cooking and warmth
7. children's loft
8. mud between logs

❓ In what ways is this frontier family self-sufficient?

Life in the Backcountry

Most of the people who settled the backcountry lived simply. Their homes were log huts with chimneys made of sticks and mud. Most homes had one room with a dirt floor and no windows. Light came through the open door in the daytime and from the fireplace at night. Families burned wood in the fireplace to cook their food and to keep warm.

At night the adults in a family spread their blankets over piles of dry leaves on the floor. The children slept in the **loft**, a part of the house between the ceiling and the roof. To get up to the loft, they climbed a ladder, which was often just wooden pegs driven into the wall.

A settler named Oliver Johnson remembered sleeping in a loft when he was a child growing up on the frontier. He wrote, "If you slept in the loft, you pulled your head under the covers during a storm. When you got up in the mornin[g], you [would] shake the snow off the covers, grab your shirt and britches [pants] and hop down the ladder to the fireplace, where it was good and warm."

People on the frontier worked hard to get food, hunting in the forests and farming in the clearings. They farmed in the Indian way. They planted corn, beans, and squash all in the same mound of soil. The cornstalks provided a stake for the beans to climb. The squash vines spread out on the ground between the mounds.

As families had done in early New England, frontier families made almost everything they needed. They churned their own butter, dyed their own cloth, and made their own soap and candles. Those who could not do things for themselves, a frontier minister observed

in 1711, would "have but a bad time of it; for help is not to be had at any rate."

Life on the frontier was full of dangers. Families had to protect themselves not only from wild animals but also from possible attacks from Indians or other settlers. Despite these dangers, people still moved farther and farther west. By the mid-1700s, English settlers had crossed the Appalachian Mountains into the Ohio Valley. The land that they moved into was also claimed by France.

REVIEW How did frontier families get the food and goods they needed?

LESSON 3
REVIEW

1 **MAIN IDEA** How did settlers meet the challenges of living on the frontier?

2 **WHY IT MATTERS** What challenges do people today face when they move to a new place?

3 **VOCABULARY** Write a sentence about frontier life, using the terms **backcountry** and **loft**.

4 **READING SKILL—Make Inferences** What do you think life was like for English settlers in the Ohio Valley if the land they lived on was also being claimed by France?

5 **HISTORY** Why did settlers move west?

6 **CRITICAL THINKING—Synthesize** Why do you think settlers of the backcountry were willing to face the hardships there?

 PERFORMANCE—Write a Journal Entry Imagine that you are a settler who has moved to the frontier in the early 1700s. Write a journal entry in which you describe your journey to the backcountry and the building of your new home.

6 Review and Test Preparation

Summary Time Line
1625 — 1650

1624
The first Dutch settlers arrive in New Netherland

USE YOUR READING SKILLS

Complete this graphic organizer by using information you have learned from the chapter to make inferences about the Middle Atlantic Colonies and the backcountry. A copy of this graphic organizer appears on page 62 of the Activity Book.

Breadbasket Colonies

WHAT YOU HAVE READ

The Middle Atlantic Colonies attracted people from many different backgrounds.

WHAT YOU KNOW

_____
_____
_____

_____
_____
_____

Moving West

WHAT YOU HAVE READ

Colonists who settled land farther west faced many challenges.

WHAT YOU KNOW

_____
_____
_____
_____

_____
_____
_____

THINK & WRITE

Write a Wise Saying Benjamin Franklin's *Poor Richard's Almanack* included many wise sayings such as, "If you have time, don't wait for time." Many of these sayings suggested that good behavior is often rewarded. Write a wise saying about the benefits of behaving well.

Write a Song Imagine the year is 1750 and your family is moving to the backcountry. Write a song about your family's journey along the Great Wagon Road. Be sure to describe the changing environment and the difficulties your family must overcome on the journey.

1675   1700   1725   1750

1664
The English take
over New Amsterdam

1682
William Penn
writes the Frame
of Government
of Pennsylvania

1710
Philadelphia
becomes the
largest city
in the Middle
Atlantic Colonies

1732
Benjamin Franklin
begins publishing
Poor Richard's Almanack

USE THE TIME LINE

Use the chapter summary time line to answer these questions.

1 When did the first Dutch settlers arrive in New Netherland?

2 When did William Penn write the Frame of Government of Pennsylvania?

USE VOCABULARY

For each pair of terms, write a sentence that explains how the terms are related.

3 **trial by jury** (p. 214), **justice** (p. 214)

4 **township** (p. 218), **militia** (p. 221)

5 **backcountry** (p. 224), **loft** (p. 226)

RECALL FACTS

Answer these questions.

6 Why did King Charles II grant William Penn the charter to Pennsylvania?

7 How did German immigrant craftworkers contribute to western settlement?

8 What was the name of the trail followed by settlers moving west from Pennsylvania?

Write the letter of the best choice.

9 **TEST PREP** The Middle Atlantic Colonies included New York, New Jersey, Pennsylvania, and—
 A Connecticut.
 B Delaware.
 C Massachusetts.
 D Virginia.

10 **TEST PREP** Farmers in the Middle Atlantic Colonies depended on market towns as places to—
 F meet with local Native American tribes.
 G sell their furs to European merchants.
 H trade their surplus farm produce for goods and services.
 J purchase naval stores.

11 **TEST PREP** Benjamin Franklin contributed to the education of others by—
 A helping start the Great Awakening.
 B designing the layout for the city of Philadelphia.
 C establishing the first subscription library in the colonies.
 D printing playing cards.

THINK CRITICALLY

12 What do you think was William Penn's greatest accomplishment as proprietor of Pennsylvania?

13 Why do you think Benjamin Franklin took such an active part in community life?

14 What do you think backcountry families did when a family member became sick?

APPLY SKILLS

Use a Circle Graph

15 Look in newspapers, magazines, or on the Internet to find an example of a circle graph. Cut out or print out the graph, and tape it to a sheet of paper. Then write a paragraph about what the graph represents.

CHESAPEAKE BAY

For hundreds of years the Chesapeake Bay has shaped the history, culture, and economy of Virginia and Maryland. The bay takes its name from the Native American word *Chesepiooc,* meaning "Great Shellfish Bay." Today, more than 15 million people live along its shores.

LOCATE IT

MARYLAND

Hooper Island

The Southern Colonies

66 Heaven and earth never agreed to frame a better place for man's habitation. 99

—John Smith, on Chesapeake Bay, 1607

CHAPTER READING SKILL

Generalize

When you **generalize,** you summarize a group of facts and show the relationship between them.

As you read this chapter, identify important facts. Then use those facts to make generalizations about the Southern Colonies.

FACT → FACT → GENERALIZATION

· LESSON ·

1

MAIN IDEA

Read to find out why selling crops was important to the success of the Southern Colonies.

WHY IT MATTERS

Selling crops or products is important to the success of many states and countries today.

VOCABULARY

indentured servant
constitution
indigo
debtor

Settlement of the South

1625 — 1750

1633–1733

In 1606 the king of England granted the Virginia Company a charter allowing settlement of the Chesapeake Bay region. In 1607 Virginia became the first permanent English colony in North America. By the 1730s the English had settled the remaining colonies in the South—Maryland, North Carolina, South Carolina, and Georgia. With its 13 colonies, the English claimed much of the Atlantic coast of North America from present-day Maine to present-day Georgia.

Maryland

Maryland was founded by the Calverts, a family of wealthy English landowners. The Calverts, who were Catholic, wanted to build a colony in North America that not only made money but also provided a refuge for Catholics. Like English Quakers, Catholics in England could not worship as they wanted.

George Calvert, the first Lord Baltimore, had been a member of the Virginia Company. He had purchased a large amount of land on the large island of Newfoundland, in what is now Canada. His goal had been to establish a colony there, but he found the climate too cold and the soil too rocky. In 1628, with Lady Baltimore,

FAST FACT The people who today live on Tangier (tan•JIR) Island in Chesapeake Bay are descendants of English colonists, who may have settled there as early as 1686. Their language and way of life have changed very little since the first settlers arrived. They speak the way people speak in parts of western England, from which most of the island's original settlers came.

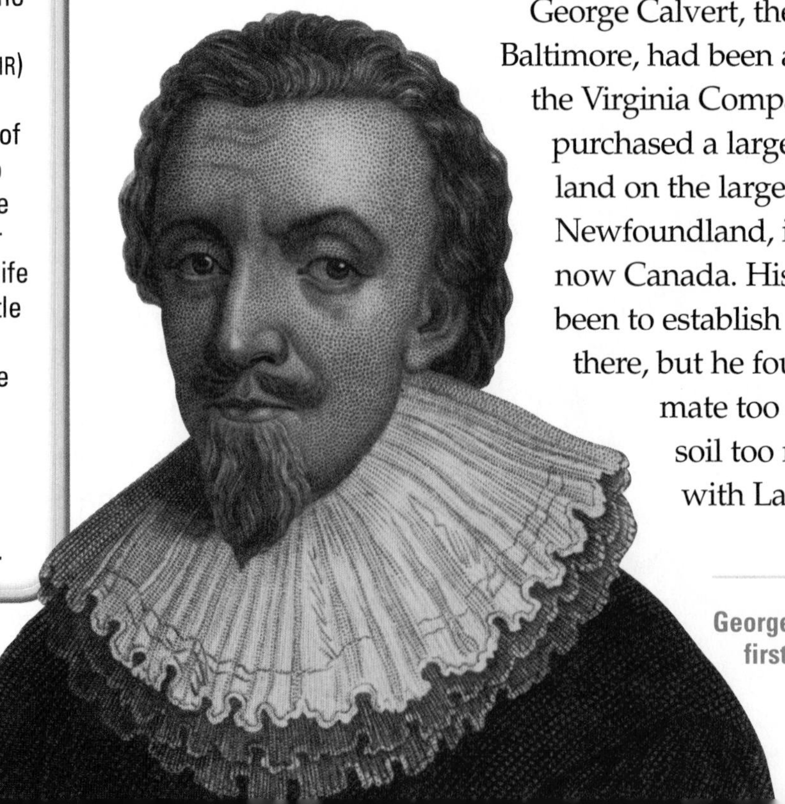

George Calvert, the first Lord Baltimore

St. Marys City

Understanding Places and Regions

St. Marys City, Maryland, is located near the mouth of the Potomac River. For most of the 1600s the town served as Maryland's first capital. Then the capital was moved to Annapolis, and the town was abandoned. Later the area was used as a tobacco plantation. In the 1970s historians and archaeologists dug up the area on which they thought the town once stood. What they discovered was a town designed in the shape of two triangles that met at a central square.

This painting by Walter Crowe shows St. Marys City in 1685.

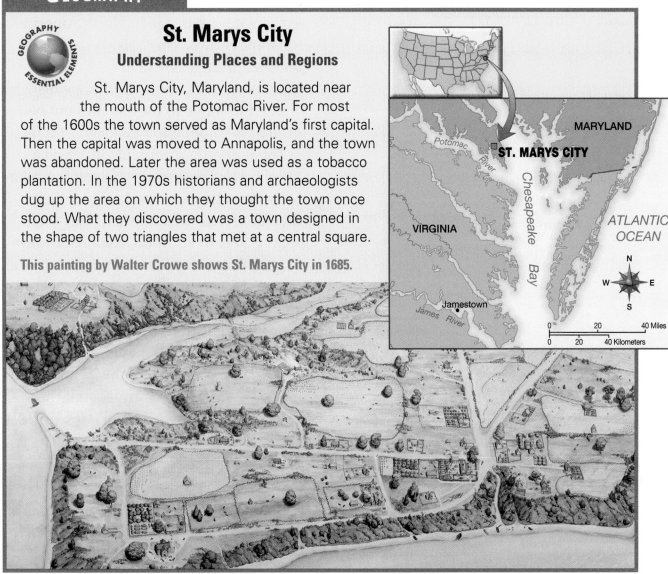

he traveled south to the Chesapeake Bay region. There they found a site where the climate was mild and the soil was rich. King Charles I signed the final colonial charter two months after George Calvert died in 1632. The king gave the grant to Cecilius Calvert, George Calvert's oldest son and the second Lord Baltimore. As proprietor, Cecilius Calvert named the new colony Maryland in honor of Queen Henrietta Maria, wife of Charles I.

In 1633 Cecilius Calvert's first group of colonists left England. "I have sent a hopeful colony to Maryland," he wrote.

The colonists established Saint Marys, later known as Saint Marys City, not far from the mouth of the Potomac River.

Cecilius Calvert appointed his brother Leonard Calvert as the governor of Maryland. Leonard Calvert had learned about the unfortunate experiences of earlier English colonists, such as those who settled early Roanoke and Jamestown. As a result, he planned ahead and prevented the Maryland colonists from suffering a period of starvation. Calvert also knew that Jamestown was nearby in case the new settlement needed supplies or help.

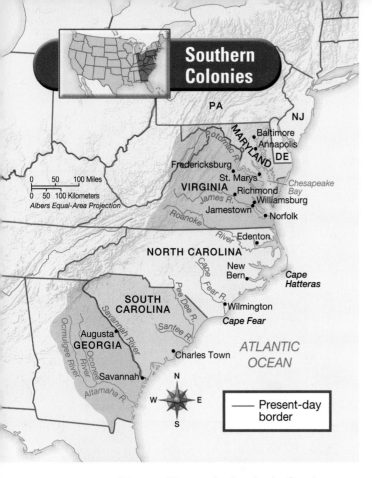

Southern Colonies

PA
NJ
Baltimore
Annapolis
DE
MARYLAND
Fredericksburg
St. Marys
Chesapeake Bay
VIRGINIA
Richmond
Williamsburg
James R.
Jamestown
Norfolk
Roanoke River
Edenton
NORTH CAROLINA
New Bern
Cape Hatteras
Cape Fear R.
Pee Dee R.
SOUTH CAROLINA
Savannah River
Wilmington
Cape Fear
Santee R.
Augusta
GEORGIA
Ocmulgee River
Oconee River
ATLANTIC OCEAN
Charles Town
Savannah
Altamaha R.

0   50   100 Miles
0   50   100 Kilometers
Albers Equal-Area Projection

N W E S

——— Present-day border

GEOGRAPHY THEME

Place **Many colonists in the Southern Colonies started plantations.**

❷ **Why do you think most of the settlements in the Southern Colonies were located in Virginia?**

The Calverts granted some colonists large pieces of land, and these colonists used the land to start tobacco plantations. However, most of the colonists going to Maryland went as indentured servants. An **indentured servant** was a person who agreed to work for another person without pay for a certain length of time in exchange for passage to North America. Most indentured servants were men between the ages of 18 and 22. Many indentured servants were Europeans who wanted to move to the colonies but had little or no money to pay for their travel.

The indentured servants in Maryland fared better than some who went to other colonies to live and work. When their time of service was finished, they were legally free. In addition, colonial leaders helped them start their own farms. They received 50 acres of land, a suit of clothes, an ax, two hoes, and three barrels of corn.

From the beginning Maryland's leaders welcomed settlers of many religions. In 1649 the Maryland assembly, a group that made laws for the colony, passed the Toleration Act. It was the first law in North America to allow all Christians to worship as they pleased. Maryland became known throughout the English colonies for its religious freedom.

REVIEW **Why did the Calverts want to build a colony in North America?**

The Carolinas

The Southern Colonies of Virginia and Maryland continued to grow during the 1600s. Then in 1663 King Charles II, the son of King Charles I, granted land for another colony, located between Virginia and Spanish Florida. The charter divided the colony, known as Carolina, among eight English nobles, known as the Lords Proprietors.

The Toleration Act allowed all Christians in Maryland to worship as they pleased.

Even before the charter was granted, colonists from Virginia had been building villages and were farming in the northern part of the area that became the Carolina Colony. After 1663, colonists from England and the Caribbean, as well as Huguenots (HYOO•guh•nahts) from France, came to settle there. The Huguenots were Protestants forced to leave their country by the French king because of their different religious beliefs.

One of the first actions the Lords Proprietors took was to set up a government for the colony. They chose a Virginian, William Drummond, to be governor. Then in 1669 the Lords Proprietors wrote a **constitution**, or written plan of government, for the colony. Their plan was called the Fundamental Constitution of Carolina. The plan allowed the colonists to make some laws for themselves, but it kept most of the authority in the hands of the king in England.

The Carolina colonists tried raising different cash crops. The climate was good for agriculture, and the soil was fertile. At first, they planted tobacco, grapes, and cotton, but these crops did not do as well as expected. They had more success in raising cattle and trapping animals for their fur, but they still searched for a cash crop. Only when they "found out the true way of raising and husking rice" did Carolina begin to prosper. The colonists also produced naval stores.

As the population grew, Carolina became more difficult to govern. In 1712 the northern two-thirds of the colony was divided into two colonies, North Carolina and South Carolina. Hilly North Carolina continued to develop as a colony of small farms. In South Carolina, however, landowners on the flat Coastal Plain created larger and larger plantations.

The main cash crop on many of South Carolina's plantations was rice. On drier land, where rice would not grow, landowners found they could grow indigo plants. From these plants they made **indigo**, which is a blue dye. The dye was widely used in the clothmaking process common in the 1700s.

Rice (left) was an important cash crop in the Carolinas. The drawing (below) shows workers in a Carolina rice field.

Indigo became an important cash crop after Eliza Lucas Pinckney, the 17-year-old daughter of a plantation owner, experimented with the plant. Using seeds from the Caribbean, Pinckney spent several years growing different kinds of indigo. By 1744 samples of the dye made from her plants were of excellent quality. Pinckney gave her indigo seeds to neighbors and friends. Within a few years South Carolina plantation owners were selling a million pounds of indigo a year to cloth makers in Europe.

The plantations of South Carolina required many workers, and since there were not enough workers available, many landowners bought enslaved Africans. The coastal settlement of Charles Town, later renamed Charleston, became the most important seaport, social center, and slave market in the Southern Colonies.

REVIEW What allowed the Carolina colonists to make some laws for themselves?

Georgia

The southern one-third of what had originally been Carolina was not settled by English colonists until 1733. A year earlier King George II had given James Oglethorpe and 19 partners a charter to settle Georgia, a colony they named for the king. Oglethorpe was an English general and lawmaker. The charter gave Oglethorpe and his partners the right to settle the region between the Savannah and Altamaha Rivers for 21 years.

Many plantations in South Carolina prospered by growing indigo plants.

Oglethorpe and his partners hoped an English colony in Georgia would strengthen England's claim to the land. At the time Spain, France, and England all claimed what became the Georgia Colony.

Oglethorpe also had the idea of bringing over **debtors**—people who were in prison for owing money—to settle the colony. In the 1700s most debtors were imprisoned as punishment for not paying back money. Oglethorpe offered each settler 50 acres of land plus a bonus of 50 acres for every debtor that the settler brought along to help with the work of starting a colony. Those who paid their own way might get up to 500 acres. Oglethorpe hoped that once the debtors were out of prison, they would better themselves through hard work. Settling them in Georgia, he thought, was the answer to this social problem.

In 1733 Oglethorpe and a group of more than 100 settlers established Savannah near the mouth of the Savannah River. During the first year, to keep the colony fairly small, Oglethorpe limited the amount of land a person could own. To avoid conflicts with the Native Americans, he forbade trading with them. He also did not allow slave traders to bring enslaved Africans to the colony. As a result, there were no plantations in Georgia, only small farms.

In 1752 control of Georgia passed from Oglethorpe and his partners back to the king, making it a royal colony. With this change in ownership also came a change to allow slavery. As a result, plantations growing cash crops quickly began to develop, and Georgia landowners began to prosper. Their way of life became similar to that in the other Southern Colonies.

Rice became the most profitable cash crop in the Georgia Colony. Some Georgia planters became so wealthy from growing rice that they were able to own a house in a nearby town in addition to the one they had on the plantation.

REVIEW What did James Oglethorpe accomplish as the leader of the Georgia Colony?

James Oglethorpe
1696–1785
Character Trait: Compassion

While working as a law-maker in England, James Oglethorpe found a special cause. He heard that a good friend of his had been sent to prison for not paying his debts. Oglethorpe hurried to the prison but arrived too late. His friend had died of smallpox from the terrible conditions in the prison. Oglethorpe made up his mind then and there to help debtors.

This 1734 engraving (below) of Savannah was used to attract settlers to the Georgia Colony.

MULTIMEDIA BIOGRAPHIES
Visit The Learning Site at
www.harcourtschool.com/biographies
to learn about other famous people.

GO ONLINE

Thirteen
English
Colonies

New England Colonies
Middle Atlantic Colonies
Southern Colonies
Present-day border

MAINE
(part of
Massachusetts)

St. Lawrence River

VERMONT
(claimed by
NY and NH)

Lake
Champlain

NEW
HAMPSHIRE

NEW
YORK

Connecticut River

MASSACHUSETTS

Lake Ontario

RHODE ISLAND

CONNECTICUT

Hudson River

Lake Erie

A P P A L A C H I A N   M O U N T A I N S

PENNSYLVANIA

Susquehanna R.

Delaware R.

NEW JERSEY

Ohio River

MARYLAND

DELAWARE

Potomac River

Chesapeake
Bay

VIRGINIA

Roanoke River

NORTH
CAROLINA

SOUTH
CAROLINA

Savannah River

GEORGIA

ATLANTIC
OCEAN

N
E
S
W

0   100   200 Miles
0   100   200 Kilometers
Azimuthal Equal-Area Projection

GEOGRAPHY
THEME

Location   The 13 English colonies were
located along the Atlantic Coast.

❧ Why do you think Georgia was the last
English colony to be founded?

Virginia Grows and Changes

By the 1730s, after all of the other
Southern Colonies had been founded, the
Virginia Colony continued to grow and
change. By 1700 Virginia had become the
largest English colony in North America.
Because the population continued to
grow, more and more settlers moved
from the coastal areas of Virginia into
the Piedmont, the Great Valley, and the
mountains of western Virginia. Settlers
from Pennsylvania also continued to
move into these areas.

In the 1700s transportation improved
throughout the Virginia Colony. It became
easier to travel between the coastal areas
and the western part of the colony. Indian
trails became small roads, over which pack
horses carried supplies. These roads soon
widened and became wagon roads.
Soon there were ferry boats that crossed
rivers to transport passengers, livestock,
tobacco, and other goods. When the fer-
ries became very busy, the Virginia
General Assembly voted to build bridges
across some of the rivers. The General
Assembly was made up of Virginia's governor, the Governor's Council, and the
members of the House of Burgesses.

While more people in Virginia were
moving west, changes were also happening along the coast. In 1699, because of
fires and other problems in Jamestown,
the House of Burgesses moved to the
nearby village of Williamsburg, which
became the colony's new capital. By the
mid-1700s Williamsburg was a large,
well-planned city. The city was soon
being compared to other important cities
of the 13 colonies, such as Boston, New
York City, and Philadelphia.

The Governor's House in Williamsburg soon became known as the Governor's Palace.

Williamsburg became the political, social, and cultural center of the Virginia Colony. It was the home of many firsts for the colony. Virginia's first theater was built there in 1716. The colony's first successful printing press was set up there in 1728.

Also, the first newspaper in the colony, the *Virginia Gazette*, was started there in 1736. Williamsburg remained Virginia's most important city for much of the 1700s.

REVIEW How did transportation change in the Virginia Colony?

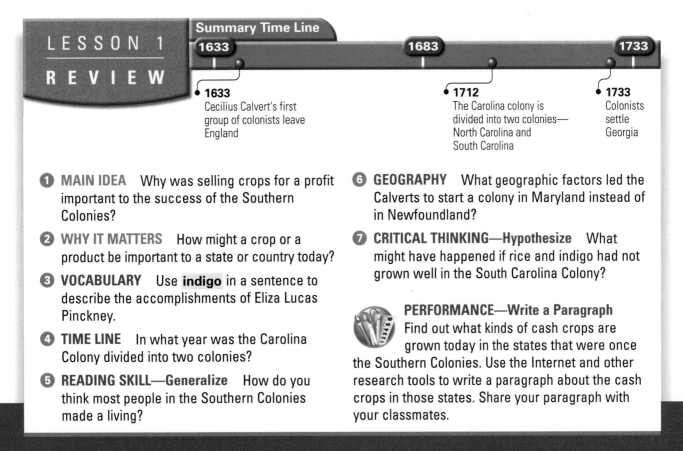

LESSON 1 REVIEW

Summary Time Line

1633   1683   1733

1633
Cecilius Calvert's first group of colonists leave England

1712
The Carolina colony is divided into two colonies— North Carolina and South Carolina

1733
Colonists settle Georgia

1. **MAIN IDEA** Why was selling crops for a profit important to the success of the Southern Colonies?

2. **WHY IT MATTERS** How might a crop or a product be important to a state or country today?

3. **VOCABULARY** Use **indigo** in a sentence to describe the accomplishments of Eliza Lucas Pinckney.

4. **TIME LINE** In what year was the Carolina Colony divided into two colonies?

5. **READING SKILL—Generalize** How do you think most people in the Southern Colonies made a living?

6. **GEOGRAPHY** What geographic factors led the Calverts to start a colony in Maryland instead of in Newfoundland?

7. **CRITICAL THINKING—Hypothesize** What might have happened if rice and indigo had not grown well in the South Carolina Colony?

PERFORMANCE—Write a Paragraph
Find out what kinds of cash crops are grown today in the states that were once the Southern Colonies. Use the Internet and other research tools to write a paragraph about the cash crops in those states. Share your paragraph with your classmates.

Tell Fact from Opinion

VOCABULARY

fact
opinion

▶ WHY IT MATTERS

Knowing how to tell a fact from an opinion can help you better understand what you hear and read. A **fact** is a statement that can be checked and proved. An **opinion** is a statement that tells what a person thinks or believes.

▶ WHAT YOU NEED TO KNOW

You have read that the Maryland Colony was founded by the Calverts. You could check whether this is a fact by looking in an encyclopedia, in other books, or on the Internet.

Facts often give dates, numbers, and other pieces of information. To tell whether a statement is a fact, ask yourself the following questions.

• Do I know this idea to be true from my own experience?
• Can the idea be proved by testing or other checking?

Other statements in this chapter give opinions. You have read John Smith's opinion about Chesapeake Bay: "Heaven and earth never agreed to frame a better place for man's habitation." There is no way to prove that Chesapeake Bay is a better place than any other place.

An opinion is what a speaker or writer believes. The following clues can help you decide whether a statement is an opinion.

• Look or listen for phrases such as *I think, I feel,* and *in my opinion.*
• Watch for words such as *best, worst, wonderful,* and *terrible.*

Historians can use facts to help them form opinions about the past.

▶ PRACTICE THE SKILL

Decide whether the following statements are facts or opinions.

1 In 1628 George Calvert traveled to the Chesapeake Bay region.

2 Saint Marys was the best settlement in the English colonies.

▶ APPLY WHAT YOU LEARNED

Many people rely on newspapers for information. Look at a recent newspaper. Underline three facts and circle three opinions. Explain how you were able to tell the facts from the opinions.

Southern Plantations

As towns and cities in the 13 English colonies grew, plantations also grew—especially in the Southern Colonies. Plantations became prosperous because plantation owners, known as **planters**, were able to grow large amounts of cash crops, more than on small farms. Planters acquired as much land as they could in order to grow more and more crops to sell.

The Plantation Economy

From the time that the first English colonists settled Jamestown, plantations became important to the economy of the Southern Colonies. As planters learned to grow more cash crops well, such as tobacco, rice, and indigo, they started even more plantations.

The earliest plantations were usually built in the rich soil of the southern tidewater. **Tidewater** is low-lying land along a coast. Waterways in the area made it easy for boats to get crops to market. Crop buyers from England traveled the waterways with English-made goods—shoes, lace, thread, farm tools, and dishes. The planters bartered, or traded, crops for these goods.

Owners of the largest plantations most often sold their cash crops through a broker. A **broker** is a person who is paid to buy and sell for someone else. Planters sent their crops to England together with a list of things they wanted the broker to buy there for them.

MAIN IDEA
Read about how southern plantations changed as plantation owners added more and more workers.

WHY IT MATTERS
Many plantation owners became important leaders in the 13 colonies.

VOCABULARY
planter
tidewater
broker
auction
overseer
spiritual
public service

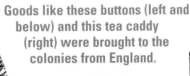

Goods like these buttons (left and below) and this tea caddy (right) were brought to the colonies from England.

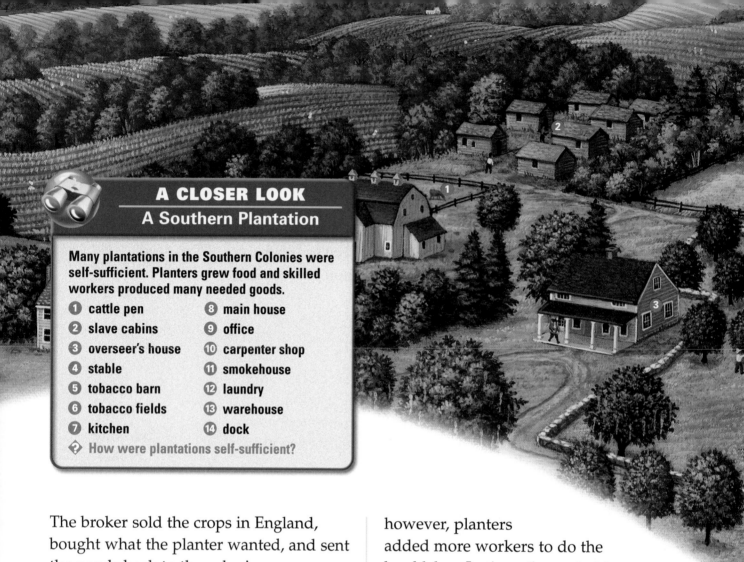

A CLOSER LOOK
A Southern Plantation

Many plantations in the Southern Colonies were self-sufficient. Planters grew food and skilled workers produced many needed goods.

1. cattle pen
2. slave cabins
3. overseer's house
4. stable
5. tobacco barn
6. tobacco fields
7. kitchen
8. main house
9. office
10. carpenter shop
11. smokehouse
12. laundry
13. warehouse
14. dock

❖ How were plantations self-sufficient?

The broker sold the crops in England, bought what the planter wanted, and sent the goods back to the colonies.

To raise more crops, planters had to keep clearing new land. Crops such as tobacco ruined the fertile soil in only a few years. As land wore out near the coast, planters began to move up the rivers to higher land. There they built even larger plantations.

REVIEW Why were the earliest plantations usually built in the southern tidewater?

Plantation Workers

On small farms every member of the family worked long hours. They worked hard, making sure that the crops were planted, harvested, stored, and shipped to market. The same was true for small plantations. As plantations grew in size, however, planters added more workers to do the hard labor. In time, the main job of the planter's family was to watch over the work of others.

Many of the earliest plantation workers came to the colonies in the South as indentured servants. However, not all indentured servants came willingly to the English colonies. Some were sent there by the English courts to work in the colonies to pay for their crimes as a form of punishment. Other indentured servants were people who had been kidnapped and then sold in the colonies against their will.

Among the first indentured servants to be sold in the English colonies were kidnapped Africans. After the mid-1600s, however, traders were bringing thousands of Africans to the English colonies not as

indentured servants but as slaves. Slaves in the colonies were sold like property at an **auction**, or public sale. Unlike indentured servants, slaves were not given their freedom after a certain length of time. They were enslaved for life. Before long, laws were passed in the colonies with a ruling that said that the children of enslaved people were also slaves.

REVIEW **Why did some people come to the colonies as indentured servants?**

A Slave's Life

There were generally two kinds of slaves—field slaves and house slaves. Field slaves worked hard in the fields, raising cash crops for the planters to sell. Some slave owners hired **overseers** to watch the field slaves as they worked and to punish them if they did not work hard.

Olaudah Equiano   1750?–1797

Character Trait: Courage

Olaudah Equiano (OHL•uh•dah ek•wee•AHN•oh) was 11 years old when he and his sister were kidnapped by slave traders. Later Equiano was separated from his sister when they were sold into slavery to different owners. Equiano's owner showed him some kindness and gave him some education. When Equiano was freed from slavery, he wrote a book about his life. In the book he told about his life in Africa and spoke out against slavery. A group of English people working against slavery used Equiano's book to help with the cause to end slavery.

Olaudah Equiano's book was published in 1789.

MULTIMEDIA BIOGRAPHIES
Visit The Learning Site at
www.harcourtschool.com/biographies
to learn about other famous people.

House slaves had more contact with the planter and the planter's family. House slaves often were clothed, fed, and housed better than field slaves. Women who were house slaves did the washing, cooking, cleaning, and sewing for the household. Male house slaves drove carriages, took care of horses, and practiced skills such as carpentry. Children of house slaves were often playmates of the planters' children, at least when they were young.

Slaves were treated well or cruelly depending on their owners. Some planters took pride in being fair and kind to their slaves. There was little protection, however, for slaves who had cruel masters. Slave owners were free to beat, whip, or insult any slave as often as they chose to do so. These slaves looked only

to escape or to resist their cruel treatment. "No day ever dawns for the slave, nor is it looked for," one enslaved African later wrote. "For the slave it is all night—all night, forever."

Laws in the colonies forbade slaves to learn to read and write. By the age of 10, most enslaved children were working alongside the adults.

Enslaved people spent very long days working. At night slaves often told stories and sang songs about their homeland. Later, the Christian religion became a source of strength for slaves as they tried to deal with the hardships of slave life. Some slaves expressed their belief in the Christian religion by singing spirituals. **Spirituals** (SPIR•ih•chuh•wuhlz) are religious songs based on Bible stories.

REVIEW What did some slaves do when their work was finished?

A Planter's Life

Plantations in the South were often far from one another and far from any towns. Weeks or months could go by without visitors and without news about the latest happenings. For this reason, visitors were always welcome.

Because people lived so far apart, there were few schools. Nevertheless, southern planters were among the best-educated people in the 13 English colonies. Some plantations had their own schools for the planters' children, and some hired teachers from Europe. Later, the planters' sons might go to Europe to complete their education. Girls stopped going to school by the age of 12 or 13 because planters' daughters were supposed to learn only basic skills and "to read and sew with their needle."

A planter and his wife were responsible for running a business and for taking care

Girls made samplers, like this one from 1675, to practice their sewing skills.

of all the people on the plantation. They had to clothe, feed, and provide medical care not only for their family but for all the members of their household. By the 1740s a large plantation household—family, servants, and slaves—often numbered in the hundreds.

Besides taking care of a plantation, a planter's duties also included public service. **Public service** is doing a job to help the community or society as a whole. Public service for a planter could mean serving as a judge or as a representative in the colonial assembly. Some planters served as advisers to the governor. Some performed all these duties. This tradition of public service may explain why so many planters became leaders in the 13 English colonies.

REVIEW How were children of planters educated?

LESSON 2 REVIEW

1 MAIN IDEA How did southern plantations change as planters added more workers?

2 WHY IT MATTERS Why did many planters become important leaders in the 13 colonies?

3 VOCABULARY Use the terms **planter** and **tidewater** to describe the plantation economy.

4 READING SKILL—Generalize What was the life of a planter like?

5 CULTURE Why were spirituals important to enslaved people?

6 CRITICAL THINKING—Analyze What were the consequences of modifying the land to grow tobacco?

PERFORMANCE—Write a Diary Entry
Suppose that you are living on a plantation in colonial times. Take on a role, and write an entry in a diary to show what a day on the plantation is like. Share your entry with a classmate.

Read a Resource and Product Map

➡ WHY IT MATTERS

A resource and product map can help you make a generalization about a place's economy. A generalization is a statement based on facts. It is used to summarize groups of facts and to show relationships between them. Symbols for resources and products, shown in the map key, tell you where they are found, made, or grown. These symbols can help you make generalizations about the areas shown on a resource and product map.

➡ WHAT YOU NEED TO KNOW

In the map key on the next page, pictures stand for resources found in the 13 colonies and goods produced there. These goods were important not only because they were sold in the 13 colonies but also because they were exported for sale in England. The map shows only some of the most important goods and resources in the colonies.

➡ PRACTICE THE SKILL

Now that you know more about the symbols in the map key, you can use these questions as a guide for making generalizations about the economy of the 13 colonies.

1 What products appear most often on the map in the New England Colonies?

2 What generalization can you make about the kinds of work most people did in the Middle Atlantic Colonies?

3 What generalization can you make about the economy of the Southern Colonies?

➡ APPLY WHAT YOU LEARNED

Look through encyclopedias, atlases, and almanacs to find an example of a resource and product map. Work with a partner to make some generalizations about the economy of the place or places shown on the map.

 Learn more about maps with the **GeoSkills CD-ROM.**

Iron was melted in furnaces like this one (left). Lumber was cut (right) and tobacco was dried (far right) before it was sent to England.

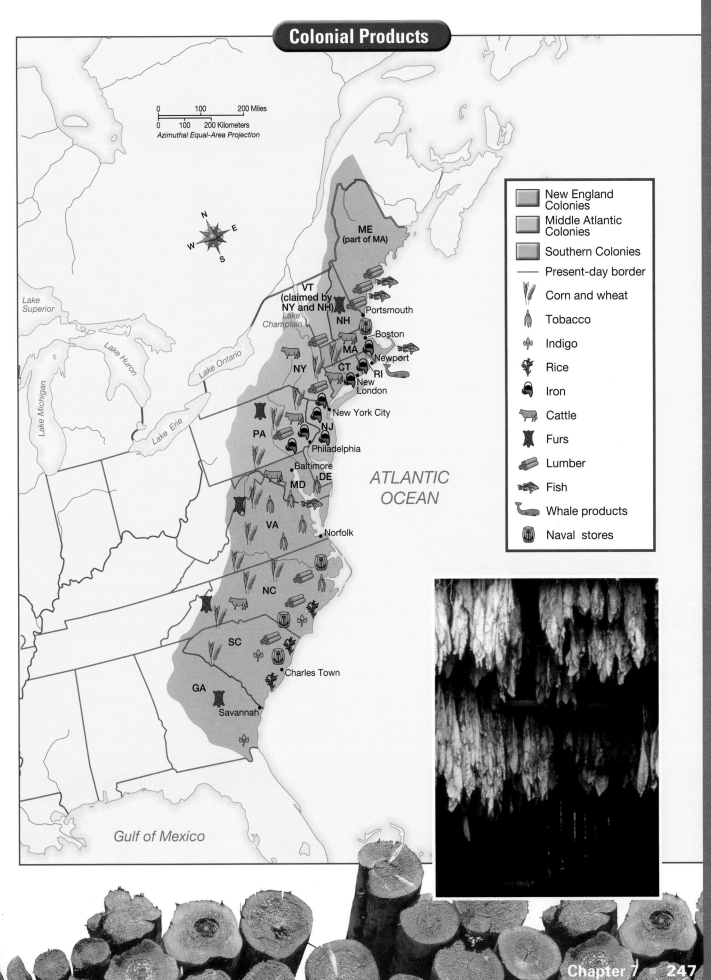

Colonial Products

Legend:
- New England Colonies
- Middle Atlantic Colonies
- Southern Colonies
- Present-day border
- Corn and wheat
- Tobacco
- Indigo
- Rice
- Iron
- Cattle
- Furs
- Lumber
- Fish
- Whale products
- Naval stores

Scale: 0 100 200 Miles / 0 100 200 Kilometers
Azimuthal Equal-Area Projection

Map labels:
Lake Superior, Lake Michigan, Lake Huron, Lake Ontario, Lake Erie
ME (part of MA), VT (claimed by NY and NH), Lake Champlain, NH, Portsmouth, Boston, MA, Newport, NY, CT, RI, New London, New York City, PA, NJ, Philadelphia, Baltimore, MD, DE, ATLANTIC OCEAN, Norfolk, VA, NC, SC, Charles Town, GA, Savannah, Gulf of Mexico

Southern Cities

| 1605 | 1655 | 1705 | 1755 |

1670–1730

MAIN IDEA

Read to learn how cities helped the Southern Colonies grow and prosper.

WHY IT MATTERS

Cities became important gathering places for people to share new ideas and new ways of doing things.

VOCABULARY

apprentice
county seat
county

The Southern Colonies generally had fewer towns and cities than did the Middle Atlantic and New England Colonies. This was because planters and farmers wanted to spread out over as much land as possible. They wanted to use the land to grow crops and were not interested in building towns.

By the mid-1700s, however, some settlements along the Atlantic coast of the Southern Colonies had grown into large towns and even cities. Among these were Charles Town, Wilmington, Norfolk, Baltimore, and Savannah. They all had good harbors, and they grew because of trade. Ships carrying imported goods arrived at these cities. After a few weeks in port, the ships sailed away loaded with exports such as tobacco, rice, and indigo.

Trade Ports

Some settlers who lived inland brought their goods to port cities, where it was easy to find buyers. They sometimes traded their goods for imports that came in on ships from Europe and other places. These imports included tea, coffee, and pepper. Luxury items such as furniture, silverware, and medicine also were imported.

FAST FACT By 1760 Charles Town had become the fourth-largest city in the 13 colonies.

Many people in southern cities worked in the trade business, which helped the cities grow. Other people in the cities worked in other kinds of businesses. Some were fishers, hatmakers, tailors, and printers. Young people learned such jobs by becoming **apprentices**. A child would move in as an apprentice with the family of a skilled worker and help in the family's business for several years. In this way, a young person learned a skill.

REVIEW How did people make a living in southern cities?

Charles Town

Charles Town, South Carolina, became the largest city in the Southern Colonies. In 1688 there were only about 300 people living there. Only 20 years later, in 1708, Charles Town's population had grown to about 6,000 people. An early visitor to the port at Charles Town predicted the city would grow when he said, "There were sixteen ships which had come to trade. The great number of ships will soon make this a busy town."

From 1670 to the mid-1700s, Charles Town was the center of life in South Carolina. During this time most of the people in South Carolina lived in Charles Town or in the area around it. Many residents of Charles Town enjoyed a social life that included dancing, seeing plays, and attending races and concerts.

Merchants and planters had the most power in Charles Town's society. Many wealthy planters in South Carolina lived in Charles Town during the months when insects infested the wetlands on the plantations where rice was grown.

REVIEW Where did most people in South Carolina live between the late 1600s and mid-1700s?

• GEOGRAPHY •

Charles Town
Understanding Places and Regions

Charles Town was located along the middle of South Carolina's coast where the Ashley and Cooper Rivers joined to form Charles Town Harbor. Until the settling of Georgia in 1733, South Carolina served as a buffer, or shield, between the Spanish in Florida and the other English colonies in North America.

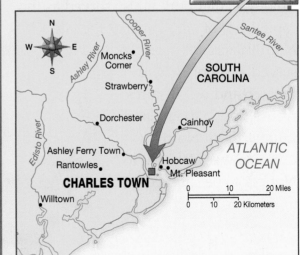

Other Southern Ports

The port city of Wilmington, North Carolina, was started in the 1720s after colonists from South Carolina began moving north along the Atlantic coast to the Cape Fear River. They were looking for fertile soil for establishing plantations. Instead, they found lots of trees. They brought in workers to cut the trees and to build sawmills. They also produced naval stores. From the port at Wilmington, the settlers shipped naval stores and lumber to England as exports.

Wilmington's location on the Cape Fear River helped it prosper. The river is deep enough to be used by large ships, and it flows directly into the Atlantic Ocean. Immigrants also helped Wilmington grow and prosper. They came from other colonies and from many parts of Europe. Some of the town's earliest settlers came from northern Scotland. The first Africans to come to Wilmington were brought as slaves. Eventually, free Africans also lived there. Some were farmers. Others worked as painters, tailors, carpenters, and blacksmiths.

Other coastal towns in the South grew quickly, too. Savannah became the Georgia Colony's chief port. It also served as the capital city of Georgia until the late 1700s. Norfolk, Virginia, grew because it served as a port where tobacco and naval stores were shipped to England. Lumber from North Carolina was also sent to Norfolk to be shipped out to England.

Baltimore's location near Chesapeake Bay helped it become a busy port city.

Baltimore, Maryland, was founded in 1729 on the Patapsco River, which flows into Chesapeake Bay. It prospered because a port was needed for the growing amounts of grain and tobacco being produced in Maryland and other nearby colonies. It quickly became a major port and a center for shipbuilding. Baltimore's shipyards later became well known for improving the way ships were built.

REVIEW How did immigrants affect the port city of Wilmington, North Carolina?

County Seats

As more people in Southern Colonies moved inland in search of more farmland, some inland towns developed and grew. Most of these towns were county seats. A **county seat** was the main town for a **county**, a large part of a colony. Over time, planters and farmers who once used

Items like this silver gravy boat could be purchased at a general store.

brokers or brought their crops to trade in coastal cities began to depend more and more on county seats as places to trade.

Several times a year plantation and farm families would pack their bags, dress in their finest clothes, and travel to the county seat. People went to church, held dances, and traded crops for goods there. Some plantation owners bought and sold slaves there. Most county seats had a general store, a courthouse, and a jail. White men who owned land and other property met at the county seat to make laws and to vote for leaders.

REVIEW Why were county seats important to people living on farms and plantations?

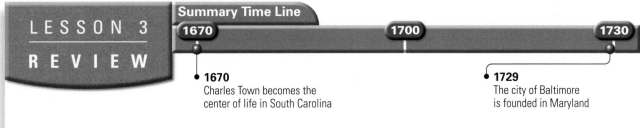

LESSON 3 REVIEW

Summary Time Line

1670 — 1700 — 1730

1670 Charles Town becomes the center of life in South Carolina

1729 The city of Baltimore is founded in Maryland

1. **MAIN IDEA** How did cities help the Southern Colonies grow and prosper?

2. **WHY IT MATTERS** In what ways have cities become important gathering places for people to share new ideas and new ways of doing things?

3. **VOCABULARY** Use the term **apprentice** in a sentence to describe how some young people learned jobs in the Southern Colonies.

4. **TIME LINE** What happened in 1670?

5. **READING SKILL—Generalize** What was life like for people who lived in cities in the Southern Colonies?

6. **ECONOMICS** What was the economic reason for colonists to settle Wilmington, North Carolina?

7. **CRITICAL THINKING—Evaluate** What were the advantages and disadvantages of building more towns in the Southern Colonies?

PERFORMANCE—Make a Map Using maps in your textbook and other sources, draw a map showing the location of the southern towns and cities that you read about in the lesson. Near each city draw pictures of products that helped that city grow and prosper.

Review and Test Preparation

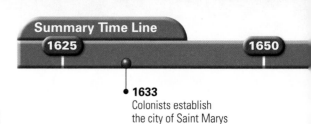

Summary Time Line

1625 ———————————————— 1650

1633
Colonists establish
the city of Saint Marys

USE YOUR READING SKILLS

Complete this graphic organizer by using facts you have
learned from the chapter to make generalizations about the
Southern Colonies. A copy of this graphic organizer appears
on page 71 of the Activity Book.

The Southern Colonies

1. Settlement Of The South

FACTS				GENERALIZATION
By 1700 Virginia is the largest English colony in North America.	___ ___ ___	___ ___ ___	→	___ ___ ___

2. Southern Plantations

FACTS				GENERALIZATION
Planters grow cash crops.	___ ___ ___	___ ___ ___	→	___ ___ ___

3. Southern Cities

FACTS				GENERALIZATION
In 20 years, Charles Town's population grows from 300 to 6,000 people.	___ ___ ___	___ ___ ___	→	___ ___ ___

THINK & WRITE

Write an Advertisement   When a
colony was first established, colonial leaders
sometimes found it difficult to attract settlers.
Write an advertisement for the Georgia
Colony, describing the benefits of moving
there.

Write a Story   During colonial times,
young people who wanted to learn a special
skill, such as hatmaking or printing, became
apprentices. Write a story about a young person who moves in with a skilled worker's
family in order to learn a skill.

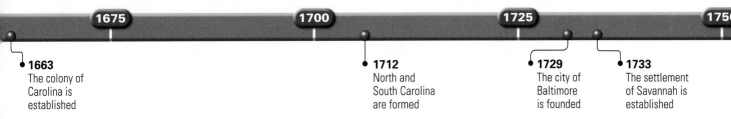

1675   1700   1725   1750

1663
The colony of
Carolina is
established

1712
North and
South Carolina
are formed

1729
The city of
Baltimore
is founded

1733
The settlement
of Savannah is
established

USE THE TIME LINE

Use the chapter summary time line to answer these questions.

1 When was the Carolina Colony established?

2 Was Baltimore founded before or after Savannah?

USE VOCABULARY

Use a term from this list to complete each of the sentences that follow.

> indentured servants
> (p. 234)
>
> constitution (p. 235)
>
> broker (p. 241)
>
> spirituals (p. 244)
>
> county seat (p. 250)

3 Southern plantation owners often sold their cash crops through a _____.

4 A _____ is a written plan of government.

5 When _____ finished their time of service, they were legally free.

6 Several times a year southern farm families would travel to their local _____.

7 Slaves often sang _____ when they gathered together at night.

RECALL FACTS

Answer these questions.

8 What was the most profitable cash crop produced by the Georgia Colony?

9 Why were there few community schools in the Southern Colonies?

10 How did the location of the city of Wilmington, North Carolina, help it prosper?

Write the letter of the best choice.

11 **TEST PREP** Planters had to start building their plantations farther up the rivers because—

  A floods often destroyed their homes.
  B their homes were sometimes attacked.
  C crops like tobacco ruined the soil.
  D the English government required it.

12 **TEST PREP** The largest southern cities were Charles Town, Wilmington, Norfolk and—

  F Boston.
  G Baltimore.
  H Philadelphia.
  J Providence.

THINK CRITICALLY

13 How do you think the demand for indigo affected South Carolina plantation owners?

14 Why were southern waterways important?

APPLY SKILLS

Tell Fact from Opinion

15 Write a news story that includes both facts and opinions. Then exchange stories with a classmate. Find three facts and three opinions in your classmate's story.

Read a Resource and Product Map

Use the map on page 247 to answer these questions.

16 What products appear most often on the map in the Middle Atlantic Colonies?

17 What generalization can you make about the kinds of work most people did in the New England Colonies?

Colonial Williamsburg

GET READY

Colonial Williamsburg is the restored and rebuilt capital of eighteenth-century Virginia. The town is a living-history museum where you can experience the sights, sounds, and smells of colonial life. You can talk with people in historical costumes who stroll the streets or tend their shops. Guides bring history to life by portraying actual citizens who lived in Williamsburg in the 1700s. In Colonial Williamsburg, history is more than just names and dates. It is the story of people just like you who lived in another time.

LOCATE IT

VIRGINIA

Colonial Williamsburg

WHAT TO SEE

Visitors to Colonial Williamsburg can take a wagon ride to see and learn about the buildings that line Duke of Gloucester Street.

Near the James Geddy House, You can take turns at hoop-rolling, stilt-walking, ninepins, and other colonial children's games.

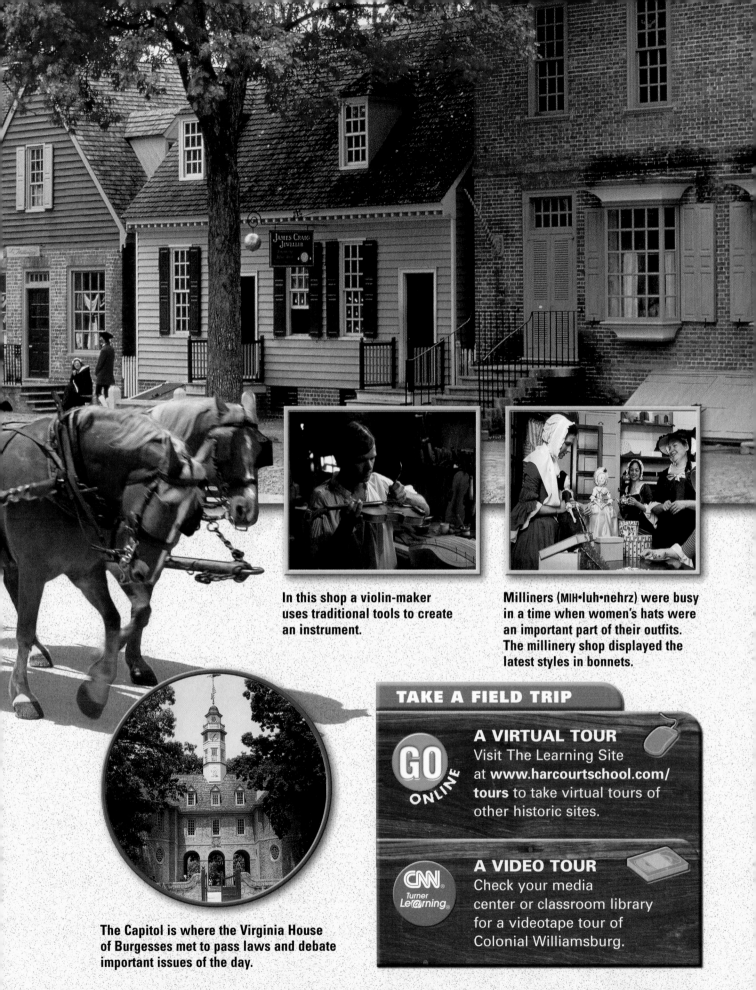

In this shop a violin-maker uses traditional tools to create an instrument.

Milliners (MIH•luh•nehrz) were busy in a time when women's hats were an important part of their outfits. The millinery shop displayed the latest styles in bonnets.

The Capitol is where the Virginia House of Burgesses met to pass laws and debate important issues of the day.

TAKE A FIELD TRIP

GO ONLINE

A VIRTUAL TOUR
Visit The Learning Site at **www.harcourtschool.com/ tours** to take virtual tours of other historic sites.

CNN
Turner
Le@rning

A VIDEO TOUR
Check your media center or classroom library for a videotape tour of Colonial Williamsburg.

3 Review and Test Preparation

USE VOCABULARY

Identify the term that correctly matches each definition.

	public office (p. 192)
	militia (p. 221)
	debtor (p. 236)
	planter (p. 241)

1 a person who was in prison for owing money

2 a person who grew large amounts of cash crops

3 a job for the community

4 a volunteer army

RECALL FACTS

Answer these questions.

5 What kinds of goods did the New England colonists produce from livestock?

6 Why were the Middle Atlantic Colonies also known as the "breadbasket" colonies?

Write the letter of the best choice.

7 **TEST PREP** Roger Williams received help from—
A Governor John Winthrop.
B French fur traders.
C Dutch merchants.
D the Narragansett Indians.

8 **TEST PREP** The triangular trade routes connected England, the English colonies in North America, and the—
F east coast of South America.
G west coast of Spain.
H west coast of Africa.
J east coast of Mexico.

Visual Summary

1625

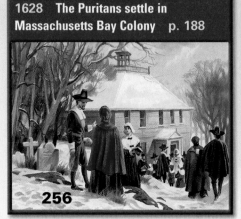

1628 The Puritans settle in Massachusetts Bay Colony p. 188

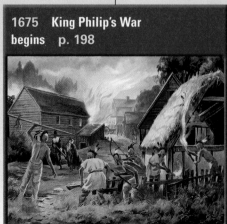

1675 King Philip's War begins p. 198

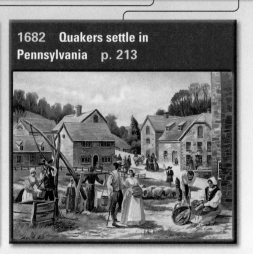

1682 Quakers settle in Pennsylvania p. 213

⑨ TEST PREP Most people in the Middle Atlantic Colonies earned a living by—

A producing naval stores.
B farming.
C fur trading.
D building ships.

THINK CRITICALLY

⑩ Why do you think England wanted its colonists to buy only English-made imports?

⑪ Why do you think the Dutch settlers in New Netherland did not try to fight the English who took over the colony in 1664?

⑫ Why do you think Virginia was the most important of the 13 colonies to England?

⑬ How would living on a plantation have been different from living in or near a town?

APPLY SKILLS

Read a Resource and Product Map
Use the map on this page to answer the following questions.

⑭ What products appear most often on the map in the Middle Atlantic Colonies?

⑮ Which two colonies produced iron?

⑯ Which two colonies produced lumber?

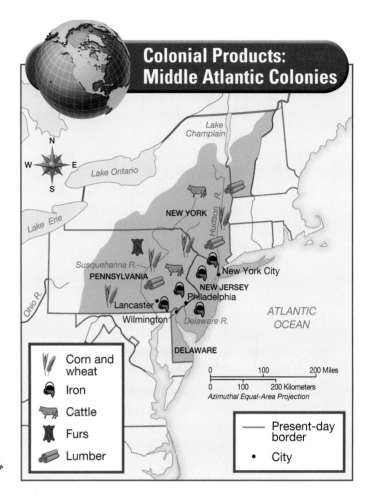

Colonial Products: Middle Atlantic Colonies

Lake Champlain
Lake Ontario
Lake Erie
NEW YORK
Hudson R.
Susquehanna R.
PENNSYLVANIA
Ohio R.
New York City
NEW JERSEY
Philadelphia
Lancaster
Wilmington
Delaware R.
ATLANTIC OCEAN
DELAWARE

🌾 Corn and wheat
🫕 Iron
🐄 Cattle
🦫 Furs
🪵 Lumber

0   100   200 Miles
0   100   200 Kilometers
Azimuthal Equal-Area Projection

—— Present-day border
• City

⑰ What generalization can you make about the colonies that produced corn and wheat?

⑱ What generalization can you make about the economy of the Middle Atlantic Colonies?

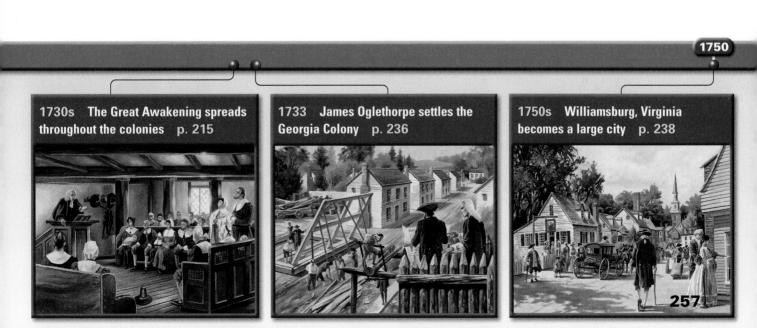

1750

1730s The Great Awakening spreads throughout the colonies p. 215

1733 James Oglethorpe settles the Georgia Colony p. 236

1750s Williamsburg, Virginia becomes a large city p. 238

257

Unit Activities

 Visit The Learning Site at
**www.harcourtschool.com/
socialstudies/activities**
for additional activities.

Design a Monument

Every colony had individuals who made important contributions to its history, such as Benjamin Franklin in Pennsylvania and Eliza Lucas Pickney in South Carolina. Work in a group to choose an individual from the unit and then design a monument to that person. Your monument can include such things as statues or gardens. Make sure your monument includes something that shows the specific contributions of the person you have chosen.

COMPLETE THE UNIT PROJECT

A Book on Colonial America   Work with a group of your classmates to complete the unit project—a book about colonial America. Review your notes on the New England Colonies, the Middle Atlantic Colonies, and the Southern Colonies. Then write a description of each region. Work together to illustrate your book with both drawings and pictures either cut out of magazines or printed from the Internet. Write captions describing the illustrations and give your book a title. Share your completed book with the rest of the class.

VISIT YOUR LIBRARY

■ *Finding Providence: The Story of Roger Williams* **by Avi. HarperCollins.**

■ *The Story of William Penn* **by Aliki. Simon & Schuster.**

■ *James Printer: A Novel of Rebellion* **by Paul Samuel Jacobs. Scholastic.**

The American Revolution

The Liberty Bell

Valley Forge National Historical Park, Pennsylvania

4

The American Revolution

**" By uniting we stand,
by dividing we fall. "**

—John Dickinson, "The Liberty Song," 1768

Preview the Content

Scan the chapter and lesson titles. Use them to make an outline of the unit. Write down any questions that occur to you about the American Revolution.

Preview the Vocabulary

Multiple Meanings   A word can often have several meanings. You may know one meaning but not another. Use the Glossary to look up each of the terms listed below. Then use each term in a sentence.

FORK ⇒ _____   OLIVE BRANCH ⇒ _____

GAP ⇒ _____   PIONEER ⇒ _____

MONOPOLY ⇒ _____   QUARTER ⇒ _____

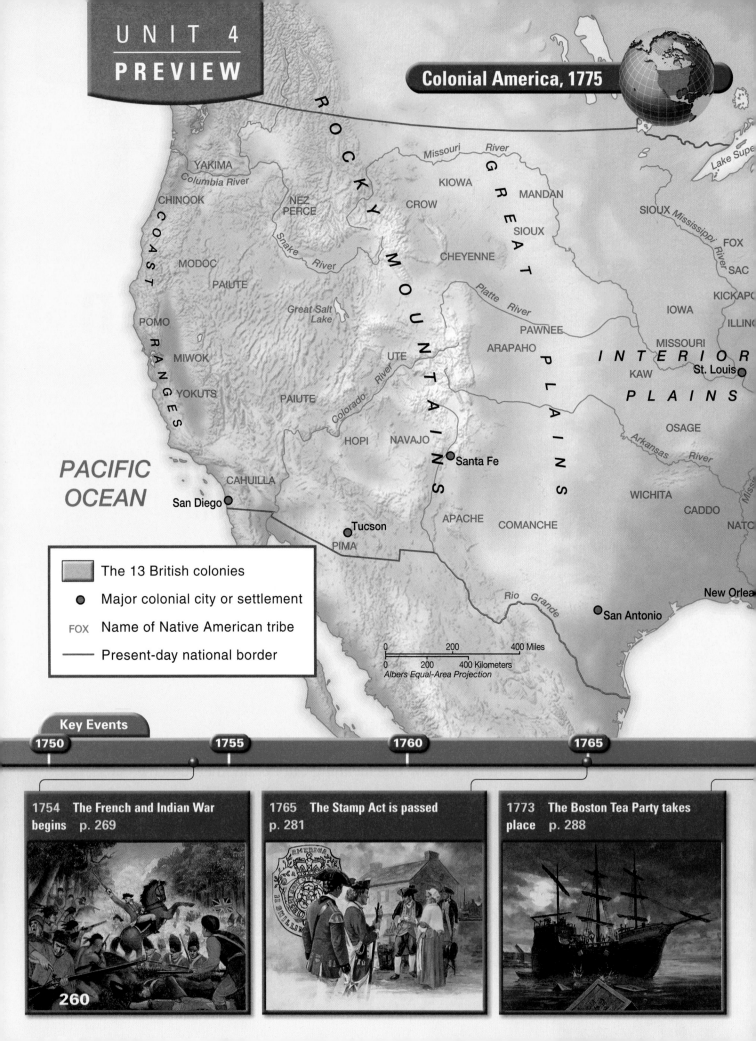

Colonial America, 1775

ROCKY MOUNTAINS

GREAT PLAINS

INTERIOR PLAINS

COAST RANGES

PACIFIC OCEAN

YAKIMA

CHINOOK

Columbia River

NEZ PERCE

Missouri River

KIOWA

CROW

MANDAN

SIOUX

MODOC

PAIUTE

Snake River

CHEYENNE

SIOUX

Mississippi River

FOX

SAC

KICKAPOO

POMO

Great Salt Lake

UTE

Platte River

ARAPAHO

PAWNEE

IOWA

ILLINOIS

MISSOURI

KAW

St. Louis

MIWOK

YOKUTS

PAIUTE

Colorado River

HOPI

NAVAJO

Santa Fe

OSAGE

Arkansas River

CAHUILLA

San Diego

WICHITA

CADDO

NATCHE

Tucson

PIMA

APACHE

COMANCHE

Rio Grande

San Antonio

New Orlea

Lake Superior

Key Events

Legend:
- The 13 British colonies
- Major colonial city or settlement
- FOX Name of Native American tribe
- Present-day national border

0   200   400 Miles
0   200   400 Kilometers
Albers Equal-Area Projection

1750   1755   1760   1765

1754 The French and Indian War begins p. 269

1765 The Stamp Act is passed p. 281

1773 The Boston Tea Party takes place p. 288

260

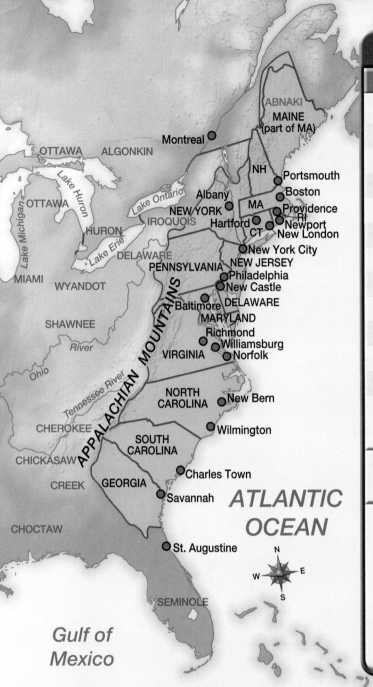

OTTAWA
ALGONKIN
OTTAWA
HURON
IROQUOIS
DELAWARE
MIAMI
WYANDOT
SHAWNEE
Ohio
CHEROKEE
CHICKASAW
CREEK
CHOCTAW
SEMINOLE

Lake Huron
Lake Michigan
Lake Erie
Lake Ontario

Montreal

ABNAKI
MAINE
(part of MA)

NH
Portsmouth
Boston
Albany
NEW YORK
MA
Providence
Hartford
RI
Newport
CT
New London
New York City
NEW JERSEY
PENNSYLVANIA
Philadelphia
New Castle
Baltimore
DELAWARE
MARYLAND
Richmond
Williamsburg
VIRGINIA
Norfolk

APPALACHIAN MOUNTAINS
Tennessee River
River

NORTH
CAROLINA
New Bern
Wilmington
SOUTH
CAROLINA
GEORGIA
Charles Town
Savannah

St. Augustine

ATLANTIC
OCEAN

Gulf of
Mexico

N
W E
S

Population of the 13 Colonies, 1750

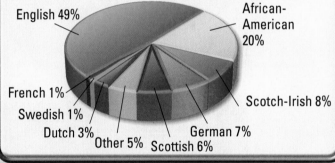

COLONY	POPULATION
Connecticut	
Delaware	
Georgia	
Maryland	
Massachusetts	
New Hampshire	
New Jersey	
New York	
North Carolina	
Pennsylvania	
Rhode Island	
South Carolina	
Virginia	

= 20,000 persons   = 16,000 persons   = 12,000 persons

= 8,000 persons   = 4,000 persons

English 49%
African-American 20%
French 1%
Swedish 1%
Dutch 3%
Other 5%
Scottish 6%
German 7%
Scotch-Irish 8%

1775   1780   1785   1790

1775 The American Revolution begins p. 291

1776 The Declaration of Independence is signed p. 306

1781 The British surrender at Yorktown, in Virginia p. 326

261

YANKEE DOODLE

People have been singing some version of "Yankee Doodle" since the 1700s. The melody is an old English tune, but no one knows for certain who wrote its original words. Some historians credit Richard Shuckburgh, a British army doctor during the French and Indian War. His words poked fun at soldiers from New England. New Englanders were sometimes called Yankees, and *doodle* means "a foolish person."

During the American Revolution, American freedom fighters sang other words to "Yankee Doodle" and often whistled the tune in battle. Their words often poked fun at the British soldiers.

In time "Yankee Doodle" became an important symbol of the United States and of what Americans believed. Read now to discover the words to a version of "Yankee Doodle" that Americans sang.

Yankee doodle went to town,
    Riding on a pony;
Stuck a feather in his hat
    And called it Macaroni.

Chorus:
Yankee Doodle keep it up,
    Yankee Doodle dandy,
Mind the Music and the step,
    And with the girls be handy.

Macaroni fancy trimming, like gold braid
dandy a fancy young man

Father and I went down to camp,
  Along with Captain Good'in,
And there we saw the men and boys
  As thick as has-ty pud-din'.

And there we saw a thousand men,
  As rich as Squire David;
And what they wasted ev'ry day,
  I wish it could be sav'ed.

And there I saw a little keg,
  Its head all made of leather,
They knocked on it with little sticks,
  To call the folks together.

hasty puddin' a thick cornmeal mush
keg small barrel

And there was Captain Washington
  Upon a slapping stallion,
A-giving orders to his men;
  I guess there was a million.

And the ribbons on his hat,
  They looked so very fine, ah!
I wanted peskily to get
  To give to my Jemima.

And there I saw a swamping gun,
  Large as a log of maple,
Upon a mighty little cart;
  A load for father's cattle.

swamping big or heavy

And every time they fired it off,
    It took a horn of powder;
It made a noise like father's gun,
    Only a nation louder.

The troopers, too, would gallop up
    And fire right in our faces;
It scared me almost half to death
    To see them run such races.

It scared me so I hooked it off,
    Nor stopped, as I remember,
Nor turned about till I got home,
    Locked up in mother's chamber.

> **hooked** to run off quickly
> **chamber** bedroom

Analyze the Literature

❶ Why do you think the British and the Americans poked fun at each other?

❷ Work with a partner to interpret the meaning of each stanza in "Yankee Doodle." Then share your interpretation with the class.

READ A BOOK

START THE UNIT PROJECT

The History Show With your classmates, plan a history show about the American Revolution. As you read this unit, take notes about the key people and events. Your notes will help you decide which people and events to use in your history show.

USE TECHNOLOGY

Visit The Learning Site at **www.harcourtschool.com/social studies** for additional activities, primary sources, and other resources to use in this unit.

MINUTE MAN NATIONAL HISTORIC PARK

Visitors to Minute Man National Historic Park can see part of the Battle Road. In April 1775 American colonists and British soldiers fought alongside this road which ran from Boston to Concord. In this photograph, reenactors are marching across Concord's North Bridge.

LOCATE IT

Boston

MASSACHUSETTS

Uniting the Colonies

" Here once the embattled farmers stood, And fired the shot heard round the world. "

—Ralph Waldo Emerson, "Concord Hymn," 1837

CHAPTER READING SKILL

Cause and Effect

A **cause** is an event or action that makes something else happen. An **effect** is what happens as a result of that event or action.

As you read this chapter, list the causes and effects of key events.

What Caused the Event	→	Event

CAUSE	→	EFFECT

The French and Indian War Begins

1750–1755

The events that led to the American Revolution began about 20 years before the 13 colonies cut ties with England, or Britain, as it became known. A **revolution** is a sudden, complete change, such as the overthrow of an established government. The first of the events was a war in North America between Britain and France that came to be called the French and Indian War. The war began as a competition between Britain and France for control of the Ohio Valley region.

Rivalry in the Ohio Valley

The Ohio Valley region stretches about 1,000 miles (1,609 km) along the Ohio River from the Appalachian Mountains to the Mississippi River. Many Native Americans lived in this region before Europeans arrived, but the French and the British each believed this land belonged to them because of earlier exploration and settlement. To the French, the Ohio Valley was an important link between France's holdings in Canada and Louisiana. The British, particularly those in the colonies of Pennsylvania and Virginia, saw it as an area for trade and growth.

By about 1750 the French had moved to make their claim to the Ohio Valley stronger.

MAIN IDEA

Read to find out why conflict over land in North America led to a war between Britain and France.

WHY IT MATTERS

The war between Britain and France determined who would control North America.

VOCABULARY

revolution
fork
ally
alliance
congress
delegate
Parliament

FAST FACT When a British soldier was hit by a bullet, his bright red uniform kept nearby soldiers from knowing he was bleeding. This helped prevent the other soldiers from getting scared and running away from the battle.

They sent soldiers into the region to drive out the British traders. They also began building a line of forts near the eastern end of the valley. The British viewed this move as an act of war and took action.

In 1753 Lieutenant (loo•TEH•nuhnt) Governor Robert Dinwiddie of Virginia sent young George Washington, then 21 years old, across the Appalachians to order the French to leave. When the French replied that they intended to stay, Dinwiddie sent a small force of soldiers from Virginia. Their orders were to build a fort at the Forks of the Ohio River, where the city of Pittsburgh, Pennsylvania, now stands. A **fork** is a place where two rivers join to form a third.

The Virginians had barely finished the fort when the French attacked it. The French drove off the Virginians and built a larger fort on that site. They called it Fort Duquesne (doo•KAYN) in honor of the Marquis (mahr•KEE) de Duquesne, the newly appointed governor general of New France. Unaware of the French attack, Dinwiddie sent young George Washington to the Forks of the Ohio River to reinforce the Virginians' fort.

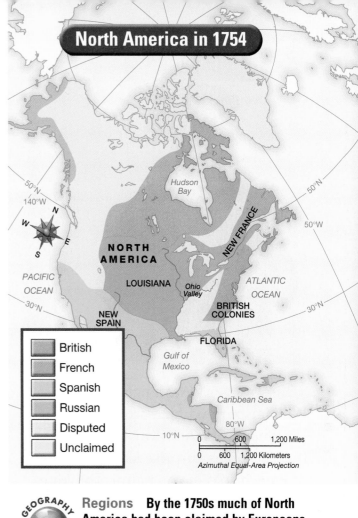

North America in 1754

Regions By the 1750s much of North America had been claimed by Europeans.

❖ Which two groups of Europeans claimed land east and west of the Ohio Valley?

LOCATE IT

PENNSYLVANIA

Fort Necessity

A re-creation of the original Fort Necessity can be seen at Fort Necessity National Battlefield near Farmington, Pennsylvania. In this photograph, reenactors take on colonial roles.

George Washington   1732–1799
Character Trait: Perseverance

The action at Fort Necessity was the first major event in the military career of George Washington. It was the only time he ever surrendered to an enemy. Washington returned to Williamsburg two weeks later, discouraged about the battle. Instead of blaming him for losing the battle, the colonists praised Washington and his soldiers for their bravery. The colonists would later praise Washington for even braver deeds as he led the colonial army in the Revolutionary War.

MULTIMEDIA BIOGRAPHIES
Visit The Learning Site at www.harcourtschool.com/biographies
to learn about other famous people.

In April 1754 Washington left Williamsburg with an army of 150 Virginians. On their way to the fort, the Virginians surprised a small group of French soldiers on patrol. Thinking "we might be attacked by considerable forces," Washington later wrote, the Virginians built a makeshift fort that they called Fort Necessity.

Within days a large force of more than 600 French soldiers and 100 of their Indian **allies**, or friends in war, attacked Fort Necessity. Outnumbered, the Virginians surrendered in what turned out to be the opening battle of the French and Indian War. The French let Washington and his soldiers return to Virginia.

REVIEW How did the French try to strengthen their claim to the Ohio Valley?

The Albany Plan of Union

As a result of Washington's defeat at Fort Necessity, the British government in London urged its colonial leaders to meet with the Iroquois. The British wanted to

be sure of the Iroquois's loyalty in the war against the French. By the mid-1700s both Britain and France had formed alliances with many of the Native American tribes in the Ohio Valley. An **alliance** is a formal agreement among nations, states, groups, or individuals. The Iroquois had become one of Britain's most important Native American allies.

In June and July of 1754, colonial leaders met at Albany, New York, in what was called the Albany Congress. A **congress** is a formal meeting of representatives. Seven colonies sent representatives,

At the time Benjamin Franklin presented his Albany Plan of Union, he was a member of the Pennsylvania Assembly.

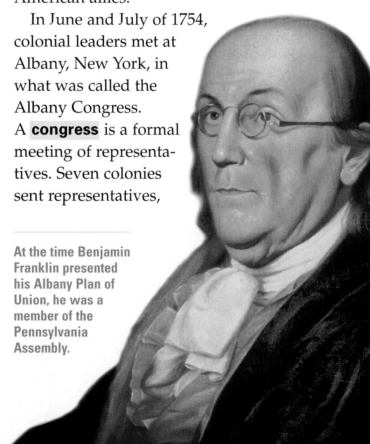

or **delegates**, including Benjamin Franklin from Pennsylvania.

Franklin and the others knew that the colonists needed more than Indian allies to defeat the French. The colonies had to be united in the fight against the French. Franklin presented his Albany Plan of Union. It was one of the first proposals for uniting all of the colonies, except for Georgia, under one government.

To get public support for his plan, Benjamin Franklin published the now famous "Join, or Die" cartoon. It first appeared in the *Pennsylvania Gazette,* one of the most widely read newspapers of that time. Franklin based the cartoon's saying on an old tale about snakes. The story said that a snake cut into pieces would come to life again if put back together before sunset.

Franklin wanted the pieces of the snake—the colonies—to come together to survive. However, in 1754, the American colonies were not yet willing to work together for a common goal.

REVIEW What was Benjamin Franklin's role in the Albany Congress?

Braddock's Defeat

As the French and Indian War continued, the British colonists soon knew that they needed more help if they were to win the war. So **Parliament**, the lawmaking body of the British government in London, sent an army to the colonies to help fight the French and their Indian allies. General Edward Braddock commanded the British forces. He invited George Washington along as an adviser.

Braddock's first goal was to capture Fort Duquesne. In April 1755 he and more than 1,800 British and colonial troops began the long march to the fort. Washington later described how the soldiers looked in their bright, colorful uniforms—British red and colonial blue—marching off against the deep green of the forest.

Not far from where Washington and his men had built Fort Necessity, the British met a force of about 900 French and Indian soldiers. For two hours the French and their Indian allies fired at the British from behind trees and boulders.

Benjamin Franklin hoped this simple cartoon would help convince the colonies to approve his Albany Plan of Union. The part of the snake labeled *N.E.* represented the New England Colonies.

General Braddock (above) and his troops panicked when the French and Indians fired on them from behind rocks and trees.

The British, trained to fight in open fields, had never fought an enemy this way. They "broke and ran," Washington later wrote, "as sheep before the hounds." When the battle ended, two-thirds of the British were dead or wounded. Braddock was one of those killed.

Braddock's loss left the British colonists in the Ohio Valley without protection. For the next two years, the French and their Indian allies carried out attacks against those colonists.

REVIEW What was a major cause of General Braddock's loss?

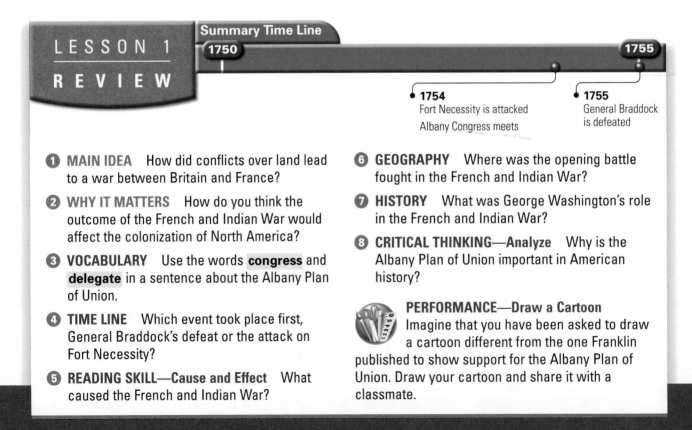

LESSON 1 REVIEW

Summary Time Line

1750

1755

1754
Fort Necessity is attacked
Albany Congress meets

1755
General Braddock is defeated

1 **MAIN IDEA**   How did conflicts over land lead to a war between Britain and France?

2 **WHY IT MATTERS**   How do you think the outcome of the French and Indian War would affect the colonization of North America?

3 **VOCABULARY**   Use the words **congress** and **delegate** in a sentence about the Albany Plan of Union.

4 **TIME LINE**   Which event took place first, General Braddock's defeat or the attack on Fort Necessity?

5 **READING SKILL—Cause and Effect**   What caused the French and Indian War?

6 **GEOGRAPHY**   Where was the opening battle fought in the French and Indian War?

7 **HISTORY**   What was George Washington's role in the French and Indian War?

8 **CRITICAL THINKING—Analyze**   Why is the Albany Plan of Union important in American history?

PERFORMANCE—Draw a Cartoon
Imagine that you have been asked to draw a cartoon different from the one Franklin published to show support for the Albany Plan of Union. Draw your cartoon and share it with a classmate.

Britain Wins North America

1750   1770   1790

1758–1763

MAIN IDEA
Read to learn that the colonists were eager to settle in Britain's newly won lands.

WHY IT MATTERS
British leaders and the colonists began to disagree over land rights and British control of the colonies.

VOCABULARY
proclamation
bill of rights
pioneer
gap

For the first two years of fighting, the French and Indian War had been only a North American conflict. In 1756, however, it became a world war, known as the Seven Years War, with battles fought in Europe and Asia, as well as in North America. To win the war, William Pitt, Britain's new leader of Parliament, decided to focus on North America. He sent more troops and more supplies there and eventually turned the war in Britain's favor.

The British Road to Victory

In 1758 the British captured three French forts—Duquesne at the Forks of the Ohio River, and Louisbourg and Frontenac, in what is now Canada. The following year they took forts at Crown Point, Niagara, and Ticonderoga in present-day New York. The British also attacked French forces near the city of Quebec in Canada. In September 1759 General James Wolfe's British troops defeated French forces under the command of the Marquis de Montcalm on the Plains of Abraham, near Quebec.

During the next year, the British closed a circle of troops and ships around French Canada.

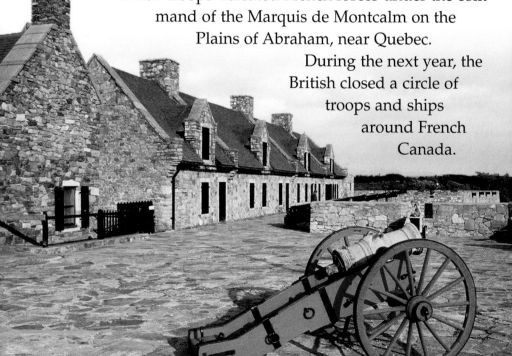

William Pitt's leadership helped the British win many battles against the French, including the one at Fort Ticonderoga (left).

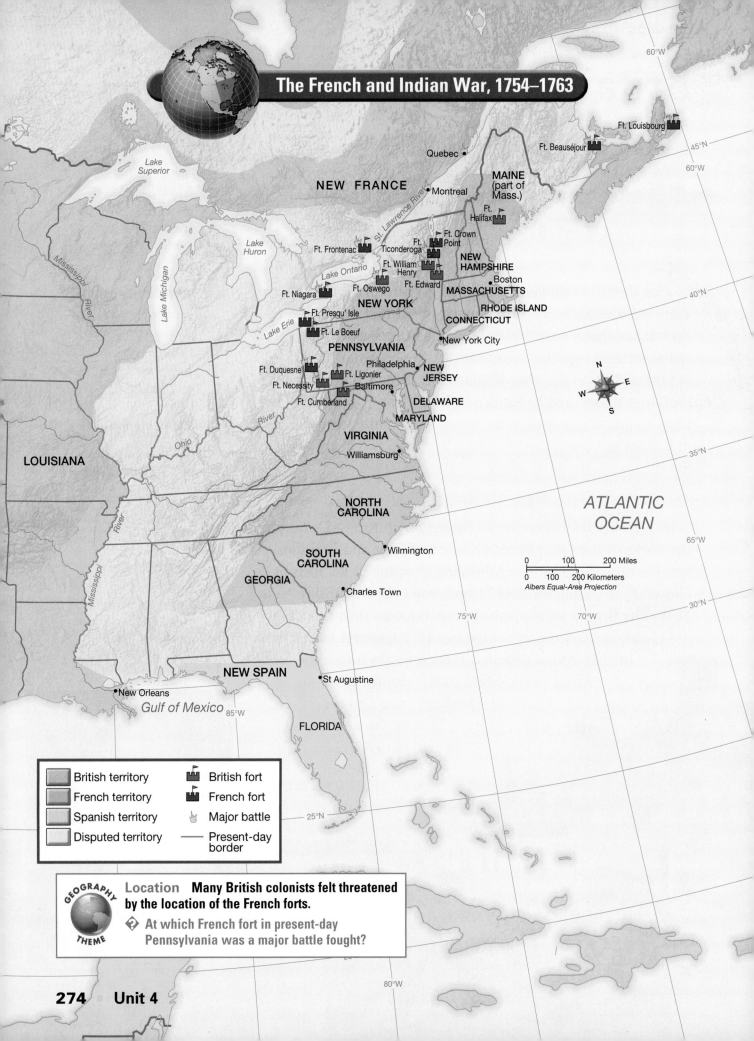

The French and Indian War, 1754–1763

Lake Superior

NEW FRANCE

Quebec

Ft. Beauséjour

Ft. Louisbourg

MAINE (part of Mass.)

Montreal

St. Lawrence River

Ft. Halifax

Lake Huron

Ft. Frontenac

Ft. Ticonderoga

Ft. Crown Point

NEW HAMPSHIRE

Lake Michigan

Lake Ontario

Ft. William Henry

Ft. Niagara

Ft. Oswego

Ft. Edward

MASSACHUSETTS

Boston

NEW YORK

RHODE ISLAND

CONNECTICUT

Lake Erie

Ft. Presqu' Isle

Ft. Le Boeuf

New York City

PENNSYLVANIA

Philadelphia

Ft. Duquesne

Ft. Ligonier

NEW JERSEY

Ft. Necessity

Baltimore

DELAWARE

Ft. Cumberland

MARYLAND

Ohio River

VIRGINIA

Williamsburg

LOUISIANA

Mississippi River

NORTH CAROLINA

ATLANTIC OCEAN

SOUTH CAROLINA

Wilmington

GEORGIA

Charles Town

200 Miles

200 Kilometers

Albers Equal-Area Projection

NEW SPAIN

St Augustine

New Orleans

Gulf of Mexico

FLORIDA

	British territory		British fort
	French territory		French fort
	Spanish territory		Major battle
	Disputed territory		Present-day border

Location Many British colonists felt threatened by the location of the French forts.

❓ At which French fort in present-day Pennsylvania was a major battle fought?

GEOGRAPHY THEME

Finally, in 1760, after the British captured Montreal, another major French city, the French gave up. Fighting, however, continued in Europe.

In the closing months of the war in North America, Spain joined with France in the fight against the British. Because of its superior sea power, however, Britain defeated Spanish forces in 1762. To make up for Spain's losses in the war, France gave Spain most of Louisiana and part of what is now Florida.

The French and Indian War finally ended in Europe and in North America in 1763, when the French and the British signed a peace treaty in Paris. Under the terms of the Treaty of Paris, France gave most of its lands in present-day Canada to Britain. France also gave up claim to most of the lands between the Appalachian Mountains and the Mississippi River. Also as a result of the Treaty of Paris, Britain received Florida from Spain.

REVIEW What parts of North America were given to Britain in the Treaty of Paris?

Pontiac's Rebellion

Now that the lands between the Appalachians and the Mississippi were under British control, many colonists began to settle there. The Native Americans who lived there, however, did not welcome these newcomers.

Chief Pontiac (PAHN•tee•ak) of the Ottawa tribe wanted to stop the loss of Indian hunting lands. So Pontiac and other Indian leaders united the tribes of the Great Lakes and Ohio Valley region to fight against the settlers.

In May 1763 Pontiac and his united tribes began attacking British forts in what is now western Pennsylvania, Ohio, Michigan, and Indiana. Most were destroyed. Two of the outposts that survived were Fort Detroit and Fort Pitt, once known as Fort Duquesne.

Pontiac and his forces attacked the forts to get guns and supplies, which in the past they had gotten from the French. However, as winter came, many Indian fighters signed peace treaties with the British and began to return to their homes. Without supplies or soldiers, Pontiac had to give up control of the British forts.

REVIEW What caused Pontiac's Rebellion?

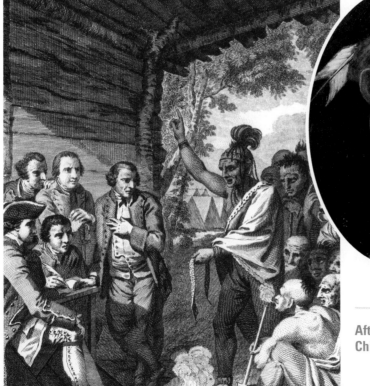

After losing a battle at Bushy Run, in Pennsylvania, Chief Pontiac refused to sign a peace treaty.

The Proclamation of 1763

Many British leaders in London blamed Pontiac's Rebellion on the back-country traders and settlers. They believed that these colonists did not have the right to claim or buy land in the region. The British government decided that stopping the westward movement of its colonists was the only way to end the fighting and prevent further trouble. To do this, the British king, George III, issued the Proclamation of 1763. A **proclamation** is an order from a country's leader to its citizens.

The Proclamation of 1763 said that British colonists could not buy land west of the Appalachians from the Indians, hunt on it, or explore it. Settlers already living there were to leave at once. George III said the lands west of the Appalachians were to be used only by the Native Americans. The king hoped the order would prevent more wars between the colonists and the Native Americans.

Indian leaders were pleased that the British king wanted to keep the colonists off their land. The colonists, however, were furious. They felt the proclamation took away their right as British citizens to travel where they wanted. As British citizens, the American colonists had the same rights as British citizens living in Britain. Those rights were listed in the English Bill of Rights which Parliament had created in 1689. A **bill of rights** is a list of rights. The English Bill of Rights said that the government could not take certain rights away from the people.

The colonists grew even more upset when the king ordered British soldiers to remain in North America to protect the newly won lands. The colonists felt this action also took away their rights. They became even angrier when the king gave his colonial governors greater authority over the colonies.

The colonists had not expected these changes. They had hoped to gain more authority to govern themselves. Instead, they now had to obey even stricter laws made by a government far away.

REVIEW What changes took place in the government of the colonies after the French and Indian War?

Americans Continue West

The Proclamation of 1763 did not stop colonial pioneers from continuing their push west into the frontier. A **pioneer** is a person who first settles a new place. Daniel Boone was one of the earliest and best-known colonial pioneers to travel west across the Appalachian Mountains.

During the French and Indian War, Boone met John Finley, a British fur trader. Finley told Boone stories about visiting a wonderful land west of the Appalachians.

Daniel Boone was born in Pennsylvania. At an early age he came to love living in the woods and hunting.

Daniel Boone leads pioneers through the Cumberland Gap in this painting by George Caleb Bingham.

In time, colonists began to call this land Kentucky, which comes from an Indian word for "meadowland."

After the war, Boone tried to reach this land, but he could not find a way over the mountains. In 1769, with Finley's help, Boone found an Indian trail that he followed across the Appalachians through what is now the Cumberland Gap. A **gap** is an opening, or low place, between mountains. The route Boone followed was later widened for wagons and became known as the Wilderness Road.

REVIEW Who was Daniel Boone?

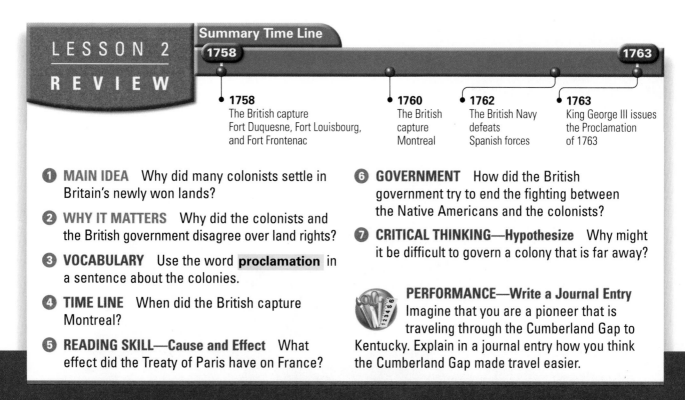

LESSON 2 REVIEW

Summary Time Line

1758 ———————————————————————————— 1763

1758
The British capture Fort Duquesne, Fort Louisbourg, and Fort Frontenac

1760
The British capture Montreal

1762
The British Navy defeats Spanish forces

1763
King George III issues the Proclamation of 1763

1 **MAIN IDEA** Why did many colonists settle in Britain's newly won lands?

2 **WHY IT MATTERS** Why did the colonists and the British government disagree over land rights?

3 **VOCABULARY** Use the word **proclamation** in a sentence about the colonies.

4 **TIME LINE** When did the British capture Montreal?

5 **READING SKILL—Cause and Effect** What effect did the Treaty of Paris have on France?

6 **GOVERNMENT** How did the British government try to end the fighting between the Native Americans and the colonists?

7 **CRITICAL THINKING—Hypothesize** Why might it be difficult to govern a colony that is far away?

PERFORMANCE—Write a Journal Entry
Imagine that you are a pioneer that is traveling through the Cumberland Gap to Kentucky. Explain in a journal entry how you think the Cumberland Gap made travel easier.

·SKILLS·

MAP AND GLOBE

Compare Historical Maps

VOCABULARY

hatch lines

➡ WHY IT MATTERS

The Treaty of Paris that officially ended the French and Indian War changed the map of North America. The historical maps on page 279 show the changes. A historical map provides information about a place at a certain time in history. Knowing how to use historical maps can help you learn how borders have changed over time.

Flags over North America

➡ WHAT YOU NEED TO KNOW

Colors are important map symbols. Sometimes colors help you tell water from land on a map. Colors on a map can also show you the areas claimed by different cities, states, or countries.

One of the color symbols on Map B has a pattern of stripes that mapmakers call hatch lines. **Hatch lines** on historical maps often show areas claimed by two or more countries. Hatch lines may also show land that has a special purpose.

The map key on Map B tells you that the region shown by hatch lines was claimed by the British. For this reason one of the colors of the hatch lines is the color used for the British. The map key also tells you that the British reserved this land for the Native Americans.

Spain

These flags were flown over different parts of North America in the mid-1700s.

France

Britain

Russia

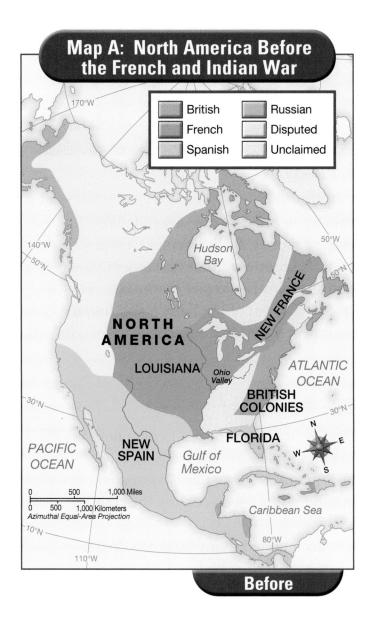

Map A: North America Before the French and Indian War

British
French
Spanish
Russian
Disputed
Unclaimed

170°W
140°W
50°N
Hudson Bay
50°W
50°N
NEW FRANCE
NORTH AMERICA
LOUISIANA
Ohio Valley
ATLANTIC OCEAN
30°N
BRITISH COLONIES
30°N
PACIFIC OCEAN
NEW SPAIN
FLORIDA
Gulf of Mexico
N
W   E
S
0   500   1,000 Miles
0   500   1,000 Kilometers
Azimuthal Equal-Area Projection
10°N
Caribbean Sea
110°W
80°W

Before

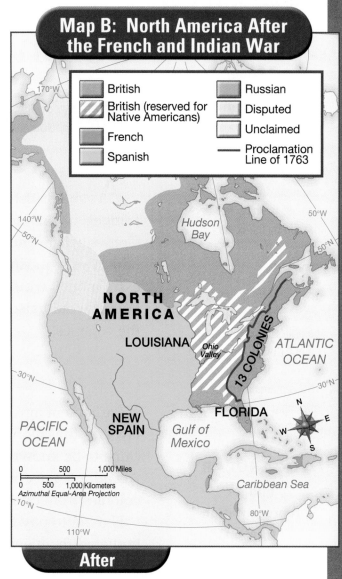

Map B: North America After the French and Indian War

British
British (reserved for Native Americans)
French
Spanish
Russian
Disputed
Unclaimed
Proclamation Line of 1763

170°W
140°W
50°N
Hudson Bay
50°W
50°N
NORTH AMERICA
LOUISIANA
Ohio Valley
13 COLONIES
ATLANTIC OCEAN
30°N
30°N
PACIFIC OCEAN
NEW SPAIN
FLORIDA
Gulf of Mexico
N
W   E
S
0   500   1,000 Miles
0   500   1,000 Kilometers
Azimuthal Equal-Area Projection
10°N
Caribbean Sea
110°W
80°W

After

▶ PRACTICE THE SKILL

Look at the map keys to learn what each color represents. Then use the maps to answer these questions.

1 What color is used to show the land claimed by the French? by the British? by the Spanish?

2 After the French and Indian War, which European country claimed the area known as Louisiana?

3 Which European country claimed Florida before the French and Indian War? after the war?

▶ APPLY WHAT YOU LEARNED

Write a paragraph that describes what these historical maps show and explains why historical maps are useful. Share your paragraph with a classmate.

MAP AND GLOBE SKILLS

Practice your map and globe skills with the **GeoSkills CD-ROM.**

MAP AND GLOBE SKILLS

Chapter 8 ▪ 279

3

MAIN IDEA

Read to learn why many colonists spoke out against the new tax laws passed by the British Parliament.

WHY IT MATTERS

The colonists believed that a government should not be able to tax its citizens unless the citizens have a voice in the government. This remains a key belief of people in the United States today.

VOCABULARY

budget
representation
treason
boycott
declaration
repeal
liberty

Colonists Speak Out

1750   1770   1790

1764–1770

As the British Parliament in London discussed its 1764 **budget**, or plan for spending money, British leader George Grenville had a suggestion. He proposed that Parliament pass new laws requiring American colonists to pay more taxes. This extra money would help pay the cost of the French and Indian War. It would also help support the British soldiers stationed in the colonies.

The Sugar Act

Parliament agreed with Grenville and began to pass new tax laws for the colonies. The first of these money-raising laws came to be known as the Sugar Act. Passed in 1764, the Sugar Act added a tax on sugar and other goods coming into the colonies from other places.

Having to pay this new tax angered many colonists. What bothered them even more was that they had had no voice in deciding on this tax law. The king and Parliament taxed the colonists without their consent, or agreement. Many colonists believed that this action violated their rights as British citizens.

One of the first colonial leaders to speak out against the Sugar Act was James Otis of Massachusetts. He called the tax "unjust." Not all colonists agreed. Some sided with the British government. Martin Howard of Rhode Island

George Grenville urged King George III (left and on British coin) and members of the British Parliament to support new taxes on sugar and other goods.

felt that the colonists should be more grateful to the king and the Parliament than they were. Without British help, Howard reminded them, they might now be under the rule of France or Spain.

REVIEW **Why were many colonists angered by the Sugar Act?**

The Stamp Act

In 1765, less than a year after the Sugar Act became law, Parliament passed a second tax law for the colonies. The Stamp Act placed a tax on newspapers, almanacs, pamphlets, all kinds of legal documents, insurance policies, licenses, and even playing cards. Each of these items had to have a special stamp on it to show that the tax had been paid. Because Parliament knew that the stamp tax might anger the colonists more than the sugar tax, it hired colonists as tax collectors.

Reaction to the Stamp Act in the colonies was the same as it had been to the Sugar Act. Once again, what really upset many of the colonists was that they had not had a voice in deciding to pass the law. They did not have a voice because they did not have any **representation** in the British Parliament.

This leather box held stamps (right) that colonists had to buy to be placed on many printed items.

POINTS OF VIEW
Taxes

THOMAS WHATELY, a member of the British Parliament

❝ We are not yet recovered from a War undertaken . . . for their [the colonists'] Protection . . . and no Time was ever so seasonable for claiming their Assistance [help]. The Distribution is too unequal, of Benefits only to the colonies, and all of the Burthens [burdens] upon the Mother Country [Britain]. ❞

SAMUEL ADAMS, a member of the Massachusetts legislature

❝ We are told to be quiet when we see that very money which is torn from us by lawless force . . . to feed and pamper a set of infamous wretches [British soldiers and officials] who swarm like the locusts of Egypt. ❞

Analyze the Viewpoints

❶ What views about taxes did each person hold?

❷ **Make It Relevant** Look at the Letters to the Editor section of your newspaper. Find two letters that express different viewpoints about the same issue. Then write a paragraph that summarizes the viewpoints of each letter.

No one was acting or speaking for them in London.

James Otis again spoke out. He told a crowd in Boston that they should refuse to pay the stamp tax until they had representation in Parliament. The colonists began repeating his words,

> **" No taxation without representation. "**

In Virginia, Patrick Henry told his fellow members of the House of Burgesses that they alone should decide what taxes Virginians would pay. Henry said that Parliament did not represent the colonies. The colonies had their own legislatures to represent them.

Members of the House of Burgesses who supported the British government

This teapot shows the colonists' unhappiness with the Stamp Act.

shouted "Treason!" during Patrick Henry's speech. By accusing Henry of **treason**, they were saying that he was working against his government. Henry is said to have answered, "If this be treason, make the most of it!" Although some members protested the decision, the House of Burgesses voted against paying any new taxes Parliament passed unless the colonists gave their consent.

More and more people in the 13 colonies decided not to buy goods that had been stamped. Many colonists also began to **boycott**, or refuse to buy, any British goods. In Boston, groups of women made thread and cloth so that colonists would not have to buy cloth

Stamp Act Protest

Analyze Primary Sources

This 1765 drawing shows colonists in New Hampshire protesting the Stamp Act.

❶ The coffin represents the colonists' wish to see the Stamp Act die.

❷ The figure made of straw represents a stamp tax collector.

❸ This angry protester prepares to throw a rock at the straw figure.

◆ Why do you think the protesters placed a straw figure high on a pole?

that had been made in Britain. In some colonies, people began drinking tea made from the local sassafras trees instead of buying tea from Britain.

Some colonists protested the Stamp Act in more violent ways. They attacked the homes of the stamp tax collectors, breaking windows and stealing property. They beat some tax collectors and chased several out of their cities and towns.

REVIEW **Why did many colonists believe that Britain had no right to tax them?**

The Stamp Act Congress

Since the time of the Albany Congress, some colonial leaders such as Benjamin Franklin and James Otis had thought that the colonies should work together instead of acting separately. In 1765 Franklin, Otis, and 25 other colonial leaders met in New York City to talk about what to do about the Stamp Act. This meeting came to be called the Stamp Act Congress. Nine colonies sent representatives.

Members of the Stamp Act Congress talked about the problems the new tax laws caused. For example, people who did not obey the Stamp Act could be tried in special courts without a jury. Trial by jury had been a right of British citizens for hundreds of years. A person accused of breaking the law had the right to be tried by a jury of fellow citizens. British citizens were also considered to be innocent until proven guilty, and their property could not be taken away without just cause. The colonists felt that these basic rights and others were now being threatened.

In response, John Dickinson from Pennsylvania proposed that a "Declaration of Rights and Grievances" (GREE•vuhn•suhz) be sent to King

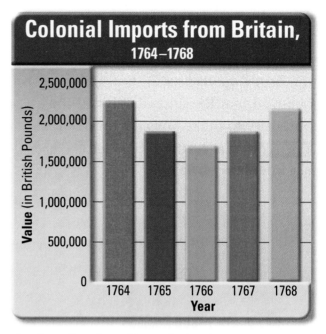

Colonial Imports from Britain, 1764–1768

Analyze Graphs After colonists began to boycott British goods in 1765, the value of colonial imports from Britain decreased.

◆ By about how much did the value of colonial imports decrease from 1764 to 1766?

George III. Such a **declaration**, or official statement, was drawn up, listing the colonists' rights as British citizens. This declaration stated that the British government had no right to tax the colonists without giving them representation. Members of the Stamp Act Congress also expressed their fears that the use of the special courts took away citizens' rights.

In Britain, merchants began to worry about how the colonists' boycott would affect their businesses. Sales of British goods had decreased by almost half in several colonies, and British merchants who depended on trade with the colonies had already started to lose money. The merchants urged Parliament to **repeal**, or cancel, the Stamp Act.

After much discussion, Parliament repealed the Stamp Act in March 1766. The next year, however, it passed some new laws called the Townshend Acts.

These laws placed taxes on lead, glass, paint, paper, and tea brought into the colonies. By passing the Townshend Acts, the British government showed it believed that Parliament still had the authority to make laws for the colonists.

REVIEW What did the Declaration of Rights and Grievances state?

· **GEOGRAPHY** ·

Boston
Understanding Places and Regions

This painting of Boston in 1770 shows the Old State House in the center. At the time it was the headquarters of His Majesty's Custom House. Taxes on trade goods were paid and collected in custom houses located in each port city in the 13 colonies. The Boston Massacre took place just east of the Boston Custom House.

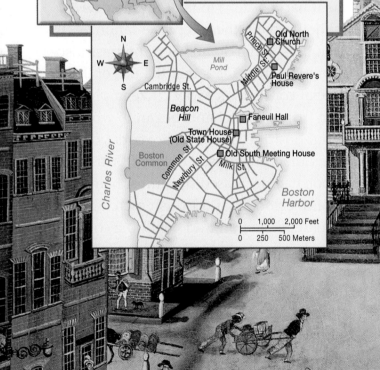

The Boston Massacre

To further show its authority over the colonists, Parliament sent more soldiers to North America. By 1770 there were more than 9,000 British soldiers in the 13 colonies. The British government said that the soldiers were there to protect the western lands won in the French and Indian War. Most of the soldiers, however, were stationed in cities along the Atlantic coast.

Having British soldiers in their cities angered many colonists. They called the soldiers "lobsters," "redcoats," and "bloody-backs," making fun of their bright red uniform jackets. Some soldiers responded to this name-calling by destroying colonial property.

As the anger between the British soldiers and the colonists grew stronger, fights broke out more and more often. Some of the worst fighting took place in Boston on March 5, 1770. In the evening a large crowd gathered near several British soldiers.

Some colonists in the crowd shouted insults at the soldiers and began to throw rocks and snowballs. As the crowd moved forward, the soldiers fired their weapons. Three colonists were killed, and two died later. Among the dead was a former slave named Crispus Attucks (A•tuhks). Many people consider Crispus Attucks the first person to be killed in the struggle for American liberty. **Liberty** means "the freedom of people to make their own laws."

Paul Revere, a Boston silversmith, made an engraving, or picture, showing the soldiers shooting at the colonists. He titled it *The Bloody Massacre*. The word *massacre* (MA•sih•ker) means "the killing

Crispus Attucks was one of the colonists killed at the Boston Massacre.

of a number of people who cannot defend themselves." The shooting in Boston was not really a massacre, but to this day the event is called the Boston Massacre.

REVIEW What was Crispus Attucks's role in the Boston Massacre?

LESSON 3 REVIEW

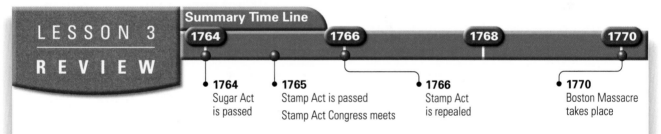

Summary Time Line

| 1764 | 1766 | 1768 | 1770 |

- **1764** Sugar Act is passed
- **1765** Stamp Act is passed / Stamp Act Congress meets
- **1766** Stamp Act is repealed
- **1770** Boston Massacre takes place

1 MAIN IDEA   Why did the new tax laws cause conflict between the colonists and Britain?

2 WHY IT MATTERS   Why do you think the idea of no taxation without representation is still important to people in the United States today?

3 VOCABULARY   Use the terms **representation** and **boycott** to describe the colonists' reaction to the Stamp Act.

4 TIME LINE   How long after the Stamp Act was passed was the law repealed?

5 READING SKILL—Cause and Effect   What caused the Boston Massacre?

6 ECONOMICS   Why did the British Parliament decide to pass new tax laws for the colonies?

7 CRITICAL THINKING—Evaluate   Do you think Parliament had the right to tax the colonists? Why or why not?

PERFORMANCE—Make a Poster
Imagine that you are a colonist. Make a poster that encourages other colonists to boycott British goods. Tell why you think the tax laws are unfair, and give reasons for the boycott.

Determine Point of View

VOCABULARY

point of view
bias

⟩ WHY IT MATTERS

You can get information from many sources—television, radio, newspapers, reference books, and the Internet. Before you use this information, however, you need to decide if you can trust its reliability.

⟩ WHAT YOU NEED TO KNOW

In the study of history, written records and pictures provide important information. They describe or show what happened. Some may show an accurate description from many points of view or from one person's point of view. A person's **point of view** is his or her set of beliefs that have been shaped by factors such as whether that person is old or young, male or female, rich or poor. Some points of view can be supported by fact, but written records and pictures showing a single point of view may bias your thinking. You show **bias** when you favor or oppose someone or something.

To find the point of view in a picture, follow these steps.

Step 1 **Identify who made the picture. Did that person see what happened or know about it only from the accounts of others? What appears to be a firsthand account may not be.**

This engraving by Paul Revere shows his view of the Boston Massacre.

Step 2 Think about the audience. For whom was this picture meant? The picture's audience may have affected what was drawn and how it was drawn.

Step 3 Check for bias. Watch for clues that show a one-sided view.

Step 4 Compare pictures of the same event, when possible. Comparing sources can give you more balanced information and help you identify bias.

▶ **PRACTICE THE SKILL**

Drawing B is based on the Boston Massacre as it was described during the trial of the British soldiers who fired at the colonists. John Adams, a lawyer from Boston, was asked by the British government to defend the British soldiers who were arrested for murder. Adams agreed to defend them because he felt the British soldiers deserved a fair trial. He argued that the soldiers had fired their weapons in self-defense. The jury agreed. It found Captain Thomas Preston and six soldiers not guilty. Two of the soldiers were found guilty of a lesser crime.

Drawing A is the engraving of the event made by Paul Revere, a colonist who worked for colonial rights. During the massacre five colonists were killed.

1 In what ways are the drawings alike? How are they different?

2 Which is more likely based on first-hand information?

3 For whom do you think Drawing A was meant? Explain.

4 Does Drawing A show bias? What details in the picture might show Revere's feeling about the British soldiers?

5 For whom do you think Drawing B was meant? Explain.

▶ **APPLY WHAT YOU LEARNED**

With a partner, preview the pictures in a magazine article. Follow the steps in What You Need to Know to study the pictures more closely. Describe the messages that the pictures convey.

This picture of the Boston Massacre is based on the descriptions given during the trial of the British Soldiers who fired at the colonists.

4

MAIN IDEA
Read to learn what actions the colonists took when Parliament passed more laws for the colonies.

WHY IT MATTERS
The colonists began to work together to find a way to respond to the growing British threat.

VOCABULARY

monopoly
blockade
quarter
intolerable
petition

The Road to War

1750	1770	1790

1773–1775

The three years following the Boston Massacre were fairly quiet in the 13 colonies. Some historians have called this time "the calm before the storm." The storm came when Parliament again angered the colonists by passing more laws.

The Boston Tea Party

In 1770 Parliament repealed all of the Townshend Acts except for the tea tax. Soon after, Parliament tried to give a monopoly on tea to the East India Company, Britain's chief tea producer. A **monopoly** is complete control of a product or service in a certain area by a single person or group. This includes control over pricing and competition.

The East India Company was able to sell tea for much cheaper. Colonial merchants could no longer make money in the tea trade. So some colonists decided to boycott tea.

In Pennsylvania, colonists did not allow ships carrying British tea to enter their ports. In Massachusetts, colonists did not want ships loaded with tea to dock at their ports either,

This painting shows one artist's idea of what happened at the Boston Tea Party. The tea leaves in the bottle on the next page are thought to be from this event.

Samuel Adams 1722–1803

Character Trait: Civic Virtue

Samuel Adams, a cousin of John Adams, helped plan the Boston Tea Party. He believed in the use of violence only when all else failed. Since the days of the Sugar Act in 1764, Adams had attempted to get people to work peacefully for their rights through committees and other meetings. In 1772 he set up a committee of correspondence in Boston. Then he got other colonists to do the same. These committees corresponded with, or wrote letters to, one another. In this way news of what was happening in one colony spread quickly to the others.

 MULTIMEDIA BIOGRAPHIES
Visit The Learning Site at www.harcourtschool.com/biographies to learn about other famous people.

but the governor, Thomas Hutchinson, gave the order to let the ships dock.

On December 16, 1773, colonists took part in what became known as the Boston Tea Party. That night, members of a group known as the Sons of Liberty boarded the ships. Disguised as Mohawk Indians, they broke open 342 tea chests and dumped the tea into the harbor.

REVIEW How did the colonists respond to the East India Company's unfair advantage in the tea trade?

Intolerable Acts

The Sons of Liberty knew that their actions would anger Parliament. After hearing about the Boston Tea Party, Parliament, now led by Lord Frederick North, passed a new series of laws to punish the colonists of Massachusetts.

The first of these laws was the Boston Port Bill, passed in March 1774. It closed the port of Boston until the colonists paid for the destroyed tea. To enforce the law,

TEA THROWN INTO BOSTON HARBOR DEC. 16. 1773.

Parliament ordered the British navy to blockade Boston Harbor. To **blockade** is to use warships to prevent other ships from entering or leaving a port.

Parliament then passed the Massachusetts Government Act. It stopped the Massachusetts legislature from making laws and banned town meetings not authorized by the governor. To further punish the colonists, the British government ordered them to **quarter** British soldiers, or to feed and provide shelter for them. Some colonists even had to take the soldiers into their homes.

In response, the colonists shouted that these laws were "intolerable acts!" The word **intolerable** means "unacceptable." The Intolerable Acts, as the new laws came to be called, led many colonists to recognize that they had a common enemy.

REVIEW What were some of the Intolerable Acts?

The First Continental Congress

Many of the colonists believed that the British government would do anything, even use its army, to make them obey the British laws. So representatives of the colonies decided to meet to discuss ways they might respond to the growing British threat. The first meeting took place in September 1774 at Philadelphia's Carpenters' Hall. Because it was the first of its kind on the North American continent, the meeting was later called the First Continental Congress.

The 56 delegates at the Congress represented the wide range of thought in the colonies. Some wanted to break away from Britain. Others wanted to find a way to get along better with Britain. Following neither extreme, the Congress agreed to develop a statement of rights. The delegates stated these rights in a **petition**, or a signed request, that they sent to Parliament.

In the petition, the Congress said that the colonists had a right to "life, liberty, and property." The Congress also stated that only the colonial legislatures had the authority to make laws "in all cases of taxation and internal polity [government]." The petition concluded by issuing a warning: "We are *for the present* only resolved to pursue . . . peaceable measures."

The Congress set May 10, 1775, as the deadline for

DEMOCRATIC VALUES
The Right to Privacy

One of the rights listed in the English Bill of Rights prevented soldiers and other government officials from entering a person's home without the owner's permission or a warrant, or order, from a court of law. As more and more British soldiers were sent to North America, however, the British government needed more places for them to live. Some colonists' homes were seized by British soldiers. These soldiers went into the people's homes and often lived there without the owner's permission.

Today, the right of privacy remains one of the most valued rights in the United States. According to the rights of United States citizens, in most cases government officials must acquire a warrant from a court of law before they can enter a person's home without permission.

Analyze the Value

❶ Why did the American colonists believe their rights had been ignored by the British soldiers?

❷ **Make It Relevant** Why do you think privacy is an important right for Americans to have?

Parliament to respond to the petition. If Parliament took no action by then, the Congress would meet again. Before ending the meeting, however, the members of the Continental Congress agreed to stop most trade with Britain.

Meanwhile, in Virginia colonial leaders such as Patrick Henry suggested that the colonists begin preparing for war. He told the House of Burgesses, "I know not what course others may take: but as for me, give me liberty or give me death!"

REVIEW Why did the First Continental Congress meet?

Patrick Henry

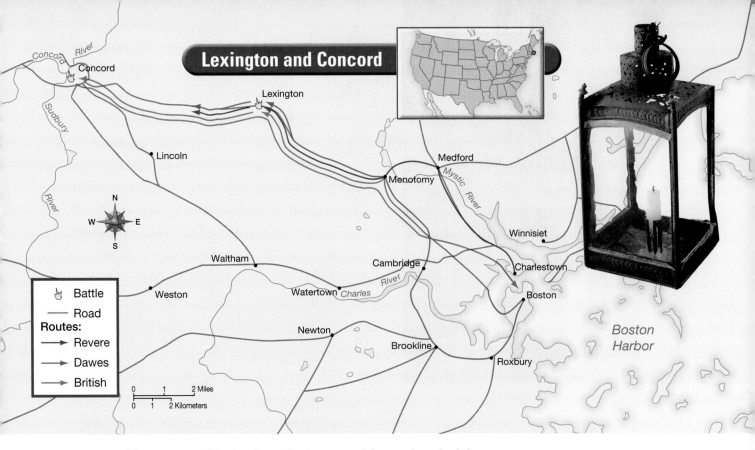

Lexington and Concord

Battle 🔥
Road —
Routes:
→ Revere
→ Dawes
→ British

0   1   2 Miles
0   1   2 Kilometers

Movement The battles at Lexington and Concord marked the beginning of a long war between the 13 colonies and Britain. The lantern (above, right) is one of the two lanterns that were hung in a church tower to signal that the British were coming by boat.

◆ What cities did Revere and Dawes ride through to warn of the British approach?

Lexington and Concord

In Massachusetts the colonists responded to the Intolerable Acts by organizing special militia units. They were called Minutemen because they could be ready in a minute to defend Massachusetts.

In April 1775 General Thomas Gage heard that two leaders of the Sons of Liberty, John Hancock and Samuel Adams, were meeting in the village of Lexington. Gage also heard that the Minutemen were storing weapons in Concord, near Lexington. The general ordered 700 British soldiers to find the weapons and arrest Hancock and Adams.

Learning of the general's order, Paul Revere, a member of the Sons of Liberty, rode his horse to Lexington to warn Hancock and Adams. Revere was joined by William Dawes and Samuel Prescott.

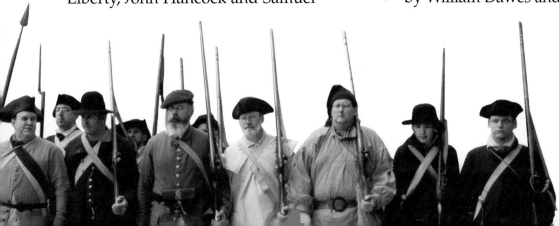

A group of men dressed as Minutemen reenact the battle at Concord at Minute Man National Historical Park in Concord, Massachusetts.

LOCATE IT

Boston

MASSACHUSETTS

This statue of Paul Revere stands near the Old North Church in Boston, Massachusetts.

From Lexington the British marched to Concord. However, the weapons they expected to find had been moved. As they marched back to Boston, the Minutemen fired at the British from the woods and fields beside the road. British losses for the day were 73 killed and 174 wounded. 93 Minutemen were killed or wounded in the fighting.

The fighting at Lexington and Concord marked the beginning of a long, bitter war between Britain and its 13 colonies. To some, it seemed a small battle, but for others it was a world event, a history-making first step in creating the United States of America. The poet Ralph Waldo Emerson would later call the shots fired at Lexington and Concord "the shot heard round the world."

REVIEW Why did the British go to Lexington and Concord?

They each rode off to Concord to warn the Minutemen that the British were on their way. When the British arrived at Lexington on April 19, 1775, they found that the Minutemen were waiting for them. Shots were fired, and eight of the Minutemen were killed. Several others were wounded.

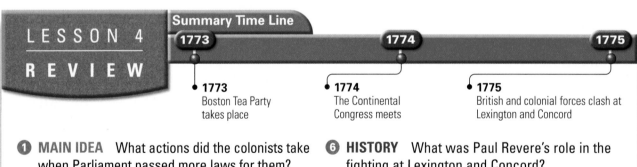

LESSON 4
REVIEW

Summary Time Line

1773 — 1774 — 1775

1773
Boston Tea Party takes place

1774
The Continental Congress meets

1775
British and colonial forces clash at Lexington and Concord

1 **MAIN IDEA** What actions did the colonists take when Parliament passed more laws for them?

2 **WHY IT MATTERS** How did colonists work together to respond to the British Parliament?

3 **VOCABULARY** Use the terms **monopoly** and **blockade** in a paragraph about the Boston Tea Party.

4 **TIME LINE** When was the fighting at Lexington and Concord?

5 **READING SKILL—Cause and Effect** What caused the Boston Tea Party?

6 **HISTORY** What was Paul Revere's role in the fighting at Lexington and Concord?

7 **CRITICAL THINKING—Analyze** Why were the shots fired at Lexington and Concord referred to as "the shot heard round the world"?

PERFORMANCE—Make a Poster Draw a poster that encourages people to join a colonial militia. Use words that you think will convince people to fight for liberty. Share your poster with your classmates.

The Second Continental Congress

1750   1770   1790

1775

MAIN IDEA
As you read, look for ways colonial leaders prepared for war with Britain and fought the first major battle of the Revolutionary War.

WHY IT MATTERS
As the colonies pushed closer to a final break with Britain, more colonists began to think of themselves as Americans instead of as British citizens.

VOCABULARY
commander in chief
earthwork
olive branch
mercenary

N ews of the fighting at Lexington and Concord quickly spread throughout the 13 colonies. As a result, the Second Continental Congress was called to meet in Philadelphia on May 10, 1775. Colonial leaders gathered at the Pennsylvania State House to decide what the colonies should do. Only Georgia failed to send representatives.

Hope for Peace, Plan for War

Once again, delegates were divided in their views, or opinions. Some called for war against the British. Others, such as John Dickinson, tried to persuade the group to avoid fighting. Dickinson believed that the "cause of liberty should not be sullied [soiled] by turbulence and tumult [commotion and uproar]." By June, however, the Congress had agreed that the colonies should at least begin to prepare for war.

The first step was for the Congress to form an army. This new "Continental Army" would have full-time, regular soldiers in addition to the part-time militia that each colony already had. The Continental Army was the first united colonial army. It would become the main army that would be assisted by the state militias.

On June 15, 1775, Congress, at the suggestion of John Adams and others, asked George Washington to lead the new Continental Army. Adams suggested Washington because of his "skill and experience as an officer, . . . great talents and universal character." Adams believed that Washington not only understood soldiers but that he knew how to fight a war.

The Second Continental Congress chose George Washington, shown here in his military uniform, to lead the Continental Army.

The next day Washington humbly accepted the role of **commander in chief**, the leader of all the military forces.

To supply the Continental Army, the Congress asked each colony to contribute money to pay for guns, bullets, food, and uniforms. The Congress also decided to print its own paper money, which came to be known as Continental currency. The Congress paid the soldiers in bills that they called continentals.

By the time George Washington left Philadelphia to take charge of the Continental Army, which was already in Massachusetts, the first major battle of the Revolutionary War had already been fought. The Battle of Bunker Hill took place near Boston on June 17, 1775.

REVIEW How did the Second Continental Congress prepare for war?

The Battle of Bunker Hill

After the fighting at Lexington and Concord, angry citizens in Massachusetts started to build **earthworks**, or walls of earth and stone, near Boston. These earthworks would help the colonists defend themselves if there were another battle with the British soldiers.

Meanwhile, Boston had become the only safe place for the British. The Minutemen had taken control of the surrounding countryside. The only way the British could enter or leave Boston was by sea.

After dark on June 16, 1775, some colonists began to build new earthworks on Breed's Hill, across the Charles River from Boston. When General Gage learned of this the next morning, he ordered British ships in the harbor to open fire on the colonists. Gage also sent General William Howe and 2,400 British soldiers to capture Breed's Hill. Shortly after noon,

Bunker Hill

Breed's Hill

colonial forces

earthworks

lines of British soldiers marched up Breed's Hill to the roll of drums. When the British drew close to the earthworks, the 1,600 colonists inside let loose a deadly hail of shot. The fighting was so fierce that, to save bullets, colonial commander Israel Putnam said to his soldiers,

> 66 **Don't fire until you see the whites of their eyes.** 99

The colonists drove the British back twice before running out of gun powder. The British finally took the hill but at great cost. More than 1,000 of the 2,400 British soldiers were killed or wounded. About 350 colonists died or were wounded.

The battle at Breed's Hill was mis-named for nearby Bunker Hill. Although the colonists were driven from the field, they were proud of how well they had done. The British had learned that fighting the colonists would not be easy.

REVIEW What was the cause of the Battle of Bunker Hill?

A CLOSER LOOK
The Battle of Bunker Hill

The first major battle of the Revolutionary War, the Battle of Bunker Hill, was fought on June 17, 1775. The British won the battle, but they suffered the heaviest losses of the entire war.

❶ British forces first landed near Morton's Point and formed battle lines.

❷ British forces marched up Breed's Hill to attack the colonists.

❸ Colonists fired on the British from behind earthworks on Breed's Hill.

❖ Why do you think the colonists chose to build earthworks on top of Breed's Hill?

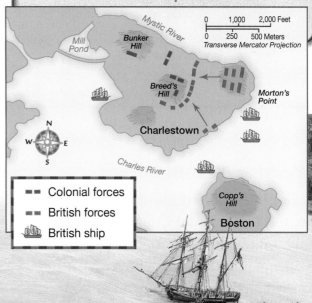

Mystic River

Mill Pond

Bunker Hill

0   1,000   2,000 Feet
0   250   500 Meters
Transverse Mercator Projection

Breed's Hill

Morton's Point

Charlestown

Charles River

- - - Colonial forces
- - - British forces
🚢 British ship

Copp's Hill

Boston

Mystic River

Morton's Point

British ships

main landing site

❶

reinforcements

❷

British forces

295

Phillis Wheatley   1753?–1784

Character Trait: Patriotism

Phillis Wheatley was one of the best-known poets of her time. She was born in Africa and brought to Massachusetts as a slave. Unlike most enslaved people, however, Wheatley learned to read and write. She was later freed upon the death of her owner.

Wheatley's poetry was first published in 1770, while she was still a teenager. In October 1775 Wheatley wrote a poem honoring George Washington on his being named commander in chief of the Continental Army.

"Proceed, great chief, and with virtue on thy side,
Thy ev'ry action let the goddess guide.
A crown, a mansion, and a throne that shine,
With gold unfading, Washington! be thine."

MULTIMEDIA BIOGRAPHIES

Visit The Learning Site at **www.harcourtschool.com/biographies** to learn about other famous people.

A Foreign War

Hoping to avoid more fighting, the Second Continental Congress agreed on July 5, 1775, to send another petition to King George III. This petition came to be known as the Olive Branch Petition because it expressed the colonists' desire for a peaceful end to the fighting. The **olive branch** is an ancient symbol of peace.

In London, the Battle of Bunker Hill had further angered British leaders. Lord North advised King George III to think of the fighting in the colonies as a foreign war. On August 23 the king issued a proclamation of rebellion. In it, he promised to use every measure to crush the rebellion and "bring the traitors to justice." As a result, by the time the Olive Branch Petition reached British leaders in London on August 24, it was already a lost cause.

To fight the colonists, the king called for the British army in the colonies to be enlarged. To accomplish this, he ordered the hiring of mercenaries (MER•suhn•air•eez) from Germany. A **mercenary** is a soldier who serves for pay in the military of a foreign government. Many of the German mercenaries were Hessians, from the Hesse region of Germany.

The king also called on Britain's Iroquois and other Native American allies for help. He knew that many Indian tribes hated the colonists for ignoring the Proclamation of 1763 and settling the lands west of the Appalachians. Because of this the king believed that many Native Americans would help the British fight the colonists.

Meanwhile, the Second Continental Congress also prepared for war. In October the Congress created a navy, which at first was nothing more than a few fishing boats. In November the Congress established a marine corps, or "army of the sea." It also set up a committee to seek alliances with various Native American tribes.

Earlier that fall, in September 1775, Georgia had agreed to join the Second Continental Congress and support the Revolutionary War. Many of the delegates could now agree with what Patrick Henry had told them during the First Continental Congress,

> 66 The distinctions between Virginians, Pennsylvanians, New Yorkers are no more. I am not a Virginian, but an American. 99

Finally, the Continental Congress stood for all 13 colonies.

REVIEW How did the Battle of Bunker Hill change Britain's view of the fight with the colonies?

In addition to their leather boots (right), some German mercenaries also wore bright metal helmets like the one shown here.

LESSON 5 REVIEW

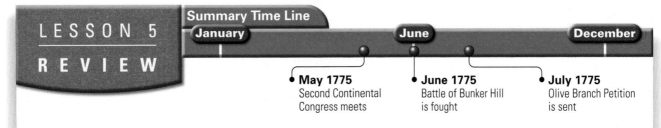

Summary Time Line

January	June	December
May 1775 Second Continental Congress meets	June 1775 Battle of Bunker Hill is fought	July 1775 Olive Branch Petition is sent

1. **MAIN IDEA** How did colonial leaders prepare for war with Britain?

2. **WHY IT MATTERS** How might the colonists' attitudes toward Britain have changed as more began to think of themselves as Americans instead of as British?

3. **VOCABULARY** Write a letter to King George III using the terms **olive branch** and **mercenary**.

4. **TIME LINE** Was the Battle of Bunker Hill fought before or after King George III received the Olive Branch Petition?

5. **READING SKILL—Cause and Effect** What were the causes and effects of the Second Continental Congress?

6. **HISTORY** What was George Washington's role in the Continental Army?

7. **GEOGRAPHY** Where was the Battle of Bunker Hill fought?

8. **CRITICAL THINKING—Hypothesize** What do you think might have happened if the Olive Branch Petition had reached London before King George III issued a proclamation of rebellion?

PERFORMANCE—Write a Diary Entry Write a diary entry from the viewpoint of either a colonist or a British soldier who fought at the Battle of Bunker Hill. Then compare your diary entry to those of classmates.

Review and Test Preparation

Summary Time Line

1750		1755

1754
French and Indian
War begins

Albany Plan of
Union is proposed

USE YOUR READING SKILLS

Complete this graphic organizer to show that you understand the causes and effects of some of the key events that helped unite the colonies. A copy of this graphic organizer appears on page 82 of the Activity Book.

Events Unite the Colonies

Cause	→	Effect

	→	
The British Parliament needs extra money to pay for the French and Indian War.	→	_____ _____
_____ _____	→	**The Boston Tea Party takes place in Boston Harbor in December 1773.**
The British Parliament passes the Intolerable Acts to punish the colonists.	→	_____ _____
_____ _____	→	**The Second Continental Congress is held in Philadelphia in May 1775.**
The Battle of Bunker Hill takes place near Boston on June 17, 1775.	→	_____ _____

THINK & WRITE

Write a Persuasive Letter Think about how the Stamp Act Congress asked all colonists to boycott British goods. Write a letter to a delegate of the congress, explaining why you do or do not support the boycott.

Report a News Event Suppose that you are a newspaper reporter who has been asked to write about the fighting at Lexington and Concord. Write a short newspaper article in which you describe the events of April 19, 1775.

| 1760 | | 1765 | | 1770 | | 1775 | | 1780 |

1763
French and Indian
War ends

1765
Stamp Act
Congress

1770
Boston
Massacre

1773
Boston
Tea Party

1775
Fighting breaks out
at Lexington and Concord

Battle of Bunker Hill

USE THE TIME LINE

Use the chapter summary time line to answer these questions.

1 When did the French and Indian War begin and end?

2 How many years after the Boston Massacre did the Boston Tea Party take place?

USE VOCABULARY

Identify the term that correctly matches each definition.

alliance (p. 270)
budget (p. 280)
boycott (p. 282)
monopoly (p. 288)
mercenary (p. 296)

3 to refuse to buy

4 a soldier who serves for pay in the military of a foreign government

5 a formal agreement among nations, states, groups, or individuals

6 the complete control of a product or service in a certain area by a single person or group

7 a plan for spending money

RECALL FACTS

Answer these questions.

8 The French and Indian War began as a competition for control of what region?

9 How did most colonists react to the Proclamation of 1763?

10 Why was the Wilderness Road important to the pioneers?

Write the letter of the best choice.

11 **TEST PREP**   Colonists were upset about the Stamp Act because—
A they had no representation in Parliament.
B it was the second tax law.
C they had to boycott British goods.
D many had to work as tax collectors.

12 **TEST PREP**   The Second Continental Congress tried to make peace by—
F sending a delegate to Britain.
G sending the Olive Branch Petition.
H uniting the 13 colonies.
J refusing to fight for the British.

THINK CRITICALLY

13 How might history have been different if the Albany Plan of Union had been approved by the colonies?

14 Imagine that you are a colonist. Will you speak out against the Sugar Act, or will you side with the British? Explain.

APPLY SKILLS

Compare Historical Maps

15 Use the maps on page 279 to name the countries that received land that was once claimed by the French.

Determine Point of View

16 In a magazine or newspaper, find a photograph showing a recent event. Tell what the photograph shows, and describe the photographer's point of view.

MORRISTOWN NATIONAL HISTORICAL PARK

During the harsh winter of 1779–1780, no one was sure if the Continental Army would survive to the following spring. That winter in Morristown, New Jersey, George Washington's soldiers suffered many hardships. Many soldiers had to sleep out in the open in the snow until tents arrived and huts were built. Today, visitors can visit the places where these soldiers camped more than 220 years ago.

LOCATE IT

Morristown National Historical Park

NEW JERSEY

The Revolutionary War

66 These are the times that try men's souls. 99

—Thomas Paine, *The American Crisis,* December 23, 1776

CHAPTER READING SKILL

Sequence

A **sequence** is the order in which events occurred.

As you read this chapter, put events about the American Revolution in the correct sequence.

FIRST → NEXT → LAST

MAIN IDEA
Read to learn why the colonists cut ties with the British government and formed their own country.

WHY IT MATTERS
The ideas expressed about freedom in the Declaration of Independence continue to guide Americans today.

VOCABULARY

public opinion
independence
allegiance
resolution
preamble
grievance

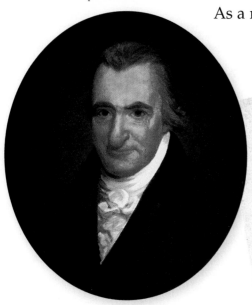

Thomas Paine argued that the colonies should claim their independence.

Independence Is Declared

1776–1781

Although the colonies were already at war with Britain, many Americans still believed that their problems with the king and Parliament could be settled. They hoped the British government would change its view and allow them to take part in making laws. By 1776 that thinking began to change.

Common Sense

One of the people who did the most to change public opinion in the colonies was Thomas Paine. **Public opinion** is the point of view held by most people. In January 1776 Paine published a pamphlet, or short book, titled *Common Sense*.

In his pamphlet Paine questioned the right of any king to rule over anyone. Paine wrote that people should rule themselves, "A government of our own is a natural right." Paine called for a revolution, and he challenged the colonists to cut their ties with the British government.

People in the 13 colonies read and talked about *Common Sense*. As a result, many began to urge **independence**. Having the

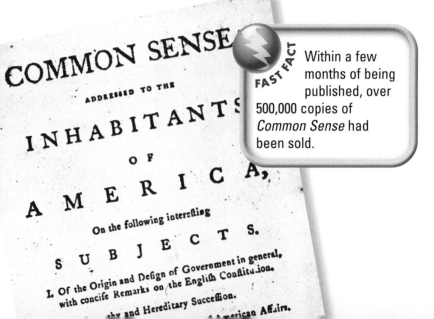

FAST FACT Within a few months of being published, over 500,000 copies of *Common Sense* had been sold.

Thomas Jefferson 1743–1826

Character Trait: Individualism

Thomas Jefferson was a very skilled person. He is best known as the chief writer of the Declaration of Independence and later as the third President of the United States. But Jefferson did many other things in his life. He was an eager reader, an inventor, and a student of mathematics, science, agriculture, and architecture. In 1768 he designed his own house, which he called Monticello. Monticello is near Charlottesville, Virginia.

MULTIMEDIA BIOGRAPHIES
Visit The Learning Site at www.harcourtschool.com/biographies to learn about other famous people.

---

freedom to govern themselves was the only way, they said, to have liberty.

Richard Henry Lee of Virginia gave a speech to the delegates of the Second Continental Congress on June 7, 1776. Lee said that the colonies no longer owed **allegiance** (uh•LEE•juhns), or loyalty, to the king. At the end, he suggested a **resolution**, a formal statement of the feelings of a group about an important topic. This resolution read, "Resolved: That these united colonies are, and of right ought to be, free and independent States."

The Congress debated the resolution for a few days, but not all the colonies were ready to vote for independence. They needed more time before taking such a dangerous action. The Congress decided to wait almost a month before calling for a vote.

REVIEW Why did Richard Henry Lee suggest that the colonies become independent?

Writing the Declaration of Independence

The delegates of the Second Continental Congress hoped that the month's wait would help all 13 colonies decide to vote as one in favor of independence. In the meantime, the Congress chose a committee to write the group's view on independence. The committee consisted of Benjamin Franklin of Pennsylvania, John Adams of Massachusetts, Robert R. Livingston of New York, Roger Sherman of Connecticut, and Thomas Jefferson of Virginia.

Thomas Jefferson was a 33-year-old lawyer. He had studied government and had already written about the colonies' problems with British rule.

Jefferson's travel desk holds the first draft of the Declaration of Independence.

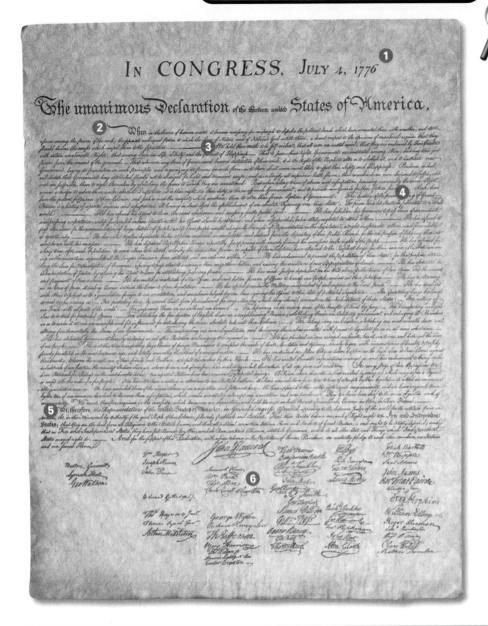

The Declaration of Independence includes the idea that a government gets its power from the consent of the people.

1 date

2 Preamble

3 the statement of rights

4 charges against the king

5 statement of independence

6 signers of Declaration

❖ What was included in the Declaration of Independence?

Two years before, Jefferson had written a pamphlet titled *A Summary View of the Rights of British America*. In it he had listed for the First Continental Congress the changes the colonies wanted in their government.

The members of the writing committee added their ideas, but Jefferson did most of the writing. Every evening for about 17 days, he wrote—and rewrote—what became the Declaration of Independence.

Thomas Jefferson planned the Declaration in several parts. In the **preamble**, the first part or introduction, he stated why the Declaration was needed. He said that sometimes a group of people finds that it has no choice but to form a new nation.

In the second part, he described the colonists' main ideas about government. These words have become some of the most famous in United States history.

> **"** We hold these truths to be self-evident, that all men are created equal, that they are endowed [provided] by their Creator with certain unalienable Rights, that among these are Life, Liberty and the pursuit of Happiness. **"**

In the third and largest part of the Declaration, Jefferson listed the colonists' **grievances**, or complaints, against the British king and Parliament. He also listed the ways the colonists had tried to settle their differences peacefully. In the last part of the Declaration, Jefferson wrote that the colonies were free and independent states.

REVIEW What did Jefferson describe in each part of the Declaration of Independence?

Approving the Declaration

When he finished writing the Declaration of Independence, Thomas Jefferson gave a draft of it to the whole Congress. On June 28, it was read aloud. For several days it was discussed, and changes were made. Then, on July 2, the delegates returned to vote on Richard Henry Lee's resolution to cut ties with Britain. That morning the resolution was approved. The American colonies now considered themselves free and independent states.

On July 4, 1776, the Congress voted to give its final approval for the Declaration. Delegates of only 12 colonies voted. New York's delegates had not yet received the authority to vote.

John Trumbull's painting of the signing of the Declaration of Independence shows the Second Continental Congress in what is today Independence Hall.

On July 8, 1776, the bell on top of Independence Hall called the citizens of Philadelphia to hear the first public reading of the Declaration of Independence. Many of the members of the Second Continental Congress stood and listened, too, as Colonel John Nixon read the document. The joy shown by the crowd so pleased John Adams that he wrote about it in a letter to his wife, Abigail. Independence Day, he said, should be celebrated "from this time forward for evermore."

By August 2, a formal copy of the Declaration of Independence was ready to be signed by members of the Second Continental Congress. The first to sign it was John Hancock, president of the Congress. He said that he wrote his name large enough so that King George could read it without his glasses. The way he signed the document became so famous that the term *John Hancock* now means "a person's signature."

REVIEW How did the people of Philadelphia react to the first reading of the Declaration of Independence?

Forming a New Government

The work of the Second Continental Congress was not completed with the final approval of the Declaration of Independence. John Hancock organized a second committee to report on how to unite the former colonies into a new country. With independence, a new government had to be formed. Congress chose John Dickinson, of Pennsylvania, to

Independence Hall

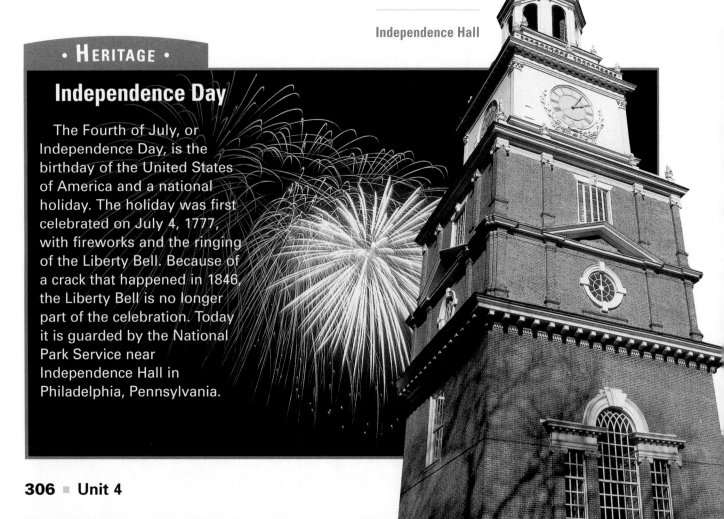

Independence Day

The Fourth of July, or Independence Day, is the birthday of the United States of America and a national holiday. The holiday was first celebrated on July 4, 1777, with fireworks and the ringing of the Liberty Bell. Because of a crack that happened in 1846, the Liberty Bell is no longer part of the celebration. Today it is guarded by the National Park Service near Independence Hall in Philadelphia, Pennsylvania.

head the committee to write the plan of government.

Dickinson's committee decided that the new states—the former colonies—should unite into a confederation. This Confederation of the United States of America would bring together the 13 independent states into "a firm league of friendship."

On July 12, 1776, Dickinson presented his committee's report to the Congress. The delegates discussed it off and on for more than a year. They finally approved the plan on November 15, 1777. The first constitution for the new country was called the Articles of Confederation. But the last state did not

John Dickinson helped write the Articles of Confederation.

approve this plan for a central government until March 1, 1781.

Under the Articles, voters of each state elected leaders. These leaders then chose representatives to a national legislature called the Congress of the Confederation. Each state, whether large or small, had one vote in the new Congress. Under the Articles of Confederation, this Congress served as the government of the United States. For eight years, it made laws for the new nation. It led the states during the last years of the Revolutionary War.

REVIEW What were the Articles of Confederation?

LESSON 1 REVIEW

Summary Time Line

1776 ————————————————— 1781

1776
The Declaration of Independence is approved

1781
Congress approves the Articles of Confederation

1 **MAIN IDEA** Why did many delegates feel that the colonies should cut their ties with Britain?

2 **WHY IT MATTERS** What are some of the ideas listed in the second part of the Declaration of Independence that are still important today?

3 **VOCABULARY** Use the words **preamble** and **grievance** in a letter to a friend about the Declaration of Independence.

4 **TIME LINE** When was the Declaration of Independence approved?

5 **READING SKILL—Sequence** Which was approved first, the Declaration of Independence or the Articles of Confederation?

6 **HISTORY** What was the name of Thomas Paine's pamphlet?

7 **CRITICAL THINKING—Synthesize** Why do you think the Declaration of Independence is still important today?

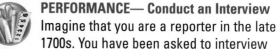

PERFORMANCE— Conduct an Interview Imagine that you are a reporter in the late 1700s. You have been asked to interview someone who attended the first reading of the Declaration of Independence. Write a list of questions you will ask during your interview.

MAIN IDEA
Read to learn why people in the United States had different views about independence.

WHY IT MATTERS
Americans disagreed over whether to support the Americans or the British.

VOCABULARY
Patriot
Loyalist
neutral
pacifist
regiment

Americans and the Revolution

The approval of the Declaration of Independence showed that the colonies had united against Britain. But the colonists themselves were not united. Whether to support independence or to remain loyal to the British king was a difficult decision for many Americans.

Taking Sides

Many people in the 13 colonies supported independence. They called themselves **Patriots**. Others however, remained loyal to the king and called themselves **Loyalists**, or Tories. Friendships, neighborhoods, and families sometimes were torn apart as people chose to take either the Patriot side or the Loyalist side.

The fighting became as much a civil war, or war between people of the same country, as it was a war with the British. In her book *If You Were There in 1776*, author Barbara Brenner describes life at the time of the Revolution. "If you were part of

Thomas Hutchinson was a governor of the Massachusetts Colony and a Loyalist.

A British flag

a Patriot family, you might have been one of the children throwing garbage or stones at the British soldiers. If your family supported the king, you could have been on the receiving end of some serious violence. Your home might have been broken into. Someone you know who was a Tory [Loyalist] could have been tarred and feathered, or ridden on a rail."

Some colonists, however, chose to be **neutral** (NOO•truhl). They took neither side. Those who were neutral were willing to accept whatever the outcome of the war would be.

REVIEW How did colonists view the decision to declare independence from Britain?

Churches and the War

Like other colonists, people in churches were divided on whether they supported the Patriots or the Loyalists or remained neutral. John Peter Muhlenberg, a young Lutheran minister, told his followers in a sermon, "There is a time to pray and a time to fight." Then, before their eyes, he tore off his church robes to show that he was wearing the uniform of a Patriot militia officer. His father, the colonies' Lutheran leader, was shocked. He himself was a Loyalist. The Lutherans, like the people of other church groups, were divided between Patriots and Loyalists.

Taking sides was especially hard for Anglican Church members. The British king was the head of the Anglican Church, as the Church of England was called in the colonies. Many Anglicans in the New England and Middle Atlantic Colonies were loyal to the king. Many of those in the Southern Colonies worked for independence.

Most Congregationalists, members of the largest church group in the New England Colonies, worked for independence. So, too, did many Baptists and northern Presbyterians. Many southern Presbyterians, however, were Loyalists.

Members of the Society of Friends, also called Quakers, would not fight at all.

John Peter Muhlenberg was a Patriot militia officer.

An early United States flag

Quakers are against all wars because they believe that fighting for any reason is wrong. These **pacifists**, or believers in peaceful settlement of disagreements, wrote pamphlets calling for an end to the war.

> **REVIEW** Why was taking sides especially hard for members of the Anglican Church?

African Americans, Free and Enslaved

At the start of the war, 1 out of every 5 people living in the 13 British colonies was of African descent. Most of these people lived in the Southern Colonies as slaves. African Americans everywhere in the colonies, however, viewed the Declaration of Independence with hope and excitement. It had, after all, stated that "all men are created equal."

Free African Americans were as quick to take sides as many of their white neighbors. Peter Salem was among at least five African Americans who fought at Concord as a Minuteman. A few weeks later he and other African Americans, some free and some enslaved, fought at the Battle of Bunker Hill. About 5,000 African Americans fought in the Continental Army.

Enslaved African Americans who joined the Continental Army were promised freedom after the war as a reward for their service. Many were so filled with the idea of freedom, or liberty, that they changed their names. Among the names listed in Continental Army records are Cuff Freedom, Dick Freedom, Ned Freedom, Peter Freedom, Cuff Liberty, and Pomp Liberty.

In November 1775 the royal governor of Virginia also had promised freedom to enslaved African Americans if they ran away from their owners and fought for the British. As a result, he raised a regiment of more than 300 African American soldiers. A **regiment** is a large, organized group of soldiers. These soldiers wore uniforms that had patches reading *Liberty to Slaves*.

> **REVIEW** What promise caused some enslaved African Americans to take sides in the war?

As a young man James Armistead (right) spied on the British army. This proclamation (far right), issued in Virginia, promised freedom to all enslaved people who joined the British army.

Mercy Otis Warren

Sarah Franklin Bache

Abigail Adams

Martha Washington

Women and the War

Many women in the colonies took part in the Patriots' war effort. Some ran farms and businesses. Others formed groups to raise money for the war and to collect clothing for the soldiers. Esther Reed started the Philadelphia Association in 1780 to help the Continental Army. When Reed died, Sarah Franklin Bache (BAYCH), Benjamin Franklin's daughter, took over the Association.

Hundreds of women took part in the fighting. These women, often with children, followed their husbands from battle to battle. In army camps they cooked food and washed clothes. Some nursed the sick and wounded. On the battlefield, women carried water to the soldiers. Others served as spies or messengers.

Some women used their talents to support the Patriot cause. Mercy Otis Warren wrote poems and plays. In her plays Warren often wrote about women heroes in the struggle for freedom in other countries. Later, she wrote a history of the American Revolution, the first by a woman.

Not all women were Patriots, however. There were Loyalist women in every colony. Some of them fought for the British. Many others gave the British food and other supplies.

REVIEW How did women on both sides take part in the war?

People in the Western Lands

Despite the Proclamation of 1763, settlers had continued to move onto the land King George III had reserved for Native Americans. Some Indian groups grew angry about these settlers, but many came to depend on both the Americans and the British as trading partners. The Patriots and the British each hoped that the Indians would take their side or, if not, stay out of the fighting.

Most of the Native American groups had decided to stay out of the fighting.

Thayendanegea, (Joseph Brant)
1742–1807

Character Trait: Self-discipline

Thayendanegea was born in what is now Ohio and as a young man became a friend of British General William Johnson. As a result of that friendship, Thayendanegea attended school in Connecticut, where he became a Christian and took the name Joseph Brant. Until the war Brant had been a missionary in the Ohio Valley. After the war he continued his missionary work among the Native Americans of Canada.

MULTIMEDIA BIOGRAPHIES
Visit The Learning Site www.harcourtschool.com/
biographies to learn about other famous people.

The loyalties of others, however, were divided, just as they had been during the French and Indian War. Some Iroquois, such as the Mohawk leader Thayendanegea (thay•en•da•NEG•ah), known as Joseph Brant, fought for the British. Others fought for the Patriots.

At first, most Americans on the frontier remained neutral. They wanted to be free of any government—British or American.

After a while their feeling began to change. Although they did not support the Patriot cause, they did want to drive the British out of the western lands. They felt that if they did not help the Patriots drive out the British, the British would probably keep the western lands even if the Americans won the war.

REVIEW **Why did many settlers in the western lands decide to help the Patriots?**

LESSON 2
REVIEW

1 **MAIN IDEA** Why did Americans have different views about independence?

2 **WHY IT MATTERS** Why do some people refer to the American Revolution as a civil war?

3 **VOCABULARY** What was the difference between a **Patriot** and a **Loyalist**?

4 **READING SKILL—Sequence** Were enslaved African Americans given their freedom when they joined the Continental Army or after the war?

5 **HISTORY** Which side did most of the Native American groups support?

6 **GEOGRAPHY** Which side did most of the Americans living on the frontier support?

7 **CRITICAL THINKING—Hypothesize** How might the war have been different if all Americans had supported the same side?

PERFORMANCE— Write a Dialogue
Write a dialogue that might have taken place between a Patriot and a Loyalist. Be sure to include what their viewpoints on independence might have been. Share this dialogue with a classmate.

Make a Decision

VOCABULARY

consequence

⬛ WHY IT MATTERS

At the time of the Revolutionary War, colonists had to make many difficult decisions. These decisions often had lasting consequences. A **consequence** is what happens because of an action. The decisions you make can have good or bad consequences. To make a thoughtful decision, you need to think about the consequences before you act.

⬛ WHAT YOU NEED TO KNOW

Here are some steps you can use to help you make a thoughtful decision.

Step 1 **Know that you have to make a decision.**

Step 2 **Gather information.**

Step 3 **Identify choices.**

Step 4 **Predict consequences and weigh those consequences.**

Step 5 **Make a choice and take action.**

⬛ PRACTICE THE SKILL

Imagine that you are living in one of the 13 colonies at the time of the American Revolution. You have to decide whether to join the Patriots, join the Loyalists, or stay neutral. Make thoughtful decisions based on the roles described below. Explain the steps you followed in making each decision.

1 Your family owns a plantation in North Carolina.

2 You are a merchant in Boston.

3 You are a minister in Pennsylvania.

4 You are a settler on the frontier.

⬛ APPLY WHAT YOU LEARNED

Think about a decision you made at school this week. What steps did you follow? What choices did you have? What were the consequences of your choices? Do you think your decision was a thoughtful one? Explain.

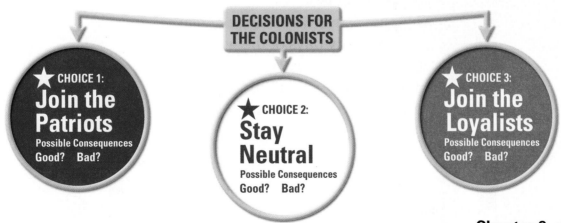

DECISIONS FOR THE COLONISTS

★ CHOICE 1:
Join the Patriots
Possible Consequences
Good?   Bad?

★ CHOICE 2:
Stay Neutral
Possible Consequences
Good?   Bad?

★ CHOICE 3:
Join the Loyalists
Possible Consequences
Good?   Bad?

MAIN IDEA
Read to learn how the Continental Army overcame great obstacles to turn the war in its favor.

WHY IT MATTERS
The Continental Army won a battle that prompted other countries to send soldiers and supplies.

VOCABULARY
enlist
turning point

Fighting the Revolutionary War

1750   1770   1790

1775–1778

George Washington arrived in Massachusetts to meet the Continental Army in July 1775, less than three weeks after the Battle of Bunker Hill. The 14,500 soldiers wore no uniforms—only their everyday clothes. Many had no guns, so they carried spears and axes. With little money and not much training, the Continental Army went to war against one of the most powerful armies in the world, the British army.

Comparing Armies

The soldiers who stood before George Washington that summer day in 1775 had never fought as an army before. Some of them had fought in the French and Indian War, but most had no military experience. Washington quickly had to make rules for the soldiers and get them trained to fight against the British.

Unlike the Continental Army, the British army was made up of professional soldiers. They had the best training and the most experienced officers. But the British had problems, too. It was difficult to fight a war more than 3,000 miles (4,828 km) from home. They often had trouble delivering soldiers and supplies across the Atlantic Ocean.

In the early days of the war, the British army's greater numbers gave it an advantage over the Continental Army. The British had more than

Many soldiers in the Continental Army (left) faced shortages of food and other supplies. British soldiers (right) had plenty of supplies.

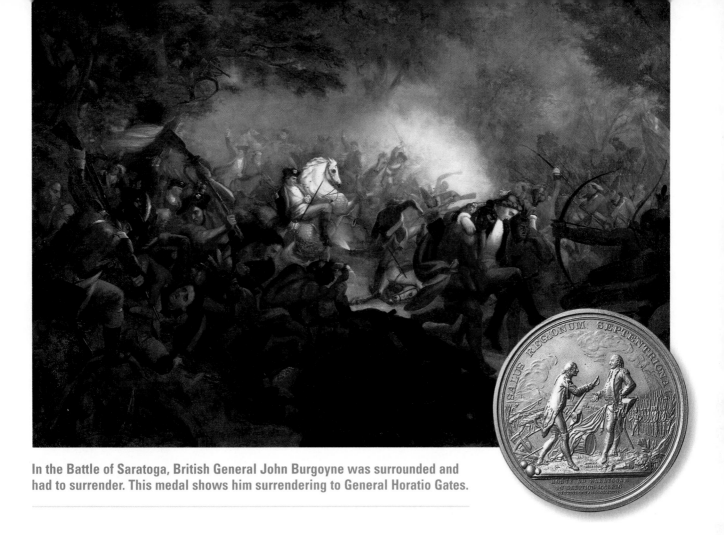

In the Battle of Saratoga, British General John Burgoyne was surrounded and had to surrender. This medal shows him surrendering to General Horatio Gates.

50,000 soldiers in the colonies. General Washington usually had no more than 15,000 soldiers in his army.

REVIEW How was the British army different from the Continental Army?

The War in the North

By the spring of 1776, Washington and his ragged army had moved south from Massachusetts to New York. By the fall the British had defeated the Americans in several battles, including the Battle of Long Island. Now the British were chasing Washington and what was left of the Continental Army.

Most of the Americans **enlisted** in, or joined, the army for almost one year at a time. They might stay that long or longer, or they might not. At harvesttime, some of the Continentals went home to their farms. Washington and the Continentals who stayed with him did their best to keep moving to avoid capture by the British. By winter they had marched through New Jersey to Pennsylvania.

Most of the British army had been sent back to New York for the winter. When Washington learned that the Hessian mercenaries stationed at Trenton, New Jersey, were not prepared for an attack, he decided to move against them. On Christmas Day 1776, Washington and his army crossed the ice-choked Delaware River in boats. By night in freezing weather, the shivering soldiers silently marched toward Trenton. At daybreak the Americans made a surprise attack. More than 900 Hessians were taken as prisoners.

William B. T. Trego's painting *The March to Valley Forge* shows the hardships Washington (on white horse) and his army faced. This knapsack (right) was carried by one of the soldiers at Valley Forge.

The new year brought more good news for Washington and his army. The best news came in October 1777 with an American victory at Saratoga in New York. There the Americans defeated a British army of more than 5,000 soldiers led by British General John Burgoyne (ber•GOYN). The British plan had called for Burgoyne to move south from Canada, while British General William Howe moved north from Philadelphia. The two armies were to cut the colonies in two. Instead, Howe failed to support Burgoyne, and the British had one of their worst defeats of the war. On October 17, 1777, Burgoyne surrendered his entire army to American General Horatio Gates.

Patriots everywhere were overjoyed at the news. The Battle of Saratoga became a turning point in the war. A **turning point** is a single event that causes important and dramatic change.

REVIEW **When was the Battle of Saratoga fought?**

Winter at Valley Forge

The Continental Army was encouraged by its victory at Saratoga. But it still faced hardships. In December 1777, General Washington set up headquarters at Valley Forge, Pennsylvania, near Philadelphia. That winter his ragtag Continental Army was almost destroyed by cold and hunger. Many men were ill, and many died.

In these hard times a German soldier named Friedrich von Steuben (vahn SHTOY•buhn) reported to Washington at Valley Forge. Von Steuben was one of many soldiers from other countries who believed in the Patriots' cause and helped them. Two Polish officers, Casimir Pulaski (puh•LAS•kee) and Thaddeus Kosciuszko (kawsh•CHUSH•koh), and the 20-year-old Marquis de Lafayette (lah•fee•ET) from France also supported the Patriots. Washington liked the young Lafayette and immediately gave him important duties.

At Valley Forge, von Steuben's job was to organize and drill the Continental Army so that it could move quickly on command. This would allow it to attack and retreat faster. Von Steuben also taught the American soldiers how to use bayonets. A bayonet is a knifelike weapon attached to a rifle. Bayonets were standard equipment for European soldiers. By the spring of 1778, Washington's soldiers were marching well.

REVIEW Who came to offer help to the Continental Army?

The Marquis de Lafayette, a French noble, was eager to help the Continental Army.

Help from Other Countries

While the Continental Army was suffering the harsh, cold winter at Valley Forge, Benjamin Franklin was working in Paris, France. Franklin was there to ask the French leaders to join the war.

• BIOGRAPHY •

Haym Salomon   1740–1785
Character Trait: Loyalty

Haym Salomon was a banker who worked for the cause of American freedom. Born in Poland, he came to New York in 1772. When the British captured the city, he stayed there and spied for the Patriots. In 1778 he fled the city with his wife and child and went into business as a banker in Philadelphia. Salomon worked to get money to pay for the Revolution.

MULTIMEDIA BIOGRAPHIES
Visit The Learning Site at **www.harcourtschool.com/biographies** to learn about other famous people.

The French wanted the Americans to win the war and weaken their longtime rival, the British. The French, however, felt that the Americans did not have much chance of winning.

Franklin talked with the French leaders for months without success. Then news of the Americans' victory at Saratoga reached France. This victory showed the French that the Americans now stood a chance of winning the war. As a result, the French sent supplies and soldiers to help the Patriots. After the victory at Saratoga, people from other places helped the Americans, too. Bernardo de Gálvez (GAHL•ves), the governor of Spanish Louisiana, sent guns, food, and money. Later, he led his own soldiers in capturing several British forts. Spanish-born Jorge Farragut (FAIR•uh•guht) fought in the Continental Army and also in the navy.

REVIEW **Why did the French decide to help the Patriots?**

Mary Ludwig Hays McCauley is shown loading a cannon at the Battle of Monmouth.

American Heroes

During the war the Americans cheered as they heard news about the deeds of many brave people from all over the United States. Their acts of courage helped make Americans sure that they could win the war.

In the mountains of the Northeast, Ethan Allen led the Green Mountain Boys. Allen and his soldiers from what is now Vermont won one of the first American victories in the war. They captured Fort Ticonderoga in New York.

When General George Washington asked for volunteers to spy on the British in New York City, a young man named Nathan Hale from Connecticut came forward. Dressed as a Dutch schoolteacher, Hale obtained the information Washington needed. As he returned to the American side, the British captured him. According to legend, Hale told the British soldiers before they hanged him, "I only regret that I have but one life to lose for my country."

In the Ohio Valley, George Rogers Clark helped protect the frontier lands claimed by many American settlers as theirs. Leading a small army, he marched through the western lands, defending settlers from attacks by the British and their Indian allies.

From bases in the swamps of South Carolina, Francis Marion led daring raids against the British. The British called him the Swamp Fox because they could never catch

This statue of Nathan Hale was built in 1914 to honor him.

NATHAN HALE
1755–1776
CLASS OF 1773

him and his soldiers. At sea John Paul Jones, a navy commander, battled larger and better-equipped British ships. In one famous battle in the North Sea near Britain, the British asked Jones to surrender. He replied, "I have not yet begun to fight." Jones kept fighting until the British ship gave up.

Many women also won fame for their bravery during the war. Mary Slocomb joined her husband at the Battle of Moores Creek Bridge in 1776. Mary Ludwig Hays McCauley earned the name Molly Pitcher by carrying water to the troops during the Battle of Monmouth in New Jersey in 1778. When her husband was wounded, she took his place firing the cannons.

REVIEW Who defended settlers in the western lands?

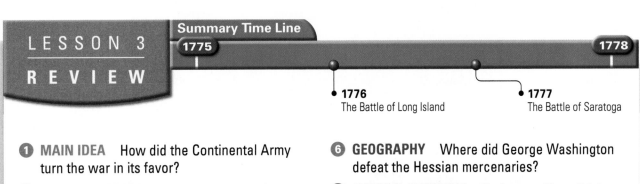

LESSON 3
REVIEW

Summary Time Line

1775

1776
The Battle of Long Island

1777
The Battle of Saratoga

1778

① **MAIN IDEA** How did the Continental Army turn the war in its favor?

② **WHY IT MATTERS** What other countries gave help to the Patriots?

③ **VOCABULARY** Write a paragraph describing the **turning point** of the war.

④ **TIME LINE** When did the British suffer one of their worst defeats of the war?

⑤ **READING SKILL—Sequence** Which battle was fought first, Saratoga or Long Island?

⑥ **GEOGRAPHY** Where did George Washington defeat the Hessian mercenaries?

⑦ **CRITICAL THINKING—Evaluate** How did the military training of the Continental soldiers affect the war?

 PERFORMANCE—Write a Song Write a song about some of the heroes of the American Revolution. Share your song with the class.

Washington's Mess Chest

During much of the Revolutionary War, George Washington and his troops lived in tents or other shelters. To prepare and eat his meals, Washington used this camp kitchen, or mess chest. It was equipped with all the pots, pans, and utensils he needed.

**FROM THE SMITHSONIAN INSTITUTION
NATIONAL MUSEUM OF AMERICAN HISTORY**

Glass storage jars used for storing water or tonics

Kettles used for heating food on the gridiron over an open flame

Kettles stacked inside each other to save space

One of three tin platters used for preparing and serving meals

Lift-out storage bins used for storing dry goods such as breads, flour, or grain

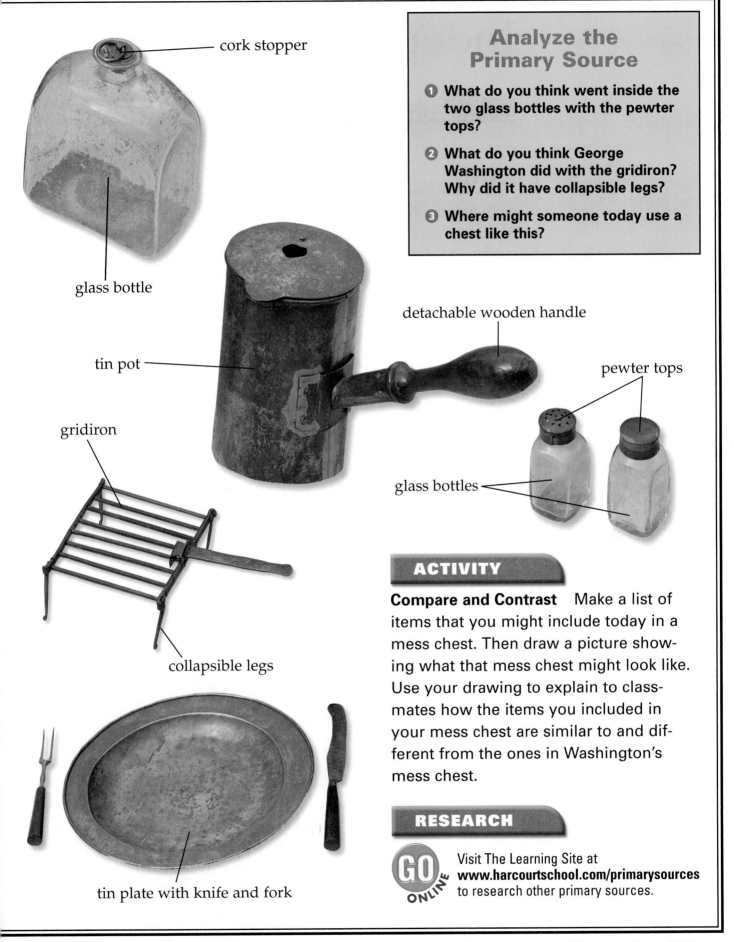

cork stopper

glass bottle

tin pot

gridiron

collapsible legs

tin plate with knife and fork

detachable wooden handle

pewter tops

glass bottles

Analyze the Primary Source

❶ What do you think went inside the two glass bottles with the pewter tops?

❷ What do you think George Washington did with the gridiron? Why did it have collapsible legs?

❸ Where might someone today use a chest like this?

ACTIVITY

Compare and Contrast Make a list of items that you might include today in a mess chest. Then draw a picture showing what that mess chest might look like. Use your drawing to explain to classmates how the items you included in your mess chest are similar to and different from the ones in Washington's mess chest.

RESEARCH

GO ONLINE Visit The Learning Site at **www.harcourtschool.com/primarysources** to research other primary sources.

4

MAIN IDEA

Read to learn how the Americans finally won their independence.

WHY IT MATTERS

The United States became the first country in the history of the world to overthrow a monarchy and establish a democracy.

VOCABULARY

traitor

negotiate

principle

Independence Is Won

1750   1770   1790

1778–1783

When the British government learned that the French were helping the Americans, British army leaders shifted the fighting. The British had already captured important cities in the North—Boston, Philadelphia, and New York. They hoped now to defeat the Patriots once and for all. So they concentrated on the South, where there was greater Loyalist support.

The War in the South

In 1778 the British captured Savannah, Georgia. In 1780, they captured the city of Charles Town, later known as Charleston, in South Carolina. From there, they attacked and defeated the Americans at Camden, also in South Carolina. This victory gave the British new hope of quickly defeating the Continental Army and winning the war.

As the British tried to stamp out the fire of independence in one place, they found that it only sprang up in another place. "We fight, get beat, rise, and fight again," General Nathanael Greene wrote. Greene commanded the Continental Army in the Southern Colonies. Under Greene's leadership General Daniel Morgan won the battle at Cowpens, South Carolina, in 1781.

The battle at Cowpens, South Carolina, was a major victory for the Americans. This photograph shows what the battlefield looks like today.

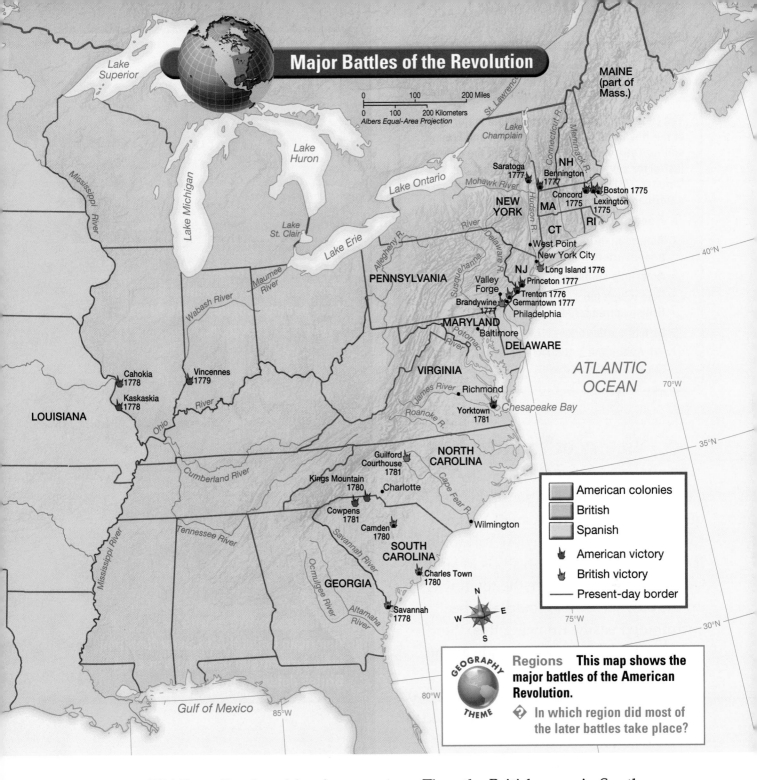

Major Battles of the Revolution

0   100   200 Miles
0 100   200 Kilometers
Albers Equal-Area Projection

American colonies
British
Spanish
🔥 **American victory**
🔥 **British victory**
— **Present-day border**

Regions This map shows the major battles of the American Revolution.

❖ In which region did most of the later battles take place?

Early in 1781 Benedict Arnold, a former Continental Army officer, led the British army's attacks on Virginia towns. Arnold was a **traitor**, or someone who acts against his or her country. Earlier, he had given the British the plans to the American fort at West Point, New York, in exchange for money and a high rank in the British army.

Then the British army in South Carolina pushed into North Carolina. There, in March 1781, the Americans suffered a terrible defeat at Guilford Courthouse. The British, however, still could not win the war, because no one city or town was the heart of America.

REVIEW What battle gave the British hope of winning the war?

French Blockade
The French navy prevented British ships from getting supplies to the British soldiers at Yorktown.

Fighting in the Trenches
American Colonel Alexander Hamilton led a large group of soldiers against British defenses at Yorktown.

Victory at Yorktown

By late summer of 1781, British General Charles Cornwallis had set up his headquarters at Yorktown, a small Virginia town on Chesapeake Bay. At Yorktown, it was easy for the British ships to land supplies. However, since the town was on the bay, the British could also be surrounded easily. Knowing this, the French and the Americans made a plan to defeat Cornwallis at Yorktown.

The French army joined the Continental Army near New York City and marched south to Virginia in order to surround Yorktown. At the same time, the French navy took control of Chesapeake Bay. Now the British navy could not get supplies to the British army or leave the area. Cornwallis was trapped.

In late September, Cornwallis sent word to his commander in the North. "If you cannot relieve me very soon," he said, "you must be prepared to hear the worst."

Scuttled Ships

Cornwallis ordered his troops to scuttle, or sink, his own ships to block the French navy from attacking Yorktown.

The painting by John Trumbull shows the British surrender at Yorktown. George Washington is shown in front of the American flag.

The worst happened. Surrounded and under attack for weeks from both land and sea, Cornwallis surrendered. A person who was there wrote, "At two o'clock in the evening Oct. 19th, 1781, the British army, led by General Charles O'Hara, marched out of its lines, with colors cased [flags folded] and drums beating a British march." When the French and American soldiers heard the drums, they stopped their fire. The British soldiers then marched out of Yorktown and laid down their weapons.

In Yorktown a British military band reportedly played a popular tune of the time. It was fittingly called "The World Turned Upside Down." When news of the surrender at Yorktown reached

The drum was used in the Battle of Yorktown.

Philadelphia, the Liberty Bell rang out the news of the American victory.

Though fighting dragged on in some places for more than two years, it was clear that the war had been decided at Yorktown in 1781. The Patriots had won after a long, hard fight.

REVIEW **What problem did the British face at Yorktown?**

The Treaty of Paris

The Battle of Yorktown did not officially end the war. The Treaty of Paris did that. Work on the treaty began in April 1782, when the British and Americans sent representatives to Paris.

There the representatives stated the American terms— that is, what the Americans wanted in the treaty. They wanted the British king and Parliament to accept American independence and to remove all British soldiers from American soil. They also asked that the British pay the Americans whose property had been destroyed in the war.

The British, in turn, asked that Loyalists who chose to remain in the United States be treated fairly. Many Loyalists had fled to Nova Scotia and other parts of Canada and to the Bahamas. Some returned to Britain but were sorry they did. Most of them could not find jobs and soon became very poor. The British government ignored them.

British and American representatives **negotiated**, or talked with one another to work out an agreement. After more than a year of such talks, the representatives signed the Treaty of Paris on September 3, 1783.

The Treaty of Paris officially named the United States of America as a new coun-try and described its borders. The United States reached to Florida on the south. The northern border would be an imaginary line through the Great Lakes. The Mississippi River formed its western border. The Treaty of Paris was just as much a victory as winning at Yorktown had been. Independence was now a fact.

REVIEW What were the American terms of the Treaty of Paris?

Washington's Farewell

Soon after the Treaty of Paris was signed, General Washington and his offi-cers had made their headquarters in New York City. Though joyful about their vic-tory, the American military leaders were sad to say good-bye to one another after the long war.

In early December 1783, Washington and his officers met at Fraunces Tavern in New York City for a farewell dinner.

This painting by Benjamin West shows—from left to right—John Jay, John Adams, and Benjamin Franklin negotiating a peace agreement with British representatives in Paris. The negotiations led to the signing of the Treaty of Paris.

At a meeting of Congress in Annapolis, Maryland, George Washington resigns from his position as commander in chief of the Continental Army.

Near the end of the meal, Washington stood up. "With a heart full of love and gratitude, I now take my leave of you," he said. One by one, each man at the dinner went up to say good-bye to the general. Tears streaming down his cheeks, Washington hugged each one. "Such a scene of sorrow and weeping I have never before seen," wrote one of the officers.

After saying his farewells, Washington started home to Virginia. On the way he stopped in Annapolis, Maryland, where Congress was then meeting. He told the representatives that, with peace, his work was done. "Having now finished the work assigned me, I retire from the great theater of action," Washington said. He was leaving public service forever, he thought.

REVIEW Why did Washington think his work was done?

Effects of the War

Wars cause change, and the Revolutionary War was no different. The American states were no longer a source of raw materials and agricultural produce just for Britain, as they had been in colonial times. Dutch, French, Spanish, and Portuguese trading ships soon began leaving American ports loaded with American goods.

After the end of the war, more Americans moved west. From Philadelphia one person wrote, "I can scarcely walk a square without meeting [someone] . . . whose destination is principally [mainly] Ohio and Indiana." Many predicted that by the 1800s most of the people in the United States would be living in the West, which at the time was the region between the Appalachian

Mountains and the Mississippi River. Land companies were organized to sell the new lands.

To help defend the new nation's far-reaching borders, leaders later established a regular, full-time army. Since that time a regular army has been added to by the National Guard or the Reserves. To provide leaders for the military, the government established schools to train officers. On July 4, 1802, the United States Military Academy opened at West Point, New York. In 1845 the Naval School, later the United States Naval Academy, opened at Annapolis, Maryland.

The Revolutionary War was not just another war. It was a milestone in human history. The American Revolution became a model for later revolutions, including those in South America. "Government by the consent of the governed" became a guiding principle. A **principle** is a rule that is used in deciding how to act.

REVIEW What effect did the Revolutionary War have on the American economy?

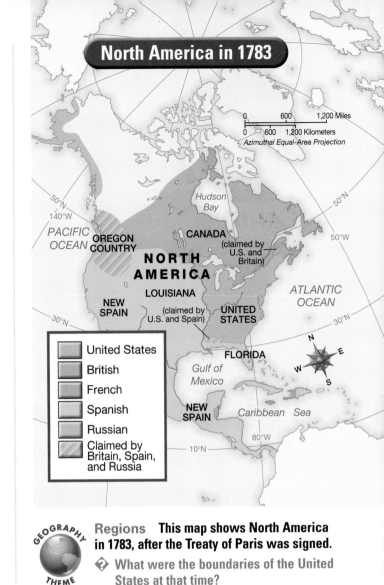

North America in 1783

Regions This map shows North America in 1783, after the Treaty of Paris was signed.

❓ What were the boundaries of the United States at that time?

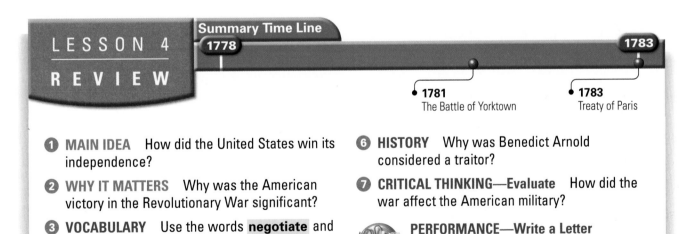

LESSON 4 REVIEW

Summary Time Line

1778

1781 — The Battle of Yorktown

1783 — Treaty of Paris

1783

❶ **MAIN IDEA** How did the United States win its independence?

❷ **WHY IT MATTERS** Why was the American victory in the Revolutionary War significant?

❸ **VOCABULARY** Use the words **negotiate** and **principle** in a sentence about independence.

❹ **TIME LINE** When was the Treaty of Paris signed?

❺ **READING SKILL—Sequence** What battle prompted General Cornwallis to surrender his troops?

❻ **HISTORY** Why was Benedict Arnold considered a traitor?

❼ **CRITICAL THINKING—Evaluate** How did the war affect the American military?

PERFORMANCE—Write a Letter
Imagine that you are an American in 1782. Write a letter to Benjamin Franklin in Paris describing what you think the terms of the Treaty of Paris should be. Share your letter with a classmate.

· SKILLS · CHART AND GRAPH

Compare Graphs

▶ WHY IT MATTERS

Suppose you want to prepare a report on trade during the American Revolution. You want to show a lot of information in a brief, clear way. One way you might do this is by making graphs. Knowing how to read and make different kinds of graphs can help you compare large amounts of information.

▶ WHAT YOU NEED TO KNOW

Different kinds of graphs show information in different ways. A bar graph uses bars and is especially useful for quick comparisons. The bar graph on page 331 shows the chief exports of the United States in 1790. A circle graph can help you make comparisons. The circle graph on page 331 shows the main trading partners of the United States in 1790. A line graph shows change over time. The line graph shows that the amount of goods the Americans exported changed over time.

This map of the world was drawn in the mid-1700s. The exchange table (bottom) was used to compare the values of the many kinds of money that were used in the American colonies.

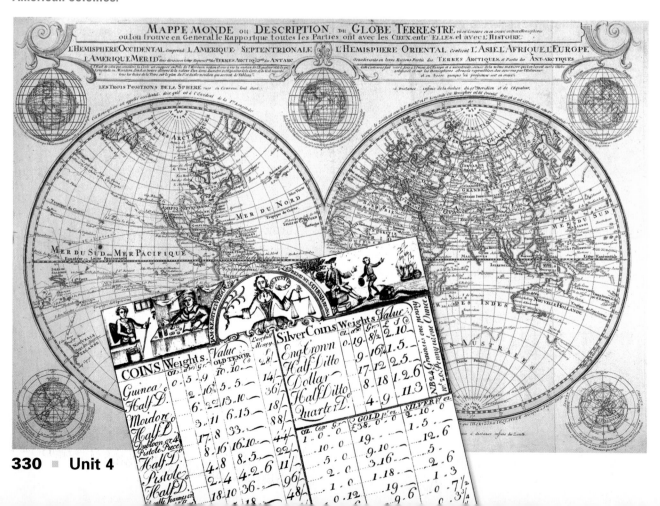

Compare the information in the bar, circle, and line graphs by answering the following questions. Think about the advantages and disadvantages of each kind of graph.

1 Look at the circle graph. Who were the main trading partners of the United States?

2 Who did the United States export most of its goods to?

3 Did the United States export more goods to Spain or to Portugal?

4 Look at the bar graph. What did the United States export?

5 Did the United States export more corn or more wheat?

6 How much lumber did the United States export?

7 Look at the line graph. How did the amount of exports to Britain change over time?

8 Why do you think the amount of exports to Britain changed over time?

► APPLY WHAT YOU LEARNED

Use the graphs on this page to write a paragraph summarizing information about trade during the late 1700s. Share your paragraph with a partner, and compare your summaries.

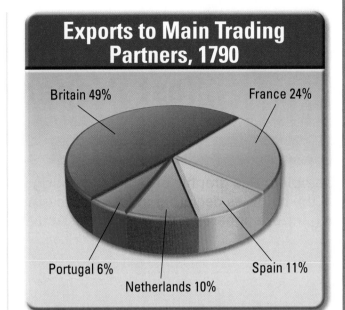

Exports to Main Trading Partners, 1790

Britain 49% France 24% Spain 11% Netherlands 10% Portugal 6%

Chief U.S. Exports, 1790

Value (in Dollars): Corn, Fish, Flour, Indigo, Lumber, Rice, Tobacco, Wheat

Products

U.S. Exports to Britain, 1760–1790

Value (in British Pounds)

Year: 1760, 1770, 1780, 1790

Summary Time Line
1775

1776
Independence
from the British
is declared

1777
The Battle
of Saratoga

USE YOUR READING SKILLS

Complete this graphic organizer by filling in the events that led to the colonies declaring independence. A copy of this graphic organizer appears on page 92 of the Activity Book.

Independence is Declared

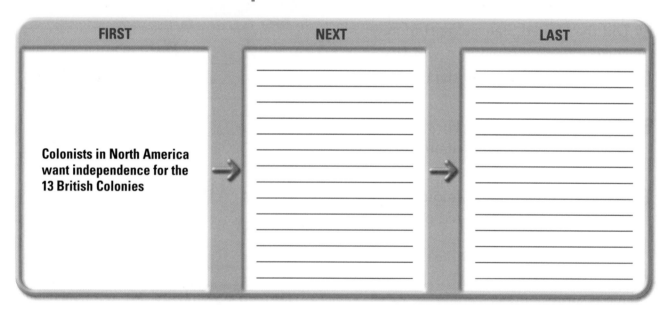

FIRST	NEXT	LAST
Colonists in North America want independence for the 13 British Colonies		

THINK & WRITE

Write a News Story Imagine the year is 1776 and you are a newspaper reporter in Philadelphia. On July 8 you attend the first public reading of the Declaration of Independence. Write a news story about the event and the reactions of those present.

Write a Speech One of the Continental Army's hardest tests was during the winter of 1777. That winter, soldiers who were camped at Valley Forge had to endure extreme cold and hunger. Write a speech to inspire the troops at Valley Forge.

1780			1785

1781
The British army
is defeated in
the Battle of
Yorktown

1783
The Treaty
of Paris is
signed

USE THE TIME LINE

Use the chapter summary time line to answer these questions.

1 When did the colonies declare their independence from Britain?

2 Did the Battle of Yorktown take place before or after the Battle of Saratoga?

USE VOCABULARY

Use these terms to write a story about the American Revolution.

public opinion (p. 302), **allegiance** (p. 303)

neutral (p. 309), **enlist** (p. 315),

turning point (p. 316)

RECALL FACTS

Answer these questions.

3 Why was the Declaration of Independence written?

4 How did Mercy Otis Warren contribute to the Patriot cause?

5 What schools were set up by the government to train military officers?

Write the letter of the best choice.

6 TEST PREP Thomas Jefferson's greatest contribution to the American Revolution was—
   A commanding American forces at the Battle of Saratoga.
   B convincing France to support the United States.
   C writing the Declaration of Independence.
   D writing *Common Sense*.

7 TEST PREP The most important effect of the Battle of Saratoga was—
   F France's decision to support the United States.
   G the defeat of more than 900 Hessian mercenaries.
   H the capture of Benedict Arnold.
   J the British army's decision to surrender.

THINK CRITICALLY

8 Why do you think so many people in the colonies read *Common Sense*?

9 What do you think would have happened if American forces had lost the Battle of Saratoga?

10 How did the military training of Continental soldiers affect the war?

11 What do you think was George Washington's greatest contribution to the American Revolution?

APPLY SKILLS

Make a Decision

12 Imagine that the year is 1777 and a friend has asked you to allow your home to be used as a shelter for Patriot soldiers. What steps might you follow to come to a decision?

CITIZENSHIP SKILLS

Compare Graphs

13 Look in an encyclopedia or on the Internet for two population graphs of your state. Make copies of the graphs or print them out. Then write a paragraph explaining the differences between the two.

CHART AND GRAPH SKILLS

Chapter 9 ■ 333

VISIT THE *Freedom Trail*

The Freedom Trail is a $2\frac{1}{2}$-mile (4-km) walking trail that weaves its way through the city of Boston. The trail connects landmarks that played an important role in America's struggle for independence. Along the Freedom Trail you can stop at places such as Faneuil Hall, where Bostonians protested British taxation policies. You can also visit the Old North Church, where on April 8, 1775, two lanterns were hung to warn Paul Revere and other colonists of incoming British troops. The Freedom Trail is more than just a path between places. Each stop on the trail tells a story about our nation's independence.

LOCATE IT

Boston

MASSACHUSETTS

WHAT TO SEE

The Freedom Trail is marked by red bricks. It gives visitors the opportunity to follow paths once walked by America's first patriots.

A Freedom Trail Marker

Faneuil Hall

King's Chapel Burying Ground

Bunker Hill Monument

Statue of Samuel Adams at Faneuil Hall

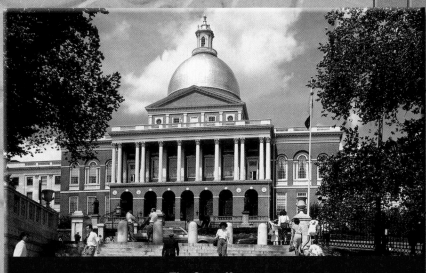

The State House

Paul Revere's house

TAKE A FIELD TRIP

GO **ONLINE**

A VIRTUAL TOUR
Visit The Learning Site at **www.harcourtschool.com/tours** to take virtual tours of other historic sites in the United States.

CNN Turner Le@rning

A VIDEO TOUR
Check your media center or classroom library for a videotape tour of the Freedom Trail.

4 Review and Test Preparation

VISUAL SUMMARY

Write a Paragraph Study the pictures and captions below to help you review Unit 4. Then choose one of the events shown. Write a paragraph that describes what happened and how that event affected the American Revolution.

USE VOCABULARY

For each pair of terms, write a sentence or two that explains how the terms are related.

1 **revolution** (p. 268), **independence** (p. 302)

2 **proclamation** (p. 276), **declaration** (p. 283)

3 **boycott** (p. 282), **blockade** (p. 289)

RECALL FACTS

Answer these questions.

4 What was the Albany Plan of Union?

5 Why did Parliament pass new tax laws for the American colonists after the French and Indian War?

Write the letter of the best choice.

6 **TEST PREP** The Stamp Act Congress met to—
   A discuss the problems the new tax laws had caused.
   B vote on the Stamp Act.
   C form an American Parliament.
   D choose a new mayor for New York City.

7 **TEST PREP** What did the British learn from the Battle of Bunker Hill?
   F Earthworks would help them.
   G The colonists had many bullets.
   H The colonists printed their own money.
   J Fighting the colonists would not be easy.

8 **TEST PREP** Which battle of the American Revolution brought about the end of the war?
   A the Battle of Yorktown
   B the Battle of Moores Creek Bridge
   C the Battle of Saratoga
   D the Battle of Long Island

Visual Summary

1750   1755   1760   1765

1754 The French and Indian War begins p. 269

1765 The Stamp Act is passed p. 281

1773 The Boston Tea Party takes place p. 288

9 Why do you think the British government believed that it had the right to make the colonists pay taxes?

10 Do you think the British could have avoided war with the colonists? Explain.

11 Why do you think some colonists chose to remain loyal to Britain during the American Revolution?

12 What do you think Nathan Hale meant when he said, "I only regret that I have but one life to lose for my country"?

APPLY SKILLS

Compare Historical Maps
Use the two historical maps on this page to answer the following questions.

13 Which map would you use to determine who claimed the 13 colonies?

14 Which map shows the land that was claimed by both Spain and the United States?

15 What areas shown on the two maps changed very little between 1763 and 1783?

16 Most of the British land that was reserved for Native Americans in 1763 became a part of what country by 1783?

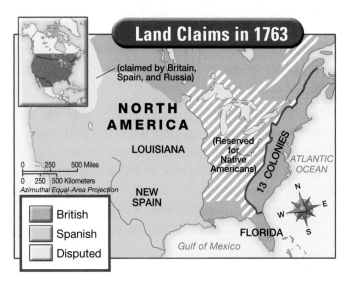

Land Claims in 1763

(claimed by Britain, Spain, and Russia)

NORTH AMERICA

LOUISIANA

(Reserved for Native Americans)

ATLANTIC OCEAN

13 COLONIES

NEW SPAIN

FLORIDA

Gulf of Mexico

0 250 500 Miles
0 250 500 Kilometers
Azimuthal Equal-Area Projection

British
Spanish
Disputed

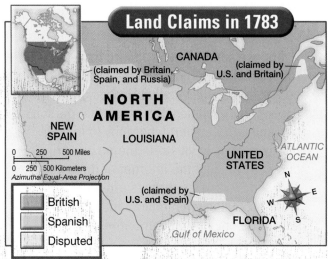

Land Claims in 1783

CANADA

(claimed by Britain, Spain, and Russia)

(claimed by U.S. and Britain)

NORTH AMERICA

NEW SPAIN

LOUISIANA

UNITED STATES

ATLANTIC OCEAN

(claimed by U.S. and Spain)

FLORIDA

Gulf of Mexico

0 250 500 Miles
0 250 500 Kilometers
Azimuthal Equal-Area Projection

British
Spanish
Disputed

17 Which map would you use to determine the location of the land that was reserved for Native Americans?

18 Who claimed Florida in 1763? in 1783?

1775 · 1780 · 1785 · 1790

1775 The American Revolution begins p. 291

1776 The Declaration of Independence is signed p. 306

1781 The British surrender at Yorktown, in Virginia p. 326

Unit Activities

Create a Time Line

Work in a group to make a large time line to display on a classroom wall. The time line should show either the important events leading up to the American Revolution or the key events that took place during and after the war. Use the time line as you take turns describing each of the events shown.

Honor Your Hero

Choose someone you admire from the American Revolution to be the subject of a poster for a display called Heroes of the American Revolution. Research that person's life, and write a short biography to include on the poster. To illustrate the poster, print out pictures from the Internet or draw your own. Add words or phrases around the pictures, telling what made that person a hero. Present your poster to the class.

Visit The Learning Site at
www.harcourtschool.com/
socialstudies/activities
for additional activities.

VISIT YOUR LIBRARY

■ *The Boston Tea Party* by Laurie A. O'Neill. Troll Associates.

■ *Thomas* by Bonnie Pryor. Morrow Junior Books.

■ *The World Turned Upside Down: George Washington and the Battle of Yorktown* by Richard Ferrie. Holiday House.

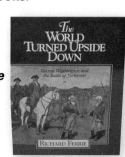

COMPLETE THE UNIT PROJECT

The History Show   Work with a group of classmates to finish the unit project—a history show about the American Revolution. Decide which key events and people you want to include in your show. Then write a script, create any needed illustrations or costumes, and choose the presenters. Videotape your show and invite other students to watch it, or perform the show "live" for them.

A New Nation

Inkwell from the Assembly
Room at Independence Hall

Independence Hall, Philadelphia, Pennsylvania

5

A New Nation

" *E pluribus unum* " (Out of many, one)

—Motto on the Seal of the United States, adopted on June 20, 1782

Preview the Content

Read the title and the Main Idea for each lesson in the unit. Then use what you have read to make a web for each chapter. Write down words or phrases that will help you identify the main topics to be covered in the unit.

MAIN TOPIC

Preview the Vocabulary

Context Clues   Context clues are words that can help you figure out the meaning of a word that is unfamiliar. Scan the unit and find the terms **inflation, commerce,** and **investor.** Write a sentence explaining how these words relate to one another.

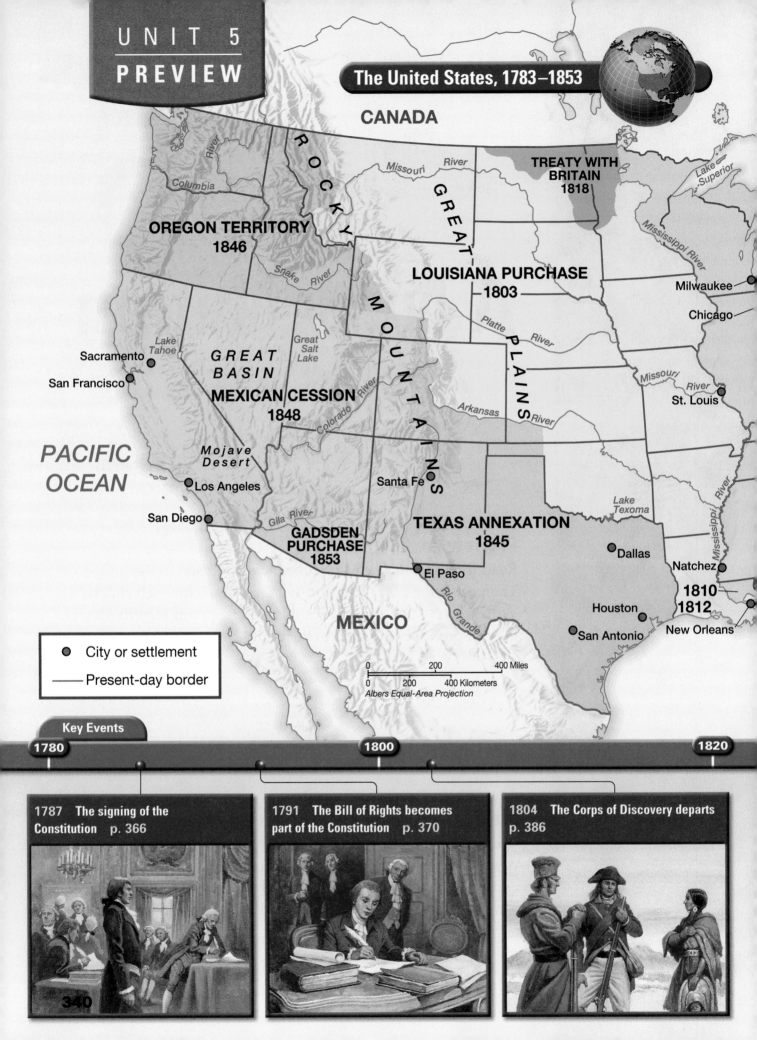

The United States, 1783–1853

CANADA

TREATY WITH BRITAIN 1818

ROCKY

GREAT

MOUNTAINS

PLAINS

Columbia *River*

Missouri *River*

OREGON TERRITORY 1846

Snake *River*

Lake Tahoe

Great Salt Lake

GREAT BASIN

LOUISIANA PURCHASE 1803

Platte *River*

Milwaukee

Chicago

Sacramento

San Francisco

MEXICAN CESSION 1848

Colorado *River*

Arkansas *River*

Missouri *River*

St. Louis

PACIFIC OCEAN

Mojave Desert

Gila *River*

Los Angeles

Santa Fe

TEXAS ANNEXATION 1845

Lake Texoma

Natchez

San Diego

GADSDEN PURCHASE 1853

El Paso

Rio Grande

MEXICO

Dallas

1810 1812

Houston

San Antonio

New Orleans

Mississippi *River*

Key:
- ● City or settlement
- —— Present-day border

0   200   400 Miles
0 200 400 Kilometers
Albers Equal-Area Projection

Key Events

1780

1800

1820

1787 **The signing of the Constitution** p. 366

1791 **The Bill of Rights becomes part of the Constitution** p. 370

1804 **The Corps of Discovery departs** p. 386

CANADA

TREATY WITH
BRITAIN
1842

St. Lawrence River

Lake Champlain

Lake Huron

Lake Michigan

Lake St. Clair

Lake Ontario

Lake Erie

Allegheny River

Portland
Portsmouth
Boston
Troy
Albany
Providence
Hartford
Buffalo
Hudson River
New York City

Detroit
Cleveland
Pittsburgh
Indianapolis

Philadelphia
Wilmington
Baltimore
Annapolis
Washington, D.C.

UNITED
STATES
1783

APPALACHIAN MOUNTAINS

Ohio River

Louisville

Richmond
Norfolk

Nashville

Tennessee River

New Bern

Wilmington

Atlanta
Birmingham
Charleston
Savannah

ATLANTIC
OCEAN

Jacksonville
St. Augustine

1813

FLORIDA
1819

Lake Okeechobee

Gulf of Mexico

N
W E
S

Population of the 10 Largest Cities in the United States, 1850

CITY	POPULATION
New York, NY	(icons representing population)
Baltimore, MD	(icons)
Boston, MA	(icons)
Philadelphia, PA	(icons)
New Orleans, LA	(icons)
Cincinnati, OH	(icons)
Brooklyn, NY	(icons)
St. Louis, MO	(icons)
Spring Garden, PA	(icons)
Albany, NY	(icons)

= 25,000 persons   = 20,000 persons   = 15,000 persons

= 10,000 persons   = 5,000 persons

1840   1860

1836   The Battle of the Alamo
p. 403

1847   The Mexican-American War
begins   p. 407

1849   The California Gold Rush
begins   p. 409

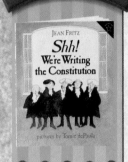

Shh! We're Writing the Constitution

by Jean Fritz
pictures by Tomie dePaola

The job of turning the 13 former British colonies into a new nation was not an easy one. The biggest problem was getting people to think of themselves as citizens of a country. Until this time most Americans thought of themselves as citizens of their states—Connecticut, Delaware, Georgia, Maryland, Massachusetts, New Hampshire, New Jersey, New York, North Carolina, Pennsylvania, Rhode Island, South Carolina, or Virginia.

———————☆———————

After the Revolutionary War most people in America were glad that they were no longer British. Still, they were not ready to call themselves Americans. The last thing they wanted was to become a nation. They were citizens of their own separate states, just as they had always been: each state different, each state proud of its own character, each state quick to poke fun at other states. To Southerners, New Englanders might be "no-account Yankees." To New Englanders, Pennsylvanians might be "lousy Buckskins." But to everyone the states themselves were all

important. "Sovereign states," they called them. They loved the sound of "sovereign" because it meant that they were their own bosses.

George Washington, however, scoffed at the idea of "sovereign states." He knew that the states could not be truly independent for long and survive. Ever since the Declaration of Independence had been signed, people had referred to the country as the United States of America. It was about time, he thought, for them to act and feel united.

Once during the war Washington had decided it would be a good idea if his troops swore allegiance to the United States. As a start, he lined up some troops from New Jersey and asked them to take such an oath. They looked at Washington as if he'd taken leave of his senses. How could they do that? they cried. New Jersey was their country!

So Washington dropped the idea. In time, he hoped, the states would see that they needed to become one nation, united under a strong central government.

But that time would be long in coming.

Analyze the Literature

❶ Why was the idea of "sovereign states" important?

❷ How was George Washington's point of view about the nation different from that of most other Americans?

READ A BOOK

START THE UNIT PROJECT

A Growing Nation Time Line
With your classmates, create an illustrated time line. As you read, make a list of the key events, people, and places you learn about. This list will help you decide which items to include on your time line.

USE TECHNOLOGY

Visit The Learning Site at **www.harcourtschool.com/ socialstudies** for additional activities, primary sources, and other resources to use in this unit.

Few places in the United States have been home to as many historic events as the Assembly Room of Independence Hall in Philadelphia. In this room, the Declaration of Independence was adopted, the design for the American flag was chosen, and the Constitution was debated and written.

LOCATE IT

PENNSYLVANIA

Philadelphia

10

The Constitution

" We the people of the United States . . . "

—Constitution of the United States,
Preamble, September 17, 1787

CHAPTER READING SKILL

Summarize

When you **summarize,** you give a shortened version of what you have read.

As you read this chapter, summarize the lessons about the Constitution and the early national government.

Summarize the Events

TOPIC OR EVENT	IMPORTANT DETAILS	SUMMARIZE
	What?	
	Who?	
	Where?	
	How?	
	Why?	

MAIN IDEA
Read to learn about the problems and successes of the first government of the United States.

WHY IT MATTERS
Government leaders developed ways to govern the nation's new lands.

VOCABULARY
republic
inflation
arsenal
territory
ordinance

The Confederation Period

1781–1787

In 1781, before the war with Britain had ended, the 13 former colonies—now independent states—approved the Articles of Confederation. This plan for a central government made the United States of America a republic. A **republic** is a form of government in which people elect representatives to govern the country. People hoped that under the Articles of Confederation, all 13 states could act together as one nation when needed. Under the Articles, however, the central government was weak. It was, as George Washington called it, "a half-starved, limping government."

Problems from the Start

Under the Articles of Confederation, the representatives met in a Congress. However, there often were not enough representatives present to allow Congress to take action. To make an important decision, representatives from at least 9 of the 13 states had to agree. Even when enough representatives were present, the states seldom agreed on anything. No state wanted to be under the control of the other states.

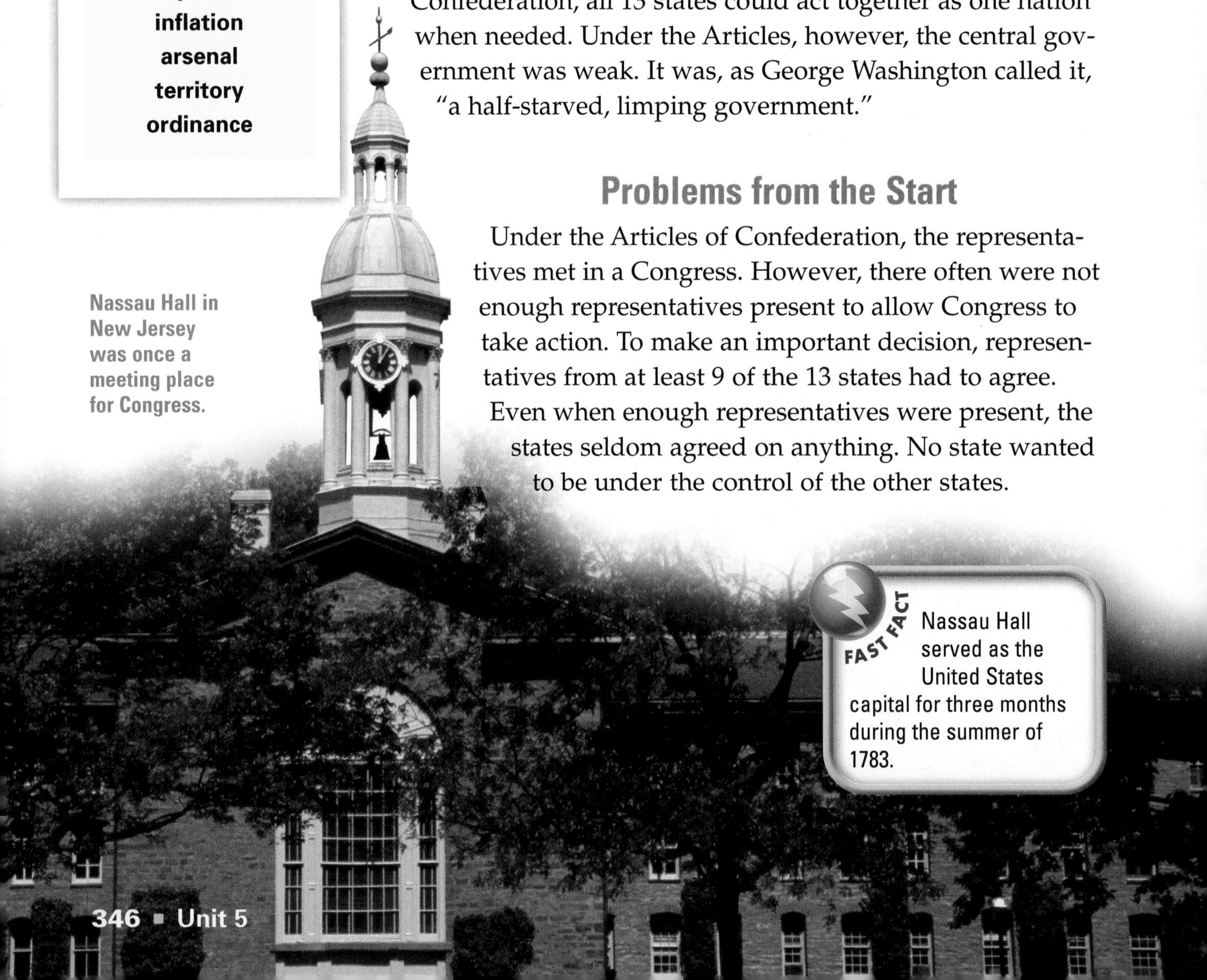

Nassau Hall in New Jersey was once a meeting place for Congress.

FAST FACT Nassau Hall served as the United States capital for three months during the summer of 1783.

Congress printed many paper bills known as Continentals. They had so little value that some Americans used the phrase *not worth a continental* to describe things that were worthless.

The new government had to face other challenges, too. Congress did not have a building of its own, so representatives had to hold meetings in many different cities and states. Also, the Articles limited the powers of the central government. For example, Congress could declare war, make treaties, and borrow money, but it could not collect taxes.

To get some of the money it needed, Congress asked each state to contribute money to help support the central government. Congress could not force the states to pay, though. State leaders could refuse to send money. They could also refuse to pay debts that they owed.

The central government could raise funds by printing and coining money. However, Congress caused inflation by printing too much money. **Inflation** occurs when the value of a government's money falls because there is too much of it. This meant that people needed more money to buy the same goods and services. During this time goods that used to cost two cents cost twenty dollars!

The Articles also stated that Congress could not raise a large army without the permission of the states. State leaders were afraid that a large army could be used to enforce unfair laws. This meant that raising an army to defend the nation against attack was difficult.

REVIEW What happened when Congress tried to print money to raise funds?

Shays's Rebellion

Economic problems during the 1780s made life difficult for many Americans. Some former soldiers still had not been paid for fighting during the Revolutionary War. Although they were poor, they had to pay high state taxes. To buy tools and seeds for planting, many farmers had to borrow money and go into debt.

Going into debt caused more problems for poor Americans. If people could not pay their debts or their taxes, the courts of some states would take away their farms. In 1786 and 1787, poor farmers protested by refusing to let the courts meet. Some of these protests, such as Shays's Rebellion in Massachusetts, turned violent.

The rebellion was named for Daniel Shays, a captain in the Continental army. During the fall of 1786, some farmers rebelled against the laws of Massachusetts.

Shays led the group in attacks against the courthouses. The farmers hoped that they could stop the courts from taking their land. Then, in January 1787, Shays led an attack on a United States arsenal located in Springfield, Massachusetts. An **arsenal** is a building that is used for storing weapons.

The arsenal at Springfield belonged to the central government, but Shays and his group attacked it anyway. Shays declared, "That crowd [the members of Congress] is too weak to act!" Congress did not have an army to defend the arsenal. Instead, the governor of Massachusetts called out state troops to stop Shays. During the fighting, four of Shays's followers died. Soon the rebellion had come to an end.

Shays's Rebellion showed that many Americans were unhappy with the state governments. Under the Articles of Confederation, Congress did not have an army to defend United States property. State governments had to defend their own lands. Americans feared that the states could not stop all the unrest.

REVIEW **Why did Daniel Shays and other farmers rebel against the government?**

The Western Lands

In spite of such problems, Congress was still responsible for many important decisions. One was about how to divide and govern the nation's new lands west of the Appalachians. In the years after the United States

The governor of Massachusetts issued the Proclamation of 1786 (below) to explain that acts such as Shays's Rebellion (left) would not be tolerated.

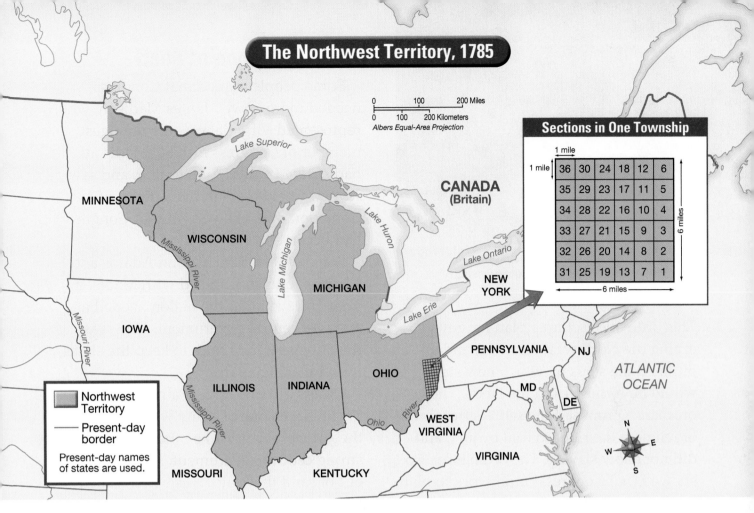

The Northwest Territory, 1785

0   100   200 Miles
0   100   200 Kilometers
Albers Equal-Area Projection

Sections in One Township

36	30	24	18	12	6
35	29	23	17	11	5
34	28	22	16	10	4
33	27	21	15	9	3
32	26	20	14	8	2
31	25	19	13	7	1

1 mile / 1 mile / 6 miles / 6 miles

CANADA (Britain)

Lake Superior, Lake Huron, Lake Michigan, Lake Ontario, Lake Erie

MINNESOTA, WISCONSIN, MICHIGAN, NEW YORK, IOWA, ILLINOIS, INDIANA, OHIO, PENNSYLVANIA, NJ, MD, DE, WEST VIRGINIA, VIRGINIA, MISSOURI, KENTUCKY

Mississippi River, Missouri River, Ohio River

ATLANTIC OCEAN

Northwest Territory
Present-day border
Present-day names of states are used.

GEOGRAPHY THEME

Regions This map shows how the Northwest Territory was divided into townships with many sections.

❓ How might the township system have helped settlers?

gained its independence, many settlers moved to the western lands. These lands had previously been set aside for Native Americans. Some of those settlers moved to lands north of the Ohio River, an area that had become known as the Northwest Territory. A **territory** is land that belongs to a national government but is not a state and is not represented in Congress.

At first, there was no plan in place for how the land should be divided among the settlers. It was difficult to tell where each person's property ended. As a result, many boundary disputes occurred.

In 1785 Congress passed a land **ordinance**, or set of laws, that created a system to survey, or measure, the west-

ern lands. The land was divided into squares that were called townships. A township measured 6 miles (10 km) long on each side, and its land was divided into 36 smaller squares, or sections. One of these sections was set aside for public schools. Then the central government sold the rest of the squares for at least one dollar per acre. This system of surveying by townships was so successful that most of the land west of the Mississippi River was divided that way. Township and section lines are still used in many parts of the United States today.

Two years later, in 1787, Congress passed the Northwest Ordinance.

Members of Congress (above) discussed the possibility of a stronger central government.

This ordinance set up a plan for governing the Northwest Territory, and it outlined the steps by which new states would be formed from the lands. The ordinance promised the settlers freedom of religion, the right to trial by jury, and did not allow slavery. The ordinance also showed that Congress could work to plan the growth of the nation.

REVIEW Which ordinance set up a plan for governing the Northwest Territory?

A Rope of Sand

Some people argued that Congress needed more power. James Madison, who represented Virginia, was the youngest member of Congress in 1780. Madison had studied ways of governing, and saw several weaknesses in the Articles of Confederation. He worried that Congress had become "a rope of sand."

Some others, such as John Adams and Thomas Jefferson, agreed with Madison. They believed that the nation needed a stronger central government. That was the only way, they said, to keep the states from breaking apart.

Others did not agree. Patrick Henry of Virginia was one of many who favored the Articles. Henry, like others, feared a strong central government. A rope made out of sand they said, was better than a rope made out of iron.

REVIEW Why did James Madison and others want a stronger central government?

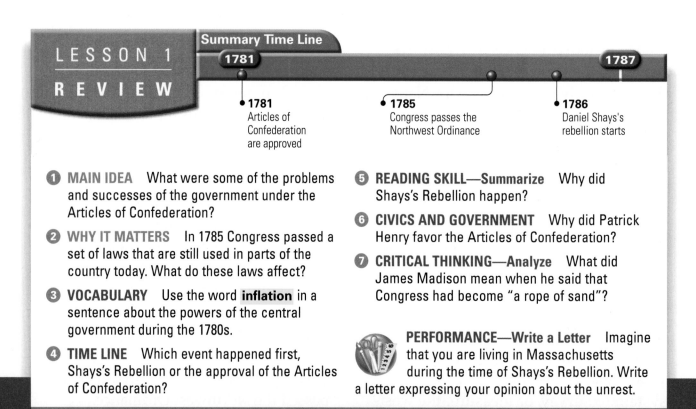

LESSON 1 REVIEW

Summary Time Line

1781 ———————————————— 1787

- **1781** Articles of Confederation are approved
- **1785** Congress passes the Northwest Ordinance
- **1786** Daniel Shays's rebellion starts

1. **MAIN IDEA** What were some of the problems and successes of the government under the Articles of Confederation?

2. **WHY IT MATTERS** In 1785 Congress passed a set of laws that are still used in parts of the country today. What do these laws affect?

3. **VOCABULARY** Use the word **inflation** in a sentence about the powers of the central government during the 1780s.

4. **TIME LINE** Which event happened first, Shays's Rebellion or the approval of the Articles of Confederation?

5. **READING SKILL—Summarize** Why did Shays's Rebellion happen?

6. **CIVICS AND GOVERNMENT** Why did Patrick Henry favor the Articles of Confederation?

7. **CRITICAL THINKING—Analyze** What did James Madison mean when he said that Congress had become "a rope of sand"?

PERFORMANCE—Write a Letter Imagine that you are living in Massachusetts during the time of Shays's Rebellion. Write a letter expressing your opinion about the unrest.

The Constitutional Convention

1780   1800   1820   1840   1860

1786–1787

Governing the country under the Articles of Confederation became very difficult. In 1786 some leaders called on the states to hold a **convention**, or an important meeting, to discuss trade among the states. It was held at Annapolis, Maryland, in September 1786.

The Annapolis Convention

Only five states—Delaware, New Jersey, New York, Pennsylvania, and Virginia—sent representatives in time to attend the Annapolis Convention. Chief among the delegates' concerns was **commerce**, or trade. Under the Articles, each state had the authority to print its own paper money. However, money from one state was usually not accepted in another state.

The delegates to the convention talked briefly before deciding that a stronger national government was needed in order to regulate commerce.

MAIN IDEA
Read to find out what leaders had to do before they could decide on a new plan of government.

WHY IT MATTERS
Through discussion and understanding, people often overcome personal differences and make decisions that benefit everyone.

VOCABULARY
convention
commerce
federal system
bill

The Annapolis State House in Maryland is the oldest state capitol still in use. Shown below is an eight-dollar banknote from Massachusetts.

EIGHT DOLLARS.
State of Maſſachuſetts-Bay.

No.25480   EIGHT DOLLARS.
THE Poſſeſſor of this Bill ſhall be paid
EIGHT Spaniſh milled DOLLARS by the Thirty firſt
Day of December, One Thouſand Seven Hundred and Eigh-
ty-ſix, with Intereſt in like MONEY, at the Rate of Five
per Centum per Annum, by the State of MASSACHU-
SETTS-BAY, according to an Act of the Legiſlature of the ſaid
State, of the Fifth Day of May, 1780.

This meant that the Articles of Confederation had to be changed. To change the Articles, however, all the states had to agree.

The delegates sent a letter to Congress, asking it to call another convention. Representatives from all the states could meet to discuss all their problems. They could also decide whether changing the Articles might help solve those problems.

At first Congress did not want to call a convention, but after Shays's Rebellion it agreed to participate. Each state was asked to send delegates to a convention to be held in Philadelphia in the spring of 1787. Rhode Island was the only state that refused to send a delegate. Its leaders feared a strong national government. They believed that such a government would be a threat to the rights of citizens.

REVIEW What decision did delegates reach at the Annapolis Convention?

The Philadelphia Convention

The delegates to the convention began to gather in Philadelphia in May 1787. One of the first to arrive was George Washington of Virginia. In 1787 Washington was 55 years old and the most highly honored hero of the Revolutionary War. The first action the delegates took was to elect Washington president of the convention.

Benjamin Franklin, representing Pennsylvania, made the most colorful entrance. Franklin was 81 years old, and he was unable to walk far or ride in a bumpy carriage. He arrived in a Chinese sedan chair carried by prisoners from the Philadelphia jail.

In all, 55 delegates from 12 of the states met in the Pennsylvania State House, which later became known as Independence Hall. The delegates were mostly lawyers, planters, and merchants. Some, such as Roger Sherman and

· BIOGRAPHY ·

James Madison   1751–1836
Character Trait: Civic Virtue

James Madison's Virginia Plan provided the basic framework for the Constitution. Because of his efforts in planning the Constitution and winning its final approval, Madison is remembered as the Father of the Constitution. Madison, however, often dismissed this title by saying the Constitution was not "the off-spring of a single brain" but "the work of many heads and many hands." Madison later served as an official in the United States government. In 1808 he was elected fourth President of the United States.

MULTIMEDIA BIOGRAPHIES
Visit The Learning Site at **www.harcourtschool.com/biographies**
to learn about other famous people.

GO ONLINE

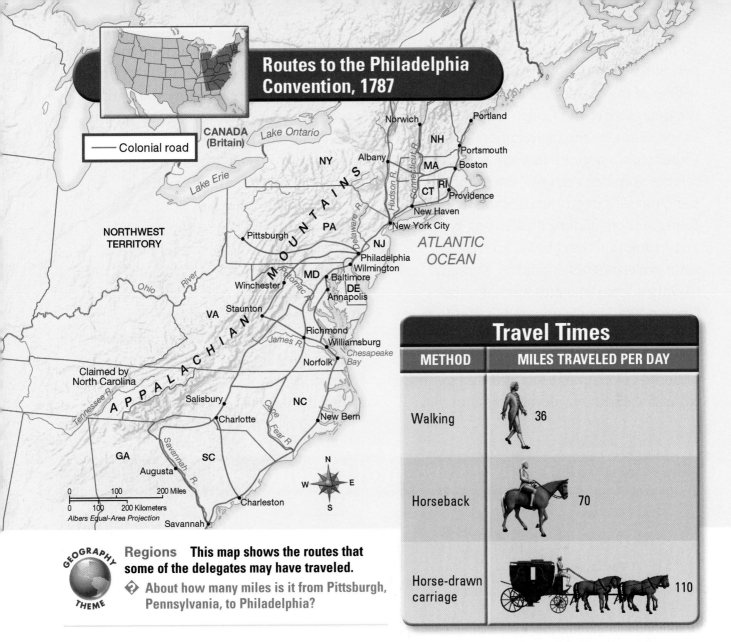

Routes to the Philadelphia Convention, 1787

— Colonial road

CANADA (Britain)

Lake Ontario

Lake Erie

NORTHWEST TERRITORY

NY

Albany

Norwich

Portland

NH

Portsmouth

MA

Boston

CT

RI

Providence

New Haven

New York City

ATLANTIC OCEAN

Pittsburgh

PA

NJ

Philadelphia

Wilmington

MD

Baltimore

Winchester

DE

Annapolis

VA

Staunton

Richmond

Williamsburg

Chesapeake Bay

Norfolk

James R.

Ohio River

Potomac R.

Tennessee R.

Claimed by North Carolina

Salisbury

Charlotte

NC

New Bern

Cape Fear R.

GA

SC

Savannah R.

Augusta

Charleston

Savannah

APPALACHIAN MOUNTAINS

Hudson R.

Connecticut R.

Delaware R.

0   100   200 Miles
0   100   200 Kilometers
Albers Equal-Area Projection

N S E W

Travel Times

METHOD	MILES TRAVELED PER DAY
Walking	36
Horseback	70
Horse-drawn carriage	110

GEOGRAPHY THEME

Regions This map shows the routes that some of the delegates may have traveled.

❓ About how many miles is it from Pittsburgh, Pennsylvania, to Philadelphia?

Benjamin Franklin, had been signers of the Declaration of Independence.

Some famous people were not delegates. Thomas Jefferson, who had written the Declaration of Independence, was in Paris as ambassador to France. John Adams was in London as ambassador to Britain. His cousin Samuel Adams was in ill health, and John Hancock was too busy as governor of Massachusetts to attend. Patrick Henry refused to take part because he did not believe that a stronger national government was a good idea.

REVIEW Who was elected president of the convention?

The Work Begins

From the beginning, the delegates agreed to conduct their meetings in secret. They believed that secret meetings would allow them to make the best decisions. Windows in the State House were covered, and guards stood at the doors.

As the convention began, some of the delegates offered ideas that they thought would improve the Articles of Confederation. Almost immediately, however, they reached a surprising decision. An entirely new plan of government—a new constitution—needed to be written.

To do this, the delegates worked diligently for the next four months.

One of the first issues discussed by the delegates to the Constitutional Convention, as the Convention in Philadelphia became known, was the relationship between the states and the national government. Some delegates thought there should be a strong national government. Others believed that the state governments should be stronger.

Only a few delegates agreed with George Read of Delaware. He said that the states should be done away with. Even most of those who wanted a strong national government thought that getting rid of the states would be going too far.

Instead, the delegates agreed to create a **federal system**, one in which the right to govern would be shared by the national government and the state governments. The states would keep some rights, and share some rights with the national, or federal, government. The national government would keep all power over matters that affected the nation as a whole.

The states would keep power over their own affairs, set up state and local governments, make state laws, and conduct state and local elections. However, the states would no longer print money, raise armies and navies, or make treaties with other countries, as they had done under the Articles of Confederation.

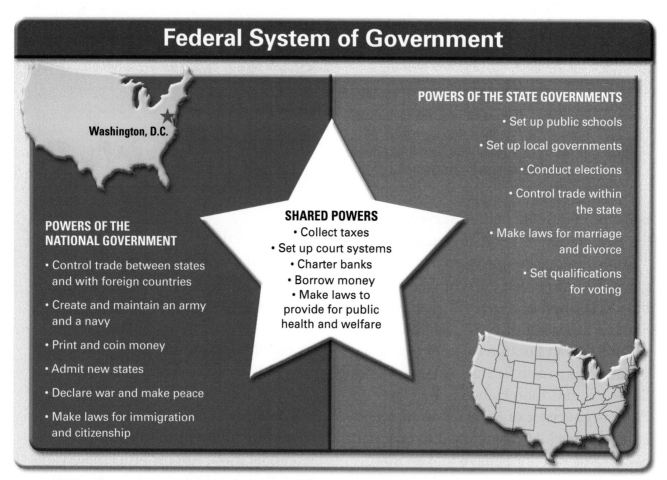

Federal System of Government

Washington, D.C.

POWERS OF THE NATIONAL GOVERNMENT

- Control trade between states and with foreign countries
- Create and maintain an army and a navy
- Print and coin money
- Admit new states
- Declare war and make peace
- Make laws for immigration and citizenship

SHARED POWERS
- Collect taxes
- Set up court systems
- Charter banks
- Borrow money
- Make laws to provide for public health and welfare

POWERS OF THE STATE GOVERNMENTS
- Set up public schools
- Set up local governments
- Conduct elections
- Control trade within the state
- Make laws for marriage and divorce
- Set qualifications for voting

Analyze Charts This chart illustrates the relationship between the national and state governments.

❖ Compare the powers of the national and state governments.

Three delegates to the Constitutional Convention—Edmund Randolph of Virginia, Roger Sherman of Connecticut, and William Paterson of New Jersey—presented ideas for the new government that started great debate and compromise.

Both the states and the national government would be able to set up their own court systems and to raise money by taxing citizens. The delegates made it clear that, under this federal system, the new rules of government would be "the supreme law of the land." They called these new rules the Constitution of the United States of America.

REVIEW How is the power to govern shared in a federal system?

Debate and Compromise

During their work, the delegates to the convention often failed to agree with one another. The new Constitution came into being only because the delegates were willing to agree to several compromises. The delegates often had to give up some of what they wanted in order to reach an agreement. As compromises were made, decisions were written down and the Constitution took shape.

One important compromise resolved the delegates' differences over how each state would be represented in the new Congress. Some people called this agreement the Great Compromise.

Edmund Randolph and the other Virginia delegates, including James Madison, thought the number of representatives that a state would have in the new Congress should be based on the number of people living in that state. Under this Virginia Plan, as it was called, states with more people would have more representatives and more votes in Congress. This plan would favor the large states of Virginia, Massachusetts, and Pennsylvania, which had many people.

"Not fair!" replied the delegates from the small states. William Paterson of New Jersey said that he would "rather submit to a monarch, to a despot [ruler with unlimited power], than to such a fate." Paterson then offered his own plan.

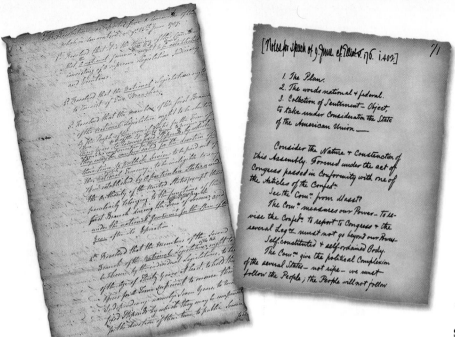

The Virginia Plan, supported by Edmund Randolph, called for representation based on population. The New Jersey Plan, offered by William Paterson, favored an equal number of representatives for each state.

Under this plan, called the New Jersey Plan, the new Congress would have one house, in which each state would be equally represented. This plan would give the small states the same number of representatives as the large states.

For weeks the delegates argued about how states should be represented in Congress. "We are now at a full stop," wrote Roger Sherman of Connecticut. The convention decided to set up a committee to work out a compromise.

In a committee meeting, Sherman presented a new plan, which became known as the Great Compromise. It was based on the idea of a two-house Congress. In one house, representation would be based on the population of each state, as in the Virginia Plan. In the other house, each state would be equally represented, as in the New Jersey Plan. Either house could present a **bill**, or an idea for a new law, but both had to approve it before it became a law.

Committee members from the large states did not like the compromise. They believed that it gave too much power to the small states. The committee added another idea. The house in which representation was based on population would have the sole authority to propose tax bills. In the end, the committee presented its plan to the whole convention. The delegates soon came to understand that if they did not agree to the Great Compromise, there would be no new plan of government.

Another compromise had to do with slavery. Delegates from the northern and southern states argued about whether enslaved African Americans should be counted when figuring each state's population. Population would affect a state's taxes and its representation in Congress.

Because the northern states had fewer enslaved African Americans than the southern states, the northern states did not want slaves to be counted for representation. After all, the delegates argued, slaves were not citizens under the Articles of Confederation and they would not become citizens under the Constitution. For tax purposes, however, the northern states did want slaves to be counted.

Delegates from the southern states wanted slaves to be counted for representation. That way they could count more

This painting by Thomas Coram shows slave quarters on a South Carolina plantation. The issue of slavery sparked heated debates among northern and southern delegates.

people and get more representatives in Congress. For tax purposes the southern states did not want slaves counted.

The delegates finally reached a compromise by counting three-fifths of the total number of slaves. This Three-fifths Compromise moved the delegates closer to forming a new government.

REVIEW What idea was called the Great Compromise?

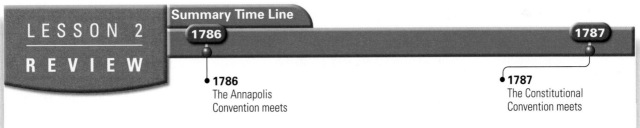

LESSON 2 REVIEW

Summary Time Line

1786 — 1787

• **1786**
The Annapolis Convention meets

• **1787**
The Constitutional Convention meets

1 **MAIN IDEA** What did delegates to the Constitutional Convention have to do before they could decide on a new plan of government?

2 **WHY IT MATTERS** Why do you think that discussion and understanding are important in making decisions?

3 **VOCABULARY** Explain the meaning of the term **federal system**.

4 **TIME LINE** Which event happened first, the Annapolis Convention or the Constitutional Convention?

5 **READING SKILL—Summarize** What is the Great Compromise and how was it reached?

6 **CIVICS AND GOVERNMENT** Under the new Constitution, what rights would the states keep?

7 **CRITICAL THINKING—Evaluate** Delegates attending the Constitutional Convention conducted their meetings in secret. If such meetings were held today, do you think they should be—or could be—kept secret? Explain.

PERFORMANCE—Write a News Story Imagine that you are a newspaper reporter in 1787. Write a brief news story about the Constitutional Convention. Share your report with classmates.

3

MAIN IDEA
Read to learn about
the three branches of the
United States government.

WHY IT MATTERS
Dividing government into
three branches keeps any
one branch from having
too much power.

VOCABULARY
census
electoral college
veto
impeach
justice
checks and balances

Gouverneur Morris (right)
was responsible for much
of the wording of the
Constitution (below).

Three Branches of Government

The delegates to the Constitutional Convention, wrote the Constitution with great care. Gouverneur (guh•ver•NIR) Morris of Pennsylvania spent long hours writing down and polishing each sentence. The delegates gave him the job of recording all the ideas that had been approved during the convention.

The Preamble

In the Preamble to the Constitution, Morris began with the words

❝We the people of the United States . . . ❞

He had originally written "We the people of the States of New Hampshire, Massachusetts, . . ." Morris changed the words because he wanted the American people to know that the Constitution would make them citizens of a nation first and citizens of separate states second. This change also helped link the Constitution with the idea in the Declaration of Independence that a government should get its power from the consent of the people.

Morris went on to explain in the Preamble that the purpose of the Constitution was to create

a better plan of government. This government would work toward fairness and peace. It would allow the nation to defend itself and it would work toward the nation's well-being.

Morris also wrote that the Constitution would provide "the blessings of liberty" for the American people. These words let the citizens of the United States know that the Constitution would make sure that they remained a free people.

REVIEW Why did Gouverneur Morris change the wording in the Preamble to the Constitution?

The Legislative Branch

In Article I of the Constitution, Gouverneur Morris described the law-making, or legislative, branch of the new government. The Congress could make tax laws, regulate commerce between states and with other countries and Indian tribes, and raise an army and a navy. It would also have power to declare war and coin money.

Congress would have two houses—the House of Representatives and the Senate. Either house could propose most bills, but tax bills could be proposed first only in the House of Representatives. For any bill to become law, the majority of those voting in each house would have to vote for it.

The number of members each state sent to the House of Representatives would depend on the state's population. A **census**, or population count, would be taken every ten years to find out the number of people in each state. Today the total number of members in the House of Representatives is limited to 435. That number is divided among the states, based on their populations. In the Senate each state has two senators.

For more than 200 years, the United States Capitol building has been home to the legislative branch of the federal government.

James Madison thought that the voters of each state should elect the members of both houses of Congress. Other delegates disagreed. Some felt that most citizens were not informed enough to have a say in government. After a long debate, the delegates agreed that citizens should vote directly for members of the House of Representatives. Senators would be selected by their state legislatures. Today, however, citizens vote directly for members of both houses of Congress.

In Article I, the delegates also outlined other rules for Congress that are still in effect. Members of the House of Representatives are elected to 2-year terms. They must be at least 25 years old, must have been citizens of the United States for at least 7 years, and must live in the state they represent. Senators are elected to 6-year terms. They must be at least 30 years old, must have been citizens of the United States for at least 9 years, and must live in the state they represent.

REVIEW **What are the main responsibilities of Congress?**

The Executive Branch

Once Congress makes the laws, it is the job of the executive branch, according to Article II of the Constitution, to carry them out. The delegates had many long arguments about whether this branch should be headed by one person or by a group of people. Some delegates believed that one person should be the chief executive, or leader. Others worried that a single executive would be too much like a monarch.

The delegates finally decided on a single chief executive called the President. The President is elected to a 4-year term. To be elected President, a person must be at least 35 years old and must have been born in the United States, or have parents who are United States citizens. The President must also have lived in the United States for 14 years.

The delegates decided that citizens would vote for electors, who, in turn, would vote for the President. This group of electors is called the **electoral college**.

The White House is the official residence of the President of the United States.

Housed in this building since 1935, the Supreme Court is the highest court in the United States.

The delegates also had long debates about how much power the President should have. They eventually decided that the President should be able to **veto**, or reject, bills that are passed by Congress.

The delegates decided that the President would represent the nation in dealing with other countries. The President would also be commander in chief of the military. The President's chief responsibility, however, would be to "take care that the laws be faithfully executed." If these duties were not carried out according to law, Congress could **impeach** the President, or accuse the President of crimes. The President could then be tried by the Senate and removed from office if found guilty.

REVIEW What is the President's main responsibility?

The Judicial Branch

Once laws are made and carried out, the judicial branch, according to Article III of the Constitution, must decide if they are working fairly. The judicial branch is the court system.

The states had always had their own courts. Now the delegates agreed on the need for a federal court system. These courts would decide cases that dealt with the Constitution, treaties, and national laws. They would also decide cases between states and between citizens of different states.

The delegates made most of their decisions about the highest court in the United States, which they called the Supreme Court. The delegates decided that the President would nominate the Supreme Court **justices**, or judges.

The Senate would vote whether to approve them. It was decided that a Supreme Court justice would stay in office for life. In this way, justices could make decisions without worrying about losing their jobs.

No decision was made as to how many justices would be on the Supreme Court. Congress decided on that number later. At first there were six justices on the Supreme Court. Today there are nine.

REVIEW **What are the duties of the federal courts?**

The Branches Work Together

None of the delegates wanted any one branch of the new government to have too much power. So they gave each branch some ways to check, or limit, the power of the other two branches.

Congress, for example, can check the power of the President if two-thirds of each house votes to override, or cancel, the President's veto. If that happens, a bill becomes a law even if the President

Analyze Diagrams This diagram shows the checks and balances within the three branches of the federal government.

◆ How can the President check the authority of Congress?

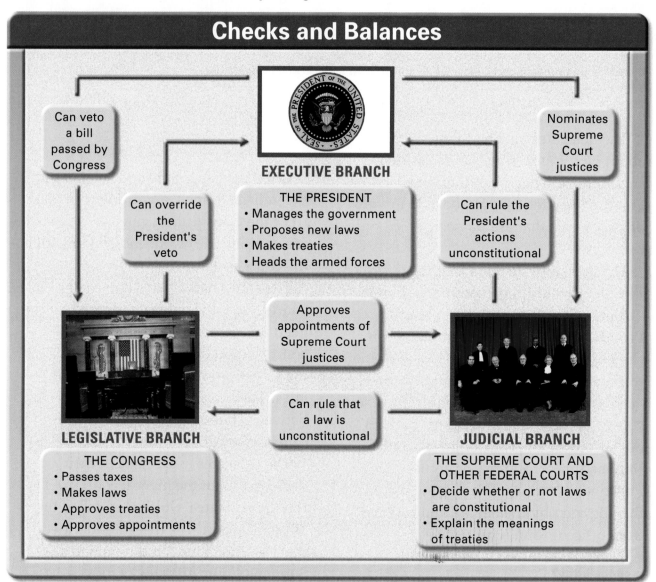

Checks and Balances

EXECUTIVE BRANCH

Can veto a bill passed by Congress

Nominates Supreme Court justices

Can override the President's veto

THE PRESIDENT
• Manages the government
• Proposes new laws
• Makes treaties
• Heads the armed forces

Can rule the President's actions unconstitutional

Approves appointments of Supreme Court justices

Can rule that a law is unconstitutional

LEGISLATIVE BRANCH

THE CONGRESS
• Passes taxes
• Makes laws
• Approves treaties
• Approves appointments

JUDICIAL BRANCH

THE SUPREME COURT AND OTHER FEDERAL COURTS
• Decide whether or not laws are constitutional
• Explain the meanings of treaties

Delegates to the Constitutional Convention set up a system of checks and balances so that no branch of the federal government would have too much power.

objects. The Supreme Court can check the power of Congress by ruling that a law does not follow the Constitution.

The President can check the power of the Supreme Court by nominating its justices, and Congress can check the power of the President by either approving or not approving the President's choices. Congress can check the power of the Supreme Court by suggesting constitutional amendments, by impeaching and convicting justices of wrongdoing, and removing them from the Court.

The delegates set up these checks to keep a balance of authority among the three branches. This system of **checks and balances** keeps any one branch from becoming too powerful or using its authority wrongly. It helps all three branches work together.

REVIEW Why was the system of checks and balances outlined in the Constitution?

LESSON 3
REVIEW

1 MAIN IDEA What are the three branches of the United States government?

2 WHY IT MATTERS Why are the powers of the United States government separate from one another?

3 VOCABULARY Explain how the terms **veto**, **impeach**, and **checks and balances** are related.

4 READING SKILL—Summarize Summarize the powers given to each branch of government.

5 CIVICS AND GOVERNMENT How can the Supreme Court check the power of Congress?

6 CRITICAL THINKING—Analyze Why is the White House a symbol of the United States?

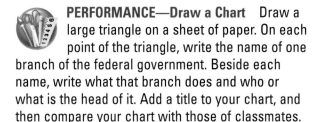 **PERFORMANCE—Draw a Chart** Draw a large triangle on a sheet of paper. On each point of the triangle, write the name of one branch of the federal government. Beside each name, write what that branch does and who or what is the head of it. Add a title to your chart, and then compare your chart with those of classmates.

Read a Flow Chart

VOCABULARY
flow chart

▶ WHY IT MATTERS

Have you ever read something and had a difficult time understanding its meaning? Sometimes information is better understood when it is presented in a different way—as in a flow chart. A **flow chart** is a drawing that shows the order in which things happen. It uses arrows to help you to read the drawings, or steps, in the correct order.

▶ WHAT YOU NEED TO KNOW

The flow chart on page 365 shows how the federal government makes new laws for the United States. The top box on the flow chart shows the first step in the process of a bill becoming a law. In this step a member of the House of Representatives or Senate introduces a bill. If the bill is a tax bill, however, only members of the House may first introduce it.

In the second step, the bill is sent to a smaller

This early gavel was used in the Senate to open and close meetings.

group called a committee, where it is reviewed. This committee is made up of members of either the House of Representatives or the Senate. The committee members study the bill, and if they decide that the bill would make a good law, they tell the rest of the House and Senate. You can find out what happens next by reading the remaining steps shown on the flow chart.

▶ PRACTICE THE SKILL

Use the flow chart on page 365 to answer these questions.

❶ What happens after both the House and the Senate approve the bill?

❷ What happens if the President signs a bill?

❸ Where does a bill go if the President vetoes it?

❹ How can a bill become a law if the President vetoes it?

▶ APPLY WHAT YOU LEARNED

With a partner, make a flow chart that explains to your classmates how something works. Write each step on a strip of paper. When you have finished, glue the steps—in order—on a sheet of posterboard. Then connect the strips with arrows. Give your flow chart a title, and present it to your classmates.

How a Bill Becomes a Law

A member of either the House or Senate can introduce a bill, but only a member of the House can introduce a tax bill.

COMMITTEES

The bill is reviewed by committees.

The House and Senate vote to approve the bill.

The bill goes to the President.

SIGN

If the President signs the bill, it becomes a law.

VETO

If the President vetoes the bill, it returns to Congress.

LAW

If the bill gets a two-thirds majority vote in both the House and Senate, it becomes a law.

Approval and the Bill of Rights

1787–1791

On September 17, 1787, the Constitution was complete. There were 42 delegates still present at the Constitutional Convention, and all but 3 of them—Elbridge Gerry, George Mason, and Edmund Randolph—signed their approval. As delegates were signing the document, Benjamin Franklin spoke of the confidence he felt in the nation's future. During the convention, Franklin had often looked at the chair used by George Washington. Its high back had a carving of a sun on it. Franklin had not been able to decide if the sun shown was supposed to be rising or setting. Afterward, he said, "I have the happiness to know that it is a rising and not a setting sun."

A Struggle to Ratify

Despite Franklin's words, the Constitution that he and the other delegates had approved was not yet the law of the land. According to Article VII, 9 of the 13 states had to **ratify**, or approve, the Constitution before it would go into effect. After the document was signed, the Convention sent it to the Congress of the Confederation. Congress, in turn, sent copies to the states. In each state, voters elected delegates to a state convention.

This sun design is on the chair used by George Washington.

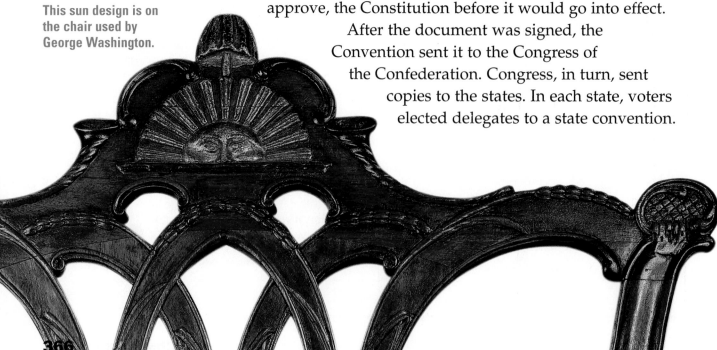

This painting shows George Washington (standing at right) addressing the delegates.

These delegates would vote for or against the Constitution.

At the state conventions, arguments began again. Patrick Henry in Virginia and George Clinton in New York told their conventions that the new national government was too strong. Some delegates did not like the way the Preamble began with "We the people." They thought it should say "We the States."

There was one point, however, on which most delegates agreed. They felt the Constitution also should protect the powers of the states and the basic rights of the people. The state delegates wanted to protect the freedoms they had won in the Revolutionary War. They did not want the new national government to have the power to limit freedoms, as the British government had done.

Many delegates to the state conventions said they would be more willing to approve the Constitution if a bill, or list, of rights were to be added. Supporters of the Constitution promised that after the Constitution was ratified, a bill of rights would be added.

REVIEW What would adding a bill of rights to the Constitution do?

The Vote

The first state to call for a vote on the Constitution was Delaware. In December 1787, all the Delaware state delegates voted to ratify the Constitution. Later that month, state delegates in Pennsylvania and New Jersey also voted to approve the Constitution. In January 1788, state delegates in Georgia and Connecticut voted to ratify. Still, eight states had not yet voted. Among those were the states of Virginia and New York. Citizens worried that the new government could not possibly work if some of the nation's largest states voted against it.

From January to June 1788, those who favored the Constitution and those against it both tried to get the backing of people in the states that had not yet voted.

Those citizens who favored the constitution came to be called **Federalists**. Federalists wanted a strong national, or federal, government. Those who did not became known as **Anti-Federalists**. Because the Constitution did not yet contain a bill of rights, the Anti-Federalists feared the document made the national government too strong.

Throughout America the two sides used the newspapers to tell what they thought and why. In New York, Alexander Hamilton, James Madison, and John Jay wrote essays defending the Constitution. These essays were later published as a book called *The Federalist*.

Citizens who could read followed the argument in the newspapers. Others heard the arguments at community meetings and even at church services. Some people saw the Constitution as the work of "lawyers, and men of learning, and moneyed men that talk so finely . . . to make us poor, illiterate people swallow down the pill." Others thought that having a new government was a good idea. They also trusted the promise of a bill of rights.

No one was certain how all the arguing would affect the vote in the state conventions. In Massachusetts, however, the promise of changes to the Constitution

CITIZENSHIP

POINTS OF VIEW
For or Against the Bill of Rights

THOMAS JEFFERSON to James Madison—December 20, 1787

❝Let me add that a bill of rights is what the people are entitled to against every government on earth, general or particular, and what no just government should refuse . . .❞

JAMES MADISON to Thomas Jefferson—April 22, 1788

❝Should this [the demand for a bill of rights] be carried in the affirmative, . . . I think the Constitution, and the Union will both be endangered.❞

Analyze the Viewpoints

❶ What viewpoint about a bill of rights did each person hold?

❷ Why do you think Jefferson and Madison held these views?

❸ **Make it Relevant** James Madison eventually changed his view about the need for a bill of rights. Can you think of a time when you changed your view on a subject? Why did you change your view?

Ratification of the Constitution

United States

1787 Year of ratification

Present-day border

0   100   200 Miles
0   100   200 Kilometers
Albers Equal-Area Projection

MAINE
(part of MA)

CANADA
(Britain)

NEW HAMPSHIRE
1788

(claimed by NY and NH)

MASSACHUSETTS
1788

NEW YORK
1788

Lake Ontario

RHODE ISLAND
1790

CONNECTICUT
1788

Lake Erie

PENNSYLVANIA
1787

NEW JERSEY
1787

DELAWARE
1787

MARYLAND
1788

VIRGINIA
1788

NORTH CAROLINA
1789

SOUTH CAROLINA
1788

ATLANTIC OCEAN

GEORGIA
1788

FLORIDA
(Spain)

Gulf of Mexico

helped change the minds of some very important people. Samuel Adams and John Hancock went to the state convention as Anti-Federalists. They returned home as Federalists. As a result, Massachusetts decided to ratify the Constitution in February 1788.

Maryland and South Carolina followed Massachusetts's example that spring. Then, on June 21, 1788, New Hampshire became the ninth state to ratify the Constitution. That was the number of states needed to put it into effect. Four days later Virginia ratified it, and New York followed in July. By the spring of 1789 the new government was at work.

GEOGRAPHY THEME

Place The map and table show when the Constitution was ratified by each of the 13 states. The table also lists the number of votes for and against the Constitution.

❖ In which state was the vote closest to being a tie?

Constitution Ratification Vote

STATE	DATE	VOTES FOR	VOTES AGAINST
Delaware	Dec. 7, 1787	30	0
Pennsylvania	Dec. 12, 1787	46	23
New Jersey	Dec. 18, 1787	38	0
Georgia	Jan. 2, 1788	26	0
Connecticut	Jan. 9, 1788	128	40
Massachusetts	Feb. 6, 1788	187	168
Maryland	April 28, 1788	63	11
South Carolina	May 23, 1788	149	73
New Hampshire	June, 21, 1788	57	47
Virginia	June 25, 1788	89	79
New York	July 26, 1788	30	27
North Carolina	Nov. 21, 1789	194	77
Rhode Island	May 29, 1790	34	32

Later that year North Carolina approved the Constitution. Rhode Island finally gave its approval in 1790.

REVIEW What group favored the Constitution and wanted a strong national government?

The Bill of Rights

As promised, not long after the states had ratified the Constitution, ten **amendments**, or changes, were added to protect the rights of the people. These ten amendments, called the Bill of Rights, became part of the Constitution in 1791.

The Bill of Rights was influenced by the Magna Carta and the English Bill of Rights of 1689. The **Magna Carta** was a charter granted by the king of England in the year 1215. It listed the rights of the upper class and limited the power of the king. The English Bill of Rights listed the rights of English citizens.

The Virginia Declaration of Rights also had a major influence on the United States Bill of Rights. Written by George Mason, the Virginia Declaration of Rights had been adopted by Virginia's state constitutional convention in June 1776. It said that "all men are by nature equally free and independent and have certain inherent rights." These rights were "the enjoyment of life and liberty, with the means of acquiring and possessing property." The Declaration also protected some rights by name, including freedom of the press, freedom of religion, and trial by jury.

The First Amendment to the Constitution gives people the freedom to follow any religion they choose.

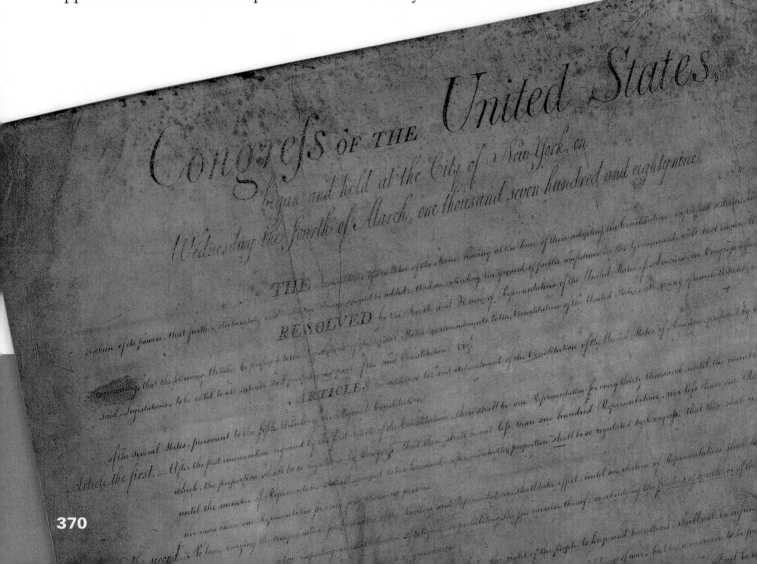

It also says the government cannot promote or financially support any religion.

Many people believe that the Virginia Statute for Religious Freedom influenced the First Amendment. This statute, written by Thomas Jefferson, supported complete religious freedom. It became law in Virginia in 1786, due in large part to the leadership and support of James Madison.

The First Amendment also protects freedom of speech and freedom of the press. It further says that people can hold meetings to discuss problems and they can petition, or ask, the government to correct the wrongs.

The Second Amendment protects people's right to carry arms or weapons. It says, "A well-regulated militia being necessary to the security of a free State, the right of the people to keep and bear arms shall not be infringed [taken away]."

The Third Amendment says that government cannot force citizens to quarter soldiers in peacetime. Before the Revolutionary War, many colonists had to house and feed British soldiers.

The Bill of Rights (left) lists the basic rights of the people. During the late 1700s, the printing press (below left) was the main tool for spreading news and opinions. The Seventh Amendment gives people accused of crimes the right to a trial by jury (right). The First Amendment allows people to publicly debate ideas (bottom).

The bald eagle became a symbol of the United States in 1782.

Under the Fourth Amendment, the government cannot search a person's home or take his or her property without that person's permission or the approval of a judge.

The Fifth through Eighth Amendments deal with **due process of law**. This means that people have the right to a fair public trial to be decided by a jury. They do not have to testify against themselves in court. They have the right to have a lawyer defend them. If they are found innocent of a crime they cannot be put on trial a second time for that same crime. They also cannot be sentenced to any cruel and unusual punishments.

The Ninth Amendment says that people have many other rights not specifically listed in the Constitution. These include the "unalienable rights" of "Life, Liberty and the pursuit of Happiness" described in the Declaration of Independence.

As a final protection for citizens, the Tenth Amendment says that the national government can do only what is listed in the Constitution. This means that all other authority, called the **reserved powers**, belongs to the states or to the people.

REVIEW Why is the Bill of Rights an important part of the Constitution?

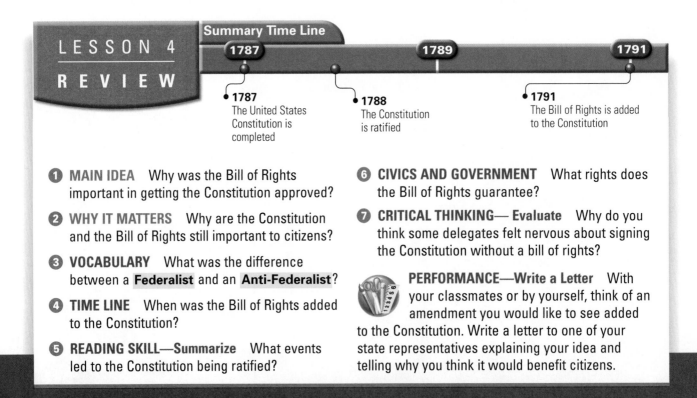

LESSON 4 REVIEW

Summary Time Line

1787 — 1789 — 1791

- **1787** The United States Constitution is completed
- **1788** The Constitution is ratified
- **1791** The Bill of Rights is added to the Constitution

1. **MAIN IDEA** Why was the Bill of Rights important in getting the Constitution approved?

2. **WHY IT MATTERS** Why are the Constitution and the Bill of Rights still important to citizens?

3. **VOCABULARY** What was the difference between a **Federalist** and an **Anti-Federalist**?

4. **TIME LINE** When was the Bill of Rights added to the Constitution?

5. **READING SKILL—Summarize** What events led to the Constitution being ratified?

6. **CIVICS AND GOVERNMENT** What rights does the Bill of Rights guarantee?

7. **CRITICAL THINKING— Evaluate** Why do you think some delegates felt nervous about signing the Constitution without a bill of rights?

PERFORMANCE—Write a Letter With your classmates or by yourself, think of an amendment you would like to see added to the Constitution. Write a letter to one of your state representatives explaining your idea and telling why you think it would benefit citizens.

Act As a Responsible Citizen

▶ WHY IT MATTERS

Responsible citizens know what is happening in their country, choose wise leaders, and take part in government. Citizens and leaders must also think about public service.

▶ WHAT YOU NEED TO KNOW

Before the Constitution could be ratified, citizens elected delegates to vote for or against the Constitution. Many of these delegates did not feel they could vote for a plan of government that did not protect the rights of the states and citizens. Here are some steps delegates may have used to act as responsible citizens:

Step 1 **They learned about the problem—some of the rights of the states and of individuals might not be protected.**

Step 2 **They thought about ways to solve the problem that would be good for the whole country.**

Step 3 **They worked together to bring about change.**

▶ PRACTICE THE SKILL

Imagine that you are a delegate to your state convention. Will you vote for the Constitution? Explain your decision and the steps you followed to act as a responsible citizen.

▶ APPLY WHAT YOU LEARNED

Some acts of citizenship, such as voting, can be done only by adults. Others can be done by citizens of almost any age. Use the steps above to decide on ways you might act as a responsible citizen of your school.

Election day in Philadelphia, Pennsylvania

373

MAIN IDEA
Read to learn how the nation's new leaders worked together despite their growing differences.

WHY IT MATTERS
Government leaders must often overcome differences to work for the common good of the nation.

VOCABULARY
Cabinet
political party
candidate

The New Government Begins

1780   1800   1820   1840   1860

1780–1800

The first elections under the new Constitution began in 1788. Voters elected members of the United States House of Representatives. Each state legislature chose two senators for the United States Senate. They also chose people who would serve in the electoral college and elect the first president.

The New Leaders

In 1789 George Washington was elected as the nation's first President. John Adams became the first Vice President. His job was to help President Washington carry out his duties. When

Americans painted pictures and sewed samplers to pay tribute to their new President.

Washington was elected, Congress planned to meet in New York City. On April 30, 1789, George Washington stood on the balcony of Federal Hall in New York City. There he recited the President's oath of office, "I do solemnly swear (or affirm) that I will faithfully execute the office of President of the United States, and will, to the best of my ability, preserve, protect, and defend the Constitution of the United States."

One of Congress's first actions was to pass the Judiciary Act. This act set up the federal judicial branch and decided the number of Supreme Court justices. President Washington named John Jay of New York as the first chief justice.

President Washington also chose advisers to help him carry out the main responsibilities of the executive branch. These people would serve as the secretaries, or heads, of executive departments that included the State Department, the Treasury Department, and the War Department.

The President asked Thomas Jefferson to serve as the nation's first secretary of state. Jefferson helped the President deal with other countries such as Spain, France, and Britain. Washington also asked Alexander Hamilton to serve as secretary of the treasury. Hamilton worked to set up a new banking system and to pass new tax laws.

Henry Knox, who had been a general in the Revolutionary War, served as secretary of war. Knox began building a national army of 1,000 soldiers to defend the nation. Another important adviser was Edmund Randolph. He became the new President's legal adviser, now called the attorney general. He

The First President

Analyze Primary Sources

This print from 1789 celebrates George Washington and the new nation. Thirteen of the circles around Washington show the 13 state coats of arms. The top circle is the nation's Great Seal.

1 The Great Seal of the United States.

2 State coats of arms.

3 President George Washington.

◆ Why do you think the artist placed the 13 state coats of arms in a circle around President Washington?

A DISPLAY of the UNITED STATES of AMERICA

explained the laws and the powers of the Constitution.

Together, Jefferson, Hamilton, Knox, and Randolph became known as the **Cabinet**, a group of the President's most important advisers. Every President since Washington has relied on such a group. Over time, however, the number of Cabinet members has grown.

REVIEW Who were the members of Washington's Cabinet?

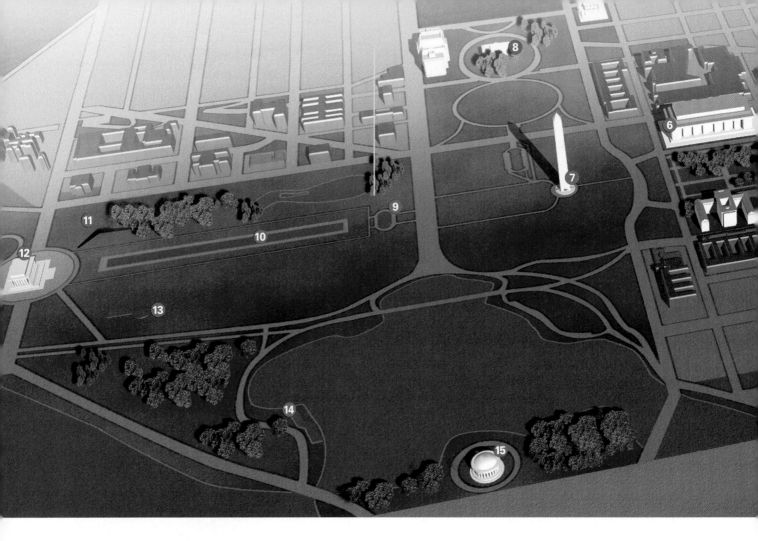

• BIOGRAPHY •

Benjamin Banneker
1731–1806

Character Trait: Inventiveness

Our nation's capital was built by the work of people such as Benjamin Banneker. In 1791 and 1792, he worked with Andrew Ellicott, the chief surveyor, to plan Washington, D.C. Banneker later became famous as the author of his own almanac, and he sent a copy to Thomas Jefferson. Banneker included a letter that asked Jefferson to help work for the rights of African Americans.

Banneker was also successful in other ways. He taught himself astronomy and mathematics. At a time when many African Americans were still enslaved, Banneker became a famous scientist.

MULTIMEDIA BIOGRAPHIES
Visit The Learning Site at **www.harcourtschool.com/biographies**
to learn about other famous people.

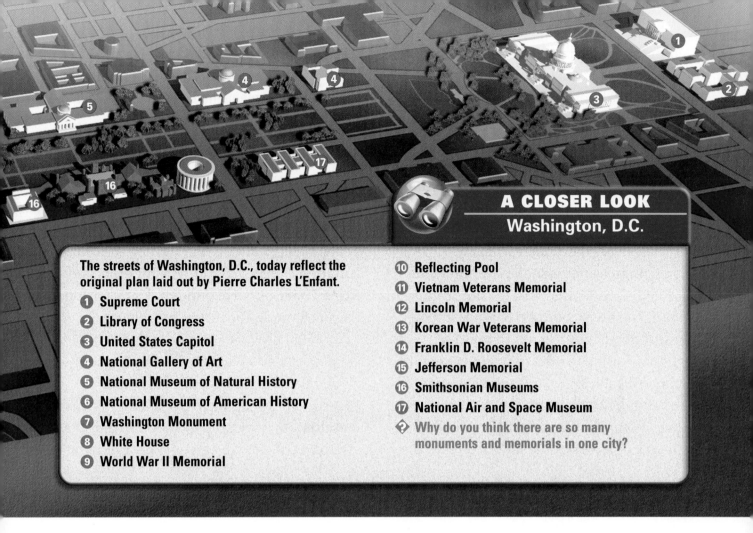

A CLOSER LOOK
Washington, D.C.

The streets of Washington, D.C., today reflect the original plan laid out by Pierre Charles L'Enfant.

1 Supreme Court
2 Library of Congress
3 United States Capitol
4 National Gallery of Art
5 National Museum of Natural History
6 National Museum of American History
7 Washington Monument
8 White House
9 World War II Memorial
10 Reflecting Pool
11 Vietnam Veterans Memorial
12 Lincoln Memorial
13 Korean War Veterans Memorial
14 Franklin D. Roosevelt Memorial
15 Jefferson Memorial
16 Smithsonian Museums
17 National Air and Space Museum

❓ Why do you think there are so many monuments and memorials in one city?

Political Parties

Before long, two of Washington's top advisers, Alexander Hamilton and Thomas Jefferson, began to argue about what was best for the United States. Hamilton wanted to have a strong national government. He favored setting up a national bank to be run by the central government. This bank would be responsible for issuing national money. Hamilton also wanted the United States to become friendly with Britain and to make use of Britain's large trading network.

Jefferson did not agree with these ideas. He thought that there should be as little central government as possible. He also believed that the United States should become friendly with France instead of with Britain. Jefferson argued that France had been an ally of the United States during the Revolutionary War.

From their disagreements, the nation's first political parties were formed. A **political party** is a group whose members try to elect government officials who share the party's point of view about many issues.

Hamilton's followers formed what became known as the Federalist party. It included people who had supported the Constitution during the state ratifying conventions. Like Hamilton, they were in favor of a strong national government. John Adams and Henry Knox became members of the Federalist party.

Jefferson's supporters, such as James Madison and Patrick Henry formed the Democratic-Republican party. They believed that the powers of the national government should be limited to those listed in the Constitution. Members of the Democratic-Republican party were sometimes called the Jeffersonian Republicans. This political party, however, was not the same as today's Republican party.

In Congress, Jeffersonian Republicans and Federalists often had to compromise so that the laws could be passed. In one compromise, they agreed to build a national capital for the new government. George Washington chose the location for the capital city that came to carry his name. Both Maryland and Virginia agreed to give up some land to create the District of Columbia (D.C.).

REVIEW What two political parties formed as a result of disagreements between Alexander Hamilton and Thomas Jefferson?

A Change in Leadership

George Washington served as President for two terms, each of which was four years long. Many people wanted him to run for a third term, but Washington said that two terms were enough. His decision set an example for future presidents.

By 1796, however, the growth of political parties had changed the way the electoral college chose the President. Instead of making its own list of **candidates**, or people to choose from, the electoral college was given a list by each

George Cooke painted this picture of the nation's capital in 1833. At that time, Washington D.C. was a much smaller city than it is today.

political party. In the election of 1796, the Federalist party backed John Adams. The Jeffersonian Republican party backed Thomas Jefferson instead. When the votes were counted, Adams won by three votes. Jefferson became Vice President.

On March 4, 1797, John Adams became the second President of the United States. He took the oath of office at Congress Hall, in Philadelphia. This was an important day in history. It was the first time that the nation had changed leaders by means of a peaceful election.

When John Adams started his term as President, Congress met in Philadelphia. Three years later, in November 1800, the federal government moved to the District of Columbia. When John Adams and his family moved to the new capital city, they lived in a special house built for the President. At first it had many names, including the President's House and the Executive Mansion. By the early 1900s,

John Adams was the first President to live in what is now the White House. Abigail Adams, his wife, wrote that the house was "built for ages to come."

however, this building was known as the White House—the name by which it is known today.

REVIEW Why did John Adams's taking the oath of office mark an important day?

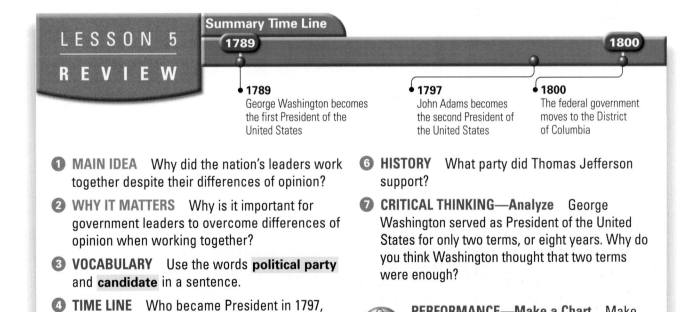

LESSON 5 REVIEW

Summary Time Line

1789 ————————————————————————— 1800

1789
George Washington becomes the first President of the United States

1797
John Adams becomes the second President of the United States

1800
The federal government moves to the District of Columbia

① **MAIN IDEA** Why did the nation's leaders work together despite their differences of opinion?

② **WHY IT MATTERS** Why is it important for government leaders to overcome differences of opinion when working together?

③ **VOCABULARY** Use the words **political party** and **candidate** in a sentence.

④ **TIME LINE** Who became President in 1797, John Adams or George Washington?

⑤ **READING SKILL—Summarize** Summarize the differences between the Federalist party and the Democratic-Republican party.

⑥ **HISTORY** What party did Thomas Jefferson support?

⑦ **CRITICAL THINKING—Analyze** George Washington served as President of the United States for only two terms, or eight years. Why do you think Washington thought that two terms were enough?

PERFORMANCE—Make a Chart Make a chart that shows what the Federalist party and the Democratic-Republican party believed in. Then explain the differences between the two parties to a classmate.

10 Review and Test Preparation

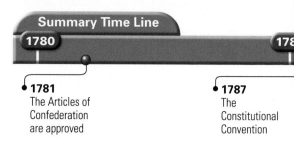

Summary Time Line

1780   178

1781
The Articles of
Confederation
are approved

1787
The
Constitutional
Convention

USE YOUR READING SKILLS

Complete this graphic organizer by summarizing the facts about the writing and ratification of the United States Constitution. A copy of this graphic organizer appears on page 101 of the Activity Book.

A New Form of Government

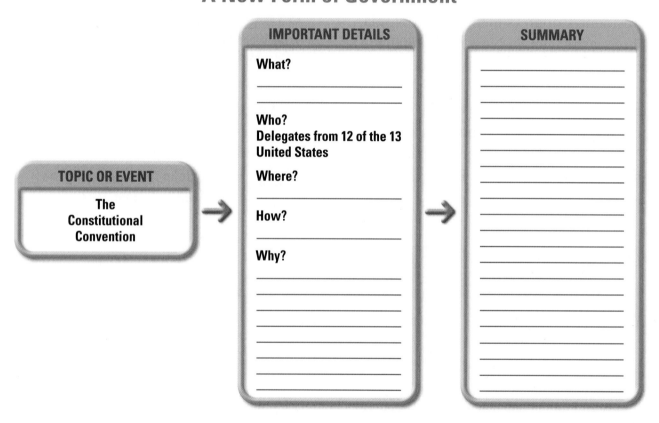

TOPIC OR EVENT

The Constitutional Convention

IMPORTANT DETAILS

What?

Who?
Delegates from 12 of the 13 United States

Where?

How?

Why?

SUMMARY

THINK & WRITE

Write a Conversation   Write a conversation that could have taken place between James Madison, William Paterson, and Roger Sherman during the Constitutional Convention. The three leaders should discuss the issue of representation.

Write an Explanation   The Bill of Rights protects the individual freedoms of all Americans. Many people place a special value on certain rights. Choose one right from the Bill of Rights and explain why it is important to you.

1788
The United States Constitution is ratified

1789
George Washington is elected the first President of the United States

1791
The Bill of Rights is added to the Constitution

1797
John Adams is elected the second President of the United States

USE THE TIME LINE

Use the chapter summary time line to answer these questions.

1 When did the Constitutional Convention take place?

2 Was George Washington elected President before or after the Bill of Rights was added to the Constitution?

USE VOCABULARY

For each pair of terms, write a sentence that explains how the terms are related.

3 **veto** (p. 361), **checks and balances** (p. 363)

4 **amendment** (p. 370), **reserved powers** (p. 372)

5 **political party** (p. 377), **candidate** (p. 378)

RECALL FACTS

Answer these questions.

6 How did Roger Sherman contribute to the creation of the Constitution?

7 What is the purpose of the Constitution according to its preamble?

Write the letter of the best choice.

8 **TEST PREP** The main function of the legislative branch of the federal government is—
  A to carry out laws.
  B to decide whether or not laws follow the Constitution.
  C to make laws.
  D to select members of the Cabinet.

9 **TEST PREP** George Washington set an example for future American Presidents by—
  F greatly increasing taxes.
  G taking the President's oath of office in Philadelphia.
  H serving only two terms.
  J allowing Congress to select his Cabinet.

THINK CRITICALLY

10 What do you think was James Madison's greatest contribution to the creation of the Constitution?

11 How might representation have been different if African Americans had been counted the same way white citizens were counted?

APPLY SKILLS

Read a Flow Chart
Study the flow chart on page 365. Then answer the following questions.

12 What happens after a bill is introduced?

13 What happens if the President vetoes a bill?

14 What happens if the President signs the bill?

Act as a Responsible Citizen

15 Identify a person who you think is a responsible citizen. Write a paragraph explaining why you think that person is acting responsibly.

CHIMNEY ROCK NATIONAL HISTORIC SITE

For settlers journeying on the Oregon Trail, Chimney Rock was an important landmark. It marked the place where the prairies ended and the ground became more rugged, heading west toward the Rocky Mountains. From 1812 to 1866, nearly half a million settlers passed Chimney Rock on their journey west.

LOCATE IT

NEBRASKA

Chimney Rock
National Historic Site

The Nation Grows

" Go west, young man, go west. "

—John B.L. Soule, editorial in the
Terre Haute Express, 1851

MAIN IDEA
Read to learn how the United States grew west of the Mississippi River.

WHY IT MATTERS
The new lands gotten by the United States doubled its size and opened up a new territory for exploration and settlement.

VOCABULARY

inauguration
pathfinder
trespass

After the Louisiana Purchase, soldiers at the fort at New Orleans replaced the French flag with the United States flag. The French artist, who mistakenly added hills and cactus to the area, had probably never been to New Orleans.

The Louisiana Purchase

| 1780 | 1800 | 1820 | 1840 | 1860 |

1800–1806

By 1800 Vermont, Kentucky, and Tennessee were added to the original 13 states, and the Northwest Territory was divided into the territories of Ohio and Indiana. Americans were moving west in greater numbers. Some Americans even began to look beyond the Mississippi to the land the French had named Louisiana. France had given Spain this huge region after France lost the French and Indian War in 1763. At this time Spain also controlled all the lands along the Gulf coast.

The Louisiana Purchase

On March 4, 1801, Thomas Jefferson became the third President of the United States. At his **inauguration** (ih•naw•gyuh•RAY•shuhn), or taking office, Jefferson spoke of his hopes for the young nation. He called the United States "a rising nation, spread over a wide and fruitful land." He knew, however, that the nation faced some serious problems.

The United States had no ports of its own on the Gulf of Mexico. Farmers who lived in Kentucky, Tennessee, and the Northwest Territory had to ship their goods down the Mississippi River to New Orleans. From there they could sell the goods to ships sailing for ports in Europe or along the Atlantic coast of the United States.

The Louisiana Purchase

Place **The Louisiana Purchase doubled the size of the United States.**

◈ What natural features of the territory made it easy to explore?

Spain once had allowed American farmers to load and unload their goods free of charge at New Orleans. That changed, however, and it became more costly for farmers to sell their products. Jefferson worried that people in the western United States might not stay loyal to the government if they had no way to ship their products to market.

Soon after Jefferson became President, he learned that Spain had given Louisiana back to France. The French leader, Napoleon Bonaparte (nuh•POH•lee•uhn BOH•nuh•part), hoped to once again establish French power in North America. However, Jefferson knew that having the French in control of Louisiana could prevent the United States frontier from moving farther west.

Jefferson sent representatives to France to ask Bonaparte to sell the land along the east bank of the Mississippi River, including New Orleans, to the United States. With this land, the United States would have a port on the Gulf of Mexico.

At this time France was getting ready for war with Britain. People in the French colony of St. Domingue (SAN daw•MANG) in the Caribbean had also rebelled against French rule. Bonaparte needed money to fight two wars. He offered to sell *all* of Louisiana— more than 800,000 square miles (2,071,840 sq km)— to the United States for about $15 million.

The agreement to buy Louisiana was made on April 30, 1803. The sale of this huge territory became known as the Louisiana Purchase.

REVIEW Why did Jefferson want to buy the land along the east bank of the Mississippi?

Lewis and Clark

Few people in the United States knew much about the Louisiana Purchase. It was a huge region, reaching from the Mississippi River to the Rocky Mountains and from New Orleans north to Canada. Americans had never explored it, so President Jefferson asked Congress for money to pay for an expedition to find out more about it.

Jefferson chose Meriwether Lewis to lead the expedition. Lewis had been an army officer and had served in the Northwest Territory. Jefferson also chose William Clark, a good friend of Lewis and brother of the Revolutionary War hero George Rogers Clark, to help lead the expedition.

Meriwether Lewis and William Clark put together a group of about 30 soldiers. They called their group the Corps of

Discovery. One member of the Corps of Discovery was York, William Clark's African American slave who was skilled in hunting and fishing.

In May 1804 the group left its camp near present-day St. Louis and traveled up the Missouri River by boat. By October the expedition had reached present-day North Dakota. With winter coming on, they built a small camp near a Mandan Indian village. They named their camp Fort Mandan.

At Fort Mandan, Lewis and Clark hired a French fur trader to interpret some Indian languages for them. The fur trader was married to a Shoshone (shoh•SHOH•nee) Indian woman named Sacagawea

Meriwether Lewis (far right) and William Clark (right) led the Corps of Discovery through the Louisiana Purchase. The painting shows Sacagawea using sign language to communicate with the Chinooks during the expedition.

(sa•kuh•juh•WEE•uh). Sacagawea agreed to guide the expedition when it reached the land of the Shoshones.

In the spring of 1805, the Lewis and Clark expedition set out again. They moved farther up the Missouri River toward the Rocky Mountains. With Sacagawea's help, the expedition got horses from the Shoshones and continued their journey through the mountain passes of the Rockies. Once over the mountains, the explorers built boats and rowed down the Clearwater, Snake, and Columbia Rivers toward the Pacific coast.

Finally, in November 1805, after traveling for more than a year and covering more than 3,000 miles (about 4,800 km), the Lewis and Clark expedition reached the Pacific Ocean. Clark wrote in his journal,

66 Great joy in camp. We are in view of the . . . great Pacific Octean [Ocean], which we have been so long anxious to see, and the roreing [roaring] or noise made by the waves brakeing [breaking] on the rockey [rocky] shores (as I may suppose) may be heard distinctly. 99

In March the Corps of Discovery began the long journey back to St. Louis. They reached the settlement in September 1806. The expedition had collected many facts about the Louisiana Purchase. They brought back seeds, plants, and even living animals. They could tell what the people and the land were like, and they had drawn maps to show where mountain passes and major rivers were. In later years the work of these pathfinders helped American settlers find their way to the Pacific coast. A **pathfinder** is someone who finds a way through an unknown region.

REVIEW Who led the first expedition to the Louisiana Purchase?

The Pike Expedition

As the Lewis and Clark expedition made its way back to St. Louis in 1806, another expedition was exploring the southwestern part of the Louisiana Purchase. This small group of pathfinders was led by Captain Zebulon Pike.

By the winter of 1806, the Pike expedition had reached a huge prairie in present-day Kansas. As the expedition traveled farther west, Pike saw what he described as a "blue mountain" in the distance. Today that blue mountain is called Pikes Peak, for the explorer.

The expedition followed the Rocky Mountains south to what Pike thought was the Red River, one of the rivers that led into the Mississippi River. It was really the northern part of the Rio Grande. The expedition had wandered out of the Louisiana Purchase and into Spanish land.

Spanish soldiers soon reached the small fort that the Americans had built along the river. The soldiers took Pike and the others to Santa Fe, the capital of the Spanish colony of New Mexico. The explorers were put in jail for **trespassing**, or going onto someone else's property without asking. In Santa Fe the Spanish governor asked Zebulon Pike if the United States was getting ready to invade the Spanish lands. Pike answered no.

When the Spanish set him free several months later, Pike reported that the people of Santa Fe needed manufactured goods. Soon American traders were heading for New Mexico.

Zebulon Pike

REVIEW Why did Spanish soldiers put Captain Zebulon Pike and the rest of his explorers in jail?

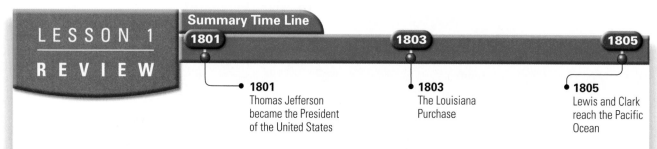

LESSON 1 REVIEW

Summary Time Line

1801 — 1801 Thomas Jefferson became the President of the United States

1803 — 1803 The Louisiana Purchase

1805 — 1805 Lewis and Clark reach the Pacific Ocean

❶ **MAIN IDEA** Why did the United States grow west of the Mississippi River?

❷ **WHY IT MATTERS** How did this expansion benefit the United States?

❸ **VOCABULARY** What is a **pathfinder**?

❹ **TIME LINE** In what year did the Louisiana Purchase take place?

❺ **READING SKILL—Draw Conclusions** Why do you think the Lewis and Clark expedition brought back plants and living animals?

❻ **GEOGRAPHY** What area did the Louisiana Purchase cover?

❼ **CRITICAL THINKING—Evaluate** How was the Lewis and Clark expedition important to American settlement out west?

PERFORMANCE—Draw a Map Imagine that you have been chosen to explore the Louisiana Purchase. Draw a map of the United States that shows the Louisiana Purchase. Then trace a route through the territory that shows the areas you would like to explore.

The War of 1812

1805–1825

As Meriwether Lewis, William Clark, and Zebulon Pike were exploring the Louisiana Purchase, American settlers were pushing the frontier farther and farther west. As settlers moved west, however, they ran into many angry Native Americans who tried to stop them from taking their lands. The Indians were helped by the British in Canada, who sold them guns and encouraged them to fight the Americans. Before long, troubles in the western lands helped push the United States into a second war with Britain—the War of 1812.

War Fever

Americans were angry with the British for other reasons, too. To stop Americans from trading with the French and other Europeans, the British navy stopped American merchant ships at sea. They even forced sailors off American merchant ships and put them to work on British navy ships. Taking workers against their will this way is called **impressment**.

MAIN IDEA
Read to learn why the United States once again found itself at war with Britain.

WHY IT MATTERS
As a result of this war, the United States became a major world power.

VOCABULARY

impressment
war hawk
national anthem
siege
nationalism
annex
doctrine

This engraving shows impressment of American sailors by the British in Boston.

Members of Congress from Ohio, Kentucky, and Tennessee, as well as the southern states, wanted war with Britain. Those who wanted war became known as **war hawks**. The war hawks thought the way to deal with the British was simple—take over Canada and drive the British out of North America. Many war hawks also believed that the United States should take over Florida, which was held by Spain, to get even more land. Congress member Henry Clay of Kentucky, one of the best-known war hawks, said the United States should "take the whole continent."

The desire for war grew strong in much of the nation. In June 1812 James Madison, the fourth President of the United States, asked Congress to declare war on Britain. Congress quickly voted for war.

As the fighting began, Britain had the strongest navy in the world. Yet the small United States Navy, with only 16 ships, won two important battles early in the war. One was on the Atlantic Ocean and the other on the Great Lakes.

On August 19, 1812, the United States warship *Constitution* fought the British ship *Guerrière* (gair•YAIR) off the coast of Nova Scotia and won. After the two ships had shot cannonballs at each other, the *Guerrière* was in bad shape. Cannonballs, however, could not pierce the hard oak sides of the *Constitution*. Legend has it that a crew member said, "Her sides are made of iron." After that, the *Constitution* was nicknamed Old Ironsides.

On September 10, 1813, the Battle of Lake Erie became an early turning point in the war. Ships commanded by American Captain Oliver Hazard Perry beat the British. This allowed General William Henry Harrison to lead 4,500 soldiers across Lake Erie into Canada. At the Battle of the Thames (TEMZ) on October 5, 1813, the American forces beat the British and their Indian allies. Among the dead was Tecumseh (tuh•KUHM•suh), the Shawnee leader of an Indian group that had tried to stop Americans from taking Indian lands. From that time on, settlers in the Northwest Territory were free of conflicts with Indians.

REVIEW **What victory allowed General Harrison to lead his troops into Canada?**

The Battle of Lake Erie was a clash between American and British ships that lasted more than three hours.

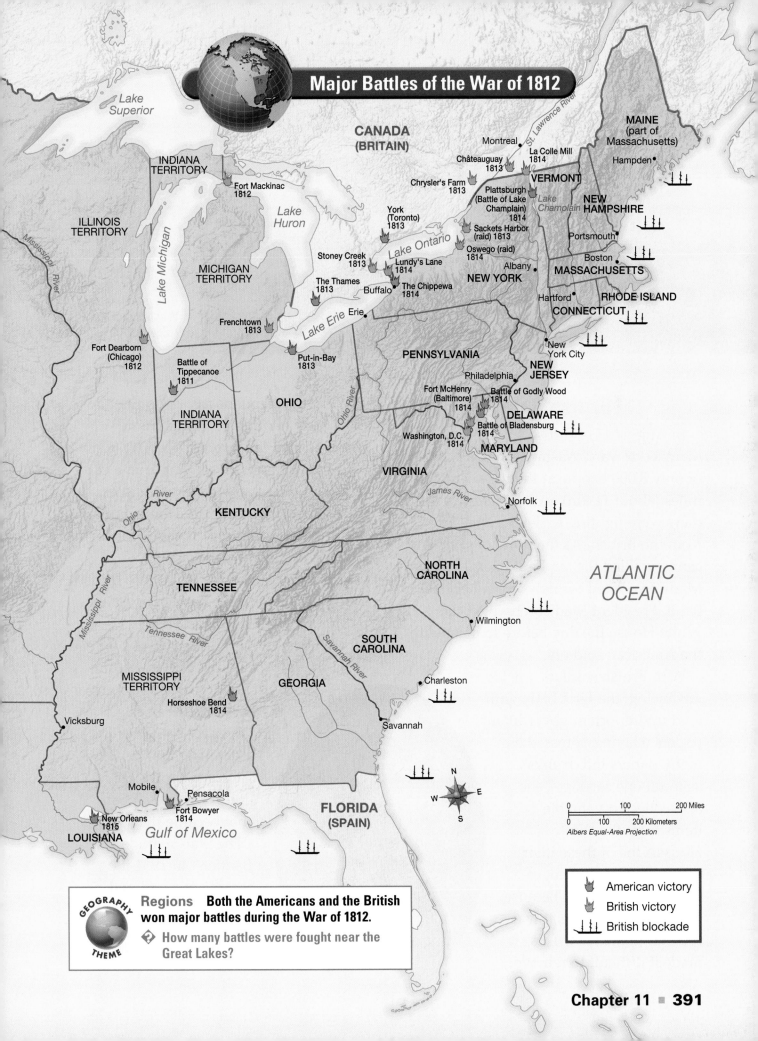

Major Battles of the War of 1812

Lake Superior

Lake Huron

Lake Michigan

CANADA (BRITAIN)

Montreal

St. Lawrence River

MAINE (part of Massachusetts)

Hampden

Châteauguay 1813

La Colle Mill 1814

Chrysler's Farm 1813

Plattsburgh (Battle of Lake Champlain) 1814

VERMONT

NEW HAMPSHIRE

INDIANA TERRITORY

Fort Mackinac 1812

York (Toronto) 1813

Lake Champlain

Lake Ontario

Sackets Harbor (raid) 1813

Oswego (raid) 1814

Portsmouth

Boston

ILLINOIS TERRITORY

MICHIGAN TERRITORY

Stoney Creek 1813

Lundy's Lane 1814

Albany

NEW YORK

MASSACHUSETTS

Mississippi River

The Thames 1813

Buffalo

The Chippewa 1814

Hartford

RHODE ISLAND

CONNECTICUT

Frenchtown 1813

Lake Erie

Erie

New York City

NEW JERSEY

Fort Dearborn (Chicago) 1812

Put-in-Bay 1813

PENNSYLVANIA

Battle of Tippecanoe 1811

OHIO

Ohio River

Philadelphia

Fort McHenry (Baltimore) 1814

Battle of Godly Wood 1814

DELAWARE

INDIANA TERRITORY

Washington, D.C. 1814

Battle of Bladensburg 1814

MARYLAND

River

Ohio River

VIRGINIA

KENTUCKY

James River

Norfolk

TENNESSEE

Tennessee River

NORTH CAROLINA

ATLANTIC OCEAN

Wilmington

MISSISSIPPI TERRITORY

SOUTH CAROLINA

Horseshoe Bend 1814

GEORGIA

Savannah River

Charleston

Vicksburg

Savannah

N
W   E
S

Mobile

Pensacola

Fort Bowyer 1814

New Orleans 1815

LOUISIANA

Gulf of Mexico

FLORIDA (SPAIN)

0   100   200 Miles
0   100   200 Kilometers
Albers Equal-Area Projection

🔥 American victory

🔥 British victory

⟊⟊⟊ British blockade

GEOGRAPHY THEME

Regions Both the Americans and the British won major battles during the War of 1812.

❓ How many battles were fought near the Great Lakes?

This engraving shows the White House damaged by fire after the British attack on Washington, D.C., in August 1814.

British Raids

In August 1814 British soldiers marched toward Washington, D.C., a city of only 8,000 people at the time. Just 7 miles (about 11 km) away, American soldiers were fighting to defend the city from the British. As the noise of guns and cannons filled the air, First Lady Dolley Madison waited for news from her husband. President Madison had left the White House the day before to meet with the American soldiers.

With British soldiers quickly advancing, the First Lady gathered up important government papers. Having "pressed as many papers into trunks as to fill one carriage" she also collected valuable items from the White House. One of these items was a life-size portrait of George Washington. Because of the portrait's size, it was secured to the wall. This made it difficult to remove.

With the enemy nearly upon her, the First Lady had the portrait's frame smashed and the canvas rolled up. Only after everything was safely put in a carriage did First Lady Dolley Madison finally leave Washington. That evening the British set fire to the White House, the Capitol, and other buildings.

With Washington in flames, the British sailed up Chesapeake Bay to Baltimore. Baltimore was protected by Fort McHenry. Although British ships bombed the fort for hours, the Americans would not give up. The sight of the huge American flag waving over the fort after the battle made Francis Scott Key very happy. He quickly wrote a poem that became the song "The Star-Spangled Banner." In 1931 it became our national

Dolley Madison rescued important items from the White House in the War of 1812.

anthem. A **national anthem** is a song of praise for a country that is recognized as the official song of that country.

When they could not beat the Americans at Baltimore, the British sailed south to New Orleans. American soldiers under the command of General Andrew Jackson were waiting for them there. Earlier that year, with the help of the Cherokees, Jackson had defeated the Creeks at the Battle of Horseshoe Bend in present-day Alabama. The Creeks were allies of the British.

When word came to General Jackson that the British might attack New Orleans, his troops hurried to defend the city. There they lived through a 10-day siege by British soldiers. A **siege** is a long-lasting attack. After fierce fighting, Jackson's soldiers finally forced the British out. Upon learning this, Jackson said, "By the Eternal, they shall not sleep on our soil!"

Americans would later learn that the Battle of New Orleans had not been necessary. On December 24, 1814—two weeks *before* the battle—the British and Americans had signed a peace treaty in Europe. Because news traveled so slowly at that time, word that the war was over had not reached New Orleans in time.

REVIEW What inspired Francis Scott Key to write "The Star-Spangled Banner"?

· HERITAGE ·

"The Star-Spangled Banner"

Originally a poem titled "The Defense of Fort McHenry" the song known today as our national anthem was first performed in October of 1814. Quickly renamed, the song was issued as a handbill, or flyer, and soon became a favorite of American troops. By 1904 American military bases were required to perform the song every time the national flag was raised or lowered. In 1931 Congress voted to officially make "The Star-Spangled Banner" the national anthem of the United States.

Francis Scott Key

Oh, say can you see by the dawn's early light
What so proudly we hail'd at the twilight's last
  gleaming,
Whose broad stripes and bright stars through the
  perilous fight
O'er the ramparts we watch'd were so gallantly
  streaming?
And the rockets' red glare, the bombs bursting in air,
Gave proof through the night that our flag was still
  there.
Oh, say does that star-spangled banner yet wave
O'er the land of the free and the home of the brave?

The Era of Good Feelings

Neither side was clearly the winner in the War of 1812. However, Americans were proud that the United States had stood up to Britain. After the war a wave of **nationalism**, or pride in the country, swept over the land. For this reason the years from 1817 to 1825 have been called the Era of Good Feelings.

National pride could be seen in the strong way the government acted with other countries. James Monroe, the fifth President of the United States, negotiated a new boundary line between the United States and British Canada. He also got Spain to give up its claims to West Florida, which had been **annexed**, or added on, to the United States earlier. In another treaty, Spain agreed to sell East Florida to the United States, too.

President Monroe knew that if the United States wanted to keep growing, it had to stop the growth of Spanish, French, Russian, and British colonies in the Americas. So on December 2, 1823, President Monroe announced a **doctrine**, or government plan of action. It came to be called the Monroe Doctrine.

In the Monroe Doctrine, President Monroe acknowledged Europe's colonies in the Western Hemisphere. However, the doctrine closed the hemisphere to any future colonization by European countries.

REVIEW What did President Monroe do to stop the growth of European colonies in the Americas?

President Monroe sent a strong warning to European nations that had interests in the Western Hemisphere.

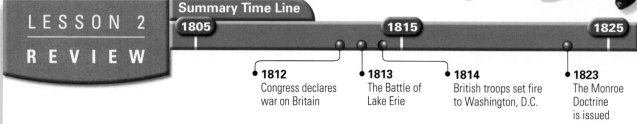

LESSON 2
REVIEW

Summary Time Line

1805 — 1815 — 1825

● **1812** Congress declares war on Britain

● **1813** The Battle of Lake Erie

● **1814** British troops set fire to Washington, D.C.

● **1823** The Monroe Doctrine is issued

① **MAIN IDEA** Why did the United States go to war with Britain?

② **WHY IT MATTERS** Why was the United States considered a world power after the war?

③ **VOCABULARY** What clues can you use to remember the meaning of **nationalism**?

④ **TIME LINE** When was the Battle of Lake Erie?

⑤ **READING SKILL—Draw Conclusions** Why do you think settlers in the West would support the idea of going to war with Britain?

⑥ **HISTORY** Why did President Monroe want to end European colonization in the Americas?

⑦ **CRITICAL THINKING—Evaluate** Why do you think that someone who was a war hawk would support the Monroe Doctrine?

PERFORMANCE—Use the Internet Research the War of 1812 on the Internet to gain more information about it. Then share what you learned with your classmates.

The Age of Jackson

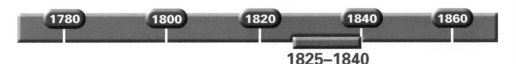

1780   1800   1820   1840   1860

1825–1840

MAIN IDEA
Read to learn about the main events that took place while Andrew Jackson was President.

WHY IT MATTERS
The right of people to make decisions about their lives and government grew to include more Americans.

VOCABULARY
democracy
ruling

The year 1826 marked the fiftieth anniversary of the Declaration of Independence. In that time the country had grown from the original 13 states to 24 states. Its land area had more than doubled in size. Ideas about democracy also were growing with the nation. In a **democracy** the people rule, and they are free to make choices about their lives and government.

Democracy Grows

In the early days of the country, voting was usually limited to property owners. In most of the new western states, such as Kentucky and Tennessee, this changed. Those states gave the vote to all white men, not just to those who owned property. This practice soon spread to all states. No other country in the world was so democratic, even though women and most free African Americans could not vote and Native Americans were not counted as citizens.

Once all white men could vote, there was a change in the kind of person elected. People elected as public officials were no longer always wealthy, well-educated men who owned property. Some, in fact, had little money or schooling. Davy Crockett, from Tennessee, was an example of this new kind of leader. Many people felt the frontier spirit of the United States was reflected in Davy Crockett's motto.

Davy Crockett started his political career in Lawrence County, Tennessee. The sketch shows the office he had there.

Chapter 11   395

His motto was "Be always sure you're right—then go ahead!"

Davy Crockett held several local and state offices in Tennessee before winning a seat in the House of Representatives. When Crockett first ran for office, he had to say he knew nothing about government. "I had never read even a newspaper in my life," he said. Crockett learned about government by being part of it.

Andrew Jackson

REVIEW How did government change once all white men could vote?

The Election of Andrew Jackson

In 1828 Andrew Jackson of Tennessee was elected the seventh President of the United States. The six Presidents before him had all come from families from either Massachusetts or Virginia. Now for the first time a person from a western state had been elected. It was also the first election in which all white American men could vote. Many of the new voters liked Jackson because they felt he was a "common man," like them.

Jackson was born in the backcountry of South Carolina to a poor family living in a log cabin. Tough and stubborn, Jackson taught himself law by reading books. In time he became a successful lawyer and later a judge.

While serving in the military, Jackson got the nickname "Old Hickory"—hickory being a very hard wood. "He's tough," said his soldiers, "tough as hickory." As a general during the War of 1812, Jackson became a national hero after his

This picture shows the excitement of the crowd outside the White House during President Jackson's inaugural celebration.

troops beat the British at the Battle of New Orleans.

When Jackson became President on March 4, 1829, his followers were overjoyed. Thousands had streamed into Washington, D.C., for the inauguration. Many of them later showed up at the White House for the party that followed. Rough-and-tumble people from the frontier stood in their muddy boots on the satin-covered chairs to get a look at their hero. To keep from being crushed by the crowd, Jackson had to escape by a back door.

As President, Andrew Jackson continued to be both tough and stubborn. He fought to bring about an end to the Second Bank of the United States. In Jackson's eyes the bank was a "hydra of corruption." A hydra is a many-headed monster from Greek mythology.

The troubled First Bank of the United States, which had been created while George Washington was President, had closed after the War of 1812. Another bank, the Second Bank of the United States, was started in 1816. This bank was influential, and it played an important role in the United States economy.

In spite of its success, President Jackson believed the bank was too powerful. It

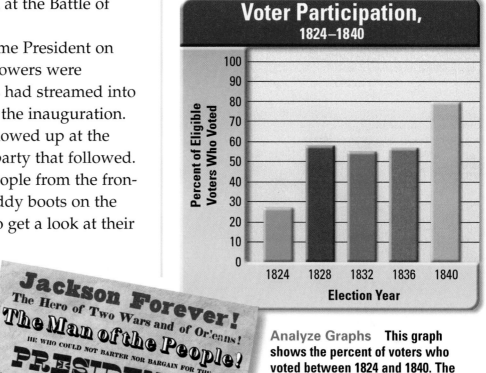

Voter Participation, 1824–1840

Percent of Eligible Voters Who Voted / Election Year

Analyze Graphs This graph shows the percent of voters who voted between 1824 and 1840. The poster (left) helped persuade people to vote for Andrew Jackson.

❖ About what percent of voters voted in the election of 1828?

controlled one-fifth of all the bank notes in the United States and one-third of all the nation's gold. Jackson argued that the bank put too much money power in the hands of the wealthy bank owners and a few rich customers and did not care about the needs of the general public.

Saying "The bank is trying to kill me, but I will kill it," Jackson vetoed a bill that would have given the bank a new charter, or contract. Government should not help the rich get richer, Jackson believed. Instead it should "shower its favors alike on the high and the low, the rich and the poor."

REVIEW How did Andrew Jackson differ from earlier Presidents of the United States?

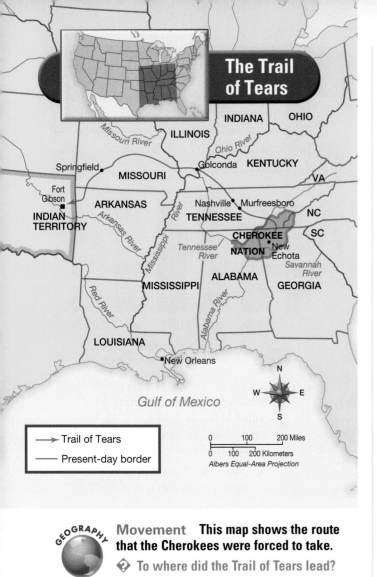

The Trail of Tears

INDIANA · OHIO
ILLINOIS
Missouri River
Ohio River
Springfield · MISSOURI · Golconda · KENTUCKY
Fort Gibson · ARKANSAS · Nashville · Murfreesboro · VA
INDIAN TERRITORY · TENNESSEE · NC
Arkansas River · CHEROKEE · SC
Mississippi River · Tennessee River · NATION · New Echota
Savannah River
Red River · Alabama River · ALABAMA · GEORGIA
MISSISSIPPI
LOUISIANA
New Orleans
Gulf of Mexico

N W E S

→ Trail of Tears
— Present-day border

0   100   200 Miles
0 100 200 Kilometers
Albers Equal-Area Projection

GEOGRAPHY THEME

Movement **This map shows the route that the Cherokees were forced to take.**

❓ To where did the Trail of Tears lead?

Indian Removal

Jackson's toughness also meant harsh and unfair treatment of the Native Americans who lived east of the Mississippi River. In 1830 Congress passed the Indian Removal Act. It had been Jackson's idea. This act said that all Indians east of the Mississippi had to leave their lands and move west to the Indian Territory. This area spread across most of what is now the state of Oklahoma.

Many tribes refused to leave their homelands. Instead, some chose to stay and fight against the soldiers sent to remove them. Led by Chief Black Hawk,

the Sauk and Fox Indians in the Great Lakes region fought United States troops and Illinois militia in the Black Hawk War. In the southeastern United States, the Seminoles of Florida, led by Osceola and helped by runaway slaves, also fought United States troops. In both wars, many Native Americans were either killed or forced to leave their homeland.

Instead of fighting on the battlefield, the Cherokee nation chose to fight for its homeland in the United States courts. Led by Chief John Ross, the Cherokees were one of the richest tribes in the United States. They had many towns and villages throughout the Southeast, including New Echota (ih•KOH•tuh), Georgia, the capital of the Cherokee nation.

In a treaty signed in 1791, the United States government had recognized the Cherokee nation's independence. In 1828, however, the state of Georgia said that Cherokee laws were no longer in effect. As a result, when gold was discovered on Cherokee lands a year later, settlers were free to pour in and stake their claims.

By 1832 the Cherokees' case had gone all the way to the United States Supreme Court. There Chief Justice John Marshall gave the Court's **ruling**, or decision. He said that Georgia had no say over the Cherokee lands. The Court's ruling, however, was ignored, and federal troops were ordered to remove the Cherokees.

In late 1838 federal troops forced the last large group of Cherokees to leave their lands. They traveled from North Carolina and Georgia through Tennessee, Kentucky, Illinois, Missouri, and Arkansas—more than 800 miles (about 1,300 km)—to the Indian Territory. By the time their journey ended in March 1839,

This painting by Cherokee artist Troy Anderson shows a group of Cherokees on the Trail of Tears. The Cherokees were forced to walk a great distance to the Indian Territory during the cold winter months.

more than 4,000 Cherokees had died of cold, disease, and lack of food. The Cherokees called their long journey the "Trail Where They Cried." It later became known as the Trail of Tears.

REVIEW How was the way in which the Cherokees fought the loss of their land different from that of other Indian tribes?

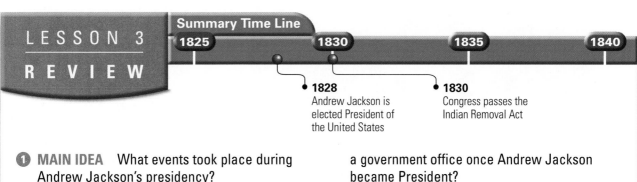

LESSON 3 REVIEW

Summary Time Line

1825 — 1830 — 1835 — 1840

1828 Andrew Jackson is elected President of the United States

1830 Congress passes the Indian Removal Act

① **MAIN IDEA** What events took place during Andrew Jackson's presidency?

② **WHY IT MATTERS** Why did more Americans get involved with the government?

③ **VOCABULARY** Write a description of a **democracy**.

④ **TIME LINE** When was Andrew Jackson elected as the President of the United States?

⑤ **READING SKILL—Draw Conclusions** Why do you think more people in the West might run for a government office once Andrew Jackson became President?

⑥ **HISTORY** What was the Trail of Tears?

⑦ **CRITICAL THINKING—Analyze** How did democracy grow during Jackson's presidency?

PERFORMANCE—Write a Biography Use library or Internet resources to write a biography of Andrew Jackson. Share the biography with a classmate.

PRIMARY SOURCES

Audubon's Paintings

John James Audubon was a gifted artist born in 1785 in what is now Haiti. During his life, Audubon observed and painted hundreds of pictures of birds and other wildlife. Some, such as those pictured on these pages, are now extinct. Audubon's attention to detail gives people today the opportunity to see animals they can no longer find in North America. Audubon's work inspired George Bird Grinnell to establish the National Audubon Society in 1886. The society works to conserve nature.

 FROM THE EWELL SALE STEWART LIBRARY AND THE ACADEMY OF NATURAL SCIENCES

John James Audubon

Carolina Parrot
Because they were used as a source for feathers to decorate hats, Carolina parrots were extinct by 1920.

Pied Duck
The last recorded sighting of a pied, or labrador, duck was in 1878 in Elmira, New York.

Passenger Pigeon
Hunted for food, the last passenger pigeon died in 1914.

![ACTIVITY]

Compare and Contrast Keep a journal for one week of the kinds of birds that you notice in your yard or on the schoolgrounds. Write or draw details that are unique to each kind of bird you see. Share your observations with the class. How are your observations alike? How are they different?

Audubon kept drawings in this box.

Analyze the Primary Source

❶ **What do the paintings tell you about the environment in which each bird lived? Look at the bills of each of the birds shown here. Why might different birds need bills that are suited for their different environments?**

❷ **Why do you think people chose to use the feathers from the Carolina Parrot?**

❸ **Why do you think people might be interested in studying Audubon's bird paintings?**

Great Auk
The Great Auk was the last flightless seabird of the Northern Hemisphere. The last two confirmed adults were killed in 1844.

RESEARCH

Visit The Learning Site at
www.harcourtschool.com/primarysources
to research other primary sources.

From Ocean to Ocean

1780   1800   1820   1840   1860

1820–1850

Americans in the early 1800s began to push beyond the nation's borders. They looked to the Spanish colony of Texas, to the Oregon Country in the Pacific Northwest, and to other western lands. In 1845 the words **manifest destiny** were heard for the first time. These words referred to the belief shared by many Americans that the United States should one day stretch from the Atlantic Ocean to the Pacific Ocean.

Americans in Early Texas

In 1820 a Missouri businessperson named Moses Austin asked Spanish leaders in Mexico to let him start a colony in Texas so that people from the United States could settle there. The Spanish leaders agreed to let Austin start a colony, but he died before he could carry out his plan. Stephen F. Austin, Moses Austin's son, took up his father's plan and started the colony. He chose an area between the Brazos and Colorado Rivers. Americans began to settle there in 1821.

That same year Mexico won its independence from Spain. At first the new Mexican government left the Americans alone. As more Americans arrived in Texas, however, the Mexican government became worried. In 1830 it passed a law stopping more Americans from settling in Texas. Mexican leaders also insisted that settlers already in Texas obey Mexico's laws and pay more taxes. This made the Americans angry.

In 1834 General Antonio López de Santa Anna took over the Mexican government and made himself **dictator**, a leader who has complete control of the government. Santa Anna sent troops to Texas to enforce Mexican laws. The American settlers, called Anglos, and many Tejanos (tay•HAH•nohs)—the

Stephen F. Austin started the first American colony in Texas. In the colony's early years, he served as leader, lawmaker, judge, and commander of the military. Present-day Austin, Texas, was named for him.

settlers from Mexico who lived in Texas—were angered by Santa Anna's actions. As a result, fighting broke out. Both groups living in Texas revolted against the Mexican government.

On November 3, 1835, Texas leaders met to organize a temporary government. They wanted to drive out Santa Anna's army, so they ordered Texas soldiers to attack the Mexican troops at San Antonio on December 5, 1835. After four days of fighting, the Mexican troops gave up. Santa Anna was so angry that he marched to San Antonio himself with thousands of soldiers to take back the city.

Texans in San Antonio took shelter behind the walls of a Spanish mission called the Alamo. Among them were Americans who had come to Texas to help them in their fight for freedom. They included James Bowie, Davy Crockett, and their commander, William B. Travis.

Santa Anna's forces attacked the Alamo on February 23, 1836. When it finally fell on March 6, all 189 Texans and their supporters had been killed. Only women and children survived.

On March 2, as the battle at the Alamo raged on, Texas leaders met to declare their independence and set up the Republic of Texas. They chose David G. Burnet as president of the new nation and Sam Houston as commander of the army.

On April 21, 1836, Houston's army took the Mexicans by surprise at the Battle of San Jacinto (hah•SEEN•toh). With the battle cry "Remember the Alamo!" the Texans beat the Mexican army and captured Santa Anna. In return for their sparing his life, Santa Anna agreed to grant Texas its independence. Texas remained an independent republic until it became part of the United States in 1845.

REVIEW **When did Texas become a republic?**

At the Alamo fewer than 200 Texans faced more than 2,000 Mexican soldiers. In this painting Davy Crockett swings his rifle at the enemy after having run out of ammunition.

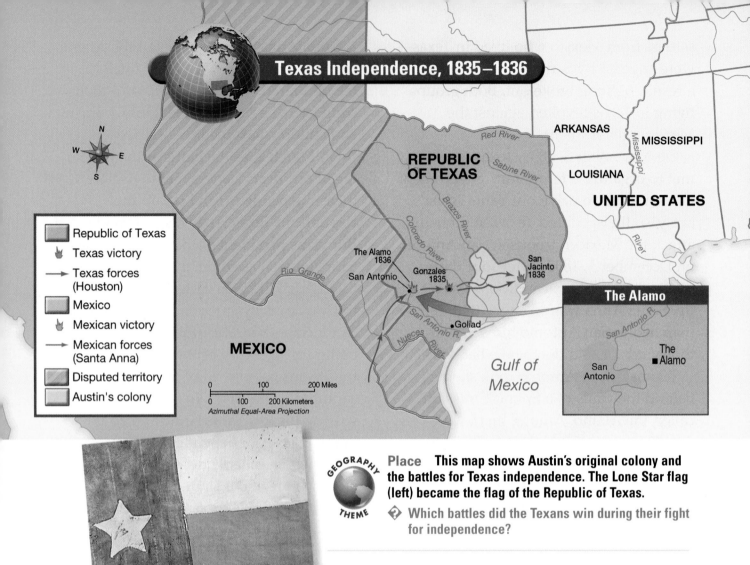

Texas Independence, 1835–1836

Legend:
- Republic of Texas
- 🔥 Texas victory
- → Texas forces (Houston)
- Mexico
- 🔥 Mexican victory
- → Mexican forces (Santa Anna)
- Disputed territory
- Austin's colony

0   100   200 Miles
0   100   200 Kilometers
Azimuthal Equal-Area Projection

ARKANSAS
MISSISSIPPI
LOUISIANA
UNITED STATES
REPUBLIC OF TEXAS
Red River
Sabine River
Brazos River
Colorado River
The Alamo 1836
San Antonio
Gonzales 1835
San Jacinto 1836
Rio Grande
MEXICO
San Antonio R.
Nueces River
Goliad
Gulf of Mexico
Mississippi R.
River

The Alamo
San Antonio R.
San Antonio
■ The Alamo

GEOGRAPHY THEME

Place This map shows Austin's original colony and the battles for Texas independence. The Lone Star flag (left) became the flag of the Republic of Texas.

❖ Which battles did the Texans win during their fight for independence?

Trails West

The same year that the first settlers from the United States traveled to Texas, a Missouri trader named William Becknell opened the Santa Fe Trail. This trail ran from Independence, Missouri, to the city of Santa Fe in New Mexico and covered a distance of 780 miles (1,255 km). By the 1850s, many people were using the trail to travel west. A new part of the trail, called the Old Spanish Trail, linked Santa Fe to Los Angeles in California.

In 1834 Christian missionaries pushed into the Oregon Country. This region in the Pacific Northwest was claimed by both the United States and Britain. It included what are now Oregon, Washington, Idaho, western Montana, and western Wyoming.

In 1836 Marcus and Narcissa Whitman and Henry and Eliza Spalding set up missions near the Walla Walla Valley, where they taught Christianity to the Cayuse (KY•yoos) Indians. In letters to her family, Narcissa Whitman told about the beautiful valleys and rich soil of the Oregon Country. Her letters were later published, and by 1842 they had attracted the first large group of American settlers to the region. Thousands more soon followed.

Travelers to the Oregon Country usually gathered in St. Louis, Missouri. From St. Louis they traveled up the Missouri River to Independence, Missouri. In Independence they joined wagon trains to cross the Great Plains and the Rocky Mountains.

The route they followed came to be called the Oregon Trail. It led northwest from Independence to the Platte River. From the Platte, it cut through the Rocky Mountains and crossed the Continental Divide. Then the trail followed the Snake and Columbia Rivers and ended at the Willamette (wuh•LA•muht) Valley in present-day Oregon.

The Oregon Trail was more than 2,000 miles (about 3,200 km) long. The journey could take as long as six months, and there were many hardships along the way. Yet many reached Oregon, and settlements there grew quickly.

The United States wanted to set up a clear border between itself and British Canada. For a long time, it looked as if arguments over the Oregon Country

This painting shows settlers gathered in St. Louis, Missouri, which came to be called the Gateway to the West.

might cause yet another war between the United States and Britain. Finally, in 1846, President James K. Polk agreed to divide the Oregon Country with Britain and signed a treaty fixing the 49th parallel as the dividing border.

REVIEW Where did the Oregon Trail begin and end?

• BIOGRAPHY •

Narcissa Prentiss Whitman   1808–1847

Character Trait: Courage

Narcissa Whitman was one of the first white women to travel west along what would become the Oregon Trail. While on her travels, she began to write her family a series of letters describing her new life. The letters, covering a span of 11 years, told of Narcissa's adventures—both good and bad—living in the American West. Upon her death these letters were published, inspiring young women across America to make the journey on the Oregon Trail.

GO ONLINE

MULTIMEDIA BIOGRAPHIES
Visit The Learning Site at www.harcourtschool.com/
biographies to learn about other famous people.

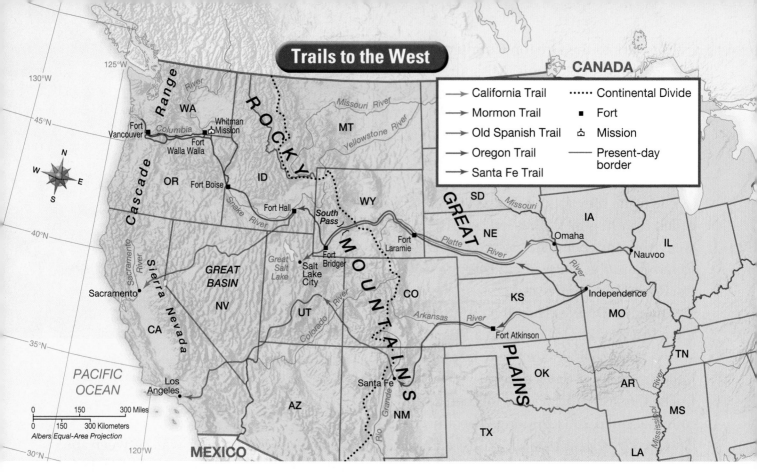

Trails to the West

Legend:
- → California Trail
- → Mormon Trail
- → Old Spanish Trail
- → Oregon Trail
- → Santa Fe Trail
- ⋯⋯ Continental Divide
- ■ Fort
- ⌂ Mission
- — Present-day border

Movement **This map shows the trails that settlers followed to the West.**

❖ Which trail led to Sacramento, California?

Mormons Settle Utah

In the 1840s the Mormons, or members of the Church of Jesus Christ of Latter-day Saints, joined the many Americans traveling west. The Mormons and their leader, Joseph Smith, had settled in the town of Nauvoo (naw•VOO), Illinois. Their beliefs caused problems with other settlers, however, and in 1844 an angry crowd killed Joseph Smith.

When Brigham Young became the new leader of the Mormons, he decided that they should move to a place where no one would bother them. In 1846 Young and the first group of

Mormons set out for the Rocky Mountains. In July 1847 the Mormons reached the Great Salt Lake in the Great Basin. Young said, "This is the place!"

The Great Basin was such a harsh land that Brigham Young thought no other settlers would want it. He used words from the Bible to tell his followers, "We will make this desert blossom as the rose." To do so, one of the first things the Mormons did was build irrigation canals. The canals brought water from the surrounding mountains and made the dry land suitable for farming.

Brigham Young

406 ■ **Unit 5**

The Great Salt Lake region grew fast. It soon became known as the Utah Territory. Brigham Young became the territory's first governor.

REVIEW What was one of the first things the Mormons did once they settled in the Great Basin?

War with Mexico

The land the Mormons settled and the rest of the lands west of Texas belonged to Mexico. Only a few months later, most of those places would become part of the United States.

The United States and Mexico did not agree on where the border between Texas and Mexico was. The United States wanted the Rio Grande as the border, but Mexico believed its lands went farther north. When Mexican troops crossed the Rio Grande in April 1846 and fought with an American patrol, President James K. Polk asked Congress to declare war on Mexico.

The United States invaded Mexico in 1847. Federal troops led by General Winfield Scott captured Mexico City.

After more than a year of fighting, the United States won the war.

In February 1848 the United States and Mexico formally ended the war by signing the Treaty of Guadalupe Hidalgo (gwah•dah•LOO•pay ee•DAHL•goh). Under the treaty's terms, Mexico had to give up all claims to southern Texas and give the United States a huge region known as the Mexican Cession. A **cession**, or concession, is something given up. The Mexican Cession included all of present-day California, Nevada, and Utah and parts of Arizona, Colorado, New Mexico, and Wyoming. In return, the United States paid Mexico $15 million.

In 1853 James Gadsden, the United States minister to Mexico, arranged to buy more of Arizona and New Mexico. This land became known as the Gadsden Purchase. The Gadsden Purchase brought the continental United States, or the part of the United States between Canada and Mexico, to its present size. It also set the current border between the United States and Mexico.

REVIEW How did the United States benefit from the Treaty of Guadalupe Hidalgo?

During the Mexican-American War, American forces captured the Spanish town of Monterey, California.

Marshall Gold Discovery State Historic Park

Understanding Places and Regions

While building a sawmill in the winter of 1848, James Marshall discovered gold in a nearby riverbed. By 1849, Marshall's find set off one of the largest migrations in history—the California gold rush of 1849. People came from all over the United States in wagons. Some even sailed around the southern tip of South America to reach California.

In time, people from all over the world knew of Marshall's discovery, moving to California with the hope of striking it rich. Today, the site of Marshall's discovery is located inside the Marshall Gold Discovery State Historic Park in Coloma, California.

The California Gold Rush

In the 1840s California was a land of large ranches and a few small towns, such as Monterey and Los Angeles. By 1847 San Francisco had only 800 people. However, that quickly changed when gold was found.

Gold was found in California not long before the treaty with Mexico was signed. In January 1848 James Marshall and several other workers were building a waterwheel for John Sutter's new sawmill along the American River near present-day Sacramento. Suddenly, something was seen glittering in the water. No one is sure who first laid eyes on or picked up the stone that was half the size of a pea, but James Marshall said that he was the one.

This painting shows people digging for gold during the California gold rush. Looking for gold was hard work.

OR
ID
NV
UT
Coloma
MARSHALL GOLD DISCOVERY STATE HISTORIC PARK
Sacramento
San Francisco
CALIFORNIA
PACIFIC OCEAN
Los Angeles
AZ
MEXICO

0   150   300 Miles
0   150   300 Kilometers
Albers Equal-Area Projection

"It made my heart thump, for I was certain it was gold," he remembered.

The finding of gold in California set off a **gold rush**, a sudden rush of new people to an area where gold has been found. Within a year, more than 80,000 gold seekers arrived in California. They came from Europe and Asia as well as from other parts of the United States.

The gold seekers began calling themselves **forty-niners** because they had arrived in the year 1849. Many forty-niners made their way west on the Oregon Trail, cutting south on the Old Spanish Trail across the Nevada desert and through the passes of the Sierra Nevada. This trip often took three months or longer. Others traveled to California by sailing around Cape Horn

The discovery of gold brought many people to California.

at the southern tip of South America and then north along the Pacific coast. That journey often took six to eight months. Clipper ships, the fastest ships of the time, could make the same trip in just three to four months. However, travel by clipper ship cost too much for most forty-niners.

A few lucky forty-niners struck it rich, but most did not. While some returned home empty-handed, many stayed and settled in California. It is estimated that California's population grew by 100,000 people by the end of 1849. In 1850, only two years after Marshall's discovery of gold at Sutter's Mill, California became a state.

REVIEW Why did gold seekers in California call themselves forty-niners?

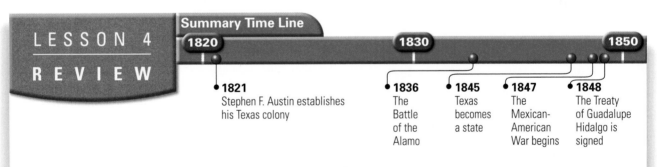

LESSON 4 REVIEW

Summary Time Line

1820 — 1830 — 1850

1821 Stephen F. Austin establishes his Texas colony

1836 The Battle of the Alamo

1845 Texas becomes a state

1847 The Mexican-American War begins

1848 The Treaty of Guadalupe Hidalgo is signed

1. **MAIN IDEA** How did the United States expand its borders in the 1800s?

2. **WHY IT MATTERS** Why did people move to the Pacific coast?

3. **VOCABULARY** Make a word web that shows how **gold rush** and **forty-niner** are related.

4. **TIME LINE** What happened in 1836?

5. **READING SKILL—Draw Conclusions** How might people traveling west influence the kinds of items that were manufactured?

6. **HISTORY** What caused the conflicts between the settlers in Texas and the Mexican government?

7. **CRITICAL THINKING—Hypothesize** What might have happened if gold had not been discovered in California?

 PERFORMANCE—Write a List Imagine that you are going to travel on the Oregon Trail. Make a list of items that you will take on your journey.

Identify Changing Borders

➡ **WHY IT MATTERS**

Historical maps give important information about places as they were in the past. By studying a historical map, you can see how a place and its borders have changed over time. Seeing those changes on a historical map can help you better understand the changes and how they came about.

➡ **WHAT YOU NEED TO KNOW**

In this chapter you read about the United States and the different countries that have controlled lands west of the Mississippi River. You also read about events that changed borders in the continental United States over time. The map on page 411 uses different colors to show how those borders changed over nearly 70 years. It uses labels to identify the different regions and to give the year in which each one became a part of the United States.

➡ **PRACTICE THE SKILL**

Use the historical map on page 411 to answer the following questions.

① What color shows land that was acquired by the United States in 1803?

② In what year did the United States win control of the Oregon Territory?

③ When did the United States get the land where the states of California and Nevada are now?

The Treaty of Guadalupe Hidalgo ended the Mexican-American War. Mexico agreed to give up the lands that came to be called the Mexican Cession, and, in return, the United States agreed to pay Mexico $15 million.

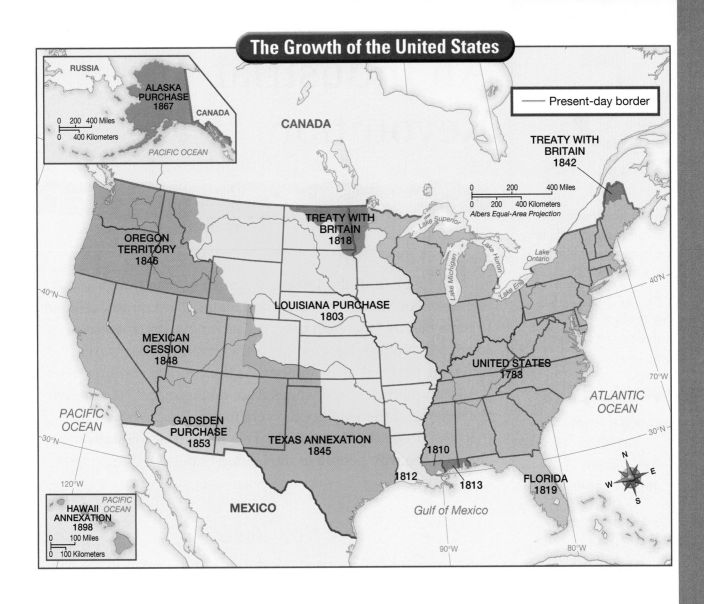

The Growth of the United States

RUSSIA

ALASKA PURCHASE 1867

CANADA

0   200   400 Miles
0   400 Kilometers

PACIFIC OCEAN

CANADA

—— Present-day border

TREATY WITH BRITAIN 1842

0   200   400 Miles
0   200   400 Kilometers
Albers Equal-Area Projection

OREGON TERRITORY 1846

TREATY WITH BRITAIN 1818

Lake Superior

Lake Michigan
Lake Huron
Lake Ontario
Lake Erie

40°N

40°N

LOUISIANA PURCHASE 1803

MEXICAN CESSION 1848

UNITED STATES 1783

70°W

PACIFIC OCEAN

30°N

GADSDEN PURCHASE 1853

TEXAS ANNEXATION 1845

ATLANTIC OCEAN

30°N

120°W

1810

1812

1813

FLORIDA 1819

N
W   E
S

HAWAII ANNEXATION 1898

PACIFIC OCEAN

MEXICO

Gulf of Mexico

0   100 Miles
0   100 Kilometers

90°W

80°W

Questions

4 What area did the United States get in 1842 as the result of a treaty with Britain?

5 In what year did the Gadsden Purchase become part of the United States?

6 In what year did the Texas Annexation take place?

7 When did Alaska become part of the United States?

▶ APPLY WHAT YOU LEARNED

The map on this page lets you identify the changing borders of the United States. You can also see changes by comparing two maps. On a sheet of paper, draw a map showing the borders of the United States in 1803. Then draw another map showing the borders of the United States in 1848. Find the information in this chapter that explains the difference between the two maps.

MAP AND GLOBE SKILLS

Practice your map and globe skills with the **GeoSkills CD-ROM.**

MAIN IDEA
Read to find out how the development of new technology changed life in the United States in the first half of the 1800s.

WHY IT MATTERS
The development of new technologies often brings other changes with it.

VOCABULARY
industrial revolution
investor
textile
interchangeable parts
mass production
supply
cotton gin
demand
patent

An Industrial Revolution

1780　　1800　　1820　　1840　　1860

1810–1850

The first half of the 1800s saw a rush of new things and a feeling of confidence in the United States. The country seemed to have met its "manifest destiny," as it now stretched from sea to sea. Nothing seemed too difficult as Americans over-came one problem after another. As the country continued to grow, other important changes were taking place. New inventions changed the way goods were made. People began using machines instead of hand tools. This **industrial revolution** changed the way people in the United States lived, traveled, and worked.

New Roads

Americans badly needed good roads in the early 1800s. Most roads were dirt paths full of tree stumps and holes. When it rained, these roads sometimes turned into "rivers."

Just before Ohio became a state in 1803, Congress voted to build a road to Ohio. The road would be used to transport goods and help settlers reach the new state. This route became known as the National Road. It was the nation's first important highway joining the eastern United States and places west of the Appalachian Mountains.

The National Road was built using the best technology of the day. It was level, and it was paved with stones and tar. The first part of the National Road opened in 1818. It ran from

This mile marker once guided people on the National Road in Maryland.

Maryland to present-day West Virginia. By 1841 the National Road was open through Ohio. It ended in Vandalia, Illinois.

By 1860 there were more than 88,000 miles (about 142,000 km) of roads in the United States. Traveling by road, however, still cost a lot and took a long time. Most wagons could carry only small amounts of goods and travelers often had to make several trips to carry their loads.

REVIEW Why was the National Road important?

Canal Building

Because road travel cost so much and took so much time, people turned to canals. Traveling on canals, boats or

barges could carry larger loads at less cost than wagons could on land. One of the most important canals built during these years was the Erie Canal in New York.

People living near the Great Lakes, however, still had to transport products to and from cities in the eastern United States by wagon. Goods could not be moved on boats because the Appalachian Mountains separated rivers flowing into the Great Lakes from rivers flowing into the Atlantic Ocean. Only one river, the St. Lawrence, flowed from the Great Lakes into the Atlantic Ocean. However, rapids and shallows kept boats from sailing its whole length.

In 1817 the state of New York voted to build a "Grand Canal" to Lake Erie.

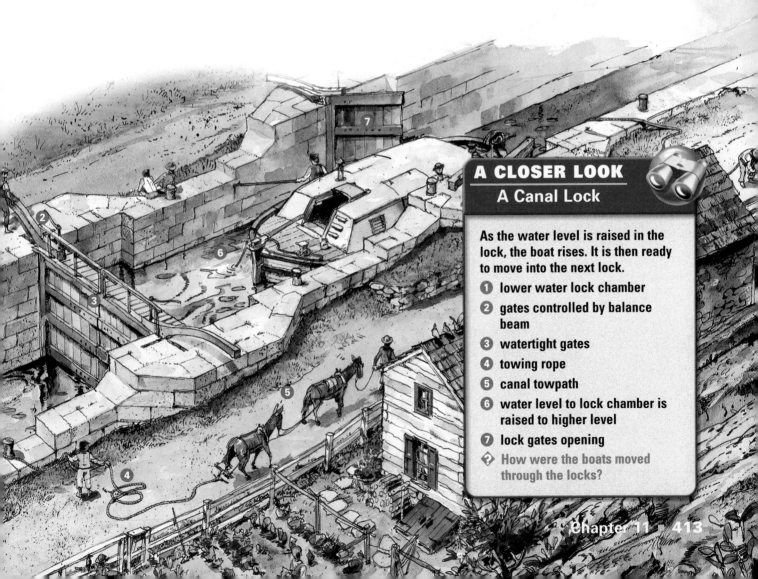

A CLOSER LOOK
A Canal Lock

As the water level is raised in the lock, the boat rises. It is then ready to move into the next lock.

1. lower water lock chamber
2. gates controlled by balance beam
3. watertight gates
4. towing rope
5. canal towpath
6. water level to lock chamber is raised to higher level
7. lock gates opening

❓ How were the boats moved through the locks?

It would start at the Hudson River and be 363 miles (584 km) long. To pay for building it, the governor of New York, DeWitt Clinton, asked investors to buy stock in the canal. An **investor** is a person who uses money to buy or make something that will yield a profit. By the summer of 1817, Clinton had enough investors to pay for the digging of the canal.

Most of the Erie Canal was dug by about 3,000 Irish immigrants who used only hand tools. The Irish came to the United States to get jobs working on the canal. Workers were paid 80 cents a day and were given meals and housing. These wages were three times what the immigrants could earn in Ireland.

After eight years of hard work, the Erie Canal opened in 1825. It cut the price of shipping goods between New York City and Buffalo on Lake Erie from $100 a ton to less than $10 a ton. It also helped make New York City the leading center of trade

This decorative hat box shows a scene on the Erie Canal.

in the United States at the time. The success of the Erie Canal set off a canal-building boom. By the 1830s, canals were being dug all over the country. Pennsylvania developed a system of canals connecting Philadelphia to other parts of the state. Ohio and Indiana built canals joining the Great Lakes and the Ohio River.

REVIEW **Why was the Erie Canal built?**

Steamboats and Railroads

Canal building lasted only a short time in the United States. New and faster methods of carrying goods and people soon took over. Steamboats quickly became the main form of river travel, and railroads changed the way people and goods moved on land.

The steam engine was invented in Britain by Thomas Newcomen in the

The *Tom Thumb* was made famous in a race with a horse. The locomotive was small, but powerful for its day. The first locomotives went about 10 miles (16 km) per hour.

early 1700s. It used the steam produced by boiling water to power its moving parts. Over the years the steam engine was improved and applied to various uses. Robert Fulton of New York used the steam engine to power a boat. In 1807 Fulton amazed people when his steamboat, the *Clermont*, chugged up the Hudson River from New York City to Albany. It was a 150-mile (241-km) trip, and it took 32 hours. Until this time, boats had not been able to travel easily upstream, or against the flow of the river.

Steamboat builders soon wanted to outdo each other as the new boats grew in popularity. Builders began to build bigger and faster boats. Greater speed meant that more cargo and passengers could be delivered in a shorter amount of time. This meant a bigger profit for cargo companies and their customers.

Soon steamboats were being used in other parts of the country, especially on the Ohio and Mississippi Rivers. By 1860 there were more than 1,000 great paddle-wheel steamboats in the United States. They traveled on most of the country's large rivers and lakes.

About the same time that steam engines were being used to power steamboats, they were also being used to power locomotives, or railroad engines. The first locomotive made in the United States was the *Tom Thumb*. A manufacturer named Peter Cooper built it in 1830 for the Baltimore and Ohio Railroad.

The company had been using railroad cars pulled by horses for its route.

Transportation in the East, 1850

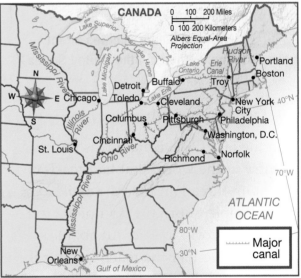

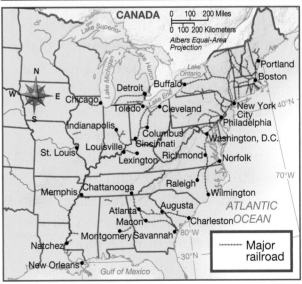

Movement These maps show major transportation links that had been built by 1850.

❓ Why do you think few links had been built west of the Mississippi River?

To prove that a locomotive could pull a heavy load faster than a horse, Cooper raced his *Tom Thumb* against a railroad car pulled by a horse. The locomotive broke down before the finish line and lost the race. Even so, it was clear that the steam-powered locomotive had better pulling power than a horse.

The number of railroads grew quickly after 1830. By 1850 about 9,000 miles (about 14,500 km) of track crossed the nation, mostly joining cities in the East. Railroads made it easier and cheaper to move heavy loads of raw materials and manufactured goods to all regions of the country. As the railroads grew, so did manufacturing in the United States.

REVIEW How did steam engines affect transportation methods in the United States?

Growth in Manufacturing

In the late 1700s Britain was the only country in the world that had machines that spun thread and wove **textiles**, or cloth. People in Britain did not want the rest of the world to find out about these machines. Neither the machines nor the plans for building them were allowed out of the country. Even the textile workers were not allowed to leave. Samuel Slater, however, carefully studied the machines in the British cotton mill where he worked. He memorized how each iron gear and wooden spool worked.

Wearing a disguise and using a different name, Slater left Britain and took what he knew to the United States. With money from an investor named Moses Brown, Slater built from memory machines like the ones he had used in Britain. In 1790 Slater and Brown started the first American spinning mill in Pawtucket, Rhode Island. This mill marked the beginning of large-scale manufacturing in the United States.

Early mills, like Slater's, were all built next to rushing rivers. These mills used the water to turn waterwheels, which in turn powered the machines connected to them. Later, steam engines were used to power the machines. Steam engines were more reliable than water power, so they allowed production to expand. Steam engines also made it possible for textile mills and other kinds of factories to be built in more places.

Instead of working at home, as most people had done in the past, more people began to go to work in factories. These workers did not need the same skills as workers who made goods by hand. In factories, machines made the goods. Factories needed workers who could be trained to run the machines. Many of these workers were women, children, and immigrants. They worked first in the mills and then later in other industries.

Francis Cabot Lowell of Massachusetts developed a new system of organizing factories. Lowell put the entire process of turning cotton into cloth under one roof at his factory in Waltham, Massachusetts. Before that time, factory workers made the thread, but other workers used hand looms in their homes to weave the thread into cloth. Lowell's system, known as the Waltham system, was also different because it provided boardinghouses for its workers. Lowell provided good living conditions for his workers. However, not all factory owners followed his lead.

Early textile mills used water power to run their machines. The water of a rushing river or waterfall turned the waterwheel. The waterwheel turned gears connected to belts that made the machines run.

1 river turns water wheel and gears

2 spinning cotton fibers into yarn

3 warping, or lining up side by side, the strands of yarn to prepare them for weaving

4 weaving the yarn into cloth

? How does the waterwheel make the machines in the mill run?

Another idea also had changed American manufacturing. In 1800 Eli Whitney developed a new system of interchangeable parts to make guns. **Interchangeable parts** were parts that were exactly alike. If one part of a gun was damaged, another part of the same kind could be put in its place. In the past, skilled workers were needed to make most products. Now anyone could put together machine-made parts and do it faster than a craftworker.

Eli Whitney invented the cotton gin (bottom), a machine that removed seeds from cotton fibers.

This idea made **mass production** possible. This is a system of producing large amounts of goods at one time. Over time many goods were made this way.

Because of mass production, the supply of manufactured goods rose sharply. In business, the **supply** is the amount of a good or service available for sale. When the supply of a product is high, prices generally fall. As a result, more expensive handmade goods were quickly replaced by cheaper ones made by machine.

REVIEW How was Lowell's system of organizing factories different from other systems?

Inventions Bring Change

In 1793 Eli Whitney developed a machine called the cotton gin, or engine. The **cotton gin** removed the seeds from cotton fibers much faster than workers could by hand. With the cotton gin, cotton could be prepared for market in less time. This made it possible for plantations to grow more cotton. In turn, this allowed plantations to supply more cotton to textile mills. Planters in the southern states sold their cotton to textile mills in the northern states and in Europe. Worldwide demand for cotton made both southern planters and northern textile-mill owners rich. In business, a **demand** is the need or want for a good or service by people who are willing to pay for it. When the demand for a product is high, its price usually goes up. Because the price of a product goes up, people are usually willing to make more of it. That means the supply of a good usually rises or falls to meet the demand.

Other useful inventions also made farming on a large scale possible in the

Cast-Steel Plow

As a blacksmith in Grand Detour, Illinois, John Deere was always repairing the wooden and cast-iron plows of farmers. The heavy, damp prairie soil stuck to these plows, and farmers had to stop and clean them every few minutes. Deere and his partner, Major Leonard Andrus, designed a plow that could easily cut through the soil. The blade of the new plow was made of cast steel. The moldboard, or the part of the plow used for lifting and turning the soil, was made of wrought iron. Both parts were then polished so smooth that the damp prairie soil could not stick to them.

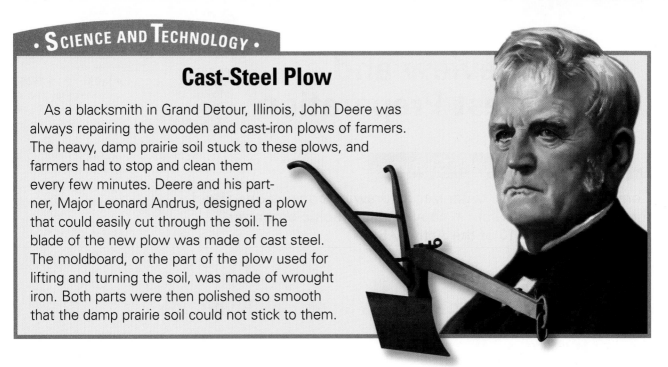

United States. In 1832 Cyrus McCormick invented a mechanical reaper for harvesting grain. With this invention farmers could cut as much wheat in one day as they had been able to cut in two weeks using hand tools. In 1837 John Deere developed the first cast-steel plow in the United States. This plow made tilling the soil easier.

As the need for finding new ways of solving problems arose, the number of inventions increased. In 1800 there were 309 **patents**, or licenses to make, use, or sell new inventions, registered with the United States Patent Office. By 1860 there were more than 40,000 patents.

REVIEW How did Cyrus McCormick's mechanical reaper help farmers?

LESSON 5 REVIEW

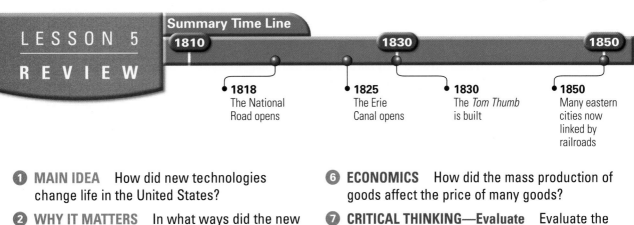

Summary Time Line

1810 — 1830 — 1850

• **1818** The National Road opens

• **1825** The Erie Canal opens

• **1830** The *Tom Thumb* is built

• **1850** Many eastern cities now linked by railroads

① **MAIN IDEA** How did new technologies change life in the United States?

② **WHY IT MATTERS** In what ways did the new technologies of the 1800s have lasting effects?

③ **VOCABULARY** How are **supply** and **demand** related?

④ **TIME LINE** When did the Erie Canal open?

⑤ **READING SKILL—Draw Conclusions** Do you think the number of inventions has grown or decreased since 1860? Explain.

⑥ **ECONOMICS** How did the mass production of goods affect the price of many goods?

⑦ **CRITICAL THINKING—Evaluate** Evaluate the effects of supply and demand on plantations.

PERFORMANCE—Make an Invention Booklet Use information from the lesson and from library sources to make a booklet about the items that were invented in the 1800s. Share your booklet with the class.

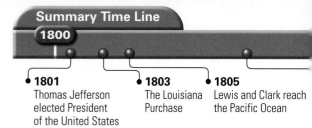

Summary Time Line

1800

● **1801**
Thomas Jefferson
elected President
of the United States

● **1803**
The Louisiana
Purchase

● **1805**
Lewis and Clark reach
the Pacific Ocean

USE YOUR READING SKILLS

Complete this graphic organizer by drawing conclusions about
the Industrial Revolution. A copy of this graphic organizer
appears on page 110 of the Activity Book.

America and the Industrial Revolution

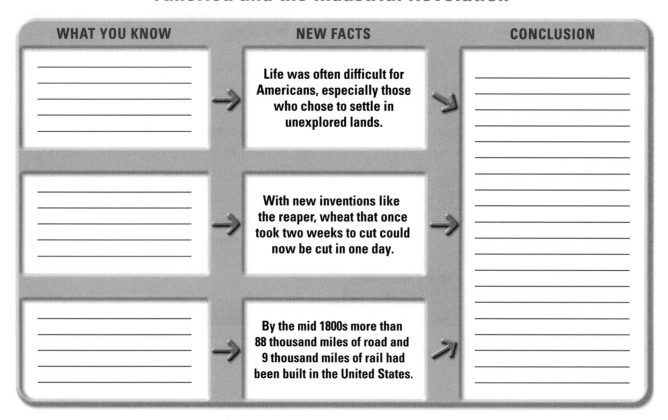

WHAT YOU KNOW	NEW FACTS	CONCLUSION
	Life was often difficult for Americans, especially those who chose to settle in unexplored lands.	
	With new inventions like the reaper, wheat that once took two weeks to cut could now be cut in one day.	
	By the mid 1800s more than 88 thousand miles of road and 9 thousand miles of rail had been built in the United States.	

THINK & WRITE

Write a Journal Entry   During the Lewis
and Clark expedition, many members of the
expedition kept journals. Imagine you are a
member of the expedition and are journeying
through the Rocky Mountains. Write a journal
entry describing your environment.

Write a Persuasive Letter   Imagine the
year is 1820 and you are trying to raise money
to open a textile factory. Write a persuasive
letter to a potential investor, explaining why
that person should consider investing in your
factory.

1812
The War of
1812 begins

1828
Andrew Jackson
is elected President
of the United States

1830
Congress passes the
Indian Removal Act

1836
The Battle
of the Alamo

1845
Texas
becomes
a state

1847
The Mexican-American War

USE THE TIME LINE

Use the chapter summary time line to answer these questions.

1 How many years after the Louisiana Purchase did Lewis and Clark reach the Pacific Ocean?

2 Was Andrew Jackson elected President before or after Texas became a state?

USE VOCABULARY

Use a term from this list to complete each of the sentences that follow.

> inaugurated (p. 384)
> siege (p. 393)
> annexed (p. 394)
> dictator (p. 402)
> investors (p. 414)

3 After the War of 1812 the United States _____ West Florida.

4 Andrew Jackson's soldiers survived a ten-day _____ during the Battle of New Orleans.

5 To pay for the Erie Canal, DeWitt Clinton brought in _____ from Europe.

6 In 1801 Thomas Jefferson was _____ as President.

7 Antonio López de Santa Anna made himself _____ of Mexico in 1834.

RECALL FACTS

Answer these questions.

8 What event caused the United States to double in size in 1803?

9 Why did many Americans want to go to war with the British in 1812?

10 How did John Deere's cast-steel plow help prairie farmers?

Write the letter of the best choice.

11 **TEST PREP**   The Lewis and Clark expedition was helped by a Shoshone Indian guide named —
A Dakota.
B Mandan.
C Metacomet.
D Sacagawea.

12 **TEST PREP**   Samuel Slater and Moses Brown helped begin the American—
F steel industry.
G railroad industry.
H textile industry.
J banking industry.

THINK CRITICALLY

13 Why do you think the United States did not surrender to the British after they invaded Washington, D.C., during the War of 1812?

14 What kind of compromise could Andrew Jackson have negotiated with Native American tribes instead of forcing them to leave their homelands?

15 Do you think many Americans welcomed the changes brought about by the Industrial Revolution? Why or why not?

APPLY SKILLS

Identify Changing Borders
Study the map on page 411. Then answer the following questions.

16 What color shows land that was acquired by the United States in 1846?

17 What present-day states would form the western border of the United States if the nation had not expanded after 1788?

VISIT

OLD IRONSIDES

GET READY

The USS *Constitution*, built in the 1790s, has a new life as a floating museum in Boston Harbor. Shipbuilders working with the original plans of designer Joshua Humphreys have restored "Old Ironsides" to like-new condition.

When you step aboard the old sailing vessel, you will be stepping back in history. Members of the United States Navy, dressed as sailors of the early 1800s, will take you on a tour. As the ship sways on the ocean's waves, you will feel what it was like to be a sailor during the war of 1812.

LOCATE IT

Boston

MASSACHUSETTS

WHAT TO SEE

The USS *Constitution* earned the nickname Old Ironsides during battle. Astonished sailors noticed that cannon balls could not break through the ship's sturdy sides.

Dressed in a historic uniform, the captain of the USS *Constitution* welcomes visitors aboard.

Navy officers aboard the ship slept in beds like these. The beds are attached to the ceiling by ropes so that they move with the swaying of the ship.

TAKE A FIELD TRIP

GO ONLINE

A VIRTUAL TOUR
Visit The Learning Site at **www.harcourtschool.com/tours** to take virtual tours of other historical museums.

CNN Turner Le@rning

A VIDEO TOUR
Check your media center or classroom library for a videotape tour of the USS Constitution.

VISUAL SUMMARY

Write a Paragraph Study the pictures and captions below to help you review Unit 5. Then choose one of the events shown. Write a news story about that event and how it affected the country.

USE VOCABULARY

Identify the term that correctly matches each definition.

arsenal (p. 348)

census (p. 359)

due process of law (p. 372)

doctrine (p. 394)

patent (p. 419)

1 a population count

2 a government plan of action

3 a building used for storing weapons

4 a person's right to a fair public trial

5 a license to make, use, or sell new inventions

RECALL FACTS

Answer these questions.

6 What was Shays's Rebellion?

7 Who was Benjamin Banneker?

8 How did Dolley Madison assist her country during the War of 1812?

Write the letter of the best choice.

9 **TEST PREP** The Constitutional Convention delegate who actually wrote the Constitution was—
A Roger Sherman.
B Benjamin Franklin.
C Elbridge Gerry.
D Gouverneur Morris.

10 **TEST PREP** The term *manifest destiny* referred to a belief that the United States should—
F stretch from the Atlantic Ocean to the Pacific Ocean.
G avoid involvement in all foreign conflicts.
H close the Western Hemisphere.
J ratify the Constitution.

Visual Summary

1780   1800   1820

1787 The signing of the Constitution   p. 366

1791 The Bill of Rights becomes part of the Constitution   p. 370

1804 The Corps of Discovery departs   p. 386

11 What do you think might have happened if the United States had decided to keep the Articles of Confederation?

12 Do you think the United States could have avoided war with Britain in 1812? Explain your answer.

13 How do you think Americans viewed the Monroe Doctrine? How do you think Europeans viewed the Monroe Doctrine?

14 Why do you think the Cherokee nation chose to fight for its homeland in the courts instead of on a battlefield?

15 How do you think the introduction of factory work changed family life in the United States?

APPLY SKILLS

Identify Changing Borders
Use the historical map on this page to answer the following questions.

MAP AND GLOBE SKILLS

16 Was Austin's original colony in eastern or western Texas?

17 Was Austin's colony larger or smaller than the Republic of Texas?

18 What river forms part of the western border of the state of Texas?

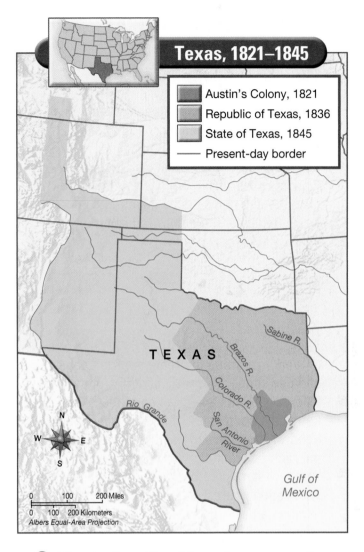

Texas, 1821–1845

Austin's Colony, 1821
Republic of Texas, 1836
State of Texas, 1845
Present-day border

TEXAS

Sabine R.
Brazos R.
Colorado R.
Rio Grande
San Antonio River

Gulf of Mexico

N W E S

0 100 200 Miles
0 100 200 Kilometers
Albers Equal-Area Projection

19 Was the Republic of Texas larger or smaller than the state of Texas today?

20 How did the state border of Texas change from 1845 to the present day?

1840

1860

1836 **The Battle of the Alamo**
p. 403

1847 **The Mexican-American War**
begins p. 407

1849 **The California Gold Rush**
begins p. 409

Unit Activities

GO ONLINE Visit The Learning Site at www.harcourtschool.com/socialstudies/activities for additional activities.

Produce a Speech

Work in a group to produce a speech that might have been given by one of these people: James Madison, Benjamin Banneker, Sacagawea, or Davy Crockett. Divide the work of researching, writing, and editing the speech. Then select a member of your group to deliver the completed speech before the class.

Create a Newspaper Front Page

Work in a group to create the front page of a newspaper that will cover one of the following events: the opening of the Erie Canal, the completion of the National Road, Robert Fulton's voyage on the *Clermont*, or the race between the *Tom Thumb* and a horse. First, research and write your story. Then, add pictures. Next, arrange your front page on a posterboard. Finally, present your completed front page to the class.

VISIT YOUR LIBRARY

■ *The Santa Fe Trail* by David Lavender. Holiday House.

■ *By the Dawn's Early Light: The Story of the Star-Spangled Banner* by Steven Kroll. Scholastic.

■ *Woman of Independence: The Life of Abigail Adams* by Susan Provost Beller. Shoe Tree Press.

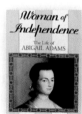

COMPLETE THE UNIT PROJECT

A Growing Nation Time Line   Work with a group of classmates to finish the unit project—a time line that shows the economic and territorial growth of the United States through the 1800s. Illustrate the events that appear on your time line by using drawings or pictures printed from the Internet. Present your completed time line to the class. Then explain why your group selected the events that it did.

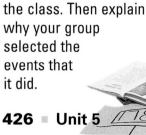

426 ■ Unit 5

Civil War Times

President Abraham Lincoln's Hat

The Lincoln Memorial, Washington, D.C.

Civil War Times

> " A house divided against itself cannot stand. "
> —Abraham Lincoln, Republican
> State Convention, Springfield, Illinois, June 16, 1858

Preview the Content

Scan the unit and read the chapter and lesson titles. Use what you have read to make a unit outline. Once you have finished, write down any questions you may have about the Civil War.

Preview the Vocabulary

Compound Words   A compound word is a combination of two or more words that form a new word when put together. For each term listed below, use the meanings of the smaller words to figure out the meaning of the compound word. Then look up each word in the Glossary to check its meaning.

ORIGINAL WORD		ORIGINAL WORD		COMPOUND WORD	POSSIBLE MEANING
under	+	ground	=	**underground**	_____
rail	+	road	=	**railroad**	_____
share	+	cropping	=	**sharecropping**	_____
carpet	+	bagger	=	**carpetbagger**	_____

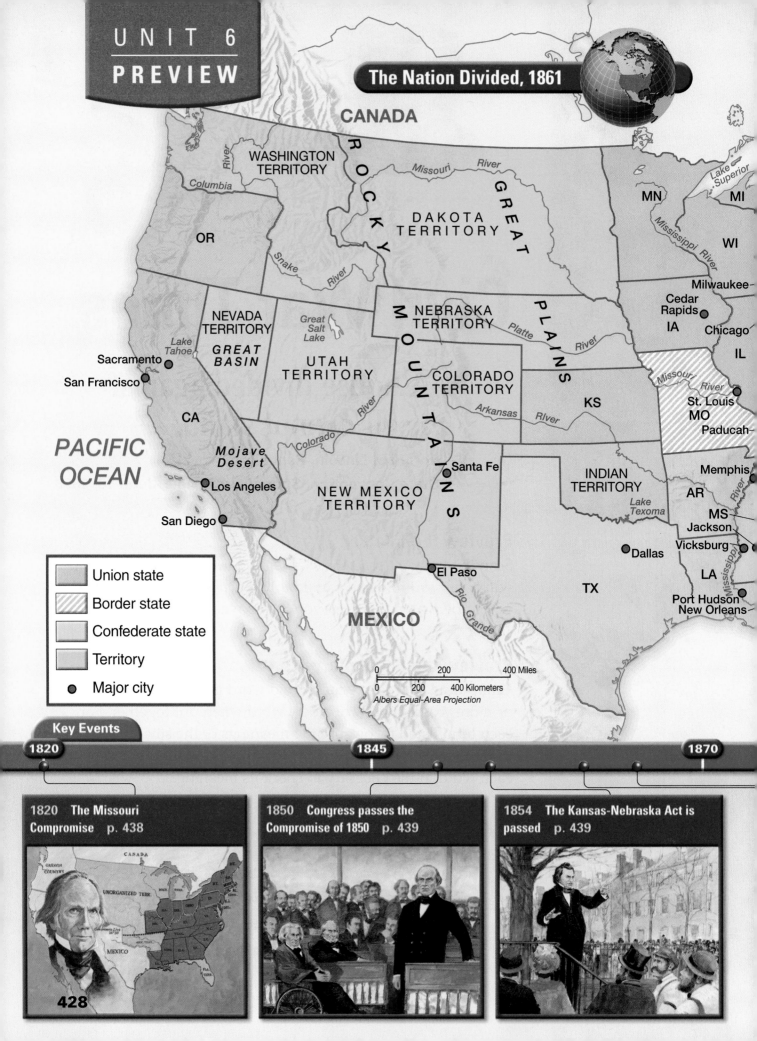

The Nation Divided, 1861

CANADA

WASHINGTON TERRITORY

Columbia River

ROCKY

Missouri River

GREAT

DAKOTA TERRITORY

MN

MI

OR

Snake River

PLAINS

WI

Milwaukee
Cedar Rapids
IA
Chicago
IL

NEVADA TERRITORY

GREAT BASIN

Great Salt Lake

NEBRASKA TERRITORY

Platte River

MOUNTAINS

Lake Tahoe

UTAH TERRITORY

COLORADO TERRITORY

Mississippi River

St. Louis
MO
Paducah

Sacramento
San Francisco

CA

Colorado River

Arkansas River

KS

Santa Fe

Missouri River

Memphis

PACIFIC OCEAN

Mojave Desert

Los Angeles

NEW MEXICO TERRITORY

INDIAN TERRITORY

AR

Lake Texoma

MS
Jackson

San Diego

El Paso

Dallas

Vicksburg
LA

TX

Port Hudson
New Orleans

Rio Grande

MEXICO

0   200   400 Miles
0   200   400 Kilometers
Albers Equal-Area Projection

Union state
Border state
Confederate state
Territory
Major city

Key Events

1820

1845

1870

1820 The Missouri Compromise p. 438

1850 Congress passes the Compromise of 1850 p. 439

1854 The Kansas-Nebraska Act is passed p. 439

428

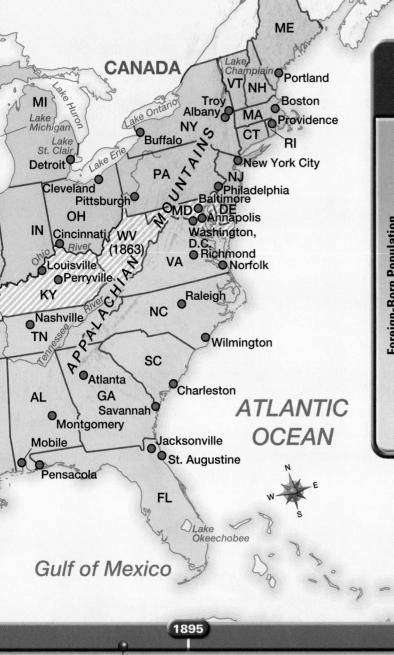

CANADA

Lake Huron
Lake Michigan
Lake St. Clair
Lake Erie
Lake Ontario
Lake Champlain

MI
Detroit
Cleveland
Pittsburgh
OH
IN
Cincinnati
Louisville
Perryville
KY
Nashville
TN

Ohio River

APPALACHIAN MOUNTAINS

WV (1863)

Tennessee River

ME
Portland
VT NH
Troy
Albany
MA
Boston
Providence
RI
Buffalo
NY
New York City
PA
NJ
Philadelphia
Baltimore
MD DE
Annapolis
Washington, D.C.
VA
Richmond
Norfolk
Raleigh
NC
Wilmington
SC
Charleston
Atlanta
GA
Savannah
AL
Montgomery
Mobile
Pensacola
Jacksonville
St. Augustine
FL
Lake Okeechobee

ATLANTIC OCEAN

Gulf of Mexico

N W E S

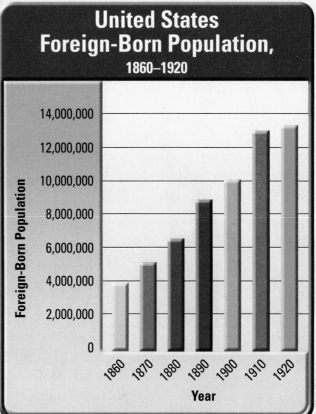

United States Foreign-Born Population, 1860–1920

Foreign-Born Population

14,000,000
12,000,000
10,000,000
8,000,000
6,000,000
4,000,000
2,000,000
0

1860 1870 1880 1890 1900 1910 1920

Year

1895

1920

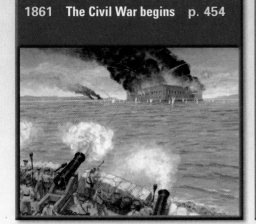

1861 The Civil War begins p. 454

1865 General Lee surrenders at Appomattox Court House p. 469

1890 The steel industry is big business in the United States p. 496

429

All for the Union

THE CIVIL WAR DIARY AND LETTERS OF ELISHA HUNT RHODES

edited by Robert H. Rhodes

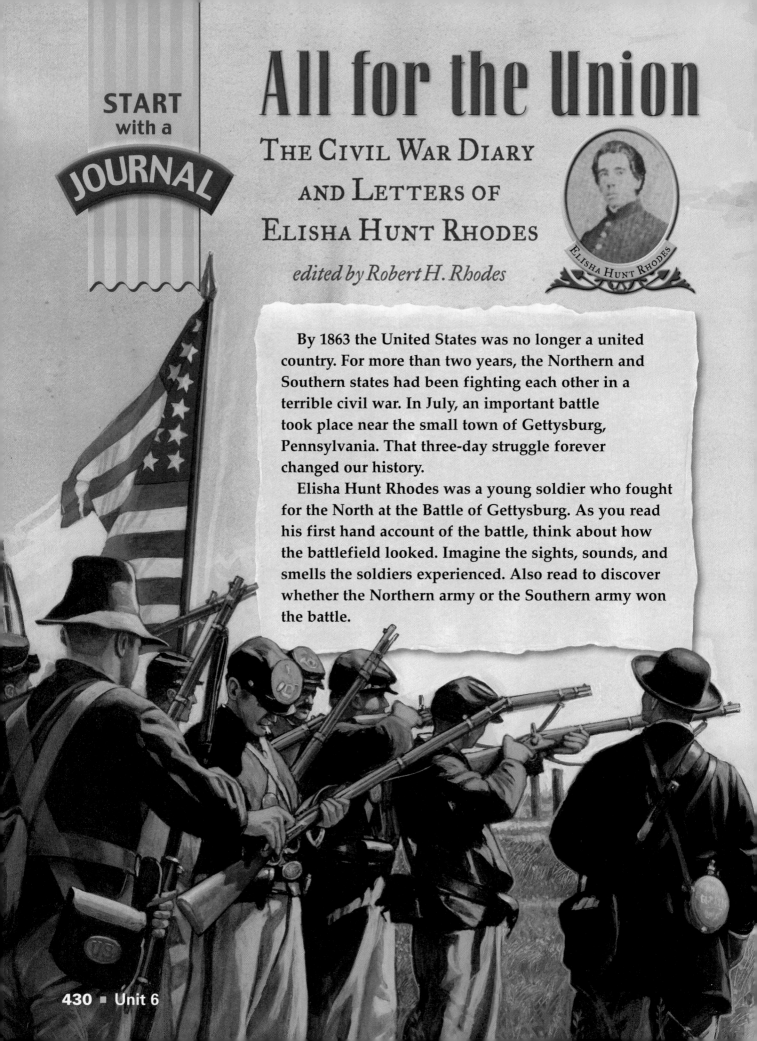

By 1863 the United States was no longer a united country. For more than two years, the Northern and Southern states had been fighting each other in a terrible civil war. In July, an important battle took place near the small town of Gettysburg, Pennsylvania. That three-day struggle forever changed our history.

Elisha Hunt Rhodes was a young soldier who fought for the North at the Battle of Gettysburg. As you read his first hand account of the battle, think about how the battlefield looked. Imagine the sights, sounds, and smells the soldiers experienced. Also read to discover whether the Northern army or the Southern army won the battle.

July 3rd 1863—This morning the troops were under arms before light and ready for the great battle that we knew must be fought. The firing began, and our <u>Brigade</u> was hurried to the right of the line to reinforce it. While not in the front line yet we were constantly exposed to the fire of the <u>Rebel</u> Artillery, while bullets fell around us. We moved from point to point, wherever danger to be <u>imminent</u> until noon when we were ordered to report to the line held by Gen. Birney. Our Brigade marched down the road until we reached the house used by General Meade as Headquarters. The road ran between ledges of rocks while the fields were strewn with boulders. To our left was a hill on which we had many <u>batteries</u> posted. Just as we reached Gen. Meade's Headquarters, a shell burst over our heads, and it was immediately followed by showers of iron. More than two hundred guns were belching forth their thunder, and most of the shells that came over the hill struck in the road on which our Brigade was moving. Solid shot would strike the large rocks and split them as if exploded by gunpowder. The flying iron and pieces of stone struck men down in every direction. It is said that this fire continued for about two hours, but I have no idea of the time. We could not see the enemy, and we could only cover ourselves the best we could behind rocks and trees. About 30 men of our Brigade were killed or wounded by this fire. Soon the Rebel yell was heard, and we have found since that the Rebel General Pickett made a charge with his Division and was <u>repulsed</u> after reaching some of our batteries. Our lines of Infantry in front of us rose up and poured in a terrible fire. As we were only a few yards in rear of our lines we saw all the fight. The firing gradually died away, and but for an occasional shot all was still. But what a scene it was. Oh the dead and the dying on this bloody field. The 2nd <u>R.I.</u> lost only one man killed and five wounded. One of the latter belonged to my Co. "B". Again night came upon us and again we slept amid the dead and dying.

Brigade a large body of troops
Rebel the Southern army or a Southern soldier
imminent ready to take place

batteries groupings of big guns
repulsed driven back
R.I. Rhode Island

July 4, 1863— Was ever the Nation's Birthday celebrated in such a way before. This morning the 2nd R.I. was sent out to the front and found that during the night General Lee and his Rebel Army had fallen back. It was impossible to march across the field without stepping upon dead or wounded men, while horses and broken Artillery lay on every side. We advanced to a sunken road (Emmitsburg Road) where we deployed as skirmishers and lay down behind a bank of earth. Berdan's Sharpshooters joined us, and we passed the day in firing upon any Rebels that showed themselves. At 12 M. a National Salute with shotted guns was fired from several of our Batteries, and the shells passed over our heads toward the Rebel lines. At night we were relieved and went to the rear for a little rest and sleep.

| **skirmishers** scouts |

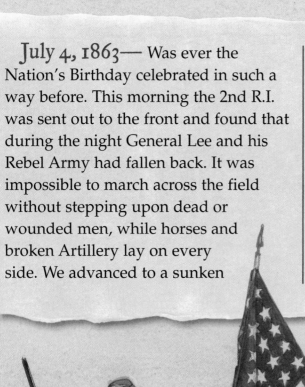

July 5th 1863— Glorious news! We have won the victory, thank God, and the Rebel Army is fleeing to Virginia. We have news that Vicksburg has fallen. We have thousands of prisoners, and they seem to be <u>stupified</u> with the news. This morning our Corps (the 6th) started in pursuit of Lee's Army. We have had rain and the roads are bad, so we move slow. Every house we see is a hospital, and the road is covered with the arms and equipments thrown away by the Rebels.

stupified stunned

Analyze the Literature

1 **What brigade did Elisha Hunt Rhodes belong to?**

2 **Where did the Southern army flee after losing the Battle of Gettysburg?**

3 **How can reading a first hand account of a historical event help you better understand it?**

READ A BOOK

START THE UNIT PROJECT

The Hall of Fame With your classmates, create a Hall of Fame about the key people in the unit. As you read take notes on the contributions key people made. Your notes will help you create your Hall of Fame.

USE TECHNOLOGY

Visit The Learning Site at **www.harcourtschool.com/ socialstudies** for additional activities, primary sources, and other resources to use in this unit.

ANTIETAM NATIONAL BATTLEFIELD

The Battle of Antietam claimed more American lives in a single day than any other one day battle in United States history. Nearly 4,700 Union and Confederate soldiers were lost on September 17, 1862. Visitors to Antietam National Battlefield can tour over 90 monuments built to honor those fallen soldiers.

LOCATE IT

MARYLAND

Antietam National Battlefield

The Nation Divided

❝ Yes, we'll rally 'round the flag, boys, we'll rally once again, Shouting the battle cry of freedom. ❞

—George Frederick Root,
The Battle Cry of Freedom, 1863

CHAPTER READING SKILL

Categorize

To **categorize** is to classify information by category. You can place people, places, and events into categories to make it easier to find facts.

As you read this chapter, categorize information about regional conflicts and the Civil War.

| UNION ARMY | CONFEDERATE ARMY |

MAIN IDEA
Read to learn how regional differences caused conflict between Northern and Southern states.

WHY IT MATTERS
If regional differences are strong enough, they can tear a nation apart.

VOCABULARY
sectionalism
tariff
states' rights
free state
slave state

People in the South used money from the cash crops they sold to buy goods from Europe.

Regional Disagreements

1820–1860

As the United States expanded its borders in the first half of the 1800s, strong differences developed among the various regions. Because of those differences, it was difficult for Americans to agree on many issues. In Congress, representatives from the North, South, and West often made decisions based on helping their own section, or region, rather than the country as a whole. This regional loyalty is called **sectionalism** (SEK•shuhn•uh•lih•zuhm), and the disagreements it caused threatened to tear the country apart.

Debate over State Authority

Sectionalism in the United States became a serious problem in 1828, when Congress set a high **tariff**, or tax, on some imports. The tariff made goods from Europe cost more than goods made in the United States. This protected factory owners and workers in the United States from foreign competition and made it easier for factories to sell their products.

The tariff helped the North because most of the nation's factories were located there. However, it did little to help the South, which remained mostly an agricultural region. People in the South sold many of their cash crops to businesses in Europe. In return, they bought many European manufactured goods. Southerners generally opposed the tariff because they did not like having to pay higher prices for those goods.

In 1829 Andrew Jackson became President, and John C. Calhoun of South Carolina became Vice President. Calhoun argued against the tariff. He believed in **states' rights**, or the idea that the states, not the federal government, should have the final authority over their own affairs. Calhoun believed that states had the right to refuse to accept a law passed by Congress.

Although President Jackson was known to support states' rights, he still believed that the federal government had the constitutional right to collect the tariff, even if South Carolina thought it was too high. President Jackson made his feelings clear when he spoke at a dinner honoring the memory of former President Thomas Jefferson. Jackson, looking straight at Calhoun, firmly said, "Our Federal Union—It must and shall be preserved!" Calhoun, who was just as determined, answered, "The Union, next to our liberty most dear. May we all remember that it can be preserved only by respecting the rights of the states."

The debate over states' rights continued after Congress passed another tariff in 1832. Sectionalism grew stronger, and it further divided the people of the United States.

REVIEW Why did most people in the South oppose tariffs?

Division over Slavery

Another issue that had long divided the nation was slavery. Northern and Southern states had argued about it since the writing of the Constitution. The same argument flared up again with the rapid settlement of the western frontier. As settlers moved west into territories such as Arkansas, Illinois, Iowa, and Missouri, they took with them their own ways of life. For settlers from the North, this meant a way of life without slavery. For settlers from the South, this meant taking along their enslaved workers.

Arguments soon broke out over the spread of slavery to the West. Most

For political advice Jackson sometimes relied on a group of unofficial advisers, whom many referred to as Jackson's "Kitchen Cabinet."

Northerners thought that slavery should go no farther than where it already was—in the South. Most Southern slave owners believed that they had the right to take their slaves wherever they wanted. As the new western territories grew, settlers there asked to join the Union as new states. In each case, the same question arose. Would the new state be a free state or a slave state? A **free state** did not allow slavery. A **slave state** did.

For a time there were as many free states as slave states. This kept a balance between the North and the South in the Senate. Then, in 1819, settlers in the Missouri Territory, a part of the Louisiana Purchase, asked to join the Union as a slave state. If this happened, slave states would outnumber free states for the first time since the founding of the country.

The Missouri Compromise, 1820

CANADA

OREGON COUNTRY

UNORGANIZED TERRITORY

MICHIGAN TERRITORY

MAINE
VT
NH
NEW YORK
MA
CT
RI

PENNSYLVANIA
NJ
MD DE

INDIANA OHIO

ILLINOIS

MISSOURI
KENTUCKY

VIRGINIA

NORTH CAROLINA

TENNESSEE

ARKANSAS TERRITORY

SOUTH CAROLINA

ATLANTIC OCEAN

MEXICO

MISSISSIPPI
ALABAMA GEORGIA

LOUISIANA

FLORIDA TERRITORY

Gulf of Mexico

Legend:
- Free state
- Free territory
- Admitted as a free state
- Slave state
- Slave territory
- Admitted as a slave state
- Missouri Compromise line

0   200   400 Miles
0   200   400 Kilometers
Albers Equal-Area Projection

Regions
The Missouri Compromise line divided lands that could join the Union as free states from lands that could join as slave states.

◈ Which two states were admitted to the Union as part of the compromise?

The Missouri question was debated in Congress for months. Henry Clay, a member of Congress from Kentucky, found himself in the middle of these heated arguments about slavery. Clay himself owned slaves, but he did not want to see the issue of slavery divide the country. He worked day and night to help solve the problem. Finally, in 1820, Clay persuaded Congress to agree to a plan known as the Missouri Compromise.

Under this plan Missouri would be allowed to join the Union as a slave state. Maine, which had also asked to become a state, would join as a free state. This would keep the balance between free states and slave states. Then a line would be drawn on a map of the rest of the lands gained in the Louisiana Purchase. Slavery would be allowed in places south of the line. It would not be allowed in places north of the line.

REVIEW How did the Missouri Compromise keep the balance between free states and slave states?

Henry Clay became known as the Great Compromiser because of his work to settle differences between the North and the South.

A New Compromise

The Missouri Compromise kept the peace for nearly 30 years. During this time six new states joined the Union. The number of free states and slave states remained equal. Then, in 1848, the United States gained new lands after winning the war with Mexico. Settlers in California, a part of these new lands, asked to join the Union as a free state. Once again arguments about the spread of slavery broke out. The Missouri Compromise did not apply to lands outside of the Louisiana Purchase.

Henry Clay again worked toward a compromise—the Compromise of 1850. Under this compromise, California joined the Union as a free state. The rest of the lands gained from Mexico were divided into two territories—New Mexico and Utah. The people in those territories would decide for themselves whether to allow slavery.

Henry Clay, who became known as the Great Compromiser, died in 1852. He never gave up hope that the country would find a peaceful way to settle its differences. On his grave marker in Lexington, Kentucky, are the words *I know no North—no South—no East—no West*. Two years after Clay's death, however, bad feelings between free states and slave states turned to violence.

REVIEW **Who became known as the Great Compromiser?**

Bleeding Kansas

In 1854 Congress passed the Kansas–Nebraska Act, which changed the rules of the Missouri Compromise. Under the Missouri Compromise, slavery would not have been allowed in the territories of Kansas and Nebraska. Under the Kansas–Nebraska Act, however, people in those territories were given the opportunity to decide for themselves whether to allow slavery. They would decide by voting.

The Kansas Territory quickly became the center of attention in the nation. People for and against slavery rushed into the territory. They hoped to help decide the outcome by casting their votes.

Compromise of 1850

Free state
Free territory
Slave state
Indian territory
Decision on slavery left to territory

GEOGRAPHY THEME

Regions Henry Clay's compromise brought California into the Union as a free state.

♦ What states were later formed from the Utah territory?

Kansas–Nebraska Act

🔍 Analyze Primary Sources

This poster was used to announce a meeting of those who supported the Kansas–Nebraska Act.

1. The headline states what type of meeting was being held.

2. The date shows when the meeting was held.

3. The phrase indicates that many people were to attend the meeting.

◈ Why do you think quotations are included on the poster?

"UNION IS STRENGTH."

FREE STATE CONVENTION!

① All who are favorable to union

BIG SPRING, THIRD DISTRICT,

② On Wednesday, September 5th,

③ **Mass Meeting**

"United we stand; divided we fall."

It was not long before fighting broke out between the two sides. More than 200 people were killed in the bitter conflict that is known as "Bleeding Kansas."

Kansas eventually joined the Union as a free state, but the bloodshed there was a sign of things to come. Many people on both sides of the slavery issue no longer saw compromise as a possible solution. Some in the South began to speak of leaving the Union.

REVIEW What did the Kansas–Nebraska Act do?

The Dred Scott Decision

In 1857 the United States Supreme Court decided the case of an enslaved African American named Dred Scott. Scott had asked the Court for his freedom. The Court said no.

Scott was the slave of an army doctor. His owner moved often and always took Scott with him. For a time they lived in Illinois, a free state. Then they lived in

Regions The Kansas–Nebraska Act allowed people in the Kansas and Nebraska territories to decide by voting whether they would be free or slave territories.

◈ How many territories could now decide for themselves whether to allow slavery?

Free state
Free territory
Slave state
Indian territory
Decision on slavery left to territory

WASHINGTON TERRITORY
OREGON TERRITORY
MINNESOTA TERRITORY
WISCONSIN
CANADA
MAINE
VT
NH
NEW YORK
MA
CT
RI
MICHIGAN
NEBRASKA TERRITORY
IOWA
PENNSYLVANIA
NJ
UTAH TERRITORY
ILLINOIS
INDIANA
OHIO
MD
DE
CALIFORNIA
KANSAS TERRITORY
MISSOURI
KENTUCKY
VIRGINIA
NEW MEXICO TERRITORY
INDIAN TERRITORY
ARKANSAS
TENNESSEE
NORTH CAROLINA
SOUTH CAROLINA
ATLANTIC OCEAN
TEXAS
MISSISSIPPI
ALABAMA
GEORGIA
LOUISIANA
FLORIDA
Gulf of Mexico

0 200 400 Miles
0 200 400 Kilometers
Albers Equal-Area Projection

Wisconsin, a free territory under the Missouri Compromise.

After his owner died, Scott took his case to court. He argued that he should be free because he had once lived on free land. The case moved up through the federal court system until it reached the Supreme Court. There, Chief Justice Roger B. Taney (TAH•nee) said that because Scott was a slave, he had "none of the rights and privileges" of an American citizen. Having lived in a free territory did not change that.

Taney also declared that Congress had no right to forbid slavery in the Wisconsin Territory. He felt that the United States Constitution protected the right of people to own slaves. Slaves, he wrote, were property. He believed that the Missouri Compromise was keeping people from owning property. This, Taney wrote, was unconstitutional.

Many people had hoped the Dred Scott decision would finally settle the disagree-

In 1857 the Supreme Court decided that Dred Scott should not be given his freedom.

ments among sections of the country over slavery once and for all. Instead, it made the problem worse.

REVIEW Why did the Supreme Court deny freedom to Dred Scott?

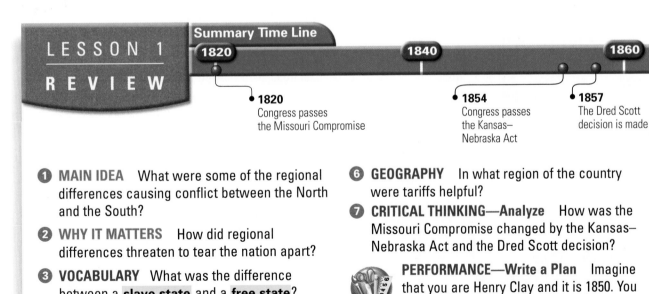

LESSON 1
REVIEW

Summary Time Line

1820 — 1840 — 1860

● **1820** Congress passes the Missouri Compromise

● **1854** Congress passes the Kansas–Nebraska Act

● **1857** The Dred Scott decision is made

① **MAIN IDEA** What were some of the regional differences causing conflict between the North and the South?

② **WHY IT MATTERS** How did regional differences threaten to tear the nation apart?

③ **VOCABULARY** What was the difference between a **slave state** and a **free state**?

④ **TIME LINE** When was the Kansas–Nebraska Act passed?

⑤ **READING SKILL—Categorize** What states were affected by the Missouri Compromise?

⑥ **GEOGRAPHY** In what region of the country were tariffs helpful?

⑦ **CRITICAL THINKING—Analyze** How was the Missouri Compromise changed by the Kansas–Nebraska Act and the Dred Scott decision?

PERFORMANCE—Write a Plan Imagine that you are Henry Clay and it is 1850. You need to write a plan that will help the country find a peaceful way to settle its differences. Describe in your plan how the country can settle its regional disagreements without tearing itself apart. Share your plan with the rest of the class.

Identify Frame of Reference

VOCABULARY

frame of reference

▶ WHY IT MATTERS

When you read something that people have written about an event or listen to them tell about it, you need to consider their **frame of reference**—where they were when the event happened or what role they played in it. A person's frame of reference can influence how he or she sees an event or feels about it. It can also influence how a person describes an event. Considering a person's frame of reference as you read or listen can help you better understand what happened.

▶ WHAT YOU NEED TO KNOW

In the 1800s, people's opinions about slavery and other issues were often influenced by where they lived. People who lived in the South, North, and West all had different frames of reference.

SENATOR JAMES HENRY HAMMOND, South Carolina, 1858

❝The greatest strength of the South arises from the harmony of her political and social institutions. This harmony gives her a frame of society, the best in the world, and an extent of political freedom, combined with entire security, such as no other people ever enjoyed upon the face of the earth. . . . In all social systems there must be a class to do the menial [unskilled] duties.❞

The statements on these pages were made in 1858 by Senator James Henry Hammond of South Carolina and Senator William Seward of New York. Senator Hammond owned a cotton plantation and had served as governor of South Carolina in 1842. Senator Seward was born, raised, and educated in New York State. He served as governor of New York from 1839 to 1843 and established a strong antislavery stand.

As you read the statements, consider how each senator's frame of reference might have affected what he said.

▶ PRACTICE THE SKILL

Answer these questions.

1 What was Senator Hammond's position on slavery? How might his frame of reference have affected it?

2 How was Senator Seward's position on slavery different from the one held by Senator Hammond? In what way was Seward's frame of reference different?

3 How might a Southerner's opinion of Senator Seward's description of the "slave system" be different from that of a person from the North? of a person from the West?

▶ APPLY WHAT YOU LEARNED

Think about a present-day example of how frames of reference cause differences in opinions and beliefs. Write a paragraph that describes this present-day example and explains why the people involved may think the way they do. Share your paragraph with a classmate.

SENATOR WILLIAM SEWARD, New York, 1858

❝The slave system is one of constant danger, distrust, suspicion, and watchfulness. It debases those whose toil [work] alone can produce wealth and resources for defense to the lowest degree of which human nature is capable . . . and this wastes energies which otherwise might be employed in national development and aggrandizement [the act of making greater].❞

MAIN IDEA
Read to learn what some
people did to try to end
slavery.

WHY IT MATTERS
As conflict over slavery
grew, divisions between
the North and the South
became deeper.

VOCABULARY

emancipation

resist

code

fugitive

underground

abolitionist

equality

Slavery and Freedom

1820–1860

By 1860 there were nearly 4 million slaves in the United States, an increase from 900,000 in 1800. This growth of slavery was due chiefly to the growing importance of cotton as a cash crop in the South. The worldwide demand for cotton had made many Southern planters rich. It had also created a demand for more enslaved workers.

The Slave Economy

Slavery had been a part of American life since colonial days. Some people thought that slavery was wrong. Other people could not make money using enslaved workers. The cost of feeding, clothing, and housing slaves was too great.

In the South, however, slavery continued because owners had come to depend on the work of enslaved people. Slaves were made to work as miners, carpenters, factory workers, and house servants. Some, however, were taken to large plantations. There they raised many acres of cotton and other cash crops, such as rice, tobacco, and sugarcane.

Many slaves had to wear identification badges (above). This scene (right) shows a plantation on the Mississippi River.

While wealthy planters owned more than half the slaves in the South, most white Southerners owned no slaves at all. By 1860 one of every four white Southern families owned slaves.

REVIEW **Why was slavery important to the South?**

Slavery and the Law

Until the 1820s most people in the South thought slavery was wrong but necessary. In 1832, members of the Virginia legislature even debated **emancipation** (ih•man•suh•PAY•shuhn), or the freeing of slaves, in their state.

The debate started because many Virginians had been frightened by a slave rebellion the year before. The rebellion took place in Southampton County, Virginia. A slave named Nat Turner led an attack that killed more than 50 people, among them his owner. In turn, slave owners trying to end the rebellion killed more than 100 slaves.

Most slaves never took part in such rebellions, but they did whatever they could to **resist**, or act against, slavery. They broke tools, pretended to be sick, or acted as if they did not understand what they had been told. Such actions were dangerous, however, and slaves had to be careful to avoid punishment.

The Virginia legislature voted not to end slavery. To prevent future uprisings, Virginia joined with other slave states who had passed laws that put more controls on slaves. These laws were called slave codes. Under these **codes**, or sets of laws, slaves were not allowed to leave their owners' land, to meet in groups, or to buy or sell goods. Most slaves were not allowed to learn to read or write, and speaking against slavery became a crime.

The federal government also passed laws about slavery. One of these laws was called the Fugitive Slave Act. A **fugitive** is a person who is running away from something. Under this law, anyone caught helping a slave escape could be punished. People who found runaway slaves had to return them to the South.

REVIEW **What were slave codes?**

Analyze Graphs **Many people did not own slaves.**

⧉ **What percent of Southerners owned no slaves?**

Southern Slaveholders in 1860

75% Owned no slaves

3% Owned 20 or more slaves

4% Owned 10–19 slaves

5% Owned 1 slave

13% Owned 2–9 slaves

The Underground Railroad

By 1860 there were more than 500,000 free African Americans living in the United States. Some had been born to parents who were free. Some had bought their freedom or had been freed by their owners. Others had escaped slavery by running away.

Over the years thousands of slaves tried to gain their freedom by running away. Some ran away alone. Others tried to escape with their families or friends.

Once away from their owners' land, runaway slaves had to find safe places to hide. Many slaves helped each other along the way. Native American groups helped slaves by giving them shelter. Some slaves hid in forests, swamps, or mountains, sometimes for years.

Many runaway slaves continued moving for months until they reached Canada or Mexico or free states in the North. Some found helpers who led the way— the brave men and women of the Underground Railroad. The word **underground** is often used to describe something done in secret.

The Underground Railroad was a system of secret escape routes leading to free

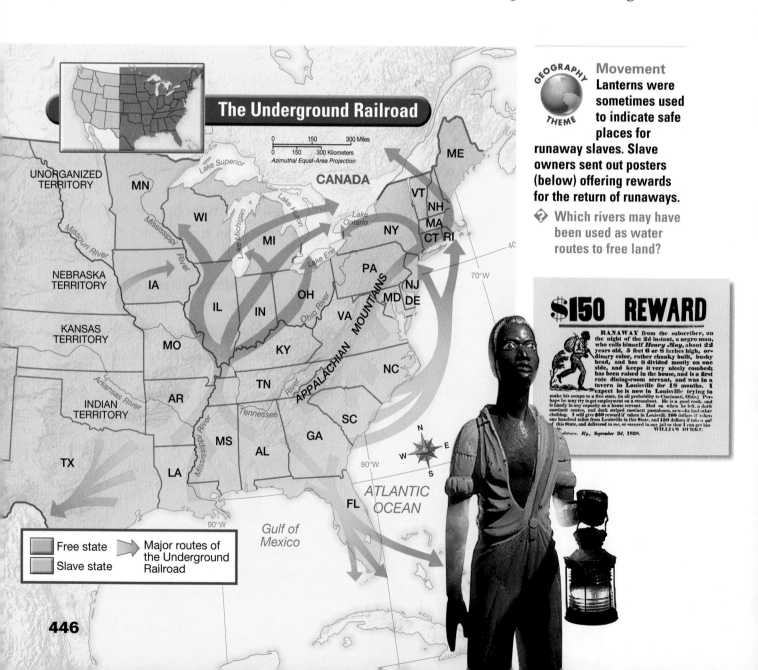

The Underground Railroad

0   150   300 Miles
0   150   300 Kilometers
Azimuthal Equal-Area Projection

UNORGANIZED TERRITORY

NEBRASKA TERRITORY

KANSAS TERRITORY

INDIAN TERRITORY

CANADA

Lake Superior

Lake Michigan

Lake Huron

Lake Ontario

Lake Erie

Missouri River

Mississippi River

Ohio River

Arkansas River

Tennessee River

Mississippi River

APPALACHIAN MOUNTAINS

ATLANTIC OCEAN

Gulf of Mexico

ME, VT, NH, MA, CT, RI, NY, PA, NJ, MD, DE, VA, OH, IN, IL, MI, WI, MN, IA, MO, KY, TN, NC, SC, GA, AL, MS, AR, LA, TX, FL

Free state
Slave state
Major routes of the Underground Railroad

Movement
Lanterns were sometimes used to indicate safe places for runaway slaves. Slave owners sent out posters (below) offering rewards for the return of runaways.

Which rivers may have been used as water routes to free land?

$150 REWARD

RANAWAY from the subscriber, on the night of the 2d instant, a negro man, who calls himself *Henry May*, about 22 years old, 5 feet 6 or 8 inches high, ordinary color, rather chunky built, bushy head, and has it divided mostly on one side, and keeps it very nicely combed; has been raised in the house, and is a first rate dining-room servant, and was in a tavern in Louisville for 18 months. I expect he is now in Louisville trying to make his escape to a free state, (in all probability to Cincinnati, Ohio.) Perhaps he may try to get employment on a steamboat. He is a good cook, and is handy in any capacity as a house servant. Had on when he left, a dark cassinett coatee, and dark striped cassinett pantaloons, new—he had other clothing. I will give $50 reward if taken in Louisville; 100 dollars if taken one hundred miles from Louisville in this State, and 150 dollars if taken out of this State, and delivered to me, or secured in any jail so that I can get him again.

...dstown, Ky., September 3d, 1838.   WILLIAM BURKE.

lands. Most routes led from the South to free states in the North or to Canada. Some led to Mexico and to islands in the Caribbean Sea.

Working mostly at night, conductors, or helpers along the Underground Railroad, led runaway slaves from one hiding place to the next along the routes. These hiding places—barns, attics, storage rooms—were called stations. There the runaways could rest and eat, preparing for the journey to the next station.

Most conductors were free African Americans and white Northerners who opposed slavery. Harriet Tubman, an African American who had escaped from slavery herself, was one of the best-known conductors of the Underground Railroad. During the 1850s Tubman returned to the South 20 times and guided about 300 people to freedom. She proudly claimed, "I never lost a single passenger."

REVIEW **What was the Underground Railroad?**

Harriet Tubman helped enslaved African Americans escape to free lands.

Women Work for Change

Many of the people who worked to free slaves were themselves not entirely free. White women, many of whom spoke out against slavery, were generally not accepted as men's equals. They could not vote, hold public office, or sit on juries.

In 1840, a group of American women went as delegates to a world antislavery convention in London, England. They were denied the right to participate and could only watch the proceedings from the balcony.

One of the women who took part in the convention in London also played an important role at another convention eight years later. Elizabeth Cady Stanton, a defender of the rights of both women and slaves, participated at the first women's rights convention, held in Seneca Falls, New York. Stanton wrote a statement listing women's grievances.

This mural by Hames Michael Newell shows runaway slaves on the Underground Railroad.

In her statement, she demanded that women "have immediate admission to all the rights and privileges which belong to them as citizens of the United States."

In 1852 Harriet Beecher Stowe worked for change by publishing a novel that turned many people against slavery. The book, *Uncle Tom's Cabin*, told the heartbreaking story of slaves being mistreated by a cruel overseer. The book quickly became a best-seller and was made into a play.

Many of the same people who fought for equal rights for women also fought to end slavery. They often united antislavery and women's rights to form a double crusade for freedom.

REVIEW What book turned many people against slavery?

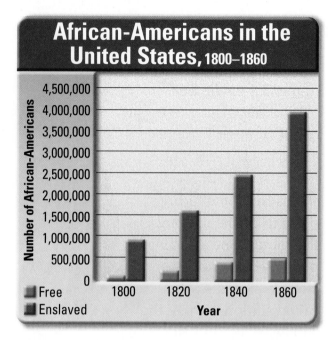

African-Americans in the United States, 1800–1860

Analyze Graphs This graph shows the numbers of free and enslaved African Americans in the United States.

◆ What trend does this graph show?

Abolitionists

People who opposed slavery worked to abolish, or end, it. Those who wanted to abolish slavery were called **abolitionists** (a•buh•LIH•shuhn•ists). Among the first to speak out, as early as the 1680s, were members of the Society of Friends,

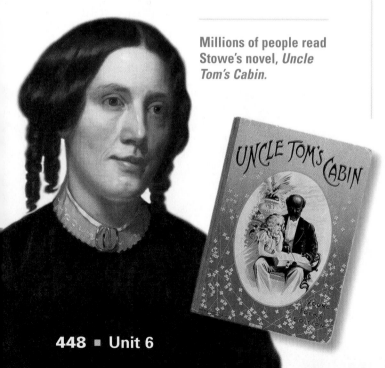

Millions of people read Stowe's novel, *Uncle Tom's Cabin.*

commonly known as the Quakers. In 1775, Quakers formed the first organized group to work against slavery.

In 1827 two free African Americans, Samuel Cornish and John Russwurm, started a newspaper that called for **equality**, or equal rights, for all Americans. The newspaper, *Freedom's Journal*, was the first to be owned and written by African Americans. In it Cornish and Russwurm wrote, "Too long have others spoken for us."

A few years later another abolitionist, William Lloyd Garrison, a white Northerner, founded a newspaper called *The Liberator*. Garrison called for a complete end to slavery, saying, "On this subject I do not wish to think, or speak, or write with moderation. I am earnest . . . I will not excuse. I will not retreat a single inch—AND I WILL BE HEARD."

While some abolitionists were writing, others were giving speeches. One of the best-known abolitionist speakers was Frederick Douglass, a runaway slave. In 1841 Douglass attended a convention of the Massachusetts Antislavery Society. He delivered a speech so moving that everyone cheered. He often told his audiences, "I appear this evening as a thief and a robber. I stole this head, these limbs, this body from my master [slave owner], and ran off with them."

Like Douglass, another former slave named Isabella Van Wagener (WAI•guh•nur) traveled the country speaking out against slavery. Van Wagener believed that God had called her to "travel up and down the land" to preach. She changed her name to reflect her path. She chose *Sojourner*, which means "traveler," for her first name and *Truth* as her last name.

Frederick Douglass was a runaway slave and an abolitionist.

Sojourner Truth believed that slavery could be ended peacefully. Other abolitionists did not. On the night of October 16, 1859, an abolitionist named John Brown and a group of followers seized a government storehouse at Harpers Ferry, in what is now West Virginia. The storehouse was filled with guns. Brown planned to give the guns to slaves so they could fight for their freedom. Brown was caught, put on trial, and hanged.

Over time, more people had come to believe that only the use of force could end slavery. By 1860 it appeared that they were right. The nation was soon to be divided by civil war.

REVIEW Who were abolitionists?

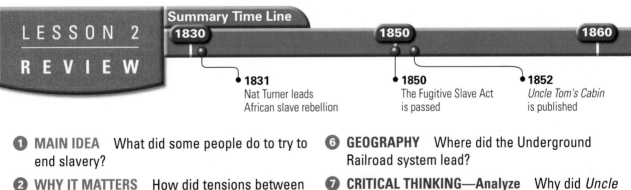

LESSON 2 REVIEW

Summary Time Line

| 1830 | 1850 | 1860 |

1831 Nat Turner leads African slave rebellion

1850 The Fugitive Slave Act is passed

1852 *Uncle Tom's Cabin* is published

1. **MAIN IDEA** What did some people do to try to end slavery?

2. **WHY IT MATTERS** How did tensions between the North and South grow as the conflict over slavery grew?

3. **VOCABULARY** Use the words **fugitive** and **resist** in a sentence about slavery.

4. **TIME LINE** In what year was *Uncle Tom's Cabin* published?

5. **READING SKILL—Categorize** Why did abolitionists work for change?

6. **GEOGRAPHY** Where did the Underground Railroad system lead?

7. **CRITICAL THINKING—Analyze** Why did *Uncle Tom's Cabin* have such a strong influence on the people who read it?

PERFORMANCE—Write a Report Use library sources to learn more about the Underground Railroad or how abolitionists worked for change. Then write a report about what you have learned and share it with the rest of your classmates.

The Union Breaks Apart

1820   1870   1920

1855–1865

MAIN IDEA
Read to learn how the election of 1860 affected the United States.

WHY IT MATTERS
The outcomes of elections often have long-lasting consequences.

VOCABULARY

secede
Confederacy

In the 1850s, new national leaders, such as Abraham Lincoln, began to speak out on the slavery issue. Abraham Lincoln was not an abolitionist, but he was against the spread of slavery. He did not think that the federal government had the right to abolish slavery in the United States. Instead, he hoped that if slavery were not allowed to spread, it would one day die out.

Young Abe Lincoln

Abraham Lincoln was named for his grandfather, who had been a friend of Daniel Boone. Lincoln's grandfather had followed Boone to Kentucky, on the western frontier. He had a son named Thomas, who eventually married Nancy Hanks. They lived in a small log cabin with a dirt floor. Abraham Lincoln was born in that cabin in 1809.

The Lincolns left their home in Kentucky in 1816 and moved to the Indiana Territory. One reason they left Kentucky was that many people there owned slaves. Because slaves did most of the work, there were few paying jobs available. The Lincolns

People today can visit a replica of Abraham Lincoln's boyhood home at the Lincoln Boyhood National Memorial near Little Pigeon Creek, Indiana.

LOCATE IT

INDIANA
Indianapolis

Lincoln Boyhood
National Memorial

Stephen Douglas and Abraham Lincoln held seven debates in 1858. This painting shows Lincoln (standing) and Douglas (to Lincoln's right) debating in Charleston, Illinois.

lived in Indiana for 14 years. By then, Indiana seemed crowded to them, so they moved to the Illinois Territory.

As a young man, Abraham Lincoln held several jobs. All the while, he studied law. In the 1830s he became a lawyer and opened a law office in Illinois.

In 1834 Abraham Lincoln entered public service. He served first in the Illinois legislature. Later, in 1846, he was elected to the United States Congress, where he served one term in the House of Representatives. After returning to Illinois, Lincoln became concerned about the spread of slavery to the West. He joined a new political party formed to fight the spread of slavery. This party was called the Republican party.

In 1858 Lincoln decided to run again for government office. On June 17, Lincoln was nominated, or chosen, by the Republican party to be its candidate for the United States Senate. In his acceptance speech, Lincoln used words from the Bible to explain his beliefs about the spread of slavery and the future of the United States. He said, "A house divided against itself cannot stand. I believe this government cannot endure permanently half slave and half free." Lincoln hoped that his strong stand would not cost him the election.

REVIEW What newly formed political party did Abraham Lincoln join?

Lincoln and Douglas

Abraham Lincoln ran against Senator Stephen A. Douglas, the person who had written the Kansas–Nebraska Act. Lincoln and Douglas were very different from each other. Abraham Lincoln was very tall and thin, while Stephen Douglas was heavy and a full foot shorter than Lincoln.

Because Douglas was already serving in the Senate, he was well known across the country. Few people in places other than Illinois had ever heard of Lincoln.

Despite their differences, Lincoln and Douglas were alike in one important way. Both were talented public speakers. In the summer of 1858, the two candidates traveled around the state of Illinois and debated questions that were important to voters. Huge crowds turned out to listen to them, and newspapers printed what each man had to say.

Stephen Douglas argued that each new state should decide the slavery question for itself. That was what the nation's founders had allowed, he said, and that was what the new Kansas–Nebraska Act allowed.

THE UNION, CONSTITUTION AND THE FLAG MUST AND SHALL BE UPHELD.

Posters in the North were made to show people's support for the Union.

Abraham Lincoln responded that "the framers of the Constitution intended and expected" slavery to end. The problem, Lincoln pointed out, was more than a question of what each state wanted. It was a question of right and wrong. Slavery should not spread to the West, Lincoln said, because slavery was wrong.

Although Stephen Douglas won reelection to the Senate for another term, people all over the country now knew who Lincoln was. Two years later, in 1860, the two men faced each other in another election. This one would decide the next President of the United States.

REVIEW How were the positions of Lincoln and Douglas on the spread of slavery different?

The Election of 1860

In the 1860 election for the presidency Abraham Lincoln represented the Republican party, which firmly opposed the spread of slavery. The Democratic party was divided in its views. Some members of the party supported Stephen Douglas, who continued to argue that western settlers should decide for themselves whether to allow slavery. Other

The first notice of South Carolina's secession was printed in the *Charleston Mercury*. Jefferson Davis (left) was elected president of the Confederacy.

members, mostly Southerners, backed John Breckinridge of Kentucky. Breckinridge thought that the federal government should allow slavery everywhere in the West.

The division within the Democratic party made Lincoln's election almost certain. Although Lincoln promised not to abolish slavery in the South, he said he hoped it would end there one day. Many Southerners feared that Lincoln was attacking their whole way of life. Some leaders in the South said that their states would **secede** from, or leave, the Union if Lincoln became President. Like most Southerners, they believed that states could freely leave the Union since the states had created the Union in the first place.

On Election Day in November 1860, Lincoln did not win a single state in the South. However, he won enough states in the North and the West to win the presidency. Southern leaders did not wait long before carrying out their threat to secede. On December 20, South Carolina seceded from the Union.

Five other states—Alabama, Florida, Georgia, Louisiana, and Mississippi—soon followed. Together these six states formed their own government at Montgomery, Alabama, early in February 1861. They called themselves the Confederate States of America, or the **Confederacy**. Jefferson Davis, a United States senator from Mississippi, was elected president. Alexander Stephens of Georgia became vice president. That month Texas seceded and later joined the Confederacy.

REVIEW What did seven Southern states do after Lincoln was elected President?

POINTS OF VIEW
Union or Secession

JOHN C. CALHOUN, a senator from South Carolina

66 What is the cause of this discontent? It will be found in the belief in the people of the Southern States. . . that they can not remain, as things are now. . . . If you who represent the stronger portion [the North], can not agree to settle [these differences] on the broad principle of justice and duty, say so; and let the states we both represent agree to separate and part in peace. 99

SAM HOUSTON, the governor of Texas

66 I tell you that, while I believe with you in the doctrine of State's Rights, the North is determined to preserve this Union. They are not a fiery, impulsive people as you are, for they live in colder climates. But when they begin to move in a certain direction. . . they move with the steady momentum and perseverance of a mighty avalanche. 99

Analyze the Viewpoints

1 What views about secession did each Southerner hold?

2 What other viewpoints might Southerners have held on the matter of secession?

3 **Make it Relevant** Look at the Letters to the Editor section of your newspaper. Find two letters that express different viewpoints about the same issue, and summarize the viewpoints of each letter.

A CLOSER LOOK
Fort Sumter Prior to the War

Fort Sumter was one of many forts built by the United States after the War of 1812.

1. stair tower
2. soldiers' barracks
3. officers' quarters
4. wall facing Charleston
5. fort lantern
6. mess hall
7. cannons
8. wharf

❖ Why do you think cannons were placed on nearly every side of the fort?

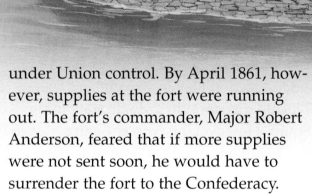

Crisis at Fort Sumter

On March 4, 1861, Abraham Lincoln took the oath of office as President of the United States. In his inauguration speech, he declared, "I have no purpose directly or indirectly to interfere with the institution of slavery in the states where it exists." Yet he firmly stated, "No state, upon its own mere action, can lawfully get out of the Union." Like many Northerners, Lincoln believed the United States could not be divided.

For one month after Lincoln's inauguration, the tension built. Americans everywhere wondered what Lincoln would do about the seceding states. Some people thought he should let them go. Others said that he should accept the Southern position on the slavery question and hope that the Southern states would return. Still others felt that Lincoln should use the army to end the revolt. The country's fate was soon determined at Fort Sumter, which is located on an island off the coast of South Carolina.

When the Southern states seceded, they had taken over post offices, forts, and other federal government property within their borders. Fort Sumter was one of the few forts in the South that remained under Union control. By April 1861, however, supplies at the fort were running out. The fort's commander, Major Robert Anderson, feared that if more supplies were not sent soon, he would have to surrender the fort to the Confederacy.

Lincoln had promised to hold onto all property that belonged to the United States. He sent supply ships to the fort and waited to see how the Confederate leaders would react. On April 12, 1861, Confederate leaders demanded that Union forces surrender. When Major Anderson refused, Confederate troops fired their cannons on the fort. They bombarded the fort for the next 34 hours, until the Union troops surrendered.

Learning of the fall of Fort Sumter, President Lincoln called for 75,000 Americans to join an army to stop the Southern rebellion and preserve the United States. Four more states—Arkansas, North Carolina, Tennessee, and Virginia—seceded and joined the

Confederacy. This brought the number of Confederate states to 11. Tensions between the Union and the Confederate States—the North and the South—had reached their breaking point. The Civil War had begun.

REVIEW Who was in command of Fort Sumter when it was fired upon?

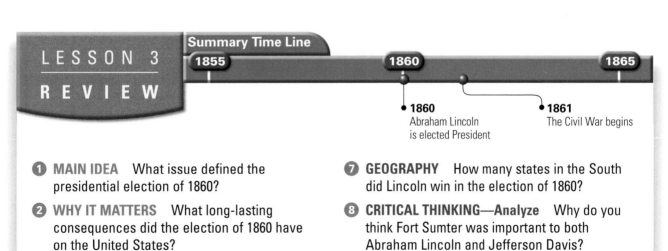

LESSON 3
REVIEW

Summary Time Line

1855   1860   1865

1860
Abraham Lincoln is elected President

1861
The Civil War begins

1. **MAIN IDEA** What issue defined the presidential election of 1860?

2. **WHY IT MATTERS** What long-lasting consequences did the election of 1860 have on the United States?

3. **VOCABULARY** Use the words **Confederacy** and **secede** in a sentence.

4. **TIME LINE** When did the Civil War begin?

5. **READING SKILL—Categorize** What states made up the Confederacy?

6. **HISTORY** What event led South Carolina's leaders to secede from the Union?

7. **GEOGRAPHY** How many states in the South did Lincoln win in the election of 1860?

8. **CRITICAL THINKING—Analyze** Why do you think Fort Sumter was important to both Abraham Lincoln and Jefferson Davis?

PERFORMANCE—Write a Newspaper Headline Write two newspaper headlines, one from a Northern newspaper and one from a Southern newspaper, as they would have appeared the day after the election of 1860. Think about what each paper might have printed as a headline.

Compare Maps with Different Scales

▶ WHY IT MATTERS

Have you ever helped your family plan a trip? You may have wanted to know how far you had to travel.

A map scale helps you find out how far one place is from another. The map scale compares a distance on a map to a distance in the real world. Map scales are different depending on how much area is shown. This means that different maps are drawn to different scales. Knowing about map scales can help you choose the best map for gathering the information you need.

▶ WHAT YOU NEED TO KNOW

Look at the map below and the map on page 457. They both show Fort Sumter and the surrounding area, but with different scales. On Map A, Fort Sumter looks larger. For that reason the scale is said to be larger. When the map scale is larger, more details can be shown. On Map B, Fort Sumter appears smaller, and the scale is said to be smaller.

Although they have different scales, Maps A and B can both be used to measure the distance between the same two places.

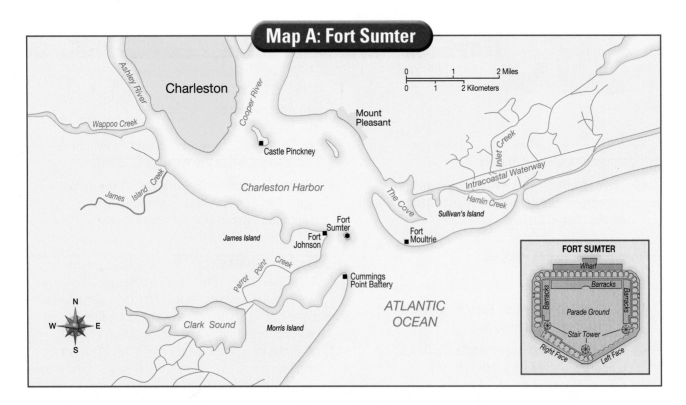

Map A: Fort Sumter

PRACTICE THE SKILL

On April 12, 1861, Confederate troops opened fire on Fort Sumter from Fort Moultrie, Fort Johnson, Castle Pinckney, and various batteries around Charleston Harbor. This act signaled the beginning of the Civil War.

Use the maps below to find the real distance in miles between Fort Sumter and Castle Pinckney.

1 On Map A, use a ruler to measure the exact length of the scale, or use a pencil to mark off the length on a sheet of paper. How long is the line that stands for one mile?

2 Still using Map A, find Fort Sumter and Castle Pinckney. Using the ruler or the sheet of paper you marked, measure the distance between these two places. What is the real distance in miles between Fort Sumter and Castle Pinckney?

3 Now go through the same steps for Map B. How long is the scale length that stands for one mile? Use that scale length to measure the distance between Fort Sumter and Castle Pinckney on the map. What is the real distance in miles? Are the real distances you found on the two maps the same? You should see that even when map scales are different the real distances shown on the maps are the same.

APPLY WHAT YOU LEARNED

Find two maps with different scales—perhaps a map of your state and a map of a large city within your state. Compare the real distances between two places that are on both maps.

Practice your map and globe skills with the **GeoSkills CD-ROM**.

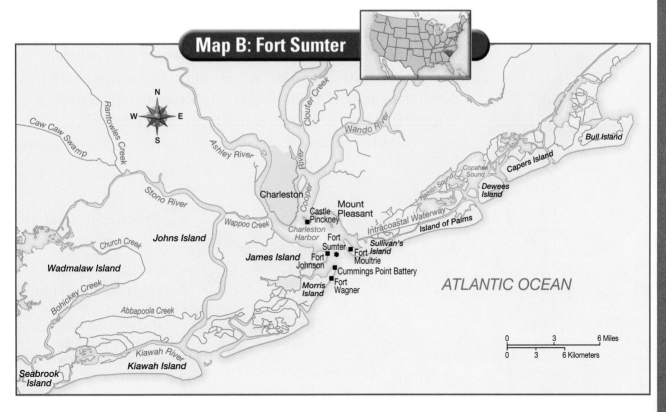

Map B: Fort Sumter

Caw Caw Swamp
Rantowles Creek
Ashley River
Clouter Creek
Wando River
Stono River
Charleston
Cooper River
Mount Pleasant
Castle Pinckney
Charleston Harbor
Wappoo Creek
Johns Island
Church Creek
Fort Sumter
Fort Johnson
James Island
Fort Moultrie
Sullivan's Island
Cummings Point Battery
Wadmalaw Island
Bohickey Creek
Morris Island
Fort Wagner
Abbapoola Creek
Intracoastal Waterway
Island of Palms
Hamlin Sound
Copahee Sound
Capers Island
Dewees Island
Bull Island
ATLANTIC OCEAN
Kiawah River
Kiawah Island
Seabrook Island

0   3   6 Miles
0   3   6 Kilometers

MAP AND GLOBE SKILLS

MAIN IDEA
Read to learn about the key events that happened in the early years of the Civil War.

WHY IT MATTERS
As the war continued, the North hoped to end slavery in the Confederate states as well as save the Union.

VOCABULARY

retreat
border state
strategy
casualty

Civil War

1820   1870   1920

1861–1863

After Confederate troops fired on Fort Sumter, hopes for peace between the North and the South ended. Both the Union and the Confederacy prepared for war. Men and boys eagerly joined regiments made up of their neighbors and friends.

The Fighting Begins

The first of the major battles between the Union and the Confederacy was fought in July 1861. The battle took place at Bull Run, a stream near the town of Manassas Junction, Virginia. On the day of the battle, crowds of enthusiastic sight-seers came in carriages from nearby Washington, D.C. They brought picnic lunches as if to watch a sporting event. A Union soldier said, "We thought it wasn't a bad idea to have the great men from Washington come out to see us thrash the Rebs [Confederate troops]."

At Bull Run two untrained armies clashed in a confusing battle. At first it appeared that the Union army would win. Then, as the Confederate army started to **retreat**, or fall back, new troops arrived. At their head was Thomas Jackson, a skilled Confederate general from Virginia. Jackson managed to stop the retreat. "There's Jackson standing like a stone wall," shouted another general as the Confederates turned and again

General Thomas Jackson

FAST FACT
The Union named battles after the nearest streams, and the Confederates named battles after the nearest towns. That is why the Battle of Manassas (shown here) is also known as the Battle of Bull Run.

Northern soldiers wore blue uniforms.

Advantages in the Civil War

NORTHERN ADVANTAGES
Advanced industry
Advanced railroad system
Strong navy

SOUTHERN ADVANTAGES
Large number of military leaders
Troops experienced in outdoor living
Familiar with the environment of the South

Analyze Graphs This graph compares the advantages of the North and South.

◈ What advantages did the North have?

Southern soldiers wore gray uniforms.

attacked the Union army. From that day on, General Jackson was known as Stonewall Jackson.

The Confederates won the Battle of Manassas, also called the Battle of Bull Run. The defeat shocked the Union. The South had proved more powerful than most Northerners had expected. Americans came to realize that this war would last far longer than they had first believed.

Most Northerners supported the Union, while most white Southerners supported the Confederacy. For some Americans, however, the choice between the Union and the Confederacy was not an easy one. The war had deeply divided people in all regions. People in the **border states**—Delaware, Kentucky, Maryland, and Missouri—were especially torn between the two sides. These states, which were located between the North and the South, permitted slavery but had not seceded.

REVIEW Where did the first major battle of the Civil War take place?

Battle Plans

The Union **strategy**, or long-range plan, for winning the war was first to weaken the South and then to invade it. To weaken the South, Lincoln and his advisers came up with a strategy that some people called the Anaconda (a•nuh•KAHN•duh) Plan. An anaconda is a large snake that squeezes its prey to death. The Union would squeeze the South by not letting it ship its cotton or bring in goods. If the South could not sell its cash crops, it would not have the money to buy supplies for its army.

The purpose of the plan was to block all imports from reaching the South. The plan called for winning control of the Mississippi River and for establishing a naval blockade of Confederate ports. Not everyone in the North liked the idea of a blockade, however. Many people thought it would take too long to set up. They wanted the Union army to invade the South. "On to Richmond!" they shouted.

The Union and the Confederacy

CANADA

WASHINGTON TERRITORY

OREGON

MINNESOTA

Lake Superior

DAKOTA TERRITORY

WISCONSIN

MICHIGAN

Lake Huron

Lake Ontario

MAINE

VT

NH

70°W

NEW YORK

MA

CT

RI

40°N

40°N

NEVADA TERRITORY

UTAH TERRITORY

NEBRASKA TERRITORY

IOWA

ILLINOIS INDIANA

OHIO

PENNSYLVANIA

NJ

MD

DE

WEST VIRGINIA (1863)

VIRGINIA

Lake Erie

CALIFORNIA

COLORADO TERRITORY

KANSAS

MISSOURI

KENTUCKY

NORTH CAROLINA

PACIFIC OCEAN

30°N

120°W

NEW MEXICO TERRITORY

INDIAN TERRITORY

ARKANSAS

TENNESSEE

SOUTH CAROLINA

ATLANTIC OCEAN

30°N

GEORGIA

ALABAMA

TEXAS

MISSISSIPPI

LOUISIANA

FLORIDA

N

E

W

S

MEXICO

Gulf of Mexico

90°W

80°W

0   200   400 Miles
0   200   400 Kilometers
Albers Equal-Area Projection

Union state
Border state
Confederate state
Territory

Regions   The Civil War had divided the nation. In western Virginia, feelings for the Union were so strong that the people voted to break away from Virginia. West Virginia joined the Union in 1863.

◆ Which states were border states?

Richmond, Virginia, had become the capital of the Confederacy by this time.

At first the most important strategy of the Confederate states was simply to protect their lands. This strategy was based on the belief that Britain and France would help the South. Both countries depended on Southern cotton to keep their textile mills going. The South also hoped that the North would tire of the war. Many Southerners, however, were impatient. Cries of "On to Washington!" were soon answered with plans to invade the North.

REVIEW What was the Anaconda Plan?

The Battle at Antietam

As the Civil War dragged on into 1862, the Anaconda Plan seemed to be working. The blockade brought trade in the South to a halt, and supplies there ran

This cannon was used in the Battle of Antietam.

460 ▪ Unit 6

very low. This made life increasingly difficult for Southern troops, who became poorly equipped, fed, and clothed. Even so, many Northerners became discouraged by the long lists of war casualties. A **casualty** is a person who has been killed or wounded in a war.

Then, in September 1862, the Union and the Confederates fought a major battle at Antietam (an•TEE•tuhm) Creek, near Sharpsburg, Maryland. By that time Robert E. Lee was Confederate commander of the Army of Northern Virginia. General Lee had led his army from Virginia into Maryland, intending to reach Harrisburg, Pennsylvania. There, Lee planned to cut off railroad communication between the states in the East and those in the West. Lee also hoped to find in Pennsylvania supplies that his troops badly needed.

At Antietam Creek, Lee's army was stopped by Union troops. The battle that followed resulted in the highest number of casualties in one day of the whole war. Union casualties numbered more than 2,000 killed and 9,500 wounded. Confederate casualties totaled 2,700 killed and over 9,000 wounded. "Never before or after in all the war were so many men shot on one day," historian Bruce Catton wrote. Having lost one-fourth of his army, Lee retreated to Virginia.

Although the battle at Antietam was really a draw, or tie, it had an important result. Five days later, on September 22, 1862, President Lincoln announced his decision to issue an order freeing the slaves in areas that were still fighting against the Union.

REVIEW Why was General Lee leading his army to Pennsylvania?

The Emancipation Proclamation

To President Lincoln, the purpose of the war had been to keep the country together—to save the Union. It had not been to abolish slavery. In 1862 President Lincoln wrote a letter explaining his view to Horace Greeley, publisher of the *New York Tribune*. "My [main] object in this struggle is to save the Union, and is not either to save or destroy slavery.

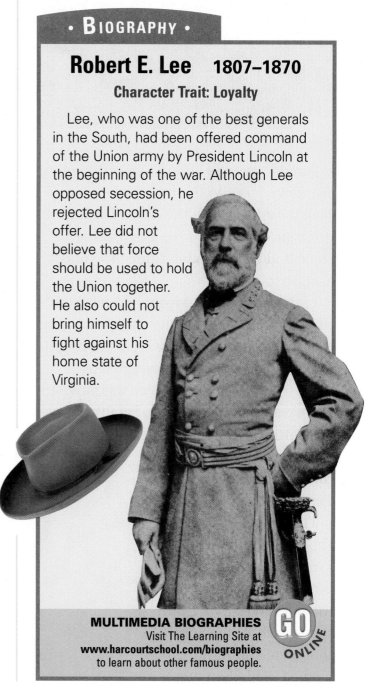

• BIOGRAPHY •

Robert E. Lee 1807–1870
Character Trait: Loyalty

Lee, who was one of the best generals in the South, had been offered command of the Union army by President Lincoln at the beginning of the war. Although Lee opposed secession, he rejected Lincoln's offer. Lee did not believe that force should be used to hold the Union together. He also could not bring himself to fight against his home state of Virginia.

MULTIMEDIA BIOGRAPHIES
Visit The Learning Site at
www.harcourtschool.com/biographies
to learn about other famous people.

GO ONLINE

This painting shows Abraham Lincoln meeting with his cabinet to discuss the Emancipation Proclamation.

If I could save the Union without freeing any slave I would do it; and if I could save it by freeing all the slaves I would do it; and if I could save it by freeing some and leaving others alone I would also do that."

Early in the war Lincoln had felt that making emancipation the main goal of the war might divide the North. It might also turn people in the border states against the Union. However, the move to end slavery grew stronger. Finally, after the Battle of Antietam Creek, Lincoln decided the time had come for an emancipation order.

The Emancipation Proclamation, which Lincoln issued on January 1, 1863, said that all slaves living in those parts of the South that were still fighting against the Union would be "then, thenceforward, and forever free." The proclamation did not give all enslaved people instant freedom. The order was meant only for the states that had left the Union, not for the border states or for areas that had already been won back by the Union.

The Emancipation Proclamation hurt the South's hopes of getting help from Britain and France. Now that the war had become a fight against slavery, most British and French citizens, who opposed slavery, gave their support to the Union. Confederate President Jefferson Davis called Lincoln's proclamation "the most execrable [terrible] measure recorded in the history of a guilty man."

To celebrate the proclamation, it was reprinted on this poster.

As the Union troops advanced farther and farther into the Confederacy, they carried out the Emancipation Proclamation. Thousands of enslaved people fled to freedom behind the Northern battle lines, where they worked as laborers or joined the Union army or navy. By allowing freed slaves to serve in the military, the Emancipation Proclamation helped ease the Union army's shortage of soldiers.

REVIEW What was the Emancipation Proclamation?

Contributions from All

In both the North and the South, only men were allowed to join the army. Women, however, found many ways to help. They took over factory, business, and farm jobs that men left behind. They sent food to the troops, made bandages, and collected supplies. Many women, such as Clara Barton and Sally Tompkins, worked as nurses. A few served as spies, and some even dressed as men, joined the army, and fought in battles.

About 180,000 African Americans eventually served in the Union army during the Civil War as well. They served in separate regiments, mostly under the command of white officers. At first they were not paid as much as white soldiers. They were also given poor equipment, and they often ran out of supplies. Despite these hardships, African American soldiers proved themselves on the battlefield. They led raids behind Confederate lines, served as spies and scouts, and fought in almost every major battle of the war.

The Union navy was open to African American men when the Civil War began. During the war the Union navy enlisted about 20,000 African American sailors. Among those who served was Robert Smalls. In 1862 Smalls and some other slaves took over a Confederate steamer in Charleston Harbor and surrendered it to Union forces.

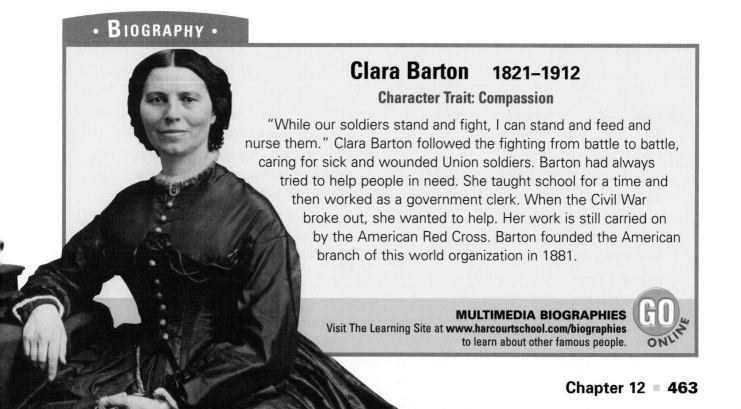

• BIOGRAPHY •

Clara Barton 1821–1912

Character Trait: Compassion

"While our soldiers stand and fight, I can stand and feed and nurse them." Clara Barton followed the fighting from battle to battle, caring for sick and wounded Union soldiers. Barton had always tried to help people in need. She taught school for a time and then worked as a government clerk. When the Civil War broke out, she wanted to help. Her work is still carried on by the American Red Cross. Barton founded the American branch of this world organization in 1881.

MULTIMEDIA BIOGRAPHIES
Visit The Learning Site at **www.harcourtschool.com/biographies**
to learn about other famous people.

GO ONLINE

African American troops (left) played a key role in support of the Union. Thousands of Hispanic Americans also took part in the war, with some fighting for the Union and others fighting for the Confederacy. Unlike African American soldiers, most Hispanic Americans served in regular army units.

European immigrants who came to this country for a better life marched off to preserve the Union, as well. There were Irishmen in the Fighting 69th, the Irish Zouaves, Irish Volunteers, and St. Patrick Brigade. Italians fought with the Garibaldi Guards and Italian Legion. Germans fought with the Steuben Volunteers, German Rifles, Turner Rifles, and DeKalb Regiment. In fact, the immigrant population in the Northern states helped the Union army replenish itself and eventually wear out a depleted Confederate army.

REVIEW How did African American soldiers help the Union during the war?

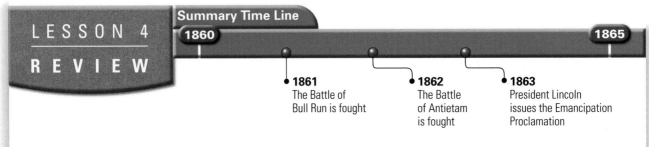

LESSON 4 REVIEW

Summary Time Line

1860 — 1865

1861 The Battle of Bull Run is fought

1862 The Battle of Antietam is fought

1863 President Lincoln issues the Emancipation Proclamation

1. **MAIN IDEA** Why did the first major battle of the Civil War shock the Union?

2. **WHY IT MATTERS** Why did Lincoln avoid making emancipation the main goal of the war?

3. **VOCABULARY** Use the word **retreat** in a sentence.

4. **TIME LINE** What Civil War battle occurred first, Antietam or Bull Run?

5. **READING SKILL—Categorize** Name the border states.

6. **HISTORY** What were the results of the Battle of Antietam?

7. **HISTORY** How did women in both the North and South help the troops?

8. **CRITICAL THINKING—Evaluate** How did the Emancipation Proclamation affect the Confederates' strategy?

PERFORMANCE—Write a Letter Imagine that you are living in the South during the Civil War. Write a letter to a friend describing how the Union's blockade is changing your life. Then share your letter with a classmate.

The Road to Union Victory

MAIN IDEA
Read to learn about the key events that led to a Union victory.

WHY IT MATTERS
A Union victory meant that the Union was preserved. The United States would remain one country.

VOCABULARY
address

1820 — 1870 — 1920

1863–1865

The Emancipation Proclamation gave new hope to enslaved people and new spirit to the North. In fact, in the months following the Emancipation Proclamation, the Union seemed to be winning the war. Across the South, younger and younger men joined the army to take the places of Confederate soldiers who had been killed or wounded. The war, however, was far from over.

Vicksburg and Chancellorsville

By May 1863 the Union army finally had a general as effective as Confederate General Robert E. Lee. His name was Ulysses S. Grant. One of Grant's first important battles began in May at Vicksburg, Mississippi, the Confederate headquarters on the Mississippi River.

Grant laid siege to the city. The Union guns pounded Vicksburg, and the Union army cut off all supplies to the city. The trapped Confederates, both soldiers and townspeople, soon ran out of food. Conditions were so bad that they had to tear down houses for firewood and dig caves in hillsides for shelter. Yet the people of Vicksburg were determined to endure whatever Grant had in store for them. One Vicksburg woman wrote, "We'll just burrow into these hills and let them batter away as hard as they please."

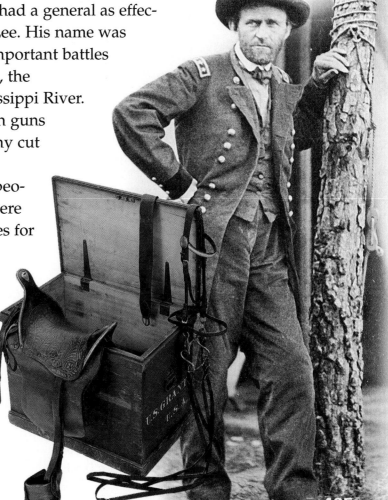

Ulysses S. Grant (right) used this box to carry his saddle and other field equipment.

465

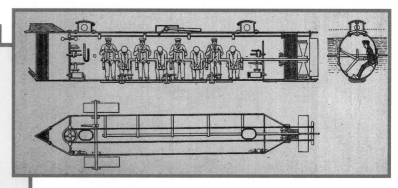

The *H. L. Hunley*

In 1864 the *H. L. Hunley* became the first submarine to sink an enemy ship during wartime. Measuring just over 39 feet (12 m) long and just under 4 feet (1 m) wide, the *Hunley* was powered by crew members who cranked a propeller by hand. The submarine was built to ram a torpedo into a target and then back away, causing a trip line to set off the explosion. The design of the *Hunley* proved to be successful when it sank the Union warship *Housatonic*.

The diagram (above) shows the inside of the Hunley (below).

However, by July 4, 1863, the people of Vicksburg could hold out no longer. They finally surrendered.

Vicksburg proved to be a key victory. Its location gave the Union control of the Mississippi River. This, in turn, cut the Confederacy into two parts. The western states of the Confederacy were no longer able to communicate easily with the states to the east or to supply many reinforcements to them.

At about the same time that Grant started to lay siege to Vicksburg, General Lee and his army defeated a Union army at Chancellorsville, Virginia. In winning, however, Lee lost one of the South's best

generals. In the confusion of battle, Stonewall Jackson was accidentally shot by one of his own troops and later died.

Despite Jackson's death, the victory at Chancellorsville gave the Confederacy confidence to try again to invade the North. The Confederates' goal was to win a victory on Northern soil.

If they could do so, the Confederates hoped people in the North would demand an end to the war. In June 1863, General Lee's troops headed north. They reached the small town of Gettysburg, Pennsylvania, on July 1.

REVIEW Why was the victory at Vicksburg so important for the Union army?

The Battle of Gettysburg

General Robert E. Lee believed that victory at Gettysburg might turn the war in favor of the Confederacy. However, after two days of fighting, victory did not seem possible. In a final attempt on July 3, 1863, Lee ordered General George Pickett's entire division—15,000 soldiers—to make a direct attack. They were to charge across open country toward a stone fence at the Union army's center.

Marching shoulder to shoulder, Pickett's troops formed a line half a mile (0.8 km) wide. Steadily, the wall of soldiers in what came to be called Pickett's Charge moved forward. As the Confederates moved closer, they were met by the fire of Union guns, which controlled the higher ground of the battlefield. "Men were falling all around us, and cannon and muskets were raining death upon us," remembered a Confederate officer. "Still on and up the slope toward the stone fence our men steadily swept."

Pickett's soldiers reached the fence but were stopped there in fierce fighting. The charge had failed, and Pickett's men retreated, leaving behind half their number dead or wounded.

The Battle of Gettysburg was one of the deadliest battles of the Civil War. In fighting between July 1 and 3, 1863, more than 3,000 Union soldiers and nearly 4,000 Confederates were killed. More than 20,000 on each side were wounded or reported missing.

The fate of the Fourteenth Tennessee Regiment tells the story. When the battle began, there were 365 men in the unit. When the battle ended, there were only 3.

The Union victory at Gettysburg marked a turning point in the war. After

This pin was worn on the hats of Civil War soldiers to indicate that they were foot soldiers.

the battle, General Lee's army retreated to Virginia. It would never again be able to launch a major attack against the Union.

REVIEW **What was Pickett's Charge?**

The Gettysburg Address

On November 19, 1863, President Lincoln went to Gettysburg to dedicate a cemetery for the Union soldiers who had died in the battle. A crowd of nearly 6,000 people gathered for the ceremony.

Lincoln gave a short speech, or **address**, that day. In fact, he spoke for less than three minutes. Lincoln's Gettysburg Address was so short that many people in the crowd were disappointed. Soon, however, people realized that this short speech was one of the most inspiring speeches ever given by a United States President.

In his address, Lincoln spoke to the heart of the war-weary North.

This scene, painted by James Walker, shows the battle at Gettysburg.

THE GETTYSBURG ADDRESS

Four score and seven years ago our fathers brought forth on this continent a new nation, conceived in Liberty, and dedicated to the proposition that all men are created equal.

Now we are engaged in a great civil war, testing whether that nation or any nation so conceived and so dedicated, can long endure. We are met on a great battlefield of that war. We have come to dedicate a portion of that field, as a final resting place for those who here gave their lives that that nation might live. It is altogether fitting and proper that we should do this.

But, in a larger sense, we can not dedicate—we can not consecrate—we can not hallow—this ground. The brave men, living and dead, who struggled here, have consecrated it, far above our poor power to add or detract. The world will little note nor long remember what we say here, but it can never forget what they did here. It is for us the living, rather, to be dedicated here to the unfinished work which they who fought here have thus far so nobly advanced. It is rather for us to be here dedicated to the great task remaining before us—that from these honored dead we take increased devotion to that cause for which they gave the last full measure of devotion—that we here highly resolve that these dead shall not have died in vain—that this nation, under God, shall have a new birth of freedom—and that government of the people, by the people, for the people, shall not perish from the earth.

He spoke of the ideals of liberty and equality on which the nation had been founded. He honored the many soldiers who had died defending those ideals. He also called on the people of the Union to try even harder to win the struggle those soldiers had died for—to save the "government of the people, by the people, for the people" so that the Union would be preserved.

REVIEW Why did Lincoln give the Gettysburg Address?

The Road to Appomattox

In March 1864 Lincoln gave command of all the Union armies to General Ulysses S. Grant. Grant soon devised a plan to invade the South and destroy its will to fight. The plan called for an army under Grant's command to march to Richmond, the Confederate capital. At the same time a second army under General William Tecumseh Sherman was to march from Chattanooga, Tennessee, to Atlanta, Georgia.

As Sherman captured Atlanta, much of the city burned to the ground. The destruction of Atlanta, a manufacturing center and junction of several railroads, was a great loss for the Confederacy.

From Atlanta, Sherman's army of 62,000 men headed toward Savannah in a march that has become known as the March to the Sea. The army cut a path of destruction 60 miles (97 km) wide and 300 miles (483 km) long. Union soldiers burned homes and stores, destroyed crops, wrecked bridges, and tore up railroad tracks. When Sherman reached Savannah on December 22, 1864, he sent a message to President Lincoln. He wrote, "I beg to present you as a Christmas gift the city of Savannah."

From Georgia, Sherman turned north and marched through South Carolina, destroying even more than he had in Georgia. At the same time, General Grant moved south into Virginia. In his pursuit of General Lee's army, Grant cut off Lee's supply lines and kept pushing the Confederates in retreat. In early April 1865, Richmond was evacuated and set on fire by retreating Confederates. More than 900 buildings were destroyed and hundreds more were badly damaged. Union troops took control of the city.

General Lee's army moved west, with General Grant in constant pursuit. Lee's men were starving, and they were now outnumbered by 10 to 1. Lee could retreat no farther, nor could he continue to fight. Lee said, "There is nothing left for me to do but to go and see General Grant, and I would rather die a thousand deaths."

On the afternoon of April 9, 1865, Lee surrendered to Grant at Appomattox (a•puh•MA•tuhks) Court House, Virginia.

This painting shows General Lee (seated at left) surrendering to General Grant (seated at right) at the home of Wilmer McLean.

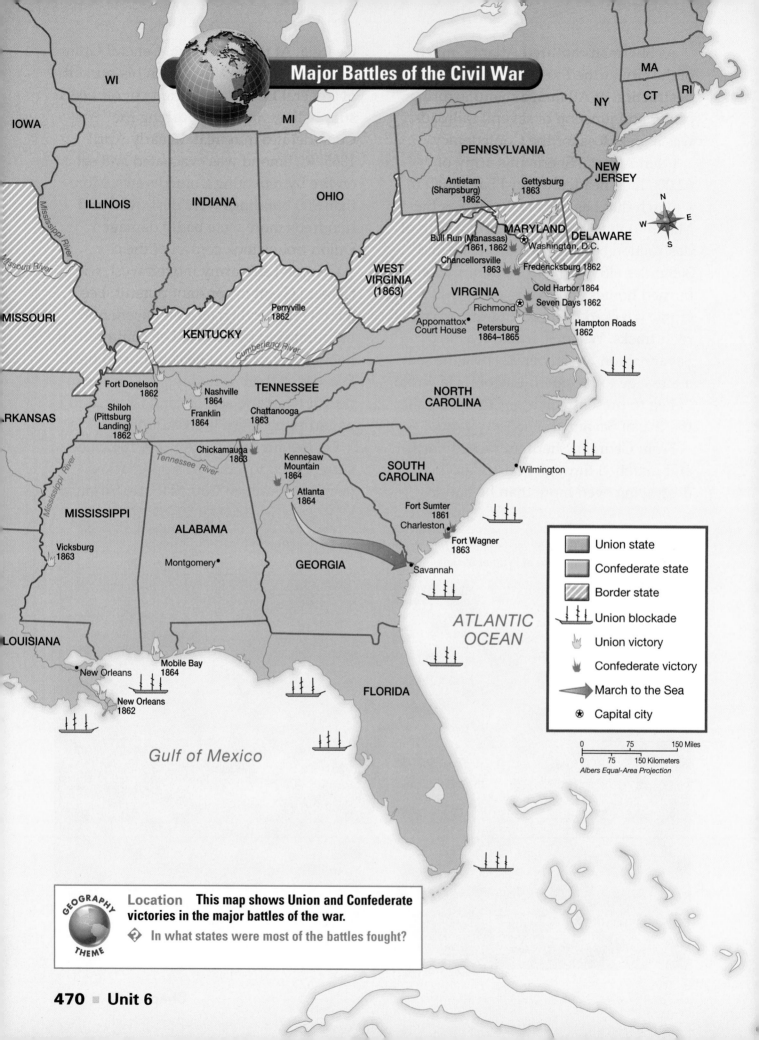

Major Battles of the Civil War

WI

MA

IOWA

MI

NY

CT

RI

PENNSYLVANIA

NEW JERSEY

ILLINOIS

INDIANA

OHIO

Antietam (Sharpsburg) 1862

Gettysburg 1863

MARYLAND

DELAWARE

Bull Run (Manassas) 1861, 1862

Washington, D.C.

WEST VIRGINIA (1863)

Chancellorsville 1863

Fredericksburg 1862

MISSOURI

Perryville 1862

VIRGINIA

Cold Harbor 1864

Seven Days 1862

Richmond

KENTUCKY

Appomattox Court House

Petersburg 1864–1865

Hampton Roads 1862

Cumberland River

ARKANSAS

Fort Donelson 1862

Nashville 1864

TENNESSEE

NORTH CAROLINA

Shiloh (Pittsburg Landing) 1862

Franklin 1864

Chattanooga 1863

Tennessee River

Chickamauga 1863

Kennesaw Mountain 1864

SOUTH CAROLINA

Wilmington

MISSISSIPPI

Atlanta 1864

Fort Sumter 1861

Vicksburg 1863

ALABAMA

Charleston

Fort Wagner 1863

Montgomery

GEORGIA

Savannah

ATLANTIC OCEAN

LOUISIANA

New Orleans

Mobile Bay 1864

FLORIDA

New Orleans 1862

Gulf of Mexico

Mississippi River

Missouri River

Legend

	Union state
	Confederate state
	Border state
	Union blockade
	Union victory
	Confederate victory
	March to the Sea
	Capital city

0   75   150 Miles

0   75   150 Kilometers

Albers Equal-Area Projection

Location This map shows Union and Confederate victories in the major battles of the war.

In what states were most of the battles fought?

Memorial Day

On May 5, 1866, people in Waterloo, New York, honored those who died in the Civil War. The people closed businesses for the day and decorated soldiers' graves with flowers. This was the beginning of the holiday known as Memorial Day, or Decoration Day. On this day Americans remember those who gave their lives for their country in all wars. Today most states observe Memorial Day on the last Monday in May.

People often celebrate this holiday by holding parades.

In a meeting at the home of Wilmer McLean, the two generals agreed to the terms of the Confederate army's surrender. After signing the surrender, Lee mounted his horse Traveller and rode back to his men.

In the next few weeks, as word of General Lee's surrender reached them, other Confederate generals surrendered, too. After four years of bloodshed the Civil War was over. The Union had been preserved, but at a horrible cost.

More than 600,000 soldiers had died during the war. Many died as a result of battle. Others, however, had died from disease. Thousands of soldiers also returned home wounded, scarred both physically and emotionally from the terrible devastation the war had brought.

REVIEW Why did Lee surrender to Grant?

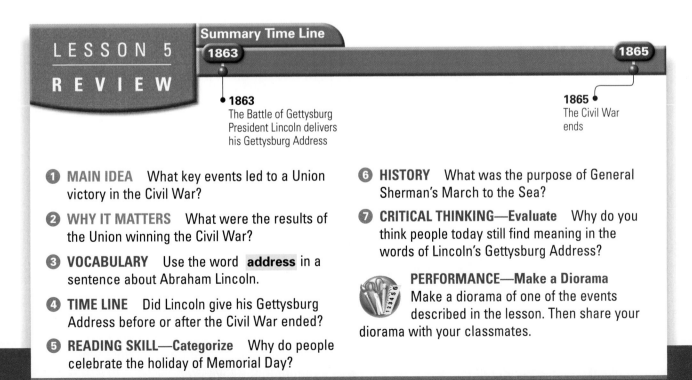

LESSON 5 REVIEW

Summary Time Line

1863 ———————————————————————— 1865

1863
The Battle of Gettysburg
President Lincoln delivers
his Gettysburg Address

1865
The Civil War
ends

1 **MAIN IDEA** What key events led to a Union victory in the Civil War?

2 **WHY IT MATTERS** What were the results of the Union winning the Civil War?

3 **VOCABULARY** Use the word **address** in a sentence about Abraham Lincoln.

4 **TIME LINE** Did Lincoln give his Gettysburg Address before or after the Civil War ended?

5 **READING SKILL—Categorize** Why do people celebrate the holiday of Memorial Day?

6 **HISTORY** What was the purpose of General Sherman's March to the Sea?

7 **CRITICAL THINKING—Evaluate** Why do you think people today still find meaning in the words of Lincoln's Gettysburg Address?

PERFORMANCE—Make a Diorama Make a diorama of one of the events described in the lesson. Then share your diorama with your classmates.

Summary Time Line
1820

● 1820
Congress
passes the
Missouri
Compromise

USE YOUR READING SKILLS

Complete this graphic organizer by categorizing important leaders and battles of the Civil War. A copy of this graphic organizer appears on page 120 of the Activity Book.

Important Leaders and Battles of the Civil War

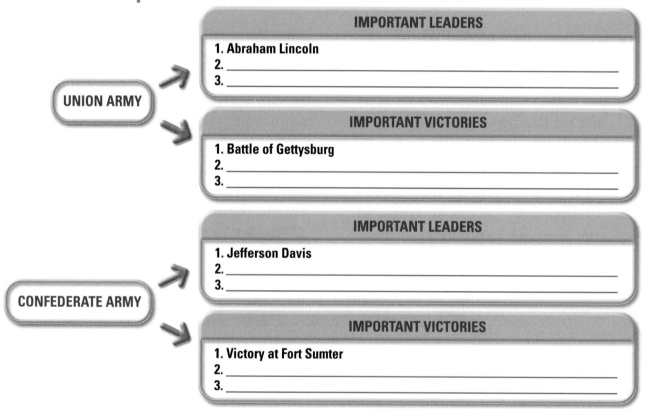

UNION ARMY

IMPORTANT LEADERS
1. Abraham Lincoln
2. _____
3. _____

IMPORTANT VICTORIES
1. Battle of Gettysburg
2. _____
3. _____

CONFEDERATE ARMY

IMPORTANT LEADERS
1. Jefferson Davis
2. _____
3. _____

IMPORTANT VICTORIES
1. Victory at Fort Sumter
2. _____
3. _____

THINK & WRITE

Write a List of Questions   Imagine you are a newspaper reporter in 1863. You have the opportunity to interview President Lincoln at the White House. Write a list of questions you would like to ask the President.

Write a Song   The Civil War inspired the writing of many patriotic American songs, such as "The Battle Hymn of the Republic." Write a song to honor the soldiers who fought in the Civil War.

1850
Congress passes the Compromise of 1850

1854
Congress passes the Kansas-Nebraska Act

1860
Abraham Lincoln is elected President

1861
The Civil War begins

1863
The Emancipation Proclamation is issued

1865
Lee surrenders at Appomattox Court House

USE THE TIME LINE

Use the chapter summary time line to answer these questions.

1 In what year did the Civil War end?

2 How many years after the Missouri Compromise did the Civil War begin?

USE VOCABULARY

Use these terms to write a story about life in the United States during the Civil War.

states' rights (p. 436),

abolitionist (p. 448),

equality (p. 448),

secede (p. 453)

Confederacy (p. 453)

RECALL FACTS

Answer these questions.

3 What effect did the Kansas-Nebraska Act have on life in the Kansas Territory?

4 How did Harriet Tubman contribute to the abolitionist cause?

5 What were some of the causes of the Civil War?

Write the letter of the best choice.

6 TEST PREP One effect of the worldwide demand for Southern cotton was that —
 A it made Southern planters want to end slavery.
 B many new public schools were built in the South.
 C it created a need for more enslaved workers.
 D many new factories were built in the South.

7 TEST PREP During the Civil War, many European immigrants helped preserve the Union by—
 F serving as members of Congress.
 G working as Union spies.
 H donating money to the war effort.
 J serving in the Union army.

THINK CRITICALLY

8 How did changes brought about by the Industrial Revolution lead to conflicts between different regions in the United States?

9 Why do you think the North and South were not able to reach a compromise over slavery in 1861?

10 What do you think would have happened if Abraham Lincoln had waited until after the Civil War to issue the Emancipation Proclamation?

APPLY SKILLS

Identify Frame of Reference

11 The debate over states' rights was one of the issues that led to the Civil War. Explain how a Southern politician's view of states' rights might have been different from a Northern politician's.

Compare Maps with Different Scales

Study the two maps of Fort Sumter on pages 456 and 457. Then answer the following question.

12 Which map would you use if you wanted to see a more detailed view of Fort Sumter and the surrounding area? Explain.

DRAYTON HALL

During the Civil War, many of the South's plantation homes were destroyed or badly damaged. Drayton Hall managed to survive the conflict and today serves as a living history museum. Visitors can learn about its various buildings, farming methods, and the daily lives of those who once lived there.

LOCATE IT

SOUTH CAROLINA

Charleston

Drayton Hall

The Nation Reunited

❝ **The war is over—the rebels are our countrymen again.** ❞

—Ulysses S. Grant, April 9, 1865, silencing his cheering troops after Robert E. Lee surrendered

CHAPTER READING SKILL

Determine Point of View

When you determine someone's **point of view** on a subject, you identify that person's way of looking at it.

As you read this chapter, determine different people's points of view about Reconstruction, industrial growth, and immigration.

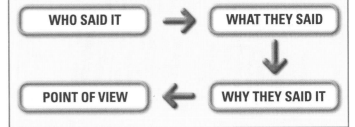

WHO SAID IT → WHAT THEY SAID

POINT OF VIEW ← WHY THEY SAID IT

1

MAIN IDEA

Read to learn how the United States government tried to rebuild the South after the Civil War.

WHY IT MATTERS

Rebuilding the South and reuniting the nation proved to be a difficult process.

VOCABULARY

Reconstruction
assassinate
black codes
acquittal

Reconstruction

1820   1870   1920

1865–1870

The end of the Civil War brought the Confederacy to its end. Now it was time to try to bring the country back together. This time of rebuilding, called **Reconstruction**, had two distinct parts. The first part was the President's plan for Reconstruction. The second part was Congress's Reconstruction plan. Before Reconstruction could begin, however, one more tragedy would add to the country's pain.

One More Tragic Death

Before the Civil War ended, Abraham Lincoln was inaugurated for a second term as President. He realized he would face a challenging task in rebuilding the country. Lincoln, however, believed the South should not be punished for the war. He wanted to bring the country back together peacefully and as quickly as possible. Lincoln spoke of his plans for Reconstruction in his second inaugural address on March 4, 1865.

> **With malice toward none, with charity for all, with firmness in the right as God gives us to see the right, let us strive on to finish the work we are in, to bind up the nation's wounds. . . .**

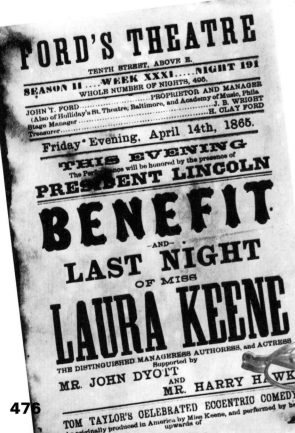

This poster announces Lincoln's plans to attend Ford's Theatre. Below are the glasses he wore that night.

FAST FACT

After shooting the President, John Wilkes Booth jumped onto the stage and cried out *Sic semper tyrannis!*, which means "Thus ever for tyrants" in Latin.

476

Following Lincoln's death, Andrew Johnson (above) was sworn in as the nation's seventeenth President. Johnson supported passage of the Thirteenth Amendment (right).

The President's plans were tragically cut short. On April 14, 1865, just five days after Lee's surrender, Lincoln went with Mary Todd Lincoln, his wife, to watch a play at Ford's Theatre in Washington, D.C. There he was **assassinated**—murdered in a sudden or secret attack—by John Wilkes Booth. Booth, an actor at Ford's Theatre, supported the Confederate cause.

Lincoln's death shocked the nation. Northerners had lost the leader who had saved the Union. Southerners had lost the leader who had promised an easy peace between the North and the South. Mary Chesnut, a Southerner, feared the worst. When she learned of Lincoln's death, Chesnut wrote in her diary, "Lincoln— old Abe Lincoln—killed. . . . I know this foul murder will bring down worse miseries on us."

REVIEW Why might many Southerners be upset by Lincoln's death?

The President's Plan

After Lincoln's death, the Vice President, Andrew Johnson, became President. Johnson returned the rights of citizenship to most Confederates who pledged loyalty to the United States. Their states then held elections, and state governments went back to work.

Johnson also said that the former Confederate states had to abolish slavery before they could rejoin the Union. To that end, the Thirteenth Amendment to the Constitution was ratified in December 1865. It ended slavery in the United States and its territories.

Such easy terms for rejoining the Union made many Northerners angry. They felt the Confederates were not being punished for their part in the war. White Southerners were again being elected to office and running state governments.

However, few people talked about the rights of the former slaves.

It was not long before the newly elected state legislatures in the South passed laws to limit the rights of former slaves. These laws, called **black codes**, differed from state to state. In most states, however, former slaves were not allowed to vote. In some they were not allowed to travel freely. They could not own certain kinds of property or work in certain businesses. They could be forced to work without pay if they could not find other jobs.

REVIEW **Why was the Thirteenth Amendment to the Constitution ratified?**

Congress's Plan

Many members of Congress were upset about what was happening in the South. As a result, Congress replaced the President's Reconstruction plan with one of its own.

As part of its plan, Congress did away with the new state governments and put the Southern states under military rule. Union soldiers kept order, and army officers were appointed to be governors. Before any Southern state could reestablish its state government, it had to write a new state constitution giving all men, both black and white, the right to vote.

Under its plan for Reconstruction, Congress sent Union troops to the Southern states. The troops in the photograph below are standing in front of a house in Atlanta, Georgia.

Johnson was the first President to be impeached. His trial in the Senate (above) drew large crowds of people.

• **BIOGRAPHY** •

Edmund G. Ross   1826–1907

Character Trait: Courage

Edmund G. Ross moved to Kansas in 1856 to lead the "free state" movement. He started two Kansas newspapers, the *Topeka Tribune* and the *Kansas State Record*, both of which supported this cause. During the Civil War, Ross became a major in the Union army. In 1866 he was appointed to the Senate, where despite pressure from other senators, he voted to acquit President Johnson.

MULTIMEDIA BIOGRAPHIES
Visit The Learning Site at
www.harcourtschool.com/biographies
to learn about other famous people.

GO ONLINE

To return to the Union, a state also had to approve the Fourteenth Amendment. The Fourteenth Amendment states that all persons born in the United States, except Native Americans, and those who later become citizens are citizens of the United States and of the state in which they live. The amendment also protects the rights of all citizens.

President Johnson was very angry about this plan and about other laws Congress had passed to limit his authority as President. After Johnson fired a popular member of his cabinet in 1868, the House of Representatives voted to impeach him. The Senate put Johnson on trial. By just one vote, the Senate failed to get the two-thirds majority needed to remove Johnson from office. The final and deciding vote for **acquittal**, or a verdict of not guilty, was cast by Senator Edmund G. Ross of Kansas. Although Andrew Johnson stayed in office, he was no longer respected as a strong leader.

REVIEW What rights are provided by the Fourteenth Amendment?

Reconstruction Governments

As the Southern states began to write new state constitutions and approve the Fourteenth Amendment, new elections were held. For the first time African Americans, such as Blanche K. Bruce and Hiram R. Revels of Mississippi, were elected to the United States Congress.

Many African Americans also served in the new Reconstruction governments in the Southern states. Jonathan C. Gibbs became secretary of state in Florida and helped set up Florida's public school system. Before this time, most schools in the South were privately run. Francis L. Cardozo, another African American, was secretary of state and, later, state treasurer in South Carolina.

Most Confederates accepted their defeat and the abolition of slavery.

This poster (left) celebrates the passage of the Fifteenth Amendment (above).

However, many were against equal rights for African Americans. They did not want African Americans to vote or to hold office, and they opposed the Reconstruction governments.

Congress then proposed the Fifteenth Amendment to the Constitution. It states that no citizen shall be denied the right to vote because of "race, color, or previous condition of servitude." This amendment, which was ratified in 1870, was designed to extend voting rights and to enforce them by law.

REVIEW **What is the Fifteenth Amendment?**

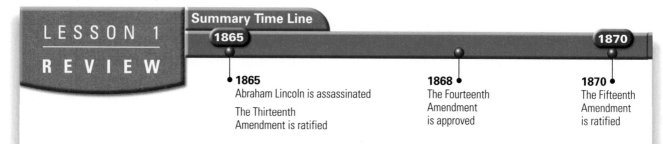

LESSON 1
REVIEW

Summary Time Line
1865 ─────────────────────────── 1870

1865
Abraham Lincoln is assassinated

The Thirteenth
Amendment is ratified

1868
The Fourteenth
Amendment
is approved

1870
The Fifteenth
Amendment
is ratified

1 **MAIN IDEA** How did the United States government try to rebuild the South after the Civil War?

2 **WHY IT MATTERS** Why was Reconstruction such a difficult process?

3 **VOCABULARY** Use the words **Reconstruction** and **black codes** in a sentence about the South after the Civil War.

4 **TIME LINE** When did the Fifteenth Amendment become part of the Constitution?

5 **READING SKILL—Determine Point of View** How did President Lincoln think the South should be treated after the Civil War ended?

6 **HISTORY** Which amendment ended slavery in the United States?

7 **CRITICAL THINKING—Evaluate** Why did many white Southerners oppose the new Reconstruction governments?

PERFORMANCE—Conduct an Interview Imagine that you are a news reporter. Write an interview with President Andrew Johnson, a senator who supports Congress's plan for Reconstruction, or an African American elected to serve in a Reconstruction government in the South. Provide both questions and answers. Then share your interview with classmates.

The South After the War

1820   **1870**   **1920**

1865–1877

MAIN IDEA
Read to learn about
the many challenges the
South faced after the war.

WHY IT MATTERS
The refusal of many white
Southerners to accept the
reconstruction of Southern
society caused conflict.

VOCABULARY
freedmen
sharecropping
carpetbagger
scalawag
secret ballot
segregation

When the Civil War ended, much of the South was in ruins. The money issued by the Confederacy was worthless, and most Confederate banks were closed. Entire cities had been burned, and many railroads, bridges, plantations, and farms had been destroyed. As one Southerner remembered, "All the talk was of burning homes, houses knocked to pieces, . . . famine, murder, desolation."

The years following the war were hard ones for all people in the South. For the more than 4 million former slaves living there, however, those years also brought new hope.

The Freedmen's Bureau

In March 1865, even before the war ended, the United States Congress set up the Bureau of Refugees, Freedmen, and Abandoned Lands—the Freedmen's Bureau, as it was called. It aided all needy people in the South, although **freedmen**—men, women, and children who had been slaves—were its main concern.

Many former slaves, like those shown outside this Freedmen's Bureau school (below), were eager to learn to read and write. Many of the teachers in those schools were Northern women.

Many former slaves were wandering through the country looking for the means to start a new life. The Freedmen's Bureau gave food and supplies to these people. It also helped some white farmers rebuild their farms. The most important work of the Freedmen's Bureau, however, was education. Newly freed slaves were eager to learn to read and write. To help meet this need, the Freedmen's Bureau built more than 4,000 schools and hired thousands of teachers.

The Freedmen's Bureau also wanted to help former slaves earn a living by providing them with land to farm, but this plan did not work. The land was to have come from the plantations taken or abandoned during the war, but the federal government decided to give those plantations back to their original owners. In the end, most former slaves were not given any land. Without money to buy land of their own, they had to find work where they could.

REVIEW Why was the Freedmen's Bureau set up?

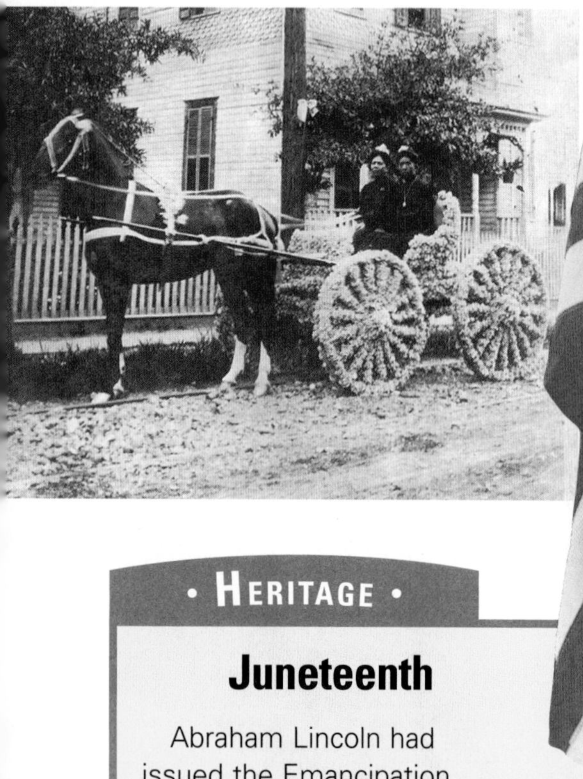

This photograph (left) shows people going to an early Juneteenth celebration. Many people, such as those participating in this parade in Austin, Texas (below), celebrate Juneteenth.

· **HERITAGE** ·

Juneteenth

Abraham Lincoln had issued the Emancipation Proclamation on January 1, 1863. But because Union troops did not control Texas at the time, the order had little effect there. On June 19, 1865, Union soldiers landed in Galveston, Texas. On that day Union General Gordon Granger read an order declaring that all slaves in Texas were free. Today people in Texas and across the country celebrate June 19, or Juneteenth, as a day of freedom. It is a holiday marked by picnics, parades, and family gatherings.

Sharecropping

In their search for jobs, many former slaves went back to work on plantations. Planters welcomed them. Fields needed to be plowed, and crops needed to be planted. Now, however, planters had to pay the former slaves for their work.

Because there was not much money available in the years following the war, many landowners paid workers in shares of crops rather than in cash. Under this system, known as **sharecropping**, a landowner gave a worker a cabin, mules, tools, and seed. The worker, called a sharecropper, then farmed the land. At harvesttime the landowner took a share of the crops plus enough extra to cover the cost of the worker's housing and supplies. What was left was the worker's share.

Sharecropping gave landowners the help they needed to work the fields. It also gave former slaves work for pay. Yet few people got ahead through sharecropping. When crops failed, both landowners and workers suffered. Even in good times, most workers' shares were very little, if anything at all.

REVIEW How were workers paid in a sharecropping system?

Carpetbaggers and Scalawags

To rebuild bridges, buildings, and railroads, the South's Reconstruction governments had to increase taxes. In Louisiana, for example, taxes almost doubled. Mississippi's taxes were 14 times higher than they had been. White Southerners blamed the higher taxes on African American state legislators and on other state government leaders they called carpetbaggers and scalawags.

Using tools like this plow, many former slaves worked as sharecroppers in the years following the Civil War.

Carpetbaggers were people from the North who moved to the South to take part in Reconstruction governments. They were called carpetbaggers because many of them carried their belongings in suitcases made of carpet material. Some of them truly wanted to help. Others were looking for an opportunity for personal gain.

James Longstreet believed that building factories would help the South rebuild its economy.

A **scalawag** (SKA•lih•wag) is a rascal, someone who supports a cause for his or her own gain. Many scalawags were white Southerners who had opposed the Confederacy. Some were thinking only of themselves. Others felt they were doing what was best for the South.

Among the most famous of the scalawags was James Longstreet, a former Confederate general. Longstreet believed that the South needed to cooperate with the North in order to prosper. He and other leading business people wanted to build factories to lessen the South's dependence on agriculture.

REVIEW How did the Reconstruction governments raise money to rebuild bridges, buildings, and railroads?

Reconstruction Ends

Many white Southerners did not want their way of life to change. Burdened by heavy taxes and a changing society, they began to organize to regain their authority. One way to do so was to control the way people voted.

In the 1860s there was no secret ballot, as there is today. A **secret ballot** is a voting method that does not allow anyone to know how a person has voted. Before the secret ballot was used, the names of voters and how they voted were published in newspapers.

Secret societies were formed to keep African Americans from voting or to make sure they voted only in certain ways. Those who joined the secret societies included white Southerners who resented the fact that African Americans were now considered their equals. Members of one secret society, the Ku Klux Klan, used violence to keep African Americans from voting or to make sure they voted as they were told.

Over time, white Southerners once again took control of their state governments and society. Despite the Fifteenth Amendment, new state laws were passed that made it very difficult, if not impossible, for African Americans to vote. African Americans also were required to go to separate schools and churches and to sit in separate railroad cars. Laws such as these led to **segregation**, or the

Many carpetbaggers who came to the South during Reconstruction carried their belongings in bags made of carpet material.

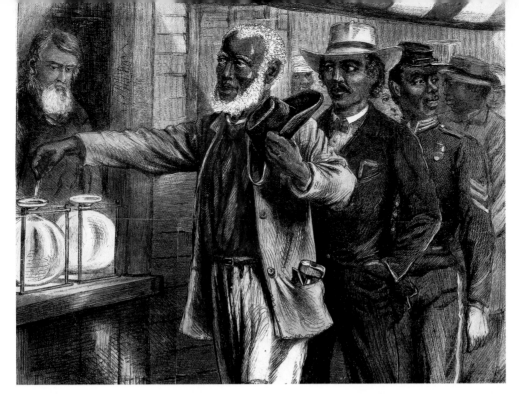

The Fifteenth Amendment guaranteed African Americans the right to vote, as seen in this illustration. With the end of Reconstruction, however, that right was again denied to most African Americans living in the South.

practice of keeping people in separate groups based on their race or culture.

Reconstruction was over by 1877. In that year the last of the Union troops left the South. The rights and freedoms that African Americans had won were again being taken away in the South. By 1900 African Americans in many of the Southern states were not allowed to vote, and few held public office.

REVIEW How did white Southerners take back control of their state governments and society?

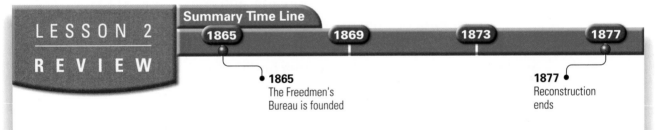

LESSON 2 REVIEW

Summary Time Line

1865 — 1869 — 1873 — 1877

1865
The Freedmen's Bureau is founded

1877
Reconstruction ends

① **MAIN IDEA** What challenges did the South face after the Civil War?

② **WHY IT MATTERS** How did the refusal of many white Southerners to accept Reconstruction cause conflict?

③ **VOCABULARY** Use the words **carpetbagger** and **scalawag** in a sentence about the South after the Civil War.

④ **TIME LINE** When did Reconstruction end?

⑤ **READING SKILL—Determine Point of View** How did members of the Ku Klux Klan feel about African Americans being allowed to vote?

⑥ **ECONOMICS** Why was it difficult for sharecroppers to get ahead?

⑦ **CRITICAL THINKING—Analyze** In what ways did the Freedmen's Bureau help African Americans? In what ways did it fail?

PERFORMANCE—Write a List Write a list of things you would have done to help rebuild the South after the Civil War. Be sure to include ways in which you would have helped the newly freed slaves, as well as the economies of the Southern states. Share your list with the rest of the class.

Settling the Last Frontier

MAIN IDEA
Read to learn why many people decided to move to the West after the Civil War.

WHY IT MATTERS
The West offered Americans a new place to explore and settle.

VOCABULARY
boom
refinery
prospector
bust
long drive
homesteader
open range
reservation

1820   1870   1920

1850–1890

The years following the Civil War saw the full-scale settlement of the West. Many Americans moved to settle this last frontier, which included the Great Plains, the Rocky Mountains, and the Great Basin.

Miners

After the California gold rush of 1849, new discoveries of gold and silver brought more miners to the West and supplied new sources of mineral wealth for the nation. Thousands of miners hurried to Colorado after gold was found near Pikes Peak in 1858. The next year, news of huge deposits of silver in the area known as the Comstock Lode drew thousands to what is now Nevada. Between 1862 and 1868, other finds in present-day Arizona, Idaho, Montana, and Alaska added to the West's **boom**, or time of fast economic or population growth.

When gold or silver was discovered in a place, miners moved into the area hoping to strike it rich. They claimed

Many stores in towns that were abandoned in the late 1800s are once again open for business. Stores, such as the one mentioned in this poster (left), were closed.

GOOD NEWS FOR MINERS.

NEW GOODS, PROVISIONS, TOOLS, CLOTHING, &c. &c.

GREAT BARGAINS!

STAR BAKERY

land and set up camps, which often grew into towns. Some towns sprang up almost overnight as people quickly started businesses and farms and built refineries. A **refinery** is a factory where metals, fuels, and other materials are cleaned and made into usable products.

Fights often broke out among the **prospectors**, or those searching for gold, silver, and other mineral resources. The towns had no sheriffs, and law and order did not exist. "Street fights were frequent," one writer reported, "and . . . everyone was on his guard against a random shot." As mining towns grew, families began to arrive. Many mining towns set up governments and started schools, hospitals, and churches.

In most places all of the gold or silver was mined in just a few years. When that happened, the miners left to look for new claims and the mining town was often abandoned. Just as quickly as a boom built a town, a **bust**, or time of fast economic decline, left a town lifeless. Some of these abandoned towns, called ghost towns, can still be seen in the West today.

REVIEW **What brought miners to the West?**

Ranchers

The West's vast grasslands attracted many ranchers to the region. Large-scale cattle ranching had begun in Texas in the early 1800s. Ranchers there raised cattle mostly for leather and for tallow, or fat, which was used for making candles and soap. After the Civil War, however, as cities in the East grew, the demand for beef increased. Cattle sold there for ten times as much as they did in Texas. Ranchers could make more money if they could get their cattle to those markets.

At first Texas ranchers drove, or herded, their cattle to port cities, such as Galveston, Texas, and Shreveport, Louisiana, for shipment to New Orleans and to cities in the East. This method was both slow and costly. In the late 1860s, a cheaper, faster method became available when the first railroads were built out West. Between 1867 and 1890, ranchers drove about 10 million head of cattle north to the railroads on **long drives**.

The long drives followed cattle trails such as the Sedalia Trail, which went from Texas to Sedalia, Missouri.

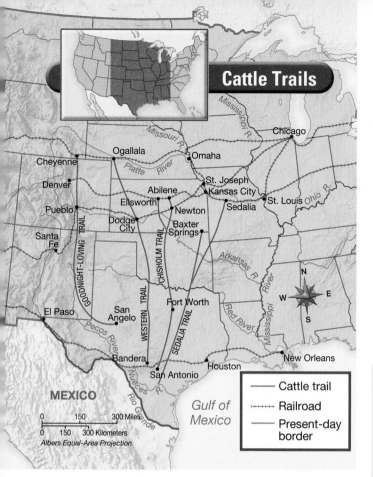

Cattle Trails

Movement **This map shows the four major cattle trails used by ranchers in the 1880s.**

◈ **Which trail led to both Abilene and Ellsworth?**

Saddles and hats like these were used by ranchers on long drives.

Other trails—the Chisholm, the Western, and the Goodnight-Loving—led to other "cow towns" along the railroads. Abilene, Kansas; Ogallala, Nebraska; and Cheyenne, Wyoming, were towns that grew at the end of cattle trails. At each town the cattle were loaded onto railroad cars and sent to Chicago. There the animals were prepared for market. The meat was then sent in refrigerated freight cars to markets in the East.

REVIEW How were railroads important to Texas ranchers?

Barbed wire was used to build fences on the Great Plains.

Homesteaders

In 1862 Congress passed the Homestead Act. This law opened the Great Plains to settlers by giving 160 acres of land to any head of a family who was over 21 years of age and who would live on the land for five years. Thousands of Americans, as well as about 100,000 immigrants from Europe, rushed to claim those plots of land called homesteads. The people who settled them were known as **homesteaders**.

Living on the Great Plains was very difficult. There were few streams for water or trees for wood. Many settlers used sod to build their houses, but sod houses were difficult to keep clean. Dirt often fell from the sod ceiling onto the furniture. Drought and dust storms were common in the summer, and homesteaders worried about prairie fires. In winter, snow and bitterly cold temperatures froze the region. Insects, too, were a problem. In 1874, grasshoppers came by the millions, turning the sky black and eating anything that was green.

Many homesteaders saw the Great Plains as a "treeless wasteland." They believed that the tough sod and dry soil were unsuited for farming, and they left. Those who stayed used new technologies to solve some of the challenges the land presented. They used an improved steel plow, invented by James Oliver of Indiana, to cut through the thick sod. They used new models of windmills to pump water from the ground. They planted Russian wheat, which needed less water, and used reapers to harvest it.

Relations with ranchers posed another problem for farmers. It was difficult to grow crops in the same area where cattle ranchers kept their herds. To keep the cattle out of their fields, farmers began using wire with steel points, known as barbed wire, to build fences. Some ranchers also built fences to keep their cattle from wandering off the ranches.

Fences often kept farmers from reaching the water they needed for their crops and kept ranchers from reaching the water they needed for their cattle. Fences also blocked some cattle from reaching the millions of acres of government land that ranchers used as **open range**, or free grazing land.

GEOGRAPHY THEME

Movement **This map shows the areas of the United States that were settled by 1870 and 1890. Among the settlers was this Nebraska family (right), who used sod to build their home.**

❓ **What happened to the frontier as settlers moved west?**

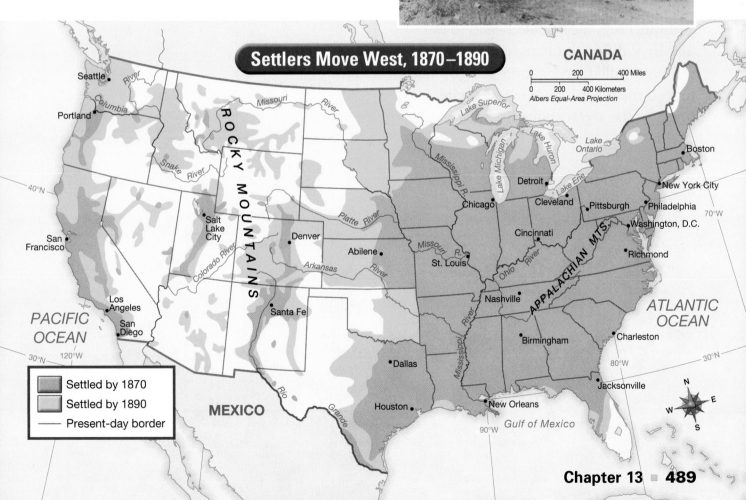

Settlers Move West, 1870–1890

Legend:
- Settled by 1870
- Settled by 1890
- Present-day border

Farmers and ranchers began cutting one another's fences. Some people even started shooting one another. These fights, called range wars, went on through the 1880s until ranchers were told they had to move their cattle off government land.

In spite of these problems, about 5 million homesteaders had migrated to the Great Plains by 1890. So many people had moved there and to lands farther west, in the Rocky Mountains and the Great Basin, that in 1890 the Census Bureau declared the last frontier "closed."

REVIEW **What hardships did homesteaders moving west face?**

Conflict in the West

Many of the Native American groups on the Great Plains had long depended on the buffalo for their basic needs. As settlers began using the land for farming and ranching, the buffalo began to die out. In addition, hunters working for the railroads killed large numbers of buffalo to feed the workers who were laying track. In the 1860s about 15 million buffalo lived on the Great Plains. Within 20 years, fewer than 1,000 were left.

With fewer buffalo and the loss of their hunting lands, many groups of Plains Indians signed treaties with the United States. Those treaties set up reservations for the Indians. A **reservation** is an area of land set aside by the government for use only by Native Americans.

· GEOGRAPHY ·

GEOGRAPHY ESSENTIAL ELEMENTS

Little Bighorn Battlefield

Understanding Places and Regions

Among the soldiers killed at the Little Bighorn Battlefield in June 1876 were five members of the Custer family—George, his two brothers Thomas and Boston, their nephew, and their brother-in-law. The Little Bighorn Battlefield was made a national military cemetery in 1879, and in 1946 it was designated a national monument.

In 1868 the Sioux Nation signed a treaty that created the Great Sioux Reservation in the Black Hills region of present-day South Dakota and Wyoming. Some Indians, however, continued to roam the lands west of the reservation in search of buffalo. After gold was discovered in the Black Hills, the United States sent soldiers to move all the Indians to reservations.

In June 1876 Lieutenant Colonel George Custer led an attack against the Sioux and their Cheyenne allies at the Little Bighorn River. Two of the chiefs leading the Sioux were Sitting Bull and Crazy Horse. As many as 2,000 Indian warriors quickly surrounded Custer and his men. In the battle that followed, about 225 soldiers were killed. Crazy Horse and

Chief Joseph

Sitting Bull were later defeated, and the Indians were forced onto reservations.

In 1877 the United States government also ordered the Nez Perce (NES PERS) Indians in eastern Oregon to move to a reservation in Idaho. The Nez Perce leader, Chief Joseph, led a group of 800 men, women, and children in an attempt to escape to Canada. They were stopped and surrendered without a fight. Chief Joseph told his people, "I am tired of fighting."

By 1880 almost all Native Americans in the United States had been moved onto reservations. In 1924 Congress granted citizenship to all Native Americans. In 1934 it gave Indians living on reservation lands the right to govern themselves.

REVIEW **Why did Custer attack the Sioux?**

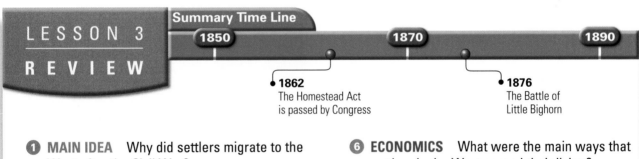

LESSON 3
REVIEW

Summary Time Line

1850   1870   1890

• **1862**
The Homestead Act
is passed by Congress

• **1876**
The Battle of
Little Bighorn

1 **MAIN IDEA** Why did settlers migrate to the West after the Civil War?

2 **WHY IT MATTERS** How did settlement of the West affect the growth of the United States?

3 **VOCABULARY** How did **prospectors** cause **booms** in some areas?

4 **TIME LINE** When was the Homestead Act passed?

5 **READING SKILL—Determine Point of View** How did ranchers and farmers think differently about cattle ranching?

6 **ECONOMICS** What were the main ways that settlers in the West earned their living?

7 **CRITICAL THINKING—Analyze** How do you think the destruction of the buffalo affected Native Americans?

PERFORMANCE—Write a List of Questions Imagine that it is 1870 and that you are going to move out West to become a homesteader. Write a list of questions that you would want to ask a homesteader or cattle rancher that will make your journey easier and help you live in an unfamiliar land.

Use a Climograph

VOCABULARY

climograph

➡ WHY IT MATTERS

In the late 1800s many Americans who moved from eastern cities to the Great Plains were surprised by much of what they found there. However, probably nothing surprised them more than the extremes of temperature and precipitation.

If you and your family were moving to another place, you would want to know more about its climate before you moved there. One way to learn about the climate of a place is to study a climograph, or climate graph. A **climograph** shows on one graph the average monthly temperature and the average monthly precipitation for a place. Comparing climographs can help you understand differences in climates.

➡ WHAT YOU NEED TO KNOW

The climographs on page 493 show the average monthly temperature and precipitation for Omaha, Nebraska, and Philadelphia, Pennsylvania. The temperatures are shown as a line graph. The amounts of precipitation are shown as a bar graph. The months are listed along the bottom of each climograph, from January to December.

Along the left-hand side of each climograph is a Fahrenheit scale for temperature. A point is shown on the climograph for the average temperature for each month. These points are connected with a red line. By studying the line, you can see which months are usually warm and which are usually cold.

Along the right-hand side of each climograph is a scale for precipitation. The average monthly amounts of precipitation are shown in inches. By studying the heights of the blue bars, you can see which months are usually dry and which are usually wet.

Pioneers who settled on the Great Plains sometimes experienced ice storms. These storms covered fences, plants, and the ground with a layer of ice.

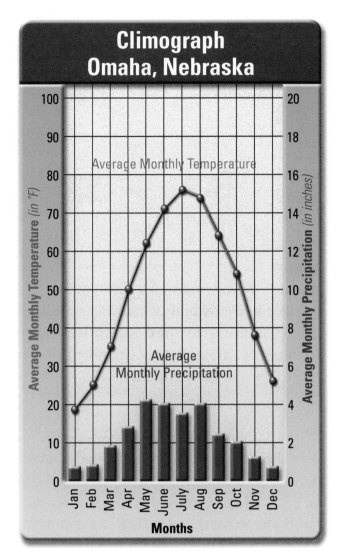

Climograph
Omaha, Nebraska

Average Monthly Temperature

Average Monthly Precipitation

Months

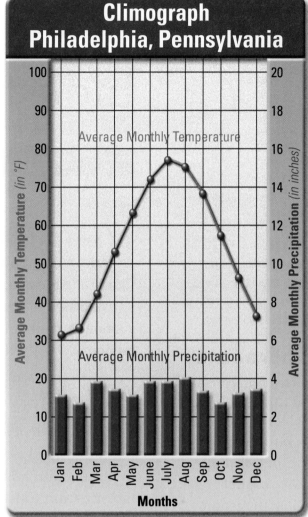

Climograph
Philadelphia, Pennsylvania

Average Monthly Temperature

Average Monthly Precipitation

Months

▶ PRACTICE THE SKILL

Use the climographs above to answer the following questions.

1 Which is the warmest month in each of these cities? Which is the coolest?

2 What is the wettest month in each city?

3 What is the driest month in each city?

4 Which city receives more precipitation during the year?

5 What is the average temperature for each place in January?

6 How much precipitation falls during January in each place?

▶ APPLY WHAT YOU LEARNED

Use an almanac, an encyclopedia, or the Internet to create a climograph for your city or for a city close to where you live. Compare your climograph with the ones shown on this page. Which place shows the greatest changes in temperature and precipitation? Share your findings with a family member or friend. Then discuss why people might need to know this kind of information.

CHART AND GRAPH SKILLS

4

MAIN IDEA
Read to learn how the United States economy grew and changed in the late 1800s.

WHY IT MATTERS
Changes in the United States economy encouraged the growth of businesses and cities.

VOCABULARY
free enterprise

transcontinental railroad

entrepreneur

petroleum

capital

human resource

FAST FACT

A train trip from New York to California on the transcontinental railroad typically took from 10 to 12 days. For $100, people could sit on plush seats in fancy cars. For $40, they had to sit on hard benches in plain cars.

The Rise of New Industries

1820   1870   1920

1860–1900

After the Civil War great changes took place in the American economy. Inventors developed new technologies that made it easier for people to travel and communicate with one another. It was an important time for **free enterprise**—an economic system in which people are able to start and run businesses with little control by the government.

The Transcontinental Railroad

From 1860 to 1900, the railroad network in the United States was built up rapidly in order to move people from place to place. Railroads were also needed to move raw materials to factories and finished products to market. By 1900 the country had more than 193,000 miles (311,000 km) of track. That included the **transcontinental railroad**, which crossed the entire continent of North America. The transcontinental railroad was actually made up of a number of different lines,

including the Union Pacific Railroad and the Central Pacific Railroad. Together they linked the Atlantic and Pacific coasts and opened the nation's vast interior to people who wanted to settle there. They also made trade between different parts of the country easier, which caused the economy to grow.

One reason for the growth of railroads was the development of new inventions that improved rail transportation. George Westinghouse's air brake made trains safer by stopping not only the locomotive but also each car. Granville T. Woods improved the air brake and also developed a telegraph system that allowed trains and stations to communicate.

The transcontinental railroad crossed both the Rocky Mountains and the Sierra Nevada. Workers had to build bridges across valleys, cut ledges on mountainsides, and blast tunnels through mountains. At Promontory, Utah, on May 10, 1869, workers laid the last of the transcontinental railroad. A ceremonial golden spike was driven into place.

REVIEW How did the transcontinental railroad help the economy grow?

The Steel Industry

Railroads needed strong, long-lasting tracks. At first, iron rails were used. With bigger and heavier locomotives, however, iron rails were no longer strong enough. Steel rails would be harder and last longer than iron, but steel was much more expensive to make.

In 1872 Andrew Carnegie, an entrepreneur (ahn•truh•pruh•NER) from Pittsburgh, Pennsylvania, visited Britain. An **entrepreneur** is a person who sets up and runs a business. In Britain, Carnegie saw a new process for making steel. Invented by Henry Bessemer, this process melted iron ore and other metals and materials together in a new kind of coal-fired furnace, called a blast furnace.

A CLOSER LOOK
Transcontinental Railroad

To complete the transcontinental railroad, workers often worked long hours in dangerous conditions. Most of the workers were Chinese and Irish immigrants.

1. Workers used tools, such as pickaxes and shovels, to clear tunnels.
2. A small locomotive powered machines that hauled dirt and rock to the surface.
3. Explosives were used to blast through rock.
4. Workers stayed behind a protective wall during tunnel blasting.
5. Workers on the transcontinental railroad laid more than 1,776 miles (2,858 km) of track.

❖ What kinds of work did immigrant workers have to do to build the transcontinental railroad?

It was called a blast furnace because blasts of air were forced through the molten metal to burn out the impurities. This process made the steel stronger.

Back in Pennsylvania, Carnegie found investors to help him build a steel mill. Western Pennsylvania and nearby areas of Ohio and West Virginia had all the resources needed to make steel. By the early 1870s, Carnegie's steel business was so successful that he built more steel mills and bought coal and iron mines to supply them. Then he bought ships to carry these natural resources to his mills. With his mines and ships, he could make a greater supply of steel at a lower cost than other mills could.

By the 1890s Andrew Carnegie had become one of the wealthiest people in the world. Carnegie, who had come to the United States as an immigrant from Scotland in 1848, gave much of his wealth to build libraries and schools.

Other industries quickly discovered new uses for steel. In the 1880s William Jenney used steel frames to build taller buildings. People called these tall buildings skyscrapers because they seemed to scrape the sky.

John Roebling, a German immigrant, used steel cables and beams to build suspended bridges. One of his bridges, the Brooklyn Bridge, still links Manhattan with Brooklyn, in New York City.

As the demand for steel increased, more steel mills were built. In the late 1800s, large deposits of iron ore were discovered in the Mesabi Range, west of Lake Superior. To be nearer to those resources, the steel industry spread to cities along the Great Lakes, such as Cleveland, Ohio, and Chicago, Illinois.

Steel Production, 1865–1900

Analyze Graphs Building projects, such as the Brooklyn Bridge (left), contributed to an increase in steel production in the United States.

❖ Between which years did steel production increase the most?

Ships and railroads carried raw materials to steel mills and carried steel to factories and cities across the nation.

REVIEW Why did the steel industry spread to cities along the Great Lakes?

The Oil Industry

For years people had been aware of the **petroleum**, or oil, that gathered on ponds in western Pennsylvania and other places. Then, in the 1840s, a Canadian scientist named Abraham Gesner discovered that petroleum burned well. When kerosene, a fuel made from petroleum, became widely used for lighting lamps, the demand for petroleum increased. This caused its price to rise.

In 1859 Edwin Drake drilled an oil well in Titusville, Pennsylvania. When the well began producing large amounts of oil, an oil boom took place. Oil towns soon sprang up all over western Pennsylvania and eastern Ohio.

John D. Rockefeller was 23 years old in 1863 when he invested money to build an oil refinery near Cleveland. The money needed to set up or improve a business is called **capital**. Rockefeller steadily invested more capital, buying up some of the other 30 refineries in the Cleveland area. In 1867 he combined his refineries into one business, which he called the Standard Oil Company.

To cut costs and be more efficient, Rockefeller bought other businesses. His company built its own barrels, pipelines, warehouses, and tank cars. As a result, it could produce and distribute oil products at the lowest prices.

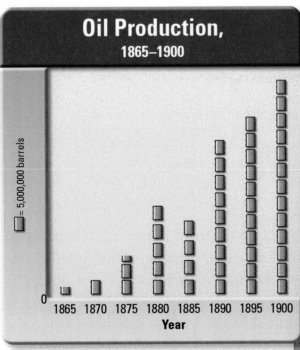

Oil Production, 1865–1900

= 5,000,000 barrels

Year: 1865, 1870, 1875, 1880, 1885, 1890, 1895, 1900

Analyze Graphs Drake's oil well (right) produced large amounts of oil. Such discoveries led to increases in oil production in the United States.

❖ About how many barrels of oil were produced in 1900?

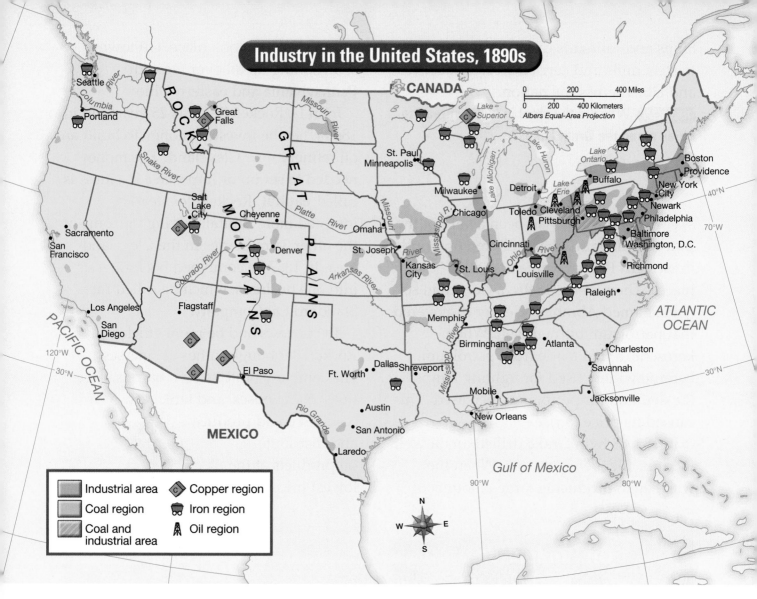

Industry in the United States, 1890s

0 200 400 Miles
0 200 400 Kilometers
Albers Equal-Area Projection

Legend:
- Industrial area
- Coal region
- Coal and industrial area
- Copper region
- Iron region
- Oil region

Regions This map shows industrial areas and resource regions in the United States about 1890.

❷ In which part of the United States were most industrial areas found?

Other companies could no longer compete and were driven out of the oil business.

By 1882 the Standard Oil Company controlled almost all of the oil refining and distribution in the United States and much of the world's oil trade as well. After the gasoline engine was invented and automobiles came into use, Rockefeller's oil refineries turned to producing gasoline and engine oil.

REVIEW What did John D. Rockefeller do to make his company more profitable?

Thomas Alva Edison

One of the most important inventors and industrial leaders in the United States was Thomas Alva Edison. Growing up, Edison had learned about the telegraph. Samuel Morse's telegraph, patented in the 1840s, was the nineteenth century's equivalent of the World Wide Web.

While studying the telegraph, Edison learned some of the practical uses of electricity. This knowledge led to his first serious invention in 1869, an electrical vote recorder for the Massachusetts State Legislature. Two years later, in 1871, Edison started a laboratory in Newark, New Jersey. At the time, Newark was known for its many fine machinists. Those machinists were just the kind of **human resources**—the workers and the ideas and skills they bring to their jobs—that Edison needed.

In 1874 Edison's laboratory developed a telegraph system that could send more than one message over a single wire. With the money he earned from selling that telegraph system, Edison opened a laboratory in Menlo Park, New Jersey, in 1876. That

laboratory averaged one patented invention every five days. The best known was the first practical electric lightbulb. Among the others was an improved telephone, an invention that Alexander Graham Bell had patented in 1876.

In 1882 Edison set up the first central power station in New York City. It made electricity available to large parts of the city. Less than 10 years later, hundreds of communities all over the United States had Edison power stations. With Edison's help, electricity soon became an important source of power for American homes, offices, and industries.

REVIEW **What was Edison's best known patented invention at Menlo Park?**

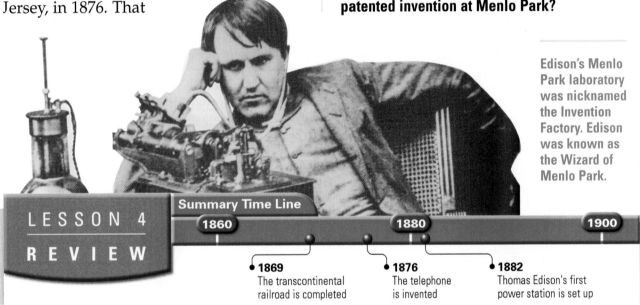

Edison's Menlo Park laboratory was nicknamed the Invention Factory. Edison was known as the Wizard of Menlo Park.

LESSON 4 REVIEW

Summary Time Line

1860 — 1880 — 1900

- **1869** The transcontinental railroad is completed
- **1876** The telephone is invented
- **1882** Thomas Edison's first power station is set up

1 **MAIN IDEA** How did the United States economy change in the years after the Civil War?

2 **WHY IT MATTERS** How did changes in the United States economy encourage growth?

3 **VOCABULARY** Use the word **entrepreneur** in a sentence about **free enterprise**.

4 **TIME LINE** When was the transcontinental railroad completed?

5 **READING SKILL—Determine Point of View** How do you think John D. Rockefeller felt about the benefits of the free enterprise system?

6 **ECONOMICS** How did the discovery of oil help the United States economy grow?

7 **CRITICAL THINKING—Analyze** How did Andrew Carnegie contribute to the growth of cities?

PERFORMANCE—Write "Who Am I" Questions Write a list of "Who Am I" questions about some of the people you read about in this lesson. Ask your classmates the "Who Am I" questions and see if they can identify who you are.

Edison's Inventions

In his lifetime, Thomas Edison obtained more than 1,000 patents, the most the United States Patent Office has ever issued to one person. Edison invented items that were just for pleasure, as well as devices to solve problems people faced in their everyday lives. These are some of the inventions Edison and his workers produced.

FROM THE HENRY FORD MUSEUM AND GREENFIELD VILLAGE AND THE SMITHSONIAN INSTITUTION NATIONAL MUSEUM OF AMERICAN HISTORY

The electric lightbulb (left) was invented in 1879. The electric pen (right) was invented in 1874.

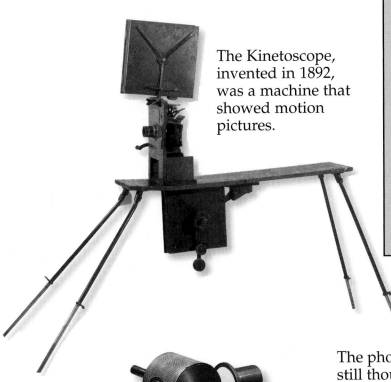

The Kinetoscope, invented in 1892, was a machine that showed motion pictures.

Analyze the Primary Source

1 **Which of these inventions looks familiar to you?**

2 **Identify the purpose of each invention. Which inventions do you think made people's lives easier?**

3 **Explain how one or more of Edison's inventions might work.**

The phonograph (left), patented in 1878, is still thought of as Edison's most original invention. The electronic stock ticker (below) was used to print out stock information.

ACTIVITY

Think Critically Make a list of tasks or jobs that you do often. Beside each item on your list, name the tools or appliances that you use to help make the task easier. Do you think you would be able to do the same tasks if the tools or appliances had not been invented?

RESEARCH

Visit The Learning Site at **www.harcourtschool.com/ primarysources** to research other primary sources.

MAIN IDEA
Read to learn about some of the problems that immigrants to the United States faced in the past.

WHY IT MATTERS
Many immigrants worked hard to overcome their problems and to make a better life for themselves in the United States.

VOCABULARY
old immigration
new immigration
advertisement
tenement
prejudice
regulation

A Changing People

| 1820 | 1870 | 1920 |

1880–1920

Like its economy, the population of the United States grew and changed after the Civil War. Between 1860 and 1910, about 23 million immigrants arrived on our shores. Those from Europe settled mostly in the cities of the East and Middle West. Those from Asia, Mexico, and parts of Central America and South America settled mostly in the West. Immigrants from all over the world played an important part in the growth of industry and agriculture in the United States.

Immigrants Old and New

European immigrants were by far the largest group to come to the United States. Before 1890 most immigrants from Europe came from northern and western Europe. They were part of the **old immigration**. That is, they came from the same parts of the world as earlier immigrants. The largest groups were from Britain, Germany, and Ireland. Others came from countries such

Between 1890 and 1920, nearly 16 million immigrants from Europe arrived in the United States. The passport below belonged to the Flinck family, from Sweden.

Irving Berlin (left) was one of the millions of immigrants who came to the United States. As a result of immigration, many cities, like New York City (above), grew very quickly.

as Denmark, Norway, and Sweden. These were the immigrants who helped build the Erie Canal and transcontinental railroad and who took part in settling the West.

Beginning about 1890, a period of **new immigration** began. People still came from the countries of northern and western Europe, but now most came from countries in southern and eastern Europe and from other parts of the world. Those from Europe came from countries such as Austria, Hungary, Italy, Greece, Poland, and Russia.

Most of the new immigrants from Europe were poor, and they had few opportunities in their homelands. They came to the United States hoping to find a better life. Many of them learned about jobs in the United States through advertisements. An **advertisement** is a public announcement that tells people about a product or an opportunity. Railroad, coal, and steel companies in the United States placed advertisements in other countries to attract new workers.

Most of the new immigrants settled in cities. They tended to live among people from their own country, with whom they shared a common language and familiar customs. Many lived with relatives, crowded together in poorly built apartment buildings called **tenements**. Wages were so low that everyone in the family—even young children—had to work to earn enough money for food.

In spite of the difficult conditions, many new immigrants succeeded. One of these people was Irving Berlin. He and his family moved to New York City from Russia in 1893. While Berlin was a boy, his father died. To help support his family, Berlin performed as a street singer and singing waiter. He began to write song lyrics and published his first song in 1907. During his life, Berlin wrote more than 800 songs, including "God Bless America," perhaps his most famous song.

REVIEW How did many immigrants learn about jobs in the United States?

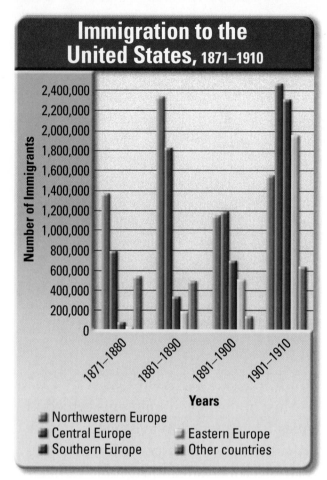

Immigration to the United States, 1871–1910

Number of Immigrants

- 2,400,000
- 2,200,000
- 2,000,000
- 1,800,000
- 1,600,000
- 1,400,000
- 1,200,000
- 1,000,000
- 800,000
- 600,000
- 400,000
- 200,000
- 0

Years: 1871–1880, 1881–1890, 1891–1900, 1901–1910

- Northwestern Europe
- Central Europe
- Southern Europe
- Eastern Europe
- Other countries

Analyze Graphs This graph compares the number of immigrants for different periods of time.

❖ When did the number of immigrants from central Europe first become larger than the number from northwestern Europe?

Immigrants from Asia

Immigrants from China first came to the United States in large numbers after the California gold rush. By 1852 about 25,000 Chinese were working in the goldfields.

As less and less gold was found, some Chinese immigrants returned home. But most stayed and looked for other kinds of work. They often worked for low wages because above all they wanted to stay in the United States. In the 1860s Chinese workers played an important part in building the transcontinental railroad. Some Chinese immigrants set up businesses in California or other parts of the West.

Immigrants from Japan and other countries in Asia also began to enter the United States and find opportunities in the West. Most found jobs in agriculture, mainly in California. Some bought their own land.

Over time, thousands of immigrants came to the United States from Asia. However, the number of Asian immigrants remained small when compared to the number of immigrants who came from Europe.

REVIEW Why did large numbers of Chinese people first come to the United States?

Reaction to Immigrants

Many people born in the United States reacted harshly to the immigrants. Some Americans felt that because many of the immigrants had little education, they were not qualified to take part in a democracy. Others worried that the newcomers would take jobs away from American workers. As a result, many immigrants faced prejudice. **Prejudice** is an unfair feeling of hate or dislike for

These three children and their families came to the United States from Asia. Most immigrants were searching for new opportunities and a better life.

members of a certain group because of their background, race, or religion.

Immigrants were sometimes taunted and called unkind names. They were denied jobs by many businesses, and certain businesses even posted signs that said things such as "Irish need not apply." Jewish immigrants were denied access to the better universities and often found it difficult to get jobs. Some immigrants also suffered physical attacks, and many were ridiculed for their religious beliefs. These anti-immigrant feelings led to the formation of groups that pressured Congress to pass laws that would limit the number of immigrants who could enter the country.

In the West there had been opposition to Asian immigrants for a long time. Their language, appearance, and customs were unfamiliar to most native-born Americans. As feelings against the Chinese grew, numerous **regulations**, or controls, were set up. Some states in the West passed laws that made life harder for the Chinese. Chinese people could not

Hiram L. Fong 1906–

Character Trait: Perseverance

Hiram Fong's parents left China to work on sugarcane plantations in Hawaii, where Hiram Fong was born. To earn money, young Hiram shined shoes and sold newspapers. He worked hard to earn enough to attend school. In time he graduated from law school. He dedicated himself to public service and was elected to Hawaii's legislature. Later he served four terms in the United States Congress as the nation's first Chinese American senator.

MULTIMEDIA BIOGRAPHIES
Visit The Learning Site at
www.harcourtschool.com/biographies
to learn about other famous people.

get state jobs, and their lawsuits would not be heard by state courts.

In 1882 the United States Congress passed the Chinese Exclusion Act. This act excluded, or kept out, all new Chinese workers. It prevented any Chinese workers from coming to the United States for ten years. By the early 1900s many Americans were calling for a stop to all immigration from Asia. Instead of passing such laws, however, the United States government persuaded Asian countries such as Japan to allow only a small number of its people to come to the United States.

REVIEW Why did many Americans react harshly to immigrants?

African Americans on the Move

Even as immigrants were moving to the United States from other countries, people within the United States were moving from place to place. This was true of many different groups of Americans, including African Americans. Many African Americans were looking for new places to live and work.

Many African Americans migrated from the South to the West. There they started farms or found job opportunities they did not have in the South. Some African Americans who had fought in the Civil War stayed in the Army and became part of units formed to fight against Native Americans in the West. The Indians gave the African American troops the name buffalo soldiers because they saw the same fighting spirit in the soldiers that they saw in the buffalo.

Most African Americans who did not move after the end of the Civil War found jobs in the South, often as sharecroppers. Few African Americans moved to the cities because they could not find work there. That changed between 1915 and 1930, however, when many African Americans moved north. This movement of people came to be known as the Great Migration.

One of the main reasons for the Great Migration was that many African Americans working on farms in the South were going through hard times. Floods had damaged many farms, and year after year an insect called the boll weevil had

This painting by artist Jacob Lawrence depicts the Great Migration. In it African Americans are shown leaving the South for cities in the North.

destroyed the cotton crop. At the same time, jobs began to open up in the North.

Many African Americans found factory jobs in large cities such as Boston, Chicago, Cleveland, Detroit, New York, Pittsburgh, Cincinnati, and St. Louis. Newspapers owned by African Americans in those cities actively encouraged this migration. "Get out of the South," advised the *Chicago Defender*. "Come north." As many as 500,000 people did.

Before the early 1900s nearly 90 percent of African Americans lived in the South. Because of the Great Migration, more than half of all African Americans now live in the North and in the Middle West. Most have parents, grandparents, or great-grandparents who were part of the huge movement north.

Jacob Lawrence's parents moved to the North in the early 1900s as part of the Great Migration.

Jacob Lawrence's parents moved north in the early 1900s. Lawrence went to art school in New York City and became a painter. He wrote in his book *The Great Migration*, "Life in the North brought many challenges, but the migrants' lives had changed for the better. The children were able to go to school, and their parents gained the freedom to vote. And the migrants kept coming. Theirs is a story of African-American strength and courage. I share it now as my parents told it to me, because their struggles and triumph ring true today. People all over the world are still on the move, trying to build better lives for themselves and for their families."

REVIEW What was the Great Migration?

LESSON 5 REVIEW

Summary Time Line

1880 ———————————————————————— 1920

● **1882** Congress passes the Chinese Exclusion Act

● **1890** A period of new immigration begins

● **1915** The Great Migration begins

1. **MAIN IDEA**   What were some of the problems immigrants to the United States faced?

2. **WHY IT MATTERS**   How did some immigrants overcome the problems associated with coming to the United States?

3. **VOCABULARY**   How did **prejudice** lead to the **regulation** of some immigrants?

4. **TIME LINE**   In what year did Congress pass the Chinese Exclusion Act?

5. **READING SKILL—Determine Point of View** How did many people born in the United States feel about immigrants?

6. **GEOGRAPHY**   Where did most people come from during the old immigration?

7. **CRITICAL THINKING—Evaluate**   How do you think African Americans felt about the Great Migration?

PERFORMANCE—Write an Advertisement Imagine that you are the owner of a railroad company in 1890. Write an advertisement to attract immigrant workers to your company. Share your advertisement with your classmates.

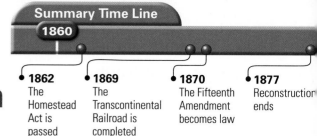

Summary Time Line
1860

● **1862**
The Homestead Act is passed

● **1869**
The Transcontinental Railroad is completed

● **1870**
The Fifteenth Amendment becomes law

● **1877**
Reconstruction ends

USE YOUR READING SKILLS

Complete this graphic organizer by describing different points of view about Reconstruction. A copy of this graphic organizer appears on page 130 of the Activity Book.

Abraham Lincoln and Reconstruction

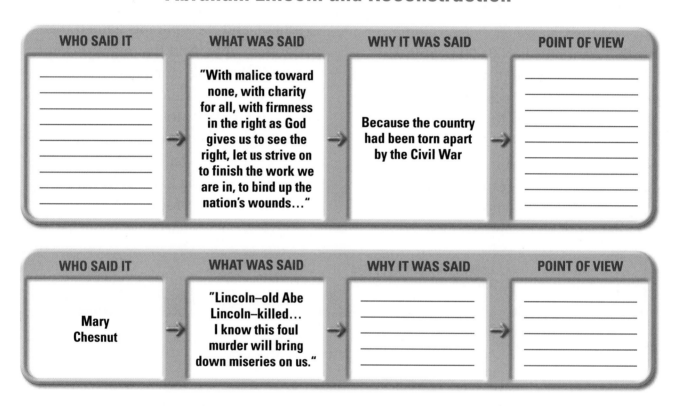

WHO SAID IT	WHAT WAS SAID	WHY IT WAS SAID	POINT OF VIEW
_____	"With malice toward none, with charity for all, with firmness in the right as God gives us to see the right, let us strive on to finish the work we are in, to bind up the nation's wounds…"	Because the country had been torn apart by the Civil War	_____

WHO SAID IT	WHAT WAS SAID	WHY IT WAS SAID	POINT OF VIEW
Mary Chesnut	"Lincoln–old Abe Lincoln–killed… I know this foul murder will bring down miseries on us."	_____	_____

THINK & WRITE

Write a Folktale   Many American folktales grew out of the nation's western experience. Imagine you are hiking in the west when you come upon a ghost town. Write a folktale about your discovery and the miners and business owners who once lived there.

Write a Letter   Immigrants to the United States have always been presented with both opportunities and challenges. Imagine you are a nineteenth century immigrant trying to adjust to your new home. Write a letter to a friend describing your situation and hopes for the future.

1915
The Great
Migration
begins

USE THE TIME LINE

Use the chapter summary time line to answer these questions.

1 When was the Transcontinental Railroad completed?

2 Did Reconstruction end before or after the Fifteenth Amendment was passed?

USE VOCABULARY

For each pair of terms, write a sentence that explains how the terms are related.

3 **freedmen** (p. 481), **segregation** (p. 484)

4 **long drive** (p. 487), **open range** (p. 489)

5 **entrepreneur** (p. 495), **capital** (p. 497)

6 **new immigration** (p. 503), **tenement** (p. 503)

RECALL FACTS

Answer these questions.

7 Why was the Fifteenth Amendment passed?

8 What challenges did Native Americans face in the years after the Civil War?

9 What was the main reason for the Great Migration?

Write the letter of the best choice.

10 **TEST PREP** The Fourteenth Amendment was passed to—
  A end slavery in the United States.
  B establish the Freedmen's Bureau.
  C give citizenship to all people born in the United States—including former slaves.
  D give every United States citizen the right to vote regardless of his or her race.

11 **TEST PREP** The most important work of the Freedmen's Bureau was—
  F to ensure voting rights for all African American males.
  G to promote African American political candidates.
  H to decide whether President Johnson should be removed from office.
  J to educate newly freed slaves.

12 **TEST PREP** The main reason oil production greatly increased in the late ninteenth century was because—
  A ranchers often traded their herds for oil.
  B people used kerosene to light their lamps.
  C homesteaders used petroleum to kill insects.
  D oil was used to fuel trains.

THINK CRITICALLY

13 Why do you think Southern state legislatures passed black codes after the Civil War?

14 How do you think the Great Migration affected the economy of the United States?

15 Why do you think many homesteaders chose to move west despite all the difficulties?

APPLY SKILLS

Use a Climograph
Study the climographs on page 493. Then answer the following questions.

CHART AND GRAPH SKILLS

16 What is the average temperature for each city in August?

17 How much precipitation falls during August in each city?

THE GETTYSBURG

NATIONAL MILITARY PARK

GET READY

The largest battle of the Civil War was fought near the town of Gettysburg, Pennsylvania. Today, nearly 6,000 acres of that battlefield have been preserved. On a visit to the Gettysburg National Military Park, a guide can lead you on an informative tour that highlights significant events of the Battle of Gettysburg. At the battlefield you can see more than 1,400 monuments and markers dedicated to the soldiers who fought and lost their lives during the three-day battle.

LOCATE IT

PENNSYLVANIA

Gettysburg
National Military Park

WHAT TO SEE

The Pennsylvania Memorial (left) is the largest monument at the Gettysburg National Military Park. It honors the Pennsylvania soldiers who fought at Gettysburg. The Gettysburg National Cemetery (below) was dedicated by President Abraham Lincoln in 1863.

Actors dressed as Union and Confederate soldiers reenact Civil War battles at the Gettysburg National Military Park.

TAKE A FIELD TRIP

GO ONLINE

A VIRTUAL TOUR
Visit The Learning Site at
www.harcourtschool.com/tours
to find virtual tours of historical
sites in the United States.

Turner Le@rning

A VIDEO TOUR
Check your media
center or classroom library for a
videotape tour of the Gettysburg
National Military Park.

6 Review and Test Preparation

VISUAL SUMMARY

Write a Letter Study the pictures and captions below to help you review Unit 6. Then choose one of the events shown. Write an informative letter to a friend describing the event and how you think it will change the country.

USE VOCABULARY

Use a term from this list to complete each of the following sentences.

tariffs (p. 436)

acquittal (p. 479)

homesteaders (p. 488)

1. Senator Edmund G. Ross cast the deciding vote for the ____ of Andrew Johnson.

2. Before the Civil War, the North and South disagreed on the issue of ____.

3. Nearly 100,000 European immigrants became ____ on the Great Plains.

RECALL FACTS

Answer these questions.

4. How did enslaved people resist slavery?

5. What is the free enterprise system?

Write the letter of the best choice.

6. **TEST PREP** The conflict that started the Civil War took place at—
   A Williamsburg, Virginia.
   B Fort Sumter, South Carolina.
   C Gettysburg, Pennsylvania.
   D Antietam Creek, Maryland.

7. **TEST PREP** One major effect of the Civil War was that—
   F the United States never again admitted a new state to the Union.
   G Northerners were not allowed to settle in the South.
   H Southerners were not allowed to vote.
   J the Southern economy suffered many hardships.

Visual Summary

1820   1845   1870

1820 **The Missouri Compromise** p. 438

1850 **Congress passes the Compromise of 1850** p. 439

1854 **The Kansas–Nebraska Act is passed** p. 439

South Carolina Coast, 1861

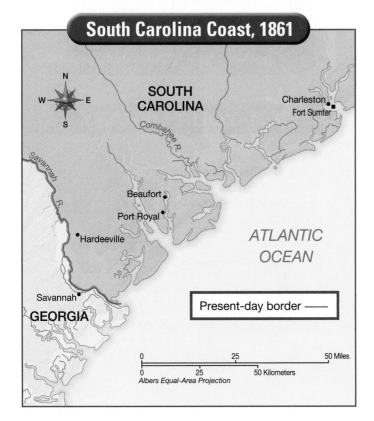

SOUTH CAROLINA

Charleston
Fort Sumter

Combahee R.

Savannah R.

Beaufort

Port Royal

Hardeeville

ATLANTIC OCEAN

Savannah

GEORGIA

N W E S

Present-day border ———

0   25   50 Miles
0   25   50 Kilometers
Albers Equal-Area Projection

8 TEST PREP During Reconstruction the Southern states were under military rule because—

A the Fourteenth Amendment to the Constitution allowed Congress to do so.

B Abraham Lincoln's assassination angered many Northerners.

C legislators began to pass laws limiting the rights of former slaves.

D it was a way to return the rights of American citizenship to most Confederates.

THINK CRITICALLY

9 Lincoln once was called "the miserable tool of traitors and rebels." Today he is thought of as a great leader. Why might someone at the time have been so critical of him?

10 What do you think would have happened if the South had won the Battle of Gettysburg?

11 How did the growth of railroads in the United States play an important role in the growth of the country? Explain your answer.

12 Why did many immigrants come to the United States?

APPLY SKILLS

MAP AND GLOBE SKILLS

Compare Maps with Different Scales

Use the map on this page and the maps on pages 456–457 to answer the following questions.

13 Compare the map on this page to Map B on page 457. Which map would you use to find the distance between Fort Sumter and the city of Charleston, South Carolina?

14 Compare the map on this page to Map A on page 456. Which map would you use to find the South Carolina–Georgia border?

1895   1920

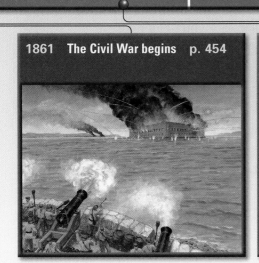

1861 The Civil War begins p. 454

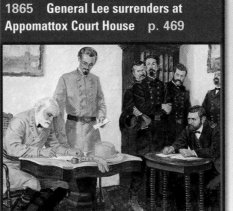

1865 General Lee surrenders at Appomattox Court House p. 469

1890 The steel industry is a big business in the United States p. 496

Unit Activities

 GO ONLINE Visit The Learning Site at www.harcourtschool.com/socialstudies/activities for additional activities.

Draw a Map

Work together to draw a map of the United States at the time of the Civil War. Use different colors for the states of the Union, the states of the Confederacy and the border states. Write the date on which each Southern state seceded. Draw diagonal lines on the border states. Label the capitals of the North and the South and the major battle sites. Use your map to tell your classmates about the Civil War.

Make a Chart

Work together in a group to make a chart titled *How New Laws Affected the Lives of Americans After the Civil War*. The first section of your chart should show how new national and state laws affected African Americans. The second section should show how new laws affected Southerners. The third section should show how new laws affected Northerners. Present your completed chart to your classmates.

VISIT YOUR LIBRARY

■ *When Jessie Came Across the Sea* by Amy Hest. Candlewick Press.

■ *Tales from the Underground Railroad* by Kate Connell. Steck-Vaughn.

■ *Across the Lines* by Carolyn Reeder. Simon & Schuster.

COMPLETE THE UNIT PROJECT

Hall of Fame Work with a group of your classmates to finish the unit project—a hall of fame honoring individuals who showed strength and bravery before, during, or after the Civil War. Your group should choose five people from this unit to include in your hall of fame. Then design a poster that includes short biographies as well as drawings or pictures of the people you have chosen. Display your group's finished poster together with those of your classmates.

The Twentieth Century

Apollo 11 mission patch

John F. Kennedy Space Center, Cape Canaveral, Florida

The Twentieth Century

" That's one small step for [a] man, one giant leap for mankind. "

—Neil Armstrong, from the
Eagle moon lander, July 20, 1969

Preview the Content

Read the lesson titles. Then fill in the first two columns of the chart with information about the twentieth century. After you have read the unit, fill in the last column.

K (What I Know)	W (What I Want to Know)	L (What I Have Learned)

Preview the Vocabulary

Related Words   Words that are related have meanings that are connected in some way. Using the vocabulary words **reform, isolation, aviation,** and **ration,** make a chart of words that are related to each vocabulary word.

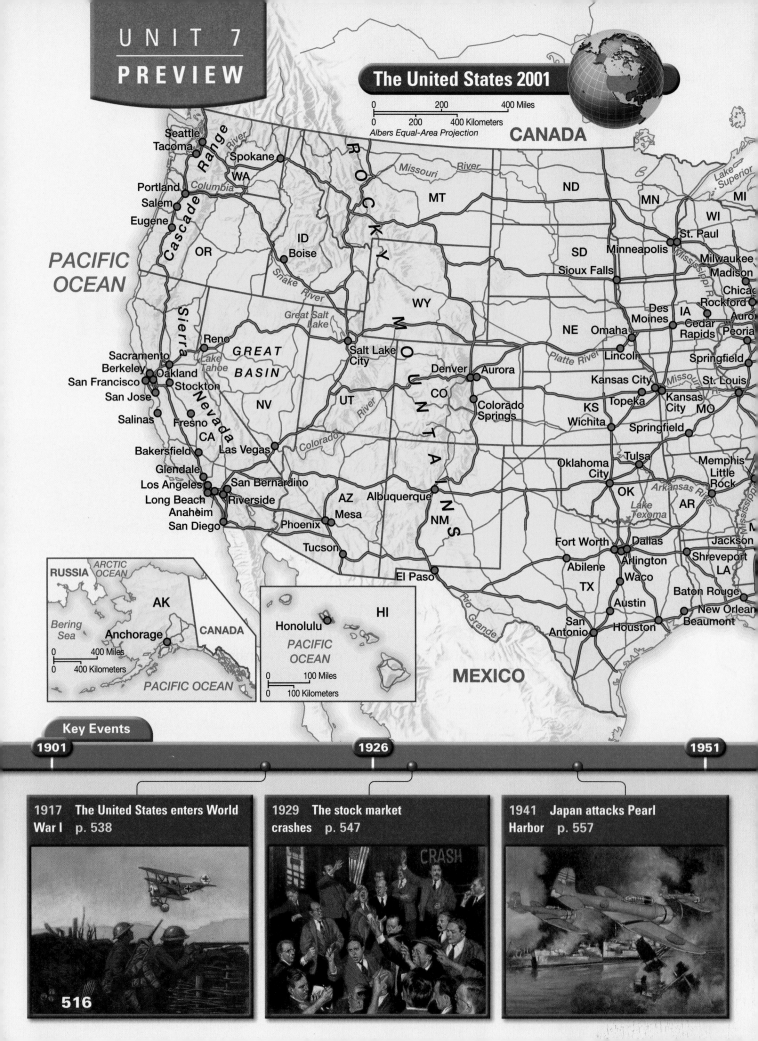

The United States 2001

200 400 Miles

200 400 Kilometers

Albers Equal-Area Projection

CANADA

PACIFIC OCEAN

Seattle
Tacoma
Spokane
WA
Portland
Salem
Eugene
OR
Columbia River
ID
Boise
Cascade Range
Snake River
MT
ND
MN
WI
St. Paul
Minneapolis
Milwaukee
Madison
Chicago
Rockford
Aurora
Peoria
Missouri River
SD
Sioux Falls
Great Salt Lake
WY
NE
Omaha
Des Moines
IA
Cedar Rapids
Lincoln
Platte River
Springfield
Reno
GREAT BASIN
Salt Lake City
Denver
Aurora
Colorado Springs
CO
Kansas City
St. Louis
Topeka
Kansas City
MO
Missouri R.
Sacramento
Berkeley
Oakland
San Francisco
Stockton
San Jose
Lake Tahoe
Sierra Nevada
NV
UT
Colorado River
KS
Wichita
Springfield
Salinas
Fresno
CA
Bakersfield
Las Vegas
Colorado
Oklahoma City
Tulsa
Memphis
Little Rock
Arkansas River
Glendale
Los Angeles
Long Beach
Anaheim
San Diego
San Bernardino
Riverside
AZ
Mesa
Phoenix
Tucson
Albuquerque
NM
OK
Lake Texoma
AR
El Paso
Fort Worth
Dallas
Arlington
Abilene
Waco
TX
Austin
San Antonio
Houston
Jackson
Shreveport
LA
Baton Rouge
New Orleans
Beaumont
Rio Grande
MEXICO
ROCKY MOUNTAINS

RUSSIA
ARCTIC OCEAN
AK
Bering Sea
Anchorage
CANADA
PACIFIC OCEAN
400 Miles
400 Kilometers

Honolulu
HI
PACIFIC OCEAN
100 Miles
100 Kilometers

Lake Superior
MI
Mississippi R.

Key Events

1901   1926   1951

1917 The United States enters World War I   p. 538

1929 The stock market crashes   p. 547

1941 Japan attacks Pearl Harbor   p. 557

CRASH

516

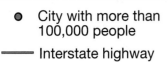

City with more than 100,000 people
Interstate highway
United States highway

CANADA

ME

Lake Champlain

Lake Michigan

Lake Huron

Lake Ontario

Lake Erie

Lake St. Clair

MI

Grand Rapids
Flint
Lansing
Ann Arbor
Detroit
South Bend
Fort Wayne
Gary
IN
Toledo
Akron
OH
Columbus
Dayton
Cincinnati
Indianapolis
Lexington
KY
Louisville
Evansville
Knoxville
Nashville
TN
Chattanooga
Huntsville
Birmingham
AL
Montgomery
Columbus
Macon
Mobile
GA
Tallahassee
FL
Tampa
St. Petersburg
Orlando
Miami
Jacksonville
Savannah

NY
Syracuse
Albany
Rochester
Buffalo
Erie
PA
Cleveland
Pittsburgh
MD
APPALACHIAN MTS.
WV
Richmond
VA
Norfolk
Newport News
Virginia Beach
Greensboro
Durham
Winston-Salem
NC
Raleigh
Charlotte
Columbia
SC
Atlanta
Ohio River

VT
NH
Worcester
Boston
MA
Hartford
CT
RI
Providence
New Haven
Bridgeport
Jersey City
Allentown
New York City
NJ
Newark
Philadelphia
Baltimore
DE
Washington, D.C.

ATLANTIC OCEAN

Lake Okeechobee

Gulf of Mexico

N E W S

Miles Traveled by Type of Transportation
1940–Present

Passenger Miles Traveled (in billions)

2,000
1,800
1,600
1,400
1,200
1,000
800
600
400
200
0

1940   1960   1980   Present*

Year

Automobile
Airplane
Train

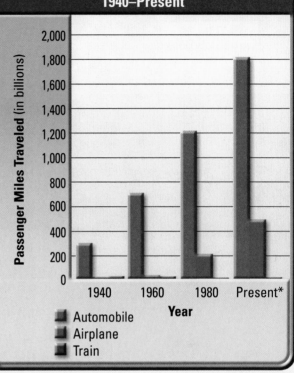

*Latest sources available

1976   2001

1964   The Civil Rights Act is passed   p. 587

1965   American combat forces arrive in South Vietnam   p. 591

1969   United States astronauts land on the moon   p. 583

The
Children's Book
of America

EDITED BY
William J. Bennett
ILLUSTRATED BY MICHAEL HAGUE

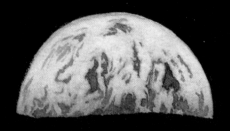

THE EAGLE HAS LANDED

Edited by William J. Bennett
Illustrated by Michael Hague

In 1962 John Glenn became the first American astronaut to orbit Earth. Then a series of explorations called the Apollo program prepared for a moon landing. In 1968 astronauts in *Apollo 8* first circled the moon. By the next year the National Aeronautics and Space Administration, or NASA, was ready to try a moon landing. On July 16, 1969, *Apollo 11* blasted off from Cape Canaveral, Florida. On board were astronauts Neil Armstrong, Edwin "Buzz" Aldrin, Jr., and Michael Collins. Once they were circling the moon, Armstrong and Aldrin climbed into the landing vehicle named the *Eagle*. Michael Collins stayed behind in case he needed to help the other two astronauts. NASA scientists at Mission Control in Houston, Texas, followed their flight closely. Now read the story of the first moon landing.

"*Eagle*, you are go for landing. Go!"

The spacecraft continued downward.

Armstrong turned to the window to look for their landing zone. He did not like what he saw. They were not where they were supposed to be.

The computer was programmed to steer the ship to a flat, smooth place for a landing. But it had overshot its target. They were plunging straight toward an area littered with deadly rocks and craters.

A light blinked on the control panel. They were running out of landing fuel.

There was no time to waste. Armstrong gripped the hand controller and took command from the computer. He had to find a place where they could set down, fast, or they would have to fire their rockets and return to space.

Gently he brought the *Eagle* under his control. The lander hovered as Armstrong searched the ground below for a level spot.

"Sixty seconds, " the voice from Mission Control warned.

Sixty seconds of fuel left.

Balanced on a cone of fire, the *Eagle* scooted over rocky ridges and yawning craters.

There was no place to land!

"Thirty seconds!"

Now there was no turning back. If the engines gulped the last of the landing fuel, there would be no time to fire the rockets that could take them back into orbit. They would crash.

The landing craft swooped across boulder fields as its pilot hunted, judged, and committed. Flames shot down as the *Eagle* dropped the last few feet. Dust that had lain still for a billion years flew up and swallowed the craft.

Back on Earth, millions of people held their breaths and waited. They prayed and listened.

Then Neil Armstrong's faint voice came crackling across the gulf of space.

"Houston, Tranquillity Base here. The *Eagle* has landed."

In a short while a hatch on the lander opened. A man in a bulky space suit backed down nine rungs of a ladder and placed his foot on the gray lunar soil. People all over the world watched the fuzzy black-and-white images on their television screens. They leaned toward their sets to catch the first words spoken by Neil Armstrong from the surface of the moon.

"That's one small step for man, one giant leap for mankind."

A few minutes later Buzz Aldrin crawled out of the *Eagle* to join his comrade. Together the astronauts planted a flag. It would never flap in a breeze on the airless moon, so a stiff wire held it out from its pole. Aldrin stepped back and saluted the Stars and Stripes.

America had made the age-old dream come true. When they departed, our astronauts left behind a plaque that will always remain. Its words proclaim:

HERE MEN FROM THE PLANET EARTH
FIRST SET FOOT UPON THE MOON
JULY, 1969 A.D.
WE CAME IN PEACE FOR ALL MANKIND

Analyze the Literature

1 Why did Neil Armstrong take control of the *Eagle*?

2 What kinds of problems do you think the scientists at NASA had to solve in building a spacecraft to carry people to the moon?

READ A BOOK

START THE UNIT PROJECT

A Class Newspaper With your classmates, create a newspaper about the 20th century. As you read the unit, make a list of key people, places, and events. This list will help you decide which people, places, and events to feature in articles in your newspaper.

USE TECHNOLOGY

Visit The Learning Site at **www.harcourtschool.com/ socialstudies** for additional activities, primary sources, and other resources to use in this unit.

SAN JACINTO STATE HISTORICAL PARK

The *USS Texas* is the only American battleship from World War I still in existence. The *Texas* was commissioned in 1914 and remained part of the United States Navy until 1948. Today, visitors to San Jacinto State Historical Park can explore many different parts of this historic vessel.

LOCATE IT

TEXAS

San Jacinto State Historical Park

35

Becoming a World Power

" Whether they will or no, Americans must now begin to look outward. "

—Alfred T. Mahan, *The United States Looking Outward,* 1890

CHAPTER READING SKILL

Make Inferences

When you make an **inference**, you use facts and your experiences to come to a conclusion about something.

As you read this chapter, make inferences about the United States' expanding role in world affairs.

FACT

INFERENCE

FACT

MAIN IDEA

Read to find out how the United States added to its land area and increased its power at the end of the 1800s.

WHY IT MATTERS

By stretching its borders, the United States gained new sources of raw materials and new markets for its goods. This helped the United States become a world power.

VOCABULARY

imperialism
armistice

Building an American Empire

1850   1900   1950
1860–1920

By the late 1800s, the western frontier had been settled and the United States was a world leader in industry and agriculture. Yet many Americans were ready to find new frontiers. They believed that setting up colonies in other parts of the world would bring the country both new sources of raw materials and new markets for its goods. The time seemed right for the United States to become a world power.

Alaska

In 1867 the United States bought Alaska from Russia for $7.2 million—about two cents an acre! At that time few Americans knew about Alaska or its peoples. Many thought it was foolish of the United States to buy land so far north. All across the country, newspapers criticized Secretary of State William

The April 1898 cover of the *Klondike News*, (left) illustrates the life of Alaskan miners, which included trekking through Klondike Valley (below).

FAST FACT
Alaska is today the largest state in the United States. It is 488 times as large as Rhode Island, and two and a half times as large as Texas.

King Kalakaua (left), and later his sister Queen Liliuokalani (right), were the last monarchs of the Hawaiian Islands (above).

Seward for agreeing to the deal. People even started calling Alaska Seward's Folly or the Polar Bear Garden.

In 1896 many people changed their opinions about Alaska after gold was found in the Klondike River valley in Canada, near Alaska. The discovery started a gold rush in the valley. From 1897 to 1899 more than 100,000 people raced to Alaska, hoping to get rich.

Most of the people who traveled to Alaska did not find gold. However, Alaska brought new wealth to the United States in other ways. Alaska was rich in natural resources, such as fish, timber, coal, and copper.

REVIEW What caused many Americans to change their opinions about Alaska?

The Hawaiian Islands

In the late 1800s, Americans also, looked to the Hawaiian Islands as a place to get more new lands. This chain of 8 major islands and 124 smaller ones lies in the Pacific Ocean about 2,400 miles (3,862 km) southwest of California. During the eighth century, Polynesian people migrated to Hawaii from other islands in the Pacific. They set up a monarchy ruled by a royal family.

Christian missionaries were among the first Americans to arrive in Hawaii. Later, American businesspeople started cattle ranches and sugar plantations on the islands. By the 1870s those Americans controlled much of the land in Hawaii.

When the Hawaiian king, Kalakaua (kah•lah•KAH•ooh•ah), tried to keep the Americans from taking over the islands in 1887, they decided to take away the king's authority. They made him sign a new constitution that left the Hawaiian monarchy without authority. In 1893 the king's sister Queen Liliuokalani (lih•lee•uh•woh•kuh•LAH•nee), tried to regain power. But the Americans took over the government and set up a republic. The United States annexed Hawaii in 1898.

REVIEW How did Hawaii become part of the United States?

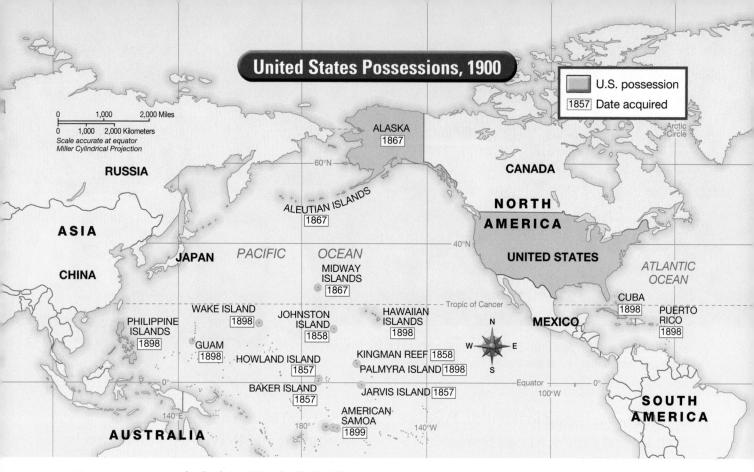

United States Possessions, 1900

U.S. possession
1857 Date acquired

0   1,000   2,000 Miles
0   1,000   2,000 Kilometers
Scale accurate at equator
Miller Cylindrical Projection

RUSSIA

ASIA

CHINA

JAPAN

PACIFIC   OCEAN

ALEUTIAN ISLANDS
1867

ALASKA
1867

CANADA

NORTH
AMERICA

UNITED STATES

ATLANTIC
OCEAN

Arctic
Circle

60°N

40°N

MIDWAY
ISLANDS
1867

WAKE ISLAND
1898

JOHNSTON
ISLAND
1858

HAWAIIAN
ISLANDS
1898

Tropic of Cancer

CUBA
1898

PUERTO
RICO
1898

PHILIPPINE
ISLANDS
1898

GUAM
1898

HOWLAND ISLAND
1857

KINGMAN REEF 1858

PALMYRA ISLAND 1898

MEXICO

N
W   E
S

BAKER ISLAND
1857

JARVIS ISLAND 1857

Equator

100°W

0°

SOUTH
AMERICA

140°E

AUSTRALIA

AMERICAN
SAMOA
1899

180°

140°W

0°

GEOGRAPHY THEME

Location   In the late 1800s the United States acquired many territories around the world.

◆ In what part of the world did the United States gain most of its new land?

War with Spain

Some people now accused the country's leaders of **imperialism**, or empire building. They believed that extending the nation's borders would cause conflict between the United States and European nations—especially Spain.

At the end of the 1800s, Spain still had two colonies—the Philippine Islands and Guam—in the Eastern Hemisphere. In the Western Hemisphere, Spain controlled Puerto Rico and Cuba. However, many Cubans wanted their island to become independent. Twice, in 1868 and again in 1895, they had rebelled against Spanish rule, but the rebellions had failed.

People in the United States watched as the conflict between Spain and Cuba con-

tinued. Many Americans, including those who had moved there to start businesses, supported the Cubans' fight for independence. Newspapers in the United States were full of stories about Spain's harsh rule of the island. Some of these stories were true, but others were not.

In 1898 President William McKinley ordered the battleship *Maine* to Havana, Cuba, to protect Americans living there. Just three weeks after the *Maine* arrived, it exploded in Havana's harbor. More than 260 sailors were killed. It was not clear why the ship blew up, but the United States blamed Spain. "Remember the *Maine*!" Americans cried, calling for action. On April 25, the United States declared war on Spain.

The first battles of the Spanish-American War were fought in the Philippine Islands. Led by Commodore George Dewey, the United States Navy destroyed the Spanish fleet there and captured Manila Bay. The fighting then shifted to Cuba.

Thousands of Americans volunteered to fight in the war. Among them was Theodore Roosevelt. He had been assistant secretary of the navy when the war started, but he quit that job to form a fighting company made up mostly of cowhands and college athletes. In Cuba, the Rough Riders, as they were called, took part in the Battle of San Juan Hill and the siege of Santiago.

On August 12, 1898, after a number of defeats, Spain signed an armistice (AHR•muh•stuhs). An **armistice** is an

This canteen was carried by a Rough Rider in Cuba.

agreement to stop fighting a war. The Spanish-American War lasted less than four months, but more than 5,000 American soldiers died. Most of them died from diseases such as malaria and yellow fever.

As a result of the Spanish-American War, the United States became a world power. Spain agreed to give the United States control of Cuba, Puerto Rico, Guam, and the Philippine Islands. Cuba and the Philippine Islands later became independent countries, but Puerto Rico and Guam remain part of the United States today.

REVIEW What lands did the United States gain as a result of the Spanish-American War?

This painting shows Roosevelt and the Rough Riders charging San Juan Hill. However, the charge was really made on foot.

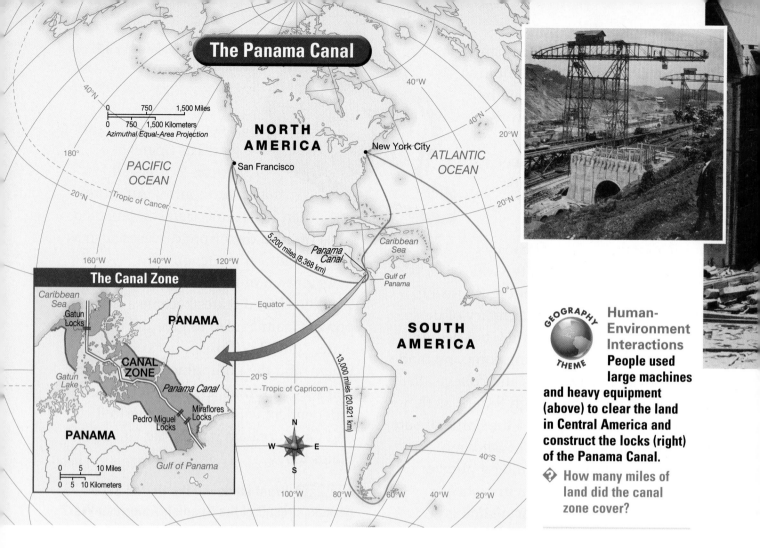

The Panama Canal

The Canal Zone

Caribbean Sea

Gatun Locks

PANAMA

CANAL ZONE

Gatun Lake

Panama Canal

Pedro Miguel Locks

Miraflores Locks

PANAMA

Gulf of Panama

0   5   10 Miles
0   5   10 Kilometers

NORTH AMERICA

PACIFIC OCEAN

New York City

San Francisco

ATLANTIC OCEAN

Tropic of Cancer

5,200 miles (8,368 km)

Panama Canal

Caribbean Sea

Gulf of Panama

Equator

SOUTH AMERICA

13,000 miles (20,921 km)

Tropic of Capricorn

0   750   1,500 Miles
0   750   1,500 Kilometers
Azimuthal Equal-Area Projection

GEOGRAPHY THEME
Human-Environment Interactions
People used large machines and heavy equipment (above) to clear the land in Central America and construct the locks (right) of the Panama Canal.

? How many miles of land did the canal zone cover?

The Panama Canal

Soon after Theodore Roosevelt came back from Cuba, he was elected governor of New York. Two years later he was elected Vice President of the United States, serving under President William McKinley. On September 6, 1901, President McKinley was shot by a person who was angry with the government. McKinley died eight days later, and Roosevelt became President.

One of President Roosevelt's main goals was to build a canal across the Isthmus of Panama, in Central America. The canal would link the Atlantic Ocean and the Pacific Ocean. This, in turn, would link American ports on the Atlantic coast with those on the Pacific

coast. "I wish to see the United States the dominant power on the shores of the Pacific Ocean," Roosevelt said.

In 1902 Congress voted to build the canal. However, the Isthmus of Panama did not belong to the United States. It belonged to Colombia. The United States offered Colombia $10 million for the right to build a canal, but Colombia rejected the offer.

Roosevelt then spread the word that he would welcome a revolution in Panama to end Colombian rule. He sent the United States Navy to protect the isthmus. If a revolution began, the navy was to keep Colombian troops from landing on shore. Within three months a revolution took place, and the people of Panama formed a new nation. Panama's

Engineers designed huge canal locks to help ships move through the waterway.

Unlike the French who had first tried to build the canal in the 1880s, American workers stayed healthy. Doctors now knew that malaria and yellow fever, the diseases that had stopped the French, were carried by mosquitoes. The Americans learned to control the mosquitoes by using insecticides and draining the swamps where the insects lived.

Building the canal took ten years and cost about $380 million. After it opened, goods could be shipped between ports on the Atlantic coast and ports on the Pacific coast in about one month. Just as the transcontinental railroad had done, the canal helped the United States economy grow. Today the canal, which is under Panama's control, continues to help move people and goods around the world.

REVIEW **Why did the United States want to build the Panama Canal?**

leaders then gave the United States the right to build the canal. The United States would control the canal and an area 5 miles (8 km) wide on each side of it.

Work on the canal began in 1904. Workers guided huge machines to cut down the trees and thick jungle growth.

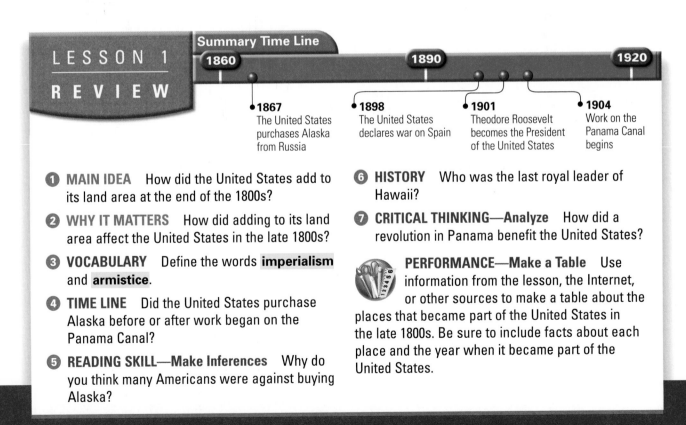

LESSON 1 REVIEW

Summary Time Line

1860 — 1890 — 1920

1867 The United States purchases Alaska from Russia

1898 The United States declares war on Spain

1901 Theodore Roosevelt becomes the President of the United States

1904 Work on the Panama Canal begins

1. **MAIN IDEA** How did the United States add to its land area at the end of the 1800s?

2. **WHY IT MATTERS** How did adding to its land area affect the United States in the late 1800s?

3. **VOCABULARY** Define the words **imperialism** and **armistice**.

4. **TIME LINE** Did the United States purchase Alaska before or after work began on the Panama Canal?

5. **READING SKILL—Make Inferences** Why do you think many Americans were against buying Alaska?

6. **HISTORY** Who was the last royal leader of Hawaii?

7. **CRITICAL THINKING—Analyze** How did a revolution in Panama benefit the United States?

PERFORMANCE—Make a Table Use information from the lesson, the Internet, or other sources to make a table about the places that became part of the United States in the late 1800s. Be sure to include facts about each place and the year when it became part of the United States.

·SKILLS·

MAP AND GLOBE

Compare Map Projections

► **WHY IT MATTERS**

Because the Earth is round and maps are flat, maps cannot represent the Earth's shape exactly. As a result, cartographers have different ways of showing the Earth on flat paper. These different views are called **projections**. All projections have **distortions**, or areas that are not accurate. But different kinds of projections have different kinds of distortions. Identifying areas on a map that are distorted will help you understand how different maps can best be used.

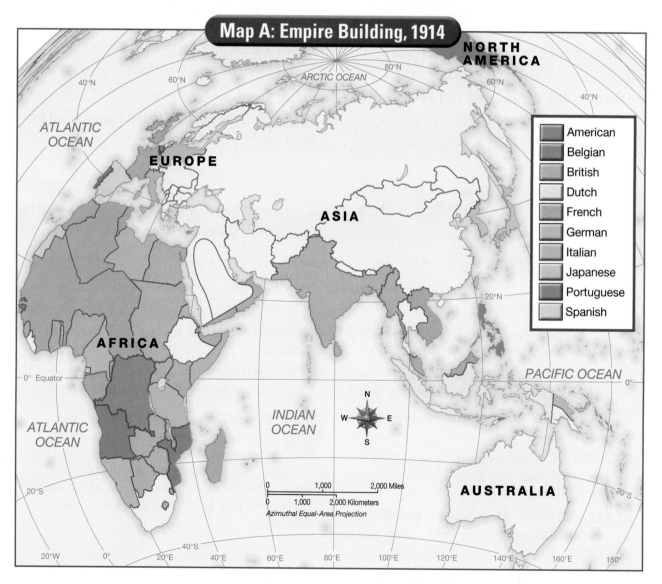

Map A: Empire Building, 1914

American
Belgian
British
Dutch
French
German
Italian
Japanese
Portuguese
Spanish

Azimuthal Equal-Area Projection

▶ WHAT YOU NEED TO KNOW

Map A and Map B show the same area, but they use different projections. Map A is an azimuthal (a•zuh•MUH•thuhl) equal-area projection. Equal-area projections show the sizes of regions in correct relation to one another, but they distort, or change, their shapes.

Map B is a Miller cylindrical projection. It is just one example of a conformal projection. Notice that the meridians on Map B are all an equal distance apart. Notice also that the parallels closer to the North and South Poles are farther apart than those near the equator. Conformal projections, like the one used on Map B, show directions correctly, but they distort sizes, especially of the places near the poles.

▶ PRACTICE THE SKILL

Use Map A and Map B to answer the following questions.

1 On which parts of Maps A and B do the shapes of the land areas appear to be the same?

2 On which map does Africa appear to be larger? On which map is the size of Africa more accurate?

▶ APPLY WHAT YOU LEARNED

Look at the maps in the Atlas on pages A4–A17 to see other map projections. Write a paragraph about the advantages and disadvantages of using equal-area and conformal projections.

Practice your map and globe skills with the **GeoSkills CD-ROM.**

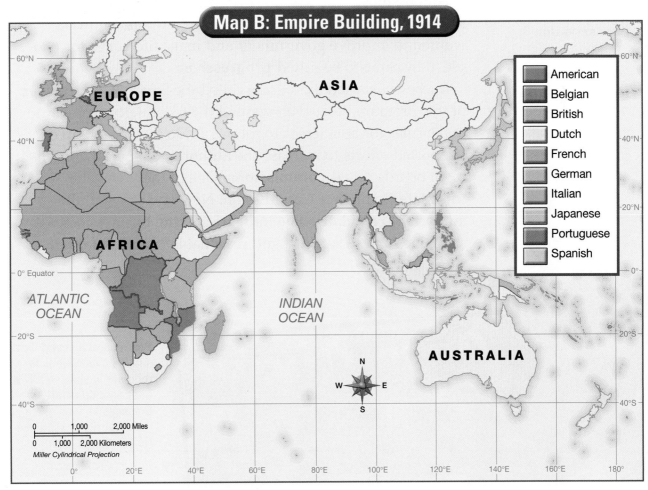

Map B: Empire Building, 1914

American
Belgian
British
Dutch
French
German
Italian
Japanese
Portuguese
Spanish

EUROPE

ASIA

AFRICA

AUSTRALIA

ATLANTIC OCEAN

INDIAN OCEAN

0° Equator

| 0 | 1,000 | 2,000 Miles |

| 0 | 1,000 | 2,000 Kilometers |

Miller Cylindrical Projection

Progressives and Reform

1901   1951   2001

1900–1920

The growing power of the United States made many Americans hopeful. But they also saw the need to **reform**, or change for the better, some parts of life in the United States. This was especially true in America's cities, which continued to grow as more and more people moved into them to work in industries.

Federal Reforms

Among those who saw the need for reform was President Theodore Roosevelt. Because Roosevelt and his followers wanted to improve government and make life better for people, they came to be called **progressives**.

Roosevelt started a program called the Square Deal. As part of this program, Roosevelt wanted the federal government to make rules for businesses to follow. To do this, he set up or supported efforts to increase the authority of special government boards called **commissions**. One of these was the Interstate Commerce Commission. New laws gave it more authority to regulate some industries doing business across state lines and to set "just and reasonable" railroad fares.

ISSUED BY THE
CENTRAL PACIFIC
RAILROAD COMPANY

ING FOR ITSELF OVER ITS OWN LINE, AND AS AGENT FOR EACH LINE NAMED
THIS TICKET AND ACCOMPANYING CHECKS, BUT ASSUMING NO RESPONSIBILITY
OND ITS OWN LINE. THIS COMPANY ASSUMES NO RISK ON BAGGAGE-EX-
T FOR WEARING APPAREL- AND LIMITS ITS RESPONSIBILITY TO ONE
DRED DOLLARS IN VALUE, UNLESS TAKEN BY SPECIAL CONTRACT.
IIS TICKET IS VOID UNLESS OFFICIALLY STAMPED AND DATED, AND
IECKS BELONGING TO THIS TICKET WILL BE VOID IF DETACHED.

Virginia & Truckee Railroad.
RENO

President Roosevelt (left) set up commissions to regulate businesses. The Interstate Commerce Commission was given the authority to set some railroad fares (right).

Labor Day

In New York City on September 5, 1882, Americans held the first Labor Day parade. Matthew Maguire, a machine worker, and Peter McGuire, a carpenter, came up with the idea of Labor Day. It is a day to honor working people and to recognize their importance to the United States. In 1894 Congress made Labor Day a legal holiday. Today, the United States and Canada celebrate Labor Day on the first Monday in September. Many other countries also honor workers with labor celebrations.

Not all people supported these changes, however. They worried that the federal government would become too powerful.

Roosevelt also wanted the federal government to make sure that foods and medicines were safe. In 1906 Congress passed the Pure Food and Drug Act. The act said that all foods and medicines had to meet government safety standards. Congress also passed the Meat Inspection Act. This act said that government-paid inspectors would visit every plant that packaged meat to make sure the meat was handled safely.

Roosevelt was also interested in conservation. **Conservation** is the protection and wise use of natural resources. Roosevelt asked Congress to set aside millions of acres of land in different parts of the country as national parks. Among these were the Grand Canyon, Mesa Verde, and Glacier national parks.

REVIEW **What did progressives want to do?**

State and Local Reforms

Progressives also worked to reform state governments. In Wisconsin, Governor Robert La Follette made so many reforms that President Roosevelt called the state, a "laboratory of democracy."

Officials in many states had been giving government jobs to people who did favors for them. To keep this from happening in Wisconsin, La Follette started a **merit system** to make sure that people were qualified for their jobs. Each person applying for a government job was given a test. The person who scored the highest on the test got the job.

Wisconsin also passed laws to help other workers. One said that a workday could be no more than ten hours. Others listed jobs for which children could not be hired and said that the state would pay workers who were hurt while working at their jobs.

THE "BRAINS"

THAT ACHIEVED THE TAMMANY VICTORY AT THE ROCHESTER DEMOCRATIC CONVENTION.

This political cartoon drawn by illustrator Thomas Nast suggests that money was used to influence political decision making in New York City.

People in other states called what La Follette was doing the Wisconsin Idea. Many states soon copied his changes.

Progressive reforms also affected city governments. At the time, many large cities were controlled by powerful leaders. These leaders—often the mayors—were called **political bosses**. People who worked for them sometimes gave money to voters so they would vote for the boss.

Some cheated in elections by counting the votes of people who were not citizens or of people who did not vote. In this way, political bosses often were elected again and again.

One of the best-known political bosses was New York City's George Plunkitt. In 1905 a journalist wrote a book based on interviews with Plunkitt. In the book, Plunkitt described how he did favors for people. Those favors, however, were always done in exchange for votes.

Progressives wanted to end boss rule. One way to do this was to change the form of city government. To keep the mayor from having all the authority, some cities set up commissions made up of several people. Each commission member oversaw a city department.

REVIEW Who were political bosses?

More Reforms

Progressives were often ordinary people trying to improve their lives or the lives of others. Jane Addams was one of these people. In 1889 Addams and Ellen Gates Starr opened a settlement house named Hull House in one of the poorest areas of Chicago.

Jane Addams (right with child) founded Hull House (below) in a poor Chicago neighborhood. It became the model for community centers throughout the country.

Janie Porter Barrett worked to educate African American children living in Virginia.

W.E.B. Du Bois worked for racial equality and was a founder of the NAACP.

A **settlement house** was a community center where immigrants and poor working people could learn new skills.

Hull House became a model for other community centers. In 1890 African American teacher Janie Porter Barrett founded a settlement house in Hampton, Virginia. Five years later, Lillian Wald started the Henry Street Settlement in New York City. By 1900 almost 100 settlement houses had opened across the country.

African American leaders also used progressive ideas to try to fight prejudice. Booker T. Washington, a former slave, led an effort to provide African Americans with more opportunities for education. In 1881 he helped found Tuskegee Institute, a trade school for African Americans, in Alabama.

In 1909 W.E.B. Du Bois (doo•BOYS) and other leaders formed the National Association for the Advancement of Colored People, or NAACP. The NAACP worked to change state laws that denied full civil rights to African Americans. **Civil rights** are the rights guaranteed to all citizens by the Constitution.

The National Urban League, founded in 1910, also worked to help African Americans. It helped the many African Americans who were moving to cities at the time find jobs and homes.

Another group of progressives, the National American Woman Suffrage Association, led the fight for women's rights. **Suffrage** refers to the right to vote. The president of the association from 1900 to 1904, and from 1915 to 1920, was Carrie Lane Chapman Catt. She had first become politically active in her home state of Iowa in the 1880s.

Due to Catt and other progressives, many states responded to women's demand. By 1915, most of the states permitted women to vote in certain elections, such as for members of school boards.

Almost a dozen states, most of them in the West, had given women full voting rights in state elections. In 1920 the Nineteenth Amendment to the United States Constitution was ratified, giving all American women the right to vote. That same year Catt founded a group called the National League of Women Voters, now called the League of Women Voters.

REVIEW What group led the fight for women's suffrage?

LESSON 2 REVIEW

Summary Time Line

1900 ——————————————— 1910 ——————————————— 1920

1909
The NAACP is founded

1920
The Nineteenth Amendment is ratified

① **MAIN IDEA** What were some of the things people did to improve life in the United States in the early 1900s?

② **WHY IT MATTERS** How do changes that began in the early 1900s continue to affect Americans today?

③ **VOCABULARY** Write a description of a **political boss**.

④ **TIME LINE** What year was the Nineteenth Amendment ratified?

⑤ **READING SKILL—Make Inferences** Why do you think President Roosevelt set aside certain areas to serve as national parks?

⑥ **HISTORY** What did Carrie Lane Chapman Catt accomplish?

⑦ **CRITICAL THINKING—Evaluate** The progressives of the early 1900s worked to improve many different things. What kinds of things are people trying to improve today?

PERFORMANCE—Deliver a Speech
Imagine that you are taking part in the first Labor Day parade. Write a speech about why people should participate in this national celebration.

The Great War

In 1914 ongoing conflicts in Europe exploded into war. At first, most Americans saw the war as a European problem. In time, however, our nation was drawn into what was then known as the Great War. It would later be called World War I.

Causes of the War

Nations across Europe had formed alliances. The members of each alliance promised to help one another if they were attacked. Europeans hoped that these alliances would prevent war, but they had the opposite effect.

Serbia, a country in southern Europe, bordered Austria-Hungary. Many Serbs, however, lived in the southern part of Austria-Hungary, and they longed to be a part of their Serbian homeland. On June 28, 1914, a Serb rebel shot and killed two members of Austria-Hungary's royal family. As a result, Austria-Hungary declared war on Serbia.

Serbia and Austria-Hungary were both members of alliances, so other European nations were quickly drawn into the conflict. On one side were the Allied Powers, or Allies.

· LESSON ·

3

MAIN IDEA
Read to learn why the United States entered World War I.

WHY IT MATTERS
World War I was just the first of many threats to democracy and world peace that Americans would face in the twentieth century.

VOCABULARY
military draft
no-man's-land
isolation

The assassination of Archduke Ferdinand and his wife led to war.

537

They included Britain, Russia, France, Italy, and Serbia. On the other side were the Central Powers—Germany, Austria-Hungary, the Ottoman Empire, and Bulgaria.

Many Americans, including President Woodrow Wilson, wanted the United States to be neutral in the war. However, that proved to be difficult. Patrolling the seas were German submarines, called *Unterseeboots*, or U-boats. On May 7, 1915, a U-boat sank the British passenger ship *Lusitania*. Almost 1,200 people were killed, including 128 Americans.

People in the United States were angry at Germany. Some began to believe the United States should enter the war on the side of the Allies. However, President Wilson still hoped to keep the United States neutral. In 1916 he was reelected President. His campaign slogan was "He kept us out of war."

REVIEW Why were many European countries drawn into World War I?

The United States Enters the War

In early 1917, German leaders said that U-boats would begin to attack all ships, including American ships, found in British waters. U-boats soon sank three American ships. On April 2, 1917, President Wilson asked Congress to declare war on Germany, saying,

> ❝The world must be made safe for democracy.❞

Four days later, the United States joined the Allied Powers.

The United States was not prepared for war. Its army was small, and it did not have many weapons. To make the army larger, Congress passed the Selective Service Act. This new law provided for a **military draft**, a way to bring people into military

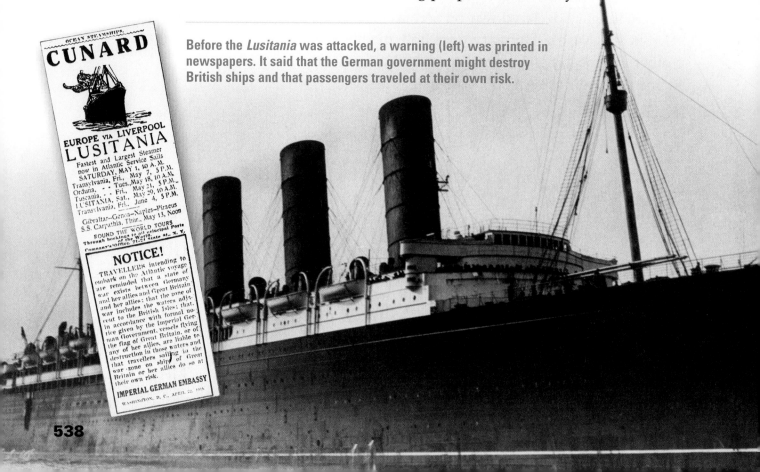

Before the *Lusitania* was attacked, a warning (left) was printed in newspapers. It said that the German government might destroy British ships and that passengers traveled at their own risk.

World War I

Allied Powers
Central Powers
Neutral countries
Major battle

FAST FACT
About 70 million people from all over the world served in the armed forces during World War I.

ICELAND (Denmark)

SWEDEN

NORWAY

RUSSIA

North Sea

•Moscow

IRELAND (BRITAIN)

BRITAIN

DENMARK

Baltic Sea

Tannenberg

0   250   500 Miles
0   250   500 Kilometers
Azimuthal Equal-Area Projection

Aral Sea

London•

NETHERLANDS

•Berlin

ATLANTIC OCEAN

BELGIUM **GERMANY**

Paris• **LUXEMBOURG**
Versailles•
Château- Argonne
Thierry Forest
SWITZERLAND

Caspian Sea

•Vienna

AUSTRIA-HUNGARY

FRANCE

ITALY Caporetto•

ROMANIA

Black Sea

Lisbon•

•Madrid

Corsica

Sarajevo•

SERBIA

MONTENEGRO
•Rome ALBANIA BULGARIA

PORTUGAL

SPAIN

Sardinia

•Constantinople
Gallipoli•

GREECE

OTTOMAN EMPIRE

ASIA

Sicily

Malta

Cyprus

MOROCCO
(FRANCE)

ALGERIA
(FRANCE)

TUNISIA
(FRANCE)

Crete

Mediterranean Sea

SPANISH
SAHARA

AFRICA

GEOGRAPHY THEME

Regions **This map shows how the war had divided Europe.**

❓ **What problems do you think Germany had because of Allied Powers on both its eastern and western borders?**

service. It required all men between the ages of 21 and 30 to sign up with draft boards. Members of the draft boards then used the lists of names to choose who would serve in the military.

Most American soldiers who arrived in Europe in 1917 were sent to France, where much of the fighting took place. Soldiers fought one another from trenches, or ditches, dug in the ground. The trenches of the two opposing sides were separated by a **no-man's-land**. This land was not controlled by either side and was filled with barbed wire and bombs buried in the ground.

Soldiers faced terrible new weapons. The Germans had developed machine guns that fired hundreds of bullets each minute. To fight against these guns, the British built tanks with steel walls. Machine gun bullets could not go through the tank walls. The most feared of the weapons was poison gas. It killed soldiers—even those in tanks—by making them unable to breathe.

REVIEW **How did the United States prepare for war?**

Changes at Home

Building an army and supplying it in a hurry were huge tasks. Goods had to be moved quickly from farms and factories to ports, where they could be shipped to Europe. To help do this, President Wilson set up the War Industries Board to oversee the production and distribution of goods. He also placed all the nation's railroads under government management.

As more and more men left their jobs to go fight in the war, there were fewer and fewer workers at home. Because of this shortage, wages generally rose, and many workers had opportunities to find better jobs. The need for workers especially helped African Americans. Between 1914 and 1919, as part of the Great Migration, half a million African Americans moved to northern cities to find jobs in the war plants there.

Thousands of women also found jobs in factories and offices. They could not have hoped to get such jobs before the war started. Some women became mechanics or worked in weapons factories.

Some went to Europe as nurses or ambulance drivers. Thousands more joined the army or navy as clerks or telegraph operators. Women, however, were not drafted or allowed to fight in the war.

REVIEW What groups of people found new job opportunities during the war?

The End of the War

American efforts made an important difference in World War I. Working together, the Americans and the other Allies began to push back the German army. Finally, on November 11, 1918, the Germans surrendered and signed an armistice that ended the fighting. Before the fighting ended, however, about 53,000 Americans had been killed. Another 230,000 had been wounded.

Allied leaders gathered in Paris, France, to make peace terms. President Wilson did not want Germany and its allies to be punished too harshly. However, the other Allied leaders wanted to weaken Germany so it could never again wage war.

During the war, women and African Americans filled jobs left by men who went overseas to serve in the military.

World leaders met at the Palace of Versailles (ver•SY), near Paris, to sign the treaty that officially ended World War I. All together, more than 8 million people died in the war.

During these talks Wilson described his idea for a League of Nations. He hoped this organization would help avoid future wars by finding peaceful ways to solve nations' conflicts. The Treaty of Versailles (ver•SY), which officially ended the war, set up the League of Nations. The United States, however, did not join. The Senate refused to approve the treaty. Many senators believed that membership in the League would involve the United States in other nations' wars. Some wanted the nation to return to a policy of **isolation**— remaining separate from other countries. Twenty years later this policy would again be challenged.

REVIEW What happened when the United States did not approve the Treaty of Versailles?

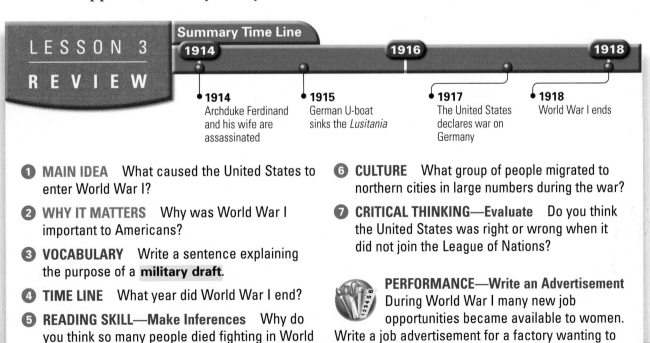

LESSON 3 REVIEW

Summary Time Line

1914 — 1916 — 1918

1914 Archduke Ferdinand and his wife are assassinated

1915 German U-boat sinks the *Lusitania*

1917 The United States declares war on Germany

1918 World War I ends

1. **MAIN IDEA** What caused the United States to enter World War I?

2. **WHY IT MATTERS** Why was World War I important to Americans?

3. **VOCABULARY** Write a sentence explaining the purpose of a **military draft**.

4. **TIME LINE** What year did World War I end?

5. **READING SKILL—Make Inferences** Why do you think so many people died fighting in World War I?

6. **CULTURE** What group of people migrated to northern cities in large numbers during the war?

7. **CRITICAL THINKING—Evaluate** Do you think the United States was right or wrong when it did not join the League of Nations?

PERFORMANCE—Write an Advertisement During World War I many new job opportunities became available to women. Write a job advertisement for a factory wanting to hire new workers.

MAIN IDEA
Read to compare life in the United States during the 1920s with life in the 1930s.

WHY IT MATTERS
The power of the federal government expanded as the good times of the 1920s were replaced by the hard times of the 1930s.

VOCABULARY
consumer good
assembly line
division of labor
industrialization
urbanization
mechanization of agriculture
stock market
depression
bureaucracy
unemployment

Good Times and Hard Times

1901   1951   2001

1900–1930

The early 1920s were good times for many Americans. People looked forward to new opportunities and wanted to enjoy themselves. For this reason, the 1920s are often called the Roaring Twenties. Many Americans thought these good times would go on forever. By the end of the decade, however, Americans again faced hard times.

New Forms of Expression

Many people in the 1920s were looking for new ways to express themselves. This new spirit of artistic freedom influenced many art forms during the Roaring Twenties. Among them was a new kind of music called jazz.

Jazz grew out of the African American musical heritage made up of music brought from West Africa and spirituals that enslaved people had sung in the United States. In the 1920s

Louis Armstrong

Nipper, the dog on RCA Victor's label, first appeared on phonographs and records in 1901. Charlie Chaplin (right) was the most popular comic actor of the time.

This is the great picture upon which the famous comedian has worked a whole year.

6 reels of Joy.

Charles Chaplin IN "THE KID"

Written and directed by Charles Chaplin

A First National Attraction

jazz musicians such as Duke Ellington and Louis Armstrong helped make this form of music popular.

Both Ellington and Armstrong often performed in the New York City neighborhood of Harlem. So many African American musicians, artists, and writers lived and worked in Harlem during the 1920s that this time came to be known as the Harlem Renaissance.

One of the best-known writers of the Harlem Renaissance was the poet Langston Hughes. He described Harlem during the 1920s as a magnet for African Americans from across the country. Writers such as Claude McKay, Countee Cullen, and Zora Neale Hurston went to Harlem to share their talents.

This time of artistic freedom also encouraged other Americans to create new ways of doing things. Frank Lloyd Wright, for example, used new designs to create unique buildings. Painter Georgia O'Keeffe created paintings about city life.

New forms of entertainment gave Americans new ways to spend their free time. The first commercial radio stations began broadcasting in the 1920s. By 1929 more than 800 stations were reaching about 10 million families. By listening to the radio, Americans could follow news and sporting events from around the country.

Another popular pastime was attending the movies. The movie business, based in Hollywood, California, started making silent films before World War I. By the late 1920s, many movies were talkies—they were made with sound.

REVIEW **What forms of entertainment were popular in the 1920s?**

Industries Bring More Changes

When World War I ended, there was no longer a demand for factories to produce weapons and other war supplies. Factories started to make products such as vacuum cleaners, washing machines, refrigerators, toasters, radios, and other new electric appliances for the home.

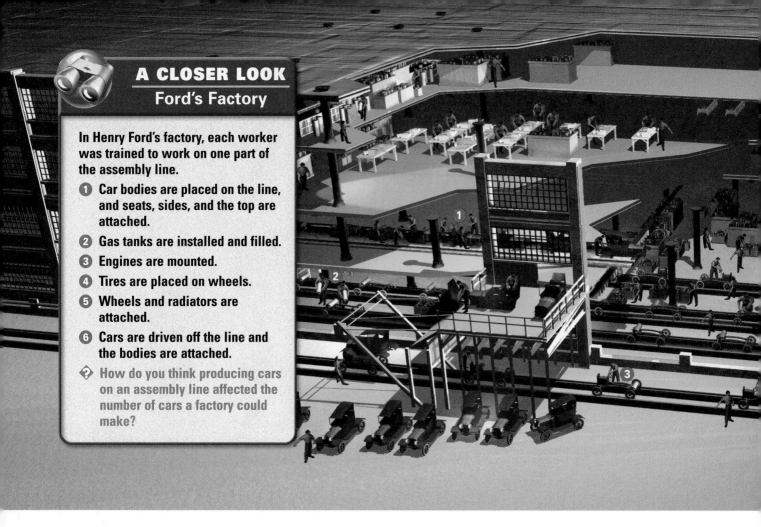

In Henry Ford's factory, each worker was trained to work on one part of the assembly line.

1. Car bodies are placed on the line, and seats, sides, and the top are attached.
2. Gas tanks are installed and filled.
3. Engines are mounted.
4. Tires are placed on wheels.
5. Wheels and radiators are attached.
6. Cars are driven off the line and the bodies are attached.

❖ How do you think producing cars on an assembly line affected the number of cars a factory could make?

These **consumer goods**—the name given to products made for personal use—were possible because more people had electricity in their homes.

Americans had a variety of consumer goods to choose from, but perhaps the most important were automobiles. The first successful gasoline-powered automobile had been built in the 1890s. By the time the United States entered World War I, companies were producing about 1 million cars a year. By 1923 they were making more than 3 million.

One of the reasons for this dramatic growth in the automobile industry was the work of a man from Michigan, named Henry Ford. Ford had developed a system of mass production that relied on a moving **assembly line**. Instead of being built one at a time, Ford's cars were assembled, or put together, as they moved past a line of workers.

Each worker at Ford's factory was trained to do only one task, such as putting in headlights or seats. Other workers along the assembly line did other tasks until the car was finished. Dividing work so that each worker does only part of a larger job is called **division of labor**. By using an assembly line and dividing the labor among his workers, Ford could produce automobiles faster and cheaper and still afford to pay his workers well. By 1925 a person could buy one of Ford's cars for about $260.

Once automobiles became more affordable, the demand for them rose sharply. This demand also affected the growth of

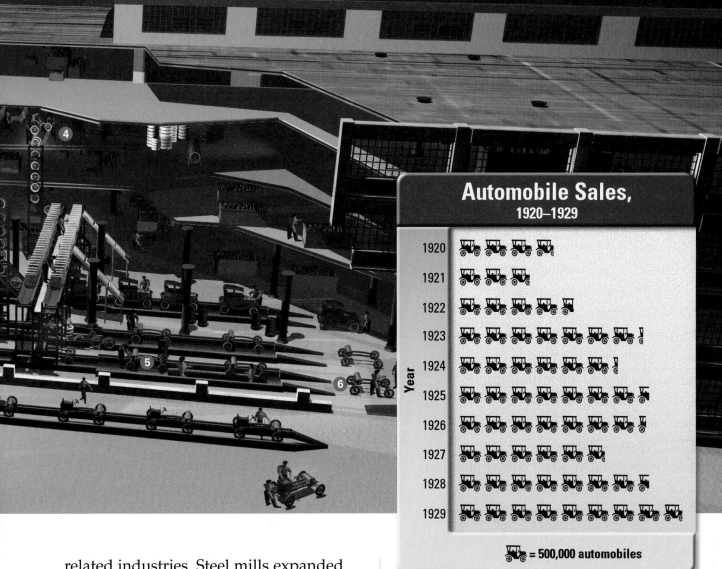

Automobile Sales, 1920–1929

Year	Sales
1920	🚗🚗🚗🚗
1921	🚗🚗🚗
1922	🚗🚗🚗🚗🚗
1923	🚗🚗🚗🚗🚗🚗🚗
1924	🚗🚗🚗🚗🚗🚗
1925	🚗🚗🚗🚗🚗🚗🚗
1926	🚗🚗🚗🚗🚗🚗🚗
1927	🚗🚗🚗🚗🚗
1928	🚗🚗🚗🚗🚗🚗🚗
1929	🚗🚗🚗🚗🚗🚗🚗🚗

🚗 = 500,000 automobiles

Analyze Graphs   Henry Ford's idea of producing cars on an assembly line helped increase sales of automobiles.

◈ About how many cars were sold in 1929?

related industries. Steel mills expanded so that they could supply more steel for making automobiles. More tires, oil, and gas were needed, too. The demand for these products increased as farmers began to use gasoline-powered tractors.

Air transportation also contributed to the nation's **industrialization** (in•duhs•tree•uh•luh•ZAY•shuhn), or the growth of industries. Two brothers, Orville and Wilbur Wright, had made the first flight in 1903 at Kitty Hawk, North Carolina. Over the years, the airplane was improved, but very few people traveled by plane.

Then, on May 20, 1927, Charles Lindbergh, an American airmail pilot, took off from New York in a small plane named the *Spirit of St. Louis*. His goal was

to be the first person to fly nonstop across the Atlantic Ocean. About 34 hours after leaving New York, Lindbergh finally arrived in Paris, France. Lindbergh's flight helped make people more interested in air travel, and soon commercial airlines were making flights.

Advances in technology in the 1920s changed American eating habits, too. George Washington Carver was an African American scientist and teacher who worked at the Tuskegee Institute.

He became well known for his work with peanuts and ways to improve farming. Carver and his students developed hundreds of new food products from peanuts, sweet potatoes, and soybeans. His advice to southern farmers to grow peanuts as a cash crop helped the region's economy.

Clarence Birdseye developed a method of freezing foods that helped preserve their original taste. His quick-frozen foods, which he sold in small packages, were an immediate success and helped change the way Americans ate.

REVIEW How did the growth of the automobile industry affect related industries?

The Growth of Cities

The continuing industrialization of the United States also affected where people lived in the 1920s. For the first time in the nation's history, more people in the United States lived in urban areas than on farms. In fact, the population of many cities doubled during the 1920s.

As a result of this **urbanization** (ur•buh•nuh•ZAY•shuhn), or movement of people to cities, cities changed in other ways. Skyscrapers and large apartment buildings became part of many city skylines. Downtown streets became crowded with cars and buses.

As cities grew, the suburbs around them also grew. Cars and buses made it possible for more people to work in cities and live in suburbs outside them.

While the population of cities increased, the number of Americans

Clarence Birdseye

living in farming communities decreased. During the 1920s more of the equipment that farmers used to prepare their fields and to plant and harvest crops became mechanized (MEH•kuh•nizd), or powered by machines. As a result of this **mechanization of agriculture**, farmers could plant more land than they could when work had to be done by hand or when equipment was powered by horses or mules. It also meant that fewer farm workers were needed. Many workers left farms and sought jobs in cities.

Improved farming equipment and farming methods sharply increased the amount of crops that were grown on American farms. However, this surplus drove down the prices paid for many crops, forcing many families to sell their farms. In growing numbers, farm families moved to urban areas in search of work.

REVIEW Why did so many people leave farming communities in the 1920s?

Many skyscrapers and apartment buildings were built in New York City as a result of urbanization.

The Great Depression

Many farmers faced hardships in the 1920s, but other Americans expected to become rich by investing money in the stock market. The **stock market** is a place where people can buy and sell stocks, or shares in businesses. If more people want to buy than sell a certain stock, the price goes up. If more people want to sell than buy, the price goes down.

During the 1920s the prices on most stocks kept going higher. People even began to borrow money to buy stocks. "How can you lose?" they asked. Before long they learned the answer.

Beginning in the fall of 1929, some people decided to take their money out of the stock market. This caused stock prices to fall. As prices fell, many investors

decided to sell, too. Soon panicked stock-holders were trying to sell all their stocks. On October 29, 1929, the stock market crashed. Nearly everyone who owned stocks lost money.

The crash of the stock market ended the good times of the Roaring Twenties. Soon people everywhere were facing hard times as businesses failed and an economic depression gripped the nation and the rest of the world. A **depression** is a time of little economic growth when there are few jobs and people have little money. This depression, which continued through the 1930s, was so bad that it became known as the Great Depression.

After the stock market crash, many people needed to spend their savings in order to live. Large numbers of them tried to take money out of the banks.

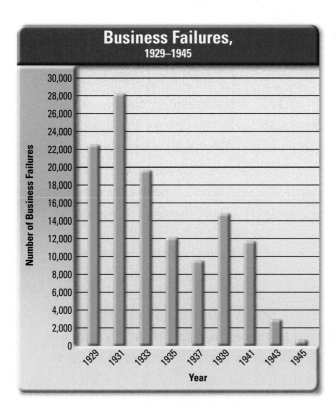

Analyze Graphs This graph shows the number of companies that went out of business from 1929 to 1945.

❖ About how many companies went out of business in 1931?

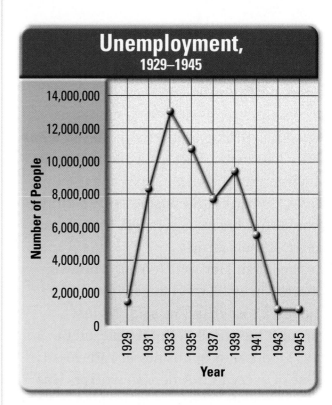

Analyze Graphs This line graph shows the number of people who lost their jobs during 1929–1945.

❖ How did the number of unemployed people change over time?

Dust Bowl Region

Understanding Environment and Society

The Dust Bowl was the name given to a section of the southern Great Plains that suffered a series of severe droughts, or periods with little or no rain, through the 1930s. The Dust Bowl region was spread out over parts of Colorado, Kansas, Texas, Oklahoma, and New Mexico. The dust storms that developed in this area were known as "black blizzards" because the swirling dirt often blocked the sun. The storms forced thousands of farm families to leave their homes.

A father and son in Oklahoma raise the fence on their property to keep it from being buried by soil.

Many banks closed. People who had money in them lost all their savings.

Because people had little money to spend, manufacturers could not sell what they had made. Factory workers then lost their jobs and could not pay what they owed to banks and businesses. So more banks and businesses failed. More farmers lost their farms.

President Herbert Hoover, who was elected in 1928, tried to give everyone hope. "Prosperity," he said, "is just around the corner." But it was not. By 1932 thousands of businesses had closed. One of every four American workers was without a job. Hungry people stood in line for bread or free meals.

REVIEW How did the Great Depression affect both manufacturers and workers?

The New Deal

In 1932 the American people elected Franklin D. Roosevelt as President. Roosevelt believed that to end the Great Depression, the federal government needed to take bold, new action. On his inauguration day, he told Americans,

❝The only thing we have to fear is fear itself.❞

Roosevelt's words gave people hope that things would improve. He quickly developed a plan to combat the effects of the Great Depression. He called his plan the New Deal. Its goal was to get people back to work.

The New Deal gave the federal government more authority. It also made it larger. This growing number of government workers formed a bureaucracy. A **bureaucracy** (byu•RAH•kruh•see) is the many workers and groups that are needed to run government programs.

One New Deal program was called the Civilian Conservation Corps, or CCC. The CCC hired thousands of young men to build bridges, plant trees, and do other helpful things. Another program, the Works Progress Administration, or WPA, hired workers to build roads, airports, and public buildings. The WPA also hired writers and artists to record life during the Great Depression.

To further growth, Congress set up the Tennessee Valley Authority, or TVA. The purpose of the TVA was to control flooding on the Tennessee River system and produce electricity with hydroelectric dams. The government would then sell the electricity at low rates to users.

President Roosevelt had high hopes for his New Deal programs.

Even with all of President Roosevelt's new programs, **unemployment**, or the number of people without jobs, remained high. But at least unemployment did not get worse.

REVIEW What was the New Deal?

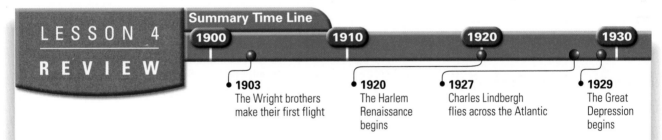

LESSON 4 REVIEW

Summary Time Line

1900 — 1910 — 1920 — 1930

1903 The Wright brothers make their first flight

1920 The Harlem Renaissance begins

1927 Charles Lindbergh flies across the Atlantic

1929 The Great Depression begins

1. **MAIN IDEA** How was life in the United States different in the 1920s compared to the 1930s?

2. **WHY IT MATTERS** How did the authority and size of the federal government change in the 1930s?

3. **VOCABULARY** How are **industrialization** and **urbanization** related?

4. **TIME LINE** In what year did the Wright brothers take flight?

5. **READING SKILL—Make Inferences** Why do you think the division of labor would cause the economy to grow?

6. **ECONOMICS** How was Henry Ford able to produce automobiles faster and cheaper?

7. **CRITICAL THINKING—Analyze** What was the relationship between the stock market crash, banks closing, and people losing their jobs?

PERFORMANCE—Write a News Story Imagine you are a newspaper reporter in 1933. You have just interviewed President Roosevelt. Write a news story about Roosevelt's plans to end the Great Depression. Share your news story with your classmates.

14 Review and Test Preparation

USE YOUR READING SKILLS

Complete this graphic organizer by making inferences about the Great Depression. A copy of this graphic organizer appears on page 139 of the Activity Book.

The Great Depression

FACT		INFERENCE
On October 29, 1929 the stock market crashed	→	_____
FACT	→	

FACT		INFERENCE
	→	Because manufacturers could not sell their products, factories shut down and more people lost their jobs
FACT	→	

THINK & WRITE

Write an Informative Letter   Imagine you are living in the Hawaiian Islands during the late nineteenth century. Write a letter to a friend explaining why some people want the United States to annex Hawaii and other people do not.

Write a Packing List   Imagine your family has decided to move from a small farming community to a large city. Write a list of items to pack for your journey and a list of things you might have to purchase when you arrive in the city.

1906
Congress passes the Pure Food and Drug Act

1915
The *Lusitania* is sunk

1917
The United States enters World War I

1920
The Nineteenth Amendment is passed

1929
The Great Depression begins

1933
President Roosevelt introduces the New Deal

USE THE TIME LINE

Use the chapter summary time line to answer these questions.

1 When was the Nineteenth Amendment passed?

2 How many years after the Great Depression began was the New Deal introduced?

USE VOCABULARY

Identify the term that correctly matches each definition.

> **suffrage (p. 535)**
>
> **isolation (p. 541)**
>
> **unemployment (p. 549)**

3 remaining separate from other countries

4 the number of people without jobs

5 the right to vote

RECALL FACTS

Answer these questions.

6 What event led to the start of World War I?

7 Why did people start to celebrate Labor Day?

8 How did Carrie Chapman Catt work for greater democracy in the United States?

Write the letter of the best choice.

9 TEST PREP One of the results of increased urbanization was that—
  A wheat production in the United States greatly decreased.
  B fewer people worked on farms.
  C the United States had to import much of its food from Europe.
  D political bosses lost all of their power.

10 TEST PREP George Washington Carver and Clarence Birdseye helped change—
  F corrupt city governments.
  G national voting laws.
  H the way Americans traveled.
  J the way Americans eat.

11 TEST PREP One event that started the Great Depression was—
  A the United States' entry into World War I.
  B the stock market crash of 1929.
  C the building of the Panama Canal.
  D the destruction of the battleship *Maine*.

THINK CRITICALLY

12 How did the Spanish-American War help make the United States a world power?

13 Why do you think Jane Addams chose to become involved in her community?

14 How do you think farm life in the 1920s was different from farm life in the 1820s?

15 What effect do you think the Great Depression may have had on other countries?

APPLY SKILLS

Compare Map Projections
Study the maps on pages 530–531. Then answer the following questions.

16 On which map are all the meridians an equal distance apart?

17 On which map does Australia appear to be larger? On which map is the size of Australia more accurate?

ARIZONA MEMORIAL

The *USS Arizona* Memorial is anchored at Pearl Harbor. It was built to honor the 1,177 sailors who lost their lives on December 7, 1941. The memorial is positioned above the sunken battleship that still lies on the ocean floor. President Dwight D. Eisenhower approved the creation of the memorial, which was dedicated in 1962.

LOCATE IT

HAWAII

USS Arizona Memorial, Pearl Harbor

Global Conflict

" Yesterday, December 7, 1941—a date which will live in infamy— "

—Franklin D. Roosevelt, December 8, 1941, in a message to Congress

---

CHAPTER READING SKILL

Cause and Effect

A **cause** is an event or action that makes something else happen. An **effect** is what happens as a result of that event or action.

As you read this chapter, determine the causes and effects of events related to World War II.

| CAUSE | | EFFECT |

MAIN IDEA
Read to find out how World War II began and why the United States became involved.

WHY IT MATTERS
World War II was the largest, the most costly, and deadliest war in history, but it preserved democracy.

VOCABULARY

concentration camp
dictatorship
civilian

German leader Adolf Hitler addresses German soldiers at Nuremberg, Germany, in 1937.

World War II Begins

1901   1951   2001

1921–1941

Franklin D. Roosevelt was reelected President in 1936. His New Deal programs had raised many people's spirits, but the worldwide depression continued. Many Europeans, still rebuilding their countries after World War I, had a hard time finding jobs to support their families. In Asia, some countries were running out of the resources needed to make their economies grow. Powerful new leaders in some European and Asian nations now promised to solve their countries' problems by force.

Worldwide Troubles

The treaty that ended World War I required Germany to pay other European countries for war damages. Germany, however, did not have enough money to pay this debt. As a result, its economy suffered. By 1923 inflation was so bad that a suitcase full of money could barely buy a loaf of bread.

FAST FACT
In 1923, inflation caused German money to become so low in value that German children were allowed to use bundles of German paper money as building blocks.

Hirohito, emperor of Japan, salutes as he inspects a group of Japanese troops. The hat (above) was worn by a Japanese officer in World War II.

Beginning in the 1920s a German World War I veteran named Adolf Hitler started giving speeches that said that Germany had not been treated fairly after the war. Hitler also said that Germans were better than all other peoples of the world. His words, however, did not apply to all Germans. He blamed the Jewish people in Germany for many of the country's problems.

Hitler became the leader of a political party in Germany called the National Socialists, or Nazis. The Nazi party promised to make Germany a powerful nation once again. It grew in power and set up a private army. Its soldiers, called storm troopers, used force to crush anyone who disagreed with them. They put many of these people in terrible prisons called **concentration camps**.

In 1933 the Nazi party took control of Germany, and Hitler began ruling as a dictator. Hitler rebuilt the nation's economy by preparing for another war. He dreamed that Germany would one day rule over all other nations.

Dictators rose to power in several other European countries, too. In Italy, Benito Mussolini (buh•NEE•toh moo•suh•LEE•nee) seized power in 1922. He wanted Italy to regain the power and glory it had in ancient times, when it was the center of the Roman Empire. With help from Hitler and Mussolini, Francisco Franco also set up a **dictatorship**—a country ruled by a dictator—in Spain. In 1924 Joseph Stalin took control of the Soviet Union, which had been formed following a revolution in Russia in 1917.

Dictators also ruled Japan, in Asia. The Japanese emperor, Hirohito (hir•oh•HEE•toh), had little authority after military officers seized the government. To get the resources Japan's industries needed, these military leaders decided to conquer other nations in Asia and the Pacific.

In the 1930s the nations of Japan, Italy, and Germany began taking over other countries. In 1931 Japan invaded Manchuria, a part of China. Then, in 1935 Italy took over the African country of Ethiopia.

German soldiers (above) march to the Polish border during Germany's invasion of Poland in 1939. American newspapers (right) announce the news.

Two years later, in 1937, Japan started a war against the rest of China. The next year, Germany took over Austria and Czechoslovakia (chehk•uh•sloh•VAHK•ee•uh), in Europe.

Because of painful memories of World War I, other countries, including the United States, did little to stop these aggressive acts. Most people hoped war could be avoided.

REVIEW What countries were ruled by dictators before World War II?

The War Begins

On September 1, 1939, German forces, numbering nearly 2 million, invaded Poland. They attacked with tanks on land and planes in the air, quickly defeating their neighbor. The Germans called this fighting style *blitzkrieg*, or "lightning war." Two days later Poland's allies,

Britain and France, responded to this attack by declaring war on Germany. World War II had begun.

German forces stormed across Europe with incredible speed. By the end of 1941, much of the continent was under German control. The only countries that remained free were Britain, Russia, and a few small neutral nations. In France, rebel armies fought to weaken Germany's grip. In the skies over Britain, German bombers continued their attacks, but Britain bravely fought on.

Germany's invasions shocked and angered most Americans. However, few Americans wanted the United States to become involved in another foreign war.

In 1940 President Roosevelt was elected to a third term. He promised to keep the United States out of the war, but he wanted the country to be prepared in case it was attacked. A military draft was begun, and the United States started making airplanes, tanks, and other war supplies. It also began to send food and war supplies to help Britain. To meet the growing demands for these goods, many businesses reopened and new ones started. Once again people were able to find jobs. The Great Depression was clearly coming to an end.

In 1940 Japanese troops invaded French Indochina, which is now made up of the countries of Laos, Cambodia, and Vietnam. Many American leaders feared that Japan would soon threaten the Philippines and other places in the Pacific. They were right.

REVIEW **What action by Germany started World War II?**

The United States Enters the War

At 7:55 A.M. on Sunday, December 7, 1941, the roar of Japanese planes shattered the early morning calm over the Hawaiian Islands. The planes dropped bombs on American ships docked at Pearl Harbor, an American naval base. World War II had come to the United States.

In less than two hours, 19 warships were sunk or damaged in the harbor. In addition, about 150 planes were destroyed at nearby Hickam Airfield. More than 2,000 sailors and soldiers and 68 civilians were killed. A **civilian** is a person who is not in the military.

The Japanese attack on Pearl Harbor caused terrible damage and loss of life.

LOCATE IT

HAWAII

Pearl Harbor

Americans were outraged by the attack on Pearl Harbor. President Roosevelt went before Congress the next day to ask that war be declared on Japan. He said,

> **❝Yesterday, December 7, 1941, a date which will live in infamy— the United States of America was suddenly and deliberately attacked by naval and air forces of the Empire of Japan. . . . I ask that the Congress declare that since the . . . attack by Japan . . . a state of war has existed between the United States and the Japanese Empire. ❞**

Three days later, Germany and Italy declared war on the United States, and Congress recognized a state of war with them, too. Germany, Italy, and Japan were known as the Axis Powers. The United States joined with the Allies, which included Britain, France, and the Soviet

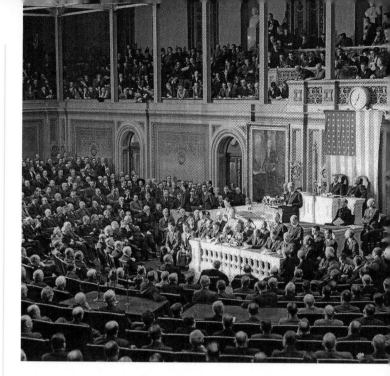

President Franklin D. Roosevelt asks Congress for a declaration of war on Japan.

Union. The Soviet Union had joined the Allies after Germany invaded it in the summer of 1941.

REVIEW **What event led the United States to enter the war?**

LESSON 1 REVIEW

Summary Time Line

1921 — 1931 — 1941

1933 Nazi party takes control of Germany's government

1939 Germany invades Poland

1941 Japanese forces attack Pearl Harbor

1. **MAIN IDEA** What caused World War II?

2. **WHY IT MATTERS** Why was World War II such an important war?

3. **VOCABULARY** What is a **dictator**?

4. **TIME LINE** Did Germany invade Poland before or after the Japanese attacked Pearl Harbor?

5. **READING SKILL—Cause and Effect** What effect did World War II have on the Great Depression in the United States?

6. **HISTORY** What major countries made up the Allied Powers? the Axis Powers?

7. **CRITICAL THINKING—Analyze** What do you think is the relationship between the rise of dictators and the coming of World War II?

PERFORMANCE—Write a Memorial Recently the United States marked the sixtieth anniversary of the attack on Pearl Harbor. Write a memorial honoring the American men and women who defended the base that day. In your memorial, also discuss the importance of the event in United States history.

·SKILLS· Predict a Historical Outcome

VOCABULARY
prediction

▶ WHY IT MATTERS

People often make **predictions**. This means they look at the way things are and decide what they think will most likely happen next. When people make predictions, they are not just guessing about what will happen in the future. They are using information and past experiences to predict a probable, or likely, outcome.

▶ WHAT YOU NEED TO KNOW

You have read about how many women worked in factories during World War I. When World War II began, American factories were again in need of many workers.

▶ PRACTICE THE SKILL

Use the following steps to predict what groups of people were employed in large numbers by American factories during World War II.

This photograph shows women working in a factory during World War II.

Step 1 Think about what you already know about the number of women who worked in American factories during World War I.

Step 2 Review the new information you learned about the beginning of World War II.

Step 3 Make a prediction about what group of people American factories began employing in large numbers during World War II.

Step 4 As you read or gather more information, ask yourself whether you still think your prediction is correct.

Step 5 If necessary, go through the steps again to form a new prediction.

After going through these steps, you should have been able to predict that factories employed many women.

▶ APPLY WHAT YOU LEARNED

Think about a prediction you made at school this week. What steps did you follow? Do you think that your prediction was a correct one?

READING SKILLS

MAIN IDEA
Read to see how World
War II brought new
challenges to the
American people.

WHY IT MATTERS
World War II was fought
mainly in other places, but
it had long-lasting effects
on the American people.

VOCABULARY
rationing
recycle
interest
relocation camp

Americans and the War

1941–1943

Supplying war materials to the Allies had already helped prepare the United States for war. After the bombing of Pearl Harbor, however, the United States suddenly had to produce even more airplanes, tanks, and other war supplies. This work provided jobs for many more Americans. Now instead of not enough jobs, there were not enough workers.

Wartime Industries

Fighting World War II led to the further growth of the federal government's authority. To produce enough war supplies, the government took control of many businesses. It set both the prices that businesses could charge for their products and the wages that they could pay their workers. The government also stopped the production of many consumer goods. Manufacturers who had produced these goods before the war were now told to make weapons or other war materials.

To produce these wartime goods, hundreds of thousands of new workers were needed. Across the country people went to

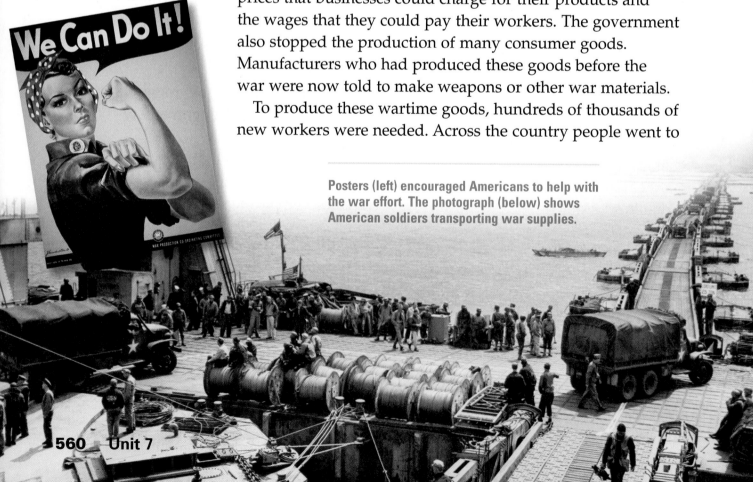

Posters (left) encouraged Americans to help with
the war effort. The photograph (below) shows
American soldiers transporting war supplies.

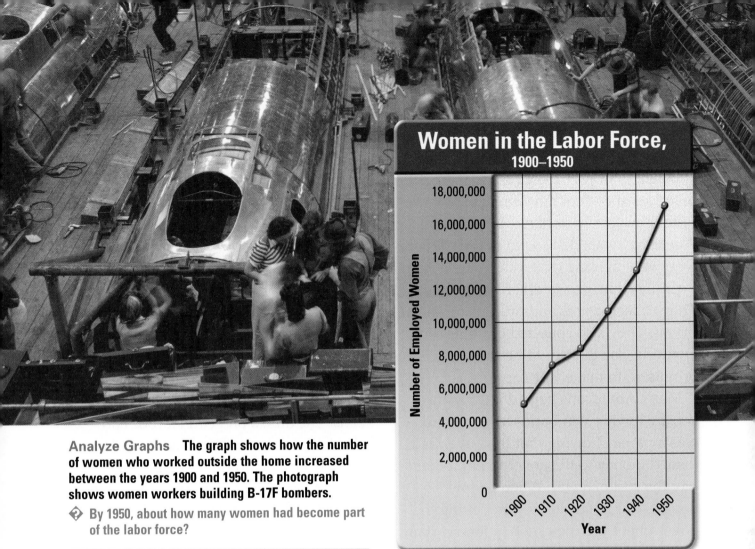

Women in the Labor Force, 1900–1950

Analyze Graphs The graph shows how the number of women who worked outside the home increased between the years 1900 and 1950. The photograph shows women workers building B-17F bombers.

◆ By 1950, about how many women had become part of the labor force?

work in factories, steel mills, shipyards, and aircraft plants. Many of these workers were women. As they had done in World War I, women took over jobs that previously had been held only by men.

Working around the clock, American workers were able to produce huge amounts of war materials at record speed. At the beginning of the war, President Roosevelt challenged American industries to produce as many as 60,000 aircraft a year. Many people believed this was an impossible goal, but in 1943 alone, American workers built almost 86,000 aircraft!

REVIEW How did the government get businesses to produce enough war supplies?

The Home Front

More than 15 million Americans served in the armed forces during World War II, including about 338,000 women. Many women in the armed forces made maps, drove ambulances, and worked as mechanics, clerks, or nurses.

To help feed the thousands of people serving in the military, farmers planted more crops and raised more livestock. This demand for food brought about prosperous times for farmers.

The war often caused shortages of goods. To make sure there were enough goods to supply soldiers, new government rules called for **rationing**, or limiting, what civilians could purchase.

To purchase certain items, such as butter, sugar, meat, and gasoline, people had to have government coupons. They could buy only the amount that the coupons allowed. That way the government could control how much of a product was sold at home, so more of it would be available to send to the soldiers who were fighting overseas.

Civilians helped in other ways, too. They collected pots and tin cans for metal drives. They also collected old tires or anything else that could be **recycled**, or reused, to make war supplies.

Many Americans helped pay for the war by buying war bonds. A war bond was a paper showing that the buyer had loaned money to the government to help pay the cost of a war. When people bought war bonds, they were letting the government use their money for a certain amount of time. After the time was up, people could turn in their bonds and get their money back with interest.

Relocated Japanese Americans had to wear identification tags like this one.

WAR RELOCATION AUTHORITY
JAMES KAWAMINAMI
14967

Interest is the money a bank or borrower pays for the use of money.

REVIEW How did Americans help pay for the war?

Japanese Americans

The war changed people's lives. It also led to terrible problems for Japanese Americans. At the time of the attack on Pearl Harbor, about 125,000 Japanese Americans lived in the United States. Most had been born there and were citizens. The attack on Pearl Harbor had shocked them as much as anyone else.

After Pearl Harbor, however, anger against Japanese Americans grew. Some United States military officials believed that Japanese Americans might even help Japan invade the United States.

In February 1942, President Roosevelt ordered the army to put about 110,000

• SCIENCE AND TECHNOLOGY •

Blood Storage

Before World War II, scientists were unable to store donated blood for long periods of time. As a result, injured people who had lost too much blood usually died. Charles Drew, an African American doctor, helped change this. Drew discovered that the plasma, or the liquid part of blood, could be separated from the red blood cells. The two could then be frozen separately and stored for long periods. When an injured or sick person needed a blood transfusion, the two parts could be combined again. During the war, Drew helped found the American Red Cross Blood Program, which saved the lives of thousands of wounded soldiers.

Charles Drew

Many of the soldiers in the 442nd Regimental Combat Team were Japanese Americans. They fought in Italy and Germany and received many service awards like the medal shown here.

Japanese Americans in what were called **relocation camps**. Japanese Americans had to wear identification tags, and they had to sell their homes, businesses, and belongings. They were moved to relocation camps in California, Arizona, Wyoming, Arkansas, and Idaho.

While their families and friends were in the relocation camps, more than 17,000 Japanese Americans served in the army. Most became members of the 442nd Regimental Combat Team.

REVIEW Why were many Japanese Americans sent to relocation camps?

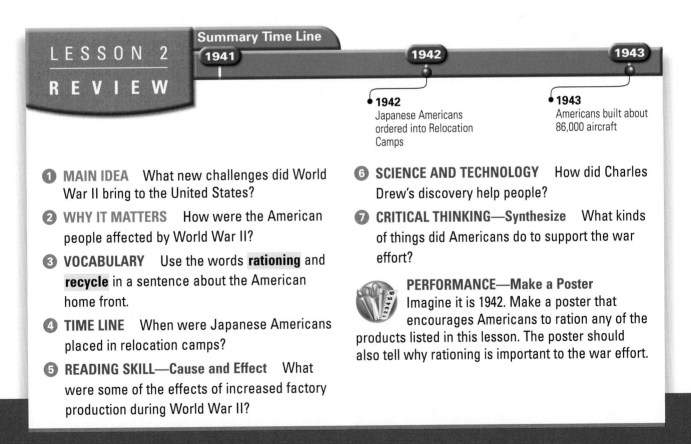

LESSON 2 REVIEW

Summary Time Line

1941

1942

1942
Japanese Americans ordered into Relocation Camps

1943

1943
Americans built about 86,000 aircraft

① **MAIN IDEA** What new challenges did World War II bring to the United States?

② **WHY IT MATTERS** How were the American people affected by World War II?

③ **VOCABULARY** Use the words **rationing** and **recycle** in a sentence about the American home front.

④ **TIME LINE** When were Japanese Americans placed in relocation camps?

⑤ **READING SKILL—Cause and Effect** What were some of the effects of increased factory production during World War II?

⑥ **SCIENCE AND TECHNOLOGY** How did Charles Drew's discovery help people?

⑦ **CRITICAL THINKING—Synthesize** What kinds of things did Americans do to support the war effort?

PERFORMANCE—Make a Poster
Imagine it is 1942. Make a poster that encourages Americans to ration any of the products listed in this lesson. The poster should also tell why rationing is important to the war effort.

· SKILLS · CITIZENSHIP

Make Economic Choices

VOCABULARY
trade-off
opportunity cost

▶ WHY IT MATTERS

When you buy something at the store or decide what to order at a restaurant, you are making an economic choice. These choices are often difficult to make. In order to buy something you want now, you must spend money that you cannot use to buy something in the future. This is called a **trade-off**. What you give up is the **opportunity cost** of what you get. Understanding trade-offs and opportunity costs can help you make more thoughtful economic choices.

▶ WHAT YOU NEED TO KNOW

You have read that during World War II, Americans showed their support for the war effort in a number of ways. One way was by buying war bonds. Buying war bonds helped support the war effort. At the same time, the war bonds paid interest to their owners.

▶ PRACTICE THE SKILL

Imagine that you are an American factory worker in 1944. After paying your bills you have some money left over. You could use it to buy something you want now, like new work clothes or you could use it to buy war bonds.

1 Think about the trade-offs. You could use the work clothes, but you would not get any money back from this purchase. By buying war bonds, you are helping the war effort, but you would have to wait a while to earn interest on your bonds. What are the trade-offs of buying war bonds?

2 Think of the opportunity costs. You do not have enough money to buy both work clothes and war bonds, so you have to give up one. If you buy war bonds, you would be giving up something you want now, to earn money later. What are the opportunity costs of buying war bonds?

▶ APPLY WHAT YOU LEARNED

Imagine that you want to buy a book and rent a movie, but you do not have enough money for both. Explain to a partner the trade-offs and the opportunity costs of your choices.

People lined up to buy war bonds in New York in 1945.

CITIZENSHIP SKILLS

Winning the War

1901 **1951** **2001**

1942–1945

Worb War II was a new kind of war. Instead of fighting from trenches, as had been done in World War I, soldiers used tanks, ships, and airplanes to quickly move from battle to battle. Bombs dropped from larger, faster airplanes destroyed whole cities.

World War II was also fought over a much larger area than any other war—almost half the world. It was fought on two major **fronts**, or battle lines, at the same time. The first was in Africa and Europe. The second was in the Pacific. Victory on both fronts would be needed to win the war.

The Fighting in Africa and Europe

To defeat the Axis Powers in Europe, the Allies decided that they should first gain control of the Mediterranean Sea. To do that, they knew that they would have to defeat the German and Italian forces in North Africa and then invade Italy. By 1942 Adolf Hitler controlled almost all of Europe and most of North Africa.

In 1942 President Roosevelt put General Dwight D. Eisenhower (EYE•zin•how•er) in command of all the American troops in Europe. A respected leader and skilled military planner, Eisenhower led the Americans as they joined in the attack against Axis forces in North Africa. After several months of fighting, the Allies won North Africa in May 1943. They then pushed north through Italy. Although the Italian government surrendered in September 1943, heavy fighting continued in Italy until the Americans captured Rome the next year.

While the Allies were fighting in Italy, they were planning another invasion of Europe, this time on the northern coast of France. On June 6, 1944, the date known as **D day**, the Allies began the largest water-to-land invasion in history.

MAIN IDEA
Read to learn how the Allies defeated the Axis Powers.

WHY IT MATTERS
World War II changed the world greatly and made people wonder if anyone could survive another world war.

VOCABULARY
front
D day
island-hopping

General Dwight D. Eisenhower was commander of all the American troops in Europe.

General Eisenhower, who earlier that year had become the commander of all Allied forces in Europe, led the D day invasion. On the morning of June 6, he told his troops,

❝ **You are about to embark upon the great crusade. . . . The hopes and prayers of liberty-loving people everywhere march with you.** ❞

On D day about 2,700 ships sailed across the English Channel from Britain. On board were more than 175,000 troops from the United States, Britain, and Canada. The troops landed on the beaches of Normandy, in France, where German forces met them with heavy gunfire.

Many soldiers gave their lives on D day, but the invasion was successful. The Allies broke through the German lines and began moving inland from the west. By the end of June, there were about 1 million Allied troops in France. They slowly pushed the enemy back toward Germany. At the same time, forces from the Soviet Union were pushing back the German armies from the east. The Allied troops met near Berlin, Germany's capital, in April 1945. There they learned that Hitler had killed himself.

Berlin fell to the Soviets on May 2, 1945, and the German military leaders asked to surrender. On May 8 the Allies accepted Germany's surrender. This day was called V-E Day, or Victory in Europe Day. It marked the end of the war in Europe.

REVIEW **What was the D Day invasion?**

FAST FACT During World War II, battleships were named after states, submarines after fish and marine animals, cruisers after cities or territories, and destroyers after military heroes.

The Pacific Front

Although the war was over in Europe, it raged on in the Pacific. The battle plan there called for the Allies to defeat Japan by forcing its troops back from the islands they had conquered. This plan of **island-hopping** meant that Allied troops would take back the islands one at a time until they reached Tokyo, Japan's capital. At the same time, the Allies would bomb Japan from the air. The first of these attacks took place in 1942, when a surprise bombing raid was led against Tokyo and other Japanese cities.

The Japanese controlled thousands of small islands in the Pacific. The Allies decided to take back only the most important ones. Still, Allied leaders knew that island-hopping would be costly. Early battles, such as the one on the island of Guadalcanal (gwah•duhl•kuh•NAL), proved this to be true. More than 1,600 Allied troops were killed.

The Allies, under the command of Americans, General Douglas MacArthur and Admiral Chester W. Nimitz, pressed on, capturing island after island. As the Allies got closer to Japan, however, the losses grew. At Iwo Jima (EE•woh JEE•muh), an island 750 miles (1,207 km) from Tokyo, more than 4,000 American soldiers lost their lives. More than 20,000 Japanese soldiers died. At Okinawa (oh•kuh•NAH•wah), about 11,000 Americans died. The Japanese lost more than 100,000 people. The Japanese were not going to give up easily.

REVIEW Who commanded the Allied forces in the Pacific?

A CLOSER LOOK
D day Invasion at Normandy

Ships carried American, British, and Canadian soldiers across the English Channel to attack the German forces along the coast of France. This picture shows the American forces that took part.

1. German pillbox bunker
2. German soldiers
3. the English Channel
4. American soldier transports
5. American soldiers
6. American tanks
7. American tank transports
8. American destroyers and battleships
9. American fighter planes

Why do you think ships and planes were used in the Allied invasion of Normandy?

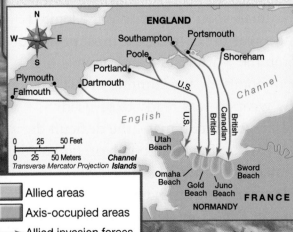

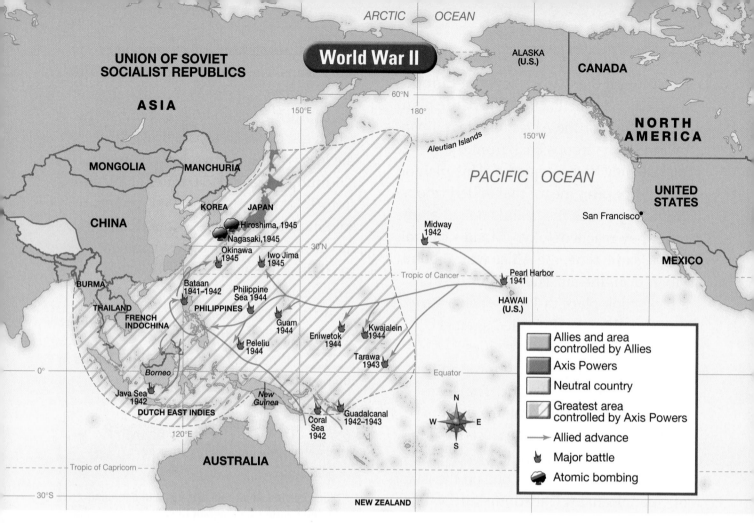

World War II

UNION OF SOVIET
SOCIALIST REPUBLICS

ALASKA
(U.S.)

CANADA

ASIA

NORTH
AMERICA

MONGOLIA   MANCHURIA

PACIFIC OCEAN

Aleutian Islands

CHINA

KOREA   JAPAN

Hiroshima, 1945

Nagasaki,1945

Okinawa
1945

Iwo Jima
1945

Midway
1942

UNITED
STATES

San Francisco

MEXICO

Pearl Harbor
1941

HAWAII
(U.S.)

Tropic of Cancer

BURMA

Bataan
1941–1942

Philippine
Sea 1944

PHILIPPINES

THAILAND

FRENCH
INDOCHINA

Guam
1944

Eniwetok
1944

Kwajalein
1944

Peleliu
1944

Tarawa
1943

Equator

Borneo

Java Sea
1942

DUTCH EAST INDIES

New
Guinea

Coral
Sea
1942

Guadalcanal
1942–1943

AUSTRALIA

Tropic of Capricorn

NEW ZEALAND

Legend:

- Allies and area controlled by Allies
- Axis Powers
- Neutral country
- Greatest area controlled by Axis Powers
- → Allied advance
- Major battle
- Atomic bombing

GEOGRAPHY THEME

Location **During the war, almost the whole world was divided between the Allied and the Axis Powers.**

❖ **Why was the location of the United States helpful?**

The War Ends

President Franklin D. Roosevelt, who had been elected to a fourth term in 1944, did not live to see the end of the war. He died on April 12, 1945. Vice President Harry S. Truman became President.

Truman soon learned that the United States was developing the most powerful bomb the world had ever known—the atom bomb. By the summer of 1945, this new weapon was ready to be used. President Truman made the difficult decision to drop the atom bomb on Japan. He wanted to end the war quickly.

On August 6, 1945, the American bomber *Enola Gay* flew over the city of Hiroshima (hir•uh•SHEE•muh), Japan. A single bomb was dropped. There was a flash like an exploding sun. The bomb flattened and burned a huge area of Hiroshima and killed more than 75,000 people.

As terrible as the atom bomb attack was, Japan did not surrender. On August 9, the United States dropped an atom bomb on Nagasaki (nah•guh•SAH•kee). Then Japan agreed to surrender. On August 15, Americans celebrated V-J Day, or Victory over Japan Day. World War II was over.

REVIEW **Why did the Japanese finally surrender?**

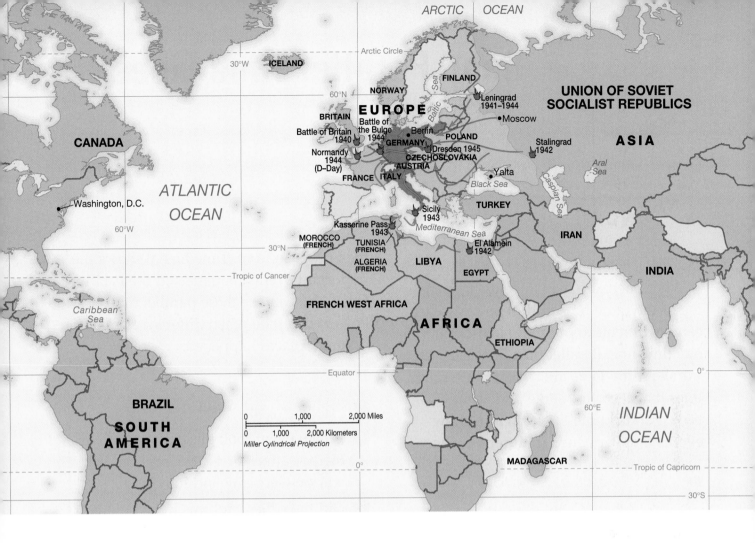

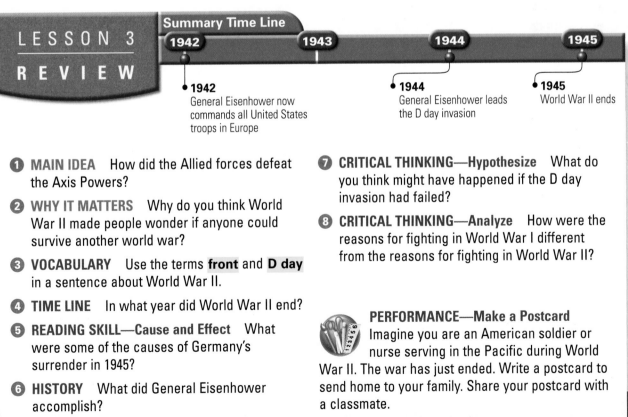

Chapter 15 ■ 569

LESSON 3 REVIEW

Summary Time Line

| 1942 | 1943 | 1944 | 1945 |

1942
General Eisenhower now commands all United States troops in Europe

1944
General Eisenhower leads the D day invasion

1945
World War II ends

❶ **MAIN IDEA**   How did the Allied forces defeat the Axis Powers?

❷ **WHY IT MATTERS**   Why do you think World War II made people wonder if anyone could survive another world war?

❸ **VOCABULARY**   Use the terms **front** and **D day** in a sentence about World War II.

❹ **TIME LINE**   In what year did World War II end?

❺ **READING SKILL—Cause and Effect**   What were some of the causes of Germany's surrender in 1945?

❻ **HISTORY**   What did General Eisenhower accomplish?

❼ **CRITICAL THINKING—Hypothesize**   What do you think might have happened if the D day invasion had failed?

❽ **CRITICAL THINKING—Analyze**   How were the reasons for fighting in World War I different from the reasons for fighting in World War II?

PERFORMANCE—Make a Postcard
Imagine you are an American soldier or nurse serving in the Pacific during World War II. The war has just ended. Write a postcard to send home to your family. Share your postcard with a classmate.

Read Parallel Time Lines

VOCABULARY

parallel time line

WHY IT MATTERS

When there are many events happening at the same time in different places, it can be difficult to put them in order on one time line. Parallel time lines can help. **Parallel time lines** are two or more time lines that show the same period of time. Parallel time lines can also show events that happened in different places.

WHAT YOU NEED TO KNOW

The parallel time lines on this page show events that took place in 1945, the last year of World War II. Time Line A shows the important events that affected the European front. Time Line B shows the important events that affected the Pacific front. You can use these parallel time lines to compare when different events in different places happened.

PRACTICE THE SKILL

1. Which event took place first, the Pearl Harbor attack or the declaration of war on Germany and Italy?

2. Did the Allies capture Guam before or after they captured North Africa?

3. Why do you think the label *Truman becomes President* is on both lines?

TIME LINE A: THE WAR IN EUROPE

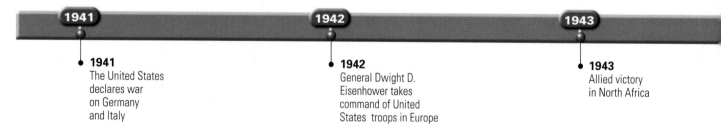

1941
1941
The United States declares war on Germany and Italy

1942
1942
General Dwight D. Eisenhower takes command of United States troops in Europe

1943
1943
Allied victory in North Africa

TIME LINE B: THE WAR IN THE PACIFIC

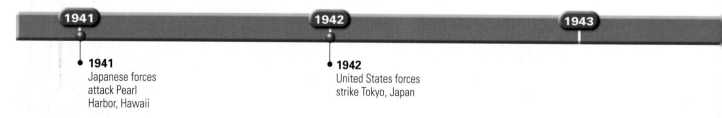

1941
1941
Japanese forces attack Pearl Harbor, Hawaii

1942
1942
United States forces strike Tokyo, Japan

1943

4 What happened in the Pacific the year that Dwight D. Eisenhower arrived to command United States forces in Europe?

The *Enola Gay* sits on a runway on Tinian Island in the Pacific after dropping an atom bomb on Hiroshima, Japan.

▶ **APPLY WHAT YOU LEARNED**

Create parallel time lines of events that have happened in your lifetime. Use one time line to show the important events in your life, beginning with the year you were born and ending with the present year. Use the other time line to show important events that have taken place in the United States during these same years.

1944

1944
D Day
Invasion

1945

1945
Harry S. Truman becomes President of the United States

V-E Day

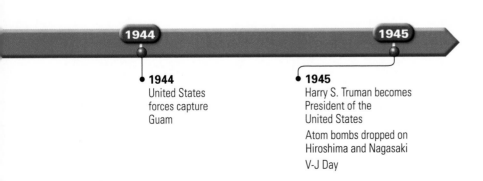

1944

1944
United States forces capture Guam

1945

1945
Harry S. Truman becomes President of the United States

Atom bombs dropped on Hiroshima and Nagasaki

V-J Day

CHART AND GRAPH SKILLS

MAIN IDEA
Read to learn how the end
of the war brought about
another threat to
democracy.

WHY IT MATTERS
Relations between the
two major powers that
emerged from the war
would shape world events
for almost the next half
century.

VOCABULARY
Holocaust
refugee
communism
free world
cold war

The Effects of the War

1945–1948

World War II caused more death and destruction than any
other war in history. About 17 million soldiers died as a result
of the war, including more than 400,000 American soldiers. No
one knows for certain how many civilians were killed, but the
number was in the millions. The end of the war also focused
the world's attention on another horror—what had happened
in the Nazis' concentration camps.

The Holocaust

Not until the war in Europe was over did people discover
everything that Hitler and the Nazis had done. As Allied
troops marched across central Europe toward Berlin, they freed
people in the Nazis' concentration camps. The Allies learned
that more than 6 million men, women, and children had been
murdered in those camps. One of the largest of them was at
Auschwitz (OWSH•vits), in Poland. About one and a half million
people were killed at this concentration camp.

The photograph below shows the harsh, barbed-wire fence that surrounded the
concentration camp at Auschwitz.

Many Nazi leaders were tried for their crimes in a court in Nuremberg, Germany.

The Nazis killed people for many reasons. Many were killed for their religious and political beliefs. Others were killed because they were ill or disabled and could not work. The largest group of victims were Jews, the people Hitler blamed for Germany's problems.

During the war more than 6 million Jewish people were murdered on Hitler's orders. This terrible mass murder of more than two-thirds of all European Jews came to be known as the **Holocaust** (HOH•luh•kawst). Hitler had called it the "final solution to the Jewish question." It was a planned attempt to destroy an entire people.

Beginning in 1945, Nazi leaders accused of committing these deeds were brought to trial by the Allies. The most important trials were held in the German city of Nuremberg. Many of the Nazi leaders were convicted and sentenced to death for their crimes.

REVIEW What was the Holocaust?

Plans for Peace

When World War II ended, cities and towns across Europe and in Japan and other places where the fighting had taken place were in ruins. In some cities more than 9 of every 10 buildings were too badly damaged to be used. Many people had no homes, no jobs, and often nothing to eat. They became **refugees**— people who seek shelter and safety elsewhere. They traveled from place to place in search of food and a safe place to live.

The United States came out of World War II as the strongest nation in the world. Americans used this strength to help feed and clothe war refugees and rebuild war-torn countries. The United States worked with other nations to create agencies that supplied food, clothing, shelter, and medical care to millions of people around the world. Much of the money spent by these agencies came from people in the United States.

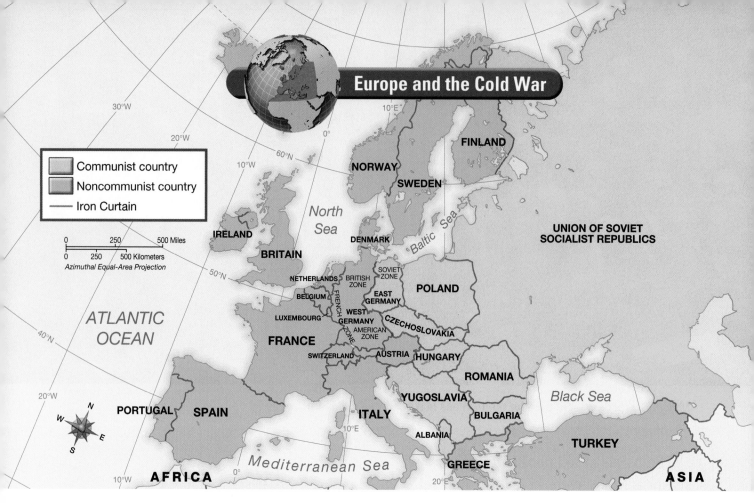

Europe and the Cold War

Communist country
Noncommunist country
—— Iron Curtain

0   250   500 Miles
0   250   500 Kilometers
Azimuthal Equal-Area Projection

FINLAND

NORWAY

SWEDEN

North Sea

IRELAND

DENMARK

Baltic Sea

BRITAIN

NETHERLANDS

SOVIET ZONE

UNION OF SOVIET SOCIALIST REPUBLICS

POLAND

BRITISH ZONE

BELGIUM

EAST GERMANY

FRENCH ZONE

WEST GERMANY

LUXEMBOURG

CZECHOSLOVAKIA

AMERICAN ZONE

FRANCE

SWITZERLAND

AUSTRIA

HUNGARY

ATLANTIC OCEAN

ROMANIA

Black Sea

PORTUGAL

SPAIN

ITALY

YUGOSLAVIA

BULGARIA

ALBANIA

TURKEY

GREECE

AFRICA

Mediterranean Sea

ASIA

Place World War II changed Europe in ways that would affect the world for years to come.

❷ What does this map show about changes that took place in Germany after World War II?

Even before the fighting ended, the United States and the other Allies had begun to make plans for peace. They decided to abolish Germany's armed forces and make the Nazi party illegal. They also decided to take some land away from Germany and divide the country into four parts. Each of the major Allies—the United States, Britain, France, and the Soviet Union—took control of one part.

Just as they had after World War I, world leaders again turned to the idea of an organization of nations. This time the United States supported the idea. In April 1945, delegates from 50 countries met in San Francisco to form the United Nations,

or UN. Today, the UN is located in New York City. The purpose of the UN is to keep world peace and promote cooperation among nations.

REVIEW What four countries took over parts of Germany after the war?

A Changed World

Even as plans for peace were being made, new conflicts were beginning. The United States and the Soviet Union had been allies during World War II. But that changed quickly once the war ended. The Soviet Union was a communist nation. **Communism** is a social and economic system in which all land and industries are owned by the government. Individuals have few rights and little freedom.

When the war ended, the Soviet Union began setting up communist governments in the eastern European countries it had invaded during the war. The **free world**—the United States and its allies in the fight against communism— saw this as a threat to freedom.

At the urging of President Truman and other leaders, such as Secretary of State George C. Marshall, the United States began to help countries fight communism by giving them military and economic aid. In 1948 the United States Congress passed the European Recovery Act, also known as the Marshall Plan. It provided $13 billion to help European countries rebuild their economies. President Truman believed that an economically healthy Europe would have little interest in communism.

Hostility, or unfriendliness, soon developed between the free world and the

President Harry S. Truman (left) meets with Secretary of State George C. Marshall (right).

communist nations. This hostility became known as the Cold War. A **cold war** is fought mostly with propaganda and money rather than with soldiers and weapons. For much of the second half of the twentieth century, the Cold War shaped many world events.

REVIEW How did the United States help countries fight communism?

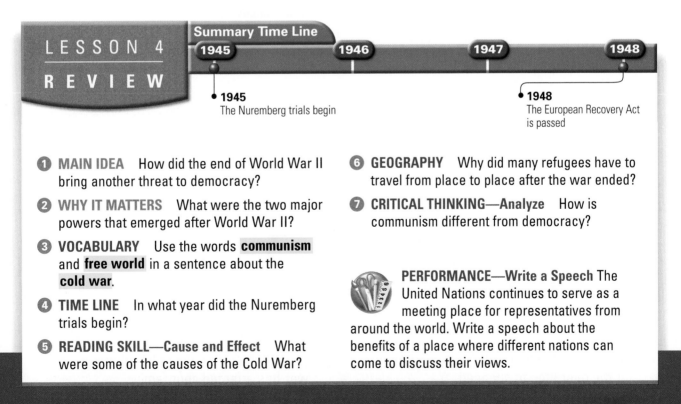

LESSON 4 REVIEW

Summary Time Line

| 1945 | 1946 | 1947 | 1948 |

● **1945**
The Nuremberg trials begin

● **1948**
The European Recovery Act is passed

1. **MAIN IDEA** How did the end of World War II bring another threat to democracy?

2. **WHY IT MATTERS** What were the two major powers that emerged after World War II?

3. **VOCABULARY** Use the words **communism** and **free world** in a sentence about the **cold war**.

4. **TIME LINE** In what year did the Nuremberg trials begin?

5. **READING SKILL—Cause and Effect** What were some of the causes of the Cold War?

6. **GEOGRAPHY** Why did many refugees have to travel from place to place after the war ended?

7. **CRITICAL THINKING—Analyze** How is communism different from democracy?

PERFORMANCE—Write a Speech The United Nations continues to serve as a meeting place for representatives from around the world. Write a speech about the benefits of a place where different nations can come to discuss their views.

15 Review and Test Preparation

USE YOUR READING SKILLS

Complete this graphic organizer by determining the causes and effects of the involvement of the United States in World War II. A copy of this graphic organizer appears on page 148 of the Activity Book.

World War II and the United States

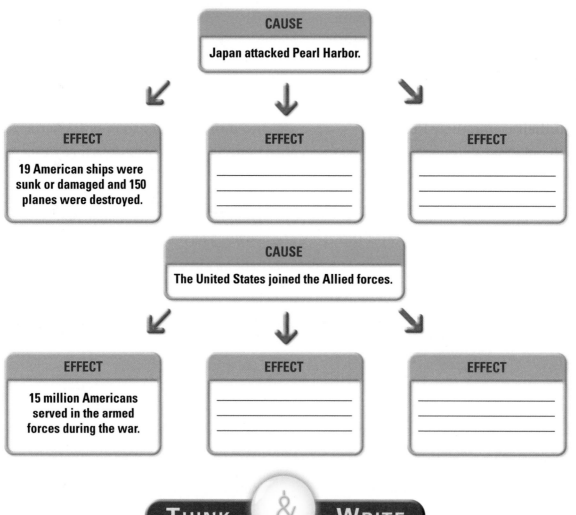

CAUSE

Japan attacked Pearl Harbor.

EFFECT

19 American ships were sunk or damaged and 150 planes were destroyed.

EFFECT

EFFECT

CAUSE

The United States joined the Allied forces.

EFFECT

15 million Americans served in the armed forces during the war.

EFFECT

EFFECT

THINK & WRITE

Write a Conversation   Write a conversation that could have taken place between Dwight D. Eisenhower and some of his advisers the night before the D day invasion. The individuals should discuss how important it is for the operation to succeed.

Write a Diary Entry   Imagine that you are living during World War II. Write a diary entry about going shopping with your family. Describe the ways the war has affected what you can buy. Also describe other ways the war has affected your family.

1939
World War II begins as German forces invade Poland

1941
The United States enters World War II

1942
Japanese Americans ordered into relocation camps

1944
The D day invasion takes place

1945
World War II ends

1948
The European Recovery Act is passed

USE THE TIME LINE

Use the chapter summary time line to answer these questions.

1 When did World War II begin?

2 How many years after the D day invasion was the European Recovery Act passed?

USE VOCABULARY

Use each term in a complete sentence that will help explain its meaning.

3 **concentration camp** (p. 555)

4 **civilian** (p. 557)

5 **interest** (p. 562)

6 **D day** (p. 565)

7 **Holocaust** (p. 573)

RECALL FACTS

Answer these questions.

8 How did the United States help Great Britain even before American forces entered World War II?

9 Why did the federal government set up a rationing program during World War II?

10 What was V-J day?

Write the letter of the best choice.

11 **TEST PREP** One major effect of the D day invasion was that—
  F it caused Germany to surrender.
  G it helped the Allies move into France.
  H it caused Japan to surrender.
  J it helped the Allies gain control of Italy.

12 **TEST PREP** After World War II, world leaders came together to form—
  A the United Nations.
  B the League of Nations.
  C the Red Cross.
  D the Works Progress Administration.

THINK CRITICALLY

13 What do you think was Franklin D. Roosevelt's greatest accomplishment?

14 What do you think was Dwight D. Eisenhower's greatest contribution to the war effort?

15 How did World War II change the world?

APPLY SKILLS

Predict a Historical Outcome
Review the information on page 559. Then answer the following question.

16 What do you predict happened to relations between the United States and the Soviet Union in the decades after World War II? Explain how you arrived at your answer.

Make Economic Choices
Review the information on page 564. Then answer the following question.

17 Describe a time when you had to think about the trade-off and opportunity cost before you made a purchase.

Read Parallel Time Lines
Review the time lines on pages 570–571. Then answer the following question.

18 Did the D day invasion occur before or after Harry S. Truman became President?

RONALD REAGAN PRESIDENTIAL LIBRARY

The Ronald Reagan Presidential Library is one of ten presidential libraries. In this photograph taken outside the library, a piece of the Berlin Wall is displayed. The original wall was 96 miles (154 km) long and divided Germany for almost 30 years. Helping bring down the wall was one of President Reagan's greatest accomplishments.

LOCATE IT

CALIFORNIA

Ronald Reagan Presidential Library

16

Into Modern Times

" Mr. Gorbachev, tear down this wall. "

—Ronald Reagan, June 12, 1987, in a speech at the Berlin Wall

---

CHAPTER READING SKILL

Predict a Likely Outcome

When people make **predictions**, they use information and past experiences to try to determine what will happen next.

As you read this chapter, predict likely outcomes for events that affected the United States in the second half of the twentieth century.

EVENTS → FACTS → PREDICTIONS → OUTCOME

1

The Early Years of the Cold War

1901   **1951**   **2001**

1950–1970

MAIN IDEA

Read to learn how the Cold War affected relations between the free world and communist nations.

WHY IT MATTERS

The race to build more powerful weapons that started during the Cold War continues to affect world affairs today.

VOCABULARY

superpower
airlift
cease-fire
arms race
satellite

The Cold War years were a frightening time for many people. The United States and the Soviet Union had become the world's most powerful nations, and conflicts developed between them. Because of the roles each country played in world events at that time, they were called **superpowers**. Even though the conflicts between these two superpowers were fought mostly with words and economic weapons, the threat of a real war was always present.

A Crisis in Berlin

The United States, Britain, and France worked to rebuild the economy of West Germany after World War II. West Germany was made up of the areas that these Western Allies had controlled since the war ended. They wanted to see West Germany become a democracy. East Germany, the area held by the Soviet Union, had a communist government.

FAST FACT American and British pilots made more than 272,000 flights over East Germany during the Berlin Airlift.

Germany After World War II

Division of Berlin

ATLANTIC OCEAN

DENMARK

American Zone

British Zone

NETHERLANDS

Berlin

Soviet Zone

EAST GERMANY

BELGIUM

French Zone

WEST GERMANY

American Zone

LUXEMBOURG

FRANCE

SWITZERLAND

AUSTRIA

HUNGARY

CZECHOSLOVAKIA

POLAND

YUGOSLAVIA

French Sector

British Sector

West Berlin

American Sector

EAST GERMANY

East Soviet Sector

Berlin

EAST GERMANY

0 150 300 Miles
0 150 300 Kilometers
Azimuthal Equal-Area Projection

N W E S

☐ Communist country
☐ Noncommunist country
— Iron Curtain — Zone border

GEOGRAPHY THEME

Regions Police stand guard (left) at the Berlin Wall that divided East and West Berlin.

❷ Which European countries were communist countries?

Berlin, the capital of Germany, had also been divided after the war. The Western Allies controlled the areas that made up West Berlin, while the Soviets controlled East Berlin.

In June 1948 the Soviet Union blocked all travel between Berlin and West Germany. The Soviets hoped this would force the Western Allies out of West Berlin. The Allies, however, refused to leave.

To get around the blockade, the Allies started the Berlin Airlift. An **airlift** is a system of moving supplies by airplane. American and British pilots carried more than 2 million tons of supplies to West Berlin. In May 1949, the Soviets lifted the blockade.

The situation in Berlin remained tense even after the blockade ended, and many people tried to leave East Berlin to escape communist rule. In 1961 the East German government, with Soviet help, built a fence to keep its people from leaving. East Germany later replaced the fence with a concrete wall. The Berlin Wall, as it came to be known, was guarded by soldiers ready to shoot those who tried to cross it.

REVIEW What was the Soviet Union's goal in blockading Berlin?

The Korean War

Like Germany, the Asian country of Korea was divided after World War II. Soviet troops occupied North Korea, and American troops occupied South Korea.

Chapter 16 ▪ 581

A Divided Korea

SOVIET UNION

CHINA

0   50   100 Miles
0   50   100 Kilometers
Conic Projection

42°N

Chongjin

NORTH
KOREA

40°N

Hŭngnam

Sea of
Japan

Pyongyang

Cease-fire
line, 1953

Prewar boundary

38°N   38°N

Panmunjom

Inchon   Seoul

Yellow

N

Sea

W   E

SOUTH

S

KOREA

36°N   36°N

Pusan   132°E

Strait

130°E

34°N

Cheju
Island

126°E   JAPAN

⊛ National capital

128°E

GEOGRAPHY THEME

Movement   The cease-fire line changed the northern boundary of South Korea.

❖ Where was the pre-war boundary?

In 1948 North Korea formed a communist government, and South Korea formed a republic.

In 1950 the North Korean army, which had been trained and equipped by the Soviet Union, invaded South Korea. North Korea wanted to make all of Korea communist.

President Truman sent more soldiers to South Korea to stop the invasion. The United Nations also sent troops. In all, about 15 countries were now fighting the Korean War.

The Korean War became a major issue in the 1952 presidential election. Dwight D. Eisenhower promised to end the war if he were elected. Soon after his election he kept his promise. By 1953 the North Korean troops had been pushed back into North Korea. A **cease-fire**, or a temporary end to the conflict, was declared and an armistice was signed. South Korea remained a republic.

REVIEW   What started the Korean War?

The Arms Race

The Cold War started an arms race between the two superpowers. In an **arms race** one country builds weapons to protect itself against another country. The other country then builds more weapons to protect itself. Both the United States and the Soviet Union believed that having the strongest weapons would keep their people safe.

Soon after the United States built the first atom bombs, the Soviet Union built its own atom bombs. In response, the United States created an even more powerful bomb—the hydrogen bomb, or the H-bomb. By the 1960s both of the superpowers had also developed missiles that could carry the new H-bombs to targets that were halfway around the world.

REVIEW Why did the arms race happen?

The Race into Space

The two superpowers also took the Cold War into space. In 1957 the Soviet Union surprised the United States by launching *Sputnik* (SPUT•nik). *Sputnik* was the world's first space **satellite**, an object that orbits Earth. Because of *Sputnik*, the United States sped its own efforts to explore space. In 1958 the National Aeronautics (air•uh•NAW•tiks) and Space Administration, or NASA, was set up to develop the nation's space program.

In 1961 John F. Kennedy became President of the United States. At his inauguration, Kennedy tried to inspire Americans to work for the good of their country. He said,

> 66 Ask not what your country can do for you; ask what you can do for your country. 99

President Kennedy soon set a new goal for the United States—to put a person on the moon by the end of the decade. In 1962 John Glenn became the first American astronaut to orbit Earth. A series of explorations called the Apollo program then prepared for a moon landing. On July 16, 1969, *Apollo 11* blasted off from Cape Canaveral, Florida. On board were astronauts Neil Armstrong, Edwin "Buzz" Aldrin, Jr., and Michael Collins. Four days later, on July 20, Armstrong became the first person to walk on the moon. President Kennedy's goal had been met.

America's interest in space exploration, however, did not end with the first moon landing. Scientists and astronomers such as Carl Sagan continued to draw people's attention with their work. In the 1960s, Sagan worked at a space observatory. There, he participated in a project trying to find signs of life on other planets. Later, Sagan helped NASA plan several crewless missions to explore and take pictures of the solar system.

REVIEW What was the Apollo Program?

Apollo 11 (far left) took astronauts into space. The plaque (above) is a replica of the plaque Armstrong and Aldrin left on the surface of the moon (left).

A Crisis in Cuba

Soon after President Kennedy took office, Cold War problems began to take up much of his time. In October 1962 Kennedy learned that the Soviet Union had built launch sites for missiles in Cuba, just 90 miles (145 km) off the southern tip of Florida. Fidel Castro had taken control of Cuba in 1959. With the help of the Soviet Union, he had formed a communist government there.

Kennedy knew that the Soviets could use the missiles in Cuba to attack the United States, so he ordered a blockade of Cuba. The United States Navy would keep Soviet ships that were carrying missiles from reaching Cuba. Americans worried as they listened to the news.

John F. Kennedy

What if the ships refused to stop? Would there be war?

Thirteen days later, the Soviet Union agreed to stop sending missiles to Cuba and to remove all the missiles that were already there. In response, the United States agreed to end the blockade and to remove American missiles from near the Soviet Union. War had been avoided.

On November 22, 1963, President Kennedy and Jacqueline, his wife, visited Dallas, Texas, to meet with supporters there. As their car drove through the streets, several shots rang out. President Kennedy was killed. A few hours later, Vice President Lyndon B. Johnson took the oath of office as the new President.

REVIEW How was the crisis in Cuba ended?

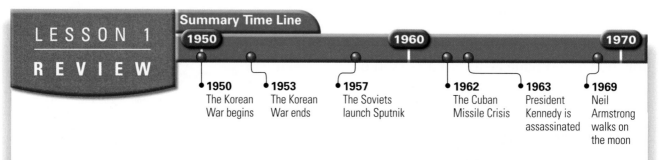

LESSON 1 REVIEW

Summary Time Line

1950 — 1960 — 1970

- **1950** The Korean War begins
- **1953** The Korean War ends
- **1957** The Soviets launch Sputnik
- **1962** The Cuban Missile Crisis
- **1963** President Kennedy is assassinated
- **1969** Neil Armstrong walks on the moon

1 **MAIN IDEA** How did the Cold War affect relations between the free world and communist nations?

2 **WHY IT MATTERS** How do weapons built during the Cold War still affect the world today?

3 **VOCABULARY** What do you think each word part of **cease-fire** means?

4 **TIME LINE** What year did the United States first land a person on the moon?

5 **READING SKILL—Predict a Likely Outcome** What do you think might have happened if the Soviet Union had not agreed to remove its nuclear missiles from Cuba?

6 **SCIENCE AND TECHNOLOGY** How did Neil Armstrong and Carl Sagan contribute to people's knowledge of space?

7 **CRITICAL THINKING—Analyze** How did the Korean War become a fight for democracy?

PERFORMANCE—Present a News Report Imagine you are a news reporter. Write a news report on the moon landing. Then read your report to the class.

Working for Equal Rights

1901   1951   2001

1960–1980

MAIN IDEA
Read to learn how individuals and groups in the United States worked to gain equal rights.

WHY IT MATTERS
The movement for equal rights made it possible for more people to participate fully in our American democracy.

VOCABULARY
nonviolence
integration
migrant worker

Working to maintain peace was not the only struggle that Americans faced after World War II. Many people across the United States continued to struggle for equal rights.

A Supreme Court Ruling

Seven-year-old Linda Brown of Topeka, Kansas, did not understand why laws in her state made African American children attend separate schools from whites. Federal laws also allowed this segregation as long as the separate schools were equal. In most cases they really were not.

In the early 1950s, Linda Brown's family and 12 other African American families decided to try to get these laws changed. The NAACP agreed to help them. One of its lawyers, Thurgood Marshall, presented their case before the United States Supreme Court.

Thurgood Marshall (left) argued against school segregation so that students, like Linda Brown (right), could get an equal education.

Rosa Parks is fingerprinted after her arrest for refusing to move to the back of the bus.

In this case, known as *Brown v. Board of Education of Topeka*, Marshall argued that separate schools did not provide an equal education.

In 1954 the Supreme Court made a decision that supported Marshall's argument. Chief Justice Earl Warren said, "In the field of education the doctrine [idea] of 'separate but equal' has no place." The Court ordered an end to segregation in public schools. However, many states were slow to obey that order. Their schools and many other public places remained segregated.

REVIEW Who was Thurgood Marshall?

A Boycott in Montgomery

On December 1, 1955, Rosa Parks got on a city bus in Montgomery, Alabama, and sat in the middle section. Under Alabama law, African Americans could sit in the middle section only if the seats were not needed for white passengers. As the bus filled up, the driver told Rosa Parks to move to the back. When she refused, the driver called the police, and Parks was arrested.

African Americans were angry when they heard what had happened. They knew the bus company needed the money it earned from them. So they passed the word—"Don't take the bus on Monday." A bus boycott began.

One of the leaders of the boycott was Martin Luther King, Jr., a young minister in Montgomery. For almost a year, King and other African Americans boycotted the buses. King said that by working together they could bring about change peacefully. Finally, in November 1956, the Supreme Court ruled that all public transportation companies had to end segregation.

REVIEW What were the effects of Rosa Parks's actions?

The Struggle for Justice

Many African Americans looked to Martin Luther King, Jr., as their leader in the fight for civil rights. King believed

in using **nonviolence**, or peaceful ways, to bring about change. He said that non-violence would change people's minds and hearts, while violence would only make matters worse.

Across the country, African Americans protested segregation. They held sit-ins at lunch counters, and at other public places. These were protests at which African Americans would not move from their seats at places that were segregated. African Americans also held marches to protest segregation and support **integration**, or the bringing together of people of all races.

In 1963 about 250,000 people gathered for a march in Washington, D.C. The marchers were there to show their support for a new civil rights law that Congress was debating. Martin Luther King, Jr., spoke to the marchers about his hopes for the future. He said, "I have a dream that one day on the red hills of Georgia the sons of former slaves and the sons of former slaveowners will be able to sit down together at the table of brotherhood. . . ."

In 1964 Congress passed the Civil Rights Act of 1964, which made segregation in public places illegal. It also said that people of all races should have equal job opportunities.

REVIEW How did Martin Luther King, Jr., work for civil rights?

Other Ideas

In 1964 Martin Luther King, Jr., won the Nobel Peace Prize for his peaceful efforts to bring about social change. However, some African American leaders disagreed with King's belief in nonviolent protest. Malcolm X was one of them. He was a member of the Nation of Islam, or the Black Muslims. He wanted change to happen faster.

Martin Luther King, Jr., (shown at center) marched in support of a new civil rights law.

When Lyndon Johnson became President, he worked hard to help ensure that the Civil Rights Act of 1964 became law. The law prohibited segregation in public places, and it created the Equal Employment Opportunity Commission (EEOC). In 1965 Johnson outlawed unfair voting rules, which led to a large increase in the number of registered African American voters.

Analyze the Value

1 What did the Civil Rights Act of 1964 do?

2 Make it Relevant Write a paragraph about why it is important that everyone is treated equally.

Malcolm X was named Malcolm Little but he changed his last name to X to stand for the unknown African name his family had lost through slavery. In his early speeches Malcolm X called for a strict separation between white people and African Americans. Only in this way, he said, could African Americans truly be free. Later, after a trip to the Islamic holy city of Mecca in 1964, he talked less about separation and more about cooperation among groups.

Malcolm X had little time to act on his new ideas. He was assassinated in 1965. Three years later, in April 1968, Martin Luther King, Jr., also was assassinated. Even though African Americans had lost two important leaders, they kept working for justice.

REVIEW How did Malcolm X's ideas change?

Cesar Chavez

Civil Rights for Other Groups

Following the lead of the African American Civil Rights movement, other groups worked for equal rights. American Indians, for example, formed groups to work for the rights that they had been promised in earlier treaties with the federal government. In many cases those treaties had not been honored. Then, in 1975, Congress passed the Self-Determination and Educational Assistance Act. For the first time, Indian tribes could run their own businesses and health and education programs.

To help improve the lives of farm workers, Cesar Chavez, Dolores Huerta (HWAIR•tah), and others organized a group that would become the United Farm Workers (UFW). Most of its members were Mexican American migrant workers. A **migrant worker** is someone who moves from place to place with the seasons, harvesting crops.

Cesar Chavez called for nonviolent action to solve problems. In 1965 he organized a strike by California grape pickers and started a nationwide boycott of grapes. His goal was to get better wages and improve working conditions for farm workers. He met this goal in 1970.

Like other groups, women organized to work for change. The Civil Rights Act of 1964 said that all people should have equal job opportunities, but many jobs were still not open to women. When men and women did have the same kind of jobs, women were often paid less than men. By the 1970s new laws had been passed saying that employers must treat men and women equally. Jobs now had to be open to both men or women.

As a result, more women began careers in jobs that were once held only by men. Some women won elections and became mayors, governors, and members of Congress. In 1981 Sandra Day O'Connor became the first woman appointed to the United States Supreme Court. In 1984 Geraldine Ferraro became the first

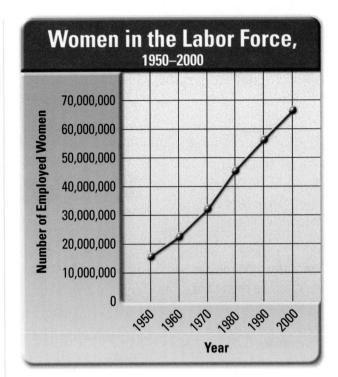

Women in the Labor Force, 1950–2000

Analyze Graphs The number of women in the labor force increased from 1950 to 2000.

◈ About how many women were employed in 2000?

woman nominated for Vice President by a major political party.

REVIEW What did Cesar Chavez accomplish?

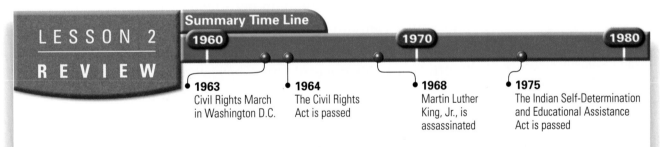

LESSON 2 REVIEW

Summary Time Line

1960 — 1970 — 1980

1963
Civil Rights March in Washington D.C.

1964
The Civil Rights Act is passed

1968
Martin Luther King, Jr., is assassinated

1975
The Indian Self-Determination and Educational Assistance Act is passed

1 **MAIN IDEA** How did individuals and groups try to gain equal rights?

2 **WHY IT MATTERS** What did the movement for equal rights make possible?

3 **VOCABULARY** Use the word integration in a sentence about Martin Luther King, Jr.

4 **TIME LINE** When was the march on Washington, D.C.?

5 **READING SKILL—Predict a Likely Outcome** What might have happened if the bus boycott had not taken place?

6 **HISTORY** How did the *Brown v. Board of Education of Topeka* case change public schools?

7 **CRITICAL THINKING—Synthesize** Why were people willing to protest for civil rights?

PERFORMANCE—Deliver a Speech
Martin Luther King, Jr.'s "I Have a Dream" speech is one of the most famous speeches in American history. Research the speech with your classmates. Then take turns reading parts of the speech aloud.

MAIN IDEA
Read to learn about the causes and effects of the Vietnam War.

WHY IT MATTERS
The Vietnam War divided the American people and caused many of them to question the role of government.

VOCABULARY
arms control
détente
scandal

The Cold War Continues

1901   1951   2001

1955–1975

While many groups in the 1960s were working for equal rights, President Lyndon B. Johnson was working on new government programs that he believed would improve life for all Americans. These programs were all part of Johnson's plans for what he called the Great Society. They included medical care for older people, money to rebuild cities, and help with education, housing, and jobs for those who needed it. At the same time, the United States was becoming deeply involved in another war in Southeast Asia. This war—the Vietnam War—sharply divided the American people.

The Vietnam War

Like Korea, Vietnam was divided into two countries after World War II. North Vietnam became a communist country, and South Vietnam became a republic. In the late 1950s, South Vietnamese communists, called the Vietcong, tried to take over South Vietnam's government. They were helped by North Vietnam. As part of its Cold War plan to stop the spread of communism, the United States sent money, war supplies, and

FAST FACT Approximately 12,000 helicopters were used by American troops in the Vietnam War.

advisers to help South Vietnam fight the Vietcong. China and the Soviet Union sent help to North Vietnam.

By the time Johnson became President in 1963, the Vietcong were winning the war. President Johnson ordered air strikes against North Vietnam. He hoped the bombing would end the war by stopping the flow of supplies from North Vietnam. But the fighting continued.

The first American ground combat forces arrived in South Vietnam in 1965. By 1968 more than 500,000 United States soldiers were serving there. The Vietnam War was now costing the United States billions of dollars each year—and thousands of lives. To pay for both the Vietnam War and the Great Society programs, the government had to raise taxes

This photograph shows President Johnson and some of his Cabinet discussing the war.

and borrow a lot of money. The country's economy began to suffer.

As the number of Americans killed in Vietnam continued to climb, more and more people began to oppose the war. Antiwar protests and marches took place all over the country.

In 1968 President Johnson shocked the nation when he suddenly announced that he would not run for reelection. Later that year, the American people elected a new President—Richard M. Nixon. Nixon called for better training for the South Vietnamese army and for the gradual withdrawal of American troops. That withdrawal began in 1969.

The next year, however, President Nixon sent American soldiers into neighboring Cambodia to destroy war supplies that the North Vietnamese had stored there. When North Vietnam launched a major attack on South Vietnam in 1972, Nixon ordered a naval blockade of North Vietnam and an increase in the bombing.

REVIEW Why did the United States become involved in Vietnam?

Analyze Graphs This graph shows how the rate of inflation has changed over time.

❖ How was the rate of inflation related to the country's changing role in the war?

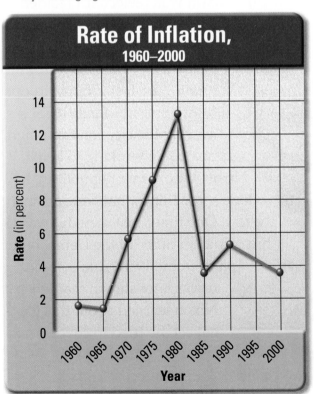

Rate of Inflation, 1960–2000

A Divided Vietnam

CHINA

BURMA

Red River

Hanoi

NORTH VIETNAM

Gulf of Tonkin

Hainan

LAOS

Vientiane

Mekong River

HO CHI MINH TRAIL

Demilitarized Zone

South China Sea

THAILAND

Bangkok

CAMBODIA

SOUTH VIETNAM

Gulf of Thailand

Phnom Penh

Saigon

Mekong Delta

0   100   200 Miles
0   100   200 Kilometers
Mercator Projection

⊛ National capital

GEOGRAPHY THEME

Movement **The Ho Chi Minh Trail was a supply route from North Vietnam to South Vietnam.**

◆ **Why did the trail go through Laos and Cambodia?**

Improved Relations

While the Vietnam War raged on, President Nixon worked to reduce Cold War tensions between the countries of the free world and the communist nations He became the first American President to visit both China and the Soviet Union.

In 1972 Nixon accepted an invitation from China's leader, Mao Zedong (MOW zeh•DOONG), to visit China. As a result of his visit, the two nations agreed to trade with each other and to allow visits from each other's scientific and cultural groups.

Three months after visiting China, Nixon flew to Moscow to meet with Soviet leader Leonid Brezhnev (BREZH•nef). The two nations agreed to increase trade and to work together on scientific and cultural projects. They also agreed on a plan for **arms control**, or limiting the number of weapons that each nation could have. This was the first of several important arms control treaties between the two nations. These agreements marked the beginning of a period of **détente** (day•TAHNT), or an easing of tensions, between the United States and the Soviet Union.

REVIEW **How did President Nixon ease tensions with China and the Soviet Union?**

Nixon Resigns and the Vietnam War Ends

In 1972 Nixon was reelected President. The next year he agreed to a cease-fire in Vietnam. He also agreed to bring the remaining American soldiers back from Vietnam. The last ground troops left Vietnam in March 1973.

During the election campaign, some people working to help Nixon, who was a Republican, had done some things that were against the law. One thing that they did was to break into an office of the Democratic party in the Watergate complex. It was later shown that when Nixon learned about this illegal act, he tried to cover it up.

A Vietnam service medal

1960-

President Nixon announces his plan to resign from office.

The Watergate scandal ended Nixon's presidency. A **scandal** is an action that brings disgrace. On August 9, 1974, Nixon became the first American President to resign. On that same day, Vice President Gerald Ford became President.

Soon after the last American ground troops had left Vietnam, fighting had broken out again. Without the support of American troops, however, South Vietnam could not continue to fight.

On April 30, 1975, South Vietnam surrendered. The war was over.

On Veterans Day in 1982, the Vietnam Veterans Memorial in Washington, D.C., was opened. Part of the memorial is a large wall of black stone. The wall lists the names of more than 58,000 American men and women who fought for their country and died or were reported missing during the Vietnam War.

REVIEW What scandal ended Nixon's presidency?

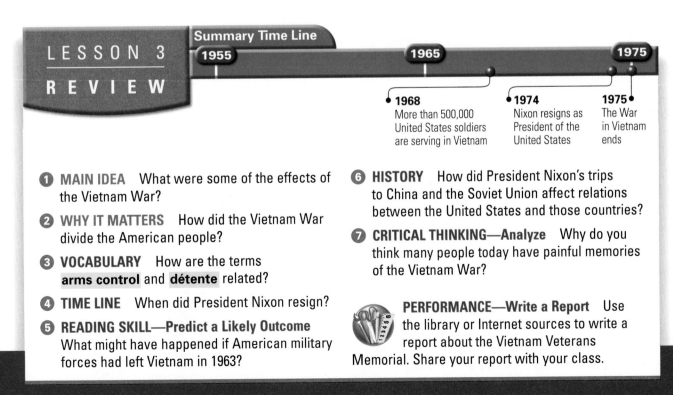

LESSON 3 REVIEW

Summary Time Line

1955 — 1965 — 1975

1968
More than 500,000 United States soldiers are serving in Vietnam

1974
Nixon resigns as President of the United States

1975
The War in Vietnam ends

1 MAIN IDEA   What were some of the effects of the Vietnam War?

2 WHY IT MATTERS   How did the Vietnam War divide the American people?

3 VOCABULARY   How are the terms **arms control** and **détente** related?

4 TIME LINE   When did President Nixon resign?

5 READING SKILL—Predict a Likely Outcome
What might have happened if American military forces had left Vietnam in 1963?

6 HISTORY   How did President Nixon's trips to China and the Soviet Union affect relations between the United States and those countries?

7 CRITICAL THINKING—Analyze   Why do you think many people today have painful memories of the Vietnam War?

PERFORMANCE—Write a Report   Use the library or Internet sources to write a report about the Vietnam Veterans Memorial. Share your report with your class.

PRIMARY SOURCES

Editorial Cartoons

Cartoons that express opinions about politics or about government are called editorial cartoons. Since the middle 1700s, editorial cartoons have been appearing in magazines and newspapers. Researchers and students can study editorial cartoons to learn more about historical events of the past. The Vietnam War is an example of an event that stirred the opinions of editorial cartoonists. In the cartoon to the right, cartoonist John Riedell expressed his political opinions about President Lyndon B. Johnson's handling of the war.

 AAEC EDITORIAL CARTOON DIGITAL COLLECTION AT THE UNIVERSITY OF SOUTHERN MISSISSIPPI

These editorial cartoons (above and right) drawn by Eddie Germano reflect his views. They reveal the difficulty that President Johnson faced as he worked to resolve the conflict in Vietnam.

Analyze the Primary Source

1. What words or images tell you what the cartoon means?

2. Describe the actions taking place in the cartoons.

3. In your own words, explain the messages of the cartoons.

4. What groups might agree or disagree with the cartoons' messages?

The photograph shows Eddie Germano (below) at work in his studio in the late 1960s. His editorial cartoon (left) is called Flicker of Hope.

ACTIVITY

Express an Opinion Think of an issue on which you have an opinion. Make an editorial cartoon that expresses your opinion. Write a caption to help explain the meaning of your cartoon.

RESEARCH

GO ONLINE Visit The Learning Site at **www.harcourtschool.com/primarysources** to research other primary sources.

MAIN IDEA
Read to learn how the
Cold War finally ended.

WHY IT MATTERS
The end of the Cold War
meant that the United
States was left as the
world's only superpower.

VOCABULARY
terrorism
deficit
hijack

A World of Change

1901   1951   2001

1971–2001

President Nixon had helped reduce tensions between the free world and communist nations, but the Cold War was not over. Americans continued to deal with troubling conflicts around the world. They also experienced **terrorism**, the deliberate use of violence to promote a cause.

Tensions at Home and Abroad

In 1976 Georgia Governor Jimmy Carter was elected President. Two years later, he earned worldwide praise for helping bring about a peace agreement between Israel, in Southwest Asia, and Egypt, in Northeast Africa. Those two nations had long been enemies.

Together, Southwest Asia and Northeast Africa are often called the Middle East. For centuries people in this region have been divided by religious, cultural, and political differences. In 1979, while Carter was President, a revolution took place in the Middle Eastern nation of Iran. Supporters of the revolution were angry at the United States for its support of Iran's previous leader. They attacked the United States embassy in Tehran, Iran's capital, and took 53 Americans as hostages.

For more than a year, President Carter tried, but failed, to win the release of the hostages. At the same time, the nation's economy slowed and unemployment rose.

President Carter (center) is shown shaking hands with President Sadat (suh•DAHT) of Egypt (left) and Prime Minister Begin (BAY•guhn) of Israel at the signing of their peace agreement.

Ronald Reagan   1911–

Character Trait: Individualism

Because of his ability to hold an audience's attention, Ronald Reagan was often referred to as the great communicator. Reagan developed his speaking skills by working first as a radio sportscaster and later as a movie actor. Twice, in 1980 and 1984, he was elected President. In his first inaugural address he stressed the importance of individual achievement. Reagan has always believed in the promise of the United States, once saying, "Every promise, every opportunity is still golden in this land."

MULTIMEDIA BIOGRAPHIES
Visit The Learning Site at
www.harcourtschool.com/biographies
to learn about other famous people.

GO ONLINE

Inflation remained very high, and there were fuel shortages. In many cities, lines formed at filling stations as Americans tried to buy gasoline for their cars.

Many people blamed Carter for the Iran crisis and the nation's troubles. He ran again for President in 1980 but lost the election to former California Governor Ronald Reagan. The day that Reagan became President, the Iranians finally released the hostages.

Before President Reagan took office, the future looked dim to many Americans. But Reagan helped change that. His positive attitude and strong sense of patriotism appealed to many people.

Reagan quickly won approval from Congress for large tax cuts. The economy grew stronger, and high inflation ended. At the same time, however, the government's budget **deficit**, or shortage, increased. When there is a deficit, the government spends more money than it takes in each year in taxes and other income.

REVIEW How did the nation's economy change after Ronald Reagan was elected President?

The Cold War Ends

"Peace through strength" was Ronald Reagan's motto. As President, he increased defense spending. He called the Soviet Union "an evil empire" and said that the Cold War was a "struggle between right and wrong, good and evil."

The Soviet Union continued to build more weapons, too, and it helped communist governments and rebels all over the world. Then, in 1985, a new leader named Mikhail Gorbachev (mee•kah•EEL gawr•buh•CHAWF) came to power in the Soviet Union. Nothing would be the same again.

President George Bush (seated in chair on the right) meets with his advisers, including General Colin Powell (far left and below). During the Gulf War, burning oil fields (above) were a common sight.

President Reagan said he would welcome the chance to meet the new Soviet leader in the "cause of world peace." In April 1985 Gorbachev agreed to a meeting. He said that better relations between the two nations were "necessary—and possible." This meeting marked the beginning of a real thaw in the Cold War. The two countries soon agreed to more arms control treaties.

In the Soviet Union, Gorbachev was already changing many of the old ways of doing things. He called for reforms that gave the Soviet people more of the freedoms they wanted.

Changes in the Soviet Union led to changes in other communist nations, too. People in Czechoslovakia, Poland, and Hungary also gained new freedoms. In

East Germany, leaders opened the gates of the Berlin Wall. Then, in 1989, the German people tore down the Berlin Wall. The next year they reunited their country.

In 1989 the new President of the United States, George Bush, met with Mikhail Gorbachev. The two leaders talked about the many changes taking place in Europe and the Soviet Union. The Cold War was finally ending.

REVIEW How did relations between the United States and the Soviet Union change during the 1980s?

New Challenges

Talking about the idea of a world without the Cold War, President Bush said, "Now we can see . . . the very real prospect of a new world order." By "a new world order," Bush meant a world without the conflicts of the past. Despite his hopes, new conflicts soon developed.

In August 1990 the Middle Eastern nation of Iraq, led by its dictator Saddam

Hussein (hoo•SAYN), invaded the small country of Kuwait (koo•WAYT). The Iraqi army quickly took over Kuwait, a major producer of oil in the Middle East. When Iraq refused to withdraw, allied forces from 27 countries, including the United States, attacked Iraq. The United States led this attack, known as Operation Desert Storm.

Among President Bush's advisers during Operation Desert Storm, also known as the Gulf War, was General Colin L. Powell. He was Chairman of the Joint Chiefs of Staff—the leaders of all the different branches of the military. Having commanded troops in South Korea and in the Vietnam War, General Powell used his military experience and leadership qualities to help the allied forces defeat the Iraqis and return Kuwait's leaders to power within seven months. Powell won fame during the Gulf War and became a national hero. In 2001 he became the United States secretary of state.

The early 1990s also marked the end of communism in eastern Europe. In 1991 the Soviet Union itself broke up into several independent countries, with Russia being the largest. Many countries in eastern Europe began fighting one another for power and the right to self-government. Some of the worst fighting occurred in the country once known as Yugoslavia. The civil war there has claimed thousands of lives.

REVIEW What caused the Gulf War to happen?

Toward a New Century

George Bush led the United States and its allies to victory in the Gulf War, but he lost the 1992 presidential election to Arkansas Governor Bill Clinton. As President, Clinton oversaw one of the greatest periods of economic growth in the nation's history. In the 1990s businesses created millions of new jobs, and unemployment dropped to its lowest level in decades. Working together, President Clinton and members of Congress also helped end the government's budget deficit and achieve a balanced budget.

Clinton also worked with Boris Yeltsin, the new president of Russia, to further reduce the number of nuclear weapons. In his 1995 State of the Union Address, Clinton said, "Tonight . . . is the first State of the Union Address ever delivered since the beginning of the Cold War when not a single Russian missile is pointed at . . . America."

President Clinton worked with Congress to achieve a balanced budget.

President Clinton achieved many successes, but he also experienced controversy. In 1999 he became only the second American President to be impeached. Clinton's 37-day trial for obstructing justice and lying under oath could have resulted in his removal from office. As a result of the Senate vote, however, he was able to finish his term.

REVIEW How did economic growth in the 1990s affect unemployment?

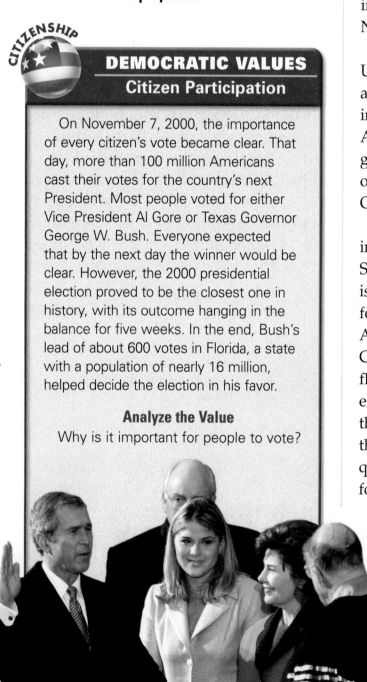

George W. Bush takes the oath of office.

Facing New Dangers

At the end of the twentieth century, the United States faced new dangers from both outside and inside its borders. The nation's military continued to defend democratic values in missions around the world—from Haiti in the Caribbean to Bosnia in Europe. The nation also experienced acts of terrorism as bombs exploded at two United States embassies in Africa and next to a United States Navy ship docked in the Middle East.

Acts of terrorism occurred inside the United States, too. In the early 1990s, a bomb rocked the World Trade Center in New York City. Then, in 1995, an American citizen who was angry with the government set off a bomb in the federal office building in Oklahoma City, Oklahoma. That blast killed 168 people.

However, the worst act of terrorism in the nation's history occurred on September 11, 2001. That morning, terrorists **hijacked**, or illegally took control of, four American commercial airplanes. Again, terrorists targeted the World Trade Center. Two of the hijacked planes were flown directly into the center's twin towers, causing tremendous explosions. The third plane was flown into the side of the Pentagon, the nation's military headquarters, near Washington, D.C. The fourth plane crashed in an empty field in Pennsylvania. Authorities believe that several passengers, acting heroically, prevented the plane from hitting another building.

Less than two hours after the attacks on the World Trade Center, both towers collapsed, killing

thousands of people. At the Pentagon, nearly 200 people lost their lives.

Just as it has done so many times in the past in the defense of liberty, the United States has again pledged to lead the world—this time in a war against terrorism. As the United States works to make our nation and the world more secure, the Constitution will continue to protect our basic freedoms as Americans. Once again the American people are united, working together to make sure that our nation and nations around the world remain strong and free.

REVIEW In what ways has terrorism affected the United States?

After the attacks, the World Trade Towers caught fire (top left). Firefighters (above) stand among the ruins and raise an American flag as a symbol of patriotism.

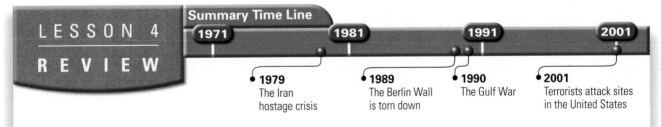

LESSON 4 REVIEW

Summary Time Line

1971 — 1981 — 1991 — 2001

1979 The Iran hostage crisis

1989 The Berlin Wall is torn down

1990 The Gulf War

2001 Terrorists attack sites in the United States

1. **MAIN IDEA** How did the Cold War finally end?

2. **WHY IT MATTERS** What did the end of the Cold War mean?

3. **VOCABULARY** What is a **deficit**?

4. **TIME LINE** In what year was the Berlin Wall torn down?

5. **READING SKILL—Predict a Likely Outcome** What do you think might have happened if the United States had not organized Operation Desert Storm?

6. **HISTORY** What was Colin Powell's role in the Gulf War?

7. **CRITICAL THINKING—Analyze** Why did the breakup of the Soviet Union cause confusion in many eastern European countries?

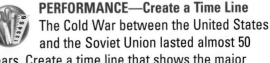

PERFORMANCE—Create a Time Line The Cold War between the United States and the Soviet Union lasted almost 50 years. Create a time line that shows the major events of the Cold War.

·SKILLS·
MAP AND GLOBE

Read a Population Map

VOCABULARY

population density

▶ WHY IT MATTERS

Like most other geographic information, population can be shown on maps in many different ways. One way is with color. Knowing how to read a population map can make it easier for you to find out the number of people who live in different areas.

▶ WHAT YOU NEED TO KNOW

Look at the key on the population map of the United States on page 603. The key tells you that the colors on the map stand for different population densities. **Population density** is the number of people who live in 1 square mile or 1 square kilometer of land. A square mile is a square piece of land. Each of its four sides is 1 mile long. A square kilometer is a square piece of land with sides that are each 1 kilometer long.

Many people today live in crowded cities (left), while others live in small, rural communities (below).

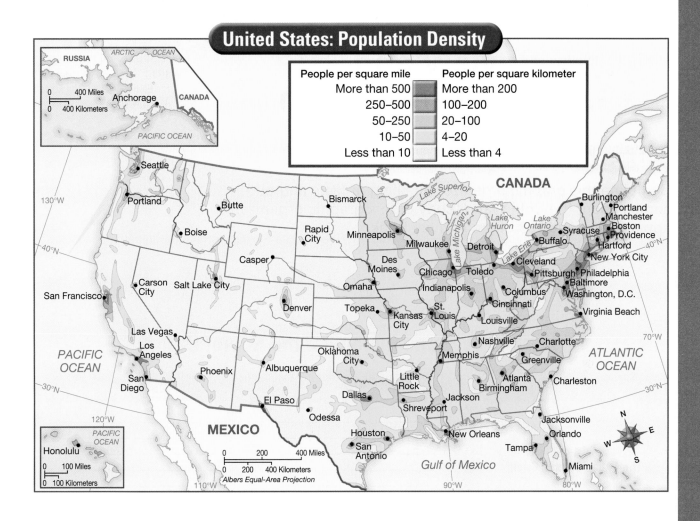

United States: Population Density

People per square mile	People per square kilometer
More than 500	More than 200
250–500	100–200
50–250	20–100
10–50	4–20
Less than 10	Less than 4

On the map, the tan color stands for the least crowded areas. Red stands for the most crowded areas. Read the map key to find the parts of the United States that have more than 500 people per square mile or less than 10 people per square mile.

➡ PRACTICE THE SKILL

Use the map to answer the following questions.

1 Find New York City on the map. What is the population density of the area in which it is located?

2 Find the dots for the cities of Jackson, Mississippi and Toledo, Ohio. Which city has more people?

3 Which city has fewer people, Miami, Florida, or Carson City, Nevada?

➡ APPLY WHAT YOU LEARNED

Study the population information given on the map. Then show some of the same information by using a chart, graph, or table. You might make a bar graph comparing the different population sizes of cities in the United States or a table showing the five states with the largest populations.

Practice your map and globe skills with the **GeoSkills CD-ROM.**

· CHAPTER ·

16 Review and Test Preparation

Summary Time Line
1940

● **1948**
The Berlin
Airlift begins

● **1950**
The Korean
War begins

USE YOUR READING SKILLS

Complete this graphic organizer by filling in facts and outcomes about the Cold War. A copy of this graphic organizer appears on page 158 of the Activity Book.

The Cold War and the end of the Soviet Union

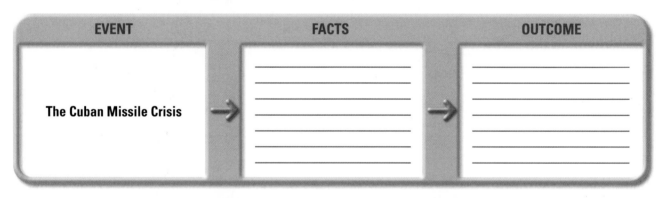

EVENT	FACTS	OUTCOME
The Cuban Missile Crisis	→	→

EVENT	FACTS	OUTCOME
Mikhail Gorbachev becomes the leader of the Soviet Union.	→	→

THINK & WRITE

Write a Radio News Report Imagine that you are living in West Berlin. The radio station you work for has asked you to report on the Berlin Airlift. Write what you will say about how the Allies are getting supplies to West Berlin.

Write Your Opinion The three astronauts aboard *Apollo 11* faced many dangers during their trip to the moon, but they also made history. Write a paragraph or two describing why you would or would not have wanted to be an astronaut on board that historic flight.

1962
The Cuban
Missile Crisis
begins

1964
The Civil
Rights Act
is signed

1968
Martin Luther
King, Jr., is
assassinated

1969
Apollo 11
astronauts
land on
the moon

1974
President
Nixon
resigns

1975
The Vietnam
War ends

1990
The Persian
Gulf War
begins

2001
Terrorists attack
sites in the
United States

USE THE TIME LINE

Use the chapter summary time line to answer these questions.

1 When did the Gulf War begin?

2 Did President Nixon resign before or after the end of the Vietnam War?

USE VOCABULARY

Use a term from this list to complete each of the sentences that follow.

superpowers (p. 580)

cease-fire (p. 582)

nonviolence (p. 587)

scandal (p. 593)

terrorism (p. 596)

deficit (p. 597)

3 Working for change by using _____ was important to Martin Luther King, Jr.

4 The United States has faced _____ both inside and outside its borders.

5 A _____ brought an end to the Korean War.

6 After World War II, the United States and the Soviet Union became the world's two _____.

7 During the 1980s the federal government's budget _____ increased.

8 A _____ forced President Nixon to resign.

RECALL FACTS

Answer these questions.

9 How did Carl Sagan contribute to Americans' understanding of space?

10 How did Rosa Parks help the Civil Rights movement?

11 How did Colin Powell contribute to the United States' victory in the Gulf War?

Write the letter of the best choice.

12 **TEST PREP** In 1958 Congress set up NASA to—
  A increase the nation's arms supply.
  B protect South Korea from North Korea.
  C protect West Berlin from East Berlin.
  D develop the nation's space program.

13 **TEST PREP** The Civil Rights Act of 1964 helped change life in the United States by—
  F giving African Americans the right to vote.
  G creating thousands of jobs for unemployed people.
  H making segregation in public places illegal.
  J calling for the building of hundreds of new schools.

THINK CRITICALLY

14 Why do you think winning the space race was important to the United States?

15 What do you think was Martin Luther King, Jr.'s greatest contribution to the Civil Rights movement?

16 Why do you think so many nations supported the United States during the Gulf War?

APPLY SKILLS

Read a Population Map
Review the map on page 603. Then answer the following questions.

17 Which city has more people—Houston or Louisville?

18 Which city has fewer people—Denver or Philadelphia?

THE BIRMINGHAM
Civil Rights Institute

GET READY

The Birmingham Civil Rights Institute celebrates the many people who worked to gain full rights for African Americans. On a visit there, you seem to travel back in time. You will see, feel, and hear what it was like in this important time in American history. After you explore the life-size scenes and watch the video presentations in the institute's different galleries, you will feel as if you lived through the events of the Civil Rights movement.

LOCATE IT

Birmingham

ALABAMA

Life-size figures and a time line walk you through important events of the Civil Rights movement.

The lunch counter exhibit at the Birmingham Civil Rights Institute illustrates a time of segregation.

TAKE A FIELD TRIP

GO ONLINE

A VIRTUAL TOUR
Visit The Learning Site at
www.harcourtschool.com/tours
to take virtual tours of other
historic sites in the United States.

Turner Le@rning

A VIDEO TOUR
Check your media
center or classroom library
for a videotape tour of the
Birmingham Civil Rights Institute.

VISUAL SUMMARY

Write a Description Study the pictures and captions below to help you review Unit 7. Then choose one of the events shown. Write a description of the event, and tell why it remains important to Americans today.

USE VOCABULARY

Use the following terms to write a story about life during the twentieth century.

military draft
(p. 538)

stock market
(p. 547)

D day (p. 565)

refugees (p. 573)

arms race (p. 582)

RECALL FACTS

Answer these questions.

1 On what fronts did World War II take place?

2 What democratic means did Cesar Chavez use to improve the lives of migrant workers?

Write the letter of the best choice.

3 **TEST PREP** The United States declared war on Germany in 1917 because—
A members of Austria–Hungary's royal family had been killed.
B Germany invaded Poland.
C 260 sailors were killed when the *Maine* exploded and sank.
D German U-boats attacked American ships.

4 **TEST PREP** The New Deal changed the federal government by—
F shifting much of its power to state governments.
G allowing the President to raise taxes without the approval of Congress.
H rewriting the Constitution.
J giving it more authority and more employees.

Visual Summary

1901   1926   1951

1917   The United States enters World War I   p. 538

1929   The stock market crashes
p. 547

1941   Japan attacks Pearl Harbor
p. 557

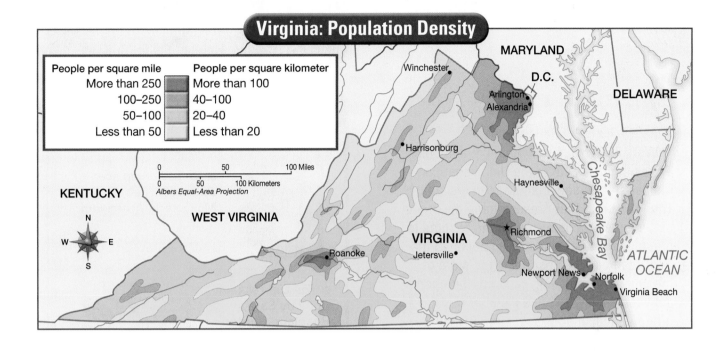

Virginia: Population Density

People per square mile
- More than 250
- 100–250
- 50–100
- Less than 50

People per square kilometer
- More than 100
- 40–100
- 20–40
- Less than 20

0   50   100 Miles
0   50   100 Kilometers
Albers Equal-Area Projection

N W E S

MARYLAND
Winchester
D.C.
Arlington
Alexandria
DELAWARE

KENTUCKY
WEST VIRGINIA

Harrisonburg

Haynesville

Chesapeake Bay

VIRGINIA

Richmond

Roanoke
Jetersville

Newport News
Norfolk
Virginia Beach

ATLANTIC OCEAN

---

5 TEST PREP World War II began in Europe when—
A Italy took over Ethiopia.
B Germany invaded Poland.
C Japan invaded Manchuria.
D Germany attacked France.

THINK CRITICALLY

6 How did mass production change the economy in the twentieth century?

7 What do you think would have happened if Germany had taken control of Britain before the United States entered World War II?

8 In what ways has the Civil Rights movement changed the United States?

APPLY SKILLS

MAP AND GLOBE SKILLS

Read a Population Map
Use the map on this page to answer the following questions.

9 Which city has a higher population density—Winchester or Virginia Beach?

10 Which city has a lower population density—Norfolk or Harrisonburg?

1976   2001

1964   The Civil Rights Act is passed   p. 587

1965   American combat forces arrive in South Vietnam   p. 591

1969   United States astronauts land on the moon   p. 583

Unit Activities

GO ONLINE Visit The Learning Site at www.harcourtschool.com/ socialstudies/activities for additional activities.

Give a Presidential Speech

Work as a group to write, edit, and deliver a Presidential State of the Union speech. Choose a President discussed in this unit. Then research that President and the important events that occurred during his time in office. Next, write and edit a speech to the American people, describing the state of the union and outlining goals for the upcoming year. Finally, select a member of your group to deliver your speech to the class.

COMPLETE THE UNIT PROJECT

Class Newspaper   Work with a group of your classmates to finish the unit project—a newspaper about the twentieth century. Review your list of key people, places, and events of the twentieth century. Then decide which of those people, places, and events you wish to feature in your newspaper. Research and write articles on the subjects you have chosen. Then draw or find pictures to go along with your articles. Arrange your articles and pictures on a posterboard. Finally, present your newspaper to the class, and discuss the subjects you featured.

VISIT YOUR LIBRARY

■ *Goin' Someplace Special* by Patricia C. McKissack. Atheneum.

■ *The Unbreakable Code* by Sara Hoagland Hunter. Northland Publishing.

■ *The Words of Martin Luther King, Jr.* Selected by Coretta Scott King. Newmarket Press.

The United States and the World

Statue of Liberty, Liberty Island,
New York

The United States and the World

" History and destiny have made America the leader of the world that would be free. **"**

—Colin Powell, Chairman of the United States Joint Chiefs of Staff, in a speech, September 28, 1993

Preview the Content

Read the title and the Main Idea for each lesson. Then write a short paragraph for each lesson, telling what you think it is about.

Preview the Vocabulary

Suffixes   A suffix is a part of a word that is added to the end of a root word. Use the root words and suffixes in the chart below to learn the meaning of each vocabulary word.

SUFFIX	ROOT WORD	VOCABULARY WORD	POSSIBLE MEANING
-ity	responsible	**responsibility**	
-ism	patriot	**patriotism**	

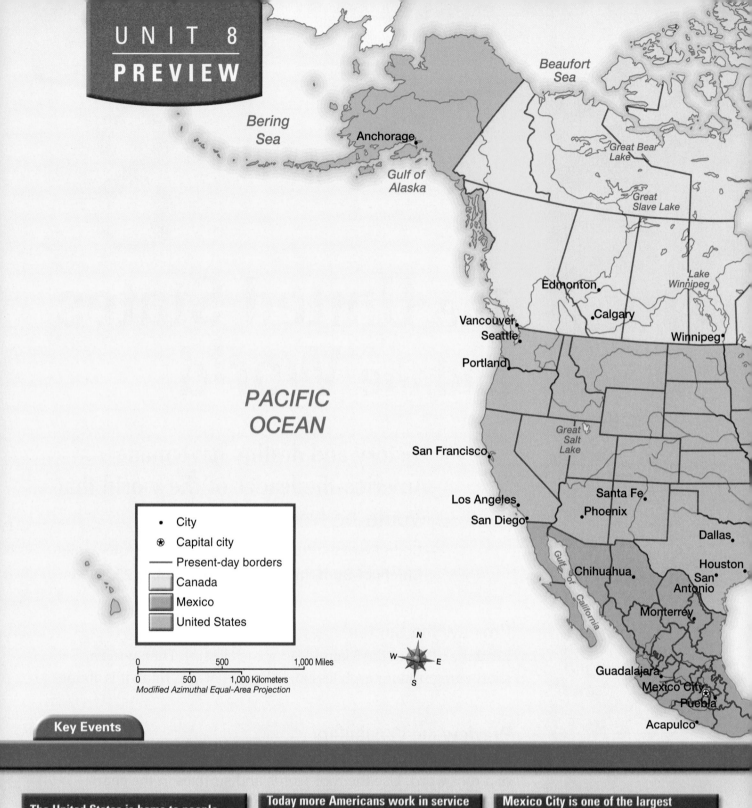

Beaufort
Sea

Bering
Sea

Anchorage

Gulf of
Alaska

Great Bear
Lake

Great
Slave Lake

Edmonton

Lake
Winnipeg

Vancouver
Seattle

Calgary

Winnipeg

Portland

PACIFIC
OCEAN

Great
Salt
Lake

San Francisco

Los Angeles

Santa Fe
Phoenix

San Diego

Dallas

Houston
San
Antonio

Chihuahua

Gulf of California

Monterrey

City
★ Capital city
— Present-day borders
Canada
Mexico
United States

0   500   1,000 Miles
0   500   1,000 Kilometers
Modified Azimuthal Equal-Area Projection

N
W   E
S

Guadalajara

Mexico City
Puebla

Acapulco

Key Events

The United States is home to people from all over the world. p. 620

Today more Americans work in service jobs than in any other kinds of jobs. p. 633

Mexico City is one of the largest metropolitan areas in the world. p. 655

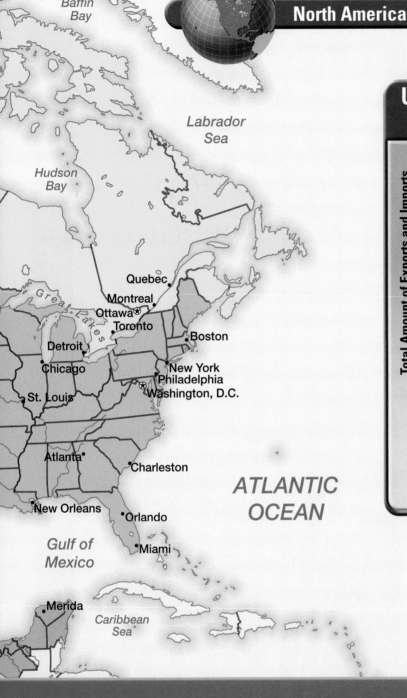

Baffin Bay

Labrador Sea

Hudson Bay

Great Lakes

Quebec
Montreal
Ottawa
Toronto
Boston
Detroit
Chicago
New York
Philadelphia
Washington, D.C.
St. Louis
Atlanta
Charleston
New Orleans
Orlando
Gulf of Mexico
Miami
Merida
Caribbean Sea

ATLANTIC OCEAN

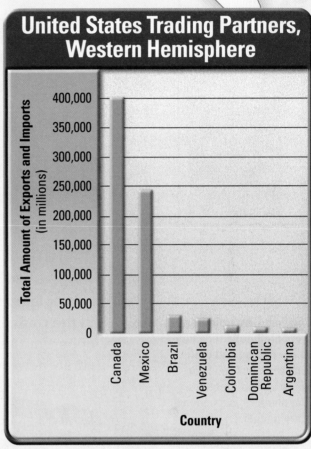

United States Trading Partners, Western Hemisphere

Total Amount of Exports and Imports (in millions)

400,000
350,000
300,000
250,000
200,000
150,000
100,000
50,000
0

Canada
Mexico
Brazil
Venezuela
Colombia
Dominican Republic
Argentina

Country

Jean-Bertrand Aristide becomes Haiti's president. p. 661

Simón Bolívar helps win independence for many present-day Latin American countries. p. 666

The St. Lawrence Seaway allows ships to travel from the Atlantic Ocean to the Great Lakes. p. 673

613

Dia's Story Cloth

The Hmong People's Journey of Freedom

by Dia Cha
stitched by Chue and Nhia Thao Cha

This hand-embroidered story cloth tells the story of the Hmong and their long journey from Laos to the United States. The name *Hmong* means "free people."

People from all over the world have come to live in the United States, and the freedoms and economic opportunities offered by our country continue to attract newcomers. Many immigrants today tell stories of how they came to the United States. Some tell their stories in letters. Others tell their stories in poems and songs. This immigrant story was inspired by a Hmong [MONG] hand-sewn story cloth. Hmong needleworkers sew pictures on cloth, using no patterns or measurements, to remember their past. The story cloth on these pages tells the story of how Dia Cha [DEE·ah CHAY] and her family left Asia, to come to the United States in 1979.

Only 15 years old when she arrived in the United States, Dia Cha found life in America very different from life in Laos.

When my people first arrived in America, most didn't speak or write English. Many families had sponsors, who picked us up at the airport.

Everything about life in America was different for the Hmong.

I was 15 years old when I came to this country. I'd never been to school, so I had to start everything from scratch. They wanted to put me in high school, but I didn't know anything. Then they wanted to put me in adult school, but the teachers said I was too young.

Shoulder baskets (left) are made in adult and child sizes for carrying crops and other items. The stool, gourd water jar, and bamboo table (right) are like those found in many Hmong households.

The Hmong are known for their beautiful needlework, which is called *pa'ndau* (pan•DOW), or "flower cloth." Each design follows a theme. Those shown above, from left to right, are called "lightning", "snail house," and "frog legs."

Finally, I started high school. Thirteen years later, I received my master's degree from Northern Arizona University. I went back to Laos as an anthropologist in 1992 to work with Hmong and Lao women in the refugee camps in Thailand.

This story cloth reminds me of the history of my family and of my people. Some of the memories it brings are good, and some are bad. But it is important for me to remember everything the Hmong have been through.

Dia Cha believes that each memory sewn into the story cloth is important. This part of the story cloth shows Cha's home in Laos.

The Hmong's heavily embroidered clothes set them apart from neighboring peoples in Asia. Hmong clothes sometimes combine green, pink, black, dark blue, and white, as seen in the child's jacket and sash above.

Hmong women in America continue to stitch new story cloths. We all have vivid memories about our lives and culture and history. The story cloth is a bridge to all the generations before us. When I show the story cloth to my niece and nephew, who were both born here in the United States, I point to different pictures and tell them that this is what it was like.

Analyze the Literature

1. What is the purpose of a Hmong story cloth?

2. Why do you think many people feel it is important to remember their past?

THE WHITE HOUSE

For over two hundred years, the White House has symbolized the executive branch. In 1800, President John Adams and his wife Abigail became the White House's first residents. Since then, the building has been home to 41 United States Presidents. On average, the White House receives nearly 5,000 visitors a day.

LOCATE IT

MARYLAND

Washington, D.C.

VIRGINIA

White House

17

The United States Today

"I pray Heaven to bestow the best of blessings on this house and all that shall hereafter inhabit it."
—John Adams, letter to Abigail Adams, November 2, 1800

CHAPTER READING SKILL

Tell Fact from Opinion

A **fact** is a statement that can be proven to be true. An **opinion** is an individual's view of something that is shaped by that person's feelings.

As you read this chapter, separate facts from opinions about the modern United States.

MAIN TOPIC

FACT OPINION

FAST FACT Today about one of every ten people in the United States was born in another country.

The American People Today

People have been coming to the Americas since before history was recorded. Over time, the United States has become a nation of many cultures. The nation has changed in other ways, too.

A Growing Nation

More than 281 million people live in the United States today, and that number is rising fast. During the 1990s alone, the population of the United States grew by almost 33 million people—the largest ten-year increase in the country's history.

The population of the United States is growing for two reasons. More people are being born in the United States, and more people are moving to this country. People who are born in the United States or who have at least one parent who is a United States citizen are automatically citizens of our country.

Many immigrants have become naturalized citizens. To become a naturalized citizen, a person must have lived in the United States for at least five years (or three if married to a citizen). Then that person must apply for citizenship and pass a test to show that he or she understands United States history and government. Finally, the person must take part in a ceremony in which he or she promises to be loyal to the United States.

Many immigrants become citizens of the United States each year.

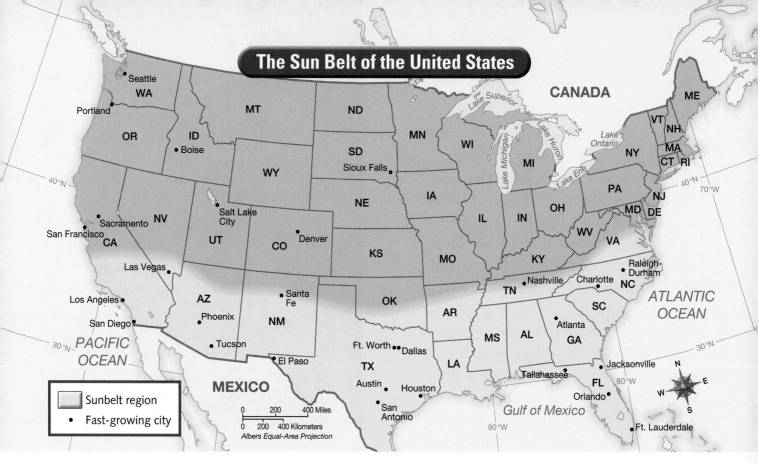

The Sun Belt of the United States

CANADA

Sunbelt region

• Fast-growing city

0 200 400 Miles
0 200 400 Kilometers
Albers Equal-Area Projection

GEOGRAPHY THEME

Regions Many Americans are attracted to the warm and sunny weather of the Sun Belt.

❓ What cities in Texas are growing fast?

In the past, most immigrants came to the United States from Europe. Today, most immigrants come from countries in Asia and Latin America. Like immigrants in the past, they come seeking freedom and new opportunities for a better life. Many seek refuge from war, weak economies, and poor living conditions in their homelands.

Most new immigrants, like most other Americans, live in metropolitan areas. In fact, about four of every five people in the United States live in metropolitan areas. About one-third of all Americans live in metropolitan areas of more than 5 million people.

More than half of the American people live in the ten states with the greatest populations—California, Texas, New York, Florida, Illinois, Pennsylvania, Ohio, Michigan, New Jersey, and Georgia. However, the population of every state is growing.

Although the population of every region of the United States is growing, different regions are growing at different rates. Much of the nation's growth has taken place in the **Sun Belt**, a wide area of the southern United States that has a mild climate all year. The Sun Belt stretches from the Atlantic coast to the Pacific coast. Places in the Sun Belt region began growing during World War II. One reason for this growth was the development of air conditioning.

Air conditioning was introduced in the early twentieth century. It was first used in movie theaters and railroad cars.

Immigrants who share a culture sometimes choose to settle in the same neighborhood. One example of this is Chinatown in San Francisco, California.

In the 1920s, the first fully air-conditioned office building, the Milam Building in San Antonio, Texas, was constructed. As air conditioning spread across the Sun Belt in the 1950s, it helped make living there more comfortable. Millions of people moved to the region, built homes and started businesses, and forever changed the environment.

The Sun Belt stretches across parts of both the South and the West. In recent years, both of these regions have grown faster than other regions of the United States. The West is the fastest-growing region of the United States, but the South has the largest population of any region. Almost 100 million people live in states in the South.

REVIEW How did the use of air-conditioning change the Sun Belt?

A Diverse Nation

The population of the United States is growing quickly. At the same time, the United States is becoming a more diverse nation. In fact, the United States has one of the world's most diverse populations in terms of ancestry. Today about 210 million Americans are of European background. Almost 35 million are African Americans, and more than 10 million are of Asian background. About two and a half million people in the United States are Native Americans.

Hispanic Americans make up the fastest-growing ethnic group in the nation. An **ethnic group** is a group of people from the same country, of the same race, or with a shared culture. A little more than 1 in 10 Americans, or about 35 million people, are of Hispanic descent. More than three-fourths of them live in the South or West. California and Texas have the largest Hispanic populations, but the state with the highest percentage of Hispanic residents is New Mexico. In New Mexico more than 4 of every 10 people are of Hispanic background.

Many Americans of Greek heritage attend Greek Orthodox churches.

Most people in the United States are either immigrants or descendants of immigrants. Some people's families have been living in the United States for hundreds of years. Others have come to live in this country only recently. Instead of arriving on ships, as immigrants often did in the past, most immigrants today arrive by plane at one of the nation's international airports.

Some people who have immigrated to this country still speak the language of the country in which they were born. So do some of their descendants. In fact, about one-fifth of all schoolchildren in the United States today speak a language other than English at home. Most of them speak Spanish.

Some Americans continue to dress in the styles of their homelands or take part in customs, celebrations, or traditions that are unique to their culture. Cultural differences among Americans can also be seen in the kinds of music people listen to, the foods they eat, and the religious groups they belong to.

Having so many different cultures has made the United States a more diverse place. At the same time, it has given Americans a richer life. Over the years, people from each culture have contributed to American life. Cultural differences help explain why people in the United States often seem so different from one another in so many ways.

Although Americans are different from one another, they also have much in common. Americans share a deep belief in individual rights. Most Americans support the government, which is based on representation and the consent of the people. Americans also value our economic system, which supports free enterprise and the ideas of competition, open opportunity, and private property. These common beliefs help unite Americans.

REVIEW In what ways can one see cultural differences among Americans?

• HERITAGE •

Epiphany

For many Hispanic families in the United States, the Christmas season does not end on December 25. It continues with Epiphany, or Three Kings Day, which is celebrated on January 6. According to tradition, 12 days after the birth of Jesus, the Three Kings, or Wise Men, arrived to present the newborn child with gifts. The night before Epiphany, many Hispanic children leave snacks out for the Kings. The children hope to find candy and presents waiting for them the next day. Other Epiphany traditions include eating special ring-shaped cakes called roscones and attending Three Kings Day parades.

Changing Ways of Life

As the United States is becoming more diverse, it is changing in other ways, too. Advances in technology, such as computers, cellular telephones, and facsimile, or fax, machines, have affected how people in the United States live, work, communicate, and travel. These machines have made it possible for people to communicate and conduct business faster and more easily.

Computers first came into widespread use after World War II. At that time computers were so big that just one would fill an entire room. Then, in 1958, scientists working independently in Texas and California each invented the silicon chip. This tiny device can now store millions of bits of computer information. Silicon chips have allowed businesses to make smaller, faster, and cheaper computers.

Today millions of computers are used in businesses and in homes and schools throughout the world. Many people even run their own businesses from their homes with the use of the Internet. The **Internet** is a network that links computers around the world for the exchange of information.

The United States Department of Defense set up a computer network in the late 1960s for military communications. The network changed and grew over the years. In 1992, the World Wide Web came into use. It allows millions of people to send and receive electronic mail, or e-mail, as well as electronic documents, pictures, and sounds.

· SCIENCE AND TECHNOLOGY ·

The Microchip

The integrated circuit, or microchip, was one of the twentieth century's greatest inventions. Introduced in 1959, the microchip helped reduce the size of all types of electronic machines. It did so by letting hundreds of electronic parts be put on a single silicon chip half the size of a paper clip. Starting in the early 1970s, microchips were used to run handheld calculators. Over the years, microchips grew more and more powerful. Today they are used in everything from personal computers to space satellites.

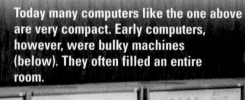

Today many computers like the one above are very compact. Early computers, however, were bulky machines (below). They often filled an entire room.

Using the Internet, people can shop for clothing, cars, or any other item online. They can check on bank accounts, transfer money, pay bills, make reservations, and do many other tasks. They can also reach government agencies, libraries, and other online sites to research almost any subject.

Another change in people's lives is the ability to travel much faster from one place to another. Each year more than 700 million people travel on jet airplanes. In just a few hours they can travel from city to city or halfway around the world to visit family members. People also travel to attend business meetings. However, people do not have to travel at all to communicate directly with others. They can hold a **teleconference**—a conference, or meeting, that uses electronic machines to connect people. Having a teleconference allows people from all over the world to

Satellites such as this one make it possible for people around the world to communicate with one another instantly.

communicate directly with one another by turning on a computer or dialing a telephone.

Advances in technology have changed people's lives in other ways, too. Doctors can use tiny video cameras attached to plastic tubes to see inside a person. Eye doctors now use laser beams to help correct eye problems. The way some automobile drivers find out how to get where they want to go has changed, too. Today, automobiles can be equipped with a Global Positioning System (GPS) receiver. These receivers use satellites to help find a driver's location anywhere on Earth. Drivers can also receive directions through the GPS.

REVIEW **What is the Internet?**

LESSON 1
REVIEW

❶ **MAIN IDEA** How have technology and diversity affected the way Americans live and work?

❷ **WHY IT MATTERS** What parts of people's lives have changed the most as a result of technology and diversity?

❸ **VOCABULARY** Write a description of the **Sun Belt**.

❹ **READING SKILL—Tell Fact from Opinion** The United States has one of the world's most diverse populations in terms of ancestry. Is this

statement a fact or an opinion? How do you know?

❺ **SCIENCE AND TECHNOLOGY** How have advances in technology helped people?

❻ **CRITICAL THINKING—Analyze** Compare and contrast today's immigrant groups and immigrant groups from 100 years ago.

PERFORMANCE—Write a Report Use library or Internet sources to research information about different cultures in the United States. Then write a report about the similarities and differences among the cultures you researched.

·SKILLS·

CHART AND GRAPH

Use a Cartogram

➤ WHY IT MATTERS

One way to show the population of different places is to use a cartogram. A **cartogram** is a diagram that gives information about places by the size shown for each place. Knowing how to read a cartogram can help you quickly compare information about different places.

➤ WHAT YOU NEED TO KNOW

Some maps of the United States base the size of each state on its land area. With a cartogram, a state's size is based on a geographical statistic. On the cartogram on page 627, size is based on population.

A population cartogram shows the states as their sizes would be if each

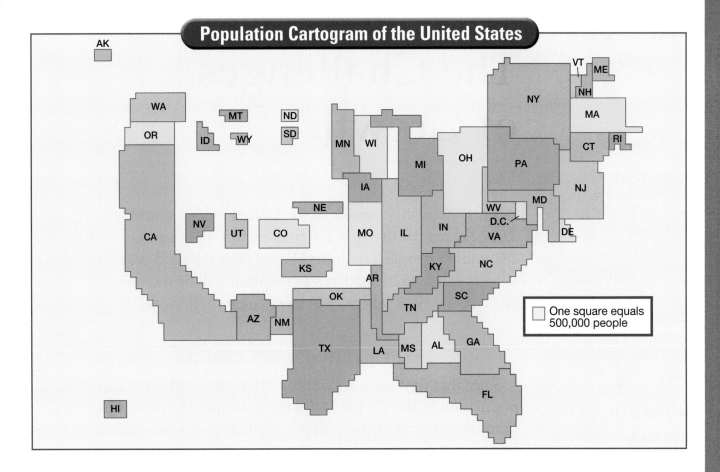

Population Cartogram of the United States

One square equals 500,000 people

person had the same amount of land. A state with many people would be much bigger than a state with few people. When states are shown this way, you can quickly compare populations around the country.

▶ PRACTICE THE SKILL

The map on page 626 is a political map of the United States. The size of each state is based on its land area. Compare the size of New Jersey with the size of South Dakota. South Dakota is larger in land area. The cartogram on this page is a population cartogram. The size of each state is based on population. Compare the sizes of New Jersey and South Dakota again. Although New Jersey has a smaller land area than South Dakota, it is shown larger than South Dakota on the cartogram because it has more people.

Continue to compare land area and population to answer these questions.

1 Which state has more land area, Pennsylvania or Montana?

2 Which of those states is shown larger on the cartogram? Why is it shown larger?

3 What does the cartogram tell about Alaska when you compare its size on the political map?

▶ APPLY WHAT YOU LEARNED

With a partner, brainstorm other ideas for cartograms. What other statistics could be shown in this way to help people compare and contrast states? Make a cartogram of the United States that is based on other statistics besides population statistics. Then prepare a list of questions that could be answered by looking at your cartogram.

The Challenges of Growth

MAIN IDEA
Read to find out how growth has affected the United States and its natural resources.

WHY IT MATTERS
A growing population creates more consumers of resources. It also creates more producers of goods and services.

VOCABULARY
rapid-transit system

In 1790 the first census of the United States counted 3,929,214 people living in the country. Today more than 281 million people live in the United States. By the year 2050, experts estimate the nation's population will be more than 400 million. With this growth have come challenges.

The Effects of Growth

Since that first census more than two hundred years ago, the population of the United States has continued to grow. Over time, quiet towns with small populations and a handful of buildings have grown into large cities. As those cities and the suburbs around them continue to grow, they often spread out over larger and larger areas. Land that was once used for farming is now used for houses, stores, office buildings, and highways.

Across the country many communities are choosing to manage urban growth by passing laws to control it. These laws not only limit where buildings may go, but what kinds of buildings may be built in an area. The laws set aside areas of land to be used only for homes, offices, or businesses, such as shopping centers. In some cases, the laws say the land cannot be used for buildings.

About eight out of every ten people live in or near large cities. Areas that were once undeveloped, such as this Florida neighborhood, are now home to large communities.

As the population grows and the spread of urban areas continues, the need for more services, such as fire protection, also increases.

Some people disagree with placing limits on how land can be used. They believe that it is unfair to restrict use of land that has valuable resources. Some believe that private ownership of land also can help to conserve it. This is because the land's owner usually wants to protect his or her land and use its resources wisely so it will remain valuable in the future.

Rapid population growth has presented many other challenges for the American people. As the nation's population has grown, so has the number of vehicles on its highways and city streets. In many places roads are often jammed with cars, trucks, and buses. This is especially true during rush hour, the time when people are going to work or going home. To help keep traffic moving, some cities now use computers to control traffic lights. Others use electronic highway signs to warn drivers of problems and to suggest other routes they can take.

To help reduce the number of vehicles on their streets, many cities have worked to improve their public transportation systems. These cities have added more bus lines and built rapid-transit systems. A **rapid-transit system** is a passenger transportation system that uses elevated or underground trains or both.

A growing population means growth in the amount of services that are needed. For example, more electricity is needed for people to run their homes and businesses. More people also means that increases are needed in other services.

Directing traffic helps keep city streets from jamming up.

Water, garbage collection, education, health care, and police and fire protection must meet the demands of a growing population.

Changes in population mean changes in government. An increase in population can affect a state's representation in Congress. When a state's population changes, the number of seats it has in the House of Representatives can change also.

Population growth also has its benefits. Having more people helps increase the number of new ideas that can lead to new inventions and new and better ways of doing things. Population growth can also help businesses grow by increasing the market for many goods and services. Having more people also encourages improvements in transportation and communication systems.

REVIEW **How have many cities reduced the number of vehicles on their streets?**

Challenges for the Environment

As the population continues to grow, so does a greater need for natural resources. As a nation it is our responsibility to use our natural resources wisely. Over the years some people's actions have damaged the country's natural resources. Water, land, and even wildlife have been affected.

However, through conservation efforts, some of the damage has been repaired. For example, at one time the American bald eagle was on the endangered species list. There were only about 417 pairs of the eagles left in the United States.

This slide is made of recycled materials. Many everyday products can be made from recycled materials.

To help save the endangered birds, laws were passed banning a chemical that was getting into the water supply. This chemical poisoned the fish eaten by the eagles. By 1998 there were more than 5,000 pairs of American bald eagles in the United States.

Another way to help preserve natural resources is to recycle. Countries with large populations, such as the United States, produce large amounts of trash. To solve this problem, many communities across the nation recycle.

Trash containing materials such as metal, glass, plastic, and paper is used to make new products. Many factories use recycled materials instead of new natural resources to make their products. Everyday items such as videocassettes, playground equipment, and clothing, can be made from recycled materials.

As in the past, Americans continue to rely on natural resources to meet their wants and needs. Today, however, most

National preserves, such as this one in Alabama, help to protect natural resources.

people understand the need to help protect the nation's natural resources for future Americans and to make sensible plans about how those natural resources are used.

REVIEW **How do many communities try to solve their trash problems?**

LESSON 2
REVIEW

① **MAIN IDEA** How has the growth of the United States population affected the land and its natural resources?

② **WHY IT MATTERS** How does a growing population create more producers of goods and services?

③ **VOCABULARY** What are the benefits of using a rapid-transit system?

④ **READING SKILL—Tell Fact from Opinion** In the lesson, find examples of one statement that is fact and one that is opinion.

⑤ **HISTORY** What helped save the American bald eagle?

⑥ **GEOGRAPHY** Why do some people disagree with placing limits on how land can be used?

⑦ **CRITICAL THINKING—Hypothesize** By the year 2050 over 400 million people may be living in the United States. What new problems do you think Americans will have in that time? How might the increase in population benefit Americans?

PERFORMANCE—Interview a Person Interview a parent, a grandparent, or someone else older than you to find out what your city or town was like when he or she was your age. Have your questions ready before the interview. Write down the answers and present them to your class.

MAIN IDEA
Read to learn how the economy of the United States has changed in recent years.

WHY IT MATTERS
Our nation's diverse economy has changed the way many Americans earn a living.

VOCABULARY
diverse economy
high-tech
Information Age
e-commerce
interdependent
international trade
free-trade agreement
global economy

The American Economy

Just as the people of the United States have become more and more diverse over time, so has the nation's economy. A **diverse economy** is one that is based on many kinds of industries. Our nation's diverse economy has created many new kinds of jobs for American workers. It has also changed the kinds of jobs that most of them do to earn a living.

A Changing Economy

Many American workers continue to do the traditional jobs that they have always done. Some people farm the land, fish the waters, cut down trees, and mine the earth for mineral resources. Others construct highways and buildings. Many others—more than 18 million—work in factories, where together they produce more manufactured goods than any other nation in the world.

While all of those jobs remain important parts of the American economy today, more Americans now work in

While some people continue to work in traditional jobs, advances in technology have increased the number of high-tech jobs available to Americans.

Analyze Graphs   The graph shows the number of Americans who work in different kinds of industries. Today more Americans, such as this doctor (below), work in the service industry than in any other kind of industry.

❖ About how many more Americans work in the service industry than in the trade and transportation industry?

Occupations in the United States by Industry

service jobs than in any other kinds of jobs. In fact, about one-third of all workers have service jobs, such as working in restaurants, repairing cars and appliances, or providing health care. If other groups of workers who provide services are included, such as government and transportation workers and people who work in stores, banks, and insurance companies, then about four of every five workers in the United States hold service jobs.

Many of the changes in the kinds of jobs that people do have come about because of advances in technology. In recent years, high-technology, or high-tech, industries have been of growing importance to the American economy. **High-tech** industries are those that invent, build, or use computers and other kinds of electronic equipment. These new devices have made it easier for businesspeople to communicate, travel, trade goods and services, and organize information.

The early 1970s marked the beginning of the **Information Age**. This period in history has been defined by the growing amount of information available to people. In fact, most of what is known about the human body has been learned in the past 40 years.

Today, organizing and storing information and getting the information to people when they need it is a major industry.

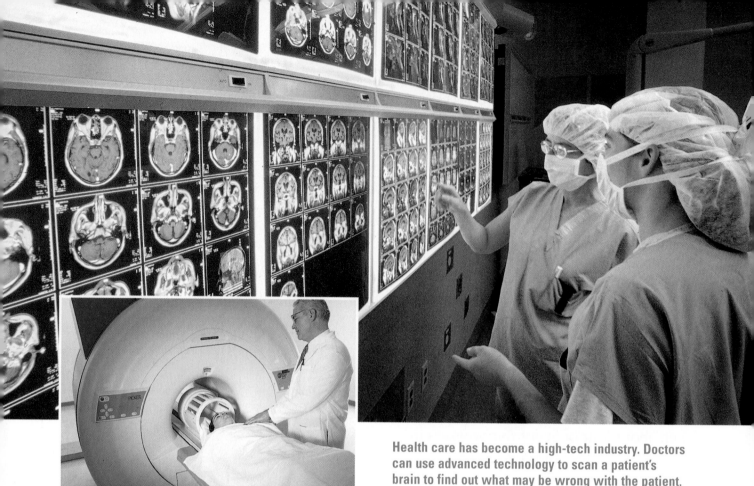

Health care has become a high-tech industry. Doctors can use advanced technology to scan a patient's brain to find out what may be wrong with the patient.

Much of this work is done electronically, through private computer networks or through public Web sites. Setting up and managing these computer systems is a growing field for workers.

New technologies are also changing the way people buy and sell goods and services. The rise of electronic commerce, or **e-commerce**, means that both large and small companies can market their products worldwide. E-commerce has greatly increased the number of goods and services available to American consumers. It has also enabled thousands of Americans to run full-time or part-time businesses from their homes. In 1999, American businesses and individual consumers spent a total of $659 billion on e-commerce purchases. More than 90 percent of this total was made up of business-to-business

sales, or businesses selling things to one another.

New technologies are also changing the part of the American economy that relates to medicine and science. High-tech advances in the field of medicine have already changed the way doctors treat disease. For example, the use of lasers in surgery has helped millions of people.

As technology and knowledge advance, the possibility of additional scientific discoveries increases. Scientific discoveries will likely change the American economy even more in time. Technology used in the area of space exploration has already given the United States many new pictures of different parts of space.

REVIEW How have new technologies changed people's lives?

A Global Economy

Each day, people in different states and in different regions of the United States exchange natural resources, finished products, and services. That is because no one state or region has all the natural resources that people and businesses there may need or want. And no one state or region can produce all the goods and services that people may need or want.

North Carolina, for example, grows too little cotton to supply all of its textile mills, so mill owners there buy cotton grown in other states, such as California and Texas. In turn, farmers in those states may buy products such as cotton blankets, towels, and clothing made by workers in mills and factories in North Carolina. In this way people in different states and regions are **interdependent**—they depend on one another for natural resources, finished products, and services.

The United States and other countries are also interdependent. Modern transportation and communication systems have made it easier for people in one country to trade with people in other countries. Goods from the United States are exported to places all over the world. At the same time, the United States imports many goods from other countries. This **international trade**, or trade among nations, allows people in the United States and in other countries to buy goods that their own countries do not make or grow. The United States' most important international trading partners are Canada, China, Britain, Germany, Japan, and Mexico.

This man is working on an American brand of automobile in a factory in Beijing, China. Below, cars in Japan await shipment overseas.

To increase international trade, many countries, including the United States, have signed free-trade agreements. A **free-trade agreement** is a treaty in which countries agree not to charge tariffs, or taxes, on goods they buy from and sell to each other. Such an agreement gives industries in each of the trading nations the chance to compete better. In 1994, Mexico, Canada, and the United States put the North American Free Trade Agreement, or NAFTA, into effect. One of NAFTA's goals has been to assist the movement of goods and services across national borders. As a result, the number of goods and services available to people in all three nations has increased.

International trade adds much to the economy of the United States. The United States also interacts with other countries in other ways. Many companies in the United States have offices and factories in other countries. Many companies from other countries also have businesses in the United States. Almost 5 million people in the United States work in businesses owned by people in other countries. This means that the nations of the world are now part of a **global economy**, the world market in which companies from different countries buy and sell goods and services.

REVIEW **What is a free-trade agreement?**

A Free Enterprise Economy

In a free enterprise economy, such as that of the United States, producers offer goods or services that consumers want to buy. Companies produce a greater supply when demand rises. Price affects demand, and demand affects price. For example, if a computer game cost $1,000, very few people would be willing to buy it. Demand for the product will be low, and the company will produce only a small number of games. If the price of the game is $10, many more people will be interested in buying it. Demand for the product will be high, and the company will produce many of the games.

In a free enterprise economy, people own and run their own businesses. In other kinds of economies, the government owns businesses. It tells factory

Many people in the United States, such as this Virginia couple, run their businesses from their homes.

Under the free enterprise system, Americans can open a wide variety of businesses, such as this store in Waitsfield, Vermont.

managers what goods to produce, how to produce them, and how much to charge for them. In the United States, these decisions are made by business owners.

The freedom that American businesses have has led to the creation of many new products. For example, some of today's largest computer companies were started in people's homes. The people who began these businesses were free to design their products any way they wished. As a result, consumers have been able to choose from a wide variety of products.

Another benefit of a free enterprise economy is that anyone, even a young person, can start a business. Some of the many businesses young people have started include everything from dog-walking services to Web site design companies.

REVIEW In what kind of economy are people allowed to own and run their own businesses?

LESSON 3 REVIEW

1 MAIN IDEA How has the economy of the United States changed in recent years?

2 WHY IT MATTERS What kinds of new jobs has our nation's diverse economy created for American workers?

3 VOCABULARY Explain how **e-commerce** is a part of the nation's **diverse economy**.

4 READING SKILL—Tell Fact from Opinion Price affects demand, and demand affects price. Is this statement a fact or an opinion? Explain.

5 HISTORY When did the Information Age begin?

6 ECONOMICS In what ways is the United States part of a global economy?

7 CRITICAL THINKING—Analyze How has e-commerce changed the American economy?

 PERFORMANCE—Conduct a Survey Survey your classmates and ask them what kind of job they would like to have when they are older. Find out how many of your classmates want to have traditional jobs and compare that to how many of your classmates want to have either high-tech or service jobs.

4

MAIN IDEA
Read to learn about the role of government and the main rights and responsibilities of American citizens.

WHY IT MATTERS
For the United States to remain strong, government and citizens must each meet their responsibilities.

VOCABULARY
responsibility
register
informed citizen
jury
volunteer
patriotism

Government and the People

The Constitution of the United States of America, which became law in 1788, set up the government for the nation. More than 200 years later, government leaders still look to the Constitution to help guide their actions. The American people also look to the Constitution to protect their rights and freedoms.

The Federal System

The federal system created by the Constitution divides political power between the national, or federal, government and the state governments. The federal government is the country's largest government system.

From the United States capital in Washington, D.C., the federal government conducts thousands of activities that affect the lives of Americans. It runs programs to help people who are poor, aged, or disabled. It tests foods and drugs for safety, conducts research on diseases, and sets

A CLOSER LOOK
The Capitol Building

The United States Capitol building in Washington, D.C. has been home to the United States Congress for more than 200 years.

1. The Senate chamber
2. Old Senate chamber
3. The dome
4. The rotunda
5. The geographical center of Washington, D.C.
6. The west front entrance
7. National Statuary Hall
8. The Hall of Columns

❖ Why do you think the United States Capitol building is an American landmark?

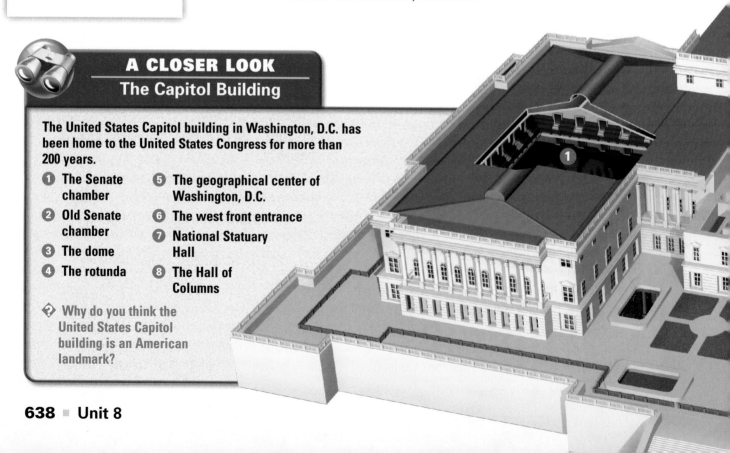

standards to control pollution. It deals with the governments of other nations, and it sets trade rules with them. The federal government is also in charge of space exploration, air travel safety, and national parks, forests, historic sites, and museums.

Many famous landmarks across the country are associated with the federal government. These include the Statue of Liberty in New York Bay, the White House in Washington, D.C., and Mount Rushmore in South Dakota. They are not just places to visit. They are patriotic symbols that remind Americans of the things that unite them as a people.

Many Americans of different backgrounds are also united by the political party to which they belong. The two main political parties are the Republican and Democratic parties. In Congress, the party with the most members in each house is known as the majority party. The party with fewer members is called the minority party.

The most powerful officer of the House of Representatives is the Speaker of the House. No member of the House may speak until called upon by the Speaker. The Speaker is always a member of the majority party and has usually served in Congress for many years.

The most powerful officers of the Senate are the majority leader and the minority leader. These people help direct the actions of their party in the Senate.

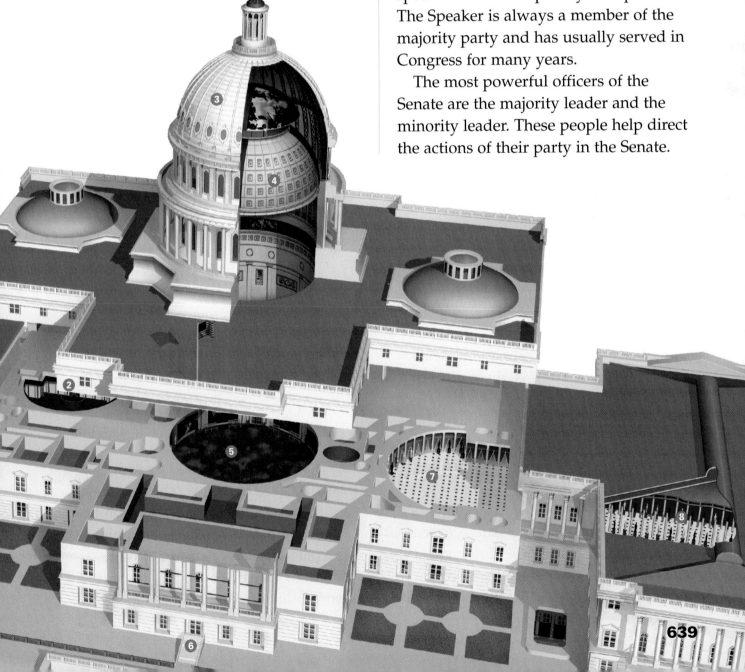

Uncle Sam

American history is filled with heroes, but only a few of them have been preserved as cartoons. During the War of 1812, Samuel Wilson, owner of a New York meat-packing business, helped supply the United States Army with beef. Wilson's supply wagons were marked with the initials *U.S.* It was reported that U.S. stood for "Uncle Sam" Wilson. In fact, the letters stood for *United States.* The name caught on and in 1868 the great political cartoonist Thomas Nast created the first Uncle Sam cartoon. In 1961 Congress passed a resolution honoring Samuel Wilson as the person who inspired America's national symbol.

I WANT YOU FOR U.S. ARMY
NEAREST RECRUITING STATION

federal treaties. Through the years, the role of the federal government has increased in traditional state government activities, such as regulating businesses and providing for public schools.

On every level of government federal, state, and local leaders attempt to fulfill their roles as government officials. Some of these leaders, such as state representatives to Congress, are elected by the voters. Others, such as federal judges, are appointed, or named, by a specific governing body. For example, in 2000 Hillary Rodham Clinton was elected to the United States Senate by the voters of New York. Supreme Court Justice Sandra Day O'Connor, on the other hand, was nominated to her position by the President of the United States.

REVIEW What are some powers that the federal and state governments share?

Civic Affairs

The Constitution says that citizens who meet the age requirements have the right to vote and the right to hold public office. All residents in the United States—citizens and noncitizens alike—have freedom of speech, freedom of the press, freedom of religion, and freedom to gather in groups. Laws passed by the United States Congress and by state governments can give people other rights, too.

With these rights come responsibilities. A **responsibility** is a duty—something that a person is expected to do. With the right to vote, for example, comes the responsibility of voting. Most state

Since most state congresses are modeled after the federal Congress, these offices also exist at the state level.

The federal and state governments both have some of the same powers. These include the rights to tax and to spend and borrow money.

Each state has its own constitution, its own laws, and its own legislative, executive, and judicial branches. However, state laws and activities must not conflict with the United States Constitution or governments say that a citizen who wants to take part in an election must **register** to vote, or show that he or she lives where the voting takes place. This is an important responsibility because every vote matters in an election. This was very clear in the 2000 Presidential election when only a few hundred votes made the difference in George W. Bush's win over Al Gore.

With freedom of speech and freedom of the press comes the responsibility of being an informed and active citizen. An **informed citizen** is one who knows what is happening in the community, the state, the nation, and the world. An informed citizen is more likely to understand why things happen and to see other people's points of view.

Citizens who feel strongly about an issue can always contact their representatives by writing letters or making phone calls. Today e-mail makes staying in touch with government leaders simpler than ever.

The responsibilities of citizens are not written in the Constitution, but they follow naturally from what is written there. For example, the Constitution says that every person charged with a crime will be judged by a jury. A **jury** is a group of citizens who decide a case in court. Citizens must be willing to be members of a jury if called upon to serve. The Constitution gives Congress the authority to raise money to run the nation. Citizens must be willing to pay taxes if the nation is to run smoothly.

Besides voting, obeying the laws, defending the nation, serving on a jury, and paying taxes, some citizens take a more active part in the government. One way citizens take action is by taking part in political campaigns.

Volunteers (right) help to register voters before the 2000 Presidential election. Other volunteers (below) work in the campaign office of California Representative Loretta Sanchez.

Some citizens go from door to door, handing out information on their candidates or on issues. Other citizens telephone voters to remind them to go to the polls on election day. Most campaign workers are **volunteers**, or people who work without pay.

The most common way citizens take part in politics is by joining a political party. Most registered voters are members of either the Republican or Democratic party. However, a growing number of voters are choosing to register as independents. These voters are not connected to any organized party.

Members of organized parties can be chosen to serve as delegates to their party's national convention. These conventions, which take place every four years, are where presidential candidates are selected. Every state sends a certain number of delegates to each convention. The greater the state's population, the more delegates it can send. These delegates then vote on who their party will nominate as its Presidential candidate.

Citizens can also be candidates themselves. One person who decided to take an active part in government is Patty Murray. As a parent volunteer, she lobbied for more money for education. In 1992 she ran for office and won, becoming the first woman to represent the state of Washington in the United States Senate.

REVIEW How can people today contact government leaders?

Working Together

The writers of the United States Constitution were not sure their government would last. No other nation had ever had a government quite like the one described by the Constitution. No other people had ever had all of the rights that

Elected officials and local citizens hold a city council meeting in Gloucester, Massachusetts.

American citizens enjoyed. But would the people be able to keep their government going and protect their freedoms over time? The country would need good citizens—citizens who would work for the common good.

Past republics, like that of ancient Rome, broke up partly because the people grew greedy and selfish. To keep the nation strong, Americans would have to keep the spirit that had given the nation its independence and its Constitution. They would need to show **patriotism**, or love of country. Patriotism is more than simply waving the American flag at special times. The writers of the Constitution knew that Americans would have to be good citizens all the time.

REVIEW **What are good citizens?**

LESSON 4
REVIEW

5 **CIVICS AND GOVERNMENT** What are some of the responsibilities that come with the rights of United States residents?

6 **CRITICAL THINKING—Analyze** What is the meaning of the Pledge of Allegiance?

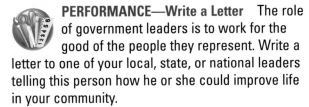

PERFORMANCE—Write a Letter The role of government leaders is to work for the good of the people they represent. Write a letter to one of your local, state, or national leaders telling this person how he or she could improve life in your community.

1 **MAIN IDEA** What are the roles of government and citizens in the United States?

2 **WHY IT MATTERS** Why must government and citizens both meet their responsibilities?

3 **VOCABULARY** Use the word **register** in a sentence about voting.

4 **READING SKILL—Tell Fact from Opinion** The most powerful officer of the House of Representatives is the Speaker of the House. Is this statement a fact or an opinion? Explain.

Identify Political Symbols

➡ WHY IT MATTERS

People often recognize sports teams, clubs, and other organizations by their symbols. The same is true for political parties, the President, Congress, the Supreme Court, and even voters. Being able to identify political symbols and what they stand for can help you better understand news reports, political cartoons, and other sources of information.

➡ WHAT YOU NEED TO KNOW

Two of the country's most famous political symbols are animals. The donkey represents the Democratic party. The elephant represents the Republican party. The donkey was probably first used to represent President Andrew Jackson, a Democrat, in the 1830s. Later the donkey became a symbol for the entire party. Cartoonist Thomas Nast introduced the elephant as a symbol of the Republican party in 1874. Both of these symbols are still used today.

One of the symbols for the national government is Uncle Sam. The bald eagle and the Statue of Liberty are other symbols for our government. Buildings are often used as political symbols. The White House is a symbol for the President, and the United States Capitol is a symbol for Congress.

When you see a political symbol, answer the following questions to help you understand its meaning.

❶ Do you recognize the symbol? Does it stand for the whole national government or only part of the national government? Does it stand for a person or group that is involved in government, such as a political party or organization?

❷ Where did you see the symbol? If it appeared in a magazine, did the writer give you any clues about its meaning?

❸ Does it include any captions or other words that help explain what the symbol means? A symbol labeled "To Protect and Serve," for example, might tell you that it stands for the police.

❹ Why do you think the symbol is a good representation of the person or group it stands for?

❺ When do you think you are most likely to see the symbol?

▶ APPLY WHAT YOU LEARNED

Look through current news-magazines, in the editorial pages of newspapers, or on the Internet. Cut or print out an example of a political symbol and paste it on a sheet of paper. Below the symbol, write a brief description of what it stands for.

The elephant (left) is the symbol of the Republican party. The donkey (below) is the symbol of the Democratic party.

CITIZENSHIP SKILLS

Political Buttons

Political candidates often think of clever ways to make themselves known to voters. They distribute buttons and other materials to rally enthusiasm and support of voters. Political buttons can list or show ideas that are important to a candidate's campaign. Many people wear political buttons to show their support for a candidate. Some people choose to wear political buttons to show they support an elected leader.

INAUGURATION DAY
JAN. 20th 1981
PRESIDENT VICE-PRESIDENT
RONALD REAGAN   GEORGE BUSH

This title identifies the button's purpose.

The photographs on this button show who was elected.

The eagle is a patriotic symbol of the United States.

The elephant is a political symbol of the Republican party.

Red, white, and blue are the colors of the American Flag.

Analyze the Primary Source

① How do you think a voter wearing a political button can help a candidate become better known? Why would a candidate or elected official want to picture their face on a political button?

② Can you think of other campaign items a candidate might use?

③ List the patriotic symbols you see on the political buttons and campaign items.

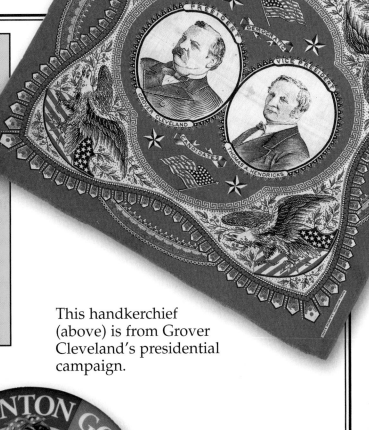

This handkerchief (above) is from Grover Cleveland's presidential campaign.

OUR CHOICE

Political buttons show a variety of information. The postcard (left) is from William Taft's presidential campaign.

ACTIVITY

Write to Explain Imagine you are running for an elected office. Design a political button for your supporters to wear. Write a paragraph that explains the information on your button.

RESEARCH

GO ONLINE Visit The Learning Site at **www.harcourtschool.com/primarysources** to research other primary sources.

17 Review and Test Preparation

USE YOUR READING SKILLS

Complete this graphic organizer by identifying facts and opinions about the United States. A copy of this graphic organizer appears on page 168 of the Activity Book.

Facts and Opinions About the United States

THE POPULATION OF THE UNITED STATES

FACT:
More than 281 million people live in the United States
→
OPINION:
_____

FACT:
_____
→
OPINION:
_____

THE UNITED STATES GOVERNMENT AND THE PEOPLE

FACT:
_____
→
OPINION:
_____

FACT:
_____
→
OPINION:
_____

THINK & WRITE

Write a List of Questions   Imagine that the President of the United States has scheduled a trip to visit your school and to spend time with your class. Write a list of questions you would like to ask the President.

Write a Poem   Many patriotic poems have been written about the United States over the course of its history. Think of the things that make the United States a great nation, and then write a poem that honors the country.

USE VOCABULARY

For each pair of terms, write a sentence that explains how the terms are related.

1 Internet (p. 624), teleconference (p. 625)

2 interdependent (p. 635), global economy (p. 636)

3 register (p. 641), informed citizen (p. 641)

RECALL FACTS

Answer these questions.

4 In what ways can people contact their representatives?

5 Why was the Pledge of Allegiance written?

Write the letter of the best choice.

6 TEST PREP   Today most new immigrants to the United States come from countries in—
  A Europe and South America.
  B Asia and Europe.
  C Asia and Latin America.
  D Africa and South America.

7 TEST PREP   Under a free enterprise system—
  F people can own and run their own businesses.
  G the government owns most businesses.
  H most people work in agriculture.
  J the government tells businesses what to charge for goods and services.

8 TEST PREP   The two main political parties in the United States today are the—
  A Republican and Federalist parties.
  B Federalist and Democratic parties.
  C Republican and Democratic parties.
  D Democratic and Whig parties.

9 TEST PREP   The most common way American citizens take part in politics is by—
  F running for office.
  G volunteering as campaign workers.
  H joining a political party.
  J serving on a jury.

THINK CRITICALLY

10 How does immigration continue to shape the United States today?

11 What do you think might happen if cities did not try to manage urban growth?

12 How have American jobs changed over the last 100 years?

13 Why do you think the United States has remained a strong nation for so long?

APPLY SKILLS

Use a Cartogram
Review the map and the cartogram in the skill on pages 626–627. Then answer the following questions.

14 Why is New Jersey shown larger than Maine on the cartogram?

15 Which West Coast state has the smallest population?

Identify Political Symbols

16 Write down the names of the last five United States Presidents. Then use the Almanac in the back of your textbook to find out their political parties. Decide which party symbol would be used to represent each President.

ORGANIZATION OF AMERICAN STATES FLAG GARDEN

The Organization of American States, or OAS, was formed in 1890. It is the world's oldest regional organization. Today, the OAS is made up of 35 Western Hemisphere nations. It has four official languages—English, Spanish, French, and Portuguese.

LOCATE IT

MARYLAND

Washington, D.C.

VIRGINIA

Organization of American States Flag Garden

Partners in the Hemisphere

 Our future cannot be separated from the future of our neighbors.
—George W. Bush, State Department speech, February 15, 2001

CHAPTER READING SKILL

Compare and Contrast

To **compare** two things is to find out how they are alike. To **contrast** them is to find out how they are different.

As you read this chapter, compare and contrast the issues and events involving the United States and its neighbors.

KEY ISSUES OR EVENTS

SIMILARITIES   DIFFERENCES

MAIN IDEA
Read to find out about the land, people, history, and economy of Mexico.

WHY IT MATTERS
As our nearest neighbor to the south, Mexico has played an important role in the history and economy of the United States.

VOCABULARY
middle class
interest rate

Mexico

1800   1900   PRESENT

In 1521 the Spanish conquistador Hernando Cortés conquered the Aztec Empire and claimed Mexico for Spain. For the next 300 years, Mexico remained under Spanish rule. Then, in 1821, a revolution ended Spain's rule, and Mexico became an independent country.

Independence, however, did not immediately bring peace. For many years afterward, the people of Mexico struggled to build an orderly society. The Mexican Constitution of 1917 reorganized the country's government and led to closer ties with the United States. Today, the two countries are major trading partners.

The Land and People of Mexico

Mexico is a land with many mountains. Two mountain ranges, the Sierra Madre Occidental on the west and the Sierra Madre Oriental on the east, stretch along Mexico's coast. Between these mountains lies the Mexican Plateau, a region of rich farmland

FAST FACT Two states in Mexico share part of their names with a state in the United States—California.

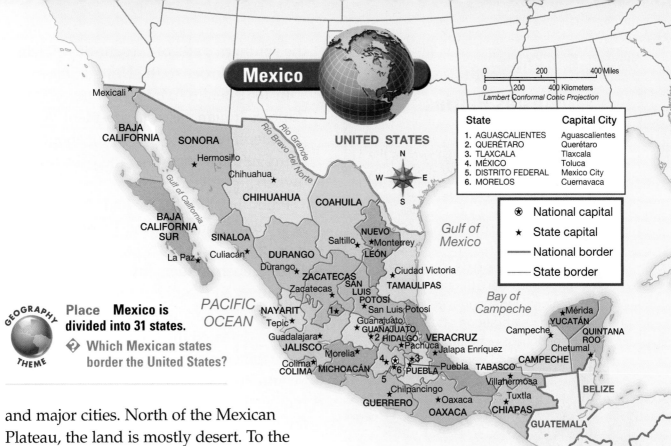

Mexico

0   200   400 Miles
0   200   400 Kilometers
Lambert Conformal Conic Projection

State	Capital City
1. AGUASCALIENTES	Aguascalientes
2. QUERÉTARO	Querétaro
3. TLAXCALA	Tlaxcala
4. MÉXICO	Toluca
5. DISTRITO FEDERAL	Mexico City
6. MORELOS	Cuernavaca

⊛ National capital
★ State capital
—— National border
—— State border

UNITED STATES

Mexicali

BAJA CALIFORNIA   SONORA
Hermosillo
Chihuahua
CHIHUAHUA   COAHUILA
BAJA CALIFORNIA SUR   SINALOA
Saltillo   NUEVO LEÓN   Monterrey
La Paz   Culiacán   DURANGO
Durango   ZACATECAS   Ciudad Victoria
Zacatecas   SAN LUIS POTOSÍ   TAMAULIPAS
PACIFIC OCEAN   NAYARIT   San Luis Potosí
Tepic   Guanajuato
Guadalajara   GUANAJUATO   HIDALGO
JALISCO   Morelia   Pachuca   VERACRUZ   Jalapa Enríquez
Colima   MICHOACÁN   PUEBLA   Puebla   TABASCO
COLIMA   Chilpancingo   Villahermosa
GUERRERO   Oaxaca   Tuxtla
OAXACA   CHIAPAS

Rio Grande / Rio Bravo del Norte
Gulf of California
Gulf of Mexico
Bay of Campeche

Mérida   YUCATÁN   QUINTANA ROO
Campeche   Chetumal
CAMPECHE

BELIZE
GUATEMALA

Place Mexico is divided into 31 states.

❓ Which Mexican states border the United States?

and major cities. North of the Mexican Plateau, the land is mostly desert. To the south on the Yucatán Peninsula, there are both rain forests and grassy plains.

Most people in Mexico today trace their cultural heritage to two main groups—Native American and Spanish. In fact, more than 60 percent of the people are mestizos, people of mixed Indian and Spanish ancestry. Mexicans continue to honor the contributions of both groups with public history displays and celebrations.

REVIEW What two groups have mainly influenced Mexico's culture and people?

These hikers (left) are in the rugged desert of Mexico's Baja Peninsula.

Mexico, a Republic

Most of the wealth and power in colonial Mexico belonged to people of pure Spanish ancestry. Other Mexicans had few opportunities. In September 1810, Father Miguel Hidalgo (mee•GAYL ee•DAHL•goh) gave a speech in his church calling for a revolution against Spain. Hidalgo's rebel army was later defeated, but his actions were not forgotten. The revolution continued, and in 1821 Mexico gained its independence.

In time, Mexico became a republic. The Mexican people, however, had little experience with self-government. Presidents were no sooner elected than they were forced out of office by their enemies. During those same years, Mexico lost most of its northern lands to the United States. Texas, which won its independence from Mexico in 1836, became part of the United States in 1845.

Fiestas Patrias

Each year the Mexican people celebrate two national holidays known as the *Fiestas Patrias*, or festivals of the country. The first of these holidays, *Cinco de Mayo*, or May 5, honors Mexico's victory over the French at Puebla on May 5, 1862. The second holiday, *Diez y Seis de Septiembre*, or September 16, is Mexico's national independence day. Both celebrations often feature speeches, patriotic songs, dances, and parades.

Three years later, following a war with the United States, Mexico agreed to give up most of its remaining northern lands to the United States. These lands included present-day California, Utah, and Nevada and parts of New Mexico, Arizona, Colorado, and Wyoming. In return, the United States paid Mexico $15 million. Mexico later sold the southern parts of present-day Arizona and New Mexico to the United States.

In 1861 Benito Juárez (HWAHR•ays), a Zapotec Indian, became president. As president, Juárez helped bring about many reforms, including the private ownership of land.

From the start, Juárez had enemies who wanted him out of office. Those enemies looked to France for help. On May 5, 1862, French soldiers invaded Mexico and attacked the city of Puebla. Though greatly outnumbered, the Mexicans at Puebla defeated the French.

Despite their loss at Puebla, the French eventually took control of Mexico and removed Juárez from office. Within a few years, however, the Mexican people rebelled. Juárez became president again.

After Juárez died, the dictator Porfirio Díaz (pour•FEER•yoh DEE•ahs) ruled for more than 30 years. Díaz ordered railroads built and factories enlarged. Díaz brought economic growth to Mexico, but problems remained. Many poor farmers lost their land. When Díaz took control, 20 percent of the people owned land. Thirty years later, only 2 percent of the people owned land.

In 1910 many Mexican farmers and other groups fought against the dictatorship. Díaz resigned, but the fighting continued in Mexico. When the fighting ended, the leaders of the revolution took control of Mexico. They wrote a new constitution that limited the time a president could serve to a six-year term.

Benito Juárez

Mexico City, like all large cities, has crowded streets. Air pollution from automobile exhaust is often a problem in the city.

LOCATE IT

Mexico City

MEXICO

Many government-owned farms were divided among farm families.

While more people owned land, they still had few political choices. For more than 70 years, a single party controlled the presidency. Candidates from other political parties were elected to the Mexican Congress, but only those from the Partido Revolucionario Institucional (PRI) became president.

The election of July 2000 changed everything. Mexicans chose Vicente Fox, from the Partido Acción Nacional (PAN), as their new president. When asked how difficult his job as president would be, Fox replied, "The challenge is gigantic, but so are our resources. In Mexico we have a saying, 'Every newborn child comes with a gift.' Democracy will bring us lots of benefits and hope."

REVIEW How does the Mexican constitution limit a president's power?

A Growing Middle Class

Mexico is divided into 31 states and one federal district. The federal district contains Mexico City, Mexico's capital. About 9 million people live in Mexico City. About 9 million more people live in its metropolitan area, making Mexico City one of the world's most populated metropolitan areas.

Mexico City is just one of the large cities that lie on the Mexican Plateau. In fact, more than half of Mexico's population lives in this region. Other large cities on the Mexican Plateau include Monterrey, Guadalajara, and Puebla. Each of these cities has more than a million people.

Many cities in Mexico have grown as people have moved from rural areas to cities to find new jobs and better wages. In recent years, many new factories have been built in northern Mexico.

George W. Bush's first international trip as President of the United States was to visit with Mexican president Vicente Fox. The trip emphasized the strong ties between the two nations.

As a result, Ciudad Juárez, Matamoros, Tijuana, and other cities near the United States border have all grown quickly.

The growth of manufacturing and other industries in Mexico also led to the growth of a large **middle class**, an economic level between the poor and the wealthy. Today, Mexico's middle class is one of the largest in the Americas.

In 1994, however, even middle-class families found buying most products difficult. The value of the peso, Mexico's basic unit of money, suddenly dropped because of inflation and the government's need to pay its debts. That caused prices in Mexico to rise sharply. Some doubled. Others tripled. **Interest rates**, the amounts that banks charge to loan money, rose as high as 80 percent. To help stabilize the Mexican economy, the United States arranged $52 billion in loans to Mexico. Had the Mexican economy collapsed, it would have had a terrible effect on the world economy.

Another major economic change occurred in 1994 when Canada, Mexico, and the United States put the North American Free Trade Agreement into effect. The year before NAFTA began, trade between the United States and Mexico totaled $80 billion a year. By 2000 that figure was $230 billion.

REVIEW Why did Mexico's middle class grow larger?

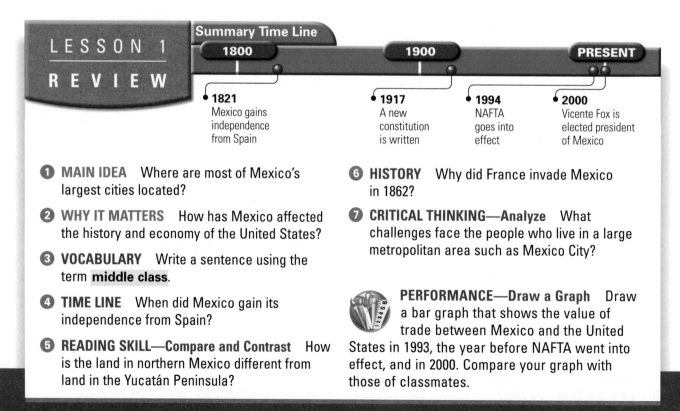

LESSON 1 REVIEW

Summary Time Line

1800 — 1900 — PRESENT

1821
Mexico gains independence from Spain

1917
A new constitution is written

1994
NAFTA goes into effect

2000
Vicente Fox is elected president of Mexico

1 MAIN IDEA   Where are most of Mexico's largest cities located?

2 WHY IT MATTERS   How has Mexico affected the history and economy of the United States?

3 VOCABULARY   Write a sentence using the term **middle class**.

4 TIME LINE   When did Mexico gain its independence from Spain?

5 READING SKILL—Compare and Contrast   How is the land in northern Mexico different from land in the Yucatán Peninsula?

6 HISTORY   Why did France invade Mexico in 1862?

7 CRITICAL THINKING—Analyze   What challenges face the people who live in a large metropolitan area such as Mexico City?

PERFORMANCE—Draw a Graph   Draw a bar graph that shows the value of trade between Mexico and the United States in 1993, the year before NAFTA went into effect, and in 2000. Compare your graph with those of classmates.

Central America and the Caribbean

1880 — 1940 — PRESENT

Like the United States, many nations in Central America and the Caribbean have a history of democracy. Costa Rica has a long democratic tradition. So does Puerto Rico, with its ties to the United States. In some places in the region, however, people continue to struggle for democracy and economic security.

The Land and People

The geography of the nations of Central America and the Caribbean is as varied as the backgrounds of the people who live there. Towering mountains, sandy beaches, dense forests, and remote islands are just some of the features that mark these two regions.

MAIN IDEA
Read to find out about the various regions, common heritages, and similar challenges facing Central American and Caribbean countries.

WHY IT MATTERS
Events in Central America and the Caribbean often affect not only the countries in those regions but also the United States.

VOCABULARY
commonwealth
embargo
free election

On the outskirts of Guatemala City, a large volcano looms.

LOCATE IT
MEXICO
GUATEMALA
Guatemala City

Central America and the Caribbean

Gulf of Mexico

Freeport

Nassau

Straits of Florida

BAHAMAS

George Town

Havana • Matanzas
• Santa Clara

CUBA

• City
⊛ Capital city
— National border

Nueva
Gerona

Camaguey
Holguin

Turks and Caicos Islands (U.K.)

ATLANTIC
OCEAN

Manzanillo

Guantanamo

DOMINICAN
REPUBLIC

Cayman Is.
(U.K.)

Santiago
de Cuba

Windward Passage

HAITI

Santiago

Virgin Is.
(U.S.)

St. Martin (FR. & NETH.)
Anguilla (U.K.)

St. Barthelemy (FR.)

Montego Bay

Hispaniola

Port-au-Prince

San
Juan

ST. KITTS
AND NEVIS

Mona Passage

JAMAICA Kingston

Santo
Domingo

• Ponce

St. Croix
(U.S.)

Puerto
Rico
(U.S.)

Basseterre

ANTIGUA
AND
BARBUDA
St. John's

Belize City
⊛Belmopan

BELIZE

Gulf of
Honduras

Monserrat (U.K.)
Guadeloupe (Fr.)

DOMINICA

Roseau⊛

GUATEMALA
Guatemala City
⊛

San Pedro Sula

HONDURAS

Caribbean   Sea

Martinique (Fr.)

ST. LUCIA

Castries

Tegucigalpa⊛

Coco River

ST. VINCENT AND
THE GRENADINES

Bridgetown

San Salvador ⊛

Aruba
(NETH.)

Curaçao
(NETH.)

Kingstown

BARBADOS

EL SALVADOR

NICARAGUA

Oranjestad•

Bonaire
(NETH.)

St. George's

Lake Managua

Managua⊛
•Granada

Willemstad

GRENADA

Lake Nicaragua

San José⊛

Port of Spain

Puntarenas•

Puerto Limon

Panama Canal

TRINIDAD
AND TOBAGO

Colon

COSTA
RICA

Panama
City⊛

PACIFIC
OCEAN

PANAMA

Gulf of
Panama

SOUTH   AMERICA

0   200   400 Miles

0   200   400 Kilometers

Lambert Conformal Conic Projection

Location   Seven countries make up the region known as Central
America, while hundreds of islands are found in the Caribbean.

❖ **Which Caribbean country lies farthest north?**

GEOGRAPHY THEME

Traveling south from Mexico, a visitor would pass through Belize (buh•LEEZ), Guatemala (gwah•tuh•MAH•luh), Honduras, El Salvador, Nicaragua (nih•kuh•RAH•gwah), Costa Rica, and Panama. These seven countries form the 202,000 square miles (523,180 sq km) called Central America. Almost all the Central American countries have mountains. Volcanoes, some still active, formed the mountains. Ash from the volcanoes made the surrounding land fertile.

The Pacific Ocean forms the western borders of all the Central American countries except Belize. The Caribbean Sea, which is part of the Atlantic Ocean, forms the eastern borders of all the Central American countries except El Salvador.

Rain forests brighten the landscapes of Guatemala and Costa Rica. Costa Rica especially wants to preserve its rain forests' rich variety of plant and animal life. About 25 percent of Costa Rica's land has been set aside as nature preserves.

The fertile land of Central America is farmed to produce crops such as bananas, sugarcane, coffee, corn, cotton, and beans. Fishing is an important industry in Belize. Some countries, such as Guatemala and Panama, also have mineral resources.

People who live on islands in the Caribbean grow many of the same kinds of crops as people in Central America, and they earn their livings in similar ways. Among the hundreds of islands in the Caribbean are Cuba, Puerto Rico, the Bahamas, Jamaica, and Hispaniola.

European explorers first visited these islands in the late 1400s and early 1500s. The beauty of the tropical islands and the rich land impressed the explorers. Today, visitors come for the islands' lovely beaches and warm climates.

Despite the beauty and the rich land, places in the Caribbean and Central America face special challenges. Earthquakes are common in Central America, and tropical storms often bring heavy rains to both regions. Hurricane Georges, for example, hit the eastern Caribbean, Haiti, and the Dominican Republic in September 1998. The storm caused more then $1.5 billion in damages. One month later, Hurricane Mitch roared into the western Caribbean, with winds that reached 180 miles (290 km) per hour. The storm then came ashore in Honduras, where its heavy rains caused mudslides in Central America. The storm killed more than 10,000 people and injured about 13,000.

Many of the people who live in Central America and the Caribbean are of Spanish and Native American descent. Many people of African descent also live in the regions. Their ancestors were brought from Africa as slaves. The main language in most of the countries is Spanish, but in some countries most people speak either English, French, or Dutch.

REVIEW What are two major challenges to living in Central America and the Caribbean?

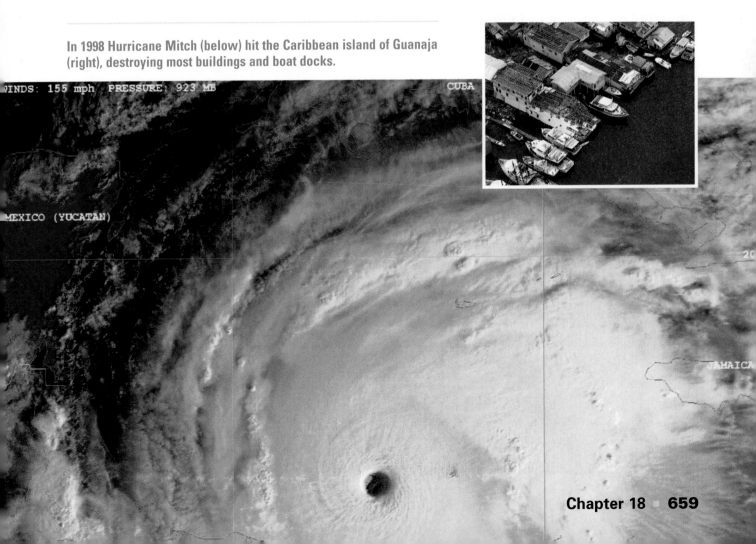

In 1998 Hurricane Mitch (below) hit the Caribbean island of Guanaja (right), destroying most buildings and boat docks.

WINDS: 155 mph PRESSURE 923 MB

CUBA

MEXICO (YUCATAN)

JAMAICA

Fidel Castro has ruled Cuba since 1959.

Government in the Regions

For the first time in recent history, almost all the nations in Central America and the Caribbean have some form of democratic government. Cuba, which is a communist dictatorship, is the exception.

Both Puerto Rico and Cuba came under United States control in 1898, after the Spanish-American War. Puerto Rico was made a United States territory, but Cuba became an independent country in 1902. In 1952 Puerto Rico became a **commonwealth**, a kind of territory that governs itself. As citizens of a territory, Puerto Ricans hold United States citizenship. The United States Virgin Islands is another United States territory in the Caribbean.

Since 1959 Fidel Castro has ruled Cuba as a communist dictator. In an effort to end communism in Cuba, the United States government set up an economic embargo against the nation in 1960. An **embargo** is one nation's refusal to trade goods with another. Cuba's economy has been weakened by the embargo, but Cuba still remains a communist nation. Meanwhile, many Cuban Americans in the United States continue to hope that Cuba will become a democracy.

At Castro's request, Pope John Paul II visited Cuba in January 1998. Although

· SCIENCE AND TECHNOLOGY ·

The Arecibo Observatory

In the late 1950s, American scientist William E. Gordon was searching for a site to build a space observatory. Because of what Gordon wished to study, the observatory had to be able to see a certain part of the sky, near the equator. The site finally chosen was Arecibo (ah•rah•SEE•boh) in northwest Puerto Rico. Today, the Arecibo Observatory has the world's largest single-dish radio telescope. The dish has a 1000-foot (305 m) diameter and covers 20 acres. The telescope has helped locate planets outside our solar system.

the Roman Catholic Church is not outlawed, its members cannot join the Communist party, which controls housing and jobs. In honor of the Pope's visit, Castro allowed Christmas to be celebrated in public for the first time in many years.

Many democratic governments in Central America and the Caribbean have struggled to survive. Costa Rica has been the most stable democracy. Like the United States, Costa Rica has three branches of government.

Despite being the second-oldest republic in the Western Hemisphere, after the United States, Haiti has had a history of military takeovers of its government. For much of its history, Haiti was ruled by dictators.

Former president of Haiti, Jean-Bertrand Aristide

At other times, however, the people of Haiti have freely elected their leaders. In 1990 Haiti held a **free election**—one that offers a choice of candidates, instead of a single candidate. Jean-Bertrand Aristide (air•ih•STEED) was elected, but military leaders soon took over. Aristide escaped to the United States. To help end military rule and return Aristide to office, the United States sent troops to Haiti in 1994. Soon Aristide returned to office.

Since that time, Haiti has held other free elections. Most people in Haiti are hopeful that their government will remain a democracy.

REVIEW What nation in the Caribbean continues to be a communist country?

LESSON 2 REVIEW

Summary Time Line

1880	1940	PRESENT

1898
Cuba, the Philippines, and Puerto Rico are under United States control

1952
Puerto Rico becomes a United States commonwealth

1990
Haiti holds free elections

1998
Pope John Paul II visits Cuba

1. **MAIN IDEA** What do all the countries in Central America and the Caribbean, except Cuba, have in common?

2. **WHY IT MATTERS** How has the United States been affected by events in Central America and the Caribbean?

3. **VOCABULARY** What is a **commonwealth**?

4. **TIME LINE** When did Puerto Rico become a commonwealth?

5. **READING SKILL—Compare and Contrast** How are the governments of Costa Rica and Cuba different?

6. **HISTORY** Why did the United States send troops to Haiti in 1994?

7. **CRITICAL THINKING—Analyze** How might an embargo affect a country?

 PERFORMANCE—Make a Mobile Make a mobile about the land and the people of Central America and the Caribbean. Include pictures that represent the regions' physical features and products. Use your mobile to describe the regions to other students.

Read Population Pyramids

VOCABULARY

population pyramid
life expectancy
median age

▶ WHY IT MATTERS

A graph that shows the division of a country's population by age is called a **population pyramid**. Each side of the graph is divided by age. One side of the graph shows the female population. The other side of the graph shows the male population.

Two factors affect the shape of the population pyramid—a country's birth rate and its death rate. The birth rate is the number of children born each year for every 1,000 people in the country. The death rate is the number of people who die each year for every 1,000 people in the country.

A population pyramid also gives a picture of a country's **life expectancy**, the number of years people can expect to live. This number varies from country to country. It tells in general how long people in a country live, but it does not say how long any one person will live.

A population pyramid also shows the country's median age. The word *median* means "middle." Half the people in the country are older than the **median age**, and half are younger.

Four generations of the same family can be seen in this photograph.

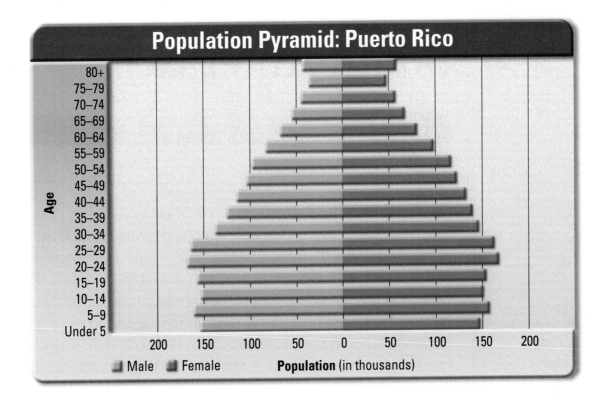

Population Pyramid: Puerto Rico

Age

| Population (in thousands) |
80+
75–79
70–74
65–69
60–64
55–59
50–54
45–49
40–44
35–39
30–34
25–29
20–24
15–19
10–14
5–9
Under 5

200   150   100   50   0   50   100   150   200

■ Male   ■ Female   **Population** (in thousands)

▶ WHAT YOU NEED TO KNOW

The population pyramid shown above gives the population of Puerto Rico. Notice how it is divided into age groups, with the youngest at the bottom and the oldest at the top. The left side of the population pyramid shows the number of males in each age group. The right side shows the number of females. If you want to know the number that a whole age group represents, add together the number of males and the number of females in that age group. For example, in the 10–14 age group, there are about 152,000 males and about 150,000 females. So there are about 302,000 persons age 10–14 in Puerto Rico.

The pyramid's shape indicates how rapidly Puerto Rico's population is growing. The very wide parts of the pyramid show that the greatest number of people are under 29 years of age. The top of the pyramid indicates that fewer people are over 70 years of age.

▶ PRACTICE THE SKILL

Use the population pyramid to answer the following questions.

1 Find your age group on the population pyramid. About how many boys in Puerto Rico are in that age group? About how many girls?

2 In which age groups are there more females than males?

3 Which age group is the largest?

4 About how many people in Puerto Rico have lived 80 years or longer?

5 What general statement can you make about Puerto Rico's population from this pyramid?

▶ APPLY WHAT YOU LEARNED

Think about the ages of people in your own family or in your class at school. Draw a population pyramid that shows the number of people of different ages in your family or class.

MAIN IDEA
Read to find out about the land and people of South America and how countries there gained independence.

WHY IT MATTERS
Countries in South America have an important effect on the world's health and economy.

VOCABULARY
standard of living
liberate
deforestation

South America

1800   1900   PRESENT

South America's diversity can be seen in its lands, climates, and resources. Across the continent, landforms range from towering mountains to broad plateaus and plains. Climates range from tropical in the north to arid and desert in the south. The continent has abundant natural resources, but some of them have not yet been fully developed. Since the countries of South America differ in their economic development, their standards of living also vary widely. A **standard of living** is a measure of how well people in a country live.

South America and Its People

South America, the fourth largest continent, covers more than twice the area of the continental United States. Only Africa has a less indented coastline than South America. Because of this, there are few good harbors along most of South America's coasts.

The Andes Mountains extend 4,500 miles (7,250 km) along the western side of South

LOCATE IT

VENEZUELA
Caracas
Angel Falls

America, from the Caribbean in the north to the continent's southern tip. East of the Andes are areas of plateaus and plains, including the Guiana Highlands in the north and the Pampus and Patagonia to the south. Three major river systems—the Río de la Plata, the Orinoco (ohr•ee•NOH•koh), and the Amazon— run like veins through the continent's lowlands. Many of these lowlands lie in the tropics. Rain forests, with unique animals and plants, cover much of the land along the Amazon and along many of the other rivers in the region.

While much of South America is hot and humid, some areas are dry and cold. West of the snowcapped Andes, along the coast of northern Chile, is the Atacama Desert. It is the world's driest desert. So little rain falls there that people have found ways to capture moisture from the early morning fogs. The southern part of the continent is cold for much of the year.

Native peoples lived in South America for thousands of years. Then, in the 1500s, Spain, Portugal, and other European countries began to build colonies there.

South America

GEOGRAPHY THEME

Location There are 13 countries on the continent of South America. Of those 13, Brazil is the largest.

❷ How are Bolivia and Paraguay different from the other countries of South America?

FAST FACT

South America has the world's highest waterfall, longest mountain range, and largest river by volume of water. Angel Falls, the Andes Mountains, and the Amazon River are three A's to remember!

The Valley of the Moon is an arid region in Chile. Angel Falls (left), in Venezuela, is the world's highest waterfall.

Simón Bolívar   1783–1830

Character Trait: Leadership

Simón Bolívar fought for nine years for his homeland's independence. In 1821, he and his troops defeated the Spanish in Venezuela. Two years earlier Bolívar had helped Colombia win its freedom. He and his troops later defeated the Spanish in Bolivia and Peru. Because of his contributions to the independence of many nations, he is known as *El Libertador*, or The Liberator.

Europeans soon ruled most of the continent.

During the late 1700s and early 1800s, political independence became a goal for many people in South America. They had observed the success of the 13 British colonies in North America in breaking free of British rule and forming the United States. In the early 1800s, colony after colony in South America declared its independence—usually through revolution.

Simón Bolívar (see•MOHN boh•LEE•var) in Venezuela and José de San Martín (sahn mar•TEEN) in Argentina were key figures in the struggle to **liberate**, or set free, these colonies. By 1828 all of Spain's and Portugal's colonies in South America had become independent. By the mid-1800s most parts of South America had been liberated.

Bolívar hoped for a single nation in South America but knew how unlikely that would be. "[South] America is separated by climatic differences, geographical diversity, conflicting interests, and dissimilar characteristics," he said. Each country developed on its own, often fighting over borders with its neighbors.

REVIEW What was the goal of many people in South America in the early 1800s?

Old Problems in New Countries

Even after independence, most of the people in South America had little say in government. Wealth was concentrated in the hands of a few landowners, and political matters were in the hands of dictators or armies. The people lacked the education necessary to make changes. They were also unschooled in the ways of self-government.

Various reformers throughout South America began working to solve these problems.

This statue of José de San Martín is in Cordoba, Argentina.

One solution was to redistribute the land so that individuals could own small farms. During the colonial period large haciendas, which were similar to plantations in the southern United States, were common. Since the 1960s, land reform supporters have enjoyed some victories, but many farmers still do not own the land on which they work.

REVIEW What were some problems the newly independent countries faced?

Many scientists are working to solve problems related to the destruction of the rain forests.

New Problems for All Countries

Many South American countries continue to face the problems of poverty, unemployment, and keeping their democracies. Land use has once again become a major issue. In some places, Indian tribes have protested land development, which they believe disturbs centuries-old patterns of life. These tribes are beginning to take legal measures to regain their ancestral lands.

In addition, many scientists are concerned over the destruction of the rain forests in some areas of South America.

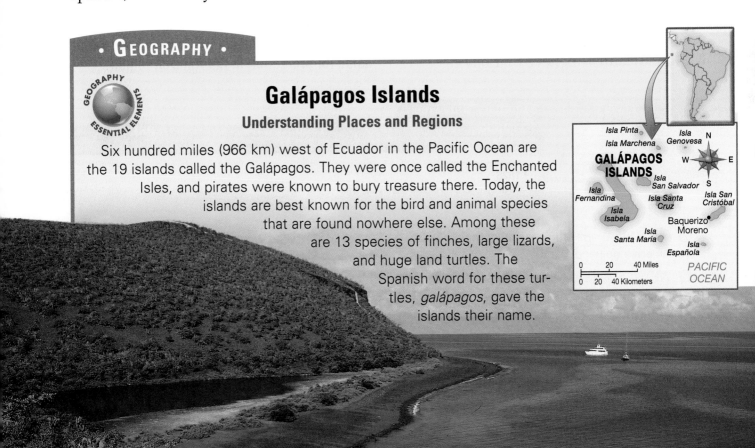

• GEOGRAPHY •

GEOGRAPHY ESSENTIAL ELEMENTS

Galápagos Islands

Understanding Places and Regions

Six hundred miles (966 km) west of Ecuador in the Pacific Ocean are the 19 islands called the Galápagos. They were once called the Enchanted Isles, and pirates were known to bury treasure there. Today, the islands are best known for the bird and animal species that are found nowhere else. Among these are 13 species of finches, large lizards, and huge land turtles. The Spanish word for these turtles, *galápagos*, gave the islands their name.

GALÁPAGOS ISLANDS

Isla Pinta
Isla Marchena
Isla Genovesa
Isla Fernandina
Isla San Salvador
Isla Santa Cruz
Isla San Cristóbal
Isla Isabela
Baquerizo Moreno
Isla Santa María
Isla Española

0   20   40 Miles
0   20   40 Kilometers

PACIFIC OCEAN

Hikers journey toward the Upsala Glacier in *Los Glaciares* National Park, Argentina. The Upsala Glacier is the largest glacier in South America.

more carbon dioxide in the atmosphere leads to warmer temperatures, which scientists term the *greenhouse effect*.

Scientists have begun to explore the use of rain forest plants for medicine. Although less than 1 percent of the plants in the rain forest have been tested for medical benefits, about 25 percent of western medicines come from rain forest plants. Destroying these plants may prevent new medicines from being discovered.

Brazil has worked to slow this **deforestation**, or the widespread cutting down of forests. Not only has the rate of cutting slowed, but lands have been set aside for protection. The Amazon region now has several plant and animal reserves, national parks, and national forests.

REVIEW **What kinds of lands have been set aside for protection in the Amazon region?**

Across South America, rain forests are cleared for their valuable wood or to build new farms, towns, and roads. As the forests are cut down, and burned, carbon dioxide is released into the atmosphere and there are fewer trees to absorb it. Some scientists believe that having

LESSON 3 REVIEW

Summary Time Line

1800 — 1900 — PRESENT

● **1828**
All of Spain and Portugal's South American colonies are independent

❶ MAIN IDEA How did most countries in South America gain independence?

❷ WHY IT MATTERS How does South America influence the world's health?

❸ VOCABULARY Use the word **liberate** in a sentence that explains its meaning.

❹ TIME LINE When did the last of Spain's and Portugal's South American colonies gain independence?

❺ READING SKILL—Compare and Contrast How is the climate of southern South America different from the climate along the Amazon?

❻ HISTORY Who were Simón Bolívar and José de San Martín?

❼ CRITICAL THINKING—Analyze Why might production increase if farmers own small plots of land, rather than having the government own all the land?

PERFORMANCE—Write a Packing List The climate and geography of parts of South America are very different. Imagine that you will be taking a trip across the continent. Tell where you will visit, and write a packing list of the clothes and supplies you might need there.

Canada

MAIN IDEA
Canada is a land of great variety and has strong ties to the United States.

WHY IT MATTERS
Canada and the United States share a long border and similar landforms. The two neighbors are also major trading partners.

VOCABULARY
province
separatist

Canada's red and white maple leaf flag is a familiar symbol to many Americans. Canada and the United States share one of the longest borders in the world, and about two-thirds of all Canadians live within 100 miles of the United States border. Geography, however, is just one reason why the two nations have such strong ties to each other.

A Varied Landscape

In land area, Canada is the second-largest country in the world. It covers more than 40 percent of North America. Canada, like the United States, stretches from the Atlantic Ocean to the Pacific Ocean, and from a 3,987-mile (6,416-km) southern border shared with the continental United States to islands in the Arctic Ocean. Canada's people may live near mountains, lakes, forests, prairies, or tundra.

A wide variety of climates and landforms can be found in Canada. Cattle graze on fertile prairie land. This glacier (inset) is in northern Alberta.

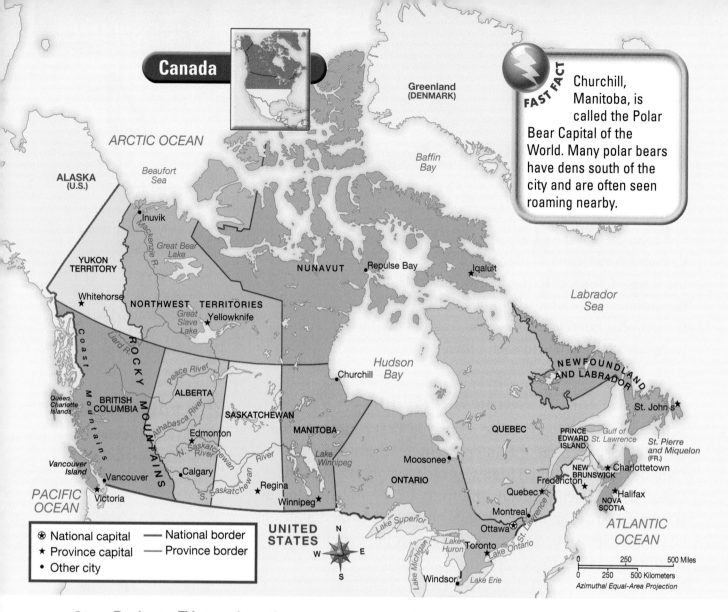

Canada

FAST FACT Churchill, Manitoba, is called the Polar Bear Capital of the World. Many polar bears have dens south of the city and are often seen roaming nearby.

Map labels:

ARCTIC OCEAN
Greenland (DENMARK)
Baffin Bay
Beaufort Sea
ALASKA (U.S.)
Inuvik
Great Bear Lake
Mackenzie R.
YUKON TERRITORY
Whitehorse
NUNAVUT
Repulse Bay
Iqaluit
Labrador Sea
NORTHWEST TERRITORIES
Great Slave Lake
Yellowknife
Liard R.
Coast Mountains
ROCKY MOUNTAINS
Peace River
Hudson Bay
Churchill
NEWFOUNDLAND AND LABRADOR
Queen Charlotte Islands
BRITISH COLUMBIA
ALBERTA
Athabasca River
SASKATCHEWAN
N. Saskatchewan River
St. John's
Edmonton
MANITOBA
QUEBEC
PRINCE EDWARD ISLAND
Gulf of St. Lawrence
St. Pierre and Miquelon (FR.)
Vancouver Island
Vancouver
Calgary
S. Saskatchewan River
Lake Winnipeg
Moosonee
NEW BRUNSWICK
Charlottetown
Fredericton
PACIFIC OCEAN
Victoria
Regina
Winnipeg
ONTARIO
Quebec
Halifax
NOVA SCOTIA
Montreal
St. Lawrence
UNITED STATES
Lake Superior
Ottawa
ATLANTIC OCEAN
Lake Michigan
Lake Huron
Toronto
Lake Ontario
Windsor
Lake Erie

Legend:
⊗ National capital
★ Province capital
• Other city
— National border
— Province border

0 250 500 Miles
0 250 500 Kilometers
Azimuthal Equal-Area Projection

N E W S (compass rose)

GEOGRAPHY THEME

Regions   This map shows the 10 provinces and 3 territories of Canada.

❖ Which Canadian province is the largest? Which territory is the largest?

Canada is a land of variety. The low Coast Mountains extend along the Pacific coast, while farther inland are the towering Rockies. The Interior Plains cover the central part of Canada. To the northeast is the Canadian Shield, a huge region of poor, rocky soil. Southeast of the Canadian Shield is the St. Lawrence Lowlands. This region has most of Canada's people and industries. The Appalachian Mountains extend into southeastern Canada.

Canada has many rivers and lakes that provide beauty and natural resources for the country. Four of the five Great Lakes help define its southern border.

Canada has 10 provinces and 3 territories. A **province** is a political region similar to a state in the United States. Each province has its own government, and it can take many actions without the approval of the national government.

REVIEW How is western Canada different from central Canada?

670 ▪ Unit 8

Journey to Self-Government

Thousands of years ago, Canada's first settlers entered the region, probably over a land bridge from Asia. Many of the descendants of these early settlers still live in Canada today. They are known as the First Nation peoples.

Canada's flag

The Vikings first explored what is now eastern Canada around A.D. 1000, but other European explorers did not reach Canada until about 500 years later. Both Britain and France wanted to control Canada's vast lands, and each nation sent explorers to claim land. After wars in Europe and North America, France lost its Canadian holdings to Britain. In the Quebec Act of 1774, Britain agreed that French settlers in Canada could keep their own laws, language, and religion.

In 1867 the British Parliament passed the British North American Act. This act, which united all of Canada into one nation, also served as Canada's first constitution. It gave Canada a representative government, but Britain held the final word in Canadian affairs.

In 1931 the British Parliament passed the Statute of Westminister. It allowed Canada to conduct its own foreign affairs, but Canada still remained partly under British rule. Canada also became a partner in the British Commonwealth of Nations, the name given to territories that give allegiance to the British crown.

Canadians wanted more control over their own government and decisions. A new constitution in 1982 permitted constitutional amendments without approval from the British Parliament.

LOCATE IT

Ottawa

ONTARIO

Great Lakes

Members of the Canadian Senate (inset) meet inside the Parliament Building, in Ottawa.

POINTS OF VIEW
Should Quebec Secede?

Almost since Britain won control of New France in 1763, Quebec has struggled to hold on to its French heritage. Some French Canadians of Quebec have tried to win Quebec's independence from Canada.

MARC-ANDRE BEDARD, a leader of the separatist movement

66 Are we a people or are we not? If we are, we should be sovereign. We should be at the table with the international community. 99

PIERRE TRUDEAU, former Canadian prime minister

66 It would be disastrous. . . . It would mean a major setback in the course of history. And the burden would lie with those who would like to break up one of history's greatest achievements—the Canadian federation. 99

Analyze the Viewpoints

❶ What views does each person hold?

❷ **Make it Relevant** Choose an issue about which the people in your class or community have different views. Find out what people think about the issue.

In Montreal (below), signs such as this one are in both French and English.

The constitution also included a Charter of Rights and Freedoms, similar to the United States Bill of Rights. Canada's independence was complete.

Canada's executive branch is still headed by Britain's monarch, who appoints a representative, the governor-general. Daily governmental affairs, however, are handled by the prime minister. He or she is a member of the ruling majority party of the House of Commons. Along with the Senate, the House of Commons makes up the Canadian Parliament.

REVIEW What did the Constitution of 1982 do?

New Solutions to Old Problems

For a long time, many Quebec citizens, called **separatists**, have wanted to form a separate country in order to preserve their French culture. In 1998, a vote to secede from Canada failed. The Canadian Supreme Court then ruled that Quebec could not secede unless the rest of Canada agreed.

Like the people of Quebec, the native peoples of Canada want to preserve their culture. In 1999 Nunavut, part of the Northwest Territories, became Canada's third territory. Most of the people who live in Nunavut are Inuit. They plan to govern the territory of Nunavut according to the traditional means of consensus, or the agreement of the community.

REVIEW Why do separatists want to secede from Canada?

A World Partner

Canada has economic partnerships with many countries, but it has the greatest cooperation with the United States. The United States and Canada are major trading partners. In 1987 the two countries signed a free trade agreement that was a forerunner to NAFTA. Today, more than 80 percent of Canada's exports go to the United States, and Canada gets about 70 percent of its imports from the United States.

One of the greatest examples of cooperation between the two neighbors was the construction of the St. Lawrence Seaway. The St. Lawrence River flows nearly 800 miles (1,287 km) from Lake Ontario to the Atlantic Ocean, but parts of the river are not deep enough for large ships to navigate. The St. Lawrence Seaway also includes the Welland Ship Canal, built between Lake Ontario and Lake Erie to bypass Niagara Falls. Construction of the

This photograph shows the first ship to enter the locks of the St. Lawrence Seaway in April of 1959.

St. Lawrence Seaway was completed in 1959. This allowed large ships to reach the Great Lakes from the Atlantic Ocean.

REVIEW What is one example of cooperation between Canada and the United States?

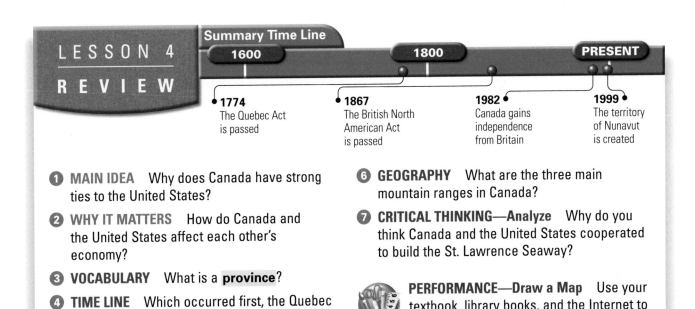

LESSON 4 REVIEW

Summary Time Line

1600	1800	PRESENT

1774 The Quebec Act is passed

1867 The British North American Act is passed

1982 Canada gains independence from Britain

1999 The territory of Nunavut is created

1 MAIN IDEA   Why does Canada have strong ties to the United States?

2 WHY IT MATTERS   How do Canada and the United States affect each other's economy?

3 VOCABULARY   What is a **province**?

4 TIME LINE   Which occurred first, the Quebec Act or the British North American Act?

5 READING SKILL—Compare and Contrast   Compare and contrast the residents of Quebec and the residents of Nunavut.

6 GEOGRAPHY   What are the three main mountain ranges in Canada?

7 CRITICAL THINKING—Analyze   Why do you think Canada and the United States cooperated to build the St. Lawrence Seaway?

PERFORMANCE—Draw a Map   Use your textbook, library books, and the Internet to draw a map of Canada. Find the location of each of Canada's major landforms, and label them on your map. Also show each of Canada's provinces and territories.

·SKILLS·

MAP AND GLOBE

Use a Time Zone Map

VOCABULARY

time zone

▶ WHY IT MATTERS

"What time is it?" The answer depends on where you are. That is because people who live in different parts of the world set their clocks at different times.

For centuries people used the sun to determine time. When the sun was at its highest point in the sky, it was noon. However, the sun cannot be at its highest point all around the Earth at the same time. As the Earth rotates, the sun is directly overhead in different places at different times. The sun is past its highest point at places east of where you are, and it has not yet reached its highest point at places west of you.

In the 1800s Charles Dowd of the United States and Sandford Fleming of Canada developed the idea of dividing the Earth into time zones. A **time zone** is a region in which a single time is used. To figure out the time in a place, you can use a time zone map like the one on page 675.

▶ WHAT YOU NEED TO KNOW

Dowd and Fleming divided the Earth into 24 time zones. A new time zone begins every fifteenth meridian, starting at the prime meridian. In each new time zone to the west, the time is one hour earlier than in the time zone before it.

The map on page 675 shows the time zones in the Western Hemisphere. Find Dallas, in the central time zone. Now find New York City. It is in the eastern time zone, which is just east of the central time zone. The time in the central time zone is one hour earlier than the time in the eastern time zone. If it is 5:00 P.M. in the central time zone, it is 6:00 P.M. in the eastern time zone.

▶ PRACTICE THE SKILL

Use the time zone map of the Western Hemisphere to answer these questions.

1 In which time zone is Los Angeles?

2 If it is 10:00 A.M. in Los Angeles, what time is it in San Antonio?

3 In which time zone is Puerto Rico?

While the sun sets in Honoina Bay, Hawaii, it is already dark in other places in the United States.

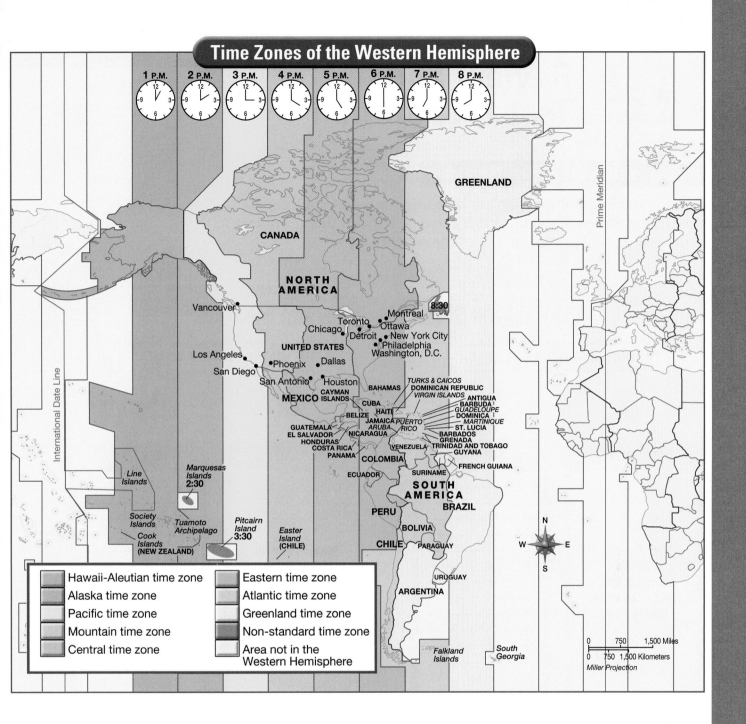

Time Zones of the Western Hemisphere

1 P.M. 2 P.M. 3 P.M. 4 P.M. 5 P.M. 6 P.M. 7 P.M. 8 P.M.

GREENLAND

Prime Meridian

CANADA

NORTH AMERICA

Vancouver

Montreal 8:30

Toronto Ottawa
Chicago Detroit New York City
Philadelphia
UNITED STATES Washington, D.C.

Los Angeles
Phoenix Dallas
San Diego
San Antonio Houston

International Date Line

BAHAMAS
TURKS & CAICOS
DOMINICAN REPUBLIC
VIRGIN ISLANDS
CAYMAN ISLANDS
MEXICO
CUBA
HAITI ANTIGUA
BELIZE BARBUDA
JAMAICA PUERTO GUADELOUPE
GUATEMALA ARUBA RICO DOMINICA
EL SALVADOR NICARAGUA MARTINIQUE
HONDURAS ST. LUCIA
COSTA RICA BARBADOS
PANAMA VENEZUELA GRENADA
TRINIDAD AND TOBAGO
COLOMBIA GUYANA

Line Islands

Marquesas Islands 2:30

ECUADOR
SURINAME FRENCH GUIANA

SOUTH AMERICA
PERU BRAZIL

Society Islands
Cook Islands (NEW ZEALAND)
Tuamoto Archipelago

Pitcairn Island 3:30

Easter Island (CHILE)

BOLIVIA
CHILE PARAGUAY

N
W E
S

URUGUAY
ARGENTINA

	Hawaii-Aleutian time zone		Eastern time zone
	Alaska time zone		Atlantic time zone
	Pacific time zone		Greenland time zone
	Mountain time zone		Non-standard time zone
	Central time zone		Area not in the Western Hemisphere

Falkland Islands
South Georgia

0   750   1,500 Miles
0 750 1,500 Kilometers
Miller Projection

---

4 If it is 3:00 P.M. in Puerto Rico, what time is it in Philadelphia? in Houston?

5 If it is 6:00 A.M. in San Diego, what time is it in Toronto?

6 Imagine that you are in Honduras. Is the time earlier than, later than, or the same as in Chicago?

▶ APPLY WHAT YOU LEARNED

Record the current time where you live. Now figure out the time in Montreal, Canada; Vancouver, Canada; Venezuela; and Argentina. Explain why it might be useful to know the time in different places.

Practice your map and globe skills with the **GeoSkills CD-ROM**.

MAP AND GLOBE SKILLS

18 Review and Test Preparation

USE YOUR READING SKILLS

Complete this graphic organizer by comparing and contrasting the United States, Canada, and Mexico. A copy of this graphic organizer appears on page 178 of the Activity Book.

The United States, Canada, and Mexico

THE UNITED STATES AND CANADA

SIMILARITIES

Both Canada and the United States were once under British Rule.

DIFFERENCES

THE UNITED STATES AND MEXICO

SIMILARITIES

Mexico and the United States each have democratic governments.

DIFFERENCES

THINK  WRITE

Write a Postcard Imagine you are traveling through South America on a family vacation. Write a postcard to a friend describing the natural wonders you have seen. Be sure to mention where these places are located.

Write a Wise Saying Having a good relationship with one's neighbors is important for both people and nations. Write a wise saying about the importance of the United States maintaining good relations with its neighbors.

1774
The Quebec Act is passed

1821
Mexico gains independence from Spain

1867
The British North American Act is passed

1917
Mexico writes a new constitution

1952
Puerto Rico becomes a United States commonwealth

1982
Canada gains independence from Britain

1990
Haiti holds free elections

1994
The NAFTA agreement is made

USE VOCABULARY

Identify the term that correctly matches each definition.

middle class (p. 656)
interest rate (p. 656)
free election (p. 661)
province (p. 670)

1 the amount that banks charge to loan money

2 a political region

3 people who are economically between the rich and the poor

4 a political race that offers a choice of candidates

RECALL FACTS

Answer these questions.

5 Why are *Fiestas Patrias* important for many Mexican Americans?

6 How is the province of Nunavut different from other Canadian provinces?

Write the letter of the best choice.

7 **TEST PREP** The purpose of NAFTA is to—
 A protect French Canadian culture.
 B continue an embargo on exports from Cuba.
 C increase trade among the United States, Canada, and Mexico.
 D bring democracy to all the nations of Central America and the Caribbean.

8 **TEST PREP** Benito Juárez was the first Native American president of—
 F Mexico.
 G Bolivia.
 H El Salvador.
 J Costa Rica.

9 **TEST PREP** Which of the following Canadian provinces has stated a wish to secede?
 A Alberta
 B New Brunswick
 C Quebec
 D British Columbia

THINK CRITICALLY

10 Why is immigration such an important issue for the United States and Mexico?

11 Why do you think some Latin American countries have had difficulty forming stable governments?

12 What might happen if Quebec decides to secede from Canada?

APPLY SKILLS

Read Population Pyramids
Review the population pyramid on page 663. Then answer the following questions.

13 What age group makes up the smallest part of the population?

14 In which age groups are there more males than females?

Use a Time Zone Map
Find the Bahamas on the time zone map on page 675. Then answer the following questions.

15 If it is 9:00 A.M. in the Bahamas, what time is it in Dallas?

16 If it is 12:00 P.M. in the Bahamas, what time is it in Vancouver?

VISIT Washington, D.C.

GET READY

Every year millions of people visit Washington, D.C. Visitors enjoy the city because, in addition to being the home of the national government, it is a beautiful city that is rich in history. If you visit Washington, D.C., you can tour important government buildings, such as the White House, where the President lives and works, and the Capitol, where Congress meets. You can visit museums, such as the National Museum of American History, or monuments, such as the Washington Monument. The many buildings, museums, and monuments of Washington, D.C. tell the story of America's past.

LOCATE IT

MARYLAND

VIRGINIA

Washington, D.C.

WHAT TO SEE

The White House

Visitors look at the *Gemini 4* space capsule at the Smithsonian National Air and Space Museum.

The Capitol

The Washington Monument

The Declaration of Independence is displayed at the National Archives.

The United States Botanic Garden has more than 10,000 varieties of plants.

TAKE A FIELD TRIP

GO ONLINE

A VIRTUAL TOUR
Visit The Learning Site at **www.harcourtschool.com/ tours** to take virtual tours of places of interest in the United States.

CNN Turner Le@rning

A VIDEO TOUR
Check your media center or classroom library for a videotape tour of Washington, D.C.

8 Review and Test Preparation

Write a Newspaper Headline Study the pictures and captions below to help you review Unit 8. Then choose one of the pictures. Write a newspaper headline that goes along with the picture you have chosen.

USE VOCABULARY

Use a term from this list to complete each of the sentences that follow.

Sun Belt (p. 621)

rapid-transit system (p. 629)

register (p. 641)

embargo (p. 660)

❶ A ____ moves passengers on an underground train.

❷ Before a citizen can vote, that person must ____.

❸ Much of the recent growth in the United States has taken place in the ____.

❹ An ____ occurs when one nation refuses to trade goods with another.

RECALL FACTS

Answer these questions.

❺ How has the Information Age affected science?

❻ How has NAFTA affected trade between the United States, Canada, and Mexico?

Write the letter of the best choice.

❼ **TEST PREP** The fastest-growing ethnic group in the United States today is—
A Hispanic Americans.
B African Americans.
C Asian Americans.
D Irish Americans.

❽ **TEST PREP** About one-third of all American workers have jobs in the—
F federal government.
G banking, insurance, and real estate industry.
H service industry.
J medical profession.

Visual Summary

The United States is home to people from all over the world.   p. 620

680

Today more Americans work in service jobs than in any other kinds of jobs.   p. 633

Mexico City is one of the largest metropolitan areas in the world.   p. 655

Time Zones of the United States

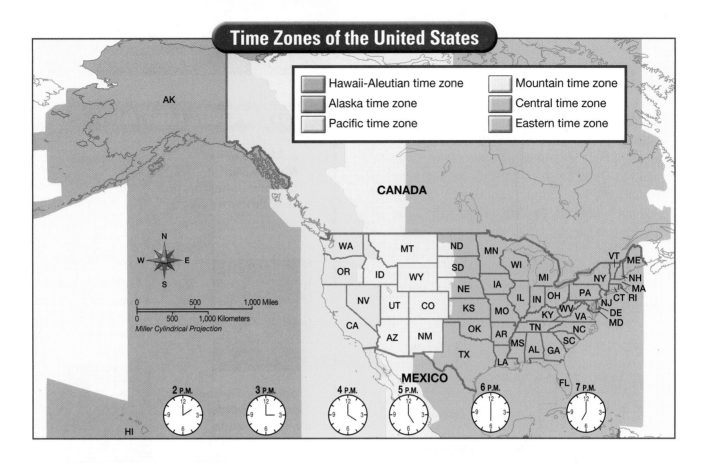

- Hawaii-Aleutian time zone
- Alaska time zone
- Pacific time zone
- Mountain time zone
- Central time zone
- Eastern time zone

AK

CANADA

N
W   E
S

0   500   1,000 Miles
0   500   1,000 Kilometers
Miller Cylindrical Projection

WA   MT   ND   MN
OR   ID   WY   SD   WI   VT ME
NV   UT   CO   NE   IA   MI   NY NH
CA   OK   KS   MO   IL IN OH PA CT RI
      AZ   NM   AR   KY   WV VA NJ
                  TX   TN   NC   DE
                        MS AL GA   SC   MD
                        LA
MEXICO
FL

HI

2 P.M.   3 P.M.   4 P.M.   5 P.M.   6 P.M.   7 P.M.

THINK CRITICALLY

9 Why is voting an important part of a citizen's responsibility?

10 Why do you think the Mexican people chose to elect Vicente Fox as president in 2000?

11 What might happen if Quebec decides to secede from Canada?

APPLY SKILLS

MAP AND GLOBE SKILLS

Use a Time Zone Map
Use the map to answer the following questions.

12 What is the time difference between New Jersey and New Mexico?

13 What is the time difference between Oklahoma and Montana?

Jean-Bertrand Aristide becomes Haiti's president. p. 661

Simón Bolívar helps win independence for many present-day Latin American countries. p. 666

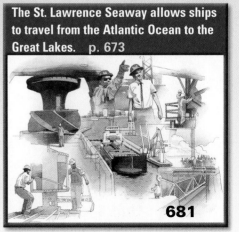

The St. Lawrence Seaway allows ships to travel from the Atlantic Ocean to the Great Lakes. p. 673

Unit Activities

 Visit The Learning Site at www.harcourtschool.com/socialstudies/activities for additional activities.

Make a Mural

Work with a group of your classmates to create a mural of famous United States monuments. First, decide which monuments you want to show on your mural. Some examples include the Washington Monument, the Lincoln Memorial, the Statue of Liberty, and Mount Rushmore. After choosing the monuments you wish to show, draw or paint them on a posterboard. Remember to label each monument. Finally, display your mural with those of your classmates.

Prepare a Newscast

Work in a group to prepare a newscast on a meeting between the President of the United States and a leader of a Western Hemisphere nation. Each member of your group should have a job, such as researcher, writer, reporter, or anchorperson. When planning your newscast, include information about the other nation and its relationship with the United States. When you are finished, present your newscast to your class.

VISIT YOUR LIBRARY

■ *My Mexico—México Mío* by Tony Johnston. G. P. Putnam's Sons.

■ *Angel Falls: A South American Journey* by Martin and Tanis Jordan. Kingfisher.

■ *Journey Through the Northern Rainforest* by Karen Pandell. Penguin Putnam Books for Young Readers.

COMPLETE THE UNIT PROJECT

A Cultural Fair Work with a group of your classmates to finish the unit project—presenting a cultural fair. Look over your notes describing the different cultures discussed in this unit. Use these notes to decide what to include in your cultural fair. Your fair may feature posters representing different art forms or styles of dress. You may also wish to feature different kinds of foods or music. Finally, hold your cultural fair.

For Your Reference

Almanac

Facts About the States

State Flag	State	Year of Statehood	Population*	Area (sq. mi.)	Capital	Origin of State Name
	Alabama	1819	4,447,100	50,750	Montgomery	Choctaw, *alba ayamule*, "one who clears land and gathers food from it"
	Alaska	1959	626,932	570,374	Juneau	Aleut, *alayeska*, "great land"
	Arizona	1912	5,130,632	113,642	Phoenix	Papago, *arizonac*, "place of the small spring"
	Arkansas	1836	2,673,400	52,075	Little Rock	Quapaw, "the downstream people"
	California	1850	33,871,648	155,973	Sacramento	Spanish, a fictional island
	Colorado	1876	4,301,261	103,730	Denver	Spanish, "red land" or "red earth"
	Connecticut	1788	3,405,565	4,845	Hartford	Mohican, *quinnitukqut*, "at the long tidal river"
	Delaware	1787	783,600	1,955	Dover	Named for Lord de la Warr
	Florida	1845	15,982,378	54,153	Tallahassee	Spanish, "filled with flowers"
	Georgia	1788	8,186,453	57,919	Atlanta	Named for King George II of England
	Hawaii	1959	1,211,537	6,450	Honolulu	Polynesian, *hawaiki* or *owykee*, "homeland"
	Idaho	1890	1,293,593	82,751	Boise	Invented name with unknown meaning

State Flag	State	Year of Statehood	Population*	Area (sq. mi.)	Capital	Origin of State Name
	Illinois	1818	12,419,293	55,593	Springfield	Algonquin, *iliniwek*, "men" or "warriors"
	Indiana	1816	6,080,485	35,870	Indianapolis	*Indian* + *a*, "land of the Indians"
	Iowa	1846	2,926,324	55,875	Des Moines	Dakota, *ayuba*, "beautiful land"
	Kansas	1861	2,688,418	81,823	Topeka	Sioux, "land of the south wind people"
	Kentucky	1792	4,041,769	39,732	Frankfort	Iroquoian, *ken-tah-ten*, "land of tomorrow"
	Louisiana	1812	4,468,976	43,566	Baton Rouge	Named for King Louis XIV of France
	Maine	1820	1,274,923	30,865	Augusta	Named after a French province
	Maryland	1788	5,296,486	9,775	Annapolis	Named for Henrietta Maria, Queen Consort of Charles I of England
	Massachusetts	1788	6,349,097	7,838	Boston	Massachusett tribe of Native Americans, "at the big hill" or "place of the big hill"
	Michigan	1837	9,938,444	56,809	Lansing	Ojibwa, "large lake"
	Minnesota	1858	4,919,479	79,617	St. Paul	Dakota Sioux, "sky-blue water"
	Mississippi	1817	2,844,658	46,914	Jackson	Indian word meaning "great waters" or "father of waters"
	Missouri	1821	5,595,211	68,898	Jefferson City	Named after the Missouri Indian tribe. *Missouri* means "town of the large canoes."

* Census 2000 figures

State Flag	State	Year of Statehood	Population*	Area (sq. mi.)	Capital	Origin of State Name
	Montana	1889	902,195	145,566	Helena	Spanish, "mountainous"
	Nebraska	1867	1,711,263	76,878	Lincoln	From an Oto Indian word meaning "flat water"
	Nevada	1864	1,998,257	109,806	Carson City	Spanish, "snowy" or "snowed upon"
	New Hampshire	1788	1,235,786	8,969	Concord	Named for Hampshire County, England
	New Jersey	1787	8,414,350	7,419	Trenton	Named for the Isle of Jersey
	New Mexico	1912	1,819,046	121,365	Santa Fe	Named by Spanish explorers from Mexico
	New York	1788	18,976,457	47,224	Albany	Named after the Duke of York
	North Carolina	1789	8,049,313	48,718	Raleigh	Named after King Charles II of England
	North Dakota	1889	642,200	70,704	Bismarck	Sioux, *dakota*, "friend" or "ally"
	Ohio	1803	11,353,140	40,953	Columbus	Iroquois, *oheo*, "great water"
	Oklahoma	1907	3,450,654	68,679	Oklahoma City	Choctaw, "red people"
	Oregon	1859	3,421,399	96,003	Salem	Unknown; generally accepted that it was taken from the writings of Maj. Robert Rogers, an English army officer
	Pennsylvania	1787	12,281,054	44,820	Harrisburg	*Penn + sylvania*, meaning "Penn's woods"

State Flag	State	Year of Statehood	Population*	Area (sq. mi.)	Capital	Origin of State Name
	Rhode Island	1790	1,048,319	1,045	Providence	From the Greek island of Rhodes
	South Carolina	1788	4,012,012	30,111	Columbia	Named after King Charles II of England
	South Dakota	1889	754,844	75,898	Pierre	Sioux, *dakota*, "friend" or "ally"
	Tennessee	1796	5,689,283	41,220	Nashville	Name of a Cherokee village
	Texas	1845	20,851,820	261,914	Austin	Native American, *tejas*, "friend" or "ally"
	Utah	1896	2,233,169	82,168	Salt Lake City	From the Ute tribe, meaning "people of the mountains"
	Vermont	1791	608,827	9,249	Montpelier	French, *vert*, "green," and *mont*, "mountain"
	Virginia	1788	7,078,515	39,598	Richmond	Named after Queen Elizabeth I of England
	Washington	1889	5,894,121	66,582	Olympia	Named for George Washington
	West Virginia	1863	1,808,344	24,087	Charleston	From the English-named state of Virginia
	Wisconsin	1848	5,363,675	54,314	Madison	Possibly Algonquian, "the place where we live"
	Wyoming	1890	493,782	97,105	Cheyenne	From Delaware Indian word meaning "land of vast plains"
	District of Columbia		572,059	67		Named after Christopher Columbus

* Census 2000 figures

Facts About the Western Hemisphere

Country	Population*	Area (sq. mi.)	Capital	Origin of Country Name
North America				
Antigua and Barbuda	66,970	171	St. Johns	Named for the Church of Santa María la Antigua in Seville, Spain
Bahamas	297,852	5,386	Nassau	Spanish, *bajamar*, "shallow water"
Barbados	275,330	166	Bridgetown	Means "bearded"—probably referring to the beard like vines early explorers found on its trees
Belize	256,062	8,867	Belmopan	Mayan, "muddy water"
Canada	31,592,805	3,851,809	Ottawa	Huron-Iroquois, *kanata*, "village" or "community"
Costa Rica	3,773,057	19,730	San José	Spanish, "rich coast"
Cuba	11,184,023	42,803	Havana	Origin unknown
Dominica	70,786	289	Roseau	Latin, *dies dominica*, "Day of the Lord"
Dominican Republic	8,581,477	18,815	Santo Domingo	Named after the capital city
El Salvador	6,237,662	8,124	San Salvador	Spanish, "the Savior"
Grenada	89,227	131	St. George's	Origin unknown
Guatemala	12,974,361	42,042	Guatemala City	Indian, "land of trees"
Haiti	6,964,549	10,714	Port-au-Prince	Indian, "land of mountains"
Honduras	6,406,052	43,277	Tegucigalpa	Spanish, "profundities" —probably referring to the depth of offshore waters
Jamaica	2,665,636	4,243	Kingston	Arawak, *xamayca*, "land of wood and water"
Mexico	101,879,171	761,602	Mexico City	Aztec, *mexliapan*, "lake of the moon"
Nicaragua	4,918,393	49,998	Managua	from *Nicarao*, the name of an Indian chief

Country	Population*	Area (sq. mi.)	Capital	Origin of Country Name
Panama	2,845,647	30,193	Panama City	From an Indian village's name
St. Kitts-Nevis	38,756	96	Basseterre	Named by Christopher Columbus—Kitts for St. Christopher, a Catholic saint; Nevis, for a cloud-topped peak that looked like *las nieves*, "the snows"
St. Lucia	158,178	238	Castries	Named by Christopher Columbus for a Catholic saint
St. Vincent and Grenadines	115,942	150	Kingstown	May have been named by Christopher Columbus for a Catholic saint
Trinidad and Tobago	1,169,682	1,980	Port of Spain	Trinidad, from the Spanish word for "trinity"; Tobago, named for tobacco because the island has the shape of a person smoking a pipe
United States of America	281,421,906	3,537,441	Washington, D.C.	Named after the explorer Amerigo Vespucci

South America

Country	Population*	Area (sq. mi.)	Capital	Origin of Country Name
Argentina	37,384,816	1,068,296	Buenos Aires	Latin, *argentum*, "silver"
Bolivia	8,300,463	424,162	La Paz/Sucre	Named after Simón Bolívar, the famed liberator
Brazil	174,468,575	3,286,470	Brasília	Named after a native tree that the Portuguese called "bresel wood"
Chile	15,328,467	292,257	Santiago	Indian, *chilli*, "where the land ends"
Colombia	40,349,388	439,735	Bogotá	Named after Christopher Columbus
Ecuador	13,183,978	109,483	Quito	From the Spanish word for *equator*, referring to the country's location
Guyana	697,181	83,000	Georgetown	Indian, "land of waters"
Paraguay	5,734,139	157,043	Asunción	Named after the Paraguay River, which flows through it
Peru	27,483,864	496,222	Lima	Quechua, "land of abundance"
Suriname	433,998	63,039	Paramaribo	From an Indian word, *surinen*
Uruguay	3,360,105	68,039	Montevideo	Named after the Uruguay River, which flows through it
Venezuela	23,916,810	352,143	Caracas	Spanish, "Little Venice"

*Census 2000 figures

Almanac

Facts About the Presidents

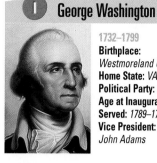

1 **George Washington**

1732–1799
Birthplace:
Westmoreland County, VA
Home State: *VA*
Political Party: *None*
Age at Inauguration: *57*
Served: *1789–1797*
Vice President:
John Adams

2 **John Adams**

1735–1826
Birthplace: *Braintree, MA*
Home State: *MA*
Political Party: *Federalist*
Age at Inauguration: *61*
Served: *1797–1801*
Vice President:
Thomas Jefferson

3 **Thomas Jefferson**

1743–1826
Birthplace:
Albemarle County, VA
Home State: *VA*
Political Party:
Democratic-Republican
Age at Inauguration: *57*
Served: *1801–1809*
Vice Presidents:
Aaron Burr,
George Clinton

4 **James Madison**

1751–1836
Birthplace:
Port Conway, VA
Home State: *VA*
Political Party:
Democratic-Republican
Age at Inauguration: *57*
Served: *1809–1817*
Vice Presidents:
George Clinton,
Elbridge Gerry

5 **James Monroe**

1758–1831
Birthplace:
Westmoreland County, VA
Home State: *VA*
Political Party:
Democratic-Republican
Age at Inauguration: *58*
Served: *1817–1825*
Vice President:
Daniel D. Tompkins

6 **John Quincy Adams**

1767–1848
Birthplace: *Braintree, MA*
Home State: *MA*
Political Party:
Democratic-Republican
Age at Inauguration: *57*
Served: *1825–1829*
Vice President:
John C. Calhoun

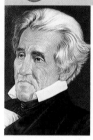

7 **Andrew Jackson**

1767–1845
Birthplace:
Waxhaw settlement, SC
Home State: *TN*
Political Party:
Democratic
Age at Inauguration: *61*
Served: *1829–1837*
Vice Presidents:
John C. Calhoun,
Martin Van Buren

8 **Martin Van Buren**

1782–1862
Birthplace: *Kinderhook,*
NY
Home State: *NY*
Political Party:
Democratic
Age at Inauguration: *54*
Served: *1837–1841*
Vice President:
Richard M. Johnson

9 **William H. Harrison**

1773–1841
Birthplace: *Berkeley, VA*
Home State: *OH*
Political Party: *Whig*
Age at Inauguration: *68*
Served: *1841*
Vice President:
John Tyler

10 **John Tyler**

1790–1862
Birthplace: *Greenway, VA*
Home State: *VA*
Political Party: *Whig*
Age at Inauguration: *51*
Served: *1841–1845*
Vice President: *none*

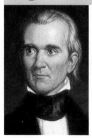

11 **James K. Polk**

1795–1849
Birthplace:
near Pineville, NC
Home State: *TN*
Political Party:
Democratic
Age at Inauguration: *49*
Served: *1845–1849*
Vice President:
George M. Dallas

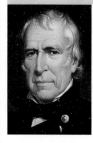

12 **Zachary Taylor**

1784–1850
Birthplace:
Orange County, VA
Home State: *LA*
Political Party: *Whig*
Age at Inauguration: *64*
Served: *1849–1850*
Vice President:
Millard Fillmore

13 **Millard Fillmore**

1800–1874
Birthplace: *Locke, NY*
Home State: *NY*
Political Party: *Whig*
Age at Inauguration: *50*
Served: *1850–1853*
Vice President: *none*

Home State refers to the state of residence when elected.

14 Franklin Pierce

1804–1869
Birthplace: *Hillsboro, NH*
Home State: *NH*
Political Party:
Democratic
Age at Inauguration: *48*
Served: *1853–1857*
Vice President:
William R. King

15 James Buchanan

1791–1868
Birthplace:
near Mercersburg, PA
Home State: *PA*
Political Party:
Democratic
Age at Inauguration: *65*
Served: *1857–1861*
Vice President:
John C. Breckinridge

16 Abraham Lincoln

1809–1865
Birthplace:
near Hodgenville, KY
Home State: *IL*
Political Party:
Republican
Age at Inauguration: *52*
Served: *1861–1865*
Vice Presidents:
*Hannibal Hamlin,
Andrew Johnson*

17 Andrew Johnson

1808–1875
Birthplace: *Raleigh, NC*
Home State: *TN*
Political Party:
National Union
Age at Inauguration: *56*
Served: *1865–1869*
Vice President: *none*

18 Ulysses S. Grant

1822–1885
Birthplace:
Point Pleasant, OH
Home State: *IL*
Political Party:
Republican
Age at Inauguration: *46*
Served: *1869–1877*
Vice Presidents:
*Schuyler Colfax,
Henry Wilson*

19 Rutherford B. Hayes

1822-1893
Birthplace:
near Delaware, OH
Home State: *OH*
Political Party:
Republican
Age at Inauguration: *54*
Served: *1877–1881*
Vice President:
William A. Wheeler

20 James A. Garfield

1831–1881
Birthplace: *Orange, OH*
Home State: *OH*
Political Party:
Republican
Age at Inauguration: *49*
Served: *1881*
Vice President:
Chester A. Arthur

21 Chester A. Arthur

1829–1886
Birthplace: *Fairfield, VT*
Home State: *NY*
Political Party:
Republican
Age at Inauguration: *51*
Served: *1881–1885*
Vice President: *none*

22 Grover Cleveland

1837–1908
Birthplace: *Caldwell, NJ*
Home State: *NY*
Political Party:
Democratic
Age at Inauguration: *47*
Served: *1885–1889*
Vice President:
Thomas A. Hendricks

23 Benjamin Harrison

1833–1901
Birthplace: *North Bend,
OH*
Home State: *IN*
Political Party:
Republican
Age at Inauguration: *55*
Served: *1889–1893*
Vice President:
Levi P. Morton

24 Grover Cleveland

1837–1908
Birthplace: *Caldwell, NJ*
Home State: *NY*
Political Party:
Democratic
Age at Inauguration: *55*
Served: *1893–1897*
Vice President:
Adlai E. Stevenson

25 William McKinley

1843–1901
Birthplace: *Niles, OH*
Home State: *OH*
Political Party:
Republican
Age at Inauguration: *54*
Served: *1897–1901*
Vice Presidents:
*Garret A. Hobart,
Theodore Roosevelt*

26 Theodore Roosevelt

1858–1919
Birthplace: *New York, NY*
Home State: *NY*
Political Party:
Republican
Age at Inauguration: *42*
Served: *1901–1909*
Vice President:
Charles W. Fairbanks

27 William H. Taft

1857–1930
Birthplace: *Cincinnati, OH*
Home State: *OH*
Political Party:
Republican
Age at Inauguration: *51*
Served: *1909–1913*
Vice President:
James S. Sherman

28 Woodrow Wilson

1856–1924
Birthplace: *Staunton, VA*
Home State: *NJ*
Political Party:
Democratic
Age at Inauguration: *56*
Served: *1913–1921*
Vice President:
Thomas R. Marshall

29 Warren G. Harding

1865–1923
Birthplace:
Blooming Grove, OH
Home State: *OH*
Political Party:
Republican
Age at Inauguration: *55*
Served: *1921–1923*
Vice President:
Calvin Coolidge

30 Calvin Coolidge

1872–1933
Birthplace:
Plymouth Notch, VT
Home State: *MA*
Political Party:
Republican
Age at Inauguration: *51*
Served: *1923–1929*
Vice President:
Charles G. Dawes

31 Herbert Hoover

1874–1964
Birthplace: *West Branch, IA*
Home State: *CA*
Political Party:
Republican
Age at Inauguration: *54*
Served: *1929–1933*
Vice President:
Charles Curtis

32 Franklin D. Roosevelt

1882–1945
Birthplace: *Hyde Park, NY*
Home State: *NY*
Political Party:
Democratic
Age at Inauguration: *51*
Served: *1933–1945*
Vice Presidents:
John N. Garner,
Henry A. Wallace,
Harry S. Truman

33 Harry S. Truman

1884–1972
Birthplace: *Lamar, MO*
Home State: *MO*
Political Party:
Democratic
Age at Inauguration: *60*
Served: *1945–1953*
Vice President:
Alben W. Barkley

34 Dwight D. Eisenhower

1890-1969
Birthplace: *Denison, TX*
Home State: *NY*
Political Party:
Republican
Age at Inauguration: *62*
Served: *1953–1961*
Vice President:
Richard M. Nixon

35 John F. Kennedy

1917–1963
Birthplace: *Brookline, MA*
Home State: *MA*
Political Party:
Democratic
Age at Inauguration: *43*
Served: *1961–1963*
Vice President:
Lyndon B. Johnson

36 Lyndon B. Johnson

1908–1973
Birthplace:
near Stonewall, TX
Home State: *TX*
Political Party:
Democratic
Age at Inauguration: *55*
Served: *1963–1969*
Vice President:
Hubert H. Humphrey

37 Richard M. Nixon

1913–1994
Birthplace: *Yorba Linda, CA*
Home State: *NY*
Political Party:
Republican
Age at Inauguration: *56*
Served: *1969–1974*
Vice Presidents:
Spiro T. Agnew,
Gerald R. Ford

38 Gerald R. Ford

1913–
Birthplace: *Omaha, NE*
Home State: *MI*
Political Party:
Republican
Age at Inauguration: *61*
Served: *1974–1977*
Vice President:
Nelson A. Rockefeller

39 Jimmy Carter

1924–
Birthplace: *Plains, GA*
Home State: *GA*
Political Party:
Democratic
Age at Inauguration: *52*
Served: *1977–1981*
Vice President:
Walter F. Mondale

40 Ronald W. Reagan

1911–
Birthplace: *Tampico, IL*
Home State: *CA*
Political Party:
Republican
Age at Inauguration: *69*
Served: *1981–1989*
Vice President:
George Bush

41 George Bush

1924–
Birthplace: *Milton, MA*
Home State: *TX*
Political Party:
Republican
Age at Inauguration: *64*
Served: *1989–1993*
Vice President:
Dan Quayle

42 William Clinton

1946–
Birthplace: *Hope, AR*
Home State: *AR*
Political Party:
Democratic
Age at Inauguration: *46*
Served: *1993–2001*
Vice President:
Albert Gore

43 George W. Bush

1946–
Birthplace: *New Haven, CT*
Home State: *TX*
Political Party:
Republican
Age at Inauguration: *54*
Served: *2001–*
Vice President:
Richard Cheney

American Documents

THE DECLARATION OF INDEPENDENCE

In Congress, July 4, 1776.
The unanimous Declaration of the
thirteen United States of America,

When in the Course of human events it becomes necessary for one people to dissolve the political bands which have connected them with another, and to assume among the powers of the earth, the separate and equal station to which the Laws of Nature and of Nature's God entitle them, a decent respect to the opinions of mankind requires that they should declare the causes which impel them to the separation.

We hold these truths to be self-evident, that all men are created equal, that they are endowed by their Creator with certain unalienable Rights, that among these are Life, Liberty and the pursuit of Happiness.

That to secure these rights, Governments are instituted among Men, deriving their just powers from the consent of the governed,

That whenever any Form of Government becomes destructive of these ends, it is the Right of the People to alter or to abolish it, and to institute new Government, laying its foundation on such principles and organizing its powers in such form, as to them shall seem most likely to effect their Safety and Happiness. Prudence, indeed, will dictate that Governments long established should not be changed for light and transient causes; and accordingly all experience hath shown, that mankind are more disposed to suffer, while evils are sufferable, than to right themselves by abolishing the forms to which they are accustomed. But when a long train of abuses and usurpations, pursuing invariably the same Object evinces a design to reduce them under absolute Despotism, it is their right, it is their duty, to throw off such Government, and to provide new Guards for their future security.

Such has been the patient sufferance of these Colonies; and such is now the necessity which constrains them to alter their former Systems of Government. The history of the present King of Great Britain is a history of repeated injuries and usurpations, all having in direct object the establishment of an absolute Tyranny over these States. To prove this, let Facts be submitted to a candid world.

He has refused his Assent to Laws, the most wholesome and necessary for the public good.

He has forbidden his Governors to pass Laws of immediate and pressing importance, unless suspended in their operation till his Assent should be obtained; and when so suspended, he has utterly neglected to attend to them.

Preamble
The Preamble tells why the Declaration was written. It states that the members of the Continental Congress believed the colonies had the right to break away from Britain and become a free nation.

A Statement of Rights
The opening part of the Declaration tells what rights the members of the Continental Congress believed that all people have. All people are equal in having the rights to life, liberty, and the pursuit of happiness. The main purpose of a government is to protect the rights of the people who consent to be governed by it. These rights cannot be taken away. When a government tries to take these rights away from the people, the people have the right to change the government or do away with it. The people can then form a new government that respects these rights.

Charges Against the King
The Declaration lists more than 25 charges against the king. He was mistreating the colonists, the Declaration says, in order to gain total control over the colonies.

The king rejected many laws passed by colonial legislatures.

He has refused to pass other Laws for the accommodation of large districts of people, unless those people would relinquish the right of Representation in the Legislature, a right inestimable to them and formidable to tyrants only.

He has called together legislative bodies at places unusual, uncomfortable, and distant from the depository of their public Records, for the sole purpose of fatiguing them into compliance with his measures.

He has dissolved Representative Houses repeatedly, for opposing with manly firmness his invasions on the rights of the people.

He has refused for a long time, after such dissolutions, to cause others to be elected; whereby the Legislative powers, incapable of Annihilation, have returned to the People at large for their exercise; the State remaining in the mean time exposed to all the dangers of invasion from without, and convulsions within.

He has endeavored to prevent the population of these States; for that purpose obstructing the Laws for Naturalization of Foreigners; refusing to pass others to encourage their migrations hither, and raising the conditions of new Appropriations of Lands.

He has obstructed the Administration of Justice, by refusing his Assent to Laws for establishing Judiciary powers.

He has made Judges dependent on his Will alone, for the tenure of their offices, and the amount and payment of their salaries.

He has erected a multitude of New Offices, and sent hither swarms of Officers to harass our people, and eat out their substance.

He has kept among us, in times of peace, Standing Armies without the Consent of our legislatures.

He has affected to render the Military independent of and superior to the Civil power.

He has combined with others to subject us to a jurisdiction foreign to our constitution, and unacknowledged by our laws; giving his Assent to their Acts of pretended Legislation:

For quartering large bodies of armed troops among us:

For protecting them, by a mock Trial, from punishment for any Murders which they should commit on the Inhabitants of these States:

For cutting off our Trade with all parts of the world:

For imposing Taxes on us without our Consent:

For depriving us in many cases, of the benefits of Trial by Jury:

For transporting us beyond Seas to be tried for pretended offenses:

For abolishing the free System of English Laws in a neighboring Province, establishing therein an Arbitrary government, and enlarging its Boundaries so as to render it at once an example and fit instrument for introducing the same absolute rule into these Colonies:

The king made the colonial legislatures meet at unusual times and places.

The king and the king's governors often dissolved colonial legislatures for disobeying their orders.

The king stopped people from moving to the colonies and into the western lands.

The king prevented the colonists from choosing their own judges. The king chose the judges, and they served only as long as the king was satisfied with them.

The king hired people to help collect taxes in the colonies.

The king appointed General Thomas Gage, commander of Britain's military forces in the Americas, as governor of Massachusetts.

The king expected the colonists to provide housing and supplies for the British soldiers in the colonies.

The king and Parliament demanded that colonists pay many taxes, even though the colonists did not agree to pay them.

Colonists were tried by British naval courts, which had no juries.

Colonists accused of treason were sent to Britain to be tried.

For taking away our Charters, abolishing our most valuable Laws, and altering fundamentally the Forms of our Governments:

For suspending our own Legislatures, and declaring themselves invested with power to legislate for us in all cases whatsoever.

He has abdicated Government here, by declaring us out of his Protection and waging War against us.

He has plundered our seas, ravaged our Coasts, burnt our towns, and destroyed the lives of our people.

He is at this time transporting large Armies of foreign Mercenaries to complete the works of death, desolation and tyranny, already begun with circumstances of Cruelty & perfidy scarcely paralleled in the most barbarous ages, and totally unworthy the Head of a civilized nation.

He has constrained our fellow Citizens taken Captive on the high Seas to bear Arms against their Country, to become the executioners of their friends and Brethren, or to fall themselves by their Hands.

He has excited domestic insurrections amongst us, and has endeavored to bring on the inhabitants of our frontiers, the merciless Indian Savages, whose known rule of warfare, is an undistinguished destruction of all ages, sexes and conditions.

In every stage of these Oppressions We have Petitioned for Redress in the most humble terms: Our repeated Petitions have been answered only by repeated injury. A Prince, whose character is thus marked by every act which may define a Tyrant, is unfit to be the ruler of a free people.

Nor have We been wanting in attentions to our British brethren. We have warned them from time to time of attempts by their legislature to extend an unwarrantable jurisdiction over us. We have reminded them of the circumstances of our emigration and settlement here. We have appealed to their native justice and magnanimity, and we have conjured them by the ties of our common kindred to disavow these usurpations, which, would inevitably interrupt our connections and correspondence. They too have been deaf to the voice of justice and of consanguinity. We must, therefore, acquiesce in the necessity, which denounces our Separation, and hold them, as we hold the rest of mankind, Enemies in War, in Peace Friends.

We, therefore, the Representatives of the united States of America, in General Congress, Assembled, appealing to the Supreme Judge of the world for the rectitude of our intentions, do, in the Name, and by Authority of the good People of these Colonies, solemnly publish and declare, That these United Colonies are, and of Right ought to be Free and Independent States; that they are Absolved from all Allegiance to the British Crown, and that all political connection between them and the State of Great Britain, is and ought to be totally dissolved; and that as Free and Independent States, they have full Power to levy War, conclude Peace, contract Alliances, establish Commerce, and to do all other Acts and Things which Independent States may of right do.

The king allowed General Gage to take military action to enforce British laws in the colonies.

The king hired Hessian mercenaries and sent them to fight the colonists.

The king's governor in Virginia promised freedom to all enslaved people who joined the British forces. The British also planned to use Indians to fight the colonists.

The Declaration explained the efforts of the colonists to avoid separation from Britain. But the colonists said that the king had ignored their protests. Because of the many charges against the king, the writers of the Declaration concluded that he was not fit to rule free people.

A Statement of Independence The writers declared that the colonies were now free and independent states. All ties with Britain were broken. As free and independent states, they had the right to make war and peace, to trade, and to do all the things free countries could do.

To support the Declaration, the signers promised one another their lives, their fortunes, and their honor.

And for the support of this Declaration, with a firm reliance on the protection of divine Providence, we mutually pledge to each other our Lives, our Fortunes and our sacred Honor.

John Hancock

NEW HAMPSHIRE
Josiah Bartlett
William Whipple
Matthew Thornton

MASSACHUSETTS
John Adams
Samuel Adams
Robert Treat Paine
Elbridge Gerry

NEW YORK
William Floyd
Philip Livingston
Francis Lewis
Lewis Morris

RHODE ISLAND
Stephen Hopkins
William Ellery

NEW JERSEY
Richard Stockton
John Witherspoon
Francis Hopkinson
John Hart
Abraham Clark

PENNSYLVANIA
Robert Morris
Benjamin Rush
Benjamin Franklin
John Morton
George Clymer
James Smith
George Taylor
James Wilson
George Ross

DELAWARE
Caesar Rodney
George Read
Thomas McKean

MARYLAND
Samuel Chase
William Paca
Thomas Stone
Charles Carroll of Carrollton

NORTH CAROLINA
William Hopper
Joseph Hewes
John Penn

VIRGINIA
George Wythe
Richard Henry Lee
Thomas Jefferson
Benjamin Harrison
Thomas Nelson, Jr.
Francis Lightfoot Lee
Carter Braxton

SOUTH CAROLINA
Edward Rutledge
Thomas Heyward, Jr.
Thomas Lynch, Jr.
Arthur Middleton

CONNECTICUT
Roger Sherman
Samuel Huntington
William Williams
Oliver Wolcott

GEORGIA
Button Gwinnett
Lyman Hall
George Walton

Members of the Continental Congress stated that copies of the Declaration should be sent to all Committees of Correspondence and to commanders of the troops and that it should be read in every state.

Resolved, That copies of the Declaration be sent to the several assemblies, conventions, and committees, or councils of safety, and to the several commanding officers of the continental troops; that it be proclaimed in each of the United States, at the head of the army.

THE CONSTITUTION OF THE UNITED STATES OF AMERICA

Preamble*

We the people of the United States, in order to form a more perfect Union, establish justice, insure domestic tranquillity, provide for the common defense, promote the general welfare, and secure the blessings of liberty to ourselves and our posterity, do ordain and establish this Constitution for the United States of America.

ARTICLE I
THE LEGISLATIVE BRANCH

SECTION 1. CONGRESS

All legislative powers herein granted shall be vested in a Congress of the United States, which shall consist of a Senate and House of Representatives.

SECTION 2. THE HOUSE OF REPRESENTATIVES

(1) The House of Representatives shall be composed of members chosen every second year by the people of the several states, and the electors in each state shall have the qualifications requisite for electors of the most numerous branch of the state legislature.

(2) No person shall be a Representative who shall not have attained to the age of twenty-five years, and been seven years a citizen of the United States, and who shall not, when elected, be an inhabitant of that state in which he shall be chosen.

(3) Representatives [*and direct taxes*]** shall be apportioned among the several states which may be included within this Union, according to their respective numbers [*which shall be determined by adding to the whole number of free persons, including those bound to service for a term of years, and excluding Indians not taxed, three-fifths of all other persons*]. The actual enumeration shall be made within three years after the first meeting of the Congress of the United States, and within every subsequent term of ten years, in such manner as they shall by law direct. The number of Representatives shall not exceed one for every 30,000, but each state shall have at least one Representative [*; and until such enumeration shall be made, the State of New Hampshire shall be entitled to choose three; Massachusetts eight; Rhode Island and Providence Plantations one; Connecticut five; New York six; New Jersey four; Pennsylvania eight; Delaware one; Maryland six; Virginia ten; North Carolina five; South Carolina five; and Georgia three*].

*Titles have been added to make the Constitution easier to read. They did not appear in the original document.

**The parts of the Constitution that no longer apply are printed in italics within brackets [ ]. These portions have been changed or set aside by later amendments.

Preamble
The introduction to the Constitution states the purposes and principles for writing it. The writers wanted to set up a fairer form of government and to secure peace and freedom for themselves and for future generations.

Congress
Congress has the authority to make laws. Congress is made up of two groups of lawmakers: the Senate and the House of Representatives.

(1) Election and Term of Members
Qualified voters are to elect members of the House of Representatives every two years. Each member of the House of Representatives must meet certain requirements.

(2) Qualifications
Members of the House of Representatives must be at least 25 years old. They must have been citizens of the United States for at least seven years. They must live in the state that they will represent.

(3) Determining Apportionment
The number of representatives a state may have depends on the number of people living in each state. Every ten years the federal government must take a census, or count, of the population in every state. Every state will have at least one representative.

(4) Filling Vacancies
If there is a vacancy in representation in Congress, the governor of the state involved must call a special election to fill it.

(5) Special Authority
The House of Representatives chooses a Speaker as its presiding officer. It also chooses other officers as appropriate. The House is the only government branch that may impeach, or charge, an official in the executive branch or a judge of the federal courts for failing to carry out his or her duties. These cases are tried in the Senate.

(1) Number, Term, and Selection of Members
Each state is represented by two senators. Until Amendment 17 was passed, state legislatures chose the senators for their states. Each senator serves a six-year term and has one vote in Congress.

(2) Overlapping Terms and Filling Vacancies
One-third of the senators are elected every two years for a six-year term. This grouping allows at least two-thirds of the experienced senators to remain in the Senate after each election. Amendment 17 permits state governors to appoint a replacement to fill a vacancy until the next election is held.

(3) Qualifications
Senators must be at least 30 years old. They must have been citizens of the United States for at least nine years. They must live in the state that they will represent.

(4) President of the Senate
The Vice President acts as chief officer of the Senate but does not vote unless there is a tie.

(5) Other Officers
The Senate chooses its other officers and a president pro tempore, who serves if the Vice President is not present or if the Vice President becomes President. *Pro tempore* is a Latin term meaning "for the time being."

(4) When vacancies happen in the representation from any state, the executive authority thereof shall issue writs of election to fill such vacancies.

(5) The House of Representatives shall choose their Speaker and other officers; and shall have the sole power of impeachment.

SECTION 3. THE SENATE

(1) The Senate of the United States shall be composed of two Senators from each state [*chosen by the legislature thereof*], for six years, and each Senator shall have one vote.

(2) [*Immediately after they shall be assembled in consequence of the first election, they shall be divided as equally as may be into three classes. The seats of the Senators of the first class shall be vacated at the expiration of the second year, of the second class at the expiration of the fourth year, and of the third class at the expiration of the sixth year, so that one-third may be chosen every second year; and if vacancies happen by resignation, or otherwise, during the recess of the legislature of any state, the executive thereof may make temporary appointments until the next meeting of the legislature, which shall then fill such vacancies.*]

(3) No person shall be a Senator who shall not have attained to the age of thirty years, and been nine years a citizen of the United States, and who shall not, when elected, be an inhabitant of that state for which he shall be chosen.

(4) The Vice President of the United States shall be President of the Senate, but shall have no vote, unless they be equally divided.

(5) The Senate shall choose their other officers, and also a President *pro tempore*, in the absence of the Vice President, or when he shall exercise the office of the President of the United States.

(6) The Senate shall have the sole power to try all impeachments. When sitting for that purpose, they shall be on oath or affirmation. When the President of the United States is tried, the Chief Justice shall preside; and no person shall be convicted without the concurrence of two-thirds of the members present.

(7) Judgment in cases of impeachment shall not extend further than to removal from office, and disqualification to hold and enjoy any office of honor, trust, or profit under the United States; but the party convicted shall nevertheless be liable and subject to indictment, trial, judgment and punishment, according to law.

SECTION 4. ELECTIONS AND MEETINGS

(1) The times, places, and manner of holding elections for Senators and Representatives shall be prescribed in each state by the legislature thereof; but the Congress may at any time by law make or alter such regulations, [*except as to the places of choosing Senators*].

(2) The Congress shall assemble at least once in every year, [*and such meeting shall be on the first Monday in December, unless they shall by law appoint a different day*].

SECTION 5. RULES OF PROCEDURE

(1) Each house shall be the judge of the elections, returns and qualifications of its own members, and a majority of each shall constitute a quorum to do business; but a smaller number may adjourn from day to day, and may be authorized to compel the attendance of absent members, in such manner and under such penalties as each house may provide.

(2) Each house may determine the rules of its proceedings, punish its members for disorderly behavior, and, with the concurrence of two-thirds, expel a member.

(3) Each house shall keep a journal of its proceedings, and from time to time publish the same, excepting such parts as may in their judgment require secrecy; and the yeas and nays of the members of either house on any question shall, at the desire of one-fifth of those present, be entered on the journal.

(6) Impeachment Trials
If the House of Representatives votes articles of impeachment, the Senate holds a trial. A two-thirds vote is required to convict a person who has been impeached.

(7) Penalty for Conviction
If convicted in an impeachment case, an official is removed from office and may never hold office in the United States government again. The convicted person may also be tried in a regular court of law for any crimes.

(1) Holding Elections
Each state makes its own rules about electing senators and representatives. However, Congress may change these rules at any time. Today congressional elections are held on the Tuesday after the first Monday in November, in even-numbered years.

(2) Meetings
The Constitution requires Congress to meet at least once a year. That day is the first Monday in December, unless Congress sets a different day. Amendment 20 changed this date to January 3.

(1) Organization
Each house of Congress may decide if its members have been elected fairly and are able to hold office. Each house may do business only when a quorum—a majority of its members—is present. By less than a majority vote, each house may compel absent members to attend.

(2) Rules
Each house may decide its own rules for doing business, punish its members, and expel a member from office if two-thirds of the members agree.

(3) Journal
The Constitution requires each house to keep records of its activities and to publish these records from time to time. The House Journal and the Senate Journal are published at the end of each session. How each member voted must be recorded if one-fifth of the members ask for this to be done.

(4) Adjournment
When Congress is in session, neither house may take a recess for more than three days without the consent of the other.

(1) Pay and Privileges
Members of Congress set their own salaries, which are to be paid by the federal government. Members cannot be arrested or sued for anything they say while Congress is in session. This privilege is called congressional immunity. Members of Congress may be arrested while Congress is in session only if they commit a crime.

(2) Restrictions
Members of Congress may not hold any other federal office while serving in Congress. A member may not resign from office and then take a government position created during that member's term of office or for which the pay has been increased during that member's term of office.

(1) Money-Raising Bills
All money-raising bills must be introduced first in the House of Representatives, but the Senate may suggest changes.

(2) How a Bill Becomes a Law
After a bill has been passed by both the House of Representatives and the Senate, it must be sent to the President. If the President approves and signs the bill, it becomes law. The President can also veto, or refuse to sign, the bill. Congress can override a veto by passing the bill again by a two-thirds majority. If the President does not act within ten days, two things may happen. If Congress is still in session, the bill becomes a law. If Congress ends its session within that same ten-day period, the bill does not become a law.

(3) Orders and Resolutions
Congress can pass orders and resolutions, some of which have the same effect as a law. Congress may decide on its own when to end the session. Other such acts must be signed or vetoed by the President.

(4) Neither house, during the session of Congress, shall, without the consent of the other, adjourn for more than three days, nor to any other place than that in which the two houses shall be sitting.

SECTION 6. PRIVILEGES AND RESTRICTIONS

(1) The Senators and Representatives shall receive a compensation for their services, to be ascertained by law and paid out of the Treasury of the United States. They shall in all cases, except treason, felony, and breach of the peace, be privileged from arrest during their attendance at the session of their respective houses, and in going to and returning from the same; and for any speech or debate in either house, they shall not be questioned in any other place.

(2) No Senator or Representative shall, during the time for which he was elected, be appointed to any civil office under the authority of the United States, which shall have been created, or the emoluments whereof shall have been increased, during such time; and no person holding any office under the United States shall be a member of either house during his continuance in office.

SECTION 7. MAKING LAWS

(1) All bills for raising revenue shall originate in the House of Representatives; but the Senate may propose or concur with amendments as on other bills.

(2) Every bill which shall have passed the House of Representatives and the Senate shall, before it become a law, be presented to the President of the United States; if he approve, he shall sign it, but if not, he shall return it, with his objections, to that house in which it shall have originated, who shall enter the objections at large on their journal, and proceed to reconsider it. If after such reconsideration two-thirds of that house shall agree to pass the bill, it shall be sent, together with the objections, to the other house, by which it shall likewise be reconsidered, and, if approved by two-thirds of that house, it shall become a law. But in all such cases the votes of both houses shall be determined by yeas and nays, and the names of the persons voting for and against the bill shall be entered on the journal of each house respectively. If any bill shall not be returned by the President within ten days (Sundays excepted) after it shall have been presented to him, the same bill shall be a law, in like manner as if he had signed it, unless the Congress by their adjournment prevent its return, in which case it shall not be a law.

(3) Every order, resolution, or vote to which the concurrence of the Senate and House of Representatives may be necessary (except on a question of adjournment) shall be presented to the President of the United States; and before the same shall take effect, shall be approved by him, or being disapproved by him, shall be repassed by two-thirds of the Senate and House of Representatives, according to the rules and limitations prescribed in the case of a bill.

SECTION 8. POWERS DELEGATED TO CONGRESS

The Congress shall have power

(1) To lay and collect taxes, duties, imposts and excises, to pay the debts and provide for the common defense and general welfare of the United States; but all duties, imposts and excises shall be uniform throughout the United States;

(2) To borrow money on the credit of the United States;

(3) To regulate commerce with foreign nations, and among the several states and with the Indian tribes;

(4) To establish an uniform rule of naturalization, and uniform laws on the subject of bankruptcies throughout the United States;

(5) To coin money, regulate the value thereof, and of foreign coin, and fix the standard of weights and measures;

(6) To provide for the punishment of counterfeiting the securities and current coin of the United States;

(7) To establish post offices and post roads;

(8) To promote the progress of science and useful arts by securing for limited times to authors and inventors the exclusive right to their respective writings and discoveries;

(9) To constitute tribunals inferior to the Supreme Court;

(10) To define and punish piracies and felonies committed on the high seas and offenses against the law of nations;

(1) Taxation
Only Congress has the authority to raise money to pay debts, defend the United States, and provide services for its people by collecting taxes or tariffs on foreign goods. All taxes must be applied equally in all states.

(2) Borrowing Money
Congress may borrow money for national use. This is usually done by selling government bonds.

(3) Commerce
Congress can control trade with other countries and between states.

(4) Naturalization and Bankruptcy
Congress decides what requirements people from other countries must meet to become United States citizens. Congress can also pass laws to protect people who are bankrupt, or cannot pay their debts.

(5) Coins, Weights, and Measures
Congress can coin money and decide its value. Congress also decides on the system of weights and measures to be used throughout the nation.

(6) Counterfeiting
Congress may pass laws to punish people who make fake money, bonds, or stamps.

(7) Postal Service
Congress can build post offices and make rules about the postal system and the roads used for mail delivery.

(8) Copyrights and Patents
Congress can issue patents and copyrights to inventors and authors to protect the ownership of their works.

(9) Federal Courts
Congress can establish a system of federal courts under the Supreme Court.

(10) Crimes at Sea
Congress can pass laws to punish people for crimes committed at sea. Congress may also punish United States citizens for breaking international law.

(11) Declaring War
Only Congress can declare war.

(11) To declare war, grant letters of marque and reprisal, and make rules concerning captures on land and water;

(12) The Army
Congress can establish an army, but it cannot vote enough money to support it for more than two years. This part of the Constitution was written to keep the army under civilian control.

(12) To raise and support armies, but no appropriation of money to that use shall be for a longer term than two years;

(13) The Navy
Congress can establish a navy and vote enough money to support it for as long as necessary. No time limit was set because people thought the navy was less of a threat to people's liberty than the army was.

(13) To provide and maintain a navy;

(14) Military Regulations
Congress makes the rules that guide and govern all the armed forces.

(14) To make rules for the government and regulation of the land and naval forces;

(15) The Militia
Each state has its own militia, now known as the National Guard. The National Guard can be called into federal service by the President, as authorized by Congress, to enforce laws, to stop uprisings against the government, or to protect the people in case of floods, earthquakes, and other disasters.

(15) To provide for calling forth the militia to execute the laws of the Union, suppress insurrections and repel invasions;

(16) Control of the Militia
Congress helps each state support the National Guard. Each state may appoint its own officers and train its own guard according to rules set by Congress.

(16) To provide for organizing, arming, and disciplining the militia, and for governing such part of them as may be employed in the service of the United States, reserving to the states, respectively, the appointment of the officers, and the authority of training the militia according to the discipline prescribed by Congress;

(17) National Capital and Other Property
Congress may pass laws to govern the nation's capital (Washington, D.C.) and any land owned by the government.

(17) To exercise exclusive legislation in all cases whatsoever, over such district (not exceeding ten miles square) as may, by cession of particular states, and the acceptance of Congress, become the seat of government of the United States, and to exercise like authority over all places purchased by the consent of the legislature of the state in which the same shall be, for the erection of forts, magazines, arsenals, dockyards, and other needful buildings; —and

(18) Other Necessary Laws
The Constitution allows Congress to make laws that are necessary to enforce the powers listed in Article I. This clause has two conflicting interpretations. One is that Congress can only do what is absolutely necessary to carry out the powers listed in Article I. The other is that Congress may stretch its authority in order to carry out these powers, but not beyond limits established by the Constitution.

(18) To make all laws which shall be necessary and proper for carrying into execution the foregoing powers, and all other powers vested by this Constitution in the government of the United States, or in any department or officer thereof.

SECTION 9. POWERS DENIED TO CONGRESS

(1) [*The migration or importation of such persons as any of the states now existing shall think proper to admit shall not be prohibited by the Congress prior to the year 1808; but a tax or duty may be imposed on such importation, not exceeding 10 dollars for each person.*]

(2) The privilege of the writ of habeas corpus shall not be suspended, unless when in cases of rebellion or invasion the public safety may require it.

(3) No bill of attainder or ex post facto law shall be passed.

(4) [*No capitation or other direct tax shall be laid, unless in proportion to the census or enumeration herein before directed to be taken.*]

(5) No tax or duty shall be laid on articles exported from any state.

(6) No preference shall be given by any regulation of commerce or revenue to the ports of one state over those of another; nor shall vessels bound to, or from, one state, be obliged to enter, clear, or pay duties in another.

(7) No money shall be drawn from the Treasury, but in consequence of appropriations made by law; and a regular statement and account of the receipts and expenditures of all public money shall be published from time to time.

(1) Slave Trade
Some authority is not given to Congress. Congress could not prevent the slave trade until 1808, but it could put a tax of ten dollars on each slave brought into the United States. After 1808, when a law was passed to stop slaves from being brought into the United States, this section no longer applied.

(2) Habeas Corpus
A writ of habeas corpus is a privilege that entitles a person to a hearing before a judge. The judge must then decide if there is good reason for that person to have been arrested. If not, that person must be released. The government is not allowed to take this privilege away except during a national emergency, such as an invasion or a rebellion.

(3) Special Laws
Congress cannot pass laws that impose punishment on a named individual or group, except in cases of treason. Article III sets limits to punishments for treason. Congress also cannot pass laws that punish a person for an action that was legal when it was done.

(4) Direct Taxes
Congress cannot set a direct tax on people, unless it is in proportion to the total population. Amendment 16, which provides for the income tax, is an exception.

(5) Export Taxes
Congress cannot tax goods sent from one state to another or from a state to another country.

(6) Ports
When making trade laws, Congress cannot favor one state over another. Congress cannot require ships from one state to pay a duty to enter another state.

(7) Public Money
The government cannot spend money from the treasury unless Congress passes a law allowing it to do so. A written record must be kept of all money spent by the government.

(8) Titles of Nobility and Gifts
The United States government cannot grant titles of nobility. Government officials cannot accept gifts from other countries without the permission of Congress. This clause was intended to prevent government officials from being bribed by other nations.

(1) Complete Restrictions
The Constitution does not allow states to act as if they were individual countries. No state government may make a treaty with other countries. No state can print its own money.

(2) Partial Restrictions
No state government can tax imported goods or exported goods without the consent of Congress. States may charge a fee to inspect these goods, but profits must be given to the United States Treasury.

(3) Other Restrictions
No state government may tax ships entering its ports unless Congress approves. No state may keep an army or navy during times of peace other than the National Guard. No state can enter into agreements called compacts with other states without the consent of Congress.

(1) Term of Office
The President has the authority to carry out our nation's laws. The term of office for both the President and the Vice President is four years.

(2) The Electoral College
This group of people is to be chosen by the voters of each state to elect the President and Vice President. The number of electors in each state is equal to the number of senators and representatives that state has in Congress.

(3) Election Process
This clause describes in detail how the electors were to choose the President and Vice President. In 1804 Amendment 12 changed the process for electing the President and the Vice President.

---

(8) No title of nobility shall be granted by the United States; and no person holding any office of profit or trust under them, shall, without the consent of the Congress, accept of any present, emolument, office, or title, of any kind whatever, from any king, prince, or foreign state.

SECTION 10. POWERS DENIED TO THE STATES

(1) No state shall enter into any treaty, alliance, or confederation; grant letters of marque and reprisal; coin money; emit bills of credit; make anything but gold and silver coin a tender in payment of debts; pass any bill of attainder, ex post facto law, or law impairing the obligation of contracts, or grant any title of nobility.

(2) No state shall, without the consent of the Congress, lay any imposts or duties on imports or exports, except what may be absolutely necessary for executing its inspection laws; and the net produce of all duties and imposts, laid by any state on imports or exports, shall be for the use of the Treasury of the United States; and all such laws shall be subject to the revision and control of the Congress.

(3) No state shall, without the consent of Congress, lay any duty of tonnage, keep troops, or ships of war in time of peace, enter into any agreement or compact with another state, or with a foreign power, or engage in war, unless actually invaded, or in such imminent danger as will not admit of delay.

ARTICLE II
THE EXECUTIVE BRANCH
SECTION 1. PRESIDENT AND VICE PRESIDENT

(1) The executive power shall be vested in a President of the United States of America. He shall hold his office during the term of four years, and together with the Vice President, chosen for the same term, be elected as follows:

(2) Each state shall appoint, in such manner as the legislature thereof may direct, a number of electors, equal to the whole number of Senators and Representatives to which the state may be entitled in the Congress; but no Senator or Representative, or person holding an office of trust or profit under the United States, shall be appointed an elector.

(3) [*The electors shall meet in their respective states, and vote by ballot for two persons, of whom one at least shall not be an inhabitant of the same state with themselves. And they shall make a list of all the persons voted for, and of the number of votes for each; which list they shall sign and certify, and transmit sealed to the seat of the government of the United States, directed to the president of the Senate. The president of the Senate shall, in the presence of the Senate and House of Representatives, open all the certificates, and the votes shall then be counted. The person having the greatest number of votes shall be the President, if such number be a majority of the whole number of electors appointed; and if there be more than one who have such majority, and have an equal number of votes, then the House of Representatives shall immediately choose by ballot one of them for President; and if no person have*

a majority, then from the five highest on the list the said House shall in like manner choose the President. But in choosing the President the votes shall be taken by states, the representation from each state having one vote: A quorum for this purpose shall consist of a member or members from two-thirds of the states, and a majority of all the states shall be necessary to a choice. In every case, after the choice of the President, the person having the greatest number of votes of the electors shall be the Vice President. But if there should remain two or more who have equal votes, the Senate shall choose from them by ballot the Vice President.]

(4) The Congress may determine the time of choosing the electors, and the day on which they shall give their votes; which day shall be the same throughout the United States.

(5) No person except a natural-born citizen [*or a citizen of the United States, at the time of the adoption of this Constitution,*] shall be eligible to the office of the President; neither shall any person be eligible to that office who shall not have attained to the age of thirty-five years, and been fourteen years a resident within the United States.

(6) [*In case of the removal of the President from office, or of his death, resignation, or inability to discharge the powers and duties of the said office, the same shall devolve on the Vice President, and the Congress may by law provide for the case of removal, death, resignation or inability, both of the President and Vice President, declaring what officer shall then act as President, and such officer shall act accordingly, until the disability be removed, or a President shall be elected.*]

(7) The President shall, at stated times, receive for his services, a compensation, which shall neither be increased nor diminished during the period for which he shall have been elected, and he shall not receive within that period any other emolument from the United States, or any of them.

(8) Before he enter on the execution of his office, he shall take the following oath or affirmation:—"I do solemnly swear (or affirm) that I will faithfully execute the office of President of the United States, and will to the best of my ability, preserve, protect, and defend the Constitution of the United States."

SECTION 2. POWERS OF THE PRESIDENT
(1) The President shall be Commander in Chief of the Army and Navy of the United States, and of the militia of the several states, when called into the actual service of the United States; he may require the opinion, in writing, of the principal officer in each of the executive departments, upon any subject relating to the duties of their respective offices, and he shall have power to grant reprieves and pardons for offenses against the United States, except in cases of impeachment.

(4) Time of Elections
Congress decides the day the electors are to be elected and the day they are to vote.

(5) Qualifications
The President must be at least 35 years old, be a citizen of the United States by birth, and have been living in the United States for 14 years or more.

(6) Vacancies
If the President dies, resigns, or is removed from office, the Vice President becomes President.

(7) Salary
The President receives a salary that cannot be raised or lowered during a term of office. The President may not be paid any additional salary by the federal government or any state or local government. Today the President's salary is $400,000 a year, plus expenses for things such as housing, travel, and entertainment.

(8) Oath of Office
Before taking office, the President must promise to perform the duties faithfully and to protect the country's form of government. Usually the Chief Justice of the Supreme Court administers the oath of office.

(1) The President's Leadership
The President is the commander of the nation's armed forces and of the National Guard when it is in service of the nation. All government officials of the executive branch must report their actions to the President when asked. The President can excuse people from punishment for crimes committed.

(2) Treaties and Appointments
The President has the authority to make treaties, but they must be approved by a two-thirds vote of the Senate. The President nominates justices to the Supreme Court, ambassadors to other countries, and other federal officials with the Senate's approval.

(3) Filling Vacancies
If a government official's position becomes vacant when Congress is not in session, the President can make a temporary appointment.

Duties
The President must report to Congress on the condition of the country. This report is now presented in the annual State of the Union message.

Impeachment
The President, the Vice President, or any government official will be removed from office if impeached, or accused, and then found guilty of treason, bribery, or other serious crimes. The Constitution protects government officials from being impeached for unimportant reasons.

Federal Courts
The authority to decide legal cases is granted to a Supreme Court and to a system of lower courts established by Congress. The Supreme Court is the highest court in the land. Justices and judges are in their offices for life, subject to good behavior.

(1) General Authority
Federal courts have the authority to decide cases that arise under the Constitution, laws, and treaties of the United States. They also have the authority to settle disagreements among states and among citizens of different states.

(2) He shall have power, by and with the advice and consent of the Senate, to make treaties, provided two-thirds of the senators present concur; and he shall nominate, and by and with the advice and consent of the Senate, shall appoint ambassadors, other public ministers and consuls, judges of the Supreme Court, and all other officers of the United States, whose appointments are not herein otherwise provided for, and which shall be established by law; but the Congress may by law vest the appointment of such inferior officers, as they think proper, in the President alone, in the courts of law, or in the heads of departments.

(3) The President shall have power to fill up all vacancies that may happen during the recess of the Senate, by granting commissions which shall expire at the end of their next session.

SECTION 3. DUTIES OF THE PRESIDENT

He shall from time to time give to the Congress information of the state of the Union, and recommend to their consideration such measures as he shall judge necessary and expedient; he may, on extraordinary occasions, convene both houses, or either of them, and in case of disagreement between them, with respect to the time of adjournment, he may adjourn them to such time as he shall think proper; he shall receive ambassadors and other public ministers; he shall take care that the laws be faithfully executed, and shall commission all the officers of the United States.

SECTION 4. IMPEACHMENT

The President, Vice President and all civil officers of the United States, shall be removed from office on impeachment for, and conviction of, treason, bribery, or other high crimes and misdemeanors.

ARTICLE III
THE JUDICIAL BRANCH
SECTION 1. FEDERAL COURTS

The judicial power of the United States shall be vested in one Supreme Court, and in such inferior courts as the Congress may from time to time ordain and establish. The judges, both of the supreme and inferior courts, shall hold their offices during good behavior, and shall, at stated times, receive for their services a compensation, which shall not be diminished during their continuance in office.

SECTION 2. AUTHORITY OF THE FEDERAL COURTS

(1) The judicial power shall extend to all cases, in law and equity, arising under this Constitution, the laws of the United States, and treaties made or which shall be made, under their authority; to all cases affecting ambassadors, other public ministers and consuls; to all cases of admiralty and maritime jurisdiction; to controversies to which the United States shall be a party; to controversies between two or more states; [*between a state and citizens of another state;*] between citizens of different states; —between citizens of the same state claiming lands under grants of different states, [*and between a state or the citizens thereof, and foreign states, citizens, or subjects.*]

(2) In all cases affecting ambassadors, other public ministers and consuls, and those in which a state shall be party, the Supreme Court shall have original jurisdiction. In all the other cases before mentioned, the Supreme Court shall have appellate jurisdiction, both as to law and fact, with such exceptions, and under such regulations as the Congress shall make.

(3) The trial of all crimes, except in cases of impeachment, shall be by jury; and such trial shall be held in the state where the said crimes shall have been committed; but when not committed within any state, the trial shall be at such place or places as the Congress may by law have directed.

SECTION 3. TREASON
(1) Treason against the United States shall consist only in levying war against them, or in adhering to their enemies, giving them aid and comfort. No person shall be convicted of treason unless on the testimony of two witnesses to the same overt act, or on confession in open court.

(2) The Congress shall have power to declare the punishment of treason, but no attainder of treason shall work corruption of blood, or forfeiture except during the life of the person attainted.

ARTICLE IV
RELATIONS AMONG STATES
SECTION 1. OFFICIAL RECORDS
Full faith and credit shall be given in each state to the public acts, records, and judicial proceedings of every other state. And the Congress may by general laws prescribe the manner in which such acts, records, and proceedings shall be proved, and the effect thereof.

SECTION 2. PRIVILEGES OF THE CITIZENS
(1) The citizens of each state shall be entitled to all privileges and immunities of citizens in the several states.

(2) A person charged in any state with treason, felony, or other crime, who shall flee from justice, and be found in another state, shall on demand of the executive authority of the state from which he fled, be delivered up, to be removed to the state having jurisdiction of the crime.

(3) [*No person held to service or labor in one state, under the laws thereof, escaping into another, shall in consequence of any law or regulation therein, be discharged from such service or labor, but shall be delivered up on claim of the party to whom such service or labor may be due.*]

(2) Supreme Court
The Supreme Court can decide certain cases being tried for the first time. It can review cases that have already been tried in a lower court if the decision has been appealed, or questioned, by one side.

(3) Trial by Jury
The Constitution guarantees a trial by jury for every person charged with a federal crime. Amendments 5, 6, and 7 extend and clarify a person's right to a trial by jury.

(1) Definition of Treason
Acts that may be considered treason are making war against the United States or helping its enemies. A person cannot be convicted of attempting to overthrow the government unless there are two witnesses to the act or the person confesses in court to treason.

(2) Punishment for Treason
Congress can decide the punishment for treason, within certain limits.

Official Records
Each state must honor the official records and judicial decisions of other states.

(1) Privileges
A citizen moving from one state to another has the same rights as other citizens living in that person's new state of residence. In some cases, such as voting, people may be required to live in their new state for a certain length of time before obtaining the same privileges as citizens there.

(2) Extradition
At the governor's request, a person who is charged with a crime and who tries to escape justice by crossing into another state may be returned to the state in which the crime was committed.

(3) Fugitive Slaves
The original Constitution required that runaway slaves be returned to their owners. Amendment 13 abolished slavery, eliminating the need for this clause.

(1) Admission of New States
Congress has the authority to admit new states to the Union. All new states have the same rights as existing states.

(2) Federal Property
The Constitution allows Congress to make or change laws governing federal property. This applies to territories and federally owned land within states, such as national parks.

Guarantees to the States
The federal government guarantees that every state have a republican form of government. The United States must also protect the states against invasion and help the states deal with rebellion or local violence.

Amending the Constitution
Changes to the Constitution may be proposed by a two-thirds vote of both the House of Representatives and the Senate or by a national convention called by Congress when asked by two-thirds of the states. For an amendment to become law, the legislatures or conventions in three-fourths of the states must approve it.

(1) Public Debt
Any debt owed by the United States before the Constitution went into effect was to be honored.

(2) Federal Supremacy
This clause declares that the Constitution and federal laws are the highest in the nation. Whenever a state law and a federal law are found to disagree, the federal law must be obeyed so long as it is constitutional.

(3) Oaths of Office
All federal and state officials must promise to follow and enforce the Constitution. These officials, however, cannot be required to follow a particular religion or satisfy any religious test.

SECTION 3. NEW STATES AND TERRITORIES

(1) New states may be admitted by the Congress into this Union; but no new state shall be formed or erected within the jurisdiction of any other state; nor any state be formed by the junction of two or more states, or parts of states, without the consent of the legislatures of the states concerned as well as of the Congress.

(2) The Congress shall have power to dispose of and make all needful rules and regulations respecting the territory or other property belonging to the United States; and nothing in this Constitution shall be so construed as to prejudice any claims of the United States, or of any particular state.

SECTION 4. GUARANTEES TO THE STATES

The United States shall guarantee to every state in this Union a republican form of government, and shall protect each of them against invasion; and on application of the legislature, or of the executive (when the legislature cannot be convened) against domestic violence.

ARTICLE V
AMENDING THE CONSTITUTION

The Congress, whenever two-thirds of both houses shall deem it necessary, shall propose amendments to this Constitution, or, on the application of the legislatures of two-thirds of the several states, shall call a convention for proposing amendments, which, in either case, shall be valid to all intents and purposes, as part of this Constitution, when ratified by the legislatures of three-fourths of the several states, or by conventions in three-fourths thereof, as the one or the other mode of ratification may be proposed by the Congress; provided that [*no amendment which may be made prior to the year 1808 shall in any manner affect the first and fourth clauses in the Ninth Section of the First Article; and that*] no state, without its consent, shall be deprived of its equal suffrage in the Senate.

ARTICLE VI
GENERAL PROVISIONS

(1) All debts contracted and engagements entered into, before the adoption of this Constitution, shall be as valid against the United States under this Constitution, as under the Confederation.

(2) This Constitution, and the laws of the United States which shall be made in pursuance thereof, and all treaties made, or which shall be made, under the authority of the United States, shall be the supreme law of the land; and the judges in every state shall be bound thereby, anything in the Constitution or laws of any state to the contrary notwithstanding.

(3) The Senators and Representatives before mentioned, and the members of the several state legislatures, and all executive and judicial officers, both of the United States and of the several states, shall be bound by oath or affirmation, to support this Constitution; but no religious test shall ever be required as a qualification to any office or public trust under the United States.

ARTICLE VII
RATIFICATION

The ratification of the conventions of nine states, shall be sufficient for the establishment of this Constitution between the states so ratifying the same.

Done in convention by the unanimous consent of the states present the seventeenth day of September in the year of our Lord one thousand seven hundred and eighty seven and of the independence of the United States of America the Twelfth. In witness whereof we have hereunto subscribed our names.

George Washington—President and deputy from Virginia

DELAWARE
George Read
Gunning Bedford, Jr.
John Dickinson
Richard Bassett
Jacob Broom

MARYLAND
James McHenry
Daniel of St. Thomas Jenifer
Daniel Carroll

VIRGINIA
John Blair
James Madison, Jr.

NORTH CAROLINA
William Blount
Richard Dobbs Spaight
Hugh Williamson

SOUTH CAROLINA
John Rutledge
Charles Cotesworth Pinckney
Charles Pinckney
Pierce Butler

GEORGIA
William Few
Abraham Baldwin

NEW HAMPSHIRE
John Langdon
Nicholas Gilman

MASSACHUSETTS
Nathaniel Gorham
Rufus King

CONNECTICUT
William Samuel Johnson
Roger Sherman

NEW YORK
Alexander Hamilton

NEW JERSEY
William Livingston
David Brearley
William Paterson
Jonathan Dayton

PENNSYLVANIA
Benjamin Franklin
Thomas Mifflin
Robert Morris
George Clymer
Thomas FitzSimons
Jared Ingersoll
James Wilson
Gouverneur Morris

ATTEST: William Jackson, secretary

Ratification
In order for the Constitution to become law, 9 of the 13 states had to approve it. Special conventions were held for this purpose. The process took 9 months to complete.

Basic Freedoms
The Constitution guarantees our five basic freedoms of expression. It provides for the freedoms of religion, speech, the press, peaceable assembly, and petition for redress of grievances.

Weapons and the Militia
This amendment protects the right of the state governments and the people to maintain militias to guard against threats to their public order, safety, and liberty. In connection with that state right, the federal government may not take away the right of the people to have and use weapons.

Housing Soldiers
The federal government cannot force people to house soldiers in their homes during peacetime. However, Congress may pass laws allowing this during wartime.

Searches and Seizures
This amendment protects people's privacy and safety. Subject to certain exceptions, a law officer cannot search a person or a person's home and belongings unless a judge has issued a valid search warrant. There must be good reason for the search. The warrant must describe the place to be searched and the people or things to be seized, or taken.

Rights of Accused Persons
If a person is accused of a crime that is punishable by death or of any other crime that is very serious, a grand jury must decide if there is enough evidence to hold a trial. People cannot be tried twice for the same crime, nor can they be forced to testify against themselves. No person shall be fined, jailed, or executed by the government unless the person has been given a fair trial. The government cannot take a person's property for public use unless fair payment is made.

AMENDMENT 1 (1791)***
BASIC FREEDOMS

Congress shall make no law respecting an establishment of religion, or prohibiting the free exercise thereof; or abridging the freedom of speech, or of the press; or the right of the people peaceably to assemble, and to petition the government for a redress of grievances.

AMENDMENT 2 (1791)
WEAPONS AND THE MILITIA

A well-regulated militia, being necessary to the security of a free state, the right of the people to keep and bear arms shall not be infringed.

AMENDMENT 3 (1791)
HOUSING SOLDIERS

No soldier shall, in time of peace, be quartered in any house, without the consent of the owner; nor in time of war, but in a manner to be prescribed by law.

AMENDMENT 4 (1791)
SEARCHES AND SEIZURES

The right of the people to be secure in their persons, houses, papers, and effects, against unreasonable searches and seizures, shall not be violated; and no warrants shall issue but upon probable cause, supported by oath or affirmation, and particularly describing the place to be searched, and the persons or things to be seized.

AMENDMENT 5 (1791)
RIGHTS OF ACCUSED PERSONS

No person shall be held to answer for a capital, or otherwise infamous crime, unless on a presentment or indictment of a grand jury, except in cases arising in the land or naval forces, or in the militia, when in actual service in time of war or public danger; nor shall any person be subject for the same offense to be twice put in jeopardy of life or limb; nor shall be compelled in any criminal case to be a witness against himself; nor be deprived of life, liberty, or property, without due process of law; nor shall private property be taken for public use without just compensation.

*** The date beside each amendment is the year that the amendment was ratified and became part of the Constitution.

AMENDMENT 6 (1791)
RIGHT TO A FAIR TRIAL

In all criminal prosecutions, the accused shall enjoy the right to a speedy and public trial, by an impartial jury of the state and district wherein the crime shall have been committed, which district shall have been previously ascertained by law, and to be informed of the nature and cause of the accusation; to be confronted with the witnesses against him; to have compulsory process for obtaining witnesses in his favor, and to have the assistance of counsel for his defense.

AMENDMENT 7 (1791)
JURY TRIAL IN CIVIL CASES

In suits at common law, where the value in controversy shall exceed 20 dollars, the right of trial by jury shall be preserved, and no fact tried by a jury shall be otherwise re-examined in any court of the United States, than according to the rules of the common law.

AMENDMENT 8 (1791)
BAIL AND PUNISHMENT

Excessive bail shall not be required, nor excessive fines imposed, nor cruel and unusual punishments inflicted.

AMENDMENT 9 (1791)
RIGHTS OF THE PEOPLE

The enumeration in the Constitution, of certain rights, shall not be construed to deny or disparage others retained by the people.

AMENDMENT 10 (1791)
POWERS OF THE STATES AND THE PEOPLE

The powers not delegated to the United States by the Constitution, nor prohibited by it to the states, are reserved to the states respectively, or to the people.

AMENDMENT 11 (1798)
SUITS AGAINST STATES

The judicial power of the United States shall not be construed to extend to any suit in law or equity, commenced or prosecuted against one of the United States or citizens of another state, or by citizens or subjects of any foreign state.

Right to a Fair Trial
A person accused of a crime has the right to a public trial by an impartial jury, locally chosen. The trial must be held within a reasonable amount of time. The accused person must be told of all charges and has the right to see, hear, and question any witnesses. The federal government must provide a lawyer free of charge to a person who is accused of a serious crime and who is unable to pay for legal services.

Jury Trial in Civil Cases
In most federal civil cases involving more than 20 dollars, a jury trial is guaranteed. Civil cases are those disputes between two or more people over money, property, personal injury, or legal rights. Usually civil cases are not tried in federal courts unless much larger sums of money are involved or unless federal courts are given the authority to decide a certain type of case.

Bail and Punishment
Courts cannot treat harshly people accused of crimes or punish them in unusual or cruel ways. Bail is money put up as a guarantee that an accused person will appear for trial. In certain cases bail can be denied altogether.

Rights of the People
The federal government must respect all natural rights, whether or not they are listed in the Constitution.

Powers of the States and the People
Any powers not clearly given to the federal government or denied to the states belong to the states or to the people.

Suits Against States
A citizen of one state cannot sue another state in federal court.

Election of President and Vice President
This amendment replaces the part of Article II, Section 1, that originally explained the process of electing the President and Vice President. Amendment 12 was an important step in the development of the two-party system. It allows a party to nominate its own candidates for both President and Vice President.

AMENDMENT 12 (1804)
ELECTION OF PRESIDENT AND VICE PRESIDENT

The electors shall meet in their respective states, and vote by ballot for President and Vice President, one of whom, at least, shall not be an inhabitant of the same state with themselves; they shall name in their ballots the person voted for as President, and in distinct ballots the person voted for as Vice President, and they shall make distinct lists of all persons voted for as President, and of all persons voted for as Vice President, and of the number of votes for each, which lists they shall sign and certify, and transmit, sealed, to the seat of government of the United States, directed to the President of the Senate; the President of the Senate shall, in the presence of the Senate and House of Representatives, open all the certificates, and the votes shall then be counted; the person having the greatest number of votes for President shall be the President, if such a number be a majority of the whole number of electors appointed; and if no person have such majority; then from the persons having the highest numbers not exceeding three on the list of those voted for as President, the House of Representatives shall choose immediately, by ballot, the President. But in choosing the President, the votes shall be taken by states, the representation from each state having one vote; a quorum for this purpose shall consist of a member or members from two thirds of the states, and a majority of all the states shall be necessary to a choice. [And *if the House of Representatives shall not choose a President whenever the right of choice shall devolve upon them, before the fourth day of March next following, then the Vice President shall act as President, as in the case of the death or other constitutional disability of the President.*] The person having the greatest number of votes as Vice President, shall be the Vice President, if such number be a majority of the whole number of electors appointed, and if no person have a majority, then, from the two highest numbers on the list the Senate shall choose the Vice President; a quorum for the purpose shall consist of two thirds of the whole number of Senators, and a majority of the whole number shall be necessary to a choice. But no person constitutionally ineligible to the office of President shall be eligible to that of Vice President of the United States.

End of Slavery
People cannot be forced to work against their will unless they have been tried for and convicted of a crime for which this means of punishment is ordered. Congress may enforce this by law.

AMENDMENT 13 (1865)
END OF SLAVERY

SECTION 1. ABOLITION

Neither slavery nor involuntary servitude, except as a punishment for crime whereof the party shall have been duly convicted, shall exist within the United States, or any place subject to their jurisdiction.

SECTION 2. ENFORCEMENT

Congress shall have power to enforce this article by appropriate legislation.

Citizenship
All persons born or naturalized in the United States are citizens of the United States and of the state in which they live. State governments may not deny any citizen the full rights of citizenship. This amendment also guarantees due process of law. According to due process of law, no state may take away the rights of a citizen. All citizens must be protected equally under law.

AMENDMENT 14 (1868)
RIGHTS OF CITIZENS

SECTION 1. CITIZENSHIP

All persons born or naturalized in the United States and subject to the jurisdiction thereof, are citizens of the United States and of the state wherein they reside. No state shall make or enforce any law which shall abridge the privileges or immunities of citizens of the United States, nor shall any state deprive any person of life, liberty, or property, without due process of law; nor deny to any person within its jurisdiction the equal protection of the laws.

SECTION 2. NUMBER OF REPRESENTATIVES

Representatives shall be apportioned among the several states according to their respective numbers, counting the whole number of persons in each state, [*excluding Indians not taxed*]. But when the right to vote at any election for the choice of electors for President and Vice President of the United States, representatives in Congress, the executive and judicial officers of a state, or the members of the legislature thereof, is denied to any of the [*male*] inhabitants of such state, being [*twenty-one years of age and*] citizens of the United States, or in any way abridged, except for participation in rebellion or other crime, the basis of representation therein shall be reduced in the proportion which the number of such [*male*] citizens shall bear to the whole number of [*male*] citizens [*twenty-one years of age*] in such state.

SECTION 3. PENALTY FOR REBELLION

No person shall be a Senator or Representative in Congress, or elector of President and Vice President, or hold any office, civil or military, under the United States, or under any state, who, having previously taken an oath, as a member of Congress, or as an officer of the United States, or as a member of any state legislature, or as an executive or judicial officer of any state, to support the Constitution of the United States, shall have engaged in insurrection or rebellion against the same, or given aid or comfort to the enemies thereof. But Congress may, by a vote of two thirds of each house, remove such disability.

SECTION 4. GOVERNMENT DEBT

The validity of the public debt of the United States, authorized by law, including debts incurred for payment of pensions and bounties for services in suppressing insurrection or rebellion, shall not be questioned. But neither the United States nor any state shall assume or pay any debt or obligation incurred in aid of insurrection or rebellion against the United States, [*or any claim for the loss or emancipation of any slave;*] but all such debts, obligations, and claims shall be held illegal and void.

SECTION 5. ENFORCEMENT

The Congress shall have power to enforce, by appropriate legislation, the provisions of this article.

AMENDMENT 15 (1870)
VOTING RIGHTS

SECTION 1. RIGHT TO VOTE

The right of citizens of the United States to vote shall not be denied or abridged by the United States or by any state on account of race, color, or previous condition of servitude.

SECTION 2. ENFORCEMENT

The Congress shall have power to enforce this article by appropriate legislation.

AMENDMENT 16 (1913)
INCOME TAX

The Congress shall have power to lay and collect taxes on incomes, from whatever source derived, without apportionment among the several states, and without regard to any census or enumeration.

Number of Representatives
Each state's representation in Congress is based on its total population. Any state denying eligible citizens the right to vote will have its representation in Congress decreased. This clause abolished the Three-fifths Compromise in Article I, Section 2. Later amendments granted women the right to vote and lowered the voting age to 18.

Penalty for Rebellion
No person who has rebelled against the United States may hold federal office. This clause was originally added to punish the leaders of the Confederacy for failing to support the Constitution of the United States.

Government Debt
The federal government is responsible for all public debts. It is not responsible, however, for Confederate debts or for debts that result from any rebellion against the United States.

Enforcement
Congress may enforce these provisions by law.

Right to Vote
No state may prevent a citizen from voting simply because of race or color or condition of previous servitude. This amendment was designed to extend voting rights to enforce this by law.

Income Tax
Congress has the power to collect taxes on its citizens, based on their personal incomes rather than on the number of people living in a state.

Direct Election of Senators
Originally, state legislatures elected senators. This amendment allows the people of each state to elect their own senators directly. The idea is to make senators more responsible to the people they represent.

Prohibition
This amendment made it illegal to make, sell, or transport liquor within the United States or to transport it out of the United States or its territories. Amendment 18 was the first to include a time limit for approval. If not ratified within seven years, it would be repealed, or canceled. Many later amendments have included similar time limits.

Women's Voting Rights
This amendment protected the right of women throughout the United States to vote.

Terms of Office
The terms of the President and the Vice President begin on January 20, in the year following their election. Members of Congress take office on January 3. Before this amendment newly elected members of Congress did not begin their terms until March 4. This meant that those who had run for reelection and been defeated remained in office for four months.

AMENDMENT 17 (1913)
DIRECT ELECTION OF SENATORS
SECTION 1. METHOD OF ELECTION
The Senate of the United States shall be composed of two Senators from each state, elected by the people thereof, for six years; and each Senator shall have one vote. The electors in each state shall have the qualifications requisite for electors of the most numerous branch of the state legislatures.
SECTION 2. VACANCIES
When vacancies happen in the representation of any state in the Senate, the executive authority of such state shall issue writs of election to fill such vacancies: *Provided*, that the legislature of any state may empower the executive thereof to make temporary appointments until the people fill the vacancies by election as the legislature may direct.
SECTION 3. EXCEPTION
[*This amendment shall not be so construed as to affect the election or term of any Senator chosen before it becomes valid as part of the Constitution.*]

AMENDMENT 18 (1919)
BAN ON ALCOHOLIC DRINKS
SECTION 1. PROHIBITION
[*After one year from the ratification of this article the manufacture, sale, or transportation of intoxicating liquors within, the importation thereof into, or the exportation thereof from the United States and all territory subject to the jurisdiction thereof for beverage purposes is hereby prohibited.*]
SECTION 2. ENFORCEMENT
[*The Congress and the several states shall have concurrent power to enforce this article by appropriate legislation.*]
SECTION 3. RATIFICATION
[*This article shall be inoperative unless it shall have been ratified as an amendment to the Constitution by the legislatures of the several states as provided in the Constitution, within seven years from the date of the submission hereof to the states by the Congress.*]

AMENDMENT 19 (1920)
WOMEN'S VOTING RIGHTS
SECTION 1. RIGHT TO VOTE
The right of citizens of the United States to vote shall not be denied or abridged by the United States or by any state on account of sex.
SECTION 2. ENFORCEMENT
Congress shall have power to enforce this article by appropriate legislation.

AMENDMENT 20 (1933)
TERMS OF OFFICE
SECTION 1. BEGINNING OF TERMS
The terms of the President and Vice President shall end at noon on the 20th day of January, and the terms of Senators and Representatives at noon on the 3rd day of January, of the years in which such terms would have ended if this article had not been ratified; and the terms of their successors shall then begin.

SECTION 2. SESSIONS OF CONGRESS

The Congress shall assemble at least once in every year, and such meeting shall begin at noon on the 3rd day of January, unless they shall by law appoint a different day.

SECTION 3. PRESIDENTIAL SUCCESSION

If, at the time fixed for the beginning of the term of the President, the President-elect shall have died, the Vice President-elect shall become President. If a President shall not have been chosen before the time fixed for the beginning of his term, or if the President-elect shall have failed to qualify, then the Vice President-elect shall act as President until a President shall have qualified; and the Congress may by law provide for the case wherein neither a President-elect nor a Vice President-elect shall have qualified, declaring who shall then act as President, or the manner in which one who is to act shall be selected and such person shall act accordingly until a President or Vice President shall be qualified.

SECTION 4. ELECTIONS DECIDED BY CONGRESS

The Congress may by law provide for the case of the death of any of the persons from whom the House of Representatives may choose a President whenever the right of choice shall have devolved upon them, and for the case of the death of any of the persons from whom the Senate may choose a Vice President whenever the right of choice shall have devolved upon them.

SECTION 5. EFFECTIVE DATE

[*Sections 1 and 2 shall take effect on the 15th day of October following the ratification of this article.*]

SECTION 6. RATIFICATION

[*This article shall be inoperative unless it shall have been ratified as an amendment to the Constitution by the legislatures of three fourths of the several states within seven years from the date of its submission.*]

AMENDMENT 21 (1933)
END OF PROHIBITION

SECTION 1. REPEAL OF AMENDMENT 18

The eighteenth article of amendment to the Constitution of the United States is hereby repealed.

SECTION 2. STATE LAWS

The transportation or importation into any state, territory, or possession of the United States for delivery or use therein of intoxicating liquors, in violation of the laws thereof, is hereby prohibited.

SECTION 3. RATIFICATION

[*This article shall be inoperative unless it shall have been ratified as an amendment to the Constitution by conventions in the several states, as provided in the Constitution within seven years from the date of the submission hereof to the states by Congress.*]

Sessions of Congress
Congress meets at least once a year, beginning at noon on January 3. Congress had previously met at least once a year beginning on the first Monday of December.

Presidential Succession
If the newly elected President dies before January 20, the newly elected Vice President becomes President on that date. If a President has not been chosen by January 20 or does not meet the requirements for being President, the newly elected Vice President becomes President. If neither the newly elected President nor the newly elected Vice President meets the requirements for office, Congress decides who will serve as President until a qualified President or Vice President is chosen.

End of Prohibition
This amendment repealed Amendment 18. This is the only amendment to be ratified by state conventions instead of by state legislatures. Congress felt that this would give people's opinions about prohibition a better chance to be heard.

Two-Term limit for Presidents
A President may not serve more than two full terms in office. Any President who serves less than two years of a previous President's term may be elected for two more terms.

Presidential Electors for District of Columbia
This amendment grants three electoral votes to the national capital.

Ban on Poll Taxes
No United States citizen may be prevented from voting in a federal election because of failing to pay a tax to vote. Poll taxes had been used in some states to prevent African Americans from voting.

Presidential Vacancy
If the President is removed from office or resigns from or dies while in office, the Vice President becomes President.

AMENDMENT 22 (1951)
TWO-TERM LIMIT FOR PRESIDENTS
SECTION 1. TWO-TERM LIMIT

No person shall be elected to the office of the President more than twice, and no person who has held the office of President, or acted as President, for more than two years of a term to which some other person was elected President shall be elected to the office of the President more than once. [*But this article shall not apply to any person holding the office of President when this article was proposed by the Congress, and shall not prevent any person who may be holding the office of President, or acting as President, during the term within which this article becomes operative from holding the office of President, or acting as President, during the remainder of such term.*]

SECTION 2. RATIFICATION

[*This article shall be inoperative unless it shall have been ratified as an amendment to the Constitution by the legislatures of three-fourths of the several states within seven years from the date of its submission to the states by the Congress.*]

AMENDMENT 23 (1961)
PRESIDENTIAL ELECTORS FOR DISTRICT OF COLUMBIA
SECTION 1. NUMBER OF ELECTORS

The District constituting the seat of Government of the United States shall appoint in such manner as Congress may direct:

A number of electors of President and Vice President equal to the whole number of Senators and Representatives in Congress to which the District would be entitled if it were a state, but in no event more than the least populous state; they shall be in addition to those appointed by the states, but they shall be considered, for the purposes of the election of President and Vice President, to be electors appointed by a state, and they shall meet in the District and perform such duties as provided by the twelfth article of amendment.

SECTION 2. ENFORCEMENT

The Congress shall have power to enforce this article by appropriate legislation.

AMENDMENT 24 (1964)
BAN ON POLL TAXES
SECTION 1. POLL TAX ILLEGAL

The right of citizens of the United States to vote in any primary or other election for President or Vice President, for electors for President or Vice President, or for Senator or Representative in Congress, shall not be denied or abridged by the United States or any state by reason of failure to pay any poll tax or other tax.

SECTION 2. ENFORCEMENT

The Congress shall have power to enforce this article by appropriate legislation.

AMENDMENT 25 (1967)
PRESIDENTIAL SUCCESSION
SECTION 1. PRESIDENTIAL VACANCY

In case of the removal of the President from office or of his death or resignation, the Vice President shall become President.

SECTION 2. VICE PRESIDENTIAL VACANCY

Whenever there is a vacancy in the office of the Vice President, the President shall nominate a Vice President who shall take the office upon confirmation by a majority vote of both houses of Congress.

SECTION 3. PRESIDENTIAL DISABILITY

Whenever the President transmits to the President pro tempore of the Senate and the Speaker of the House of Representatives his written declaration that he is unable to discharge the powers and duties of his office, and until he transmits to them a written declaration to the contrary, such powers and duties shall be discharged by the Vice President as Acting President.

SECTION 4. DETERMINING PRESIDENTIAL DISABILITY

Whenever the Vice President and a majority of either the principal officers of the executive departments or of such other body as Congress may by law provide, transmit to the President pro tempore of the Senate and the Speaker of the House of Representatives their written declaration that the President is unable to discharge the powers and duties of his office, the Vice President shall immediately assume the powers and duties of the office as Acting President.

Thereafter, when the President transmits to the President pro tempore of the Senate and the Speaker of the House of Representatives his written declaration that no inability exists, he shall resume the powers and duties of his office unless the Vice President and a majority of either the principal officers of the executive department or of such other body as Congress may by law provide, transmit within four days to the President pro tempore of the Senate and the Speaker of the House of Representatives their written declaration that the President is unable to discharge the powers and duties of his office. Thereupon Congress shall decide the issue, assembling within 48 hours for that purpose if not in session. If the Congress, within 21 days after receipt of the latter written declaration, or, if Congress is not in session, within 21 days after Congress is required to assemble, determines by two-thirds vote of both houses that the President is unable to discharge the powers and duties of his office, the Vice President shall continue to discharge the same as Acting President; otherwise the President shall resume the powers and duties of his office.

AMENDMENT 26 (1971)
VOTING AGE

SECTION 1. RIGHT TO VOTE

The right of citizens of the United States, who are 18 years of age or older, to vote shall not be denied or abridged by the United States or any state on account of age.

SECTION 2. ENFORCEMENT

The Congress shall have the power to enforce this article by appropriate legislation.

AMENDMENT 27 (1992)
CONGRESSIONAL PAY

No law, varying the compensation for the services of the Senators and Representatives, shall take effect, until an election of Representatives shall have intervened.

Vice Presidential Vacancy
If the office of the Vice President becomes open, the President names someone to assume that office and that person becomes Vice President if both houses of Congress approve by a majority vote.

Presidential Disability
This section explains in detail what happens if the President cannot continue in office because of sickness or any other reason. The Vice President takes over as acting President until the President is able to resume office.

Determining Presidential Disability
If the Vice President and a majority of the Cabinet inform the Speaker of the House and the president pro tempore of the Senate that the President cannot carry out his or her duties, the Vice President then serves as acting President. To regain the office, the President has to inform the Speaker and the president pro tempore in writing that he or she is again able to serve. But, if the Vice President and a majority of the Cabinet disagree with the President and inform the Speaker and the president pro tempore that the President is still unable to serve, then Congress decides who will hold the office of President.

Voting Age
All citizens 18 years or older have the right to vote. Formerly, the voting age was 21 in most states.

Congressional Pay
A law raising or lowering the salaries for members of Congress cannot be passed for that session of Congress.

THE NATIONAL ANTHEM

The Star-Spangled Banner

"The Star-Spangled Banner" was written by Francis Scott Key in September 1814 and adopted as the national anthem in March 1931. The army and navy had recognized it as such long before Congress approved it.

During the War of 1812, Francis Scott Key spent a night aboard a British warship in the Chesapeake Bay while trying to arrange for the release of an American prisoner. The battle raged throughout the night, while the Americans were held on the ship. The next morning, when the smoke from the cannons finally cleared, Francis Scott Key was thrilled to see the American flag still waving proudly above Fort McHenry. It symbolized the victory of the Americans.

There are four verses to the national anthem. In these four verses, Key wrote about how he felt when he saw the flag still waving over Fort McHenry. He wrote that the flag was a symbol of the freedom for which the people had fought so hard. Key also told about the pride he had in his country and the great hopes he had for the future of the United States.

(1)

Oh, say can you see by the dawn's early light
What so proudly we hail'd at the twilight's last gleaming,
Whose broad stripes and bright stars through the perilous fight
O'er the ramparts we watch'd were so gallantly streaming?
And the rockets' red glare, the bombs bursting in air,
Gave proof through the night that our flag was still there.
Oh, say does that star-spangled banner yet wave
O'er the land of the free and the home of the brave?

(2)

On the shore dimly seen through the mists of the deep,
Where the foe's haughty host in dread silence reposes,
What is that which the breeze, o'er the towering steep,
As it fitfully blows, half conceals, half discloses?
Now it catches the gleam of the morning's first beam,
In full glory reflected now shines in the stream.
'Tis the star-spangled banner, oh, long may it wave
O'er the land of the free and the home of the brave!

(3)

And where is that band who so vauntingly swore
That the havoc of war and the battle's confusion
A home and a country should leave us no more?
Their blood has wash'd out their foul footstep's pollution.
No refuge could save the hireling and slave
From the terror of flight or the gloom of the grave,
And the star-spangled banner in triumph doth wave
O'er the land of the free and the home of the brave.

(4)

Oh, thus be it ever when freemen shall stand
Between their lov'd home and the war's desolation!
Blest with vict'ry and peace may the heav'n-rescued land
Praise the power that hath made and preserv'd us a nation!
Then conquer we must, when our cause it is just,
And this be our motto, "In God is our Trust,"
And the star-spangled banner in triumph shall wave
O'er the land of the free and the home of the brave.

The Pledge of Allegiance

I pledge allegiance to the Flag
of the United States of America,
and to the Republic
for which it stands,
one Nation under God, indivisible,
with liberty and justice for all.

The flag is a symbol of the United States of America. The Pledge of Allegiance says that the people of the United States promise to stand up for the flag, their country, and the basic beliefs of freedom and fairness upon which the country was established.

Biographical Dictionary

The Biographical Dictionary lists many of the important people introduced in this book. The page number tells where the main discussion of each person starts. See the Index for other page references.

A

Adams, Abigail *1744–1818* Patriot who wrote about women's rights in letters to John Adams, her husband. p. 311

Adams, John *1735–1826* 2nd U.S. President and one of the writers of the Declaration of Independence. pp. 303, 306, 353, 377, 379

Adams, Samuel *1722–1803* American Revolutionary leader who set up a Committee of Correspondence in Boston and helped form the Sons of Liberty. pp. 281, 289, 353, 369

Addams, Jane *1860–1935* American reformer who brought the idea of settlement houses from Britain to the United States. With Ellen Gates Starr, she founded Hull House in Chicago. p. 534

Aldrin, Edwin, Jr. *1930–* American astronaut who was one of the first people to set foot on the moon. p. 583

Ali, Sunni *1400s* Ruler of African empire of Songhay from 1464 to 1492. p. 111

Allen, Ethan *1738–1789* American Patriot from Vermont who led the Green Mountain Boys. p. 318

Anderson, Robert *1805–1871* Union commander of Fort Sumter who was forced to surrender to the Confederacy. p. 454

Aristide, Jean-Bertrand (air•ih•STEED, ZHAHN bair•TRAHN) *1953–* Freely elected president of Haiti who was overthrown in 1991 but was returned to office in 1994. p. 661

Armstrong, Louis *1901–1971* Noted jazz trumpeter who helped make jazz popular in the 1920s. p. 543

Armstrong, Neil *1930–* American astronaut who was the first person to set foot on the moon. p. 583

Arnold, Benedict *1741–1801* Continental Army officer who became a traitor and worked for the British army. p. 323

Atahuallpa (ah•tah•WAHL•pah) *1502?–1533* Inca ruler who was killed in the Spanish conquest of the Incas. p. 133

Attucks, Crispus (A•tuhks) *1723?–1770* Patriot and former slave who was killed during the Boston Massacre. p. 285

Austin, Moses *1761–1821* American pioneer who wanted to start an American colony in Texas. p. 402

Austin, Stephen F. *1793–1836* Moses Austin's son. He carried out his father's dream of starting an American colony in Texas. p. 402

B

Bache, Sarah Franklin *1700s* Daughter of Benjamin Franklin; took over Philadelphia Association when Esther Reed died. p. 311

Balboa, Vasco Núñez de (bahl•BOH•uh, NOON•yays day) *1475–1519* Spanish explorer who, in 1513, became the first European to reach the western coast of the Americas—proving to Europeans that the Americas were separate from Asia. p. 123

Banneker, Benjamin *1731–1806* African American who helped survey the land for the new capital of the United States. p. 376

Barrett, Janie Porter *1865–1948* African American teacher who founded a settlement house in Hampton, Virginia. p. 535

Barton, Clara *1821–1912* Civil War nurse and founder of the American Red Cross. p. 463

Bates, Katharine Lee *1859–1929* American educator and poet. p. 17

Becknell, William *1796?–1865* American pioneer from Missouri who opened the Santa Fe Trail. p. 404

Bellamy, Francis *1800s* Writer of patriotic oath that came to be called the Pledge of Allegiance. p. 643

Berlin, Irving *1888–1989* American songwriter who moved to New York City from Russia in 1893. p. 503

Bessemer, Henry *1813–1898* British inventor of a way to produce steel more easily and cheaply than before. p. 495

Bienville, Jean-Baptiste Le Moyne, Sieur de (bee•EN•vil, ZHAHN ba•TEEST luh•MWAHN) *1680–1747* French explorer who—with his brother, Pierre Le Moyne, Sieur d'Iberville—started an early settlement at the mouth of the Mississippi River. p. 154

Birdseye, Clarence *1886–1956* American scientist who developed methods of quick-freezing foods to preserve freshness. p. 546

Black Hawk *1767–1838* Leader of Sauk and Fox Indians; led fight against U.S. troops and Illinois militia. p. 398

Bolívar, Simón (boh•LEE•var, see•MOHN) *1783–1830* Leader of independence movements in Bolivia, Colombia, Ecuador, Peru, and Venezuela. p. 666

Bonaparte, Napoleon (BOH•nuh•part, nuh•POH•lee•uhn) *1769–1821* French leader who sold all of the Louisiana region to the United States. p. 385

Boone, Daniel *1734–1820* American who was one of the first pioneers to cross the Appalachians. pp. 225, 276

Booth, John Wilkes *1838–1865* Actor who assassinated President Abraham Lincoln. p. 477

Bowie, James *1796–1836* American soldier killed at the Alamo. p. 403

Braddock, Edward *1695–1755* Commander in chief of British forces in French and Indian War; defeated in surprise attack. p. 271

Bradford, William *1590–1657* Governor of Plymouth Colony. p. 168

Breckinridge, John *1821–1875* Democrat from Kentucky who ran against Abraham Lincoln in the 1860 presidential election. p. 453

Brezhnev, Leonid (BREZH•nef) *1906–1982* Leader of the Communist Party of the Soviet Union from 1964 until his death in 1982. President Nixon's 1972 visit with him in the Soviet Union led to arms control and began a period of détente. p. 592

Brown, John *1800–1859* American abolitionist who seized a weapons storehouse to help slaves rebel. He was caught and hanged. p. 449

Brown, Linda *1943–* African American student whose family was among a group that challenged public-school segregation. p. 585

Brown, Moses *1738–1836* Textile pioneer who built the first textile mill in the United States, using Samuel Slater's plans. p. 416

Bruce, Blanche K. *1841–1898* Former slave who became U.S. senator from Mississippi. p. 479

Bruchac, Joseph Author of Native American folktales and legends. p. 14

Burgoyne, John (ber•GOYN) *1722–1792* British general who lost a battle to the Continental Army on October 17, 1777, at Saratoga, New York. p. 316

Burnet, David G. *1788–1870* First president of the Republic of Texas, when it was formed in 1836. p. 403

Bush, George *1924–* 41st U.S. President. He was President at the end of the Cold War and during Operation Desert Storm. pp. 598-599

Bush, George W. *1946–* 43rd U.S. President; son of George Bush, he won the closest election in history. pp. 600, 641, 651

C

Cabeza de Vaca, Álvar Núñez (kah•BAY•sah day VAH•kah) *1490?–1560?* Spanish explorer who went to Mexico City and told stories of the Seven Cities of Gold. p. 131

Caboto, Giovanni (kah•BOH•toh) *1450?–1499?* Italian explorer who in 1497 sailed from England and landed in what is now Newfoundland, though he thought he had landed in Asia. The English gave him the name John Cabot. p. 123

Calhoun, John C. *1782–1850* Vice President under John Quincy Adams and Andrew Jackson. He was a strong believer in states' rights. pp. 437, 453

Calvert, Cecilius *1605–1675* First proprietor of the Maryland colony; appointed his brother Leonard Calvert as governor of Maryland. p. 233

Calvert, George *1580?–1632* Member of Virginia Company and the first Lord Baltimore; bought land in Newfoundland, but found it too cold; moved to Chesapeake Bay area; father of Cecilius Calvert. p. 232

Cardozo, Francis L. *1800s* African American who became secretary of state and state treasurer in South Carolina. p. 479

Carnegie, Andrew *1835–1919* Entrepreneur who helped the steel industry grow in the United States. pp. 495, 496

Carter, Jimmy *1924–* 39th U.S. President. He brought about a peace agreement between Israel and Egypt. p. 596

Carteret, Sir George *c.1610–1680* Proprietor with Lord John Berkeley of territory between the Hudson and Delaware Rivers; named the state of New Jersey for his birthplace. p. 213

Cartier, Jacques (kar•TYAY, ZHAHK) *1491–1557* French explorer who sailed up the St. Lawrence River and began a fur-trading business with the Hurons. p. 137

Carver, George Washington *c.1864–1943* African American scientist who developed hundreds of new uses for peanuts, sweet potatoes, and soybeans. p. 545

Castro, Fidel *1926–* Leader who took over Cuba in 1959 and made it a communist nation. pp. 584, 660

Catt, Carrie Chapman *1859–1947* President of National American Woman Suffrage Association. pp. 535–536

Cavelier, René-Robert (ka•vuhl•YAY) *See* La Salle.

Champlain, Samuel de (sham•PLAYN) *1567?–1635* French explorer who founded the first settlement at Quebec. p. 151

Charles I *1500–1558* King of Spain. p. 145

Charles I *1600–1649* British king who chartered the colonies of Massachusetts and Maryland. pp. 188, 233

Charles II *1630–1685* British king who granted charters for the New Hampshire Colony and the Carolina Colony. Son of Charles I and Henrietta Maria. pp. 197, 234

Chavez, Cesar *1927–1993* Labor leader and organizer of the United Farm Workers. p. 588

Clark, George Rogers *1752–1818* American Revolutionary frontiersman who helped protect western lands and settlers. p. 319

Clark, William *1770–1838* American explorer who aided Meriwether Lewis in an expedition through the Louisiana Purchase. p. 386

Clay, Henry *1777–1852* Representative from Kentucky who worked for compromises on the slavery issue. pp. 390, 438

Clemens, Samuel Langhorne *1835–1910* American writer and steamboat pilot; he wrote under the pen name Mark Twain. p. 30

Clinton, DeWitt *1769–1828* Governor of New York who found European investors to pay for building of Erie Canal. p. 414

Clinton, George *1739–1812* American politician who helped form the Democratic-Republican party. p. 367

Clinton, Hillary Rodham *1947–* Wife of William Clinton; senator of New York. p. 640

Clinton, William *1946–* 42nd U.S. President. pp. 599–600

Collins, Michael *1930–* American astronaut who remained in the lunar orbiter during the *Apollo 11* moon landing. p. 583

Columbus, Christopher *1451–1506* Italian-born Spanish explorer who in 1492 sailed west from Spain and thought he had reached Asia but had actually reached islands near the Americas, lands that were unknown to Europeans. pp. 106, 121

Cooper, Peter *1791–1883* American manufacturer who built *Tom Thumb*, one of the first locomotives made in the United States. p. 415

Cornish, Samuel *1795–1858* African American who in 1827 helped John Russwurm found an abolitionist newspaper called *Freedom's Journal*. p. 448

Cornwallis, Charles *1738–1805* British general who surrendered at the Battle of Yorktown, resulting in victory for the Americans in the Revolutionary War. p. 324

Coronado, Francisco Vásquez de (kawr•oh•NAH•doh) *1510?–1554* Spanish explorer who led an expedition from Mexico City into what is now the southwestern United States in search of the Seven Cities of Gold. p. 131

Cortés, Hernando (kawr•TEZ) *1485–1547* Spanish conquistador who conquered the Aztec Empire. pp. 128, 652

Crazy Horse *1842?–1877* Sioux leader who fought against General George Custer. p. 491

Crockett, Davy *1786–1836* American pioneer who was killed at the Alamo. pp. 395, 403

Custer, George *1839–1876* U.S. Army general who led an attack against Sioux and Cheyenne Indians. Custer and all of his men were killed in the battle. p. 491

D

da Gama, Vasco (dah GA•muh) *1460?–1524* Portuguese navigator who sailed from Europe, around the southern tip of Africa, and on to Asia between 1497 and 1499. p. 118

Davis, Jefferson *1808–1889* United States senator from Mississippi who became president of the Confederacy. p. 453

Dawes, William *1745–1799* American who, along with Paul Revere, warned the Patriots that the British were marching toward Concord. p. 291

Deere, John *1804–1886* American industrialist who created steel plows for use on the Great Plains. p. 419

Deganawida (deh•gahn•uh•WIH•duh) *1500s* Legendary Iroquois holy man who called for an end to the fighting among the Iroquois, a view that led to the formation of the Iroquois League. p. 90

de Narváez, Pánfilo *1500s* Spanish explorer who hoped to conquer lands along the Gulf of Mexico but failed. p. 130

de Soto, Hernando (day SOH•toh) *1496?–1542* Spanish explorer who led an expedition into what is today the southeastern United States. p. 132

Dewey, George *1837–1917* American naval commander who destroyed the Spanish fleet and captured Manila Bay in the Spanish-American War. p. 527

Dias, Bartolomeu (DEE•ahsh) *1450?–1500* Portuguese navigator who in 1488 became the first European to sail around the southern tip of Africa. p. 118

Díaz, Porfirio *1830–1915* Mexican dictator. p. 654

Dickinson, John *1732–1808* Member of the Continental Congress who wrote most of the Articles of Confederation, adopted in 1781. pp. 283, 293, 306

Dinwiddie, Robert *1693–1770* British Lieutenant Governor of Virginia; sent George Washington to defend Ohio Valley from seizure by the French. p. 269

Douglas, Stephen A. *1813–1861* American legislator who wrote the Kansas-Nebraska Act and debated Abraham Lincoln in a race for a Senate seat from Illinois. p. 452

Douglass, Frederick *1817–1895* Abolitionist speaker and writer who had escaped from slavery. p. 449

Drake, Edwin *1819–1880* American pioneer in oil industry; became first to tap petroleum at its source. p. 497

Drake, Francis *1543–1596* English explorer who sailed around the world. p. 157

Drew, Charles *1904–1950* American physician who developed an efficient way to store blood plasma in blood banks. p. 562

Du Bois, W. E. B. (doo•BOYS) *1868–1963* African American teacher, writer, and leader who helped form the National Association for the Advancement of Colored People (NAACP). p. 535

E

Edison, Thomas *1847–1931* American who invented the phonograph and the electric lightbulb; he also built the first power station to supply electricity to New York City. pp. 498–499, 500–501

Eisenhower, Dwight D. *1890–1969* 34th U.S. President and, earlier, American general who led the D day invasion. pp. 565–566, 582

Elizabeth I *1533–1603* Queen of England from 1558 to 1603. p. 156

Ellington, Edward Kennedy (Duke) *1899–1974* Band leader who became well-known playing jazz during the 1920s. p. 543

Emerson, Ralph Waldo *1803–1882* American poet who wrote "Concord Hymn." pp. 267, 292

Endecott, John *1588–1665* Member of New England Company who sailed to New England in 1628 and settled at Salem. p. 188

Equiano, Olaudah (ek•wee•AHN•oh, OHL•uh•dah) *1750?–1797* African who was kidnapped from his village and sold into slavery. He later wrote a book describing his experiences. p. 244

Esteban (ehs•TAY•bahn) *1500–1539* African explorer who went with Cabeza de Vaca to Mexico City and told stories of the Seven Cities of Gold. Esteban was killed on a later expedition, the purpose of which was to find out whether the stories were true. p. 131

F

Farragut, Jorge (FAIR•uh•guht, HAWR•hay) *1755–1817* Spanish-born man who fought in the Continental Army and the navy. p. 318

Ferdinand II *1452–1516* King of Spain who—with Queen Isabella, his wife—sent Christopher Columbus on his voyage to find a western route to Asia. p. 121

Ferraro, Geraldine *1935–* First woman to be nominated as a major party's candidate for Vice President of the United States. p. 589

Finley, John Fur trader who helped Daniel Boone find the way across the Appalachian Mountains to Kentucky. p. 277

Fong, Hiram L. *1906–* Chinese immigrant who settled in Hawaii; became first Chinese American senator. p. 505

Ford, Gerald *1913–* 38th U.S. President. The Vietnam War ended during his term. p. 593

Ford, Henry *1863–1947* American automobile manufacturer who mass-produced cars at low cost by using assembly lines. p. 544

Fox, Vicente *1942–* Elected president of Mexico in 2000. p. 655

Frame, Richard *1600s* Colonist and writer. p. 209

Franco, Francisco *1892–1975* Spanish dictator. p. 555

Franklin, Benjamin *1706–1790* American leader who was sent to Britain to ask Parliament for representation. He was a writer of the Declaration of Independence, a delegate to the Constitutional Convention, and a respected scientist and business leader. pp. 221, 271, 283, 303, 318, 352, 366

Frontenac, Louis de Buade, Count de (FRAHN•tuh•nak) *1622–1698* French leader who was appointed governor-general of New France. p. 152

Fulton, Robert *1765–1815* American engineer and inventor who created the first commercial steamboat. p. 415

G

Gadsden, James *1788–1858* U.S. minister to Mexico who arranged to buy parts of present-day New Mexico and Arizona from Mexico—known as the Gadsden Purchase. p. 407

Gage, Thomas *1721–1787* Head of the British army in North America and colonial governor. pp. 291, 294

Gálvez, Bernardo de (GAHL•ves) *1746–1786* Spanish governor of Louisiana who sent supplies to the Patriots in the Revolutionary War and led his own soldiers in taking a British fort in Florida. p. 318

Garrison, William Lloyd *1805–1879* American abolitionist who started a newspaper called *The Liberator*. p. 448

Gates, Horatio *1728–1806* American general who defeated the British in 1777 at Saratoga, New York. p. 316

George II *1683–1760* British king who chartered the Georgia Colony. p. 236

George III *1738–1820* King of England during the Revolutionary War. pp. 276, 296

Gerry, Elbridge *1744–1814* Massachusetts delegate to the Constitutional Convention. p. 366

Gibbs, Jonathan C. *1800s* African American who became secretary of state in Florida; helped set up public school system. p. 479

Glenn, John H., Jr. *1921–* American astronaut who was the first person to orbit the Earth. Former U.S. senator. p. 583

Gorbachev, Mikhail (gawr•buh•CHAWF, mee•kuh•EEL) *1931–* Leader of the Soviet Union from 1985 to 1991. He improved relations with the United States and expanded freedom in the Soviet Union. pp. 597-598

Gordon, William E. *1918–* American scientist who established the Arecibo Observatory in Puerto Rico. p. 660

Gore, Albert *1948–* Vice President under President Bill Clinton. Defeated by George W. Bush in the 2000 election—the closest election in history. pp. 600, 641

Granger, Gordon Union general who read the order declaring all slaves in Texas to be free. p. 482

Grant, Ulysses S. *1822–1885* 18th U.S. President and, earlier, commander of the Union army in the Civil War. pp. 465, 468, 469, 471, 475

Greeley, Horace *1811–1872* American journalist and political leader; publisher of a newspaper called the *New York Tribune*. p. 461

Greene, Nathanael *1742–1786* Commander of the Continental Army in the Southern Colonies; forced British out of Georgia and the Carolinas. p. 322

Grenville, George *1712–1770* British prime minister who passed the Stamp Act in 1765. p. 280

Gutenberg, Johannes *1390–1468* German inventor; invented movable type. p. 109

H

Hale, Nathan *1755–1776* American Revolutionary hero who was hanged by the British for spying for the Patriots. p. 319

Hamilton, Alexander *1755–1804* American leader in calling for the Constitutional Convention and winning support for it. He favored a strong national government. pp. 368, 375, 377

Hammond, James Henry *1807–1864* Senator from South Carolina. p. 442

Hancock, John *1737–1793* Leader of the Sons of Liberty in the Massachusetts Colony. pp. 306, 353, 369

Harrison, William Henry *1773–1841* 9th U.S. President. Earlier he directed U.S. forces against the Indians at the Battle of Tippecanoe and was a commander in the War of 1812. p. 390

He, Zheng *1400s* Chinese admiral who made seven voyages between 1405 and 1433. p. 109

Henrietta Maria *1609–1669* Queen of Charles I of England. The Maryland Colony was named in her honor. p. 233

Henry *1394–1460* Henry the Navigator, prince of Portugal, who set up the first European school for training sailors in navigation. p. 115

Henry IV *1553–1610* King of France. p. 150

Henry, Patrick *1736–1799* American colonist who spoke out in the Virginia legislature against paying British taxes. His views became widely known, and Loyalists accused him of treason. pp. 282, 290, 350, 353, 367, 378

Hiawatha (hy•uh•WAH•thuh) *1500s* Onondaga chief who persuaded other Iroquois tribes to form the Iroquois League. p. 90

Hidalgo, Miguel *1753–1811* Mexican priest who called for a revolution against Spain in 1810. p. 653

Hirohito *1901–1989* Emperor of Japan from 1926 until his death. p. 555

Hitler, Adolf *1889–1945* Nazi dictator of Germany. His actions led to World War II and the killing of millions of people. p. 555

Hooker, Thomas *1586?–1647* Minister who helped form the Connecticut Colony. His democratic ideas were adopted in the Fundamental Orders. p. 196

Hoover, Herbert *1874–1964* 31st U.S. President. When the depression began, he thought that the economy was healthy and conditions would improve. p. 548

Houston, Sam *1793–1863* President of the Republic of Texas and, later, governor of the state of Texas. pp. 403, 453

Howard, Martin *1700s* Rhode Island colonist who defended Britain's right to tax the colonists. p. 280

Hudson, Henry *?–1611* Explorer who sailed up the Hudson River, giving the Dutch a claim to the area. p. 138

Huerta, Dolores *1900s* Labor leader and organizer, along with Cesar Chavez, of the United Farm Workers. p. 588

Hughes, Langston *1902–1967* African American poet and one of the best-known Harlem writers. p. 543

Hurston, Zora Neale *1903–1960* African American novelist and one of the best-known Harlem writers. p. 543

Hussein, Saddam *1937–* Leader of Iraq. p. 598

Hutchinson, Anne Marbury *1591–1643* English-born woman who left Massachusetts because of her religious beliefs. She settled near Providence, which joined with other settlements to form the Rhode Island Colony. p. 195

Iberville, Pierre Le Moyne, Sieur d' (ee•ber•VEEL) *1661–1706* French explorer who—with his brother, Jean-Baptiste Le Moyne, Sieur de Bienville—started an early settlement at the mouth of the Mississippi River. p. 154

Ibn Majid, Ahmad *1432–1500* Great contributor to study of navigation; born in what is today United Arab Emirates. p. 118

Isabella I *1451–1504* Queen of Spain who—with King Ferdinand, her husband—sent Columbus on his voyage to find a western route to Asia. p. 121

Jackson, Andrew *1767–1845* 7th U.S. President and, earlier, commander who won the final battle in the War of 1812. As President he favored a strong Union and ordered the removal of Native Americans from their lands. pp. 393, 396, 437

Jackson, Thomas (Stonewall) *1824–1863* Confederate general. pp. 458, 466

James I *1566–1625* King of England in the early 1600s. The James River and Jamestown were named after him. pp. 160, 164

Jay, John *1745–1829* American leader who wrote letters to newspapers, defending the Constitution. He became the first chief justice of the Supreme Court. pp. 368, 375

Jefferson, Thomas *1743–1826* 3rd U.S. President and the main writer of the Declaration of Independence. pp. 303, 353, 368, 371, 375, 376, 377, 384

Jenney, William *1832–1907* American engineer who developed the use of steel frames to build tall buildings. p. 496

John I *1357–1433* King of Portugal during a time of great exploration. Father of Prince Henry, who set up a school of navigation. p. 115

Johnson, Andrew *1808–1875* 17th U.S. President. Differences with Congress about Reconstruction led to his being impeached, though he was found not guilty. pp. 477, 479

Johnson, Lyndon B. *1908–1973* 36th U.S. President. He started Great Society programs and expanded U.S. involvement in the Vietnam War. pp. 584, 588, 590, 591

Joliet, Louis (zhohl•YAY, loo•EE) *1645–1700* French fur trader who explored lakes and rivers for France, with Jacques Marquette and five others. p. 152

Jones, John Paul *1747–1792* American naval officer who defeated bigger and better-equipped British ships during Revolutionary War. p. 319

Joseph *1840?–1904* Nez Perce chief who tried to lead his people to Canada after they were told to move onto a reservation. p. 491

Josephy, Alvin M., Jr. *1915–* Historian and author of books about Native Americans and the United States westward movement. p. 55

Juárez, Benito *1806–1872* Served twice as president of Mexico; made many reforms. p. 654

K

Kalakaua (kah•lah•KAH•ooh•ah) *1836–1891* Hawaiian king who tried but failed to keep Americans from taking over the Hawaiian Islands. p. 525

Kennedy, John F. *1917–1963* 35th U.S. President. He helped pass the Civil Rights Act of 1964. pp. 583–584

Key, Francis Scott *1779–1843* American lawyer and poet who wrote the words to "The Star-Spangled Banner." p. 392

King, Martin Luther, Jr. *1929–1968* African American civil rights leader who worked for integration in nonviolent ways. King won the Nobel Peace Prize in 1964. pp. 586, 587

Knox, Henry *1750–1806* Secretary of war in the first government under the Constitution. pp. 375, 377

Kosciuszko, Thaddeus (kawsh•CHUSH•koh) *1746–1817* Polish officer who helped the Patriots in the Revolutionary War. He later returned to Poland and led a revolution there. p. 317

Kublai Khan (KOO•bluh KAHN) *1215–1294* Ruler of China who was visited by Marco Polo. p. 109

L

La Follette, Robert *1855–1925* Wisconsin governor who began many reforms in his state, including a merit system for government jobs. p. 533

La Salle, René-Robert Cavelier, Sieur de (luh•SAL) *1643–1687* French explorer who found the mouth of the Mississippi River and claimed the whole Mississippi Valley for France. p. 153

Lafayette, Marquis de (lah•fee•ET) *1757–1834* French noble who fought alongside the Americans in the Revolutionary War. p. 317

Las Casas, Bartolomé de (lahs KAH•sahs, bar•toh•loh•MAY day) *1474–1566* Spanish missionary who spent much of his life trying to help Native Americans. p. 145

Law, John *1671–1729* Scottish banker who was appointed proprietor of the Louisiana region in 1717. p. 155

Lawrence, Jacob *1900s* African American artist; his parents took part in the Great Migration. p. 507

Le Moyne, Jean-Baptiste *See* Bienville.

Le Moyne, Pierre *See* Iberville.

Lee, Richard Henry *1732–1794* American Revolutionary leader who said to the Continental Congress that the colonies should become independent from Britain. p. 303

Lee, Robert E. *1807–1870* United States army colonel who gave up his post to become commander of the Confederate army in the Civil War. pp. 461, 466, 471

L'Enfant, Pierre Charles *1754–1825* French-born American engineer who planned the buildings and streets of the new capital of the United States. p. 377

Lewis, Meriwether *1774–1809* American explorer chosen by Thomas Jefferson to be a pathfinder in the territory of the Louisiana Purchase. p. 386

Liliuokalani, Lydia (lih•lee•uh•woh•kuh•LAH•nee) *1838–1917* Hawaiian queen who tried but failed to bring back the Hawaiian monarchy's authority. p. 525

Lincoln, Abraham *1809–1865* 16th U.S. President, leader of the Union in the Civil War, and signer of the Emancipation Proclamation. pp. 100, 450-455, 461, 462, 468, 476-477

Lincoln, Mary Todd *1818–1882* Wife of Abraham Lincoln. p. 477

Lindbergh, Charles *1902–1974* Airplane pilot who was the first to fly solo between the United States and Europe. p. 545

Livingston, Robert R. *1746–1813* One of the writers of the Declaration of Independence. p. 303

Longstreet, James *1821–1904* Former Confederate general who wanted the South to build more factories; considered a scalawag. p. 484

Louis XIV *1638–1715* King of France. pp. 152, 153

Lowell, Francis Cabot *1775–1817* Textile pioneer who set up an American mill in which several processes were completed under one roof. p. 416

M

MacArthur, Douglas *1880–1964* Commanded Allied forces in the Pacific during World War II. p. 567

Madison, Dolley *1768–1849* James Madison's wife and First Lady during the War of 1812. p. 392

Madison, James *1751–1836* 4th U.S. President. He was a leader in calling for the Constitutional Convention, writing the Constitution, and winning support for it. pp. 350, 352, 360, 368, 371, 378, 390

Magellan, Ferdinand (muh•JEH•luhn) *1480?–1521* Portuguese explorer who in 1519 led a fleet of ships from Spain westward to Asia. He died on the voyage, but one of the ships made it back to Spain, completing the first trip around the world. p. 124

Maguire, Matthew *1800s* Machine worker who, along with Peter McGuire, came up with the idea for Labor Day. p. 533

Mahan, Alfred T. *1840–1914* American naval officer and historian. p. 523

Malcolm X *1925–1965* African American leader who disagreed with the views of Martin Luther King, Jr., on nonviolence and integration. p. 587

Malintzin (mah•LINT•suhn) *1501?–1550* Aztec princess who interpreted for Hernando Cortés and helped him in other ways to conquer Mexico. p. 128

Mao Zedong (MOW zeh•DOONG) *1893–1976* Leader of China from 1949 until his death. President Nixon's 1972 visit with him in China led to trade and cultural exchange with the United States. p. 592

Marion, Francis *1732?–1795* Known as the Swamp Fox, he led Continental soldiers through the swamps of South Carolina on daring raids against the British. p. 319

Marquette, Jacques (mar•KET, ZHAHK) *1637–1675* Catholic missionary who knew several American Indian languages. With Louis Joliet, he explored lakes and rivers for France. p. 152

Marshall, George C. *1880–1959* U.S. Secretary of State who developed the European Recovery Program, also known as the Marshall Plan, after World War II. p. 575

Marshall, James *1810–1885* Carpenter who found gold at John Sutter's sawmill near Sacramento, California, leading to the California gold rush of 1849. p. 408

Marshall, John *1755–1835* Chief Justice of the Supreme Court in 1832; Marshall ruled that the United States should protect the Cherokees and their lands in Georgia. p. 398

Marshall, Thurgood *1908–1993* NAACP lawyer who argued the school segregation case that the Supreme Court ruled on in 1954 and, later, was the first African American to serve on the Supreme Court. p. 585

Mason, George *1725–1792* Virginia delegate to the Constitutional Convention who argued for an end to the slave trade. pp. 366, 370

Massasoit (ma•suh•SOYT) *?–1661* Chief of the Wampanoags, who lived in peace with the Pilgrims. p. 169

Mather, Cotton *1663–1728* Member of well-known family of American Congregational clergymen; published over 400 works on religious, historical, scientific, and moral subjects. p. 187

McCauley, Mary Ludwig Hays *1754?–1832* Known as Molly Pitcher, she carried water to American soldiers during the Battle of Monmouth; when her husband fell during the battle, she began firing his cannon. p. 319

McCormick, Cyrus *1809–1884* Inventor of a reaping machine for harvesting wheat. p. 419

McGuire, Peter *1800s* Carpenter who, along with Matthew Maguire, came up with the idea for Labor Day. p. 533

McKinley, William *1843–1901* 25th U.S. President. The Spanish-American War was fought during his term. pp. 526, 528

Menéndez de Avilés, Pedro (may•NAYN•days day ah•vee•LAYS) *1519–1574* Spanish leader of settlers in St. Augustine, Florida, the first permanent European settlement in what is now the United States. p. 146

Metacomet *1639?–1676* Called King Philip by the English. Son of Massasoit; leader of Wampanoags; made war upon New England settlers—called King Philip's War. p. 198

Minuit, Peter *1580–1638* A director of the New Netherland Colony who purchased Manhattan Island from the Manhattan Indians for $24. p. 211

Mongoulacha (mahn•goo•LAY•chah) *1700s* Indian leader who helped Bienville and Iberville. p. 154

Monroe, James *1758–1831* 5th U.S. President. He established the Monroe Doctrine, which said that the United States would stop any European nation from expanding its American empire. p. 394

Morgan, Daniel *1736–1802* American general who defeated the British at Cowpens in the Revolutionary War. p. 322

Morris, Gouverneur (guh•ver•NIR) *1752–1816* American leader who was in charge of the final wording of the United States Constitution. pp. 358-359

Motecuhzoma (maw•tay•kwah•SOH•mah) *1466–1520* Emperor of the Aztecs when they were conquered by the Spanish. He is also known as Montezuma. p. 129

Muhlenberg, John Peter *1746–1807* Young minister, son of the colonies' Lutheran leader, who became a Patriot militia officer. p. 309

Mussolini, Benito (moo•suh•LEE•nee, buh•NEE•toh) *1883–1945* Ruler of Italy from 1922 until 1943, most of that time as dictator. p. 555

N

Nast, Thomas *1840–1902* American cartoonist who created the "Uncle Sam" character. p. 640

Newcomen, Thomas *1663–1729* English blacksmith and inventor who invented the steam engine. p. 414

Nimitz, Chester W. *1885–1966* Commander of U.S. Pacific fleet during World War II. p. 567

Nixon, Richard M. *1913–1994* 37th U.S. President. He tried to end the Vietnam War, he reduced tensions with communist nations, and he resigned the presidency because of the Watergate scandal. pp. 591–593

Niza, Marcos de (day NEE•sah) *1495–1558* Spanish priest who was sent with Esteban to confirm stories of the Seven Cities of Gold. When he returned to Mexico City, he said he had seen a golden city. p. 131

O

O'Connor, Sandra Day *1930–* First woman to be appointed to the United States Supreme Court. pp. 589, 640

Oglethorpe, James *1696–1785* English settler who was given a charter to settle Georgia. He wanted to bring in debtors from England to help settle it. p. 236

O'Keeffe, Georgia *1887–1986* American painter who developed her own style showing abstract studies of color and light. p. 543

Osceola *1804–1838* Leader of the Seminoles in Florida. p. 398

Otis, James *1725–1783* Massachusetts colonist who spoke out against British taxes and called for "no taxation without representation." pp. 280, 282, 283

P

Paine, Thomas *1737–1809* Author of a widely read pamphlet called *Common Sense*, in which he attacked King George III and called for a revolution to make the colonies independent. pp. 301, 302

Parks, Rosa *1913–* African American woman whose refusal to give up her seat on a Montgomery, Alabama, bus started a year-long bus boycott. p. 586

Paterson, William *1745–1806* Constitutional delegate from New Jersey who submitted the New Jersey Plan, under which each state would have one vote, regardless of population. p. 355

Penn, William *1644–1718* Proprietor of Pennsylvania under a charter from King Charles II of Britain. Penn was a Quaker who made Pennsylvania a refuge for settlers who wanted religious freedom. p. 213

Perry, Oliver Hazard *1785–1819* American naval commander who won an important battle in the War of 1812. p. 390

Philip IV *1605–1665* King of Spain from 1621 to 1665. p. 143

Pickett, George *1825–1875* Confederate general who led the charge against Gettysburg; forced to retreat. p. 466

Pike, Zebulon *1779–1813* American who led an expedition down the Arkansas River to explore the southwestern part of the Louisiana Purchase. pp. 19, 388

Pinckney, Eliza Lucas *1722?–1793* South Carolina settler who experimented with indigo plants. She gave away seeds, and indigo then became an important cash crop in the colonies. p. 236

Pitt, William *1708–1778* British leader of Parliament who helped Britain win battles against the French. p. 273

Pizarro, Francisco (pee•ZAR•oh) *1475?–1541* Spanish conquistador who conquered the Inca Empire. p. 133

Plunkitt, George *1800–1900s* Political boss in New York City. p. 534

Pocahontas (poh•kuh•HAHN•tuhs) *1595–1617* Indian chief Powhatan's daughter. p. 162

Polk, James K. *1795–1849* 11th U.S. President. He gained land for the United States by setting a northern boundary in 1846 and winning a war with Mexico in 1848. pp. 405, 407

Polo, Maffeo Trader from Venice; uncle of Marco Polo. p. 109

Polo, Marco *1254–1324* Explorer from Venice who spent many years in Asia in the late 1200s. He wrote a book about his travels that gave Europeans information about Asia. pp. 109, 112

Polo, Nicolò Trader from Venice; father of Marco Polo. p. 109

Ponce de León, Juan (POHN•say day lay•OHN) *1460–1521* Spanish explorer who landed on the North American mainland in 1513, near what is now St. Augustine, Florida. p. 127

Pontiac *c.1720–1769* Ottawa Indian chief who led a rebellion against the British to stop the loss of Indian hunting lands. p. 275

Powell, Colin L. *1937–* Chairman of the Joint Chiefs of Staff during the Gulf War; became U.S. secretary of state in 2001. p. 599

Powhatan (pow•uh•TAN) *1550?–1618* Chief of a federation of Indian tribes that lived in the Virginia territory. Pocahontas was his daughter. p. 162

Prescott, Samuel *1751–1777?* American who, along with Paul Revere, warned the Patriots that the British were marching toward Concord. p. 291

Ptolemy, Claudius (TAH•luh•mee) *100s* Astronomer in ancient Egypt. p. 123

Pulaski, Casimir (puh•LAS•kee) *1747–1779* Polish noble who came to the British colonies to help the Patriots in the Revolutionary War. p. 317

Putnam, Israel *1718–1790* American Revolutionary commander who fought at the Battle of Bunker Hill. p. 295

R

Raleigh, Sir Walter (RAH•lee) *1554–1618* English explorer who used his own money to set up England's first colony in North America, on Roanoke Island near North Carolina. p. 158

Randolph, Edmund *1753–1813* Virginia delegate to the Constitutional Convention who wrote the Virginia Plan, which stated that the number of representatives a state would have in Congress should be based on the population of the state. pp. 355, 366, 375

Read, George *1733–1798* Delaware delegate to the Constitutional Convention who thought the states should be done away with in favor of a strong national government. p. 354

Reagan, Ronald *1911–* 40th U.S. President. His meetings with Soviet leader Mikhail Gorbachev led to a thaw in the Cold War, including advances in arms control. pp. 579, 597–598

Reed, Esther *1700s* American who, in 1780, started the Philadelphia Association to help the Continental Army. p. 311

Revels, Hiram R. *1822–1901* First African American elected to U.S. Senate. p. 479

Revere, Paul *1735–1818* American who warned the Patriots that the British were marching toward Concord, where Patriot weapons were stored. pp. 285, 291

Rockefeller, John D. *1839–1937* American oil entrepreneur who joined many refineries into one business, called the Standard Oil Company. pp. 497–498

Roebling, John *1806–1869* Engineer and industrialist who designed suspension bridges. p. 496

Rolfe, John *1585–1622* English colonist of the Jamestown colony whose discovery of a method of drying tobacco led to great profits. p. 163

Roosevelt, Franklin Delano *1882–1945* 32nd U.S. President. He began New Deal programs to help the nation out of the depression, and he was the nation's leader during World War II. pp. 548–549, 553, 556, 558, 568

Roosevelt, Theodore *1858–1919* 26th U.S. President. He showed the world America's strength, made it possible to build the Panama Canal, and worked for progressive reforms and conservation. pp. 527–528, 532–533

Root, George Frederick *1820–1895* American composer and teacher. p. 435

Ross, Edmund G. *1826–1907* Senator from Kansas who voted to acquit President Johnson. p. 479

Ross, John *1790–1866* Chief of the Cherokee nation. He fought in United States courts to prevent the loss of the Cherokees' lands in Georgia. Though he won the legal battle, he still had to lead his people along the Trail of Tears to what is now Oklahoma. p. 398

Russwurm, John *1799–1851* Helped Samuel Cornish found an abolitionist newspaper called *Freedom's Journal* in 1827. p. 448

S

Sacagawea (sa•kuh•juh•WEE•uh) *1786?–1812?* Shoshone woman who acted as an interpreter for the Lewis and Clark expedition. p. 386

Sagan, Carl *1934–1996* American astronomer who worked to find life on other planets and helped NASA plan missions to explore the solar system. p. 583

Salem, Peter *1750?–1816* African who fought with the Minutemen at Concord and at the Battle of Bunker Hill. p. 310

Salomon, Haym *1740–1785* Polish banker who spied for the Patriots and helped fund the Revolution. p. 317

Samoset *1590?–1653?* Native American chief who spoke English and who helped the settlers at Plymouth. p. 169

San Martín, José de (sahn mar•TEEN) *1778–1850* Leader of an independence movement in Argentina. p. 666

Santa Anna, Antonio López de *1794–1876* Dictator of Mexico; defeated Texans at the Alamo. p. 402

Scott, Dred *1795?–1858* Enslaved African who took his case for freedom to the Supreme Court and lost. p. 440

Scott, Winfield *1786–1866* American general in the war with Mexico. p. 407

Serra, Junípero *1713–1784* Spanish missionary who helped build a string of missions in California. pp. 148, 174

Seward, William H. *1801–1872* Secretary of state in the cabinet of Abraham Lincoln. p. 443

Shays, Daniel *1747?–1825* Leader of Shays's Rebellion, which showed the weakness of the government under the Articles of Confederation. pp. 347, 352

Sherman, Roger *1721–1793* One of the writers of the Declaration of Independence. Connecticut delegate to the Constitutional Convention who worked out the compromise in which Congress would have two houses—one based on state population and one with two members from each state. pp. 303, 356

Sherman, William Tecumseh *1820–1891* Union general who, after defeating Confederate forces in Atlanta, led the March to the Sea, on which his troops caused great destruction. p. 468

Sitting Bull *1831–1890* Sioux leader who fought against General George Custer. p. 491

Slater, Samuel *1768–1835* Textile pioneer who helped bring the Industrial Revolution to the United States by providing plans for a new spinning machine. p. 416

Slocomb, Mary *1700s* North Carolina colonist who fought in the Revolutionary War. p. 319

BIOGRAPHICAL DICTIONARY

Smalls, Robert *1839–1915* African American who delivered a Confederate steamer to the Union forces. p. 463

Smith, John *1580–1631* English explorer who, as leader of the Jamestown settlement, saved its people from starvation. pp. 161, 231

Smith, Joseph *1805–1844* Mormon leader who settled his people in Illinois and was killed there. p. 406

Soule, John B. L. *1815–1891* Editor of the Terre Haute (Indiana) *Express* in the mid-1800s. p. 383

Spalding, Eliza *1807–1851* American missionary and pioneer in the Oregon Country. p. 404

Spalding, Henry *1801–1874* American missionary and pioneer in the Oregon Country. p. 404

Squanto *See* Tisquantum.

Stalin, Joseph *1879–1953* Dictator of the Soviet Union from 1924 until his death. p. 555

Standish, Miles *1584?–1656* Captain who sailed with Pilgrims to America aboard the *Mayflower*. p. 167

Stanton, Elizabeth Cady *1815–1902* American reformer who organized the first convention for women's rights. p. 447

Starr, Ellen Gates *1860–1940* Reformer who, with Jane Addams, founded Hull House in Chicago. p. 534

Steuben, Friedrich, Baron von (vahn SHTOY•buhn) *1730–1794* German soldier who helped train Patriot troops in the Revolutionary War. p. 317

Stowe, Harriet Beecher *1811–1896* American abolitionist who in 1852 wrote the book *Uncle Tom's Cabin*. p. 448

Stuyvesant, Peter (STY•vuh•suhnt) *1610?–1672* Last governor of the Dutch colony of New Netherland. p. 212

Sutter, John *1803–1880* American pioneer who owned the sawmill where gold was discovered, leading to the California gold rush. p. 408

T

Taney, Roger B. (TAH•nee) *1777–1864* Supreme Court chief justice who wrote the ruling against Dred Scott. p. 441

Tapahonso, Luci *1953–* Navajo poet and author. p. 72

Tecumseh (tuh•KUHM•suh) *1768–1813* Shawnee leader of Indians in the Northwest Territory. He wanted to stop Americans from settling on Indian lands. p. 390

Thayendanegea (thay•en•da•NEG•ah) *1742–1807* Known as Joseph Brant; Mohawk leader who befriended a British general, became a Christian, and worked as a missionary. p. 312

Tisquantum *1585?–1622* Native American who spoke English and who helped the Plymouth Colony. p. 169

Tompkins, Sally *1833–1916* Civil War nurse who eventually ran her own private hospital in Richmond, Virginia. She was a captain in the Confederate army, the only woman to achieve such an honor. p. 463

Tonti, Henri de (TOHN•tee, ahn•REE duh) *1650–1704* French explorer with La Salle. p. 154

Travis, William B. *1809–1836* Commander of the Texas force at the Alamo, where he was killed. p. 403

Truman, Harry S. *1884–1972* 33rd U.S. President. He ordered the atom bomb to be dropped on Japan to end World War II; he later sent American soldiers to support South Korea in 1950. pp. 568, 575, 582

Truth, Sojourner *1797?–1883* Abolitionist and former slave who became a leading preacher against slavery. p. 449

Tubman, Harriet *1820–1913* Abolitionist and former slave who became a conductor on the Underground Railroad. She led about 300 slaves to freedom. p. 447

Turner, Nat *1800–1831* Enslaved African who led a rebellion against slavery. p. 445

Tuscalusa (tuhs•kuh•LOO•suh) *1500s* Leader of the Mobile people when they battled with Spanish troops led by Hernando de Soto. p. 132

V

Verrazano, Giovanni da (ver•uh•ZAH•noh) *1485?–1528?* Italian navigator who discovered New York Bay while searching for a water route linking the Atlantic and Pacific Oceans. p. 136

Vespucci, Amerigo (veh•SPOO•chee, uh•MAIR•ih•goh) *1454–1512* Italian explorer who made several voyages from Europe to what many people thought was Asia. He determined that he had landed on another continent, which was later called America in his honor. p. 123

W

Wald, Lillian *1867–1940* Reformer who started the Henry Street Settlement in New York City. p. 535

Waldseemüller, Martin (VAHLT•zay•mool•er) *1470–1518?* German cartographer who published a map in 1507 that first showed a continent named America. p. 123

Warren, Earl *1891–1974* Chief justice of the Supreme Court who wrote the 1954 decision against school segregation. p. 586

Warren, Mercy Otis *1728–1814* Massachusetts colonist who wrote poems and plays supporting the Patriot cause. p. 311

Washington, Booker T. *1856–1915* African American who founded Tuskegee Institute in Alabama. p. 535

Washington, George *1732–1799* 1st U.S. President, leader of the Continental army during the Revolutionary War, and president of the Constitutional Convention. pp. 269, 293, 314, 327, 352, 374

Westinghouse, George *1846–1914* American inventor who designed an air brake for stopping trains. p. 495

Wheatley, Phillis *1753?–1784* American poet who wrote poems that praised the Revolution. p. 296

White, John *?–1593?* English painter and cartographer who led the second group that settled on Roanoke Island. p. 158

Whitman, Marcus *1802–1847* American missionary and pioneer in the Oregon Country. p. 404

Whitman, Narcissa *1808–1847* American missionary and pioneer in the Oregon Country. p. 404

Whitney, Eli *1765–1825* American inventor who was most famous for his invention of the cotton gin and his idea of interchangeable parts, which made mass production possible. p. 418

Williams, Roger *1603?–1683* Founder of Providence in what is now Rhode Island. He had been forced to leave Massachusetts because of his views. p. 194

Wilson, Samuel *1766–1854* American meat packer who inspired the "Uncle Sam" national symbol. p. 640

Wilson, Woodrow *1856–1924* 28th U.S. President. He brought the country into World War I after trying to stay neutral. He favored the League of Nations, but the Senate rejected U.S. membership in the league. pp. 538, 541

Winthrop, John *1588–1649* Puritan leader who served several times as governor of the Massachusetts Bay Colony. Helped form confederation among people of New England and served as its first president. p. 189

Woods, Granville T. *1856–1910* African American who improved the air brake and developed a telegraph system for trains. p. 495

Wright, Frank Lloyd *1867–1959* American architect known for producing unusual buildings. p. 543

Wright, Orville *1871–1948* Pioneer in American aviation who—with his brother, Wilbur—made and flew the first successful airplane, at Kitty Hawk, North Carolina. p. 545

Wright, Wilbur *1867–1912* Pioneer in American aviation who—with his brother, Orville—made and flew the first successful airplane, at Kitty Hawk, North Carolina. p. 545

York *1800s* Enslaved African whose hunting and fishing skills contributed to the Lewis and Clark expedition. p. 386

Young, Brigham *1801–1877* Mormon leader who came after Joseph Smith. He moved his people west to the Great Salt Lake valley. p. 406

Yzquierdo, Pedro *1400s* Member of Columbus's first expedition to America. p. 105

Gazetteer

The Gazetteer is a geographical dictionary that will help you locate places discussed in this book. The page number tells where each place appears on a map.

A

Abilene A city in central Kansas on the Smoky Hill River; a major railroad town. (39°N, 97°W) p. 488

Adena (uh•DEE•nuh) An ancient settlement of the Mound Builders; located in southern Ohio. (40°N, 81°W) p. 65

Adirondack Mountains (a•duh•RAHN•dak) A mountain range in northeastern New York. p. 89

Africa Second-largest continent on Earth. p. 27

Alamo A mission in San Antonio, Texas; located in the southeastern part of the state; used as a fort during the Texas Revolution. (29°N, 98°W) p. 404

Alaska Range A mountain range in central Alaska. p. 20

Albany The capital of New York; located in the eastern part of the state, on the Hudson River. (43°N, 74°W) p. 212

Alberta One of Canada's ten provinces; located in western Canada. p. 670

Aleutian Islands (uh•LOO•shuhn) A chain of volcanic islands; located between the North Pacific Ocean and the Bering Sea, extending west from the Alaska Peninsula. pp. 20, 526

Alexandria Seaport on the northern coast of Egypt. (31°N, 29°E) p. 108

Allegheny River (a•luh•GAY•nee) A river in the northeastern United States; flows southwest to join the Monongahela River in Pennsylvania, forming the Ohio River. p. 341

Altamaha River (AWL•tuh•muh•haw) A river that begins in southeastern Georgia and flows into the Atlantic Ocean. p. 234

Amazon River The longest river in South America, flowing from the Andes Mountains across Brazil and into the Atlantic Ocean. p. 665

American Samoa (suh•MOH•uh) A United States territory in the Pacific Ocean. p. 526

Andes Mountains (AN•deez) The longest chain of mountains in the world; located along the entire western coast of South America. p. 665

Annapolis (uh•NA•puh•luhs) The capital of Maryland; located on Chesapeake Bay; home of the United States Naval Academy. (39°N, 76°W) p. 234

Antarctica One of Earth's seven continents. p. 27

Antietam (an•TEE•tuhm) A creek near Sharpsburg in north central Maryland; site of a Civil War battle in 1862. (39°N, 78°W) p. 470

Antigua An island in the eastern part of the Leeward Islands, in the eastern West Indies. p. 658

Appalachian Mountains (a•puh•LAY•chuhn) A mountain system of eastern North America; extends from southeastern Quebec, Canada, to central Alabama. pp. 20, 225

Appomattox (a•puh•MA•tuhks) A village in central Virginia; site of the battle that ended the Civil War in 1865; once known as Appomattox Courthouse. (37°N, 79°W) p. 470

Arctic Ocean One of Earth's four oceans; located north of the Arctic Circle. p. 27

Arkansas River A tributary of the Mississippi River, beginning in central Colorado and ending in southeastern Arkansas. pp. 29, 153

Asia Largest continent on Earth. p. 27

Atlanta Georgia's capital and largest city; located in the northwest central part of the state; site of a Civil War battle in 1864. (33°N, 84°W) pp. 470, 621

Atlantic Ocean Second-largest ocean; separates North and South America from Europe and Africa. p. 27

Austin Capital of Texas; located in south central Texas. (30°N, 97°W) p. 621

Australia A country; smallest continent on Earth. p. 27

B

Baghdad Capital of Iraq; located on the Tigris River in central Iraq. (33°N, 44°E) p. 108

Bahamas An island group in the North Atlantic Ocean; located southeast of Florida and north of Cuba. p. 658

Baja California A peninsula in northwestern Mexico extending south-southeast between the Pacific Ocean and the Gulf of California. p. 653

Baltimore A major seaport in Maryland; located on the upper end of Chesapeake Bay. (39°N, 77°W) pp. 47, 234

Barbados An island in the Lesser Antilles, West Indies; located east of the central Windward Islands. p. 658

Barbuda A flat coral island in the eastern West Indies. p. 658

Baxter Springs A city in the southeastern corner of Kansas. (37°N, 94°W) p. 488

Beaufort Sea (BOH•fert) That part of the Arctic Ocean between northeastern Alaska and the Canadian Arctic Islands. p. 20

Beijing (bay•JING) The capital of China; located on a large plain in northeastern China; once known as Khanbalik. (40°N, 116°E) p. 108

Belmopan A town in Central America; capital of Belize. (17°N, 88°W) p. 658

Benin (buh•NEEN) A former kingdom in West Africa; located along the Gulf of Guinea; present-day southern Nigeria. p. 108

Bennington A town in the southwestern corner of Vermont; site of a major Revolutionary War battle in 1777. (43°N, 73°W) p. 323

Bering Strait A narrow strip of water; separates Asia from North America. p. 57

Beringia (buh•RIN•gee•uh) An ancient land bridge that once connected Asia and North America. p. 57

Black Sea A large inland sea between Europe and Asia. p. 113

Bogotá A city in South America located on the plateau of the Andes; capital of Colombia. (4°N, 74°W) p. 665

Boise (BOY•zee) Idaho's capital and largest city; located in the southwestern part of the state. (44°N, 116°W) p. 621

Bonampak An ancient settlement of the Mayan civilization; located in present-day southeastern Mexico. (16°N, 91°W) p. 65

Boston The capital and largest city of Massachusetts; a port city located on Massachusetts Bay. (42°N, 71°W) p. 291

Boston Harbor The western section of Massachusetts Bay; located in eastern Massachusetts; the city of Boston is located at its western end. p. 291

Brandywine A battlefield on Brandywine Creek in southeastern Pennsylvania; site of a major Revolutionary War battle in 1777. (40°N, 76°W) p. 323

Brasília A city in South America on the Tocantins River; capital of Brazil. (15°S, 48°W) p. 665

Brazos River (BRAH•zuhs) A river in central Texas; flows southeast into the Gulf of Mexico. p. 404

British Columbia One of Canada's ten provinces; located on the west coast of Canada and bordered by the Yukon Territory, the Northwest Territories, Alberta, the United States, and the Pacific Ocean. p. 670

Brookline A town in eastern Massachusetts; west-southwest of Boston. (42°N, 71°W) p. 291

Brooks Range A mountain range crossing northern Alaska; forms the northwestern end of the Rocky Mountains. p. 20

Buenos Aires A city in South America; the capital of Argentina. (34°S, 58°W) p. 665

Bull Run A stream in northeastern Virginia; flows toward the Potomac River; site of Civil War battles in 1861 and in 1862. p. 470

C

Cahokia (kuh•HOH•kee•uh) A village in southwestern Illinois; site of an ancient settlement of the Mound Builders. (39°N, 90°W) pp. 65, 108

Calgary A city in southern Alberta, Canada; located on the Bow River. (51°N, 114°W) p. 670

Calicut (KA•lih•kuht) A city in southwestern India; located on the Malabar Coast. (11°N, 76°E) p. 108

Cambridge A city in northeastern Massachusetts; located near Boston. (42°N, 71°W) p. 291

Camden A city in north central South Carolina, near the Wateree River; site of a major Revolutionary War battle in 1780. (34°N, 81°W) p. 323

Canal Zone A strip of territory in Panama. p. 528

Canary Islands An island group in the Atlantic Ocean off the northwest coast of Africa. (28°N, 16°W) p. 122

Canton A port city in southeastern China; located on the Canton River; known in China as Guangzhou. (23°N, 113°E) p. 108

Canyon de Chelly An ancient settlement of the Anasazi; located in present-day northeastern Arizona. p. 65

Cape Cod A peninsula of southeastern Massachusetts, extending into the Atlantic Ocean and enclosing Cape Cod Bay. (42°N, 70°W) p. 197

Cape Fear A cape at the southern end of Smith Island; located off the coast of North Carolina, at the mouth of the Cape Fear River. (34°N, 78°W) p. 234

Cape Fear River A river in central and southeastern North Carolina; formed by the Deep and Haw Rivers; flows southeast into the Atlantic Ocean. p. 234

Cape Hatteras (HA•tuh•ruhs) A cape on southeastern Hatteras Island; located off the coast of North Carolina. (35°N, 75°W) p. 234

Cape of Good Hope A cape located on the southernmost tip of Africa. (34°S, 18°E) p. 119

Cape Verde Islands (verd) A group of volcanic islands off the western coast of Africa. (16°N, 24°W) p. 119

Caracas A city in northern Venezuela; capital of Venezuela. (10°N, 67°W) p. 665

Caribbean Sea A part of the Atlantic Ocean between the West Indies and Central and South America. p. 658

Cascade Range A mountain range in the western United States; a continuation of the Sierra Nevada; extends north from California to Washington. p. 20

Cayenne A city on the northwestern coast of Cayenne Island, in northern South America; capital of French Guiana. (5°N, 52°W) p. 665

Chaco Canyon (CHAH•koh) An ancient settlement of the Anasazi; located in present-day northwestern New Mexico. (37°N, 108°W) p. 65

Chancellorsville (CHAN•suh•lerz•vil) A location in northeastern Virginia, just west of Fredericksburg; site of a Civil War battle in 1863. (38°N, 78°W) p. 470

Charles River A river in eastern Massachusetts; separates Boston from Cambridge; flows into Boston Bay. p. 291

Charleston A city in southeastern South Carolina; a major port on the Atlantic Ocean; once known as Charles Towne. (33°N, 80°W) pp. 234, 249, 323, 470

Charlestown A city in Massachusetts; located on Boston Harbor between the mouths of the Charles and Mystic Rivers. p. 291

Charlotte The largest city in North Carolina; located in the south central part of the state. (35°N, 81°W) p. 621

Charlottetown The capital of Prince Edward Island, Canada; located in the central part of the island. (46°N, 63°W) p. 670

Chattanooga (cha•tuh•NOO•guh) A city in southeastern Tennessee; located on the Tennessee River; site of a Civil War battle in 1863. (35°N, 85°W) p. 470

Cherokee Nation (CHAIR•uh•kee) A Native American nation located in present-day northern Georgia, eastern Alabama, southern Tennessee, and western North Carolina. p. 398

Chesapeake Bay An inlet of the Atlantic Ocean; surrounded by Virginia and Maryland. pp. 29, 233

Cheyenne (shy•AN) The capital of Wyoming; located in the southeastern part of the state. (41°N, 105°W) p. 488

Chicago A city in Illinois; located on Lake Michigan; the third-largest city in the United States. (42°N, 88°W) p. 488

Chickamauga (chik•uh•MAW•guh) A city in northwestern Georgia; site of a Civil War battle in 1863. (35°N, 85°W) p. 470

Chihuahua A city and state in northern Mexico. (28°N, 85°W) p. 653

Cincinnati (sin•suh•NA•tee) A large city in southwestern Ohio; located on the Ohio River. (39°N, 84°W) p. 47

Coast Mountains A mountain range in western British Columbia and southern Alaska; a continuation of the Cascade Range. p. 20

Coast Ranges Mountains along the Pacific coast of North America, extending from Alaska to Baja California. p. 20

Coastal Plain Low, mostly flat land that stretches inland from the Atlantic Ocean and the Gulf of Mexico. p. 20

Cold Harbor A location in east central Virginia, north of the Chickahominy River; site of Civil War battles in 1862 and in 1864. (38°N, 77°W) p. 470

Colorado River A river in the southwestern United States; its basin extends from the Rocky Mountains to the Sierra Nevada; flows into the Gulf of California. p. 29

Columbia River A river that begins in the Rocky Mountains in southwestern Canada, forms the Washington–Oregon border, and empties into the Pacific Ocean below Portland; supplies much of that area's hydroelectricity. pp. 29, 385

Compostela (kahm•poh•STEH•lah) A city in west central Mexico. (21°N, 105°W) p. 129

Concord A town in northeastern Massachusetts, near Boston; site of a major Revolutionary War battle in 1775. (42°N, 71°W) pp. 291, 323

Concord River A river in northeastern Massachusetts; formed by the junction of the Sudbury and Assabet Rivers; flows north into the Merrimack River at Lowell. p. 291

Connecticut River The longest river in New England; begins in New Hampshire, and empties into Long Island Sound, New York. p. 197

Constantinople (kahn•stant•uhn•OH•puhl) A port city in northwestern Turkey. (41°N, 29°E) p. 108

Copán (koh•PAHN) An ancient settlement of the Mayan civilization; located in present-day Honduras, in northern Central America. (15°N, 89°W) p. 65

Cowpens A town in northwestern South Carolina; located near the site of a major Revolutionary War battle in 1781. (35°N, 82°W) p. 323

Crab Orchard An ancient settlement of the Mound Builders; located in present-day southern Illinois. (38°N, 89°W) p. 65

Cuba An island country in the Caribbean; the largest island of the West Indies. (22°N, 79°W) pp. 129, 526, 658

Cuzco (KOOS•koh) The ancient capital of the Inca Empire; a city located in present-day Peru, in western South America. (14°S, 72°W) pp. 108, 133

D

Dallas A city in northeastern Texas; located on the Trinity River. (33°N, 97°W) p. 621

Damascus (duh•MAS•kuhs) The capital of Syria; located in southwest Syria. p. 108

Deerfield A town in northwestern Massachusetts. (43°N, 73°W) p. 197

Delaware Bay An inlet of the Atlantic Ocean; located between southern New Jersey and Delaware. p. 212

Delaware River A river in the northeastern United States; begins in southern New York and flows into the Atlantic Ocean at Delaware Bay. p. 89

Denver Colorado's capital and largest city. (40°N, 105°W) pp. 488, 621

Des Moines (dih•MOYN) Iowa's capital and largest city. (42°N, 94°W) p. A3

Dickson An ancient settlement of the Mound Builders; located in present-day central Illinois. p. 65

Dodge City A city in southern Kansas; located on the Arkansas River; once a major railroad center on the Santa Fe Trail. (38°N, 100°W) p. 488

Dominica (dah•muh•NEE•kuh) An island and a republic in the West Indies; located in the center of the Lesser Antilles between Guadeloupe and Martinique. p. 658

Dominican Republic A country in the West Indies, occupying the eastern part of Hispaniola. p. 658

Dover (DE) The capital of Delaware; located in the central part of the state. (39°N, 76°W) p. 212

Dover (NH) A city in southeastern New Hampshire. (43°N, 71°W) p. 197

Durango A city and state in northwestern central Mexico. (24°N, 104°W) p. 653

E

Edenton (EE•duhn•tuhn) A town in northeastern North Carolina; located on Albemarle Sound, near the mouth of the Chowan River. (36°N, 77°W) p. 234

Edmonton The capital of Alberta, Canada; located in the south central part of the province on both banks of the North Saskatchewan River. (53°N, 113°W) p. 670

El Paso A city at the western tip of Texas; located on the Rio Grande. (32°N, 106°W) p. 621

Ellsworth A city in central Kansas. p. 488

Emerald Mound An ancient settlement of the Mound Builders; located in present-day southwestern Mississippi. (32°N, 91°W) p. 65

Equator Great circle of Earth that is equal distance from the North and South Poles and divides the surface into Northern and Southern Hemispheres. p. 50

Erie Canal The longest canal in the world; located in New York; connects Buffalo (on Lake Erie) with Troy (on the Hudson River). p. 415

Europe One of Earth's seven continents. p. 27

F

Falkland Islands A British colony in the Atlantic Ocean; located east of the Strait of Magellan. p. 665

Falmouth (FAL•muhth) A town in southwestern Maine. (44°N, 70°W) p. 197

Fort Atkinson A fort in southern Kansas; located on the Sante Fe Trail. (43°N, 89°W) p. 406

Fort Boise (BOY•zee) A fort in eastern Oregon; located on the Snake River and on the Oregon Trail. p. 406

Fort Bridger A present-day village in southwestern Wyoming; once an important station on the Oregon Trail. (41°N, 110°W) p. 406

Fort Christina A Swedish fort; located in present-day Wilmington, Delaware. p. 211

Fort Crèvecoeur (KREEV•ker) A fort in central Illinois; located on the Illinois River; built by La Salle in 1680. (41°N, 90°W) p. 153

Fort Crown Point A French fort; located in northeastern New York, on the shore of Lake Champlain. p. 274

Fort Cumberland A British fort located in northeastern West Virginia, on its border with Maryland. p. 274

Fort Dearborn A fort in northeastern Illinois; built in 1803; eventually became part of Chicago; site of a major battle in the War of 1812. (42°N, 88°W) p. 391

Fort Donelson A fort located in northwestern Tennessee; site of a major Civil War battle in 1862. p. 470

Fort Duquesne (doo•KAYN) A French fort in present-day Pittsburgh, Pennsylvania; captured by the British and new fort built and named Fort Pitt. (40°N, 80°W) p. 274

Fort Edward A British fort in New York, on the Hudson River; a present-day village. (43°N, 74°W) p. 274

Fort Frontenac (FRAHN•tuh•nak) A French fort once located on the site of present-day Kingston, Ontario, in southeastern Canada; destroyed by the British in 1758. (44°N, 76°W) pp. 153, 274

Fort Gibson A fort in eastern Oklahoma; end of the Trail of Tears. (36°N, 95°W) p. 398

Fort Hall A fort in southeastern Idaho; located on the Snake River, at a junction on the Oregon Trail. p. 406

Fort Laramie A fort in southeastern Wyoming; located on the Oregon Trail. (42°N, 105°W) p. 406

Fort Lauderdale A city in southeast Florida along the Atlantic coast. p. 621

Fort Ligonier (lig•uh•NIR) A British fort; located in southern Pennsylvania near the Ohio River. p. 274

Fort Louisbourg (LOO•is•berg) A French fort; located in eastern Canada on the coast of the Atlantic Ocean. (46°N, 60°W) p. 274

Fort Mackinac A fort located on the tip of present-day northern Michigan; site of a major battle in the War of 1812. (46°N, 85°W) p. 391

Fort Mandan A fort in present-day central North Dakota, on the Missouri River; site of a winter camp for the Lewis and Clark expedition. (48°N, 104°W) p. 385

Fort McHenry A fort in central Maryland; located on the harbor in Baltimore; site of a major battle in the War of 1812. (39°N, 77°W) p. 391

Fort Miamis A French fort located on the southern shore of Lake Michigan, in present-day southwestern Michigan. p. 153

Fort Necessity A British fort located in southwestern Pennsylvania; located in present-day Great Meadows. (38°N, 80°W) p. 274

Fort Niagara A fort located in western New York, at the mouth of the Niagara River. (43°N, 79°W) p. 274

Fort Oswego A British fort; located in western New York, on the coast of Lake Ontario. (43°N, 77°W) p. 274

Fort Sumter A fort on a human-made island, off the coast of South Carolina, in Charleston Harbor; site of the first Civil War battle in 1861. (33°N, 80°W) p. 470

Fort Ticonderoga (ty•kahn•der•OH•gah) A historic fort on Lake Champlain, in northeastern New York. (44°N, 73°W) p. 274

Fort Vancouver A fort in southwestern Washington, on the Columbia River; the western end of the Oregon Trail; present-day Vancouver. (45°N, 123°W) p. 406

Fort Wagner A fort near Charleston, South Carolina; site of a Civil War battle in 1863. p. 470

Fort Walla Walla A fort in southeastern Washington; located on the Oregon Trail. (46°N, 118°W) p. 406

Fort William Henry A British fort located in eastern New York. (43°N, 74°W) p. 274

Fort Worth A city in northern Texas; located on the Trinity River. (33°N, 97°W) p. 621

Fox River Located in southeast central Wisconsin; flows southwest toward the Wisconsin River, and then flows northeast and empties into Green Bay. p. 153

Franklin A city in central Tennessee; site of a major Civil War battle in 1864. (36°N, 87°W) p. 470

Fredericksburg A city in northeastern Virginia; located on the Rappahannock River; site of a Civil War battle in 1862. (38°N, 77°W) p. 470

Fredericton The capital of New Brunswick, Canada; located in the southwestern part of the province. (46°N, 66°W) p. 670

Frenchtown A town in present-day eastern Michigan; site of a major battle in the War of 1812. (42°N, 83°W) p. 391

G

Galápagos Islands Nineteen islands off the coast of Ecuador; home to many unique bird and animal species. p. 667

Gatun Lake (gah•TOON) A lake in Panama; part of the Panama Canal system. p. 528

Georgetown A city in South America; located at the mouth of the Demerara River; capital of Guyana. (6°N, 58°W) p. 665

Germantown A residential section of present-day Philadelphia, on Wissahickon Creek, in southeastern Pennsylvania; site of a major Revolutionary War battle in 1777. (40°N, 75°W) p. 323

Gettysburg A town in southern Pennsylvania; site of a Civil War battle in 1863. (40°N, 77°W) pp. 470, 510

Golconda (gahl•KAHN•duh) A city in the southeastern corner of Illinois; a point on the Trail of Tears. (37°N, 88°W) p. 398

Gonzales (gohn•ZAH•lays) A city in south central Texas; site of the first battle of the Texas Revolution. (30°N, 97°W) p. 404

Great Basin One of the driest parts of the United States; located in Nevada, Utah, California, Idaho, Wyoming, and Oregon; includes the Great Salt Lake Desert, the Mojave Desert, and Death Valley. pp. 20, 406

Great Lakes A chain of five lakes; located in central North America; the largest group of freshwater lakes in the world. p. 29

Great Plains A continental slope in western North America; borders the eastern base of the Rocky Mountains from Canada to New Mexico and Texas. pp. 20, 406

Great Salt Lake The largest lake in the Great Basin; located in northwestern Utah. pp. 29, 406

Great Wagon Road A former route used in the mid-1700s by colonists moving to settle in the backcountry. p. 225

Greenland The largest island on Earth; located in the northern Atlantic Ocean, east of Canada. p. 20

Grenada (grah•NAY•duh) An island in the West Indies; the southernmost of the Windward Islands. p. 658

Groton (GRAH•tuhn) A town in southeastern Connecticut; located on Long Island Sound. (41°N, 72°W) p. 197

Guadalajara A city in western central Mexico; capital of Jalisco state. (20°N, 103°W) p. 653

Guam (GWAHM) United States territory in the Pacific Ocean; largest of the Mariana Islands. p. 526

Guatemala City Capital of Guatemala; largest city in Central America. (14°N, 90°W) p. 658

Guiana Highlands Highland area in northern South America. p. 665

Guilford Courthouse (GIL•ferd) A location in north central North Carolina, near Greensboro; site of a major Revolutionary War battle in 1781. (36°N, 80°W) p. 323

Gulf of Alaska A northern inlet of the Pacific Ocean; located between the Alaska Peninsula and the southwestern coast of Canada. p. 29

Gulf of California An inlet of the Pacific Ocean; located between Baja California and the northwestern coast of Mexico. p. 20

Gulf of Mexico An inlet of the Atlantic Ocean; located on the southeastern coast of North America; surrounded by the United States, Cuba, and Mexico. pp. 29, 153

Gulf of Panama A large inlet of the Pacific Ocean; located on the southern coast of Panama. p. 528

Haiti A country in the West Indies; occupies the western part of the island of Hispaniola. p. 658

Halifax The capital of the province of Nova Scotia, Canada; a major port on the Atlantic Ocean; remains free of ice all year. (44°N, 63°W) p. 670

Hampton Roads A channel in southeastern Virginia that flows into Chesapeake Bay; site of a Civil War naval battle in 1862 between two ironclad ships, the *Monitor* and the *Merrimack*. p. 470

Hartford The capital of Connecticut. (42°N, 73°W) p. 197

Havana The capital of Cuba; located on the northwestern coast of the country. (23°N, 82°W) p. 129

Hawaiian Islands A state; a chain of volcanic and coral islands; located in the north central Pacific Ocean. p. 526

Hawikuh (hah•wee•KOO) A former village in southwestern North America; located on the route of the Spanish explorer Coronado in present-day northwestern New Mexico. p. 129

Hiroshima Japanese city upon which first atom bomb was dropped in World War II. p. 568

Hispaniola (ees•pah•NYOH•lah) An island in the West Indies made up of Haiti and the Dominican Republic; located in the Caribbean Sea between Cuba and Puerto Rico. pp. 129, 658

Honolulu (hahn•nuh•LOO•loo) Hawaii's capital and largest city; located on Oahu. (21°N, 158°W) p. A2

Hopewell An ancient settlement of the Mound Builders; located in present-day southern Ohio. (39°N, 83°W) p. 65

Horseshoe Bend A location in eastern Alabama; site of a battle in the War of 1812; a present-day national military park. p. 391

Houston A city in southeastern Texas; third-largest port in the United States; leading industrial center in Texas. (30°N, 95°W) p. 621

Hudson Bay An inland sea in east central Canada surrounded by the Northwest Territories, Manitoba, Ontario, and Quebec. p. 138

Hudson River A river in the northeastern United States beginning in upper New York and flowing into the Atlantic Ocean; named for the explorer Henry Hudson. p. 89

Iceland An island country in the northern Atlantic Ocean; between Greenland and Norway. p. 569

Illinois River A river in western and central Illinois; flows southwest into the Mississippi River. pp. 29, 153

Independence A city in western Missouri; the starting point of the Oregon and Santa Fe Trails. (39°N, 94°W) p. 406

Indian Ocean One of Earth's four oceans; located east of Africa, south of Asia, west of Australia, and north of Antarctica. p. 27

Iqaluit The capital of Nunavut Territory, Canada; located on the eastern coast. p. 670

Isthmus of Panama (IS•muhs) A narrow strip of land that connects North America and South America. p. 125

Iwo Jima Japanese island; site of major battles during World War II. p. 568

Jacksonville A city in northeastern Florida; located near the mouth of the St. Johns River. (30°N, 82°W) p. 621

Jamaica (juh•MAY•kuh) An island country in the West Indies; south of Cuba. pp. 129, 658

Jamestown The first permanent English settlement in the Americas; located in eastern Virginia, on the shore of the James River. (37°N, 76°W) p. 234

Jerusalem The capital of Israel; located in the central part of the country. (32°N, 35°E) p. 108

Kahoolawe (kah•hoh•uh•LAY•vay) One of the eight main islands of Hawaii; located west of Maui. p. 557

Kaskaskia (ka•SKAS•kee•uh) A village in southwestern Illinois; site of a major Revolutionary War battle in 1778. (38°N, 90°W) p. 323

GAZETTEER

Kauai (kah•WAH•ee) The fourth-largest of the eight main islands of Hawaii. p. 557

Kennebec River (KEN•uh•bek) A river in west central and southern Maine; flows south from Moosehead Lake to the Atlantic Ocean. p. 197

Kennesaw Mountain (KEN•uh•saw) An isolated peak in northwestern Georgia, near Atlanta; site of a Civil War battle in 1864. p. 470

Kings Mountain A ridge in northern South Carolina and southern North Carolina; site of a Revolutionary War battle in 1780. p. 323

Kingston A commercial seaport in the West Indies; capital of Jamaica. (18°N, 76°W) p. 658

L

La Paz A city in South America; capital of Bolivia. (16°S, 68°W) p. 665

La Venta An ancient settlement of the Olmecs; located in present-day southern Mexico, on an island near the Tonalá River. (18°N, 94°W) p. 65

Labrador A peninsula in northeastern North America; once known as Markland. p. 20

Labrador Sea Located south of Greenland and northeast of North America. p. 20

Lake Champlain (sham•PLAYN) A lake between New York and Vermont. p. 89

Lake Erie The fourth-largest of the Great Lakes; borders Canada and the United States. p. 29

Lake Huron The second-largest of the Great Lakes; borders Canada and the United States. p. 29

Lake Michigan The third-largest of the Great Lakes; borders Michigan, Illinois, Indiana, and Wisconsin. pp. 29, 153

Lake Okeechobee (oh•kuh•CHOH•bee) A large lake in south Florida. p. 29

Lake Ontario The smallest of the Great Lakes; borders Canada and the United States. pp. 29, 89

Lake Superior The largest of the Great Lakes; borders Canada and the United States. p. 29

Lake Tahoe A lake on the California-Nevada border. p. 29

Lanai (luh•NY) One of the eight main islands of Hawaii. p. 557

Lancaster A city in southeastern Pennsylvania. (40°N, 76°W) p. 212

Las Vegas (lahs VAY•guhs) A city in southeastern Nevada. (36°N, 115°W) p. 621

Lexington A town in northeastern Massachusetts; site of the first battle of the Revolutionary War in 1775. (42°N, 71°W) pp. 291, 323

Lima (LEE•mah) The capital of Peru; located on the Rímac River. (12°S, 77°W) p. 665

Lisbon The capital of Portugal; a port city located in the western part of the country. (39°N, 9°W) pp. 108, 119

Little Bighorn A location near the Little Bighorn River in southern Montana; site of a fierce battle in 1876 between Sioux and Cheyenne Indians and United States Army soldiers led by General George Armstrong Custer. p. 490

London A city located in the southern part of England; capital of present-day Britain. (52°N, 0°) p. 108

Long Island An island located east of New York City and south of Connecticut; lies between Long Island Sound and the Atlantic Ocean. p. 323

Los Adaes Site of a mission of New Spain; located in present-day eastern Texas. p. 149

Los Angeles The largest city in California; second-largest city in the United States; located in the southern part of the state. (34°N, 118°W) p. 621

Louisiana Purchase A territory in the west central United States; it doubled the size of the nation when it was purchased from France in 1803; extended from the Mississippi River to the Rocky Mountains, and from the Gulf of Mexico to Canada. p. 385

M

Machu Picchu (MAH•choo PEEK•choo) The site of an ancient Inca city on a mountain in the Andes, northwest of Cuzco, Peru. (13°S, 73°W) p. 133

Macon (MAY•kuhn) A city in central Georgia; located on the Ocmulgee River. (33°N, 84°W) p. 415

Madeira (mah•DAIR•uh) An island group in the eastern Atlantic Ocean, off the coast of Morocco. p. 122

Managua A city in Central America; capital of Nicaragua; located on the south shore of Lake Managua. (12°N, 86°W) p. 658

Manitoba (ma•nuh•TOH•buh) A province in central Canada; bordered by the Nunavut Territories, Hudson Bay, Ontario, the United States, and Saskatchewan; located on the Interior Plains of Canada. p. 670

Marshall Gold Discovery State Historic Park A historical park in eastern California located at the site where James Marshall discovered gold in 1848; setting of the California gold rush of 1849. p. 408

Massachusetts Bay An inlet of the Atlantic Ocean; on the eastern coast of Massachusetts; extends from Cape Ann to Cape Cod. p. 189

Maui (MOW•ee) The second-largest island in Hawaii. p. 557

Mecca A city in western Saudi Arabia; a holy city and chief pilgrimage destination of Islam. p. 108

Medford A city in northeastern Massachusetts, north of Boston. (42°N, 71°W) p. 291

Mediterranean Sea (meh•duh•tuh•RAY•nee•uhn) An inland sea, enclosed by Europe on the west and north, Asia on the east, and Africa on the south. p. 113

Menotomy Located in northeastern Massachusetts. p. 291

Mérida A city in southeastern Mexico; capital of Yucatán state. (21°N, 89°W) p. 653

Merrimack River A river in southern New Hampshire and northeastern Massachusetts; empties into the Atlantic Ocean. p. 197

Mesa Verde (MAY•suh VAIR•day) An ancient settlement of the Anasazi; located in present-day southwestern Colorado. (37°N, 108°W) p. 65

Mexico City A city on the southern edge of the Central Plateau of Mexico; the present-day capital of Mexico. (19°N, 99°W) pp. 149, 653

GAZETTEER

Midway Islands A United States territory in the central Pacific Ocean. p. 526

Minneapolis The largest city in Minnesota; located in the southeast central part of the state, on the Mississippi River; twin city with St. Paul. (45°N, 93°W) p. 498

Mississippi River The longest river in the United States; located centrally, its source is Lake Itasca in Minnesota; flows south into the Gulf of Mexico. pp. 29, 153

Missouri River A tributary of the Mississippi River; located centrally, it begins in Montana and ends at St. Louis, Missouri. pp. 29, 385

Mobile Bay An inlet of the Gulf of Mexico; located off the coast of southern Alabama; the site of a Civil War naval battle in 1864. p. 470

Mohawk River A river in central New York that flows east to the Hudson River. p. 89

Molokai (mah•luh•KY) One of the eight main islands of Hawaii. p. 557

Monterrey A city in northeastern Mexico; capital of Nuevo León state. (25°N, 100°W) p. 653

Montevideo A seaport city located in the southern part of the north shore of La Plata estuary; capital of Uruguay. (35°S, 56°W) p. 665

Montreal The second-largest city in present-day Canada; located in southern Quebec, on Montreal Island on the north bank of the St. Lawrence River. (46°N, 73°W) p. 274

Morristown A town in northern New Jersey; located west-northwest of Newark. (41°N, 74°W) p. 212

Moscow The capital and largest city of Russia; located in the western part of the country. (56°N, 38°E) p. 108

Moundville An ancient settlement of the Mound Builders; located in present-day central Alabama. (33°N, 88°W) p. 65

Murfreesboro A city in central Tennessee; located on the west fork of the Stones River; a site on the Trail of Tears. (36°N, 86°W) p. 398

Mystic River A short river rising in the Mystic Lakes; located in northeastern Massachusetts; flows southeast into Boston Harbor north of Charlestown. p. 291

N

Nagasaki Japanese city upon which the second atom bomb was dropped, resulting in an end to World War II. p. 568

Narragansett Bay An inlet of the Atlantic Ocean in southeastern Rhode Island. (41°N, 71°W) p. 197

Nashville The capital of Tennessee; site of a Civil War battle in 1864. (36°N, 87°W) pp. 470, 621

Nassau A city on the northeastern coast of New Providence Island; capital of the Bahamas. (25°N, 77°W) p. 658

Natchitoches (NAH•kuh•tuhsh) The first settlement in present-day Louisiana; located in the northwest central part of the state. (32°N, 93°W) p. 385

Nauvoo (naw•VOO) A city in western Illinois; located on the Mississippi River; beginning of the Mormon Trail. (41°N, 91°W) p. 406

New Amsterdam A Dutch city on Manhattan Island; later became New York City. (41°N, 74°W) p. 211

New Bern A city and port in southeastern North Carolina. (35°N, 77°W) p. 234

New Brunswick One of Canada's ten provinces; bordered by Quebec, the Gulf of St. Lawrence, Northumberland Strait, the Bay of Fundy, the United States, and Nova Scotia. p. 670

New Echota (ih•KOHT•uh) A Native American town in northwestern Georgia; chosen as the capital of the Cherokee Nation in 1819. (34°N, 85°W) p. 398

New France The possessions of France in North America from 1534 to 1763; included Canada, the Great Lakes region, and Louisiana. p. 269

New Guinea (GIH•nee) An island of the eastern Malay Archipelago; located in the western Pacific Ocean, north of Australia. p. 568

New Haven A city in southern Connecticut; located on New Haven Harbor. (41°N, 73°W) p. 197

New London A city in southeastern Connecticut; located on Long Island Sound at the mouth of the Thames River. (41°N, 72°W) p. 247

New Orleans The largest city in Louisiana; a major port located between the Mississippi River and Lake Pontchartrain. (30°N, 90°W) pp. 391, 470

New Spain The former Spanish possessions from 1535 to 1821; included the southwestern United States, Mexico, Central America north of Panama, the West Indies, and the Philippines. p. 269

New York City The largest city in the United States; located in southeastern New York at the mouth of the Hudson River. (41°N, 74°W) p. 603

Newark A port in northeastern New Jersey; located on the Passaic River and Newark Bay. (41°N, 74°W) p. 212

Newfoundland (NOO•fuhn•luhnd) One of Canada's ten provinces; bordered by Quebec and the Atlantic Ocean. p. 670

Newport A city on the southern end of Rhode Island; located at the mouth of Narragansett Bay. (41°N, 71°W) p. 197

Newton A city in south central Kansas. (38°N, 97°W) p. 488

Niihau (NEE•how) One of the eight main islands of Hawaii. p. 557

Norfolk (NAWR•fawk) A city in southeastern Virginia; located on the Elizabeth River. (37°N, 76°W) p. 234

Normandy Region of northwest France; site of Allied D day invasion on June 6, 1944. p. 569

North America One of Earth's seven continents. p. 27

North Pole The northernmost point on Earth. p. 50

Northwest Territories One of Canada's three territories; located in northern Canada. p. 670

Nova Scotia (NOH•vuh SKOH•shuh) A province of Canada; located in eastern Canada on a peninsula. pp. 151, 670

Nueces River (noo•AY•says) A river in southern Texas; flows into Nueces Bay, at the head of Corpus Christi Bay. p. 404

Nunavut Territory One of Canada's three territories; formed in 1999 and inhabited mostly by Inuit peoples. p. 670

GAZETTEER

O

Oahu (oh•AH•hoo) The third-largest of the eight main islands of Hawaii; Honolulu is located there. p. 557

Oaxaca (wuh•HAH•kuh) A city and state in southern Mexico. (17°N, 96°W) p. 653

Ocmulgee (ohk•MUHL•gee) An ancient settlement of the Mound Builders; located in present-day central Georgia. p. 65

Ocmulgee River (ohk•MUHL•gee) A river in central Georgia; formed by the junction of the Yellow and South Rivers; flows south to join the Altamaha River. p. 234

Oconee River (oh•KOH•nee) A river in central Georgia; flows south and southeast to join the Ocmulgee and form the Altamaha River. p. 234

Ogallala (oh•guh•LAHL•uh) A city in western Nebraska on the South Platte River. (41°N, 102°W) p. 488

Ohio River A tributary of the Mississippi River, beginning in Pittsburgh, Pennsylvania, and ending at Cairo, Illinois. p. 29

Old Spanish Trail Part of the Santa Fe Trail that linked Santa Fe to Los Angeles. p. 406

Omaha (OH•muh•hah) The largest city in Nebraska; located in the eastern part of the state, on the Missouri River. (41°N, 96°W) p. 406

Ontario (ahn•TAIR•ee•oh) One of Canada's ten provinces; located between Quebec and Manitoba. p. 670

Oregon Country A former region in western North America; located between the Pacific coast and the Rocky Mountains, from the northern border of California to Alaska. p. 385

Oregon Trail A former route to the Oregon Country; extended from the Missouri River northwest to the Columbia River in Oregon. p. 406

Orinoco River A river in Venezuela in northern South America. p. 665

Orlando A city in central Florida. (28°N, 81°W) p. 621

Ottawa (AH•tuh•wuh) The capital of Canada; located in Ontario on the St. Lawrence Lowlands. (45°N, 75°W) p. 670

P

Pacific Ocean Largest body of water on Earth; extends from Arctic Circle to Antarctic Regions, separating North and South America from Australia and Asia. p. 27

Pagan Ruined Asian town; capital of a powerful dynasty during the 11th–13th centuries. p. 113

Palenque (pah•LENG•kay) An ancient settlement of the Mayan civilization; located in present-day Chiapas, in southern Mexico. (18°N, 92°W) p. 65

Palmyra Island (pal•MY•ruh) One of the northernmost of the Line Islands; located in the central Pacific Ocean. p. 526

Pampas Plains of South America; located in southern part of the continent, extending for nearly 1,000 miles. p. 665

Panama Canal A canal across the Isthmus of Panama; extends from the Caribbean Sea to the Gulf of Panama. p. 528

Panama City The capital of Panama; located in Central America. (9°N, 80°W) p. 658

Paramaribo A seaport city located on the Suriname River; capital of Suriname. (5°N, 55°W) p. 665

Paraná River A river in southeast central South America; formed by the joining of the Rio Grande and the Paranaíba River in south central Brazil. p. 665

Patagonia A barren tableland in South America between the Andes and the Atlantic Ocean. p. 665

Pearl Harbor An inlet on the southern coast of Oahu, Hawaii; the Japanese attacked an American naval base there on December 7, 1941. p. 557

Pecos River (PAY•kohs) A river in eastern New Mexico and western Texas; empties into the Rio Grande. p. 488

Pee Dee River A river in North Carolina and South Carolina; forms where the Yadkin and Uharie Rivers meet; empties into Winyah Bay. p. 234

Perryville A city in east central Kentucky; site of a major Civil War battle in 1862. (38°N, 90°W) p. 470

Perth Amboy A port city in central New Jersey; located on Raritan Bay. (40°N, 74°W) p. 212

Petersburg A port city in southeastern Virginia; located on the Appomattox River; site of a series of Civil War battles from 1864 to 1865. (37°N, 77°W) p. 470

Philadelphia A city in southeastern Pennsylvania, on the Delaware River; a major United States port. (40°N, 75°W) p. 219

Philippine Islands A group of more than 7,000 islands off the coast of southeastern Asia, making up the country of the Philippines. pp. 125, 526

Phoenix Capital and largest city of Arizona; located in south central Arizona. p. 621

Piedmont Area of high land on the eastern side of the Appalachian Mountains. p. 20

Pikes Peak A mountain in east central Colorado; part of the Rocky Mountains. p. 385

Pittsburgh The second-largest city in Pennsylvania; located in the southwestern part of the state, on the Ohio River. (40°N, 80°W) p. 47

Platte River (PLAT) A river in central Nebraska; flows east into the Missouri River below Omaha. p. 406

Plattsburgh A city in northeastern New York; located on the western shore of Lake Champlain; site of a major battle in the War of 1812. (45°N, 73°W) p. 391

Plymouth A town in southeastern Massachusetts, on Plymouth Bay; site of the first settlement built by the Pilgrims, who sailed on the *Mayflower*. (42°N, 71°W) p. 189

Port Royal A town in western Nova Scotia, Canada; name changed to Annapolis Royal in honor of Queen Anne; capital of Nova Scotia until 1749. (45°N, 66°W) p. 151

Port-au-Prince A seaport located on Hispaniola Island, in the West Indies, on the southeastern shore of the Gulf of Gonâve; capital of Haiti. (18°N, 72°W) p. 658

Portland (ME) A port city in southwestern Maine; located on Casco Bay. (44°N, 70°W) p. 353

Portland (OR) Oregon's largest city and principal port; located in the northwestern part of the state on the Willamette River. (46°N, 123°W) p. 621

Port of Spain A seaport in the northwestern part of the island of Trinidad; capital of Trinidad and Tobago. (10°N, 61°W) p. 658

Portsmouth (NH) (PAWRT•smuhth) A port city in southeastern New Hampshire; located at the mouth of the Piscataqua River. (43°N, 71°W) p. 197

Portsmouth (RI) A town in southeastern Rhode Island; located on the Sakonnet River. (42°N, 71°W) p. 197

Potomac River (puh•TOH•muhk) A river on the Coastal Plain of the United States; begins in West Virginia and flows into Chesapeake Bay; Washington, D.C., is located on this river. p. 233

Prince Edward Island One of Canada's ten provinces; located in the Gulf of St. Lawrence. p. 670

Princeton A borough in west central New Jersey; site of a major Revolutionary War battle. (40°N, 75°W) p. 323

Providence Rhode Island's capital and largest city; located in the northern part of the state, at the head of the Providence River. (42°N, 71°W) p. 197

Puebla A city and state in southeastern central Mexico. (19°N, 98°W) p. 653

Pueblo (PWEH•bloh) A city in Colorado. p. 488

Pueblo Bonito (PWEH•bloh boh•NEE•toh) Largest of the prehistoric pueblo ruins; located in Chaco Canyon National Monument, New Mexico. p. 65

Puerto Rico An island of the West Indies; located southeast of Florida; a commonwealth of the United States. pp. 129, 526

Put-in-Bay A bay on South Bass Island, north of Ohio in Lake Erie; site of a major battle in the War of 1812. (42°N, 83°W) p. 391

Quebec (kwih•BEK) The capital of the province of Quebec, Canada; located on the northern side of the St. Lawrence River; the first successful French settlement in the Americas; established in 1608. (47°N, 71°W) pp. 151, 670

R

Raleigh (RAW•lee) The capital of North Carolina; located in the east central part of the state. (36°N, 79°W) p. 621

Red River A tributary of the Mississippi River; rises in eastern New Mexico, flows across Louisiana and into the Mississippi River; forms much of the Texas–Oklahoma border. pp. 29, 385

Regina (rih•JY•nuh) The capital of Saskatchewan, Canada; located in the southern part of the province. (50°N, 104°W) p. 670

Richmond The capital of Virginia; a port city located in the east central part of the state, on the James River; capital of the Confederacy. (38°N, 77°W) p. 470

Rio de Janeiro A commercial seaport in southeastern Brazil on the southwestern shore of Guanabara Bay. (23°S, 43°W) p. 665

Río de la Plata A river on the southeastern coast of South America. p. 665

Rio Grande A river in southwestern North America; it begins in Colorado and flows into the Gulf of Mexico; forms the border between Texas and Mexico. pp. 29, 385

Roanoke River A river in southern Virginia and northeastern North Carolina; flows east and southeast across the North Carolina border and into Albemarle Sound. p. 234

Rocky Mountains A range of mountains in the western United States and Canada, extending from Alaska to New Mexico; these mountains divide rivers that flow east from those that flow west. pp. 20, 385

Roxbury A residential district in southern Boston, Massachusetts; formerly a city, but became part of Boston in 1868; founded in 1630. (42°N, 71°W) p. 291

Sabine River (suh•BEEN) A river in eastern Texas and western Louisiana; flows southeast to the Gulf of Mexico. p. 404

Sacramento The capital of California; located in the north central part of the state, on the Sacramento River. (39°N, 121°W) p. 621

Sacramento River A river in northwestern California; rises near Mt. Shasta and flows south into Suisun Bay. p. 406

Salem A city on the northeastern coast of Massachusetts. (43°N, 71°W) p. 189

Salt Lake City Utah's capital and largest city; located in the northern part of the state, on the Jordan River. (41°N, 112°W) pp. 406, 621

San Antonio A city in south central Texas; located on the San Antonio River; site of the Alamo. (29°N, 98°W) pp. 404, 621

San Antonio River A river in southern Texas; flows southeast and empties into San Antonio Bay. p. 404

San Diego A large port city in southern California; located on San Diego Bay. (33°N, 117°W) pp. 149, 174, 621

San Francisco The second-largest city in California; located in the northern part of the state, on San Francisco Bay. (38°N, 123°W) pp. 149, 621

San Jacinto (hah•SEEN•toh) A location in southeastern Texas; site of a battle in the Texas Revolution in 1836. (31°N, 95°W) p. 404

San José A city in Central America; capital of Costa Rica. (10°N, 84°W) p. 658

San Juan (san WAHN) Puerto Rico's capital and largest city. (18°N, 66°W) p. 658

San Lorenzo An ancient settlement of the Olmecs; located in present-day southern Mexico. (29°N, 113°W) p. 65

San Salvador One of the islands in the southern Bahamas; Christopher Columbus landed there in 1492. p. 122

Santa Fe (SAN•tah FAY) The capital of New Mexico; located in the north central part of the state. (36°N, 106°W) pp. 149, 406, 621

Santa Fe Trail A former commercial route to the western United States; extended from western Missouri to Santa Fe, in central New Mexico. p. 406

Santee River A river in southeast central South Carolina; formed by the junction of the Congaree and Wateree Rivers; flows southeast into the Atlantic Ocean. p. 234

Santo Domingo The capital of the Dominican Republic. (18°N, 70°W) p. 658

São Francisco River A river in eastern Brazil; flows north, northeast, and east into the Atlantic Ocean. p. 665

São Paulo A city in southeastern Brazil; capital of São Paulo state. p. 665

Saratoga A village on the western bank of the Hudson River in eastern New York; site of a major Revolutionary War battle in 1777; present-day Schuylerville. (43°N, 74°W) p. 323

Saskatchewan (suh•SKA•chuh•wahn) One of Canada's ten provinces; located between Alberta and Manitoba. p. 670

Savannah The oldest city and a principal seaport in southeast Georgia; located in the southeastern part of the state, at the mouth of the Savannah River. (32°N, 81°W) pp. 234, 470

Savannah River A river that forms the border between Georgia and South Carolina; flows into the Atlantic Ocean at Savannah, Georgia. p. 234

Schenectady (skuh•NEK•tuh•dee) A city in eastern New York; located on the Mohawk River. (43°N, 74°W) p. 212

Seattle The largest city in Washington; a port city located in the west central part of the state, on Puget Sound. (48°N, 122°W) p. 621

Sedalia (suh•DAYL•yuh) A city in west central Missouri. (39°N, 93°W) p. 488

Serpent Mound An ancient settlement of the Mound Builders; located in present-day southern Ohio. (39°N, 83°W) p. 65

Shiloh (SHY•loh) A location in southwestern Tennessee; site of a major Civil War battle in 1862; also known as Pittsburg Landing. (35°N, 88°W) p. 470

Sierra Madre Occidental (see•AIR•ah MAH•dray ahk•sih•den•TAHL) A mountain range in western Mexico, running parallel to the Pacific coast. p. 20

Sierra Madre Oriental (awr•ee•en•TAHL) A mountain range in eastern Mexico, running parallel to the coast along the Gulf of Mexico. p. 20

Sierra Nevada A mountain range in eastern California that runs parallel to the Coast Ranges. p. 20

Snake River A river that begins in the Rocky Mountains and flows west into the Pacific Ocean; part of the Oregon Trail ran along this river. p. 385

South America One of Earth's seven continents. p. 27

South Pass A pass in southwestern Wyoming; crosses the Continental Divide; part of the Oregon Trail. p. 406

South Pole The southernmost point on Earth. p. 50

Spiro An ancient settlement of the Mound Builders; located in eastern Oklahoma. (35°N, 95°W) p. 65

Springfield (MA) A city in southwestern Massachusetts; located on the Connecticut River. (42°N, 73°W) p. 197

Springfield (MO) A city in southwestern Missouri; a point on the Trail of Tears. (37°N, 93°W) p. 398

St. Augustine (AW•guh•steen) A city on the coast of northeastern Florida; the oldest city founded by Europeans in the United States. (30°N, 81°W) pp. 129, 149

St. Croix (KROY) A city on the border of Maine and New Brunswick, Canada. (45°N, 67°W) p. 151

St. Ignace (IG•nuhs) A city in Michigan; located on the southeastern side of Michigan's upper peninsula. (46°N, 85°W) p. 153

St. John's A city on the southeastern coast of Canada, on the Atlantic Ocean; the capital of Newfoundland. (47°N, 52°W) p. 670

St. Joseph A city in northwestern Missouri on the Missouri River. (40°N, 95°W) p. 488

St. Lawrence River A river in northeastern North America; begins at Lake Ontario and flows into the Atlantic Ocean; forms part of the border between the United States and Canada. p. 151

St. Louis A major port city in east central Missouri; known as the Gateway to the West. (38°N, 90°W) pp. 47, 385

St. Lucia An island and an independent state of the Windward Islands; located in the eastern West Indies, south of Martinique and north of St. Vincent. p. 658

St. Marys A village in southern Maryland; the capital until 1694; present-day St. Marys City. (38°N, 76°W) p. 233

St. Paul The capital of Minnesota; located in the eastern part of the state, on the Mississippi River. (45°N, 93°W) p. 498

Strait of Magellan (muh•JEH•luhn) The narrow waterway between the southern tip of South America and Tierra del Fuego; links the Atlantic Ocean with the Pacific Ocean. p. 125

Sucre A city in Bolivia, South America. (19°S, 65°W) p. 665

Sudbury River A river in western Massachusetts; connects with the Concord River. p. 291

Suriname A country in north central South America. p. 665

Susquehanna River (suhs•kwuh•HA•nuh) A river in Maryland, Pennsylvania, and central New York; rises in Otsego Lake, New York, and empties into northern Chesapeake Bay. p. 89

T

Tallahassee Capital of Florida; located in the state's panhandle. (34°N, 84°W) p. 621

Tegucigalpa A city in Central America; capital of Honduras. (14°N, 87°W) p. 658

Tenochtitlán (tay•nohch•teet•LAHN) The ancient capital of the Aztec Empire, on the islands of Lake Texcoco; location of present-day Mexico City, in southern Mexico. (19°N, 99°W) p. 108

Tikal (tih•KAHL) An ancient settlement of the Mayan civilization; located in present-day Guatemala, in Central America. (17°N, 89°W) p. 65

Timbuktu A town in Mali; located in western Africa, near the Niger River. (17°N, 3°W) p. 108

GAZETTEER

Toledo (tuh•LEE•doh) A port city in northwestern Ohio located at the southwestern corner of Lake Erie. (42°N, 84°W) p. 498

Toronto The capital of the province of Ontario, Canada; located near the northwestern end of Lake Ontario; largest city in Canada. (43°N, 79°W) p. 670

Trail of Tears A trail that was the result of the Indian Removal Act of 1830; extended from the Cherokee Nation to Fort Gibson, in the Indian Territory. p. 398

Trenton The capital of New Jersey; located in the west central part of the state; site of a major Revolutionary War battle in 1776. (40°N, 75°W) p. 323

Tres Zapotes (TRAYS sah•POH•tays) An ancient settlement of the Olmecs; located in southern Mexico. (18°N, 95°W) p. 65

Trinidad and Tobago An independent republic made up of the islands of Trinidad and Tobago; located in the Atlantic Ocean off the northeastern coast of Venezuela. p. 658

Tucson (TOO•sahn) A city in southern Arizona; located on the Santa Cruz River. (32°N, 111°W) p. 621

Turtle Mound An ancient settlement of the Mound Builders; located on the present-day east central coast of Florida. (29°N, 81°W) p. 65

V

Valley Forge A location in southeastern Pennsylvania, on the Schuylkill River; site of General George Washington's winter headquarters during the Revolutionary War. (40°N, 77°W) p. 323

Vancouver Canada's eighth-largest city; located where the northern arm of the Fraser River empties into the Pacific Ocean. (49°N, 123°W) p. 670

Vandalia (van•DAYL•yuh) A city in south central Illinois. (39°N, 89°W) p. 415

Venice A port city in northeastern Italy; located on 118 islands in the Lagoon of Venice. (45°N, 12°E) pp. 108, 113

Veracruz (veh•rah•KROOZ) A state in Mexico; located in the eastern part of the country, on the Gulf of Mexico. (19°N, 96°W) p. 653

Vicksburg A city in western Mississippi; located on the Mississippi River; site of a major Civil War battle in 1863. (32°N, 91°W) p. 470

Victoria The capital of British Columbia, Canada; located on Vancouver Island. (48°N, 123°W) p. 670

Vincennes (vihn•SENZ) A town in southwestern Indiana; site of a Revolutionary War battle in 1779. (39°N, 88°W) p. 323

W

Wabash River (WAW•bash) A river in western Ohio and Indiana; flows west and south to the Ohio River, to form part of the Indiana–Illinois border. p. 323

Wake Island A United States territory in the Pacific Ocean. p. 526

Washington, D.C. The capital of the United States; located between Maryland and Virginia, on the Potomac River in a special district that is not part of any state. (39°N, 77°W) pp. 25, 391

West Indies The islands enclosing the Caribbean Sea, stretching from Florida in North America to Venezuela in South America. p. 202

West Point A United States military post since the Revolutionary War; located in southeastern New York on the western bank of the Hudson River. p. 323

Whitehorse The capital of the Yukon Territory, Canada; located on the southern bank of the Yukon River. (60°N, 135°W) p. 670

Whitman Mission Site of a Native American mission, established in 1836 by Marcus and Narcissa Whitman; located in present-day southeastern Washington. p. 406

Williamsburg A city in southeastern Virginia; located on a peninsula between the James and York Rivers; capital of the Virginia Colony. pp. 234, 254

Wilmington A coastal city in southeastern North Carolina; located along the Cape Fear River. p. 234

Winchester A city in northern Virginia; located in the Shenandoah Valley. (39°N, 78°W) p. 353

Winnipeg The capital of the province of Manitoba, Canada; located on the Red River. (50°N, 97°W) p. 670

Wisconsin River A river located in central Wisconsin that flows south and southeast to the Mississippi River. p. 153

Y

Yellowknife Capital of the Northwest Territories in Canada; located on the northwestern shore of Great Slave Lake at the mouth of the Yellowknife River. (62°N, 114°W) p. 670

Yellowstone River A river in northwestern Wyoming, southeastern Montana, and northwestern North Dakota; flows northeast to the Missouri River. p. 385

York Former name of Toronto, Canada; located near the northwestern end of Lake Ontario; site of a major battle in the War of 1812. p. 391

Yorktown A small town in southeastern Virginia; located on Chesapeake Bay; site of the last major Revolutionary War battle in 1781. (37°N, 76°W) p. 323

Yucatán Peninsula (yoo•kah•TAN) A peninsula in southeastern Mexico and northeastern Central America. p. 20

Yukon Territory One of Canada's three territories; bordered by the Arctic Ocean, the Northwest Territories, British Columbia, and Alaska. p. 670

GAZETTEER

Glossary

The Glossary contains important social studies words and their definitions. Each word is respelled as it would be in a dictionary. When you see this mark ´ after a syllable, pronounce that syllable with more force than the other syllables. The page number at the end of the definition tells where to find the word in your book.

add, āce, câre, pälm; end, ēqual; it, īce; odd, ōpen, ôrder; tŏŏk, pōōl; up, bûrn; yōō as u in *fuse*; oil; pout; ə as a in *above*, e in *sicken*, i in *possible*, o in *melon*, u in *circus*; check; ring; thin; <u>th</u>is; zh as in *vision*

A

abolitionist (a•bə•li´shən•ist) A person who wanted to end slavery. p. 448

absolute location (ab´sə•lŏŏt lō•kā´shən) The exact location of a place on Earth, either a postal location or its lines of latitude and longitude. p. 50

acquittal (ə•kwi´təl) A verdict of not guilty. p. 479

adapt (ə•dapt´) To adjust ways of living to land and resources. pp. 6, 70

address (ə•dres´) A formal speech. p. 467

advertisement (ad•vər•tīz´mənt) A public announcement that tells people about a product or an opportunity. p. 503

agriculture (a´grə•kul•chər) Farming. p. 64

airlift (âr´lift) A system of moving supplies by airplane. p. 581

allegiance (ə•lē´jəns) Loyalty. p. 303

alliance (ə•lī´əns) A formal agreement among nations, states, or individuals to cooperate. p. 270

ally (a´lī) A partner in an alliance; a friend, especially in times of war. p. 270

almanac (ôl´mə•nak) A yearly calendar and weather forecast that helps farmers know when to plant crops. p. 222

amendment (ə•mend´mənt) An addition or change to the Constitution. p. 370

analyze (a´nəl•īz) To look closely at how the parts of an event connect with one another and how the event is connected to other events. p. 3

ancestor (an´ses•tər) An early family member. p. 59

annex (ə•neks´) To add on. p. 394

Anti-Federalist (an´tī•fe´də•rə•list) A citizen who was against ratification of the Constitution. p. 368

apprentice (ə•pren´təs) A person who learns a trade by living with the family of a skilled worker and training for several years. p. 249

archaeologist (är•kē•o´lə•jist) A scientist who studies the culture of people who lived long ago. p. 57

arid (ar´əd) Dry. p. 36

armada (är•mä´də) A Spanish fleet of warships. p. 159

armistice (är´mə•stəs) An agreement to stop fighting a war. p. 527

arms control (ärmz kən•trōl´) A limiting of the number of weapons that each nation may have. p. 592

arms race (ärmz rās) A situation in which two or more countries build weapons to protect themselves against each other. p. 582

arsenal (är´sə•nəl) A place used for storing weapons. p. 348

artifact (är´tə•fakt) An object made by early people. p. 58

assassinate (ə•sa´sən•āt) To murder a leader by sudden or secret attack. p. 477

assembly line (ə•sem´blē līn) A system of mass production in which parts of a product, such as a car, are put together as they move past a line of workers. p. 544

astrolabe (as´tra•lāb) An instrument formerly used to calculate one's position compared to the sun, moon, and stars. p. 116

auction (ôk´shən) A public sale. p. 243

authority (ə•thôr´ə•tē) The right to control and make decisions. p. 164

B

backcountry (bak´kən•trē) The land between the Coastal Plain and the Appalachian Mountains. p. 224

barter (bär´tər) To exchange goods usually without using money. p. 77

basin (bā´sən) Low, bowl-shaped land with higher ground all around it. p. 22

bias (bī´əs) An opinion or feeling for or against someone or something. p. 286

bill (bil) An idea for a new law. p. 356

bill of rights (bil uv rīts) A list of freedoms. p. 276

black codes (blak kōdz) Laws limiting the rights of former slaves in the South. p. 478

blockade (blä•kād´) To use warships to prevent other ships from entering or leaving a harbor. p. 289

boom (bōōm) A time of fast economic growth. p. 486

border state (bôr´dər stāt) During the Civil War, a state—Delaware, Kentucky, Maryland, or Missouri—between the North and the South that was unsure of which side to support. p. 459

borderlands (bôr´dər•landz) Areas of land on or near the borders between countries, colonies, or regions that serve as barriers. p. 146

boycott (boi´kät) To refuse to buy or use goods or services. p. 282

broker (brō´kər) A person who is paid to buy and sell for someone else. p. 241

budget (bu´jət) A plan for spending money. p. 280

buffer zone (bu´fər zōn) An area of land that serves as a barrier. p. 146

bureaucracy (byŏŏ•rä´krə•sē) A system of organizing the many workers and groups that are needed to run government programs. p. 549

burgess (bûr´jəs) A representative in the legislature of colonial Virginia or Maryland. p. 163

bust (bust) A time of quick economic decline. p. 487

C

Cabinet (kab´ə•nit) A group of the President's most important advisers. p. 375

candidate (kan´də•dāt) A person running for office. p. 378

capital (ka´pə•təl) The money needed to set up or improve a business. p. 497

caravel (kâr´ə•vel) A ship that used square or triangular sails to travel long distances swiftly. p. 116

cardinal direction (kärd´nal də•rek´shən) One of the main directions: north, south, east, or west. p. A3

carpetbagger (kär´pət•ba•gər) A Northerner who moved to the South to take part in Reconstruction governments. p. 483

cartogram (kär´tə•gram) A diagram that gives information about places based on the size shown for each place. p. 626

cartographer (kär•tä´grə•fər) A person who makes maps. p. 115

cash crop (kash krop) A crop that people raise to sell rather than to use themselves. p. 163

casualty (ka´zhəl•tē) A person who has been killed or wounded in a war. p. 461

cause (kôz) An event or action that makes something else happen. p. 120

cease-fire (sēs•fīr´) A temporary end to a conflict. p. 582

census (sen´səs) An official population count. p. 359

century (sen´chə•rē) A period of 100 years. p. 60

ceremony (ser´ə•mō•nē) A series of actions performed during a special event. p. 72

cession (se´shən) Something given up, such as land. p. 407

charter (chär´tər) An official paper in which certain rights are given by a government to a person, group, or business. p. 188

checks and balances (cheks and ba´lən•səz) A system that gives each branch of government different powers so that each branch can watch over the authority of the others. p. 363

chronology (krə•nä´lə•jē) Time order. p. 2

circle graph (sûr´kəl graf) A round chart that can be divided into pieces, or parts; often referred to as a pie graph. p. 223

city-state (si´tē•stāt) A city and the surrounding area that stands as an independent state. p. 111

civic participation (si´vik pär•ti•sə•pā´shən) Being concerned with and involved in issues related to the community, state, country, or world. p. 9

civics (si´viks) The study of citizenship. p. 9

civil rights (si´vəl rīts) Rights guaranteed to all citizens by the Constitution. p. 535

civil war (si´vəl wôr) A war between two groups in the same country. p. 151

civilian (sə•vil´yən) A person who is not in the military. p. 557

civilization (si•və•lə•zā´shən) A culture that usually has cities with well-developed forms of government, religion, and learning. p. 65

claim (klām) To declare that a person or a country owns something. p. 121

clan (klan) A group of families that are related to one another. p. 78

class (klas) A group of people who are alike in some way. Classes are treated with different amounts of respect in a society. p. 65

classify (kla´sə•fī) To group. p. 171

climate (klī´mət) The kind of weather a place has most often, year after year. p. 33

climograph (klī´mə•graf) A chart that shows the average monthly temperature and the average monthly precipitation for a place. p. 492

code (kōd) A set of laws. p. 445

cold war (kōld wôr) Hostilities in which opposing nations attack each other by using propaganda and money rather than soldiers and weapons. p. 575

colonist (kä´lə•nist) A person who lives in a land ruled by a distant country. p. 144

colony (kä´lə•nē) A land ruled by a distant country. p. 144

commander in chief (kə•man´dər in chēf´) A person who is in control of all the armed forces of a nation. p. 294

commerce (kä´mərs) Trade. p. 351

commission (kə•mi´shən) A special committee that is set up to study something. p. 532

common (kä´mən) An open area where sheep and cattle graze; village green. p. 190

commonwealth (kä´mən•welth) A nation that governs itself but is a territory of another country. p. 660

communism (käm´yə•ni•zəm) A social and economic system in which all land and industries are owned by the government, and individuals have few rights and little freedom. p. 574

compact (käm´pakt) An agreement. p. 167

company (kum´pə•nē) A business. p. 138

compass (kum´pəs) An instrument used to find direction. p. 109

GLOSSARY

compass rose (kum´pəs rōz) A circular direction marker on a map. p. A3

compromise (käm´prə•mīz) An agreement in which each side in a conflict gives up some of what it wants in order to get some of what it wants. p. 91

concentration camp (kon•sən•trā´shən kamp) A guarded camp built by the German National Socialist party, or Nazis, where prisoners were held. p. 555

Confederacy (kən•fe´də•rə•sē) The group of eleven states that left the Union, also called the Confederate States of America. p. 453

confederation (kən•fe•də•rā´shən) A loosely united group of governments working together. p. 89

congress (kän´grəs) A formal meeting of government representatives who have the authority to make laws. p. 270

conquistador (kän•kēs´tə•dôr) Any of the Spanish conquerors in the Americas during the early 1500s. p. 127

consent (kən•sent´) Agreement. p. 195

consequence (kän´sə•kwens) Something that happens because of an action. p. 313

conservation (kän•sər•vā´shən) The protection and wise use of natural resources. p. 533

constitution (kän•stə•tōō´shən) A written plan of government. p. 235

consumer good (kən•sōō´mər good) A product made for personal use. p. 544

contour line (kän´tōōr līn) A line on a drawing or map that connects all points of equal elevation. p. 24

convention (kən•ven´shən) An important meeting. p. 351

cotton gin (kä´tən jin) A machine that removed seeds and hulls from cotton fibers much more quickly than workers could by hand. p. 418

council (koun´səl) A group that makes laws. p. 90

county (koun´tē) The large part of a colony or a state. p. 250

county seat (koun´tē sēt) The main town of a county. p. 250

crossroads (krôs´rōdz) A place that connects people, goods, and ideas. p. 46

cultural region (kul´chə•rəl rē´jən) An area in which people share some ways of life. p. 45

culture (kul´chər) A way of life. p. 10

current (kûr´ənt) The part of a body of water flowing in a certain direction. p. 26

D

D day (dē dā) June 6, 1944, a day on which Allied forces during World War II worked together in the largest water-to-land invasion in history. p. 565

debtor (de´tər) A person who was put in prison for owning money. p. 236

decade (de´kād) A period of ten years. p. 60

declaration (de•klə•rā´shən) An official statement. p. 283

deficit (de´fə•sət) A shortage. p. 597

deforestation (dē•fôr•ə•stā´shən) The cutting down of most or all trees in an area. p. 668

delegate (de´li•gət) A representative. p. 271

demand (di•mand´) The need or want for a product or service by people who are willing to pay for it. p. 418

demarcation (dē•mär•kā´shən) A line that marks a boundary. p. 126

democracy (di•mä´krə•sē) A form of government in which the people have power to make choices about their lives and government, either directly or through representation. p. 395

depression (di•pre´shən) A time of little economic growth when there are few jobs and people have little money. p. 547

descendant (di•sen´dənt) A person's child, grand-child, and so on. p. 58

desertion (di•zûr´shən) Leaving one's duties, such as military service, without permission. p. 132

détente (dā•tänt´) An easing of tensions, especially between countries. p. 592

dictator (dik´tā•tər) A leader who has complete control of the government. p. 402

dictatorship (dik´tā•tər•ship) A form of government where a leader has complete control of the government. p. 555

distortion (di•stôr´shən) An area that is not accurate on a map. p. 530

diverse economy (də•vûrs´ i•kä´nə•mē) An economy that is based on many kinds of industries. p. 632

division of labor (də•vi´zhən uv lā´bər) Work that is divided so that each worker does a small part of a larger job. p. 544

doctrine (däk´trən) A government plan of action. p. 394

drainage basin (drā´nij bā´sən) Land drained by a river system. p. 31

drought (drout) A long period with little or no rain. p. 36

due process of law (dōō prä´ses uv lô) The principle that guarantees the right to a fair public trial. p. 372

dugout (dug´out) A boat made from a large, hollowed-out log. p. 76

E

earthwork (ûrth´wərk) A wall made of dirt or stone. p. 294

e-commerce (ē•kä´mərs) The buying and selling of goods and services through computer connections. p. 634

economic region (e•kə•nä´mik rē´jən) An area defined by the kind of work people do or the products they produce. p. 45

economics (e•kə•nä´miks) The study of how people use resources to meet their needs. p. 8

economy (i•kä´nə•mē) The way people of a state, region, or country use resources to meet their needs. p. 8

effect (i•fekt´) The result of an event or action. p. 120

electoral college (i•lek´tə•rəl kä´lij) A group of officials chosen by citizens to vote for the President and Vice President. p. 360

elevation (e•lə•vā´shən) The height of land in relation to sea level. p. 24

emancipation (i•man•sə•pā´shən) The freeing of enslaved peoples. p. 445

embargo (im•bär´gō) The refusal of one nation to trade goods and services with another. p. 660

empire (em´pīr) The conquered lands of many people and places governed by one ruler. p. 106

encounter (in•koun´tər) A meeting. p. 106

enlist (in•list´) To join. p. 315

entrepreneur (än•trə•prə•nûr´) A person who sets up and runs a business. p. 495

equality (i•kwä´lə•tē) Equal rights. p. 448

erosion (i•rō´zhən) The wearing down of Earth's surface, usually by wind or water. p. 42

estuary (es´chə•wer•ē) The wide mouth of a river where ocean tides flow in. p. 137

ethnic group (eth´nik grōōp) A group of people from the same country, of the same race, or with a shared way of life. p. 622

expedition (ek•spə•di´shən) A journey. p. 118

expel (ik•spel´) To force to leave. p. 195

export (ek´spôrt) A product that leaves a country. p. 201

extinct (ik•stingt´) No longer in existence. p. 64

F

fact (fakt) A statement that can be checked and proved to be true. p. 240

fall line (fôl līn) A place where the elevation of the land drops sharply, causing rivers to form waterfalls or rapids. p. 31

farm produce (färm prō´dōōs) Grains, fruits, and vegetables for sale. p. 215

federal system (fe´də•rəl sis´təm) A system of government in which the authority to govern is shared by the central and state governments. p. 354

Federalist (fe´də•rə•list) After the American Revolution, a citizen who wanted a strong national government and was in favor of ratifying the Constitution. p. 368

fertilizer (fûr´təl•ĭ•zər) Matter added to the soil to make it produce more crops. p. 41

flow chart (flō chärt) A diagram that shows the order in which things happen. p. 364

fork (fôrk) A place in which a river divides. p. 269

forty-niner (fôr•tē•nī´nər) A gold seeker who arrived in California in 1849. p. 409

frame of reference (frām uv ref´rəns) A set of ideas that determine how a person understands something. pp. 3, 442

free election (frē i•lek´shən) An election that offers a choice of candidates. p. 661

free enterprise (frē en´tər•prīz) An economic system in which people are able to start and run their own businesses with little control by the government. p. 494

free state (frē´ stāt) A state that did not allow slavery before the Civil War. p. 437

free world (frē wûrld´) The United States and its allies. p. 575

freedmen (frēd´mən) Men, women, and children who had once been slaves. p. 481

free-trade agreement (frē•trād´ ə•grē´mənt) A treaty in which countries agree to charge no tariffs, or taxes, on goods they buy from and sell to each other. p. 636

front (frənt) A battle line. p. 565

frontier (frən•tir´) The land that lies beyond settled areas. p. 199

fugitive (fyōō´jə•tiv) A person who is running away from something. p. 445

fundamental (fən•də•men´təl) Basic. p. 197

G

gap (gap) An opening or a low place between mountains. p. 277

generalization (jen•ə•rə•lə•zā´shən) A statement based on facts, used to summarize groups of facts and to show relationships between them. p. 68

geography (jē•ä´grə•fē) The study of Earth's surface and the way people use it. p. 6

glacier (glā´shər) A huge, slow-moving mass of ice covering land. p. 56

global economy (glō´bəl i•kä´nə•mē) The world market in which companies from different countries buy and sell goods and services. p. 636

gold rush (gōld´ rush) A sudden rush of new people to an area where gold has been found. p. 409

government (gu´vərn•mənt) A system by which people of a community, state, or nation use leaders and laws to help people live together. p. 9

grant (grant) A sum of money or other payment given for a particular purpose. p. 127

Great Awakening (grāt ə•wā´kən•ing) A religious movement started by a Dutch minister in the Middle Atlantic Colonies that called for greater freedom of choice in religion. p. 215

grid system (grid sis′təm) An arrangement of lines that divide something, such as a map, into squares. p. A3

grievance (grē′vəns) A complaint. p. 305

hacienda (ä•sē•en′dä) A large estate where cattle and sheep are raised. p. 147

harpoon (här•pōōn′) A long spear with a sharp shell point. p. 79

hatch lines (hach līnz) A pattern of stripes used on historical maps to show areas claimed by two or more countries. p. 278

heritage (her′ə•tij) Culture that has come from the past and continues today. p. 10

high-tech (hī•tek′) The term used to describe industries that invent, build, or use computers and other kinds of electronic equipment. p. 633

hijack (hī jak′) A person who illegally takes control of something. p. 600

historical empathy (hi•stôr′i•kəl em′pə•thē) An understanding of the thoughts and feelings people of the past had about events in their time. p. 3

historical map (hi•stôr′i•kəl map) A map that provides information about a place as it was in the past. p. 112

history (hi′stə•rē) Events of the past. p. 2

hogan (hō′gän) A cone-shaped Navajo shelter built by covering a log frame with bark and mud. p. 72

Holocaust (hō′lə•kôst) The mass murder of European Jews, during World War II. p. 573

homesteader (hōm′sted•ər) A person living on land granted by the government. p. 488

human feature (hyōō′mən fē′chər) Something created by humans, such as a building or road, that alters the land. p. 6

human resource (hyōō′mən rē′sôrs) A worker who brings his or her own ideas and skills to a job. p. 499

humidity (hyōō•mi′də•tē) The amount of moisture in the air. p. 36

immigrant (i′mi•grənt) A person who comes into a country to make a new home. p. 219

impeach (im•pēch′) To accuse a government official, such as the President, of "treason, bribery, or other high crimes and misdemeanors." p. 361

imperialism (im•pir′ē•ə•liz•əm) Empire building. p. 526

import (im′pôrt) A product brought into a country. p. 201

impressment (im•pres′mənt) The taking of workers against their will. p. 389

inauguration (i•nô•gyə•rā′shən) A ceremony in which a leader takes office. p. 384

indentured servant (in•den′chərd sûr′vənt) A person who agreed to work for another person without pay for a certain length of time in exchange for passage to North America. p. 234

independence (in•də•pen′dəns) The freedom to govern on one's own. p. 302

indigo (in′di•gō) A plant from which a blue dye can be made. p. 235

industrial revolution (in•dus′trē•əl re•və•lōō′shən) The period of time during the 1700s and 1800s in which machines took the place of hand tools to manufacture goods. p. 412

industrialization (in•dəs•trē•ə•lə•zā′shən) The growth of industry. p. 545

industry (in′dəs•trē) All the businesses that make one kind of product or provide one kind of service. p. 200

inflation (in•flā′shən) An economic condition in which more money is needed to buy goods and services than was needed earlier. p. 347

Information Age (in•fər•mā′shən āj) The period in history that began in the second half of the twentieth century and is marked by the growing amount of information people can get. p. 633

informed citizen (in•fôrmd′ si′tə•zən) A citizen who knows what is happening in the community, the state, the nation, and the world. p. 641

inlet (in′let) An area of water extending into the land from a larger body of water. p. 27

inset map (in′set map) A smaller map within a larger one. p. A3

integration (in•tə•grā′shən) The bringing together of people of all races in education, jobs, and housing. p. 587

interchangeable parts (in•tər•chān′jə•bəl pärts) Identical copies of parts made by machines so that if one part breaks, an identical one can be installed. p. 418

interdependent (in•tər•di•pen′dənt) Depending on each other. p. 635

interest (in′trəst) The fee a borrower pays for the use of money. p. 562

interest rate (in′trəst rāt) The amount a bank charges to lend money. p. 656

intermediate direction (in•tər•mē′dē•it də•rek′shən) One of the in-between directions: northeast, northwest, southeast, southwest. p. A3

international trade (in•tər•na′shə•nəl trād) Trade among nations. p. 635

Internet (in′tər•net) The system that joins computers around the world for the exchange of information. p. 624

intolerable (in•täl′ər•ə•bəl) Unacceptable. p. 289

investor (in•ves′tər) A person who uses money to buy or make something that will yield a profit. p. 414

irrigation (i•rə•gā´shən) The use of canals, ditches, or pipes to move water to dry areas. p. 41

island-hopping (ī´lənd•hä´ping) The process of the Allies capturing island after island as they advanced toward Japan during World War II. p. 567

isolation (ī•sə•lā´shən) The policy of remaining separate from other countries. p. 541

isthmus (is´məs) A narrow strip of land that connects two larger land areas. p. 123

jury (jûr´ē) A group of citizens who decide a case in court. p. 641

justice (jus´təs) A Supreme Court judge. p. 361

justice (jus´təs) Fairness. p. 214

land use (land yōōs) The way in which most of the land in a place is used. p. 43

landform (land´fôrm) A physical feature, such as a plain, mountain, hill, valley, or plateau, on the Earth's surface. p. 18

legislature (le´jəs•lā•chər) The lawmaking branch of government. p. 163

liberate (li´bə•rāt) To set free. p. 666

liberty (li´bər•tē) The freedom of people to make their own laws. p. 285

life expectancy (līf ik•spek´tən•sē) The average number of years a person can expect to live. p. 662

line graph (līn graf) A chart that uses one or more lines to show changes over time. p. 205

lines of latitude (līnz uv la´tə•tōōd) Lines on a map or globe that run east and west; also called parallels. p. 50

lines of longitude (līnz uv lon´jə•tōōd) Lines on a map or globe that run north and south; also called meridians. p. 50

location (lō•kā´shən) The place where something can be found. p. 6

locator (lō´kā•tər) A small map or picture of a globe that shows where an area on the main map is found in a state, on a continent, or in the world. p. A3

lodge (läj) A circular house of the Plains Indians. p. 82

loft (lôft) The part of a house located between the ceiling and the roof. p. 226

long drive (lông drīv) A trip made by ranchers to lead cattle to the market or the railroads. p. 487

longhouse (lông´hous) A long wooden building in which several related Iroquois families lived together. p. 89

Loyalist (loi´ə•list) A person who supported the British government during the American Revolution. p. 308

Magna Carta (mag´nə kär´tə) The English charter granted in 1215 by King John. It lists the rights of the royal class and limits the rights of the king. p. 370

majority rule (mə•jôr´ə•tē rōōl) The political idea that the majority of an organized group should have the power to make decisions for the whole group. p. 168

manifest destiny (ma´nə•fest des´tə•nē) The belief, shared by many Americans, that the United States should one day stretch from the Atlantic Ocean to the Pacific Ocean. p. 402

map key (map kē) A part of a map that explains what the symbols on a map stand for. p. A2

map scale (map skā l) A part of a map that compares a distance on the map to a distance in the real world. p. A3

map title (map tī´təl) Words on a map that tell the subject of the map. p. A2

mass production (mas prə•duk´shən) A system of producing large amounts of goods at one time. p. 418

mechanization of agriculture (me•kə•nə•zā´shən uv a´grə•kul•chər) The use of machines to plant and harvest crops. p. 546

median age (mē´dē•ən āj) The average age of all the people in a country. p. 662

mercenary (mûr´sən•er•ē) A soldier who serves for pay in the military of a foreign nation. p. 296

meridian (mə•ri´dē•ən) A line of longitude that runs from the North Pole to the South Pole. p. 50

merit system (mer´ət sis´təm) A way of making sure that the most qualified people get government jobs. p. 533

metropolitan area (me•trə•pä´lə•tən ar´ē•ə) A large city and the suburbs that surround it. p. 47

middle class (mi´dəl klas) The group of people who are economically between the rich and the poor. p. 656

migrant worker (mī´grənt wûr´kər) Someone who moves from place to place with the seasons to harvest crops. p. 588

migration (mī•grā´shən) The movement of people. p. 57

military draft (mil´ə•ter•ē draft) A way to bring people into military service. p. 538

militia (mə•li´shə) A volunteer army. p. 221

millennium (mə•le´nē•əm) A period of 1,000 years. p. 60

mission (mi´shən) A small religious settlement. p. 148

missionary (mi´shə•ner•ē) A person sent out by a church to spread its religion. p. 148

modify (mä´də•fī) To change. pp. 6, 40

monarch (mä´närk) A king or queen. p. 108

monopoly (mə•no′pə•lē) The complete control of a product or service. p. 288

mountain range (moun′tən rānj) A group of connected mountains. p. 19

mutiny (myōō′tə•nē) Rebellion against the leader of one's group. p. 138

national anthem (na′shə•nəl an′thəm) A song of praise for a country that is recognized as the official song of that country. p. 393

nationalism (na′shə•nəl•i•zəm) Pride in one's country. p. 394

natural resource (na′chə•rəl rē′sôrs) Something found in nature that people can use. p. 40

natural vegetation (na′chə•rəl ve•jə•tā′shən) The plant life that grows naturally in a place. p. 33

naval store (nā′vəl stōr) A product that is used to build and repair a ship. p. 203

navigation (na•və•gā′shən) The method of planning and controlling the course of a ship. p. 115

negotiate (ni•gō′shē•āt) To talk with another to work out an agreement. p. 327

neutral (nōō′trəl) Not taking a side in a disagreement. p. 309

new immigration (nōō i•mə•grā′shən) After 1890, the large group of people who came from southern and central Europe and other parts of the world to settle in North America. p. 503

nomad (nō′mad) A wanderer who has no settled home. p. 63

no-man's-land (nō′manz•land) In a war, land that is not held by either side but is filled with obstacles such as barbed wire and land mines. p. 539

nonrenewable (nän•ri•nōō′ə•bəl) Not able to be made again quickly by nature or people. p. 41

nonviolence (nän•vī′ə•ləns) The use of peaceful ways to bring about change. p. 587

Northwest Passage (nôrth′west pa′sij) A waterway in North America thought to connect the Atlantic Ocean and the Pacific Ocean. p. 136

old immigration (ōld i•mə•grā′shən) Before 1890, people who came from northern and western Europe to settle in North America. p. 502

olive branch (ä′liv branch) An ancient symbol of peace. p. 296

open range (ō′pən rānj) Land on which animals can graze freely. p. 489

opinion (ə•pin′yən) A statement that tells what a person thinks or believes. p. 240

opportunity cost (ä•pər•tōō′nə•tē kôst) the value of the thing a person gives up in order to get something else. p. 564

oral history (ôr′əl his′tə•rē) Stories, events, or experiences told aloud by a person who did not have a written language or who did not write down what happened. p. 2

ordinance (ôr′dən•əns) A law or set of laws. p. 349

origin story (ôr′ə•jən stōr′ē) A story or set of stories by Native American people that tell about their beginnings and how the world came to be. p. 59

overseer (ō′vər•sē•ər) A hired person who watched field slaves as they worked. p. 243

pacifist (pa′sə•fist) A believer in the peaceful settlement of differences. p. 310

palisade (pa•lə•sād′) A wall made of sharpened tree trunks to protect a village from enemies or wild animals. p. 87

parallel (par′ə•lel) A line of latitude. It is called this because parallels are always the same distance from one another. p. 50

parallel time line (par′ə•lel tīm līn) Two or more time lines that show the same period of time. p. 570

Parliament (pär′lə•mənt) The lawmaking body of the British government. p. 271

patent (pa′tənt) A license to make, use, or sell a new invention. p. 419

pathfinder (path′fīn•dər) Someone who finds a way through an unknown region. p. 387

Patriot (pā′trē•ət) A colonist who was against British rule and supported the rebel cause in the American Colonies. p. 308

patriotism (pā′trē•ə•ti•zəm) Love of one's country. p. 643

permanent (pûr′mə•nənt) Long-lasting. p. 144

petition (pə•ti′shən) A signed request made to an official person or organization. p. 290

petroleum (pə•trō′lē•əm) Oil. p. 497

physical feature (fi′zi•kəl fē′chər) A land feature that has been made by nature. p. 6

piedmont (pēd′mänt) An area at or near the foot of a mountain. p. 19

pilgrim (pil′grəm) A person who makes a journey for religious reasons. p. 166

pioneer (pī•ə•nir′) A person who is first to settle a new place. p. 276

pit house (pit hous) A house that was partially built over a hole in the earth so some rooms could be underground. p. 78

plantation (plan•tā′shən) A huge farm. p. 155

planter (plan′tər) A plantation owner. p. 241

plateau (pla•tō′) A broad area of high, mostly flat land. p. 21

point of view (point uv vyōō) A person's perspective. pp. 3, 286

political boss (pə•li′ti•kəl bôs) A powerful, often corrupt leader who has many dishonest employees and who is able to control the government. p. 534

political party (pə•li′ti•kəl pär′tē) A group whose members seek to elect government officials who share the group's points of view about many issues. p. 377

political region (pə•li′ti•kəl rē′jən) An area that shares a government and leaders. p. 45

population density (po•pyə•lā′shən den′sə•tē) The number of people who live within 1 square mile or 1 square kilometer of land. p. 602

population pyramid (po•pyə•lā′shən pir′ə•mid) A graph that shows the division of a country's population by age. p. 662

population region (po•pyə•lā′shən rē′jən) An area based on where people live. p. 45

potlatch (pät′lach) A special Native American gathering or celebration with feasting and dancing. p. 78

prairie (prer′ē) An area of flat or rolling land covered mostly by grasses and wildflowers. p. 38

preamble (prē′am•bəl) An introduction; first part. p. 304

prediction (pri•dik′shən) A decision about what may happen next, based on the way things are. p. 559

prejudice (pre′jə•dəs) An unfair feeling of hate or dislike for members of a certain group because of their background, race, or religion. p. 504

presidio (prā•sē′dē•ō) A Spanish fort. p. 146

primary source (prī′mer•ē sôrs) A record of an event made by a person who saw or took part in it. p. 4

prime meridian (prīm mə•ri′dē•ən) The meridian marked 0 degrees and that runs north and south through Greenwich, England. p. 50

principle (prin′sə•pəl) A rule that is used in deciding how to behave. p. 329

proclamation (prä•klə•mā′shən) An order from a leader to the citizens. p. 276

profit (prä′fət) The money left over after all expenses have been paid. p. 115

progressive (prə•gre′siv) A person who wants to improve government and make life better. p. 532

projection (prə•jek′shən) A way of showing Earth on flat paper. p. 530

proprietary colony (prə•prī′ə•tər•e kä′lə•nē) A colony owned and ruled by one person who was chosen by a king or queen. p. 155

proprietor (prə•prī′ə•tər) An owner. p. 155

prospector (präs′pek•tər) A person who searches for silver, gold, and other mineral resources. p. 487

prosperity (präs•per′ə•tē) Economic success. p. 162

province (prä′vəns) A political region, similar to a state. p. 670

public office (pub′lik ô′fəs) A job a person is elected to do. p. 192

public opinion (pub′lik ə•pin′yən) The point of view held by the majority of people. p. 302

public service (pub′lik sûr′vəs) A job someone does to help the community or society as a whole. p. 245

pueblo (pwe′blō) A Spanish word for *village*. p. 66

Puritan (pyûr′ə•tən) A member of the Church of England who settled in North America to follow Christian beliefs in a more "pure" way. p. 188

quarter (kwôr′tər) To provide or pay for housing at no cost to another person. p. 289

rain shadow (rān sha′dō) The driest side of a mountain. p. 35

rapid (ra′pəd) The fast-moving, dangerous place in a river caused by a sudden drop in elevation. p. 138

rapid-transit system (ra′pəd tran′sət sis′təm) A passenger transportation system that uses elevated or underground trains or both. p. 629

ratify (ra′tə•fī) To approve. p. 366

rationing (rash′ən•ing) The limiting of a supply of something. p. 561

raw material (rô mə•tir′ē•əl) A resource that can be used to make a product. p. 158

Reconstruction (rē•kən•struk′shən) The time during which the South was rebuilt after the Civil War. p. 476

recycle (rē•sī′kəl) To reuse. p. 562

refinery (ri•fī′nə•rē) A factory in which materials, especially fuels, are cleaned and made into usable products. p. 487

reform (ri•fôrm′) To change for the better. p. 532

refuge (re′fyōōj) A safe place. p. 213

refugee (ref′yōō•jē) A person who leaves home to seek shelter and safety elsewhere. p. 573

regiment (re′jə•mənt) A large, organized group of soldiers. p. 310

region (rē′jən) An area of Earth in which many features are similar. p. 6

register (rej′ə•stər) To enroll as a voter. p. 641

regulation (re•gyə•lā′shən) A rule or an order. p. 505

relative location (re′lə•tiv lō•kā′shən) The position of one place in relation to another. p. 44

relocation camp (rē•lō•kā′shən kamp) A temporary settlement in which Japanese Americans were forced to live during World War II. p. 563

Renaissance (re′nə•säns) A French word meaning "rebirth," used to name a time of advances in thought, learning, art, and science. p. 109

renewable (ri•nōō′ə•bəl) Able to be made or grown again by nature or people. p. 42

repeal (ri•pēl′) To cancel, or undo, a law. p. 283

GLOSSARY

representation (re•pri•zen•tā´shən) The act of speaking on behalf of someone else. p. 281

republic (ri•pub´lik) A form of government in which people elect representatives to govern the country. p. 346

reservation (re•zər•vā´shən) An area of land set aside by the government for use only by Native Americans. p. 490

reserved powers (ri•zûrvd´ pou´ərz) Authority that belongs to the states or to the people, not to the national government. p. 372

resist (ri•zist´) To act against. p. 445

resolution (re•zə•loō´shən) A formal statement of the feelings of a group of people about an important topic. p. 303

resolve (ri•zälv´) To settle. p. 91

responsibility (ri•spän•sə•bil´ə•tē) A duty. p. 640

retreat (ri•trēt´) To fall back. p. 458

revolution (re•və•loō´shən) A sudden, great change, such as the overthrow of an established government. p. 268

royal colony (roi´əl kä´lə•nē) A colony ruled directly by a monarch. p. 152

ruling (roō´ling) A decision. p. 398

rural (rûr´əl) Like or having to do with a place away from a city. p. 46

S

satellite (sa´tə•līt) An object in orbit around Earth. p. 583

savanna (sə•va´nə) A kind of grassland that has areas with a few scattered trees. p. 39

scalawag (ska´li•wag) A rascal; someone who supports something for his or her own gain. p. 484

scandal (skan´dəl) An action that brings disgrace. p. 593

sea dog (sē dôg) A commander of English warships that attacked Spanish ships carrying treasure. p. 156

sea level (sē le´vəl) The level of the surface of the ocean. p. 21

secede (si•sēd´) To leave. p. 453

secondary source (se´kən•der•ē sôrs) A record of an event written by someone who was not there at the time. p. 5

secret ballot (sē´kret ba´lət) A voting method in which no one knows how anyone else voted. p. 484

sectionalism (sek´shən•ə•li•zəm) Regional loyalty. p. 436

sedition (si•di´shən) Speech or behavior that causes other people to work against a government. p. 196

segregation (se•gri•gā´shən) The practice of keeping people in separate groups based on their race or culture. p. 484

self-rule (self•roōl´) Control of one's own government. p. 168

self-sufficient (self•sə•fi´shənt) Able to provide for one's own needs without help. p. 147

separatist (se´pə•rə•tist) A citizen of Quebec who wants Quebec to be independent. p. 672

settlement house (se´təl•mənt hous) A community center. p. 535

sharecropping (sher´kräp•ing) A system of working the land in which the worker was paid with a "share" of the crop. p. 483

siege (sēj) A long-lasting attack. p. 393

slash-and-burn (slash•and•bûrn) A method of clearing land for farming that includes cutting and burning of trees. p. 87

slave state (slāv stāt) A state that allowed slavery before the Civil War. p. 437

slavery (slā´və•rē) The practice of holding people against their will and making them carry out orders. p. 66

society (sə•sī´ə•tē) A human group. p. 10

sod (sod) Earth cut into blocks or mats, held together by grass and its roots. p. 82

sound (sound) A long inlet often parallel to the coast. p. 28

specialize (spe´shə•līz) To work at one kind of job and do it well. p. 190

spiritual (spir´i•chə•wəl) A religious song based on Bible stories. p. 244

standard of living (stan´dərd uv li´ving) A measure of how well people in a country live. p. 664

staple (stā´pəl) Something, such as milk or bread, that is always needed and used. p. 71

states' rights (stāts rīts) The idea that the states, rather than the federal government, should have the final authority over their own affairs. p. 436

stock (stäk) A share of ownership in a business. p. 161

stock market (stäk mär´kət) A place where people can buy and sell shares of a business. p. 547

strategy (stra´tə•jē) A long-range plan. p. 459

suburban (sə•bûr´bən) Of or like the area of smaller cities or towns around a large city. p. 46

suffrage (su´frij) The right to vote. p. 535

Sun Belt (sun belt) A wide area of the southern United States that reaches from the Atlantic coast to the Pacific coast. p. 621

superpower (soō´pər•pou•ər) A nation that is one of the most powerful in the world. p. 580

supply (sə•plī´) The amount of a product or service that is available. p. 418

surplus (sûr´pləs) An amount that is more than what is needed. p. 71

T

tariff (tar´əf) A tax on goods brought into a country. p. 436

technology (tek•nä´lə•jē) The use of scientific knowledge and tools to make or do something. p. 63

teleconference (te´li•kän•frəns) A conference, or meeting, that uses electronic equipment to connect people. p. 625

tenement (te´nə•mənt) A poorly built apartment building. p. 503

tepee (tē´pē) A cone-shaped tent made from wooden poles and buffalo skins. p. 84

territory (ter´ə•tôr•ē) Land that belongs to a national government but is not a state. p. 349

terrorism (ter´ər•i•zəm) The use of violence to promote a cause. p. 596

textile (tek´stīl) Cloth. p. 416

theory (thē´ə•rē) A possible explanation. p. 57

tide (tīd) The regular rise and fall of the ocean and of the bodies of water connected to it. p. 27

tidewater (tīd´wô•tər) Low-lying land along a coast. p. 241

time line (tīm līn) A diagram that shows events that took place during a certain period of time. p. 60

time zone (tīm zōn) A geographic region in which the same time is used. p. 674

totem pole (tō´təm pōl) A tall wooden post carved with shapes of animals and people and representing a family's history and importance. p. 79

town meeting (toun mē´ting) An assembly in the New England Colonies in which male landowners could take part in government. p. 192

township (toun´ship) An area of land. p. 218

trade-off (trād´ôf) The giving up of one thing to get another. p. 564

traitor (trā´tər) One who works against one's own government. p. 323

transcontinental railroad (trans•kän•tə•nen´təl rā l´rōd) The railway line that crossed North America. p. 494

travois (trə•voi´) A device made of two poles fastened to a dog's harness, used to carry possessions. p. 85

treason (trē´zən) The act of working against one's own government. p. 282

treaty (trē´tē) An agreement between nations about peace, trade, or other matters. p. 126

trespass (tres´pas) To go onto someone else's property without asking permission. p. 388

trial by jury (trī´əl bī jûr´ē) The right of a person accused of a crime to be tried by a jury, or group, of fellow citizens. p. 214

triangular trade route (trī•ang´gyə•lər trād rōōt) A shipping route that linked England, the English colonies in North America, and the west coast of Africa, forming an imaginary triangle in the Atlantic Ocean. p. 202

tribe (trīb) A group of people who share the same language, land, and leaders. p. 64

tributary (tri´byōō•ter•ē) A stream or river that flows into a larger stream or river. p. 30

tundra (tun´drə) A cold, dry region where trees cannot grow. p. 37

turning point (tûr´ning point) A single event that causes important and dramatic change. p. 316

underground (un´dûr•ground) Done in secret. p. 446

unemployment (un•im•ploi´mənt) The number of people without jobs. p. 549

urban (ûr´bən) Of or like a city. p. 45

urbanization (ûr•bə•nə•zā´shən) The movement of people into cities. p. 546

veto (vē´tō) To reject. p. 361

volcano (väl•kā´nō) An opening in Earth, often on a hill or mountain, through which hot lava, gases, ash, and rocks may pour out. p. 23

volunteer (vä•lən•tir´) A person who works without pay. p. 642

W

wampum (wäm´pəm) Beads made from cut and polished seashells used to keep records, send messages to other tribes, barter for goods, or give as gifts. p. 88

war hawk (wôr hôk) A member of Congress who wanted war with Britain before the War of 1812. p. 390

wigwam (wig´wäm) A round, bark-covered Native American shelter. p. 88

Index

Page references for illustrations are set in italic type. An italic *m* indicates a map. Page references set in boldface type indicate the pages on which vocabulary terms are defined.

INDEX

INDEX

For permission to reprint copyrighted material, grateful acknowledgment is made to the following sources:

Atheneum Books for Young Readers, an imprint of Simon & Schuster Children's Publishing Division: Cover illustration from *Anasazi* by Leonard Everett Fisher. Copyright © 1997 by Leonard Everett Fisher. Cover illustration by Ronald Himler from *Squish! A Wetland Walk* by Nancy Luenn. Illustration copyright © 1994 by Ronald Himler. Cover illustration by Jerry Pinkney from *Goin' Someplace Special* by Patricia McKissack. Illustration copyright © 2001 by Jerry Pinkney.

Candlewick Press Inc., Cambridge, MA: Cover illustration by P. J. Lynch from *When Jessie Came Across the Sea* by Amy Hest. Illustration copyright © 1997 by P. J. Lynch.

Candlewick Press Inc., Cambridge, MA, on behalf of Walker Books Ltd., London: Cover illustration by Kevin Tweddell from *The History News: Explorers* by Michael Johnstone. Illustration copyright © 1997 by Walker Books Ltd.

Dutton Children's Books, an imprint of Penguin Books for Young Readers, a division of Penguin Putnam Inc: Cover photograph by Art Wolfe from *Journey Through the Northern Rainforest* by Karen Pandell. Photograph copyright © 1999 by Art Wolfe.

Jane Feder, on behalf of Julie Downing: Cover illustration by Julie Downing from *If You Were There in 1492* by Barbara Brenner. Illustration copyright © 1991 by Julie Downing.

Harcourt, Inc.: "If We Should Travel" from *Between Earth & Sky* by Joseph Bruchac. Text copyright © 1996 by Joseph Bruchac.

HarperCollins Publishers: Cover illustration by James Watling from *Finding Providence: The Story of Roger Williams* by Avi. Illustration copyright © 1997 by James Watling. From *Stranded at Plimoth Plantation 1626* by Gary Bowen. Copyright © 1994 by Gary Bowen. Cover illustration by Stephen Fieser from *The Silk Route: 7,000 Miles of History* by John S. Major. Illustration copyright © 1995 by Stephen Fieser. Cover illustration by Bert Dodson from *American Adventures: Thomas* by Bonnie Pryor. Illustration copyright © 1998 by Bert Dodson.

David Higham Associates Limited: Cover illustration by Martin Jordan from *Angel Falls: A South American Journey* by Martin and Tanis Jordan. Illustration copyright © 1995 by Martin Jordan. Published by Larousse Kingfisher Chambers Inc.

Holiday House, Inc.: Cover illustration by Peter Fiore from *The Boston Tea Party* by Steven Kroll. Illustration copyright 1998 by Peter Fiore.

Henry Holt and Company, LLC: From "San Salvador" by Jamake Highwater in *The World in 1492* by Jean Fritz, Katherine Paterson, Patricia and Fredrick McKissack, Margaret Mahy, and Jamake Highwater, cover illustration by Stefano Vitale. Text copyright © 1992 by The Native Land Foundation; cover illustration copyright © 1992 by Stefano Vitale.

Lee & Low Books, Inc., 95 Madison Avenue, New York, NY 10016: From *Dia's Story Cloth: The Hmong People's Journey to Freedom* by Dia Cha, illustrated by Chue and Nhia Thao Cha. Copyright © 1996 by Denver Museum of Natural History.

Robin Moore and BookStop Literary Agency: Cover illustration by Robin Moore from *Across the Lines* by Carolyn Reeder. Illustration copyright © 1997 by Robin Moore.

Northland Publishing Company: Cover illustration by Julia Miner from *The Unbreakable Code* by Sara Hoagland Hunter. Illustration copyright © 1996 by Julia Miner.

Orion Books, a division of Random House, Inc.: From *All for the Union* by Robert Hunt Rhodes. Text and photograph copyright © 1985 by Robert Hunt Rhodes.

G. P. Putnam's Sons, an imprint of Penguin Putnam Books for Young Readers, a division of Penguin Putnam Inc.: From *Shh! We're Writing the Constitution* by Jean Fritz, illustrated by Tomie dePaola. Text copyright © 1987 by Jean Fritz; illustrations copyright © 1987 by Whitebird, Inc. Cover illustration by F. John Sierra from *My Mexico—México mío* by Tony Johnston. Illustration copyright © 1996 by F. John Sierra.

Scholastic Inc.: Cover illustration by Mark Summers from *James Printer: A Novel of Rebellion* by Paul Samuel Jacobs. Illustration © 1997 by Mark Summers. Published by Scholastic Press, a division of Scholastic Inc. Cover illustration by Dan Andreasen from *By the Dawn's Early Light: The Story of the Star-Spangled Banner* by Steven Kroll. Illustration copyright © 1994 by Dan Andreasen.

Simon & Schuster Books for Young Readers, an imprint of Simon & Schuster Children's Publishing Division: Cover illustration from *The Story of William Penn* by Aliki. Copyright © 1964 by Aliki Brandenberg; copyright renewed © 1992 by Aliki Brandenberg. From "The *Eagle* Has Landed" in *The Children's Book of America*, edited by William J. Bennett, illustrated by Michael Hague. Text copyright © 1998 by William J. Bennett; illustrations copyright © 1998 by Michael Hague.

Steck-Vaughn Company: Cover illustration by Debbe Heller from *Tales from the Underground Railroad* by Kate Connell. Illustration copyright © 1993 by Dialogue Systems, Inc.

ILLUSTRATION CREDITS

Pages 12-13, Angus McBride; 13, Steve Weston; 14-15, Leland Klanderman; 28, 34, 35, Sebastian Quigley; 56-57, Tom McNeely; 62-63, Dennis Lyall; 71, Luigi Galante; 77, Inklink; 100-101, Uldis Klavins; 102-103, Dave Hendersch; 107, Steve Weston; 106-107, Studio Liddell; 116-117, Dennis Lyall; 160-161, Mike Lamble; 167, Bill Smith Studio; 180-181, Andrew Wheatcroft; 182-185, Nina Martin; 190-191, George Gaadt; 220, 226-227, Yuan Lee; 260-261, George Gaadt; 308-309, Vincent Wakerley; 324, Dennis Lyall; 324-325, Sebastian Quigley; 325, Dennis Lyall; 340-341, Gino D'Achille; 355, Vincent Wakerley; 376-377, Chuck Carter; 393, Bill Smith Studio; 412-413, Don Foley; 428-429, Cliff Spohn; 430-433, George Gaadt; 454-455, Luigi Galante; 468, Bill Smith Studio; 494-495, Dennis Lyall; 516-517, Bill Maughan; 544-545, Chuck Carter; 566-567, Dennis Lyall; 612-613, Rick Johnson; 638-639, Studio Liddell; 643, Bill Smith Studio; 644-645, Vincent Wakerley.

All maps by MapQuest.com

PHOTO CREDITS

Cover: Stephen Krasemann/DRK Photo (eagle); Roger Ressmeyer/Corbis (shuttle); The Image Bank (Mt. Rushmore); G. George Diebold/Corbis Stock Market (waves).

PLACEMENT KEY: (t) top; (b) bottom; (l) left; (c) center; (r) right; (bg) background; (i) inset

POSTER INSERT

Flag: Don Mason/Corbis Stock Market, eagle: Minden Pictures.

TITLE PAGE AND TABLE OF CONTENTS

(fg) Andria/Hendrickson; (bg) Doug Armand/Stone; iv, The Detroit Institute of Arts; v, National Maritime Museum Picture Library; vi, Historical Society of Pennsylvania, Silver Gorget, c. 1757 Artist: Joseph Richardson, Sr., S-8-120; vii, Lester Lefkowitz/Corbis Stock Market; viii, Independence National Historical Park; ix, Smithsonian Institution; x, NASA.

INTRODUCTION

1 (t) Andria/Hendrickson, (l) Doug Armand/Stone; 2 (t) Bob Daemmrich/Stock, Boston/PictureQuest; 2 (b) ChromoSohm/Sohm/Visions of America; 3 (t) Christie Parker/Houserstock, Inc.; 3 (b) Underwood & Underwood/Corbis; 4 National Park Service; 4 National Park Service; 4 National Park Service; 5 (br) John McGrail; 5 (tl) The Granger Collection, New York; 5 (inset) National Park Service; 7 (tl) Mattew Borkoski/Stock, Boston Inc./PictureQuest; 7 (tr) Andre Jenny/Focus Group/PictureQuest; 7 (cl) Peter Pearson/Stone; 7 (cr) Jeffrey Muir Hamilton/Stock, Boston Inc./PictureQuest; 7 (bl) Robert Hildebrand; 7 (br) David Young-Wolff/PhotoEdit/PictureQuest; 8 (l) Jeff Lepore/Panoramic Images; 8 (r) David Young-Wolff/PhotoEdit; 9 (bl) Joseph Sohm/Stock, Boston Inc./PictureQuest; 9 (br) Bill Bachman/PhotoEdit; 10 (t) David Young-Wolff/PhotoEdit/PictureQuest; 10 (b) Calumet Regional Archives, Indiana University Northwest.

UNIT 1

UNIT OPENER, (fg) The Detroit Institute of Arts; (bg) Tom & Susan Bean, Inc.; 11 (t) The Detroit Institute of Arts; (l) Tom & Susan Bean, Inc; 16-17 Robert Hildebrand Photography; 18-19 (b) Russ Finley; 19 (t) David Muench/Corbis; 21 (b) Dave G. Houser; 22 (b) Marc Muench/David Muench Photography, Inc.; 23 (t) David Muench; 26 (b) Stocktrek/Corbis Stock Market; 30 (t) Greg Ryan/Sally Beyer/Positive Reflections; 30 (inset) Bettmann/Corbis; 31 (br) Stock Barrow; 32 (t) David Muench; 33 (b) Mark E. Gibson Photography; 37 California Stock Photography; 39 Tom & Susan Bean; 40 Ted Streshinsky/Corbis; 41 Mark E. Gibson Photography; 43 (t) Charles Gupton/Corbis Stock Market; 44 Henry T. Kaiser/Stock Connection/PictureQuest; 46-47 (b) Mark E. Gibson Photography; 48 Place Stock Photo; 54-55 David Muench Photography; 58 (b) John Maier, Jr./JB Pictures; 58 (inset) Mercyhurst Archaeological Institute; 59 Lawrence Migdale; 63 (t) Courtesy of Arizona State Museum, AZ/Jerry Jacka Photography; 64 (tl) Harald Sund/The Image Bank; 64 (tr) Zion National Park; 65 (br) Werner Forman/Art Resource; 66-67 (t) Michael Hampshire/Cahokia Mounds Historic Site; 67 (tr) Richard A. Cooke/Corbis; 68 American Hurrah; 70 Place Stock Photo; 72-73 (b) James Cowlin/Adstock; 72 (inset) Monty Roessel; 73 (t) Fifth Generation Traders, Farmington, N.M./Jerry Jacka Photography; 74 (t) Stephen Trimble; 74 (b) Smithsonian Institution; 75 (t) Aldo Tutino/ Art Resource, NY; 75 (c) John Bigelow Taylor/Art Resource, NY; 75 (b) Gift of

of the Massachusetts Historical Society; 297 (c) Peabody Essex Museum, Salem, MA. Photo by Mark Sexton; 297 (tr) Jamestown-Yorktown Foundation; 300-301 Morristown National Park; 302 (bc) Hulton/Archive; 302 The Granger Collection; 303 (b) Smithsonian Institution; 303 (tr) Independence National Historical Park; 305 Francis G. Mayer/Corbis; 306 (br) Lee Snider Photo Images; 306 (bkgd) Scott Barrow; 307 Historical Society of Pennsylvania; 308 (bl) Courtesy of the Massachusetts Historical Society; 309 (br) Martin Art Gallery, Muhlenberg College, Allentown, Pennsylvania; 310 (b) Valentine Museum, Richmond History Center; 310 (inset) Tracey W. McGregor Library/University of Virginia; 311 (tl) Bequest of Winslow Warren/Courtesy, Museum of Fine Arts, Boston; 311 (tr) Bettmann/Corbis; 311 (tlc) Detroit Publishing Co. Photograph Collection/Library of Congress; 311 (trc) Richard Walker/New York Historical Association, Cooperstown; 312 Independence National Historical Park; 314 (br) Eliot Cohen/Janelco Photographers; 314 (bl) Russ Finley; 315 (t) Fort Ticonderoga Museum; 315 (bl) Russ Finley; 315 (inset) The Granger Collection; 316 (t) The Valley Forge Historical Society; 317 (t) Bettmann/Corbis; 317 (b) Jewish-American Hall of Fame; 318 (b) Bettmann/Corbis; 318 (tl) Hulton/Archive Photos; 318 (tc) Hulton/Archive Photos; 318 (tr) Independence National Historical Park Collection; 319 Edifice/Corbis; 320-321 American Museum of American History/Smithsonian Institution. Trans. no. 76-3259; 322 (b) David Muench Photography; 325 (br) Roy Andersen/National Geographic Society; 326 (b) Yorktown Victory Center; 326 (t) a detail, John Trumbull "The Surrender of Lord Cornwallis at Yorktown, 19 October 1781", Yale University Art Gallery, Trumbull Collection; 327 (b) Courtesy, Winterthur Museum; 328 (t) Hulton/Archive Photos; 330 (b) Royal Geographical Society, London/The Bridgeman Art Library International; 330 (inset) American Antiquarian Society; 334 (t) Peter Southwick/Stock, Boston; 334 (bc) Michael Dwyer/Stock Boston; 334 (bg) Gibson Stock Photography; 335 (br) Danilo G. Donadoni/ Bruce Coleman; 335 (tr) Tibor Bognar/Corbis Stock Market; 335 (tc) Susan Cole Kelly; 335 (cl) Dave G. Houser/Corbis; 335 (tl) Ed Young/Corbis; 335 (bl) Richard Cummins/Corbis; 335 (cr) Dave G. Houser/Corbis.

UNIT 5

UNIT OPENER; (fg) Independence National Historical Park; (bg) Independence National Historical Park; 339 (t) Independence National Historical Park; (l) Independence National Historical Park; 344-345 Johnathan Wallen Photography; 346 Roman Soumar/Corbis; 347 (tc) From the Robert H. Gore Jr. Numismatic Collection; 347 (tr) American Antiquarian Society; 348 (bl) The Granger Collection; 348 (br) The New-York Historical Society; 350 Library of Congress; 351 (bl) The Granger Collection; 351 (br) The Granger Collection; 352 Bettmann/Corbis; 355 (tl) The Library of Virginia; 355 (tc) Ralph Earl Roger Sherman (1721-1793) M. G. (Hon.) 1786 Yale University Art Gallery/Gift of Roger Sherman White, BA. 1899, L. L. B. 1902; 355 (tr) Princeton University; 356 Emmet Collection, Rare Books and Manuscripts Division, The New York Public Library, Astor, Lennox, and Tilden Foundations; 357 (t) 'Residences and Slave Quarters of Mulbery

Plantation' by Thomas Coram, The Gibbes Museum of Art, Charleston, SC; 358 (b) Joseph Sohm/Stock, Boston/PictureQuest; 358 (inset) Northwind Picture Archives; 359 O and J Heaton/Stock, Boston; 360 (b) Dave G. Houser/Houserstock, Inc.; 361 Lee Snider Photo Images; 362 (bl) Dennis Brack/Black Star Publishing/PictureQuest; 362 (br) Richard W. Strauss/Smithsonian Institute/Supreme Court Historical Society; 363 Independence National Historical Park, Phil; 365 (l) James Foote/Photo Researchers; 365 (cr) James Foote/Photo Researchers; 366 Independence National Historical Park; 367 Virginia Museum of Fine Arts, Richmond. Gift of Edgar William and Bernice Chrysler Garbisich. Photo: Ron Jennings@Virginia Museum of Fine Arts.; 368 (bl) New York Historical/The Bridgeman Art Library International; 368 (br) Colonial Williamsburg Foundation; 370 National Archives and Records Administration; 371 (c) Culver Pictures; 371 (bl) Franklin Institute; 371 (br) The Granger Collection, New York; 372 Dover Publications; 373 (b) Courtesy, Winterthur Museum; 374 (b) LM Cooks Salute to General Washington in NY Harbor, Gift of Edgar Williams & Bernice Chrysler Garbisch Board of Trustees/National Gallery of Art, Washington; 374 (inset) Museum of the City of New York, Bequest of Mrs. J. Insley Blair in Memory of Mr. and Mrs. J. Insley Blair; 375 Courtesy of the John Carter Brown Library at Brown University; 376 (b) Maryland Historical Society; 378 White House Historical Assoc.; 379 The New-York Historical Society; 382-383 David Muench Photography; 384 C. Jean/Reunion des Musees Nationaux/Art Resource, NY; 386 (t) National Park Service; 386-387 (b) Amon Carter Museum; 386 (bl) Courtesy Independence National Historical Park; 387 (br) Courtesy Independence National Historical Park; 389 Bettmann/Corbis; 390 Bettmann/Corbis; 392 (t) Library of Congress; 392 (b) Collection of the New York Historical Society; 393 (br) Corbis; 394 Bettmann/Corbis; 395 (b) Burstein Collection/Corbis; 395 (inset) Lawrence County Historical Society; 396 (t) The Granger Collection, NY; 396 (b) Library of Congress; 397 Collection of The New York Historical Society; 399 Troy Anderson; 400 (bl) National Portrait Gallery/Smithsonian Institution/Art Resource, NY; 400 (br) Academy of Natural Sciences of Philadelphia/Corbis; 401 (t) Academy of Natural Sciences of Philadelphia/Corbis; 401 (c) North Carolina Museum; 401 (br) Academy of Natural Sciences of Philadelphia/Corbis; 401 (cl) Academy of Natural Sciences of Philadelphia/Corbis, Inc.; 402 The State Preservation Board, Austin Texas; 403 (b) Friends of the Governor's Mansion, Austin, Texas; 404 H. K. Barnett/Star of the Republic Museum, Jefferson, Texas; 405 (t) The Saint Louis Art Museum; 405 Whitman Mission National Historic Society; 406 Bettmann/Corbis; 407 The Granger Collection; 408 Smithsonian American Art Museum, Washington DC/Art Resource, NY; 409 Gill C. Kenny/The Image Bank; 410 National Archives; 412 Russ Poole Photography; 414 (t) Cooper Hewitt Museum; 414 B & O Railroad Museum; 418 (tl) Art Resource, NY; 418 (bl) Bettmann/Corbis; 419 (tr) Courtesy of the John Deere Company; 419 (inset) John Deere.

UNIT 6

UNIT OPENER; (fg) Smithsonian Institution; (bg) Peter Gridley/FPG International; 427 (t) Smithsonian Institution; (l) Peter Gridley/FPG International; 430 All for the Union; 434-435

David Muench Photography; 436 The American Clock and Watch Museum; 437 Stock Montage/Hulton Archive/Getty Images; 438 Bettmann/Corbis; 441 Missouri Historical Society; 442 (bl) Courtesy of the South Carolina Library; 442 (br) Courtesy of the South Carolina Library; 443 (br) Hulton-Deutsch Collection/Corbis; 443 (br) Bettmann/Corbis; 444 (br) Scala/Art Resource, NY; 444 (cl) The Charleston Museum; 446 Library of Congress; 447 (t) Hulton/Archive Photos; 447 (b) National Museum of American Art, Washington DC/Art Resource, NY; 448 (bl) National Portrait Gallery, Smithsonian Institution/Art Resource, NY; 448 (inset) Book cover slide of "Uncle Tom's Cabin" by Harriet Beecher Stowe. Courtesy of the Charles L. Blockson Afro-American Collection, Temple University; 449 (t) National Portrait Gallery, Smithsonian Institution/Art Resource, NY; 450 (b) Morton Beebe, S.F./Corbis; 451 Courtesy of the Illinois State Historical Library; 452 (bl) National Portrait Gallery, Smithsonian Institution/Art Resource, NY; 452 (bc) Corbis; 453 (t) National Portrait Gallery, Smithsonian Institution/Art Resource, NY; 453 (b) The Granger Collection; 458 (b) Brown Military Collection, Brown University; 458 (bl) National Portrait Gallery, Smithsonian Institution/Art Resource, NY; 460 James P. Rowan Photography; 461 Library of Congress; 462 (t) National Portrait Gallery; 462 (b) Library of Congress; 463 (b) Bettmann/Corbis; 464 Chicago Historical Society; 465 (bc) Salamander Books; 465 (br) National Portrait Gallery, Smithsonian Institution, Washington, D.C.; 466 (t) Courtesy of General Dynamics Corp., Electric Boat Div.; 466 (cl) Richmond, Virginia/Katherine Wetzel; 467 (b) New Hampshire Historical Society; 469 (b) Tom Lovell©National Geographic; 471 Tom Prettyman/PhotoEdit/PictureQuest; 476 (bl) Corbis; 476 (bc) Library of Congress; 477 (t) Hulton Archive/Getty Images; 477 (inset) Library of Congress; 478 Corbis; 479 (c) Library of Congress; 479 (tl) The Granger Collection, New York; 480 (tl) American Treasures of the Library of Congress; 480 (tr) Library of Congress; 481 (bl) Corbis; 481 (br) Southern Historical Collection; 482 (br) Bob Daemmrich Photography; 482 (cl) Bob Daemmrich Photography; 483 (t) The Metropolitan Museum of Art, Morris K. Jessup Fund; 483 (inset) Smithsonian Institution, Division of Agriculture; 484 (t) Hulton/Archive/Getty Images; 484 (b) Smithsonian Institute; 485 The Granger Collection; 486 (inset) The Bancroft Library; 486-487 Joseph Sohm/Visions of America/PictureQuest; 488 (b) Jeff Greenberg/PhotoEdit; 488 (tc) William Manns Photo/Zon International Publishing; 489 Solomon D. Butcher Collection, Nebraska State Historical Society; 490 Corbis; 491 Corbis; 492 Michael Forsberg; 496 Corbis; 497 Corbis; 499 From the Collections of Henry Ford Museum & Greenfield Village; 500 (t) Transfer from the National Museum of American Art; Gift of Dr. Eleanor A. Campbell to the Smithsonian Institution, 1942.; 500 (bl) Henry Ford Museum & Greenfield Village; 500 (br) History of Technology Division, National Museum of American History, photographed by John Tsantes/Smithsonian Institution; 501 (t) Henry Ford Museum & Greenfield Village; 501 (c) Science Museum, London, UK/The Bridgeman Art Library International; 501 (br) Alfred Harrell/Smithsonian Institution; 502 (inset) "By Courtesy of the Statue of Liberty National Monument"; 503 (tl) Corbis; 504-505 (b) Corbis;